Special Education Advocacy

Special Education Advocacy

Ruth Colker
Distinguished University Professor
Heck-Faust Memorial Chair in Constitutional Law
Michael E. Moritz College of Law
The Ohio State University

Julie K. Waterstone
Director of the Children's Rights Clinic
Associate Clinical Professor of Law
Southwestern Law School

ISBN: 978–1–4224–7958–2

Library of Congress Cataloging-in-Publication Data

Special education advocacy / Ruth Colker, Julie K. Waterstone [editors].
    p. cm.
    Includes index.
    ISBN 978-1-4224-7958-2 (soft cover)
    1. Children with disabilities--Education--Law and legislation--United States. 2. Special education--Law and legislation--United States. I.
Colker, Ruth. II. Waterstone, Julie K.
    KF4209.3.S6767 2011
    344.73'0791--dc22   2011004193

NOTE TO USERS

To ensure that you are using the latest materials available in this area, please be sure to periodically check the LexisNexis Law School web site for downloadable updates and supplements at www.lexisnexis.com/lawschool.

Editorial Offices
121 Chanlon Rd., New Providence, NJ 07974 (908) 464-6800
201 Mission St., San Francisco, CA 94105-1831 (415) 908-3200
www.lexisnexis.com

MATTHEW◆BENDER

Dedication

In Memory of Janice Seiner Colker

R.C.

For Michael, who continuously inspires, supports and encourages me and for Ava and Jack, who make everything worthwhile

J.W.

Preface: An Advocacy Approach

This is a highly unusual set of materials both with respect to its content and how it was produced. In early 2010, Professor Colker began approaching clinicians who were teaching students how to be advocates for children in the special education area to see if they might be interested in developing a set of teaching materials. The response was overwhelming. Dozens of people indicated an interest in using such materials in the classroom and nine professors indicated an interest in helping to write such material. This material is a result of that collaboration. Julie Waterstone joined Ruth Colker as an editor on the overall manuscript and eight other individuals joined them as authors of discrete chapters.

Ruth Colker authored the first chapter in which she provides a brief historical overview of the development of special education law in the United States. The Appendix contains the current statute and regulations as well as thirteen of the most important cases in the field. Some of these cases provide additional historical information about the roots of special education law in the United States.

Chapter Two provides an overview of how to initiate a special education case. Yael Zakai Cannon, Practitioner-in-Residence at the Washington College of Law at American University and Laura N. Rinaldi, Clinical Instructor, Juvenile and Special Education Law Clinic, University of the District of Columbia David A. Clarke School of Law, wrote that chapter together. This chapter reflects their work at the Children's Law Center before working at special education clinics at their respective law schools.

Chapter Three discusses the "child find" and referral obligations under the Individuals with Disabilities Education Act (IDEA). It was written by Esther Canty-Barnes who is a Clinical Professor of Law and Director of the Special Education Clinic at Rutgers-Newark School of Law. She represents indigent parents and caregivers of children with disabilities in need of educational services, and teaches in this area, and has done specialized work on behalf of children in foster care.

Chapter Four discusses the definitions of disability used in the IDEA and related statutes as well as how the assessment instruments are used to classify children as disabled. Professor Colker authored this chapter drawing on her empirical work in disabilities studies as well as experience in working with parents of children with disabilities to help their children be found eligible for services under the IDEA or other federal statutes.

Chapter Five discusses the process of developing an "Individualized Educational Plan." Jane R. Wettach, Clinical Professor of Law, Duke Law School, and Brenda Berlin, a Senior Lecturing Fellow and Supervising Attorney in the Children's Law Clinic, Duke Law School, co-authored this chapter. Professor Wettach is the first director of the Law School's Children's Law Clinic and teaches Education Law. She has been working in the special education area since 1994 and brings her vast knowledge to this chapter. Before coming to Duke in 2001, Professor Berlin was Director of the Pro Bono Program and a Staff Attorney at the Legal Aid Society of the District of Columbia where she represented low-income individuals in the areas of family law, landlord and tenant law and public benefits.

Chapter Six discusses intervention for young children under Individualized Family Services Plans. This chapter was written by Jennifer N. Rosen Valverde. Professor Valverde is a Clinical Professor of Law at Rutgers-Newark School of Law. Her work with young children reflects her M.S.W. and law degree. She currently supervises law and social work students in the representation of indigent parents of children with disabilities in early intervention and special education matters.

Preface: An Advocacy Approach

Chapter Seven discusses school discipline issues for children with disabilities. It was co-authored by Professors Waterstone and Wettach. Professor Waterstone is the first director of the Children's Rights Clinic at Southwestern Law School where she focuses her work on special education and school discipline. This chapter reflects their collective experience representing children with disabilities who also have discipline issues.

Chapter Eight discusses the foster care and child welfare systems as they relate to special education. Professor Valverde worked with her colleague Randi Mandelbaum to author this chapter. Professor Mandelbaum is a Clinical Professor of Law and Director of the Child Advocacy Clinic at Rutgers-Newark School of Law where she specializes in the needs of low-income children and their families.

Chapter Nine discusses dispute resolution under the IDEA. This chapter was written by Professor Canty-Barnes. Chapter Ten was written by Professor Cannon and discusses the remedies available under the law of special education.

Chapter Eleven, authored by Joseph B. Tulman, focuses on delinquency, the criminal justice system and special education issues. Joseph Tulman is Professor of Law, University of the District of Columbia David A. Clarke School of Law, and Director of the Took Crowell Institute for At-Risk Youth. Professor Tulman directs the law school's Juvenile and Special Education Law Clinic. He has been widely recognized for his work on behalf of juveniles and brings that experience to his chapter.

In this book, we have collaborated to try to provide students and lawyers with the basic tools they need to be effective advocates in educational cases involving children with disabilities. Each of us has done some practical work in this field and has been disappointed with the materials available for teaching students how to be a child's advocate in this field. This book does not seek to offer a balanced treatment of how to represent school districts. It is designed to enhance the knowledge and skills of special education advocates who work on behalf of children.

Our perspective in developing these materials is that statutory and regulatory material is generally more useful than case law. Hearing officers usually cite few judicial decisions in their opinions and case law discussions are rare at meetings with school district personnel. The everyday tools of special education advocates are statutes, regulations and general material from educational psychology. Hence, we have collected a set of cases at the end of this book but the primary focus is on statutory and regulatory material, as well as practical examples.

This is not a "hide-the-ball" set of materials. By using examples from real cases, we hope to illuminate the major principles that are important to successful advocacy on behalf of children with special needs. We hope you find these materials helpful as well as accurate. We welcome any feedback as we strive to improve these materials over the years.

Acknowledgements

This project could not have been accomplished without the generous contributions of many individuals. The Executive Acquisitions Manager at LexisNexis, Leslie R. Levin, had the confidence in us to support our work as the sole textbook dedicated to Special Education Advocacy. Keith D. Moore, Editor of the Academic Publishing Team at LexisNexis, was a tremendously helpful editor at all stages of this project. We thank you for your support.

Throughout this project, many members of the staffs at the Ohio State University Moritz College of Law and the Southwestern Law School provided outstanding editorial and technical assistance. In Columbus, Ohio, Jenny Pursell, a Faculty Assistant, provided extensive technical assistance to Ruth Colker. Kathleen Patterson and Joseph Brown, Moritz law students, also provided important legal research. In Los Angeles, California, Jahmy Graham, Legal Clinic Assistant, also provided extensive technical assistance to Julie Waterstone. Jenny Rodriguez-Fee read countless drafts, provided invaluable feedback, and drafted the sample due process complaint. Melany Avanessians provided extensive help in organizing, cite checking, and proof reading the materials.

We also would like to thank the following faculty members who were generous enough to write chapters of this book while juggling a heavy client load in their own clinics: Brenda Berlin, Yael Zakai Cannon, Esther Canty-Barnes, Randi Mandelbaum, Laura N. Rinaldi, Joseph B. Tulman, Jennifer N. Rosen Valverde, and Jane R. Wettach.

The views herein, of course, reflect only those of the authors and contributors and not any university or law school.

Ruth Colker
Columbus, Ohio

Julie Waterstone
Los Angeles, California

November 2010

SUMMARY OF CONTENTS

Table of Contents

Preface

Table of Contents

Table of Contents

Table of Contents

Table of Contents

Table of Contents

Table of Contents

Chapter 1

A BRIEF OVERVIEW[1]

Historically, many children with disabilities received no education at all, and such results were legally sanctioned. As early as 1893, the Massachusetts Supreme Court affirmed the exclusion of a child who is "weak in mind" from the public schools. *See Watson v. City of Cambridge*, 32 N.E. 864, 864 (Mass. 1893). A Wisconsin case from 1919 was typical of the views in the early twentieth century justifying exclusion. The school district justified the exclusion of a child from the public schools merely because his paralysis was unsightly to others: "his physical condition and ailment produces a depressing and nauseating effect upon the teachers and school children." *State ex rel. Beattie v. Board of Education*, 172 N.W. 153, 153 (Wis. 1919).

When they were educated, it was typically in segregated classrooms or facilities in which little actual education took place. The number of children enrolled in segregated institutions rose from 40,000 in 1958 to 127,000 in 1966. In addition, more than 439,000 children were educated in special settings by 1948; those numbers increased by 47 percent between 1948 and 1953. *See generally* Robert L. Osgood, The History of Inclusion in the United States (2005). Investigations during the 1960s revealed that many of these institutions were deplorable and offered little or no education to children. "The wide range of ages and severity of educational functions of each became clouded by the institutions' multiple roles as school, hospital, penal institution, and warehouse." *Id.* at 155.

Advocates began to attack these practices of exclusion and substandard education through the courts and the legislature. In 1965, Congress provided some money to educate children whose families were below the poverty line as well as some children with disabilities through the Elementary and Secondary Education Act of 1965, Pub. L. 89-10, 79 Stat. 27 (1965). Disability education funding was part of what is usually termed "Title I" funds. This statute did not mandate universal access to education but did provide some funds for state-operated programs for students with disabilities. In 1970, Congress adopted the first statute to support students with disabilities in the form of the Education of the Handicapped Act, Pub. L. 91-230, 84 Stat. 175 (1970). In addition to expanding the state grant program, it also provided money for some pilot programs.

Meanwhile, some legal progress took place in attacking the way that the "mental retardation" label was used to maintain de facto racial segregation and provide inferior educational services. *See Hobson v. Hansen*, 269 F. Supp. 401, 443-449 (D.D.C. 1967). Most of the litigation, however, involved the issue of the total exclusion of children with disabilities from the educational system. Children were unilaterally excluded without a hearing or even notice.

---

[1] This chapter was written by Ruth Colker, Distinguished University Professor and Heck-Faust Memorial Chair in Constitutional Law at the Michael E. Moritz College of Law, The Ohio State University.

For example, the parents of David Tupi, a child with cognitive impairments, only learned that David was excluded from school "when the school bus which regularly brought him to school failed to show up." *Pennsylvania Association for Retarded Children v. Commonwealth of Pennsylvania*, 343 F. Supp. 279, 293 (E.D. Pa. 1972).

Two pivotal cases were decided in 1972 that set the stage for the framework that would be adopted in 1974 when Congress amended the Education of the Handicapped Act to rename it the Education for All Handicapped Children Act, Public Law 94-142. In *Mills v. Board of Education*, 348 F. Supp. 866 (D.D.C. 1972), and *Pennsylvania Association for Retarded Children v. Commonwealth of Pennsylvania*, 343 F. Supp. 279 (E.D. Pa. 1972), the lower courts approved consent decrees that provided procedural protections for parents or guardians of children with disabilities, mandated the end of exclusionary practices that kept those children from receiving any education, and instituted the expectation that these children would be educated in the regular classroom if that placement was appropriate. (These cases are both included in the Appendix. They are cited extensively by the Supreme Court, reflecting their pivotal role in the development of the law of special education.) Both the procedural guarantees and substantive standards were parallel to what Congress would adopt in 1974. The statute has been amended many times as part of the reauthorization process and was renamed the Individuals with Disabilities Education Act in 1990, Pub. L. 101-476, 104 Stat. 1103 (1990). Congress enacted major amendments in 1997 and 2004.

The basic terminology and framework, however, has remained the same since 1974. In this section, we will provide a brief overview of the IDEA's principle provisions.

The structure of the IDEA is both procedural and substantive. Various "child find" rules are used to identify children as disabled. In general, children are considered "disabled" under the IDEA if they have various diagnoses and need special education and related services. 20 U.S.C. § 1401(3). It is also possible for children who need accommodations, but not special education and related services, to be identified as disabled under the Americans with Disabilities Act or Section 504 of the Rehabilitation Act of 1973. (We will discuss the interplay between these two statutes in Chapter Four).

School districts are mandated to "find" children who are disabled, including homeless children and wards of the state, although parents often initiate the discussion about possible disability status. *See* 20 U.S.C. § 1412(a)(3). This obligation exists irrespective of the severity of the disability; all children are entitled to a free and appropriate public education.

If parents or school districts suspect that a child is disabled, then they can request that a school district conduct a multifactor evaluation of the child to determine whether the child is disabled and, if so, the educational needs of the child. 20 U.S.C. § 1414(a)(1)(C). The evaluation must take place within sixty days of the parent providing consent for the evaluation. A parent may also obtain an independent educational evaluation of the child. 20 U.S.C. § 1415(b). In some cases, the school district even has to pay for that independent evaluation.

One challenging issue is identifying the actual client, because parents or guardians are frequently making decisions on behalf of their children. We will discuss those issues in Chapter Two.

If children are identified when they are under age three, then Part C of the IDEA applies, and they receive an "individual family services plan." If identification occurs after age three, then they receive an "individualized education program." The hallmark of the IDEA is that each child is entitled to a "free appropriate public education" and that program should be identified through an individualized education program. The IEP requirements are extensively defined in 20 U.S.C. § 1414(d). The rule of thumb is that the IEP should permit the child to make "meaningful educational progress." The statute does not define how much progress is "meaningful," but the 2004 Amendments have suggested that mere advancement to the next grade does not necessarily mean that the educational progress was sufficient. *See* 34 C.F.R. § 300.101(c) ("child advancing from grade to grade").

Parents and school districts sometimes disagree about whether a child should be identified as disabled or whether the educational plan is sufficiently individualized and appropriate. When disagreements occur, a broad series of procedural protections can be invoked.

The disagreement process is typically triggered when the parent disagrees with the school district's determination of eligibility or educational program. The school may refuse to classify a child as disabled, insist on what the parent believes to be the wrong disability classification or suggest an educational program that the parent believes is inadequate or inappropriate.

When the parent disagrees, that triggers the school district's responsibility to provide what the statute calls "written prior notice." 20 U.S.C. § 1415(b)(3). That term is a historical anachronism from the days when the statute provided that parents be given notice before a child is removed from his or her educational setting. Today, such notice is required whenever the parent and school district disagree about "the identification, evaluation, or educational placement of the child, or the provision of a free appropriate public education to the child." 20 U.S.C. § 1415(b)(3). A parent is also entitled to examine all of a child's educational records. 20 U.S.C. § 1415(b)(1). Because traditional discovery does not occur at the early stages of the complaint procedures, the document examination and written notice are crucial to the development of the parent's case on behalf of his or her child.

When a parent has a disagreement with the school district, he or she must file a due process complaint with the state setting forth a description of the nature of the problem and the parent's proposed resolution. 20 U.S.C. § 1415(b)(7)(A). The state must provide the parent with an opportunity for mediation at state expense before the due process hearing takes place. If the school district has not already sent the parent its "prior written notice" then it must send such notice within ten days of receiving the parent's complaint. 20 U.S.C. § 1415(c)(2)(B). If mediation is unsuccessful, then a due process hearing is supposed to occur within 30 days of the receipt of the complaint. 20 U.S.C. § 1415(f)(1)(B)(ii). Although mediation is not supposed to "deny or delay a parent's right to a due process hearing," 20 U.S.C. § 1415(e)(2)(A)(ii), it is logistically difficult to schedule a due process hearing within 30 days if a mediation is also supposed to take place before the hearing. The purpose of the 30 day rule is to facilitate quick relief for children with disabilities. The hearing officer must render a decision within 45 days after the hearing is held. 34 C.F.R. § 300.515(a). As we will discuss, this 75 day timetable is rarely followed.

The IDEA is designed to make it possible for parents to participate in due process hearings without assistance of counsel and with little expense. In most areas of the law, an advocate must be a lawyer because advocacy is considered to be the practice of law. The IDEA provides that parents can be "accompanied and advised . . . by individuals with special knowledge or training with respect to the problems of children with disabilities." 20 U.S.C. § 1415(h)(1). Further, parents are entitled to a transcript of the hearing at no cost. 20 U.S.C. § 1415(h)(4). If parents do retain an attorney, and are successful, they can recover the cost of their attorney fees from the school district by filing a claim in federal court. 20 U.S.C. § 1415(i)(3)(B). The Supreme Court has ruled that parents are not entitled to recover the costs of expert witnesses.

Arlington Cent. School District v. Murphy, 548 U.S. 291 (2006). In practice, parents rarely prevail if they do not obtain legal counsel. The Supreme Court's determination in 2005, that parents have the burden of proof in IDEA cases, has made it even more difficult for parents to prevail without assistance of counsel. *See Schaffer v. Weast*, 546 U.S. 49, 62 (2005). (Some states, though, do allocate the burden of proof on the school district, so lawyers need to be familiar with state law on this issue.)

Aside from eligibility determinations and educational program disputes, parents and school districts sometimes have disputes over discipline issues. Removal of a child from school for more than ten days constitutes a "change in placement" that triggers various procedural protections. Even children who are excluded from school, if eligible, are entitled to special education and related services.

Hearing officers can render decisions on procedural or substantive grounds. If they rule for the child on procedural grounds, they must conclude that the procedural error impeded the child's right to a free and appropriate public education, significantly impeded the parent's participation in the process or caused a deprivation of educational benefits. 20 U.S.C. § 1415(f)(3)(E)(ii). In other words, there must be significant harm from the procedural error. Parents are unlikely to be able to recover for what might be considered minor procedural errors on the part of the school district.

With respect to the due process hearing, some states have a one-tier system and others have a two-tier system. After the state administrative process is completed, a party can appeal the decision to state or federal court. Federal district courts may hear such cases without regard to the amount in controversy and have authority to award attorney fees.

If parents pursue their rights under the Americans with Disabilities Act or Section 504 of the Rehabilitation Act, they may be able to avoid this often cumbersome state administrative process, although some courts have ruled that parents must exhaust their rights under the IDEA before pursuing their rights under Section 504 or the ADA.

In sum, the IDEA has substantial procedural and substantive safeguards and a fairly complicated process that parents must navigate to protect the rights of their children. We will now turn to a more detailed discussion of those rights.

Chapter 2

INITIATING A SPECIAL EDUCATION CASE[1]

A mother and her teenage son meet with an attorney to discuss possible legal representation in connection with the son's special education needs. If the attorney accepts the case, who will she represent? Is her client the parent, the child, or both? Are the attorney's views of what may be in the child's best interests relevant, or is the attorney limited to zealously representing the expressed interests of his or her client or clients? What happens if someone other than the biological parent is caring for the child? Figuring out who the client is may be obvious in many other areas of law, but can get murky in special education matters. In cases in which a child's interests are at stake, such as a special education matter, there can be significant ambiguity in determining which individual is serving in the client role. Nancy J. Moore, *Conflicts of Interests in the Representation of Children*, 64 Fordham L. Rev. 1819, 1827 (1995-1996).

Different Models of Representation

- Parent/Caregiver

- Joint Representation

- Child

- Best Interests of Child

I. WHO IS THE CLIENT? MODELS OF REPRESENTATION IN SPECIAL EDUCATION MATTERS

The Individuals with Disabilities Education Act (IDEA) confers rights on both the parent and the child, amplifying the ambiguity. Although the IDEA provides that the *child* has a right to a free and appropriate public education, one of the statute's stated purposes is "to ensure that the rights of children with disabilities *and parents of such children* are protected." 20 U.S.C. §§ 1400(d)(1)(A), (B) (emphasis added). In interpreting this statement, the Supreme Court explained that "The word 'rights' in the quoted language refers to the rights of parents

---

[1] This chapter was written by Yael Zakai Cannon, Practitioner in Residence, Disability Rights Law Clinic, Washington College of Law at American University, and Laura N. Rinaldi, Clinical Instructor, Juvenile and Special Education Law Clinic, University of the District of Columbia David A. Clarke School of Law. The authors would like to thank Robert Dinerstein and Joseph Tulman for their invaluable guidance and support, and Bridget Koza for her thorough assistance with research in connection with this chapter.

as well as the rights of the child; otherwise the grammatical structure would make no sense." *Winkelman v. Parma City Sch. Dist.*, 550 U.S. 516, 528 (2007). Because the statute references the rights of both the parents and the child, it may be unclear to attorneys who their client is or should be in a special education matter.

CASE STUDY

Meet Jack

Jack is twelve years old and is repeating the fifth grade. Both of Jack's parents passed away in a car accident when he was six, and he has lived with his grandmother since that time. Jack is doing poorly in school and struggles with reading and writing. His teachers say he reads on a first grade level. Jack rarely participates in class activities and never completes his homework. He has no friends at school and often gets into fights with his classmates. Jack's teachers call his grandmother at least two times a week requesting that she pick him up early from school because "he is causing too many problems in the classroom." Jack's pediatrician diagnosed him with Attention Deficit Hyperactivity Disorder (ADHD) when Jack was seven years old. He was on medication for about four months, but his grandmother took him off the medication because it made him act "like a zombie." Jack also attends grief counseling regularly with a therapist who was recommended by his pediatrician. Jack's grandmother has repeatedly asked his teachers for help so that he will not fall further behind. Periodically, Jack's teacher will spend some extra time after school helping Jack with his reading. At a recent doctor's appointment, Jack's pediatrician advised his grandmother that he should be receiving special education services.

There are various models of representation that attorneys use in special education cases. Many attorneys represent the parent or a qualified caregiver exclusively, while other attorneys represent the parent and child together. Some attorneys represent solely the child with an expressed interest model, while still other attorneys advocate for the best interests of the child. For children who are involved in either the neglect or delinquency systems, the court may appoint an attorney to handle the related special education matter. For these attorneys, there may be limitations imposed by a statute other than the IDEA, non-special education regulations, court rules, or judicial instruction as to who is the client.

A.   Parent as Client

Many attorneys choose to represent parents — or other caregivers where appropriate — exclusively in special education matters, without formally including the child as a client. There are a variety of reasons why an attorney might choose this model of representation. Generally, the Supreme Court has underscored the long-held principle of the "liberty of parents and guardians to direct the upbringing and education of children under their control." *Pierce v. Society of Sisters*, 268 U.S. 510, 534-535 (1925). The Court has also emphasized that "it is cardinal with us that the custody, care and nurture of the child reside first in the parent, whose primary function and freedom include preparation for obligations the state can neither supply nor hinder." *Prince v. Commonwealth of Massachusetts*, 321 U.S. 158, 166 (1944). Those who argue that the parent is the client might contend that parents, or caregivers in a parental role, are almost always the best situated to determine their children's interests. Christine Gottlieb, *Children's Attorneys' Obligation to Turn to Parents to Assess Best Interests*, 6 Nev. L.J. 1263, 1264 (2005-2006). Parents not only have the constitutional right, but are uniquely qualified, to make decisions on behalf of their minor child, especially where the child is involved in litigation. Moreover, protection of parental rights in decision-making is in the best interests of society because parents are simply the best decision-makers for their children. Jonathan Hafen, *Children's Rights and Legal Representation — The Proper Roles of Children, Parents, and Attorneys*, 7 Notre Dame J.L. Ethics & Pub. Pol'y 423, 427, 446 (1993). Parents typically know their children's needs, desires, strengths, weaknesses, personality and history in nuanced ways that others cannot come close to approaching. Gottlieb, *supra*, at 1264. Furthermore, "the 'liberty' specially protected by the Due Process Clause includes the right . . . to direct the education and upbringing of one's children . . . . [T]he Due Process Clause of the Fourteenth Amendment protects the fundamental right of parents to make decisions concerning the care, custody, and control of their children." *Troxel v. Granville*, 530 U.S. 57, 66 (2000). Advocates of parent-driven models of legal representation argue that parents have a legally protected right to make decisions for their children, even when an attorney may not believe that the parents are making the decisions that would be best for the child. Gottlieb, *supra*, at 1265.

A parent is in a unique position both to advocate on behalf of his or her child and to serve as an expert on the child and the child's needs, which may be especially true where the child has a disability and the parent understands the child's needs most intimately. "Children are extremely dependent on their parents for both care and support. This is even more true for disabled students. In fact, parents of disabled children literally are their lifelines. . . . These parents undoubtedly are experts in the everyday lives of children, but are they legal experts as well?" Justin M. Bathon, *Defining "Parties Aggrieved" Under the Individuals with Disabilities Education Act: Should Parents be Allowed to Represent their Disabled Child Without an Attorney?*, 29 S. Ill. U. L.J. 507, 507 (2004-2005). A parent's involvement in the entire process can also significantly influence the type and level of educational services that the student receives. Deborah Rebore & Perry Zirkel, *Transfer of Rights Under the Individuals with Disabilities Act: Adulthood with Ability or Disability*, 2000 B.Y.U. Educ. & L.J. 33, 34.

The IDEA specifically envisions the parent as the enforcer of special education rights and confers upon the parent a wide variety of procedural rights to ensure that a free and appropriate public education (FAPE) is being provided to his or her child. The IDEA explicitly provides parents with many procedural rights, including the opportunities to request an initial evaluation, provide consent for evaluations and for special education and related services, participate in decision-making about the child's educational planning and placement, examine the child's records, file a complaint for a due process hearing, and pursue various remedies should the child be denied a FAPE. 20 U.S.C. §§ 1414(a)(1)(B); 1414(a)(1)(D); 1414(e); 1415(b). Indeed, "Congress intended each parent to contribute to the educational planning as an expert on her child and to advocate for the child's needs. . . . In the end, although IDEA includes the above-described institutional enforcement mechanisms, the primary role of enforcement falls as a practical matter on parents." Patricia A. Massey &

Stephen A. Rosenbaum, *Disability Matters: Toward a Law School Clinical Model for Serving Youth with Special Education Needs*, 11 Clinical L. Rev. 271, 277 (2004-2005). Congress has recognized that the educational services received by children with disabilities depend, at least in part, on a parent's ability to advocate on their behalf, up to and including filing legal action to challenge the denied educational services. Julie F. Mead & Mark A. Paige, *Parents as Advocates: Examining the History and Evolution of Parents' Rights to Advocate for Children with Disabilities under the IDEA*, 34 J. Legis. 123, 125 (2008). There is no doubt that parents play a strong and central role under the IDEA.

The Supreme Court has further affirmed both the procedural and substantive rights of parents in the special education context, emphasizing "it is not a novel proposition to say that parents have a recognized legal interest in the education and upbringing of their child." *Winkelman*, 550 U.S. at 529. In *Winkelman*, the Supreme Court held that the IDEA provides parents with not only procedural rights, but independent, enforceable, substantive rights, which they are empowered by the IDEA to enforce on their own behalf as "real parties in interest." *Id.* at 526-33. The Court reasoned that it is beyond dispute that the relationship between a parent and child is sufficient to support a legally cognizable interest in the education of one's child. *Id.* at 535. In developing the IDEA, Congress found that "the education of children with disabilities can be made more effective by . . . strengthening the role and responsibility of parents and ensuring that families have meaningful opportunities to participate in the education of their children." *Id.* Although minor children are prohibited by the Federal Rules of Civil Procedure from bringing a civil action in federal court on their own without a representative, a parent clearly has a right to file a civil action on behalf of, or as next friend of, his or her child, or, post-*Winkelman*, on his or her own behalf. *Id.*; Fed. R. Civ. P. 17(c). Note that while the Court's decision in *Winkelman* granted parents the right to bring a special education action *pro se* on their own behalf as real parties in interest, the Court left open the question of whether parents can bring an action *pro se* on behalf of their child. *Winkelman*, 550 U.S. at 535. Subsequent lower court decisions have found that parents may not bring an action *pro se* on behalf of their child. *See* Patricia C. Hagdorn, *Winkleman v. Parma City School District: A Major Victory for Parents or More Ambiguity?*, 39 Seton Hall L. Rev. 981, 1004-1010 (2009). Moreover, following *Winkelman*, it remains unclear whether a parent and child each are able to separately litigate substantive claims under the IDEA. Logan Steiner, *Playing Lawyers: The Implications of Endowing Parents with Substantive Rights Under the IDEA in Winkleman v. Parma City School District*, 31 Harv. J.L. & Pub. Pol'y 1169, 1180 (2008). Although parents have "independent" rights, the substantive rights of parents cannot be completely divorced from those of their children because "parents have no rights under the IDEA if they do not have a disabled child seeking an education." *Collinsgru v. Palmyra Bd. of Educ.*, 161 F.3d 225, 236 (3d Cir. 1998).

A special education attorney will need to provide clarity from the outset as to the role of the parent, and the role of the child, if any, in the attorney-client relationship. When a parent retains a lawyer regarding a matter in which a child's interests are involved, the parent will often select the lawyer, retain the lawyer, and fully expect to direct the representation. Pursuant to this model, if a special education attorney represents the parent alone and the attorney and parent are clear that the parent alone will direct the representation, then there is no need for an analysis of conflicts of interest, regardless of any disagreements or other conflicts of interests between parent and child, because the parent's wishes will control. Moore, *supra*, at 1824. Conflicts of interest with the child may present challenges more broadly, but should generally not affect the representation of the parent or alter the attorney-client relationship where the parent is the client and directs the representation, as the attorney has an ethical responsibility to advocate zealously to pursue the parent's expressed wishes and his or her wishes alone. *Model Rules of Prof'l Conduct* Preamble § 2 (2009) ("As advocate, a lawyer zealously asserts the client's position."). Understanding the principles behind a parent-driven model of representation is important even if an attorney selects an alternate model of representation, because other individuals involved in addressing the child's special education needs, such as school staff or an administrative due process hearing officer, may be expecting the attorney to be taking direction from the parent as a result of these aforementioned principles. A special education attorney should be prepared to explain and clarify who is the client should there be confusion within the relationship or with other individuals as to whom the attorney represents.

1.   Who Is a "Parent"?

When an attorney chooses a model of representation that includes a parent or other caregiver, the attorney must ensure that the individual falls under the IDEA definition of a parent. A parent is defined by the IDEA as a natural, adoptive, or foster parent (unless a foster parent is prohibited by state law from serving as a parent); a guardian (although not the state if a child is a ward of the state); an individual acting in the place of a natural or adoptive parent, including a grandparent, stepparent, or other relative, with whom the child lives; an individual who is legally responsible for the child's welfare; or an individual assigned to be a surrogate parent under the IDEA. 20 U.S.C. § 1401(23); 34 C.F.R. § 300.30(a). When more than one person is qualified as the parent, the biological or adoptive parent is presumed to be the "parent" for purposes of the IDEA. 34 C.F.R. § 300.30(b)(1). However, that person may not be the parent for IDEA purposes if he or she does not have legal authority to make educational decisions for the child or a judicial decree or order identifies another specific person, who otherwise qualifies under the IDEA definition as a "parent," to act as the parent or educational decision-maker. 34 C.F.R. § 300.30(b)(2). Because the IDEA defines "parent" broadly to include a variety of different caregivers, many individuals in a care-giving role will be able to qualify as a "parent" under the IDEA and serve as the client to direct representation in a special education matter.

In certain situations, the IDEA provides for the appointment of a surrogate parent. Specifically, the state or local educational agency must have procedures in place for the assignment of an individual to act as a surrogate parent whenever the parents of a child are not known, the local or state agency cannot, after reasonable efforts, locate the parents, or the child is the ward of a state. 20 U.S.C. § 1415(b)(2)(A). The agency must have an established method for determining whether a child needs a surrogate parent and for assigning the surrogate. 34 C.F.R. § 300.519(b). The surrogate may not have any personal or professional interest that conflicts with the interest of the child, must have knowledge and skills that can ensure adequate representation of the child, and cannot be an employee of any agency involved in the education or care of the child, although he or she can be paid by the state to serve in that role. 20 U.S.C. § 1415(b)(2)(A); 34 C.F.R. § 300.519(d)-(e).

Alternatively, if the child is a ward of the State, the surrogate can be appointed by the judge overseeing the child's care, as long as the surrogate meets the requirements of the IDEA. 20 U.S.C. § 1415(b)(2)(A)(i); 34 C.F.R. § 300.519(c). The local educational agency must appoint a surrogate for an unaccompanied homeless youth, and appropriate staff of emergency shelters, independent living programs, and street outreach programs can be appointed as temporary surrogate parents, even though they may work for an agency involved in the care of the child, until a surrogate parent can be appointed who meets all of the requirements of the statute and regulations. 20 U.S.C. § 1415(b)(2)(A)(ii); 34 C.F.R. § 300.519(f). The State is responsible for ensuring that a surrogate is appointed within thirty days after a determination by a state or local educational agency that the child needs a surrogate. 20 U.S.C. § 1415(b)(2)(B); 34 C.F.R. § 300.519(h). Surrogate parents can represent the child in all matters relating to the identification, evaluation, and educational placement of the child and in all matters relating to the provision of a free appropriate public education to the student. 34 C.F.R. § 300.519(g).

Some states have separate provisions allowing for the appointment of a foster parent as the educational decision-maker. For example, New Hampshire provides that where the parental rights of the biological parents have been terminated by a court of law or by death, a foster parent in a long-term parental relationship with a child can be appointed, and such appointment would supersede that of a surrogate parent. N.H. Rev. Stat. Ann. § 186-C:14-a.

An attorney interested in providing special education representation in connection with a child for whom the parents are unknown or cannot be located, a child who is a ward of the state, or a child who is unaccompanied and homeless, should research state laws, regulations and court rules to be sure that he or she understands who may be appointed to serve as a surrogate parent for the child. The attorney should work with the appropriate entity — whether it is the state or local educational agency, a child welfare agency, or a court — to ensure that a qualified individual is appointed as a surrogate if the child requires one and no individual has yet been identified. If an individual who seeks the attorney's representation is serving in the role of a surrogate, but has not been officially appointed, the attorney should research and investigate to determine whether that individual requires any sort of formal appointment as a surrogate in order to proceed as a decision-maker. The person may not require formal appointment as a surrogate if he or she meets the definition of a parent under the IDEA, as noted above. 20 U.S.C. § 1401(23). The fact that the IDEA provides for the appointment of a surrogate where the "parent" is not identifiable underscores the importance of parental decision-making under the statute, and may provide further evidence that a parent or person in a parental or surrogate role is the natural person to serve as the attorney's client in a special education case.

a.   Involving the Student Even When He or She is Not the Client

A model of representation in which the parent, as defined by the IDEA, is the sole client, without any involvement from the student in the attorney-client relationship, is very common. However, even if this model is chosen, the student is still the subject of the representation and literally at the heart of the matter. Although the parent's wishes would control under this model of representation, it may be extremely helpful for the attorney to spend time with the student and find ways to involve the child in the representation. The attorney should try to understand the student's frustrations, needs, wishes, strengths and interests, and seek as much information as possible from the student to assist in understanding the legal violations and developing an appropriate educational program for the student. Especially if the student is an adolescent and able to communicate, she may participate in IEP meetings or otherwise voice her opinions as to her educational needs. *See, e.g.*, 20 U.S.C. § 1414(d)(1)(B)(vii) (providing that a student is a member of the IEP team whenever appropriate). If the student's views differ from the parent's views, it will be helpful for the attorney to learn about any such conflicts and prepare to handle them appropriately. Under a model of representation in which the parent alone is the client, an attorney may choose, with the parent-client's agreement, to communicate and spend time with the student, and involve the student in the representation in informal ways, so long as there is no confusion as to the fact that the parent is the ultimate decision-maker in regards to the representation.

B.   Parent and Student as Joint Clients

An attorney could choose to jointly represent both the parent and student. Joint representation can have advantages in providing both the parent and student with a voice in the special education process, especially given that both the parent and student have recognized rights and a strong stake in the special education process. An attorney who represents both the parent and student can ensure that the rights of both individuals are protected, without disenfranchising one or the other. A joint model of representation can help involve both the parent and student in playing a role in shaping the student's education, which can also serve to empower each of them to become more well-informed, effective self-advocates in the long-term even after the representation has concluded. Additionally, both the parent and student have important information, opinions, and views that can assist the attorney in providing adequate and effective representation if both parent and student serve as clients. However, an attorney should think through any risks or challenges inherent in such an arrangement before entering into joint representation.

Conflict Between Jack and His Grandmother

Assume you are the attorney for both Jack and his grandmother for purposes of getting Jack appropriate special education services. Jack's grandmother believes that Jack needs a special education placement in a residential school, and Jack adamantly wants to remain in the community and attend a local special education day school. Jack's grandmother also thinks that he needs psychotherapy services as part of his IEP, but Jack refuses to attend his counseling sessions with the psychotherapist and does not want this service to be a part of his IEP.

- How will you handle this conflict? What do you tell Jack? What do you tell Jack's grandmother? Which position do you advocate?

If a lawyer is considering representing both parent and student, a standard conflicts of interests analysis is necessary in deciding whether to enter into joint representation in the first place and if joint representation is pursued, what to do if the clients disagree during the course of representation. Moore, *supra*, at 1824. Under a standard conflicts analysis, the ethical propriety of joint representation of a parent and student is determined by identification of any potentially impermissible conflicts, deciding whether any such conflicts are waivable, and where they are waivable, obtaining voluntary consent after disclosure. *Id.* at 1831. The requirement that a client have the "legal capacity to give consent" in such situations may be problematic for a young child or a child who is severely disabled and unable to express his or her wishes. *Id.* at 1835. Where the potential for conflict seems remote, a parent is not prevented from consenting to joint representation on behalf of both herself or himself and the child. *Id.* at 1839. If the interests of both clients appear to be compatible and there is no reason to believe that the parent is not acting in the student's best interests, it may seem both unwarranted and overly intrusive to require separate legal representation. *Id.* at 1839. Nonetheless, the attorney must think through the risks and potential disadvantages of joint representation and, where selecting such a model, stay alert to changing circumstances, bring any developing conflicts to the attention of the clients, and be prepared to withdraw in the event that the positions of the clients become fundamentally antagonistic. *Id.* at 1839-1840.

Ethical conflicts of interest may arise, particularly where the student is a teenager or old enough to voice views that may diverge from the parent's views. The Model Rules of Professional Conduct provide that a lawyer should not represent a client if the representation involves a concurrent conflict of interest, which happens if the representation of one client will be directly adverse to another client or there is a significant risk that the representation of a client will be materially limited by the lawyer's responsibilities to another client. *Model Rules of Prof'l Conduct* R. 1.7(a) (2009). The lawyer can proceed with the representation of a client, despite a concurrent conflict of interest, if the lawyer reasonably believes that he or she will be able to provide competent and diligent representation to each affected client, the representation is not prohibited by law, the representation does not involve the assertion of a claim by one client against another represented by the lawyer in the same proceeding before a tribunal, and each affected client gives written informed consent. *Model Rules of Prof'l Conduct* R. 1.7(b) (2009).

The comments to Model Rule 1.7 provide more guidance that might be useful to an attorney contemplating common, multiple representation of both parent and student. In determining whether to jointly represent both the parties, the lawyer should keep in mind the potential adverse effects on either the parent or student or both if the representation fails. *Model Rules of Prof'l Conduct* R 1.7 cmt. 29 (2009). The lawyer may be forced to withdraw if the common representation is not effective. *Id.* Some attorneys may want to try to mediate between a parent and student when conflicts arise and try to maintain the common representation. The lawyer may be able to mediate such conflicts effectively, but a lawyer cannot undertake common representation when contentious negotiations between the clients are imminent or contemplated. *Id.* It may also be difficult for the lawyer to remain impartial when there are conflicts. When he or she agrees with one client more than the other and when it is unlikely that impartiality can be maintained, representation of multiple clients is improper. *Id.*

If the lawyer believes there is a concurrent conflict of interest, as defined in Model Rule 1.7(a) and discussed above, but chooses to proceed in representation and seek informed consent from both the parent and student to continue the multiple representation, the attorney needs to ensure that both parties are aware of the implications of the common representation, including possible effects on loyalty, confidentiality and the attorney-client privilege, and the advantages and risks involved. *Model Rules of Prof'l Conduct* R. 1.7 cmt. 18 (2009).

In some cases, the alternative to common representation can be that each party may have to obtain separate representation with the possibility of incurring additional costs. These costs, along with the benefits of securing separate representation, are factors that may be considered by the affected client in determining whether common representation is in the client's interests. *Model Rules of Prof'l Conduct* R. 1.7 cmt. 19 (2009). In special education cases, it may not be possible for both parent and student to secure separate representation due to the limited availability of attorneys who handle special education matters and because the student may not be able to bring a due process complaint or civil action on his or her own pursuant to the IDEA and/or state law. Although it is unclear whether a minor child could bring a due process complaint under the IDEA, a minor child is clearly prohibited by the Federal Rules of Civil Procedure from bringing his or her own civil action in federal court, as a minor child may only bring a complaint through a representative such as a next friend or guardian *ad litem*. Fed. R. Civ. P. 17(c) (detailing who may sue or defend on behalf of a minor). Therefore, to allow the attorney to pursue a due process complaint or civil action if necessary, common representation of the parent and student or primary representation of the child, with the parent still playing a limited role as "next friend," may be preferable to sole representation of a student who is a minor child.

Between commonly represented clients, the prevailing rule is that the attorney-client privilege does not attach. *Model Rules of Prof'l Conduct* R. 1.7 cmt. 30 (2009). Therefore, communications between the attorney and the parent are not confidential as to the student, and communications between the attorney and the student can similarly be shared with the parent. The parent and student will need to clearly understand this alteration to the traditional attorney-client privilege prior to agreeing to representation. Because the lawyer has an equal duty of loyalty to each client and each client has the right to be informed of anything bearing on the representation and use of that information to the client's benefit, common representation is likely to be problematic if one client asks the lawyer not to disclose to the other client information relevant to the representation. *Model Rules of Prof'l Conduct* R. 1.7 cmt. 31 (2009). As a result, if the student discloses information relevant to the representation, and asks the lawyer not to share this information with the parent, the lawyer may need to end the common representation. The same would be true if the parent discloses information relevant to the representation and requests that the lawyer not share the information with the student.

When establishing or adjusting a relationship between clients, any limitations on the scope of the representation should be fully explained to both the clients at the outset. *Model Rules of Prof'l Conduct* R. 1.7 cmt. 32 (2009). Special care should be taken to ensure that the student understands the model of representation being utilized and any limitations on the traditional attorney-client relationship that may flow from the model being used. An attorney should also check the rules of professional responsibility in his or her own state to see if those rules provide additional guidance for common representation of both parent and student. The parent and student might be in continued accord throughout the duration of the representation and open to the full sharing of information between each other, making joint, common representation more likely to succeed. However, with familial relationships, attorneys should be aware that conflicts do arise and sometimes a parent has information he does not want to share with his student or the student has information she does not want to share with her parent. In such instances, joint, common representation of parent and student in a special education case can become problematic. Close consideration should be given to the attorney's ethical responsibilities before proceeding with a model of representation in which the attorney represents both the parent and student. If common representation is not preferable or possible for whatever reason, a parent and student otherwise seeking common representation may choose to have one or the other serve as the client.

C. Student as Client

In a special education matter, the student is the subject of the case. But should the student serve as the client in a special education case? As detailed below, in most cases where the student has reached the age of majority, he or she will take over those rights that previously belonged to the parent under the IDEA and the parent will not retain any rights under the IDEA. 20 U.S.C. § 1415(m); 34 C.F.R. § 300.520. Therefore, in most situations in which a student has reached the age of majority and taken over the rights previously belonging to the parent, exclusive representation of the student, without involvement by the parent in the representation, is the clear choice. However, in deciding whether it may be possible to establish an attorney-client relationship with a minor student or an adult student to whom parental rights under the IDEA have not been transferred, the attorney can consider the student's age, maturity level, competency, and whether the child has the capacity to consent to representation and make decisions throughout the course of the case.

Even if an attorney does decide that he can represent the child, it is not clear under the IDEA whether a minor child can make decisions about his education and consent to evaluations or special education services. As described above, the IDEA and applicable regulations appear to provide these decision-making rights — and in fact all of the procedural rights provided for in the statute — to the parent or person serving in a parental role. The notion that the procedural rights under the IDEA belong to the parent is evidenced by the fact that the IDEA explicitly transfers those rights away from the parent and to the student once he reaches the age of majority in that jurisdiction. 20 U.S.C. § 1415(m).

Where filing an administrative due process complaint may be necessary, it is unclear whether a minor student may bring a due process complaint under the IDEA without any involvement from a parent or other guardian or next friend. The IDEA and applicable regulations explicitly entitle parents to file a due process complaint when they are aggrieved. 20 U.S.C. § 1415(b)(6); 34 C.F.R. § 300.507(a)(1). The regulations also reference the parent as the individual who should be provided with information about free and low cost legal services upon filing a complaint, perhaps alluding to the fact that the parent is the complainant in a due process hearing, not the student, and the parent is the party entitled to be accompanied by a legal representative if he or she chooses. 20 U.S.C. § 1415(b)(8); 34 C.F.R. §§ 300.507(a)(1), (b). Not specific to the special education context, many jurisdictions have procedural codes, court rules, or administrative rules delineating that a minor does not have the capacity to sue on her own behalf, a principle based in common law, and that a minor may only sue or be sued through a "representative, such as a general guardian" or "by a next friend or by a guardian *ad litem*." Moore, *supra*, at 1828–29. In most circumstances, minors cannot bring suit themselves, but parents are entitled to bring suit on behalf of their children, as general guardians, next friends, or guardians *ad litem*, depending on the specifics of state law. *Id.* at 1829. If a jurisdiction has specific rules relating to the ability of minors to bring suit without a representative on their own behalf in administrative hearings or local or state court proceedings, these rules should be reviewed and analyzed by the special education attorney in determining whether the child may bring a due process complaint on his own behalf.

If a complaint needs to be filed in federal court, the Federal Rules of Civil Procedure do not allow a minor child to bring a civil action without a representative. Fed. R. Civ. P. 17(c). Although a minor would need a parent or other representative to bring a special education suit in federal court on his or her behalf as next friend or guardian *ad litem*, the attorney may still be able to use a model of representation in which the child directs the representation, especially if the parent or representative consents to such a model. In other civil contexts, where parents bring cases on behalf of their children in this way, it is not necessarily clear who has the authority to make decisions during the course of the litigation. Sometimes general guardians are considered real parties in interest, whereas next friends and guardians *ad litem* are sometimes treated as nominal parties, with the minor being the real party in interest. Moore, *supra*, at 1829. If the latter situation applies, it may be possible for an attorney to represent the child exclusively if he or she is the only real party in interest in a case. However, because parents are considered real parties in interest in a special education matter pursuant to *Winkelman*, the parent may conversely not be treated as a nominal party when filing as next friend of a child. An arrangement in which an attorney represents a child exclusively, but the parent files the civil action as next friend of a child, may present complications, given that both the parent and attorney would be taking on a role as the child's representative in this type of litigation arrangement.

If an attorney represents a minor student exclusively, without including the parent in the attorney-client relationship, the attorney will need to research and reach a conclusion as to his student-client's rights in the special education context. The attorney will need to advise the student about the scope of these rights and the likely limitations on the student's right to make his own educational decisions and bring suit on his own behalf while he is still a minor. Even if the attorney determines that the student does not possess educational decision-making authority or procedural rights in the special education context, the attorney-client relationship could potentially still proceed on the understanding that the attorney will serve the role of articulating the student's wishes and trying to persuade the IEP team members on behalf of the student. If the attorney represents the child exclusively, but the parent is involved in the IEP process and takes action contrary to the child's wishes, it remains unresolved whether students can initiate administrative proceedings against their parents or school boards if their parents failed to adequately represent their interests or ignored their wishes in developing their IEPs. Charles J. Russo, *The Rights of Non-Attorney Parents Under the IDEA: Winkelman v. Parma City School District*, 221 Ed. L. Rep. 1, 15 (2007).

If the attorney does involve the parent in the representation, the student's voice can still be central, such as where a parent is willing to defer to the child to take the lead role in directing the representation, even though the parent is formally part of the attorney-client relationship or serving as a next friend in a due process complaint or civil action. The voice of the child may also be especially important where the attorney is representing an appointed surrogate who knows little about the child or what might be the best decision for him or her.

If the attorney determines that it is in fact possible to represent a minor child exclusively, this model of representation has the strong benefit of providing the child with a real voice in the special education process and a sense of agency and empowerment in making decisions in regards to his or her educational programming. Too often, the voices of children, especially those with disabilities, go unheard in matters affecting their own lives. An attorney who can effectively represent a minor child exclusively can help the child overcome this disempowerment and disenfranchisement, and make sure that the child's interests and core rights to a free and appropriate public education are truly protected.

1.   Expressed Interests or Best Interests?

Where the attorney does choose to represent the student exclusively, what position will the attorney take if the student wishes to pursue a course of action that the attorney believes to be a detriment to the student? Will the attorney pursue the student's expressed interests or the action that the attorney believes to be in the student's best interests? In other areas of law in which a child may be represented by an attorney, there may be confusion as to whether the attorney represents the child's expressed wishes or best interests. Jean Koh Peters, Representing Children in Child Protective Proceedings, 36-45 (3d ed. 2007). Traditionally, a guardian *ad litem* is charged with advocating for the best interests of the child, while counsel for a child, such as counsel appointed in a delinquency matter, will usually be charged with advocating for the child's expressed wishes. *Id.* If the attorney represents the student exclusively as his or her attorney in a special education matter, without guidance from a judge who may have appointed the attorney pursuant to a case in delinquency or dependency court or guidance from relevant court rules or practice standards, the attorney should maintain as normal an attorney-client relationship as possible, even if the child is a minor or has diminished capacity. *Model Rules of Prof'l Conduct* R. 1.14(a) (2009). This obligation means the attorney should pursue the student's expressed interests wherever possible, even if the student's capacity to make adequately considered decisions in connection with the representation is diminished, whether because of minority or disability or both. *Id.*

The American Bar Association Model Rules of Professional Conduct remind lawyers that a client with diminished capacity often has the ability to understand, deliberate upon, and reach conclusions about matters affecting the client's own well-being. *Model Rules of Prof'l Conduct* R. 1.14 cmt. 1 (2009). The Comments to Rule 1.14 specifically note that children as young as five or six, and certainly those of ten or twelve, are regarded as having opinions that are entitled to weight in legal proceedings concerning their custody. *Id.* This guidance can be useful in the special education context as well. When the lawyer reasonably believes that the client has diminished capacity; is at risk of substantial physical, financial or other harm unless action is taken; and cannot adequately act in his or her own interest, the lawyer can take reasonably necessary protective action, including consulting with individuals or entities that have the ability to take action to protect the client and, in appropriate cases, seek the appointment of a guardian *ad litem*, conservator or guardian. *Model Rules of Prof'l Conduct* R. 1.14(b) (2009). In taking any protective action, the lawyer should be guided by the wishes and values of the client to the extent known and the client's best interests and ensure that any intrusion into the client's decision-making autonomy is as minimal as possible, maximizing client capacities and respecting the client's family and social connections. *Model Rules of Prof'l Conduct* R. 1.14 cmt. 5 (2009). This approach may involve the attorney utilizing "substituted judgment," or making a decision on behalf of an incompetent client based on what the client would decide if he or she were competent. Kristin Henning, *Loyalty, Paternalism, and Rights: Client Counseling Theory and the Role of Child's Counsel in Delinquency Cases*, 81 Notre Dame L. Rev. 245, 303 (2005). When an attorney substitutes her own judgment for that of a child, she should do so as thoughtfully as possible, given that such decision-making involves a high degree of speculation, as well as arbitrariness. *Id.* at 305.

If a legal representative has already been appointed for the client, the lawyer should ordinarily look to the representative for decisions on behalf of the client where protective action is required. *Model Rules of Prof'l Conduct* R. 1.14 cmt. 4 (2009). In matters involving a minor, whether the lawyer should look to the parents or natural guardians may depend on the type of proceeding or matter in which the lawyer is representing the minor. *Id.* In a special education matter, depending on the attorney's interpretation of the IDEA, the parent may already be the recognized representative of the student under the statute, meaning the lawyer would look to the parent if protective action is required. Generally, the unique significance of the parent under special education law further complicates the lawyer's assessment of whether he may represent the student independently without involvement of the parent and without regard to the wishes of the parent.

Where the attorney represents a student independently and exclusively, the student client may still choose to have parents, family members, or other individuals participate in discussions with the lawyer. When necessary to assist in the representation, the presence of such persons generally does not affect the applicability of the attorney-client evidentiary privilege. *Model Rules of Prof'l Conduct* R. 1.14 cmt. 3 (2009). Nevertheless, the lawyer must keep the client's interests foremost and must look to the student and not his or her family members, to make decisions on the client's behalf. *Id.* Even where the client is exclusively the student, with the student's permission, the lawyer may improve the effectiveness of his or her representation by communicating with parents or caregivers, who often are the most important individuals in the student's life. Gottlieb, *supra*, at 1273.

Some authors argue that school boards should seek the appointment of a guardian *ad litem* for a special education student whose desires conflict with those of their parents, essentially attempting to sever the interests of the children from those of their parents. Russo, *supra*, at 10. Such a system would potentially ensure that the substantive interests of students are more adequately represented at IEP meetings, although guardians *ad litem* are not necessarily charged with advocating for the expressed desires of a child. Instead, guardians *ad litem* usually pursue the best interests of the child, which are grounded in the guardian *ad litem*'s own views of the child's best interests.

Some attorneys use a model of representation in which the attorney advocates for the best interests of the child, rather than the expressed interests of either the parent or child. For example, the Juvenile Division of the Los Angeles County Superior Court has established protocols providing for the appointment of an education attorney in delinquency and dependency cases "to represent the *best educational interests* of the minor," not those of the Educational Rights Holder, the term used by the court to describe the parent, caregiver, or designated individual who holds the educational decision-making rights for the child. *Rights and Responsibilities of Education Attorney/Advocate and Rights and Responsibilities of Educational Rights Holder Pursuant to WIC § 317(e) or CRC § 5.663 Appointment for Education Advocacy and Acknowledgement of Receipt*, Juvenile Division, Superior Court of Los Angeles County (emphasis added). Within this "best interests" model, the protocols allow the educational attorney to disclose information to the proper authorities if he or she feels that the actions of the Educational Rights Holder are not in the best of interest of the minor. The educational attorney can also seek a court order to remove that individual and have a new Educational Rights Holder appointed. *Id.* Courts in other jurisdictions may similarly provide for appointment of an educational attorney to advocate for the best interests of a child involved in family court proceedings.

2.   Students Who Have Reached the Age of Majority

Under the IDEA, when a student reaches the age of majority, depending on state law, he or she may become the educational decision-maker and retain all of the rights that his or her parent previously possessed under Part B of the IDEA. 20 U.S.C. § 1415(m); 34 C.F.R.

§ 300.520. States have discretion as to whether to allow the transfer of rights to occur at the age of majority, and that age is based on the laws in each individual state. *Id.* In many jurisdictions, such as the District of Columbia and North Carolina, the age of majority is eighteen. *Policies Governing Services for Children with Disabilities*, N.C. § 1504-1.21(a); 5 D.C.M.R. § E-3023. The rights accorded to parents also transfer to children who are incarcerated in an adult or juvenile, state or local correctional institution. 20 U.S.C. § 1415(m)(1)(D); 34 C.F.R. § 300.520(a)(2). If the rights previously belonging to the parent under the IDEA have transferred to a student, it is likely that the attorney will represent the student exclusively, especially given that the parent does not retain any rights under the IDEA in that situation.

Not later than one year before the student reaches the age of majority, the school district must inform the student of those rights under the IDEA, if any, that will transfer when the student reaches the age of majority. The IEP must also include a statement that the student was informed about this transfer. 34 C.F.R. § 300.320(c); 20 U.S.C. § 1414(d)(1)(A)(i)(VIII)(cc). Specifically, all of the rights accorded to the parent under Part B of the IDEA transfer to the student. This transfer includes, but is not limited to, the right to participate in IEP meetings, the right to participate in placement decisions, the right to provide informed consent for evaluations, and the right to present a complaint for a due process hearing. When the transfer of rights occurs, the school district is required to provide notice of the transfer to both the student and the parent. Once the transfer of rights occurs, the school district must continue to provide legally required notices to the parent and also provide them to the adult student. This obligation includes notices such as prior written notices and notices about IEP meetings. 20 U.S.C. § 1415(m)(1)(A).

The IDEA explicitly provides that the rights accorded to parents do not transfer to a child who has been determined incompetent under state law when he or she reaches the age of majority. 20 U.S.C. § 1415(m)(1). Moreover, even where a child has not been deemed incompetent under state law, if that child does not have the ability to provide informed consent with respect to his or her educational program, there must be state-established procedures for appointing the parent of the child or, where unavailable, another appropriate individual, to represent the child's educational interests when the child reaches the age of majority through the duration of his or her special education eligibility. 20 U.S.C. § 1415(m)(2); 34 C.F.R. § 300.520(b). Neither the IDEA nor its accompanying regulations provides a standard for making this determination. For a comprehensive analysis of the transfer of rights at age of majority, including the exceptions for students found incompetent or unable to provide informed consent with respect to their educational programs, see Rebore & Zirkel, *supra.*

Attorneys should check their local statutes and regulations to determine if their jurisdiction has adopted the transfer of rights provision of the IDEA. If the transfer of rights is applicable in the attorney's jurisdiction, then the attorney needs to know the specific age of majority and how an individual is deemed incompetent in that state. In some states, like North Carolina, the standard for the determination of competency is included in the state's special education statutes or regulations. *Policies Governing Services for Children with Disabilities*, N.C. § 1504-1.21(b). If this information is not included in a state's special education statute and regulations, then the attorney will have to refer to different statutes, such as those that provide for the appointment of a guardian for an individual deemed incompetent, to ascertain this information.

Because a student to whom rights are transferred at the age of majority becomes the holder of educational rights instead of the parent, an attorney providing special education representation in this situation should strongly consider representing the student exclusively. Moreover, if the attorney is representing the parent exclusively or the parent and student jointly and there is a possibility that the representation may be ongoing when the student reaches the age of majority, the attorney should consider planning with the parent and student at the outset of the representation for how the representation will change, if at all, when the student reaches the age of majority. For example, the attorney and parent may decide that the attorney will cease representing the parent at that time and begin representing the student exclusively or the parties may agree that the student would seek separate representation from another attorney at that time. In determining with the parties if and how the representation might change once the student reaches the age of majority, the attorney should also consider any relevant conflicts issues that may affect the determination.

D.   Court-Appointed Special Education Attorneys

Just as the Los Angeles County Superior Court has provided for the appointment of a special education attorney where appropriate, other family courts may similarly provide for the appointment of a special education attorney in connection with a child's delinquency or dependency case. As in Los Angeles County, these jurisdictions may have statutory or regulatory provisions, court rules, or practice standards that designate the role of the special education attorney, and specify the model of representation that the attorney should employ. *See, e.g.*, Superior Court of the District of Columbia, Family Court Attorney Practice Standards for Special Education Attorneys, 5, 13 (2009) (providing that the parent is the client of a special education attorney appointed by the Family Court because the right to make educational decisions on behalf of the child belongs to the parent under federal law, except where counsel decides to represent both the parent and student pursuant to a retainer agreement in cases where the parent's interests do not conflict with those of the child). In some jurisdictions, the family court may order the attorney to represent a particular adult or caregiver. *Id.* at 13 (providing that the appointment order will inform the special education attorney and other parties who the client (educational decision maker) is for purposes of the special education representation). Sometimes, even court-appointed attorneys are faced with significant ambiguity as to their role and the identification of a client in a special education matter. If an attorney is appointed through a family court proceeding, it is critical to understand any requirements or guidance that may apply in that jurisdiction or particular proceeding.

Legal Representation in Jack's Case

You are an attorney who handles special education cases. Jack's grandmother calls you to find out if you can provide the family with legal representation to help them secure appropriate special education services for Jack.

- If you accept the case, who will you represent and why?

- How do you explain the model of representation to Jack's grandmother?

II. RETAINERS

Given the different models of representation that an attorney could use in the special education context and the conflicts of interest that may arise, it is critical that the attorney understand exactly which individual or individuals she is and is not representing. The parent and student must also be clear as to their roles, and as to which individual is charged with making decisions in the course of the representation. The retainer agreement between the attorney and client(s) can serve to clarify these issues. The person or persons serving in the client role should sign the retainer to acknowledge informed consent. The retainer agreement, which is sometimes referred to as a contract for legal services, can also describe any fee arrangement, which should be communicated to the client in writing. *Model Rules of Prof'l Conduct* R. 1.5(b) (2009). Retainer agreements can also help to clearly define the scope of the representation for the client. For example, if the attorney agrees to pursue an administrative due process hearing on behalf of the client, but is not prepared to agree at the outset of the attorney-client relationship to representation of the client in an appeal of the administrative hearing decision should an appeal be necessary, the retainer agreement can clarify this limitation and clearly identify the contours of the representation.

Retainer for Jack

You have agreed to provide legal assistance to help Jack and his grandmother secure appropriate special education services. Because Jack's grandmother has a very low income, you have decided to represent Jack and his grandmother pro bono. You know you have the time and resources to pursue a due process hearing for the family if a hearing becomes necessary, but you are not sure at this time whether you will have the resources to appeal the case by filing a civil action in court if the administrative due process hearing is not successful.

- Based on the model of representation you selected for Jack's family and the above facts, what information will you include in the retainer agreement?

- Consider using an alternative model of representation. How will this different model of representation alter the retainer agreement?

The following are three sample retainers used by legal clinics that provide representation in special education matters. The Children's Rights Clinic at Southwestern Law School typically uses a joint retainer that is signed by both parent and student, while the Juvenile and Special Education Law Clinic at the University of the District of Columbia David A. Clarke School of Law uses one type of retainer for representation of a student who has reached the age of majority and another type for representation of the parent.

CHILDREN'S RIGHTS CLINIC

Date:

Address:

Dear:

The Children's Rights Clinic at Southwestern Law School ("CRC") has agreed to provide you with legal representation. We are pleased to agree to this representation on the following terms and conditions:

1. Scope of Services. The scope of our engagement will be:

2. Limitation on Services. The scope of the project may be altered or expanded only by written agreement between you and CRC.

3. Joint Representation. It is the policy of CRC to act in the "best interest" of the child regardless of whether the parent or guardian is the person who seeks CRC's advice. For this reason, CRC enters into an agreement with the student and the parent/guardian.

4. Cost of Services. CRC will not charge a fee for its services. You will, however, if determined that you are able, be responsible for costs and expenses incurred by CRC in its representation including, but not limited to, filing fees, copying, and expert witnesses.

5. Client Responsibilities. As a client of the CRC, you understand that you have the responsibility to cooperate fully with CRC on all matters regarding the representation, including, but not limited to:

   a. Keeping CRC informed of any changes in your circumstances, including, but not limited to, any change of address, telephone number, or income;

   b. Promptly informing CRC about any documents or other communications related to the matters upon which CRC is providing representation;

   c. Responding to correspondence and other communications and requests, including, but not limited to, requests for information or the production of documents in a timely manner;

   d. If the student has a Dependency or Delinquency case open, CRC may have to communicate with the Dependency or Delinquency Attorney representing the Child or the Dependency or Delinquency Court regarding the education issue;

   e. You may be interviewed numerous times by the students. You agree to make yourself available for those interviews at a mutually convenient time. You further agree to arrive at all scheduled interviews in a timely fashion and to notify the office as soon as you learn that you will be unable to make a scheduled appointment; and

   f. The students may videotape or audiotape their interviews and mock hearings with you for educational purposes. You agree to permit such tapings.

6. Confidentiality. CRC shall maintain all its client records and information in confidence. CRC will not reveal information relating to your representation without your permission unless required to do so by law. However, CRC may reveal information when necessary to further your interests, which may include revealing confidential information to staff members of CRC, students in CRC, or other legal advocacy groups or experts who may consult on the case. Such staff members and other organizations or individuals outside of CRC are bound by the same duty not to reveal confidential information without your permission unless there is a legal duty to do so. This duty of confidentiality continues after your representation has been terminated.

7. Policy Regarding Client Files. CRC's policy is that it will destroy the client's file, including all original documents, seven years after the client's matter is closed. You understand that you have the right to obtain a portion or your entire file from CRC.

8. Termination.

   a. You may terminate our representation at any time without cause. If you choose to terminate the representation, you must notify CRC in writing.

   b. Pursuant to the rules of professional conduct and responsibility, CRC may withdraw from this representation, after taking reasonable steps to avoid prejudice to your rights, including first giving you notice of intention to withdraw. If permission for withdrawal is required by a court, CRC will promptly apply for such permission. CRC may withdraw if, in the Clinic's judgment:

      i. You are not cooperating with CRC or your conduct makes it unreasonably difficult for the Clinic to carry-out the representation effectively or efficiently;

      ii. You insist that we engage in conduct that is contrary to our judgment and advice or is contrary to law;

      iii. Continued representation would result in a violation of the rules of ethics and professional responsibility then applicable in the jurisdiction of CRC's practice;

      iv. You are no longer financially eligible for legal services free of charge because of a material change in your resources or alteration in your objectives. Financial eligibility shall be determined solely by CRC; or

      v. There is other good cause under applicable law or ethical rules to justify withdrawal.

9. Student Representation. You will be represented in this matter by the second year law students under the direct supervision of licensed attorneys. The Children's Rights Clinic provides representation by certified third year law students under the supervision of an attorney, as permitted by the California Rules Governing the Practical Training of Law Students. By signing this Agreement, you agree to that representation. In some instances, the Children's Rights Clinic may make changes in your representation based on changes in students participating in the Children's Rights Clinic.

If these arrangements are satisfactory, please sign the enclosed copy of this letter and return it to me. Please contact us if you have any questions.

Sincerely,

[Name]
[Title]

ACCEPTED AND AGREED:

By Parent/Guardian: _____
Date: _____
By Student: _____
Date: _____

_____

UNIVERSITY OF THE DISTRICT OF COLUMBIA

David A. Clarke School of Law

4200 Connecticut Avenue, N.W. Bldg. 38

Washington, D.C. 20008

RETAINER

I, Julius Minelli, hereby retain the Juvenile and Special Education Law Clinic ("the Clinic") of the University of the District of Columbia David A. Clarke School of Law (UDC-DCSL) in Washington, D.C. to advise me and to advocate on my behalf regarding any and all matters related to identifying and/or obtaining appropriate, educational services/programs for my daughter, Liza Minelli, and matters pertaining to the protection of due process rights pursuant to the Individuals With Disabilities Education Act (IDEA) and the District of Columbia Municipal Regulations.

I understand and agree that this representation is limited to efforts to obtain educational (and particularly special education) services for my daughter, Liza, and extends to those legal matters which are necessarily and reasonably related thereto. The attorney and law student advocates in the Clinic may not be able to address special education and other legal issues outside of the District of Columbia.

Initially, this agreement applies to advocacy at, and leading to, the administrative hearing level and, without explicit agreement, does not include an appeal of a hearing officer's special education determination to a court or enforcement of a hearing officer's determination in a court. The attorney and law student advocates in the Clinic will discuss at any appropriate point with me whether an appeal or enforcement action in federal court or in Superior Court regarding special education rights is warranted.

I further understand and agree that any qualified student, consultant and/or employee of UDC-DCSL may assist the attorney and law student advocates in the development of the aforementioned legal matters to the extent necessary and permitted by law in this jurisdiction.

I understand that the Clinic is part of UDC-DCSL, a law school, and that the law student advocates work on special education cases as a part of their training. I understand that it is likely that each semester Professor Justice will assign new law student advocate(s) to the case, and I also understand that Professor Justice supervises the work of the law student advocates.

I agree to allow Professor Justice to use information from my case to inform lawyers, judges, educators, and others about the need to provide special education services to students who are in the delinquency system or the criminal system and about the need to accommodate people with disabilities (and not to discriminate against people with disabilities) who are in the delinquency system or in the criminal system. I understand that, in his work to inform people about these issues, Professor Justice will not use information from my case that will identify me.

_____

Julius Minelli

_____

Date

_____

Professor Justice

_____

Date

_____

UNIVERSITY OF THE DISTRICT OF COLUMBIA

David A. Clarke School of Law

4200 Connecticut Avenue, N.W. Bldg. 38

Washington, D.C. 20008

RETAINER

I, Raymond Student, hereby retain the Juvenile and Special Education Law Clinic ("the Clinic") of the University of the District of Columbia David A. Clarke School of Law (UDC-DCSL) in Washington, D.C. to advise me and to advocate on my behalf regarding any and all matters related to identifying and/or obtaining appropriate, educational services/ programs for me, and matters pertaining to the protection of due process rights pursuant to the Individuals With Disabilities Education Act (IDEA) and the District of Columbia Board of Education Rules.

I understand and agree that this representation is limited to efforts to obtain educational (and particularly special education) services for me and extends to those legal matters which are necessarily and reasonably related thereto. The attorney and law student advocates in the Clinic may not be able to address special education and other legal issues outside of the District of Columbia.

Initially, this agreement applies to advocacy at, and leading to, the administrative hearing level and, without explicit agreement, does not include an appeal of a hearing officer's special education determination to a court or enforcement of a hearing officer's determination in a court. The attorney and law student advocates in the Clinic will discuss at any appropriate point with me whether an appeal or enforcement action in federal court or in Superior Court regarding special education rights is warranted.

I further understand and agree that any qualified student, consultant and/or employee of UDC-DCSL may assist the attorney and law student advocates in the development of the aforementioned legal matters to the extent necessary and permitted by law in this jurisdiction.

I understand that the Clinic is part of UDC-DCSL, a law school, and that the law student advocates work on special education cases as a part of their training. I understand that it is likely that each semester Professor Justice will assign new law student advocate(s) to the case, and I also understand that Professor Justice supervises the work of the law student advocates.

I agree to allow Professor Justice to use information from my case to inform lawyers, judges, educators, and others about the need to provide special education services to students who are in the delinquency system or the criminal system and about the need to accommodate people with disabilities (and not to discriminate against people with disabilities) who are in the delinquency system or in the criminal system. I understand that, in his work to inform people about these issues, Professor Justice will not use information from my case that will identify me.

_____

Raymond Student

_____

Date

_____

Professor Justice

_____

Date

_____

III. INTRODUCTORY LETTER TO A CLIENT AND AUTHORIZATION FOR RELEASE OF INFORMATION AND RECORDS

Soon after accepting a case, an attorney should contact the client if he or she has not already done so to make an introduction and set up a meeting in which the attorney will interview the client and gather more information. While the initial introductory conversation will often take place over the phone, a written introduction in addition to any telephone conversation can help to provide the client with formal documentation that the relationship is beginning, and to provide the client with the attorney's contact information in writing. A sample introductory letter to a client can be found below. When communicating with the client, in writing or verbally, the attorney should consider the client's communication needs. If the client is not proficient in English, the attorney may need to make arrangements for an interpreter not only for meetings, but also for telephone calls, as well as translation for any written documents. If the client has limited reading abilities, the attorney should consider the implications for any written correspondence or documentation the attorney might need to exchange with the client or provide to him or her. Some clients may not have completed high school or may read at a low grade level. Other clients may have disabilities that make reading difficult for them. Regardless of these factors, clients will not have the legal education to understand sophisticated legalese, legal terminology or acronyms. It is important for attorneys to keep these factors in mind, as well as any unique communication needs a client might have, when corresponding with the client, whether in writing, over the telephone, or in person.

An introductory letter to a client can also be used to outline any next steps that the attorney and client might be taking together, such as the date, time and location of an upcoming initial client interview meeting that the attorney and client may have arranged. The sample letter below illustrates one way to approach an introductory letter to a client.

October 8, 2010

Ms. Ivy Washington
123 Client St.
Anyplace, Nowhere 12345

Re: Simon Washington

Dear Ms. Washington:

Thank you for contacting the Greatest Law School Education Legal Clinic regarding legal representation for the educational placement of your son, Simon. I am writing to inform you that the Greatest Law School Education Legal Clinic has made a decision to provide you with legal representation to obtain appropriate special education services for Simon.

I am attaching an "Authorization for Release of Information and Records" form. By signing this form, you are providing permission to Simon's school to provide me with the records and information I need to assist you with Simon's special education needs. Please sign this form and return it to me in the enclosed stamped, addressed envelope. Also, if you have any of Simon's school or medical records at home that you think may assist us in representing you, please mail these to us as well.

As you know, we have arranged to meet on October 16, 2010 at 2:00pm for our first meeting at my office at the Greatest Law School Education Legal Clinic located at 222 West Street. Please bring any additional school or medical records for Simon with you to our meeting.

It is important that you keep me updated regarding any new information regarding Simon's education, as well as inform me of any concerns or issues that you may face with him or his school. In addition, please do not hesitate to contact me at 222-222-2222 if you have any further questions or wish to provide me with any further information.

Sincerely,

Betty Johnson

Law Student Attorney

In addition to providing a client with the attorney's contact information and serving as a formal introduction of the relationship, an initial introductory letter to a client can also be used to make a request for the client to gather documents that the client may have in his or her possession that would be useful for the attorney to have. The attorney may choose to include an authorization for release of information and records form with the introductory letter to the client, along with a stamped envelope addressed to the attorney if possible, so that the client can sign the release forms and send them back to the attorney as soon as possible. This practice is especially necessary in situations where there might be some delay before the attorney and client can meet face to face for the client to complete them. In the authorization form, the client provides written authorization to outside parties such as school officials or a child's therapist to release documentation and provide information verbally or in writing to the attorney and/or individuals working with the attorney. If any forms, such as the authorization for release of information and records forms, are included with the letter, the letter should include an explanation of those forms and specific instructions on what the client should do with the forms. The attorney should use clear, simple and concise language and avoid using legalese and complex terms when communicating with the client in writing. It is important to review relevant statutes that protect the confidentiality of educational and health information in determining what language to include in an authorization for release of information, such as the federal Family Educational Rights and Privacy Act (FERPA) and Health Insurance and Portability and Accountability Act (HIPAA). Family Educational Rights and Privacy Act, 20 U.S.C. § 1232g; Health Insurance and Portability and Accountability Act, 42 U.S.C. § 1320d *et seq.*.

Below are several sample authorization forms for release of records and information that reflect different approaches.

CHILDREN'S RIGHTS CLINIC

Student's Name:
D.O.B.:
Parent/Guardian/Surrogate Name:
Address:
Telephone Number:

AUTHORIZATION TO RELEASE INFORMATION/RECORDS

I authorize any person, governmental agency, corporation or other agency to release to Julie Waterstone and her students in the Children's Rights Clinic at Southwestern Law School any and all information pertaining to _____ education, developmental, social service, and/or mental health needs. Such information shall include medical, psychological, social, vocational, rehabilitative, educational, and law enforcement records, reports, assessments, and evaluations. The authorization includes the release of all records or documents deemed confidential and extends to all documents otherwise considered confidential under any Federal or State privacy laws.

This authorization shall include, but not be limited to, the right to inspect, copy, or otherwise utilize said records as may be deemed fit and to obtain whatever clarification or opinion on said records that Julie Waterstone shall deem necessary to the proper disposition of my case.

I understand that this authorization, except for action already taken, is subject to revocation by me at any time. I also understand a photocopy or facsimile copy of this authorization has the same effect as the original.

Please forward all records regarding the above-named minor within five (5) days of receipt of this form to:

Southwestern Law School

Children's Rights Clinic
Attn: _____
3050 Wilshire Blvd.
Los Angeles, CA 90010

Person Authorizing Release of Information/Records:

[Specify: Parent/Guardian/Surrogate] _____

Signature_____ Date: _____

University of the District of Columbia
David A. Clarke School of Law
4200 Connecticut Avenue, N.W.
Building 38, 2nd Floor
Washington, D.C. 20008

RELEASE

TO WHOM IT MAY CONCERN:

Upon receipt of this Release, or a photocopy thereof, you are authorized to allow any representative of the U.D.C. David A. Clarke School of Law including, but not limited to Laura N. Rinaldi and Joseph B. Tulman, Attorneys, and, Student Attorney(s) _____, to examine, inspect, make, and retain notes from, or make and retain photocopies of, any and all records and information, related to a student named_____, whose date of birth is _____. This Release covers any and all records and information in your possession, custody, or control, including medical, psychiatric, legal, financial, employment, military, and educational records and information.

This Release further authorizes any person familiar with or having or acquiring knowledge about _____ related to any of the above subject matters to freely discuss such information, records, or non-recorded information with any of the above-named persons or representatives from the U.D.C. David A. Clarke School of Law.

A photocopy of this Release should be given the same effect as the original.

Dated: _____
Signed: _____
Address: _____
Relationship to the Above-Referenced Student:

Disability Rights Law Clinic
American University Washington College of Law
4801 Massachusetts Ave., NW Suite 417 • Washington, DC 20016
Phone: (202) 274-4147 • Fax: (202) 274-0659

Authorization to Disclose Protected Health and Mental Health Information

I, _____, authorize the disclosure of my protected health information as described below. I understand that this authorization is voluntary. I also understand that, if the person(s) or organization(s) that I authorize to receive my protected health information are not subject to federal and state health information privacy laws, subsequent disclosure by such person(s) or organization(s) may not be protected by these laws.

1. I authorized the following person(s) and/or organization(s) to disclose my protected health information:

    Name/Organization: _____

    Address: _____

2. I authorize the following person(s) and/or organizations to request and receive my protected health information, as disclosed by the person(s) and/or organization(s) above:

    Name/Organization: _____

    Address: _____

3. I authorize disclosure of the following specific information (authorization to disclose psychotherapy notes must be separate):

4. The information is to be used for the following purpose:

5. I understand that I may revoke this authorization in writing at any time, except to the extent that the person(s) and/or organization(s) named above have taken action in reliance on this authorization.

6. I understand that this information may not be re-disclosed without my authorization and that the law requires this notice: "THE UNAUTHORIZED DISCLOSURE OF MENTAL HEALTH INFORMATION VIOLATES THE PROVISIONS OF THE DISTRICT OF COLUMBIA MENTAL HEALTH INFORMATION ACT OF 1978. DISCLOSURE MAY ONLY BE MADE PURSUANT TO A VALID AUTHORIZATION BY THE CLIENT, OR AS PROVIDED IN TITLES III AND IV OF THAT ACT. THE ACT PROVIDES FOR CIVIL DAMAGES AND CRIMINAL PENALTIES FOR VIOLATION."

7. This authorization expires on _____, not to exceed 365 days from the date of this authorization.

I have had the opportunity to read and consider the contents of the authorization. I confirm that the contents are consistent with my direction.

Signed: _____   Date: _____
Name: _____
Address: _____
Telephone: _____   D.O.B.: _____

IV. CLIENT INTERVIEW

Sometimes the attorney providing the representation in a special education matter will have conducted an initial intake with the parent or caregiver, and other times another attorney, an administrative assistant, a paralegal, an intake specialist, or another individual will have completed an initial intake conversation with the client. An initial intake can provide helpful information in determining whether to accept a case for representation. There are many ways to structure an initial intake with a potential client, which can take place over the phone or in person. Below is a checklist for special education intakes, as well as a sample completed intake used by the Children's Rights Clinic at Southwestern Law School. These samples present one way that an attorney or support professional can approach an initial intake.

CHILDREN'S RIGHTS CLINIC
Education Intake Check List

Special Education

√ Is the Child in Special Education?

√ Has the child ever been evaluated?

√ Is there an IEP?

√ Initial IEP Date?

√ What services is the student receiving?

√ Student's Eligibility? [Mental Retardation; Orthopedic Impairment; Visual Impairment; Leaning Disabled; Autism; Emotional Disturbance; Speech/Language Impairment; Traumatic Brain Injury; Other (ADD/ADHD); Multiple Disabilities]

√ Current Placement? [General Ed with RSP; Residential School; Special Day Class; Non Public School]

√ Most Recent IEP Date?

√ IEP Coming Up?

√ Date of Last Evaluation?

504 Plan

√ Is there currently a 504 Plan?

√ Has s/he ever been evaluated for 504 services?

√ How does the student qualify?

√ 504 Plan Meeting?

√ What 504 accommodations is the student receiving?

Discipline

√ Is the student in trouble?

√ What happened? Details.

√ Discipline Used? [O.T., Suspension, Expulsion]

√ Pre-Suspension Conference?

√ Pre-Expulsion Conference?

√ Manifestation Determination IEP? When?

√ Expulsion Hearing? When?

√ With O.T, was there a DRT meeting or any other Team meeting ?

CHILDREN'S RIGHTS CLINIC
EDUCATION INTAKE

Intake Date: 10.16.10   **Conducted by:** J. Waterstone
         Result: _____

Brief Description of Case:

Lisa called that her 7 year old son was suspended from school for 5 days for telling the executive director that he is going to burn her. She has requested an IEP so that her son can be tested for social and behavioral problems.

Parent/Guardian Information:

First Name: Lisa   Last Name: Jones
Age:_____ Date of Birth: _____ Sex: M ☐F✓
Ethnicity: Asian-American   Disabled: Yes☐ No✓
Language (if other than English):   Household Income:
_____   _____

Address:_____
Home Phone: _____   Other Phone:_____
Email Address: _____
Foster parent: Yes☐ No☐

Client/Child's Information:

First Name: Chris   Last Name: Jones
Age: 7 Grade: 1ˢᵗ Date of Birth: 8.25.03 Sex: M ✓F☐
Ethnicity: Asian-American   Disabled: Yes☐ No☐
Language (if other than English):   Foster child: Yes☐ No☐
_____

Address: _____
Home Phone: _____   Other Phone:_____
Current School: Has been attending New School Academy for three days
Address: _____
District: Charter School
         Contacts: (Adults, Social Worker, Referral Source, etc.)

First Name:_____   Last Name:_____
Relationship to client:_____
Age:_____ Date of birth:_____ Sex: M ☐F☐
Ethnicity:_____
Disabled: Yes☐ No☐ No   Language (if other than
                                      English):_____
Address:_____
Home phone: _____   Other phone:_____

_____

Notes:

Lisa called in on October 16, 2010. Her son has been suspended from New School Academy for five days and is now facing expulsion. He has been suspended from school because he threatened the executive director. He told the director that he was going to burn her. Ms. Jones has requested an IEP with the school. Chris was attending Primary School throughout preschool and kindergarten. He had an IEP for speech and language as well as social delays. When he started this academic year at Primary, he had a lot of behavioral issues. In one incident, he told the principal that he was going to kill her with a gun. In another incident, he pinched the principal. After that incident, the school administrators decided that they were going to provide Chris with counseling. Ms. Jones asked for an IEP, but no action was taken. She then transferred Chris to New School Academy. Before transferring him, she informed the school of all of his behavioral problems. They accepted him anyway. He was attending school for 3 days when he told the ED that he was going to burn her. He has been suspended since then. Ms. Jones requested an IEP and was told that she needed to wait until Monday.

She believes that her son may have some social and emotional problems and wants him reassessed. She is very concerned and doesn't want her son to be expelled.

Regardless of whether the attorney herself conducted the initial intake and regardless of how comprehensive the initial intake may or may not have been, the attorney providing the actual representation will need to conduct a full interview directly with the client after the case is accepted to get the additional information needed to initiate the case and proceed with representation. An effective client interview can accomplish a great deal early in the case. Such a meeting provides a face-to-face opportunity to gather information from the client, learn about a client's goals, and make sure the client understands how the attorney-client relationship will work. An interview also gives the attorney a chance to build rapport with the client and establish a good working partnership from the start. In a special education case, the initial client interview provides an opportunity for the attorney to collect any records from the client that have not yet been provided to the attorney during the intake phase.

When scheduling the interview, an attorney should consider the client's scheduling needs and the best location for the interview. Some clients may have constraints, such as transportation or child care needs, that the attorney should take into account. The initial client interview should be conducted in a language that the client can understand. For some clients, this may mean that an interpreter will be necessary, and arrangements should be made in advance to secure an interpreter. For a helpful discussion of considerations related to working with a language interpreter, see Angela McCaffrey, *Don't Get Lost in Translation: Teaching Law Students to Work with Language Interpreters*, 6 Clinical L. Rev. 347 (2000). During the course of the interview, the attorney should also explain lawyer-client confidentiality to the client.

A.   Active Listening

Active listening is an approach that can assist attorneys in interviewing any client, whether adult or child. Active listening describes a range of approaches through which an attorney can acknowledge facts, emotions and positive qualities of character expressed by the client through such strategies as summarizing the facts relayed by the client, paraphrasing the factual content and attaching an emotional feeling, and validation, or directly stating an understanding of the client's situation or some portion of those feelings. Ellmann et al., *supra*, 27-28. An effective active listening response will often reflect back to the speaker the substance, as well as the emotional content, of the speaker's statement. Joseph B. Tulman, *The Special Education Process: Investigating and Initiating the Special Education Case, in* Special Education Advocacy under the Individuals with Disabilities Education Act (IDEA) for Children in the Juvenile Delinquency System, 7-4 (Joseph B. Tulman & Joyce A. McGee eds., 1998). These approaches not only show the client that the attorney is engaged in the conversation, has heard more of the client's concerns than just the facts, and is empathetic to the client's situation, but also allows the attorney to ensure that he has accurately heard what the client has said or, if not, then to seek clarification from the client. Ellmann et al., *supra*, at 27-28.

Moreover, if the attorney is taking written notes during the interview, which is often not only helpful but necessary, the attorney may want to explain to the client why he or she is writing during the conversation. An explanation of why the attorney is taking notes can make a client feel more comfortable with the attorney writing while he or she is speaking, as unexplained note-taking can be confusing, intimidating or worrisome to some clients. An attorney who is taking notes during an initial client interview should still remember to utilize active listening approaches to ensure that the attorney is validating the client's concerns and that the client knows the attorney is fully engaged in the conversation.

B.   Interviewing the Student

Regardless of the model of representation selected by the lawyer and client, it is almost always helpful to interview the student who is the subject of the representation, or at least interact with him or her in some way. Attorneys gain an understanding of the student's strengths and needs from such interaction unequaled by a review of documentation describing the student. Moreover, if the student is able to communicate with the attorney, an interview of the student can provide the attorney with important information necessary not only in building the factual evidentiary record in a special education matter, but in helping the client to determine the appropriate remedies to pursue and the course of action to achieve those remedies.

When interviewing a student, lawyers may need to vary their interviewing techniques as a result of a client's special circumstances, such as cognitive limitations, age limitations, or emotional or psychological limitations. Ellmann et al., *supra*, at 113. Where the student is a client, an attorney should, as far as reasonably possible, maintain a normal lawyer-client relationship with the client. *Model Rules of Prof'l Conduct* R. 1.14(a) (2009). Even a client with a diminished capacity "often has the ability to understand, deliberate upon, and reach conclusions about matters affecting the client's own well-being." *Model Rules of Prof's Conduct* R. 1.14 Cmt. [1] (2009). Even if the student is not the actual client, these principles are helpful for the lawyer to keep in mind to guide his interactions with the student, including interactions during the course of an interview of the student.

To conduct an effective interview of the child, the attorney may want to review some of the extensive research on interviewing children. While much of this literature focuses on the child welfare and criminal justice contexts, many of the principles remain the same. For example, open-ended questions are preferable because closed-ended questions tend to lead children to respond with no more information than the answer requires. Thomas D. Lyon, *Investigative Interviewing of the Child, in* Child Welfare Law and Practice: Representing Children, Parents and State Agencies in Abuse, Neglect, and Dependency Cases 2-3 (D.N. Duquette & A.M. Haralambie, eds. 2010). It is also important to give the child plenty of time to respond to questions, particularly at the beginning of the interview. *Id.* at 13. Especially if a student's special education needs are not being met, school may be an unpleasant topic. "Wait-time," in which children are allowed plenty of time to think about a question before an assumption is made that they do not know the answer, can be effective in enabling the child to build up the courage to discuss even difficult subjects. *Id.*

Attorneys may want to consult the Handbook on Questioning Children (hereinafter "ABA Handbook") produced by the American Bar Association Center on Children on the Law. Anne Graffam Walker, Handbook on Questioning Children, ABA Center on Children and the Law (2d. ed 1999). The ABA Handbook provides guidance for interviewing children in different development stages. For example, the book cautions that even adolescents between the ages of eleven and eighteen may not have acquired adult narrative skills, may not understand time as a historical concept and are likely to lose track of long, complex questions. *Id.* at 4-5. While some of these materials on interviewing children, such as the ABA Handbook, provide guidance to attorneys based on a child's age range, children with disabilities may not have reached the developmental milestones and, therefore, information for attorneys in these materials that are based on age or age range may not be applicable to every child. Therefore, attorneys should avoid making assumptions about the capabilities and capacity of a student before beginning an interview and try to garner from other sources prior to the interview and from the student at the start of the interview the student's actual communication abilities. Regardless, the use of active listening and openness of mind can assist the lawyer in understanding a child or adolescent client. Ellmann et al, *supra*, at 128.

C.   Developing a Preparation Plan for the Client Interview

Prior to conducting an interview of a client, an attorney should prepare adequately to ensure that the interview is effective. A thorough review of any documentation that the attorney already has in her possession serves as a good starting point. The attorney should consider how to best organize and structure the interview. For example, the attorney may choose to ask questions in a way that gathers information chronologically, which can assist the parent and child in remembering the pertinent information and answering questions accurately, and can provide the attorney with a framework for understanding the student's history. An effective interviewer will assist the interviewee in presenting the history completely. This task can be accomplished by the attorney asking open-ended questions, providing verbal prompting, and helping to orient the client so that he or she presents the history of the problem comprehensively. Tulman, *supra*, at 7-4. In preparation for the interview, the attorney may want to prepare a written plan for the interview. A preparation plan for an interview can include issue areas to cover and specific questions within those issue areas. Below are a number of key issue areas that, if effectively explored in an interview where applicable, can help the attorney gather the initial information he or she needs to proceed with further investigation, begin to develop a case theory, and counsel the client on possible courses of action.

1.   General Overview of Parent's Concerns

It is often helpful to learn from the outset what concerns the parent has about the child that prompted the parent to seek legal representation. A general, open-ended question aimed at eliciting the parent's concerns can help an attorney understand not only what legal violations may have occurred, but also the parent's point of view and the concerns that are driving and motivating the parent. Clients have stories to tell that not only elucidate the problems they are facing, but include "the reasons for, hesitation or excitement about, and fear of whatever prompted their need for legal help." Ellmann et al., *supra*, at 139. Open-ended questions that provide the client with an opportunity to tell his or her story can serve as an effective opening to an interview.

2.   Student's Developmental History

Information about the child's developmental history can sometimes help a lawyer understand whether he or she had or continues to have unmet special education needs. Were there any delays in reaching developmental milestones that might signal an unidentified disability or unmet need? Does the child have any medical or psychiatric diagnoses? Has he or she been prescribed any medications, psychotropic or otherwise? Has the child ever experienced a head trauma? Has the child's pediatrician ever expressed concerns about any developmental delays or the child's need for certain services, such as early intervention or special education services? Sometimes gathering information about the child's home setting, and the child's siblings, including their ages, school histories and any special needs they might have, can also help an attorney understand the child and the family. The attorney may also want to gather contact information for the child's pediatrician or other relevant health professionals in the child's life.

3.   Student's Educational History

The interviewer should try to learn as much as he or she can about the student's educational history in order to begin to develop a chronology, which can be supplemented by information gained through other means of investigation, as discussed below. Did the student receive early intervention services? Did the student attend pre-school? What schools has the child attended? What academic or behavioral deficiencies did the parent or the child's teachers observe during each school year? Some special education students may have attended several schools because either their parents have moved them from school to school in search of an appropriate placement or the school system has transferred them out of various schools because they are unable to meet the child's needs. For these students especially, but indeed for all students, it will be helpful to garner information for each school year about the school the child attended that year, the grade the child was in, the name of the child's teachers, and any concerns or information about the child's academic progress related to that school year. The attorney will also want to understand the child's history of special education evaluations and services, if any, during each school year. This information will be useful in beginning to develop a visual school chronology, whether through a list, outline, chart, or other means, as discussed below.

In interviewing the parent about the child's special education background and chronology, it is important to gather as much information as possible, where applicable, about the child's history of evaluations, eligibility classifications, Individualized Educational Program (IEP) history, special education services, and school placements. For example, has the student been referred for special education evaluations? When? By whom? Were special education evaluations conducted? What types of evaluations? Was the student found eligible for special education? Under which disability classifications? Does the student have a current IEP? How many hours of specialized instruction does the IEP call for? Is the student receiving the required number of hours per week? What related services are included in the IEP? Is the student receiving the required services? Has the parent been satisfied with the child's school placements? The answers to these and other related questions will help the attorney begin to flag legal violations and develop a plan for further investigation.

4.   Information About the Student's Needs and Interests Outside of School

In addition to developing a thorough understanding of a child's needs related to his or her education, it is helpful in a special education case to understand a child's needs and interests more generally, as well as the services a child is receiving or might require outside of school. Information related to any difficulties the child might be experiencing in settings other than school, such as with homework, chores, following directions, memory, sustaining concentration, sitting still, communication, or expression, can help an attorney determine whether the child may have needs related to a disability that are not being appropriately addressed by the child's school. For example, if the parent reports that her child has great difficulty following directions, sustaining concentration, or sitting still, that child may have unmet needs related to Attention Deficit Hyperactivity Disorder that could be manifesting in challenges during the school day and could mean that the child requires special education services or accommodations to address those needs. Similarly, significant behavioral problems at home or other settings outside of school could be a sign that there are unmet needs during the school day.

An attorney conducting an initial interview should also try to ascertain whether the child is receiving any relevant services outside of school, such as counseling or psychiatric services, speech/language therapy, occupational therapy, or physical therapy, which may relate to the child's special education needs. Moreover, those service providers may be able to provide useful information, observations or recommendations about the child. Therefore, the attorney will want to gather contact information for any relevant service professionals for possible additional investigation. The attorney may similarly want to inquire about other adults in the child's life, such as other family members, day care workers, camp counselors, coaches, or mentors, who may have regular interaction with the child and could provide information to the attorney about the child's educational needs.

The attorney should also explore the child's strengths, successes, talents, and interests. Some advocates might miss or minimize these components. Tulman, *supra*, at 7-4. A child's deficits are too often the focus of programming and decision-making in special education. However, an approach to legal advocacy in a special education case that incorporates a child's strengths and interests can serve to empower the child and parent in a system that sometimes feels disempowering to families.

5.   Parent's Efforts to Obtain Help from the School or Other Agencies

An attorney should try to discern what, if any, attempts the parent has made in the past to seek assistance related to the child's unmet needs. This information will help the attorney not only in constructing an accurate educational chronology, but also in flagging potential legal violations, such as a school's failure to provide the parent with prior written notice of its refusal to provide special education evaluations following a parent's request for evaluations. 20 U.S.C. § 1415(b)(3)(B). The attorney might ask the parent more generally whether he or she ever expressed any concerns to any school officials about the child's academic performance. More specifically, did the parent make any specific requests for evaluations or services? Were any interventions or services promised? Were these interventions ever implemented? Has the parent previously filed a due process complaint related to the child's special education needs? If so, what was the outcome? Did the parent seek any assistance from other government agencies for the child? From any private agencies? If the attorney learns of any attempts that the parent has made to express concern to the school or to obtain assistance in remedying the situation, it is helpful to know which individual or individuals the parent contacted, whether in writing or verbally, when the contact or correspondence occurred, and what, if any, response the parent received.

It is also useful to know whether an attorney previously represented the parent in connection with the child's special education needs. An attorney may have represented a parent in the past and helped the parent to resolve a prior issue, but the parent has sought representation from the new attorney on a more recent issue. It is important to ensure that representation by any attorneys in previous special education matters has been properly terminated in order for the new attorney to proceed with representation. In addition, it is helpful to know about prior representation because the previous attorney may have records and information that could prove useful to the new attorney. Representation by multiple attorneys in the past on the same issue may signal a potential problem of which the attorney might want to be aware. Finally, there may be reasons why the prior representation ended, such as the parent's dissatisfaction with the previous attorney that could help the new attorney understand the parent's needs and concerns as a client, if that information is shared.

Interviewing Jack and His Grandmother

You have an initial client interview scheduled with Jack and his grandmother.

- What are the goals of your interview?

- Develop a preparation plan for your interview. How will you structure your interview? What questions do you want to ask Jack in your interview? What questions do you want ask his grandmother?

---

6.   School Discipline

Historically, students with special education needs have been disproportionately excluded from the classroom through informal and formal suspensions and through expulsions, sometimes in violation of their rights. If a child has been excluded from the classroom, whether through formal or informal discipline processes, the attorney should try to gather as much information as possible related to the alleged behavior and the disciplinary action initiated by the school. For example, it will be helpful for the attorney to understand details such as the nature of the alleged behavior that gave rise to the disciplinary action, the nature of the disciplinary action, the period of time for which the student was excluded from the classroom or school, the nature of any education or special education services provided to the child during the period of exclusion, the date and form of any notice that may have been provided to the parent about the disciplinary action and the contents of any such notice, whether the school held a manifestation determination meeting, and whether a multi-disciplinary team convened to discuss the behavioral problems. Information about school discipline actions can help an attorney understand whether the child had any unmet special education needs and whether any legal violations occurred or continue to occur related to the parent and child's due process and special education rights.

D.   Ascertaining the Client's Goals

Any client-centered interview will also focus on ascertaining the client's goals. Here, the attorney may garner the parent's or child's goals by asking the parent and/or the child to describe the ideal school situation for the child. What would an appropriate classroom or school look like? What would an ideal school day for the child include? The attorney should review the client's goals carefully to ensure that the attorney properly understands them.

More seasoned attorneys may be able to include a discussion of the law and client counseling about possible options in an initial interview. New attorneys and even more experienced attorneys may want to consider focusing the initial interview on the establishment of rapport and fact-gathering, and instead save a discussion of the law and counseling about potential options for future meetings. This strategy will give the attorney time to engage in legal research and additional fact investigation before attempting to explain the legal framework to the client or counsel the client on possible next steps. Prematurely providing information to a client about his or her legal options could confuse the client or provide inaccurate information or false hope. For example, if a parent tells the attorney that his child was suspended for getting into a fight, the attorney may have some sense that there are additional protections to which children in special education are entitled before certain types of suspensions can occur. However, if the attorney counsels the client about his child's rights and explains that the parent has a strong chance of getting the suspension overturned before the attorney understands the law related to those protections for special education students or before knowing all of the facts, the attorney might be giving the client inaccurate and confusing information or false hope. After an initial client interview, it is often helpful to conduct additional legal research and fact investigation, and then prepare thoroughly for a later counseling discussion about the client's legal rights and his or her possible courses of action.

Below are general instructions for several client interviewing simulations. Confidential instructions are provided separately in the teacher's manual.

SOUTHWESTERN LAW SCHOOL
CHILDREN'S RIGHTS CLINIC: INTERVIEWING EXERCISE
GENERAL FACTS FOR THE INTERVIEWER*

INSTRUCTIONS:

This same set of facts has been provided to both the interviewer and the child. The child has additional confidential facts. Your job is to interview this child to get an understanding of what occurred and any other pertinent information to your representation of this child.

PERTINENT FACTS:

The client calls and tells you that their child, James, is facing expulsion. The client isn't entirely clear on the story. The school called her said that her child has sexually assaulted another child and that he was found with drugs. The client tells you that her son has never been in trouble before and doesn't do drugs. The mother and child are coming to your office. You have already told the mother to wait in the waiting room and that you want to meet with the child alone.

University of the District of Columbia David A. Clarke School of Law

CLIENT INTERVIEW SIMULATION

(Handout for Interviewer/Lawyer)

Ms. Betty Snipes has retained the Juvenile and Special Education Law Clinic for legal representation in order to get her son, Jack, back into school. You will be conducting the initial client interview with Ms. Snipes today in order to gather case-related information from her. From the intake documents that contain information provided by Ms. Snipes, you know the following:

1) Jack is a seventeen-year-old African American student.

2) Jack is in the 9th grade at a school in Washington, D.C.

3) Jack's school told Ms. Snipes that Jack couldn't return to his school because they found him with drugs.

4) At the time of the interview, Jack has been out of school for two weeks.

5) Jack has always struggled in school and his first year of high school has been really difficult.

6) Jack used to be in special classes when he was younger.

7) Ms. Snipes is frustrated and doesn't know what to do about Jack.

8) Ms. Snipes is worried that if Jack doesn't get back into school soon he will drop out of school altogether or go to jail.

Disability Rights Law Clinic
American University Washington College of Law
4801 Massachusetts Ave., NW Suite 417 • Washington, DC 20016
Phone: (202) 274-4147 • Fax: (202) 274-0659

Client Interview Simulation

Written by Robert D. Dinerstein

Lawyer Instructions — Goodman Interview

* Confidential Instructions for Mr./Ms. Goodman and additional Confidential Instructions for the Lawyer can be found in the teacher's manual

You are a law student in the Disability Rights Law Clinic. As a result of the intake process, a prospective client, **Audrey (Arthur) Goodman**, has made an appointment to see you today. The intake information from the clinic's administrative assistant is that the potential client wants to see you concerning a legal matter related to her son Roger's special education. Ms. Goodman is a resident of Northeast Washington, DC. Roger is a 12 year-old child with learning disabilities and the matter apparently relates to some misbehavior in which Roger became involved, leading to his possible suspension or expulsion from the middle school he attends. Ms. Goodman first thought she could handle the matter on her own, but now believes she should consult a lawyer to find out what her legal options are. You traded phone messages with Ms. Goodman, and though you've not spoken with her directly, you both agreed that she would come to the clinic's offices for the first interview. Additional information you have learned through your legal research can be found in separate confidential instructions for you. Ms. Goodman, your prospective client, will also receive separate confidential instructions.

V. INVESTIGATION

Investigation is a fundamental component of a special education case and the attorney should never leave any stone unturned. Investigation is necessary even if the attorney's case does not end up in litigation against the school system. Careful and comprehensive investigation is critical for educational planning, IEP meeting preparation, and advising clients, as well as for litigation. The attorney must collect as much information as possible about the child's educational experience and educational needs. The attorney may uncover legal violations of which the client was unaware and the attorney will want to compile evidence for his or her case, whether he or she ultimately decides to file a state complaint, pursue a due process hearing, or advocate for his or her client at an IEP meeting.

Investigation in a special education case includes three main activities — obtaining documents, interviewing key individuals (who may also be potential witnesses), and observing the student. Before beginning any of these investigation activities, the attorney will have interviewed the client, as described above, to obtain information about where to get documents, who to interview, and where to observe the student. The attorney should begin investigation on day one of the case and should continue investigation activities throughout the life of the case. Investigation does not happen all at once and the timing of a particular investigation activity will vary based on the particular circumstances of the case. The attorney can also consider engaging an education expert at this point or at any point moving forward in the case.

A.   Obtaining Documents

Collecting and reviewing documents is an essential part of gathering evidence for the attorney's case. An attorney should request documents as soon as he or she opens a case, if the attorney has not already requested documents during the intake phase. Depending on the length of a case and the particular activities in that case, the attorney may need to request documents more than once. For example, if the attorney opens the case in November (which is generally the middle of the school year) and does not file a due process complaint until the following summer, the attorney should request educational records at the outset of the case and periodically throughout the school year. This strategy is important because the attorney can see whether the student is progressing, whether any academic or behavioral concerns persist, cease, or develop, and whether the school has convened any IEP meetings or conducted any evaluations of the student. The attorney should consult local laws and procedures in advance of requesting documents to ensure the request is being made in the proper manner and to the proper entity.

Ways to Obtain Records:

1)   Written Request

2)   In-Person Request

3)   Freedom of Information Act (FOIA) Request

4)   Subpoena (if there is any court involvement)

1. Educational Records

Parents have an explicit right to gain access to their child's educational records. Specifically, parents have a right to inspect and review their child's records any time a request is made. 34 C.F.R. § 300.613. The school must provide access to the records without unnecessary delay, but not more than 45 days after the parent makes the request. *Id.* Also, the school must provide the requested records to the parent prior to any upcoming IEP meeting, dispute resolution session, or due process hearing. *Id.* A parent has a right not only to inspect records but actually to receive copies of those records if failure to provide the copies would effectively prevent the parent from gaining access to and inspecting the records. *Id.* This right extends to any representative of the parent, including the parent's lawyer. *Id.*

Examples of Educational Records to Obtain from School:

- Report Cards
- Progress Notes from teachers and related service providers (i.e., counselors, speech/language pathologist)
- Teacher's Notes or Comments
- Individualized Education Programs (IEPs), including if appropriate:
  - Transition Plans
  - Behavior Intervention Plans (BIPs)
- IEP Meeting Notes
- Prior Written Notices
- Evaluations, including if appropriate:
  - Functional Behavior Assessments (FBAs)
  - Screenings for Evaluations
- Standardized Test Scores
- Encounter Tracking Forms from Related Service Providers
- Disciplinary Records
- Attendance Records
- Samples of Student's Schoolwork

When requesting educational records, the attorney should put the request in writing and provide a copy of the authorization of release of information and records signed by the parent to the school, as described above. The time period it takes school districts to comply with records requests varies by jurisdiction, but an attorney could expedite the process by going to the school in person to review the records or by offering to copy the records or pick up the records in person from the school.

There are a wide variety of educational records an attorney should obtain and review for his or her case. These records can generally be grouped into one of three categories: Cumulative (or General) Records, Disciplinary Records, and Special Education Records. Some schools maintain all of these records together, and other schools may keep them separately or even have different custodians for different types of records. An attorney should inquire about how the record keeping system is organized and to whom records requests should be directed at a particular school so that she can obtain a complete copy of the student's educational records. Also, it is important for an attorney to obtain educational records not only for the current school year, but for the student's entire educational career.

To ensure that the attorney receives the requested documents, she should carefully choose the language to include in the records request letter. The attorney may elect to make a general request for all educational records, but the school may respond by providing only a portion of what the attorney is seeking. For example, the school may provide only the student's cumulative file and fail to provide any special education records. In the alternative, the attorney may choose to make a more specific request and list all of the documents he or she wants from a certain time period. This approach may ensure that the attorney receives more of the documents that he or she is seeking. This more specific approach, however, may preclude the attorney from receiving additional documents that may exist in the student's file that the attorney did not know were there. The best approach is a combination of the general and specific approach, where the attorney makes a general request for the educational records and then indicates that the request "includes, but is not limited to" specifically listed documents. This approach will help to guarantee that the school provides the attorney with as many records as possible, including those specific documents of which the attorney is already aware.

Below are two sample records requests to a school, which reflect different levels of detail and different approaches. An authorization for release of records and information, signed by the parent or caregiver, should be attached to any records request letter, as reflected in the language in the sample letters below, and sent to the school or the custodian of educational records.

August 10, 2010

Stevie Wonder
Special Education Coordinator
Jones Elementary School
22 Smith Road
Walkerville, Any State 22222

Re: Request for School Records for Frank Sinatra (DOB 1/22/02)

Dear Mr. Wonder:

I am writing to request a complete copy of any and all school records that you have for Frank Sinatra (DOB 1/22/02). This request includes, but is not limited to, the following documents:

- attendance records
- report cards and/or progress reports
- results of standardized testing
- disciplinary reports or records
- IEPs and multidisciplinary team (MDT) meeting notes
- progress notes
- prior notices and other relevant special education notifications
- any evaluations that may have been conducted on the child.

I have enclosed an authorization for release of records signed by Frank's mother, Ms. Sinatra. Please let me know when the records are available for pick up or please mail them to me at the address on my letterhead. Thank you for your timely response. If you have any questions, please do not hesitate to contact me at 222-333-4444.

Sincerely,

Sammy Davis, Jr.

Student Attorney

October 2, 2010

Loretta James, Special Education Coordinator

ABC Elementary School

123 4th Street

Plainville, State 11111

Re: Records Request for John Doe (Date of Birth 5/15/00)

Dear Ms. James,

I am writing on behalf of my client, Jane Doe, to request the full school records file for her son, John Doe (DOB: 5/15/00). Please include copies of his main file including report cards and progress reports, his special education file including IEPs, evaluations and progress reports, his disciplinary files, and any medical records that you have.

I have attached an Authorization for Release of Information and Records, signed by Ms. Doe.

Please fax the information to me as soon as possible at 123-555-1234, sent to my attention. Otherwise, I can come to the school to pick them up.

Thank you in advance for your time and attention. If you have any questions, please do not hesitate to contact me at 123-555-4321, x123 or via e-mail at greatattorney@helpingmyclient.org.

Regards,

Alan Attorney

Counsel for Jane Doe

2.   Medical Records, Including Mental Health Records

Medical records can sometimes provide critical evidence in a special education case. Health and education are inextricably linked. If a child has a purely medical disability, it is clear why medical records would be important. However, if the child has a learning disability or an emotional disturbance, the medical records are likely to still be important in a case. Depending on the doctor-patient relationship, doctors can obtain a variety of information about their patients. Doctors may identify certain developmental, academic, or mental health concerns, and then make recommendations for evaluations or services. Moreover, parents may speak to their child's doctor about educational concerns, such as their child's difficulty reading, their child's behavioral issues, or their child's difficulty with fine motor skills. The doctor may order an evaluation or refer the parent to a specialist. Or the doctor may simply make a note in the medical file that a concern exists or indicate that the child should receive special education. Any of these indications in a medical document by a doctor may be useful evidence at a due process hearing or relevant information to provide at an IEP meeting. In addition, medical documents may also contain evaluations that could be useful to the special education case. Medical records can also be useful in helping the attorney to develop the educational history of the student, which should also include a history of the child's early developmental milestones — which can often be found in medical records. An attorney should make medical record requests to a child's primary care doctor and to any specialists the child may have seen, including mental health providers.

Examples of Medical Records:

General:

- Well-child Visit Reports

- Developmental Evaluations

- Records of Referrals to Other Providers for Services or for Evaluations

- Sick Visit Reports

- Emergency Room Records

- Medication History

- Specialist Reports and Evaluations

Mental Health Records:

- Evaluations

- Treatment Plans

- Treatment Notes

- Diagnostic and Assessment Information

- Medication History

- Risk Assessment

Mental health records, a type of medical record, can play an important role in a special education case, especially when the case involves a child with behavioral issues in the classroom setting. Children with behavioral or social-emotional issues may have a mental health provider in the community who the attorney can contact to obtain records. Some examples of mental health providers are a counselor, psychiatrist, therapist, social worker, and psychologist. Information obtained in mental health records could be used to inform the attorney about the child's mental health history, the services the child has received in the past, or the services the child currently requires.

3.   Records from Outside Services Providers and Other Sources

If the student participates in activities or receives services outside of school, the attorney should request these records too. As described above in the initial client interview, the attorney should seek to learn about and obtain contact information for other providers who interact with the child so that when it is time to request these records, the attorney will know who to contact. Outside service providers could include mental health providers (as discussed above in medical records), tutors, mentors, non-clinical social workers, camp counselors, and athletic coaches. The documentation obtained from any of these providers could provide extra support for the attorney's case. For example, an independent tutor may keep progress notes for each tutoring session. These progress notes may contain information about the student's progress, lack of progress or behavior during tutoring sessions. The attorney could use this information to corroborate other information obtained on the student. Or in contrast, the attorney could use this information to impeach the credibility of information provided by the school. For example, if the student is scoring high marks on a report card from school, but the tutoring records indicate that the student cannot complete basic age-appropriate skills, the attorney can call into question the reliability of the school records.

If the student is involved in a neglect or delinquency matter, the attorney should consider obtaining documents from the court file. The court files can often contain relevant information for a special education case. The attorney should consult her local laws and court rules and procedures to determine if she is permitted to gain access to the court files and, if she is, how to go about doing so. The attorney, as discussed in later chapters, can also consider at this stage how to utilize the various court systems to further advance the client's objectives in the special education case and how to use the special education case to obtain better outcomes in any court matters.

As part of the investigation stage, the attorney can also obtain other documents and information that is not specifically related to the student but that is still relevant to the case. Such documents may include policy statements issued by the school system, memoranda of understanding between the school system and other government agencies, information about a particular school or educational program, and statements about procedures and best practices within the special education system. The attorney should consider engaging different strategies to obtain these documents. The attorney may be able to submit a simple request to the custodian of a certain document or find the information posted on the internet, or the attorney may need to submit a request under the Freedom of Information Act to obtain the information. In conjunction with collecting documents or subsequent to their collection, the attorney will also need to seek out key individuals in the case to interview.

Records for Jack

You just started working on Jack's case and one of your first tasks is to create an investigation plan for the case. One of the activities in the investigation plan is to obtain records for Jack to support your case.

- What kind of records would you request for Jack?

- Are there any specific documents you want to request? If so, which ones?

- To whom would you make each of these requests?

B.   Investigative Interviewing

Interviewing key individuals in a special education case is a critical part of any investigation plan. Attorneys can obtain a wealth of useful information from a variety of individuals, who are also potential witnesses in a due process hearing or civil action or potential IEP team members. For purposes of this chapter, key individuals who an attorney will want to interview in connection with a special education case are referred to as "witnesses." Some witnesses will prove to be more helpful than others. Some witnesses will turn out to be ideal witnesses to testify at a due process hearing, while others will not. Some witnesses may provide the attorney with useful information about the case that can help the attorney in developing a case theory or in advancing the client's objectives. Other witnesses may not provide the attorney with information directly about the case, but may provide the attorney with names of other people who the attorney will want to interview or ideas about additional documents to obtain.

Potential Witnesses in A Special Education Case — People the Attorney Should Consider Interviewing

- Student and Parent (as discussed above)

- General Education Teachers

- Special Education Teachers

- Mentor

- Tutor

- Classroom Aide

- Volunteers at School

- Special Education Coordinators or Supervisors

- School Administrators

- Related Service Providers (i.e., Counselors, Speech and Language Therapists, and Occupational Therapists)

- General Pediatrician

- Developmental Pediatrician

- Specialty Doctors (i.e., Neurologist, Psychiatrist)

- Nurse (from school or private practice)

- Family Member or Friend with Relevant Knowledge

- Classmate or Friend of Student

- Educational Expert

- Coach

- Outside Service Providers (as discussed above)

At the outset of a special education case, the attorney should brainstorm a list of witnesses that he or she wants to interview. A good starting point is to create a list of possible witnesses based on the information the attorney obtains from the client, the student, and from the document review. The attorney should then create an investigation plan to make certain that the attorney can interview as many witnesses as possible. Prior to meeting with the witness, the attorney should prepare for the interview by deciding what the attorney wants to find out from the witness. The attorney should outline and sequence the topics that he or she wants to cover in the interview and prepare specific questions to ask the witness. Prior to the interview, the attorney may also want to do some preliminary research on the witness if the attorney is unfamiliar with the witness. The research can be cursory or more detailed, depending on the situation. Cursory research on a witness can sometimes be accomplished through using basic Internet search engines, such as Google, or through legal research databases, such as Lexis or Westlaw. The attorney may uncover interesting facts about the witness that can help the attorney to build rapport with the witness. For example, if the attorney learns that the psychiatrist has written an article about alternatives to medication for children who suffer from depression, she could mention that she is familiar with the article and use it as an icebreaker at the outset of the interview. Or, the attorney may find information about the witness that will signal to the attorney that the witness may be problematic or that the witness has a history of negative behavior, such as information showing that the special education teacher is not properly certified or the therapist has a criminal record. Once the attorney is prepared for the interview, she will have to decide how to contact the witness and arrange the interview. The attorney can choose to contact the witness in advance via telephone or electronic mail to set up a time to meet or the attorney can choose to show up unexpectedly to interview the witness. The attorney should weigh the pros and cons of each method for every individual witness because the effectiveness of a particular approach will vary by witness.

Discussion Questions

Assume Jack's elementary school is part of a public school district, which is represented by its own Office of General Counsel. Taking into account Rule 4.2 of the American Bar Association's Model Rules on Professional Conduct and the accompanying comments, which provide guidelines for an attorney's communication with a represented party, can the attorney interview Jack's teacher? What about the special education coordinator at Jack's school who has decision-making authority related to the provision of special education services at the school? What about the assistant superintendent for the school district? Does your answer change for any of the preceding questions if there is pending litigation?

Interviewing a witness is different from interviewing the client or the student. First, the attorney does not work for the witness as the attorney does for the client. Second, there is no lawyer-client confidentiality. This absence of confidentiality could make it more difficult for the attorney to create trust with the witness, and the witness may not be as apt to provide information during the interview. Third, the witness may not continue to be available throughout the life of the case, and the attorney may only have one opportunity to interview a witness. Lastly, there are generally three types of witnesses, and the style of the interview will more than likely be dictated by the type of witness you are interviewing.

A witness can be hostile, neutral, or friendly. *See* Stefan H. Kreiger & Richard K. Neuman, Jr., Essential Lawyering Skills: Interviewing, Counseling, Negotiation, and Persuasive Fact Analysis 9 (3d ed. 2007). A hostile witness is someone who is adverse to your client or to the legal case. *Id.* It may be difficult to obtain information from a hostile witness, and he or she may not be willing to spend much time talking to the attorney, if the hostile witness is willing to talk to the attorney at all. An example of a hostile witness may be a school administrator who thinks that the client's child has too many behavioral problems or who has had prior clashes with the parent. A friendly witness is someone who may be sympathetic with the parent, the child or the legal case or may have an alliance with the parent or the child. *Id.* The child's longstanding pediatrician who believes that the school is not providing the child with the appropriate services and agrees with the due process complaint the attorney may be initiating against the school is an example of a friendly witness. A neutral witness is a person who may not want to spend time getting interviewed and sees the time spent as an inconvenience. *Id.* The neutral witness does not have a particular alliance to either side or may not want to get caught in the middle of a lawsuit. *Id.* An example of a neutral witness would be the student's tutor who works over sixty-five hours a week and is a fulltime graduate student. The tutor understands the student's learning difficulties and does not think that the school is providing the appropriate services, but the tutor also has a longstanding contract with the child's school and is friends with many of the student's teachers.

Discussion Questions

In interviewing each of the witnesses discussed above — the pediatrician, the school administrator, and the tutor — which of the different approaches can the attorney use in preparing for, scheduling, and conducting the interview for each witness? Why should the attorney choose these particular approaches?

When interviewing witnesses, the attorney should take care in the conduct of the interview so that she can obtain the best possible information from a particular witness. It is important to make the witness feel comfortable during the interview. When conducting an interview, the attorney should be friendly and use non-legalese language. The attorney may want to consider dressing for the interview in a particular way, such as in a business casual style, for the interview to ensure both that she is taken seriously and that she is not intimidating to the witness. The attorney should be mindful of where the interview is conducted and, to the best extent possible, make sure there are minimal distractions. To ensure an effective interview, the attorney should also use active listening skills and empathetic, non-judgmental responses, as discussed in detail in the above section "Client Interview."

Witnesses for Jack

- What witnesses would you interview in connection with Jack's case?
- What information would you want to try to obtain from each of these witnesses?

The attorney also needs to decide how he or she is going to document any valuable information obtained from the witness. The attorney may want to use any valuable information obtained from the witness at a subsequent due process hearing or IEP meeting and will need to preserve the information for future use. This is especially important for due process hearings, given that the attorney will not be able to testify herself at the hearing. The attorney can consider one of four approaches. First, the attorney can bring along another person such as an investigator or paralegal. Second, the attorney can send an investigator to interview the witness in lieu of the attorney. In both of these approaches, the investigator will serve as a witness to the statements made and then can subsequently testify about the information at the hearing. While hearsay is not generally admissible in court, in some jurisdictions, strict rules of evidence do not apply for due process hearings and thus hearsay may be admissible evidence. In jurisdictions where there are prohibitions against admitting hearsay, the information could still be introduced into evidence to impeach a witness or as one of the exceptions to the hearsay rule. Third, the attorney can summarize the conversation in a letter to a witness and send the letter to that witness as a written confirmation of the statement he or she made. The attorney will need to determine whether the letter will be admissible in a due process hearing before relying on this approach. The fourth approach, obtaining a written witness statement, can be used by itself or in conjunction with one of the other approaches.

Obtaining a written statement from a witness is the paramount way to preserve information from a witness. If the attorney (or the investigator or paralegal) is interviewing a witness and the witness provides information that supports the case, then the attorney should write down what the witness is saying in a clear, accurate, and easy-to-read format. When taking the statement, the attorney should number each page of the statement, record the name of the person making the statement, the name of the person writing the statement, the time of the statement, and the location where the statement was made. When the statement is complete, for accuracy purposes, the attorney should read the statement aloud back to the witness and have the witness read over the statement. The attorney should then have the witness initial each page and provide his or her signature along with the date at the end of the statement. It is important to use language prior to the signature that indicates that the witness is affirming the truth and accuracy of the statement. Once this written statement is obtained, the attorney may be able to use it as evidence at a due process hearing, for impeachment purposes at a due process hearing, or for review at an IEP meeting. Below is a sample template for a witness statement.

WITNESS STATEMENT

This is the statement of Janet Johnson. This statement was given by Janet Johnson (DOB: 5/22/84) in the presence of Outstanding Student Investigator of the Best Law School Special Education Legal Clinic at 1234 Main Street, U.S.A. on December 19, 2010 at 8:35 PM.

_____

_____

_____

I have reviewed and read this statement. I have had this statement read to me. I have initialed each page of this statement. I declare under penalty of perjury under the laws of the District of Columbia that the above is true and correct.

Executed this 19th day of December, 2010

_____

Signature of Janet Johnson

_____

Witness

---

1.   Consultation with Experts or Providers from Other Disciplines

Part of the attorney's investigation may include consultation with experts or providers from other disciplines. Special education law practice implicates many disciplines other than law — education, psychology, psychiatry, and developmental pediatrics are just a few. The attorney may want to consult with these professionals for variety of reasons. First, the attorney may be considering using an expert to advocate on behalf of the student. The expert may provide testimony at a due process hearing or participate at an IEP meeting in support of the parent's case. The expert may provide an evaluation, written progress report, or letter with recommendations that can be used at any point in the case, such as at a hearing or an IEP meeting, or as part of settlement negotiations. Second, the attorney may need to develop some expertise in a certain area to better understand the legal case. For example, the attorney may want to consult with an educational expert so that the attorney can understand what an optimal inclusion setting looks like for a child with an emotional disturbance. The attorney may want to consult with a neurologist to understand how traumatic brain injury can affect a child's learning processes. Or, the attorney may want to consult with a psychologist regarding the results of a psycho-educational evaluation. The attorney may choose to consult with the evaluator who completed the testing or a different evaluator, depending on the circumstances of the case.

Consulting Experts in Jack's Case

What experts should you consult with in Jack's case?

What is the purpose for consulting with each of the experts?

What information do you want to obtain from each of the experts?

Third, the attorney may want to consult with an expert to advocate with that expert on behalf of the student. For example, the attorney may consider accompanying the client and the student on the next visit with the student's psychiatrist. The attorney may want to advocate with the psychiatrist at the appointment to consider an alternative type of treatment for the student's Attention Deficit Disorder, such as incorporating school interventions into the student's treatment plan. The attorney should consider, at the outset and throughout the life of a case, which experts he or she wants to contact and for what reason. The attorney should recognize in a special education case that he or she should rely on the knowledge and expertise of professionals in other disciplines to gain a better understanding of the case and to obtain successful outcomes for the client. In fact, experts are sometimes required in order to effectively litigate certain issues, such as the need for a particular compensatory education plan, in some jurisdictions.

C.   Observing the Student

Visiting the student's school and observing the student during the school day is a vital part of any investigation plan in a special education case. If the student is involved in an after-school program or any other activities, the attorney should also consider observing the student in a setting apart from the classroom. The student's behavior and performance and the support and services the student is receiving can be compared and contrasted across settings. The attorney can rely on documents and second-hand information about the student's educational performance, but this information is not a substitute for a first-hand opportunity to observe the student's educational experiences. For reasons discussed above in the section on interviewing witnesses, the attorney should consider arranging for another individual, such as an investigator, to accompany the attorney when conducting the observation. Alternatively, the attorney can send another individual to complete the observation, such as an investigator or an educational expert. If the attorney sends someone to complete the observation, the attorney should provide the observer with background information about the student and the case, as well as information the attorney would like the observer to collect.

Items to Note During a School Visit/Observation:

- Number of students in the class

- Age and functioning level of students (if you are able to obtain this)

- Certification of teachers

- Student-teacher ratio

- Length of class periods

- Behavior interventions used by the teacher

- Type of work being done by class and by client's child

- Participation of client's child in class

- Interaction between client's child and classmates and teacher

- Lunch period

- Size of entire school

- Environment of classroom

- Teaching methodologies used

- Special resources or accommodations available

- Structure of classroom (free time vs. instruction time)

- Teacher's experience with special education students

There is a vast amount of information that the attorney can obtain from observing the student and visiting the school. The attorney will be able to compare the information she receives first-hand with information she has learned through documents and interviews. In this way, the observations can test the reliability of other information obtained. When conducting a school observation, the attorney should consider the time of day the observation is taking place. Is it early in the morning when the student may be at his or her best or is it late in the day when the student's attention starts to wane? The attorney should also try to complete the observation over an extended period so that the student is observed with more than one teacher, in more than one class, or learning about more than one subject matter. A student's behavior and performance can vary widely across these different realms and it is important to take note of any consistencies and discrepancies.

Subsequent to the school visit, it is good practice for the attorney to record the information obtained from the visit and observation. The attorney, or other individual who completes the observation, should draft a memo to the case file describing the visit and observation. It is important for the memo to be as detailed as possible, providing the names of people encountered (such as teachers or administrators), the time of visit, the description of the environment, and the specifics about what was observed. The attorney can also consider sending a letter to the school detailing any concerns about the child's education and/or requesting the school to remedy any problems observed. The attorney may be able to introduce either the memo or the letter into evidence at a due process hearing, depending on the evidentiary rules for administrative hearings in the attorney's jurisdiction.

Visit to Jack's School

- Should you visit Jack's school as part of the investigation in your case?

- If so, what information do you want to collect and why?

The attorney may choose to complete any combination of the three investigation major tasks — obtaining documents, interviewing witnesses, and observing the student — when going to visit the school. For example, while at the school, the attorney can pick up school records and ask to view samples of the student's recent schoolwork, observe the student in class, and take some time while in the class to interview the teacher. The attorney should also consider going to observe the student more than one time over the course of the case. Visiting the school and observing the student is an invaluable investigative task that may provide critical evidence at a due process hearing, relevant facts for an IEP meeting, or information from which the attorney can further develop his or her case.

VI. DEVELOPING AN EDUCATIONAL CHRONOLOGY

After the attorney embarks on investigation and begins obtaining information about the case and the student, the attorney should review and organize the information. Careful and detailed review of all investigative information is essential, and the attorney should become intimately familiar with the facts of the case. Developing a visual educational chronology for the student will assist the attorney with moving the case forward. Creating a chronology will provide the attorney with an overall picture of the student's educational history, which will be useful for developing a case theory as discussed in the section below. The attorney can see at what point the student began to struggle or at what point the school system failed in its legal obligations. The attorney can also see if there are any gaps in the investigation and assess whether further information needs to be obtained from the client or from any secondary sources. Moreover, the attorney can consider using the visual chronology as demonstrative evidence or as an illustrative aid at a due process hearing to assist the decision-maker in understanding the child's educational history and the failures of the school system. Hines & Tulman, *supra*, at 7-3.

The sample below, borrowed from Joseph Tulman and Joyce McGee's Special Education Advocacy Under the Individuals with Disabilities Education (IDEA) for Children in the Juvenile Delinquency System (1998) (p. 7-5 to 7-6), is one example of a method for organizing an educational chronology. This chart format organizes extensive information about the student's school history. The attorney can also consider developing outlines, timelines, or lists in lieu of a chart. In addition, the attorney can develop a separate chronology of the child's IEPs, evaluations, or developmental history to supplement a more comprehensive educational chronology, such as the one below. These types of chronologies are useful because the attorney can chart progress, regression, or stagnation in a particular area over an extended period of time. For example, when the attorney lays out the chronology of the IEPs, she may find that the student had the same or similar goals on the IEPs for multiple school years (indicating a possible lack of educational progress or denial of FAPE). Or, when the attorney creates a chronology of the evaluations, she may find that the same cognitive assessments administered at different periods yielded substantially different results or that the student's achievement tests scores have not improved over the past several years. When reviewing information obtained from investigation, the attorney should consider the most logical and practical way to organize the information so that she can reference and use it throughout the course of the case. Once investigation is underway and the attorney creates an educational chronology for the student, she can begin to analyze the facts and develop a legal theory (or multiple theories) for the case.

SCHOOL YEAR	SCHOOL ATTENDED	REPORT CARD GRADES	STANDAR-DIZED TEST SCORES	REPORTED CONDUCT OR BEHAVIOR	REPORTED ATTEN-DANCE	REPEATED GRADE?

TEACHER COMMENTS	DISCIPLI-NARY AC-TIONS?	PARENT/ SCHOOL CONTACT	PARENT INQUIRIES/ HELP RE: CHILD'S LACK OF PROGRESS	REQUEST MADE FOR SPECIAL ED. EVALUA-TIONS?	EVALUA-TION COMPLE-TED?	RE-EVALUA-TION COM-PLETED?

VII.   DEVELOPING A THEORY OF THE CLIENT'S CASE

Early in the case, the attorney should develop a legal theory for the case in preparation for achieving the client's objectives. The purpose of developing a case theory in a special education case is to create a persuasive story about the client so that the attorney can convince the school system or the IEP team to provide the student with an appropriate education or the judge or hearing officer to order the school system to provide the appropriate education to the student. Creatively combining the facts of the case to the relevant law is the foundation of developing a case theory. Creating a case theory involves more than simply making a conclusory statement, such as "the school failed to provide Jack with a FAPE," but instead involves a several-step process. David F. Chavkin, Clinical Legal Education: A Textbook for Law School Clinical Programs 48 (2002). First, the attorney should assess the facts obtained from the client and the investigation. Taking all of the critical facts about the case, the attorney should create a story. *Id.* The attorney should deal with both the good and bad facts of the case — emphasizing the good facts and explaining and mitigating the bad facts. Second, the attorney should identify the relevant special education law. The attorney should apply the facts of the case (the story) to the relevant law, and engage the facts in a legal analysis. *Id.* Finally, the attorney should reach a conclusion based on the legal analysis that has the likelihood of achieving the client's objectives. *Id.*

The attorney may choose to develop the case theory early in the case prior to conducting extensive investigation. Drafting a case theory can help an attorney determine which facts are necessary to support the legal theory and therefore prove useful in crafting an investigation plan. The case theory is dynamic and likely to change as the attorney learns more facts through investigation. The case theory should be malleable while still serving as a guiding anchor for the attorney throughout the life of the case.

---

8 Elements to Creating a Good Theory of the Case in the Special Education Context

A good case theory should:

- be consistent with the client's wishes;

- be consistent with the client's objectives;

- be consistent with the facts of the case;

- be consistent with the law;

- be persuasive;

- be credible;

- be appealing emotionally; and

- tie everything together and be comprehensive.

Chavkin, *supra*, at 48-50.

In special education cases, case theory will fall into one of two major categories. Tulman, *supra*, at 7-1 to 7-110. The first category is for students who have never received special education services. In these cases, the attorney will have to assess whether the student is entitled to special education services under the law. *Id.* The second category is for students who are already in the special education system. The attorney in these cases will have to assess whether the special education services and programming are appropriate to meet the student's needs and whether, historically, the services and programming were appropriate for the student. *Id.*

In a special education case, there may be many legal violations, especially if the attorney is assessing the case for violations over more than one school year. In preparing to develop a case theory, the attorney should read all of the documents and review all information with a critical eye to identify all plausible legal violations. The attorney should assess the facts of the case for both procedural and substantive violations of the law. For example, when reviewing an IEP document, the attorney will want to see if all necessary participants were present at the meeting. The attorney will also want to see if the type and frequency of a particular related service is appropriate to meet the student's needs. When reviewing evaluations, the attorney will want to see if the evaluations were completed in a timely fashion. The attorney will also want to determine whether all of the evaluator's recommendations were incorporated into the student's IEP and if they were not, the reasons why they were not included. As the attorney reads the subsequent chapters in this book, where each stage of the special education process is discussed in detail, the attorney will be able to more comprehensively assess the facts in her case to determine all of the legal violations that exist and to develop a good theory of the case.

Legal Issue/ Violation	Elements	Facts	Documents	Witnesses

The legal issue chart above, used in the Juvenile and Special Education Law Clinic at the University of the District of Columbia David A. Clarke's School of Law, is an example of one way for the attorney to chart out the legal issues in the case. Completing this chart can serve to create the foundation on which the attorney will develop the theory of the case. This chart is also helpful for the attorney to use in preparation for litigating a case. The attorney can assess whether he or she is missing any evidence to support all the factual contentions in the case. After completing the legal issue chart for the case or similar mapping of the legal issues and facts, the attorney can begin to develop a winning case theory, which she can use — and modify as necessary — as the case proceeds.

VIII.   CLIENT COUNSELING

After the attorney has conducted legal research and factual investigation, and developed a sound theory of the case, the attorney can prepare to counsel the client on various courses of action in the case. Client counseling includes a discussion of options, consequences of each, and a decision as to the course of action. Effective counseling will assist a client in selecting a legal method of resolution that will best satisfy the client's goals and values. Ellmann et al., *supra*, at 50. Because the student's educational needs are constantly evolving, the attorney should consider counseling the client throughout the course of the case. Below are general instructions for two client counseling simulations. Confidential instructions for the various roles for each simulation will be provided in the teacher's manual.

Special Education Practicum

Counseling Session Between Parent and Advocate (A) & (B)

Joint Instructions for Maria Martinez and Advocate

*Confidential instructions for each role can be found in the teacher's manual

Participants:

1. **Parent**

2. **Advocate**

Elena Martinez is in the fourth grade and attends Crestview Elementary. Specialists at Children's Hospital diagnosed Elena with attention deficit hyperactivity disorder (ADHD) and a speech-language impairment when she was in first grade. At the request of her mom and her second grade teacher, school staff administered a multi-factored evaluation (MFE) to Elena at the beginning of Elena's third grade year. As a result of that evaluation, the evaluation team deemed Elena eligible for special education services under the category of "other health impairment" (OHI). Since that time, Elena has had an individualized education plan (IEP).

The second grading period for Elena's fourth grade year ended on October 28. According to her most recent report card, Elena is struggling both academically and behaviorally. She received an A in physical education, a B- in Math, an F in reading, and D's in all other subjects. The report card also identified problems with Elena's behavior at school. That information, included under the "personal development" section of the report card, noted problems with the following issues: displaying self control, staying on task, being prepared, bringing necessary supplies, organizing school work and personal belongings, working carefully and neatly, and working independently.

The school principal disciplined Elena numerous times over the last few months for "insubordination" in the classroom. This discipline includes frequent removals from the classroom and multiple early removals and suspensions from the school building. Suspension means that a student is removed from school for a certain number of days, depending on the type of school violation. At Crestview Elementary, as with most schools, on the days a child is removed from school for behavior, the school principal contacts the child's parent and requests that the parent immediately pick up his or her child from school. The child cannot return to school for the remainder of the day in which he or she was removed in addition to the number of designated suspension days.

Elena's academic background up until her current fourth grade year is summarized below:

Kindergarten

Elena performed reasonably well in kindergarten, with a few minor incidents.

First Grade

In first grade, Elena struggled with reading. She was also frequently disciplined for not doing her work, for routinely having a messy desk, for talking to her neighbors during reading time, for not remaining in her seat during work time, and for calling out answers without raising her hand. Her report card indicated that she needed improvement in all subjects. Her mother requested that the school provide Elena with special education services. The school principal informed her mother that Elena did not qualify for an IEP.

Second Grade

By second grade Elena was significantly behind her peers in reading. She spent a considerable amount of time at her desk with her head down during recess because she was constantly getting in trouble for the same reasons as in first grade.

Third Grade

Elena's behavior progressively worsened during her third grade year. Mrs. Johnson, Elena's third grade teacher, wholeheartedly believed in the school's zero tolerance policy. She used a demerit system to address misbehavior in the classroom. Each day, the first time a student was not doing what she was supposed to do, the teacher gave the student a warning. The second time a student was not doing something she was supposed to do, the student missed recess, and the third time the student was sent to the principal's office.

Elena was sent to the office at least twice each week in third grade during reading time or for leaving the room without asking, not paying attention while the teacher was talking, not completing assignments, getting up out of her seat when she was told to stay seated, playing with toys in her desk, and not turning in completed assignments. Elena was regularly ridiculed by her classmates because they said she was dumb. The principal became irritated that Elena was always taking up his time, so half way through the second grading period he instituted a policy that she would receive an out of school suspension for every third time she was sent to his office. The week after the principal made this decision, Elena was suspended. As the year went on, Elena was suspended more and more frequently.

During Elena's third grade year, her mom asked the teacher for additional help for Elena during every parent-teacher conference. She also asked the principal about having her tested for special education services frequently throughout the year as she received calls to come and pick Elena up early due to insubordination. The principal told her that Elena's only problem was stubbornness and an unwillingness to follow rules.

Before Thanksgiving, Elena's mom ran into another parent who advised her to put her request for an evaluation in writing. Maria put her request in writing and sent a copy of the letter to the school with a letter from the doctor stating that Elena had been diagnosed with ADHD and a speech impairment. The evaluation was finally completed and an IEP was put into place.

The IEP that was put in place has some suggestions for improving Elena's organizational skills by giving her check lists at her desk to help her keep on track with her work. She also gets one thirty minute session of speech-language therapy a week. The subsequent IEP provided the same services.

Disability Rights Law Clinic
American University Washington College of Law
4801 Massachusetts Ave., NW Suite 417 • Washington, DC 20016
Phone: (202) 274-4147 • Fax: (202) 274-0659

Client Counseling Simulation — Goodman

Written by Robert D. Dinerstein

Joint Instructions for Lawyer and Mr./Ms. Goodman

* Confidential Instructions for Mr./Ms. Goodman and Confidential Instructions for the Lawyer can be found in the teacher's manual

This client counseling session follows the Interviewing Simulation based on the same facts, which you should have conducted prior to conducting this counseling session. This counseling session builds on the facts you learned in your Interviewing Simulation instruction sheets and that you learned in the course of conducting the Interviewing Simulation. As you recall, the status of the case at the time of the first interview was that the principal was planning to send Roger to an interim alternative educational setting for up to 45 school days before any hearing on his misbehavior in class. Assume it is two weeks since the client interview took place. Confidential instructions for both the Lawyer and Mr./Ms. Goodman will be provided separately in the teacher's manual.

IX. CONCLUSION

In conclusion, an attorney initiating a special education case should begin by thoughtfully identifying his or her model of representation, and reflecting the arrangement as to who will serve as the client within a clearly drafted retainer agreement. The attorney will need to draft an authorization for release of information and records, and obtain the client's signature in order to be able to request records. The attorney may also wish to send the client a letter introducing herself and laying out any next steps. Early in the representation, the attorney will need to prepare for and conduct a thorough client interview, which should include an interview of both the parent and student, whenever possible, regardless of which individual is serving in the client role. The attorney will also need to conduct a comprehensive investigation into the special education case, including obtaining documents, interviewing key individuals (who are also potential witnesses), including any experts the attorney wishes to consult, and observing the student. The information that the attorney gathers in the course of interviewing the client and conducting the investigation should be used to develop an educational chronology for the student. The attorney will also need to develop a guiding, but dynamic, case theory that tells a persuasive story about the client, reflecting the law and relevant facts, in support of the client's objectives. Identifying the legal issues, the elements within each legal issue, the supporting facts, and the sources for those facts will also help the attorney further develop his or her case. Once the attorney has identified the legal violations and the various courses of action that the client can consider going forward, the attorney will need to counsel the client in selecting a method of resolution that will satisfy the client's goals. These various steps in initiating a special education case will help prepare the lawyer to effectively advocate for the protection of her client's special education rights throughout the course of the case.

Chapter 3

CHILD FIND[1]

I. INTRODUCTION

Each state accepting federal funds under IDEA is responsible for having in effect policies and procedures to ensure that all children with disabilities are "identified, located and evaluated," and "a practical method is developed and implemented to determine which children are currently receiving needed special education and related services." 34 C.F.R. § 300.111(a). This is called the "child find" obligation of IDEA. 20 U.S.C. § 1412(a)(3). The state educational agency (SEA) bears the ultimate responsibility to ensure compliance with the IDEA. 20 U.S.C. § 1412(a)(3), (11). Local education agencies (LEAs) are primarily responsible for complying with state policies and procedures as a condition of receiving IDEA funds. 20 U.S.C. § 1413(a)(1). This includes the child find obligation of IDEA. 20 U.S.C. § 1412(a)(3).

The child find provision encompasses "all children residing in the State" and includes children with disabilities who are homeless, wards of the state, and children with disabilities attending private schools, regardless of the severity of their disability, and who "are in need of special education and related services." 34 C.F.R. § 300.111(a). Child find also applies to those children who are "highly mobile," such as migrant and homeless children, as well as those who are "suspected of being a child with a disability" and in need of special education, even if they are being promoted to the next grade level. 34 C.F.R. § 300.111(a)(1)(i), (c). For those children who are "highly mobile," such as migrant and homeless children, IDEA requires that LEAs cooperate in ensuring the linkage of health and educational records for "electronic exchange" with other states. 20 U.S.C. § 1413(a)(9); 34 C.F.R. § 300.111(c).

In implementing the child find requirements, a state may adopt a definition of the term "developmental delay" to establish eligibility under IDEA that applies to children "aged three through nine, or to a subset of that age range (*e.g.*, ages three to five)." 34 C.F.R. § 111(b)(1). Moreover, "early identification and assessment" of children's disabilities is included as related services. 34 C.F.R. § 300.34(a). This means that a state may use IDEA funds for "implementation of a formal plan for identifying a disability as early as possible in a child's life." 34 C.F.R. § 300.34(c)(3).

The IDEA and its implementing regulations do not indicate to what extent the state and LEAs must ensure that the child find obligation must be met or carried out for children who are enrolled in public schools. Thus, states are left to develop and implement their plans to ensure that children are located, identified and evaluated in accordance with the IDEA. Activities that the LEA must conduct have been explained in the comments to the implementing regulations to:

---

[1] This chapter was written by Esther Canty-Barnes, Director, Special Education Clinic, Rutgers-Newark School of Law.

[I]nclude, but is not limited to, such activities as widely distributing informational brochures, providing regular public service announcements, staffing exhibits at health fairs and other community activities, and creating direct liaisons with private schools.

71 Fed. Reg. 46593 (2006).

Extensive requirements apply to children who are enrolled in private schools. 34 C.F.R. § 300.130 to 300.144. Each LEA must locate, identify and evaluate all children with disabilities who are placed in private schools by their parents. 34 C.F.R. § 300.131(a). Private schools include "religious, elementary and secondary schools." 20 U.S.C. § 1412(a)(10)(A)(ii)(I). The LEA where the private school is located is responsible for conducting a "thorough and complete child find process to determine the number of parentally placed children with disabilities attending private schools located in the local educational agency." 20 U.S.C. § 1412(a)(10)(A)(i)(II). The child find process must be designed to ensure "equitable participation" of parentally placed children in private schools and to obtain an accurate count of these children. 34 C.F.R. § 300.131(b). Costs may not be considered in determining if the LEA has carried out its child find mandate. 34 C.F.R. § 300.131(d). The LEA where the private school is located must conduct "activities similar to activities undertaken" for public school children to ensure that the timelines are consistent with those for public school children. 34 C.F.R. § 300.131(c).

II. ELIGIBLE CHILDREN

Eligible Children under Part B of the IDEA must be between the ages of three and twenty-one and meet the definition of a "child with a disability." 20 U.S.C. § 1401(3). A child with a disability is defined as a child with 1) mental retardation, 2) hearing impairments, 3) speech or language impairments, 4) visual impairments, 5) serious emotional disturbances, 6) orthopedic impairments, 7) autism, 8) traumatic brain injury, 9) other health impairments, or 10) specific learning disabilities; and as a result, "needs special education and related services." 20 U.S.C. § 1401(3)(A). At the discretion of each state, a "child with a disability" may also include children between the ages of three through nine, including the preschool aged group of three to five, who are experiencing developmental delays in one or more of the following areas: physical development, cognitive development, communication development, social emotional development, or adaptive development; and "by reason thereof, needs special education and related services." 20 U.S.C. § 1401(3)(B)(i)-(ii). Since the definition of a "child with a disability" may vary somewhat from state to state, it is important to review state statutes, regulations and standards to determine whether a child meets the eligibility criteria of a particular state. This topic is discussed in greater depth in the Chapter 4.

III. PROCEDURES FOR IDENTIFICATION AND REFERRALS

Each state must establish procedures for identifying, referring and evaluating children with disabilities and ensuring that procedural protections of the parent and the child are consistent with federal laws. 20 U.S.C. § 1414(a)(1)(C)(i). Moreover, each state must also have procedures to determine if a child meets the criteria for a "child with a disability" and to determine the educational needs of the child. 34 C.F.R. § 300.301(c)(2). The procedures for referring or identifying children with a disability may vary from state to state, however, the process typically begins with a referral.

A referral is a written request for an initial evaluation to determine whether the child qualifies as a child with a disability. N.J. Admin. Code § 6A:14-1.3; Cal. Educ. Code § 56029 (2009). "[A] parent of a child, or a State educational agency, other State agency, or local educational agency may initiate a request for an initial evaluation to determine" whether the child is an eligible child with a disability. 20 U.S.C. § 1414(a)(1)(B). Each public agency must conduct a "full and individual initial evaluation" in compliance with the IDEA before the "initial provision of special education." 34 C.F.R. § 300.301(a).

The initial evaluation must consist of procedures to determine whether a child is a child with a disability within sixty days of receipt of parental consent or a timeframe within which the evaluations must be conducted as established by the state. 34 C.F.R. § 300.310(c)(1).

The sixty day timeframe does not apply if the parent of the child "repeatedly fails to produce the child for the evaluation" or the "child enrolls in another public agency after" the sixty day timeframe and before a determination is made as to whether the child meets the eligibility criteria. 34 C.F.R. § 300.301(d). If a child is enrolled in another district during the identification process, the second exception applies "only if the subsequent public agency is making sufficient progress to ensure prompt completion of the evaluation," and the parties agree to a specific time when the evaluations are to be completed. 34 C.F.R. § 301.301(e).

A parent or public agency may initiate a request for an evaluation. 34 C.F.R. § 300.301(b). If a LEA requests an evaluation, some states require the use of interventions prior to referral. Ohio Operating Standards, § 3301-51-06(A)(2) (2008); N.J. Admin. Code § 6A:14-3.3(b)-(c) (2010). However, interventions may not be used to unnecessarily delay the evaluation. N.J. Admin. Code § 6A:14-3.3(e) (2010). Where a parent requests the referral, the public agency must act upon the request within a reasonable time as designated by state law. *Id.* The parent must be given an opportunity to participate in identification and referral meetings and given prior written notice regarding the meetings. 34 C.F.R. § 300.501(b)(1)(i), (b)(2). Moreover, the parent must be given the opportunity to review and inspect the child's educational records during the process. 34 C.F.R. § 300.501(a)(1).

The timelines and procedures for the referral and identification process vary from state to state. In New Jersey, a school district must respond to the parent's request for an evaluation within twenty days and give prior written notice at least fifteen days in advance of any action when it "proposes" or "refuses" to implement a change in the identification, evaluation, placement or the provision of a FAPE. N.J. Admin. Code § 6A:14-2.3(h)(1), (5) (2010). In California, unless the parent or guardian agrees to an extension, "a proposed assessment plan shall be developed within 15 calendar days of referral for assessment," excluding holidays and vacations. Cal. Educ. Code § 56043(a) (2009). The parent or guardian has fifteen days after receiving the proposed assessment plan or changes to an existing plan, to either consent or refuse the plan. Cal. Educ. Code § 56043(b) (2009). In Ohio, within thirty days of receipt of a request for a referral, the public agency must obtain parental consent for an initial evaluation or provide prior written notice stating that the school does not suspect a disability. Ohio Operating Standards § 3301-51-06(B)(3) (2008).

PRACTICE TIPS:

- Timelines are incredibly important in the referral process. Be sure to keep track of all dates (*e.g.*, when a request for evaluation was made, the date the assessment plan was signed, and when the sixty day timeframe expires).

- Check your state laws for the timeframe for creation of an assessment plan after consent to assess is given.

- Keep track of the date that a request for an evaluation was made and mark your calendar with the appropriate deadline by which the LEA must generate an assessment plan based on your state's timeframe.

- Then, mark your calendar for sixty days from the date that parental consent was given. That is the date by which the LEA must assess the student, unless otherwise agreed to by both parties.

IV. PROCEDURAL SAFEGUARDS NOTICE

The parent must be given the procedural safeguards notice "upon initial referral or parent request for an evaluation." 34 C.F.R. § 300.504(a)(1). The procedural safeguards notice must include a "full explanation" of the parent's many procedural rights, including those relating to independent evaluations, prior written notice, parental consent, access to education records, disclosure of evaluations results, and the opportunity to present and resolve complaints. 34 C.F.R. § 300.504(a)(1), (c).

V. PRIOR WRITTEN NOTICE

There are several instances where a LEA must provide prior written notice[2] to the parent of a child with a disability. 34 C.F.R. § 300.503(a). Prior written notice must be given a "reasonable time before" the public agency "proposes to initiate or change" or "refuses to initiate or change" the "identification" or "evaluation" of a child with a disability. 34 C.F.R. § 300.503(a). The written notice must include:

1) A description of the action proposed or refused by the agency;

2) An explanation of why the agency proposes or refuses to take action;

3) A description of each evaluation procedure, assessment, record, or report the agency used . . . ;

---

[2] The term "prior written notice" is an anachronism from a time when the requirement was only triggered if the child was to be removed from the regular classroom. Written notice was required before such a change could take place. Now, this term is used as a catch-all phrase whenever the school district is acting contrary to the parent's request or expectations. It simply serves as an explanation for the school district's conduct.

4) A statement that the parents . . . have protection under the procedural safeguards
. . . ;

5) Sources the parents may contact to obtain additional assistance in understanding the
provisions . . . ;

6) A description of other options that the IEP Team considered and the reasons why
those options were rejected; and

7) A description of other factors that are relevant to the agency's proposal or refusal.

34 C.F.R. § 300.503(b). The notice must be written in language understandable by the general
public and provided in the parent's native language or mode of communication unless it is not
feasible to do so. 34 C.F.R. § 300.503.

Prior written notice is a very important procedural step in the IDEA process because it
gives the parent an understanding of why a school district took a particular action, such as
refusing to identify a child as disabled, so that the parent can file a due process complaint, if
appropriate. As stated above, prior written notice is required when the agency "refuses to take
action." Therefore, a refusal to identify a child as disabled can trigger the prior written notice
requirement.

REMEMBER:

It is critical to have the school district put any proposed action in writing. This is
what you will use as your basis to challenge a school district's action.

VI. INFORMED CONSENT

Before eligibility can be determined, there must be informed consent by the parent of the
child for the initial evaluation. 20 U.S.C. § 1414(a)(1)(D)(i)(I). Informed consent means that the
parent 1) has been "fully informed" in his or her "native language or mode of communication"
of all relevant information concerning the activity for which the school district requests
consent; 2) "understands and agrees in writing" to the activity; and 3) understands that consent
is voluntary and may be revoked at any time. 34 C.F.R. § 300.9(a)-(c). The consent must be in
writing and describe the activity for which consent is requested and list the records, if any, that
are to be released, and the persons to whom they are to be released. 34 C.F.R. § 300.9(b).

Subsequent to the parent's consent, the LEA has sixty days in which to complete the
evaluation, unless otherwise indicated by state law. Where the parent refuses to consent to the
initial evaluation or fails to respond, the LEA will not be considered to be in violation of IDEA
or required to provide a FAPE. 20 U.S.C. § 1414(a)(1)(D)(ii)(III). Under these circumstances,
the LEA may file a request for due process or mediation if appropriate. 34 C.F.R.
§ 300.300(a)(3)(i). A LEA does not violate its obligations under IDEA if it declines to obtain an
evaluation through due process or mediation. 34 C.F.R. § 300.300(a)(3)(ii).

Where a child is a ward of the state, the LEA must make reasonable efforts to obtain the consent of the parent for the initial evaluation. 20 U.S.C. § 1414(a)(1)(D)(iii). Nonetheless, the LEA is not required to obtain informed consent from a parent if: 1) the whereabouts of the parents cannot be determined after "reasonable efforts;" 2) the parents' rights have been terminated; or 3) the parents' rights to make educational decisions "have been subrogated by a judge" and "consent for an initial evaluation has been given by an individual appointed by the judge to represent the child." 20 U.S.C. § 1414(a)(1)(D)(iii)(II).

VII. CHARTER SCHOOLS AND IDEA

Children who attend public charter schools and their parents retain their rights under IDEA. 34 C.F.R. § 300.209(a). Public charter schools, as a part of their affirmative obligation to provide FAPE to those eligible students, are not exempt from the child find mandate of IDEA. Rebekah Gleason, *Looking Back and Moving Forward: New Approaches to Legal Advocacy in the 21st Century: Charter Schools and Special Education: Part of the Solution or Part of the Problem?*, 9 USC-DCSL L. Rev. 145, 162 (2007). For-profit charter schools are not eligible for funding under IDEA. *Ariz. State Bd. of Charter Sch. v. U.S. Dept. of Educ.*, 464 F.3d 1003, 1008 (9th Cir. 2006). Because federal IDEA funding is specifically limited to "nonprofit" institutions, including nonprofit charter schools, the child find obligations for charter schools that are designated as for-profit would rest with the LEA where the for-profit charter school is located. 34 C.F.R. § 300.131(a).

Public charter schools are considered elementary and secondary schools within the meaning of the IDEA and are eligible for IDEA funding. 20 U.S.C. § 1401(6), (27); 20 U.S.C. § 7801(18), (36). An elementary or secondary school means a "nonprofit institutional day or residential school, including a public elementary charter school" or a "public secondary charter school." *Id.* A LEA is defined by IDEA as a "public board of education or other public authority legally constituted within a State for either administrative control or direction of, or to perform a service function for, public elementary schools or secondary schools." 20 U.S.C. § 1401(19)(A).

Where charter schools are a part of a LEA, the LEA must serve children with disabilities "in the same manner" it serves children in its other schools, "including providing supplementary and related services." 20 U.S.C. § 1413(a)(5)(A). In such cases, the LEA provides funds to the charter schools "on the same basis as the local education agency provides funds" to its other public schools including "proportional distribution" based on enrollment of children with disabilities. 20 U.S.C. § 1413(a)(5)(B). Unless state law provides otherwise, the LEA is responsible for ensuring that the requirements of the IDEA are met. 34 C.F.R. § 300.209(b)(2)(ii).

In cases where the public charter school is an individual LEA, separate and apart from the public school district in which it is located, and receives state funds, the charter school is responsible for ensuring that the requirements of IDEA are met, unless otherwise indicated by state law. 20 U.S.C. § 1413(a); 34 C.F.R. § 300.209(c). Where a public charter school is not considered a LEA or a part of a LEA and is receiving IDEA funds, the SEA is responsible for ensuring compliance with the provisions of the IDEA. 34 C.F.R. § 300.209(d).

(Initial Referral Request Form Letter)

Jane Smith
Address of Parent
Anywhere, USA 12345
Phone Number (Day)
Phone Number (Evening)

_____
School Name

_____
School Address

_____
City, State, Zip Code

Dear _____:
    Child Study Team Member

I am the parent of [name of child] , who was born [date of birth] .

My child is in the _____ grade and attends School at [name of school] .

    My child is having academic difficulty and is not progressing well in school. I believe that s/he needs special education services and supports. I am writing to request a child study team evaluation to determine if s/he is eligible for special education services. I understand that you must schedule a meeting within _____ calendar days of the time you receive this letter to determine if an evaluation is needed. Please contact me as soon as possible to let me know the time and date of the evaluation meeting.

    Thank you for your time and assistance in my child's education

Very truly yours,

_____
Parent/Caregiver's Name

SAMPLE NOTICE: INVITATION TO AN IDENTIFICATION MEETING

Date:

Name
Address
City, State 00000

Dear (*parent's name or name of adult student*):

You are invited to attend a meeting [*regarding your child*, _____]. The purpose of this meeting is to determine whether an evaluation will be conducted to determine if your child is eligible for special education and related services. If it is determined that an evaluation will be conducted, the members of the team will determine the nature and scope of the assessments to be conducted.

Your participation in planning for [*your educational needs*] **or** [*the educational needs of your child*] is important. The meeting is scheduled for:

Date: **Time:**   **Location:**

If this is not a convenient time or place, or should you have any questions, please contact me (*or name of other person*) by (*date*) at (*phone*) to discuss rescheduling the meeting or to discuss your questions.

The following individuals will be participating in the meeting:

Title:

_____School psychologist

_____Learning disabilities teacher-consultant

_____School social worker

_____General education teacher

_____Other: _____

The agency representative is:

_____ Case manager

_____ Other: _____

If you have any questions, please contact me at (*phone*).

Sincerely,

(Name)
(Position)

Attachment: Parental Rights In Special Education (PRISE)

N.J. Department of Education website - http://www.nj.gov/education/specialed/form/

SAMPLE NOTICE FOLLOWING AN IDENTIFICATION/EVALUATION PLANNING MEETING

Date: _____

Parent's Name: _____

Address: _____

City, State ZIP Code: _____

Dear (*parent's name*): _____

As the result of an identification and evaluation planning meeting held with you on (date), the (*school district*) proposes to evaluate your child for special education and related services. Therefore, the district proposes to conduct the following assessment(s) of your child and requests your consent to conduct the assessment(s):

Areas of Suspected Disability:

Assessment Procedures: **Evaluators (by discipline):**
_____ Standardized Test(s):
        _____   _____
        _____   _____

_____ Functional Assessment(s)[3]:
        _____   _____
        _____   _____
        _____   _____
        _____

_____ Related (Therapy) Services
        _____   _____
        _____   _____

_____ Other: (Please specify)
        _____   _____

_____

The following is a description of any other options discussed (when other options were considered) and the reasons why they were rejected:

PROCEDURAL SAFEGUARDS STATEMENT:

As the parent of a student with disabilities, you have rights regarding the identification, evaluation, classification, the development of an IEP, placement, and the provision of a free, appropriate public education under the New Jersey Administrative Code for Special Educa-

---

[3] A functional assessment includes assessment of academic performance and where appropriate, assessment of: behavior, language needs for LEP students, communication needs and the need for assistive technology. A functional assessment consists of an observation, interviews, record review, a review of interventions in general education and one or more informal measures.

tion, N.J.A.C. 6A:14. A description of these rights, which are called procedural safeguards, is contained in the document, *Parental Rights in Special Education (PRISE)*. This document is published by the New Jersey Department of Education.

A copy of *PRISE* is provided to you one time per year and upon referral for an initial evaluation, when you request a due process hearing or complaint investigation and when a disciplinary action that constitutes a change of placement is initiated. In addition you may request a copy by contacting (*name of office or district personnel*) at (*phone*).

For help in understanding your rights, you may contact any of the following:

- (*name of school district representative*) (*phone*)

- Statewide Parent Advocacy Network (SPAN) at 1(800) 654-7726

- New Jersey Protection and Advocacy, Inc. at 1(800) 922-7233

- The New Jersey Department of Education through the (*name of*) County Office, (*name of county supervisor of child study*), (*phone*)

If you have any questions regarding this notice, please contact me.

Sincerely,

(Name)
(Position)
(Phone Number)
Attachments: New Jersey Administrative Code, (N.J.A.C.) 6A:14, Special Education

New Jersey Administrative Code (N.J.A.C.) 1:6A, Office of Administrative Law, Special Education Program

N.J. Department of Education website — http://www.nj.gov/education/specialed/form/

In light of this material, consider the following hypothetical. Did the district violate its child find obligations and, if so, what recourse do her parents have?

Sally

Sally has attended public school since kindergarten and is a high functioning student academically. She has excellent grades and an SAT score of over 1400. In high school, her classes were primarily advanced placement honors classes.

She began to experience psychiatric problems during her sophomore year, and her mother managed to obtain treatment for her. During her junior year, she began to deteriorate and was unable to handle the public school system. By June of her junior year, she had missed at least sixty days of school. Despite Sally's absences and bouts with major depression, the school district promoted her to her senior year. During her senior year, Sally's depression continued to the extent that she could not attend school after October of her senior year. From October through December, she received home instruction in math and language arts. Home instruction was discontinued when Sally could no longer function and was hospitalized for her depression and suicidal thoughts. Her hospitalization continued for a period of four months or until May of her senior year. While hospitalized, Sally received academic instruction totaling five hours per week. The course work included general instruction in math, history and English.

In May, the school district advised Sally's parents that Sally was eligible for graduation. The social worker attempted to arrange for Sally to be placed in a residential school for students who were high functioning academically, but Sally's school district refused. Graduation is scheduled for June 23 and Sally's parents have come to you for advice to determine what options are available for their daughter.

When do you think the school district should have suspected that Sally may potentially be a child with a disability? In considering the advice you would give Sally's parents, would your response be the same if the hospital was located in a different city or town? If Sally was attending a private boarding school in another state when she was hospitalized, what would her options be?

Chapter 4

EDUCATIONAL EVALUATIONS AND ASSESSMENTS[1]

Educational evaluations and assessments are a crucial component of compliance with the IDEA. Advocates need to have a solid understanding of how to interpret test scores in order to assist children and their families. This chapter will seek to provide an overview of how to read and interpret test scores and then discuss each of the categories of disabilities potentially covered under the IDEA as well as the Americans with Disabilities Act (ADA) and Section 504 of the Rehabilitation Act of 1973. The emphasis of the chapter will be the IDEA definitions, but some brief discussion of the ADA and Section 504 will also be included.

I. IDEA AND ADA OVERVIEW

A. IDEA

Under the IDEA, the term "child with a disability" means a child —

(i)   with mental retardation, hearing impairments (including deafness), speech or language impairments, visual impairments (including blindness), serious emotional disturbance (referred to in this title as "emotional disturbance"), orthopedic impairments, autism, traumatic brain injury, other health impairments, or specific learning disabilities; and

(ii)   who, by reason thereof, needs special education and related services.

20 U.S.C. § 1401(3)(A).

School districts have the flexibility to use a more expansive definition of disability for young children, which will be discussed below. School districts have an obligation to identify, locate and evaluate which children meet this definition and are entitled to special education and related services. *See* 20 U.S.C. § 1412(a)(3) (Child find provision). A school district is obligated to use "a variety of assessment tools and strategies to gather relevant functional, developmental, and academic information, including information provided by the parent" to determine whether a child is a child with a disability. *See* 20 U.S.C. § 1414(b). Thus, advocates for children need to have a good grasp of assessment tools in order to enter into discussions concerning whether a child should be covered by the IDEA as a child with a disability.

B. ADA and Section 504

Under the ADA and Section 504, the term disability means, with respect to an individual —

---

[1] This chapter was written by Ruth Colker, Distinguished University Professor & Heck-Faust Memorial Chair in Constitutional Law, Michael E. Moritz College of Law, The Ohio State University.

(A)   a physical or mental impairment that substantially limits one or more major life activities of such individual;

(B)   a record of such an impairment; or

(C)   being regarded as having such an impairment.

42 U.S.C. § 12102(1) (ADA).

Only the first definition is typically relevant to school-age children with disabilities. The ADA and Section 504 have an identical definition of disability. Title II of the ADA covers public entities and has nearly identical coverage as Section 504. Hence, the two statutes can be used interchangeably in this context.

The important definitional question with respect to coverage under the ADA and Section 504 is whether there is a substantial limitation in a "major life activity." Congress amended these statutes in 2008 to clarify that major life activities include "speaking, learning, reading, concentrating, thinking and communicating." Hence, students with learning disabilities and ADHD (as well as other conditions) are clearly covered by the ADA and Section 504. Unlike the IDEA, the ADA and Section 504 do not include the requirement that the student "needs special education services." Hence, a child with a learning disability or ADHD who does not need special education services but who does need an accommodation such as extended time on tests would be covered by the ADA and Section 504 but not the IDEA. Because the amendment to the ADA and Section 504 did not go into effect until January 1, 2009, many school districts have not modified their practices to accommodate children who are disabled but do not qualify for special education services under the IDEA.

The ADA and Section 504 provide a different set of remedies than the IDEA. The IDEA is very procedurally driven with prior written notice requirements and an elaborate state administrative process for filing complaints. The IDEA also contains various discipline protections when behavior is a manifestation of a disability. Hence, if you pursue an ADA/Section 504 remedy for a child, you need to be aware of the set of procedural rules that apply to that statute in contrast to the IDEA.

II.   AN EVALUATION PRIMER

A.   Standard Deviations and Errors of Measurement

Evaluation instruments can be used to measure a wide variety of characteristics such as hearing, vision, intelligence, speech, physical agility or fine motor skills. Some evaluation instruments use paper and pencil tests, others use structured observations, and others record attempts at various physical activities such as standing on one leg.

There are many, many different kinds of assessments. One type of assessment — often administered under No Child Left Behind[2] — is a basic competency or proficiency test. The purpose of the assessment is to determine whether the child is performing at grade level (as defined by state rules and regulations). On such an assessment, every child in the class could attain a score of "proficient." There could also be a score for "below proficient" and "above

---

[2] No Child Left Behind Act is the popular name for the Elementary and Secondary Education Act of 1975, as amended by Public Law 107-110 (requiring every child to be proficient in reading and math by 2014).

proficient" (or gradations within those categories). Again, every child in the class could be in one of these three categories because the assessment is not comparative in nature. The standards for these competency exams are often quite low. A child could be deemed "competent" under a particular state standard but, on a comparative basis, be well below the norms for that classroom or school district. These proficiency exams do not typically play a big role in determining whether a child is in need of special education and related services, although they can confirm that a child is not performing up to grade level expectations for that school district or state. The 2004 Amendments to the IDEA clarify that children can be entitled to special education services even if they are advancing from grade to grade. *See* 34 C.F.R. § 300.101(c)(1) ("Each State must ensure that FAPE [free appropriate public education] is available to any individual child with a disability who needs special education and related services, even though the child has not failed or been retained in a course or grade, and is advancing from grade to grade."). Thus, the mere fact that a child attains a "proficient" score on a state assessment does not preclude the child from being identified as disabled under the IDEA.

The more typical kinds of assessments that are used to determine eligibility under the IDEA consist of "normed" tests in which someone's score is compared to that of the general population. The most well-known normed tests are IQ tests in which an average score (at the 50th percentile) is 100. A score is often reported as a numeric normed score (such as 70 or 100 or 130) and also reported as a certain number of "standard deviations" below or above the mean. A score of 70 is typically two standard deviations below the mean, a score of 100 is at the mean itself, and a score of 130 is typically two standard deviations above the mean.

The concept of "standard deviations" is a way to express how far someone is below (or above) the averages for the population using a normal bell-shaped curve to express the distribution in the population. If someone is at the 50th percentile on a measurement, then the person is at the "zero" standard deviation — in other words, the person does not "deviate" at all from the population averages. On a typical IQ test, the score for the "zero" standard deviation level is 100. Hence, we say that someone with a 100 IQ has a score that is average for the population.

Because IQ tests are scored on a bell shape curve, two standard deviations below the mean is the 2nd percentile and reported as a 70. One standard deviation below the mean is the 16th percentile and reported as an 85. The mean itself is the 50th percentile and reported as a 100. Similarly, one standard deviation above the mean is the 84th percentile and reported as a 115. Two standard deviations above the mean is the 98th percentile and reported as a 130. The 98th percentile is typically used for gifted identification and the 2nd percentile for intellectually disabled identification.

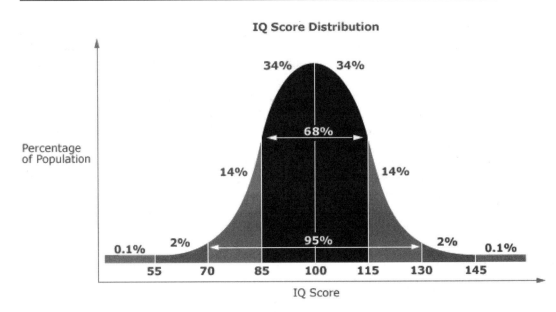

The bell shaped curve displayed above provides a visual example of how to interpret IQ tests. The area of each quadrant under the bell shaped curve reflects how many people in the population have scores in that range. Because it is a "normal" distribution, the scores are bunched near the mean, and far fewer people have scores at each end of the curve. Thus, 34% of the population would have a score between 85 and 100. Similarly, 34% of the population would have a score between 100 and 115. But only 2 percent of the population would have a score between 0 and 70, or 130 and 200. The range between 85 and 115 describes 68% of the population and is often described as the "normal" range. When a person is two standard deviations below (or above) the mean, he or she is in the bottom (or top) two percentile of the population. Because that person is so far from the mean, we say that that difference is statistically significant. In other words, factors other than chance are likely to explain those scores. If two people, by contrast, had IQ scores of 98 and 102, we should say that we do not know if they genuinely have different IQs because their scores are not statistically different. Chance factors may explain that difference and, in fact, if they retook the test we might expect their scores to flip. For identification purposes, then, a score of 70 is meaningful because it is statistically "different" than a score of 100. Thus, a score of 70 is usually considered a meaningful indicator of an intellectual impairment (assuming the test was an appropriate and fair test given under appropriate conditions).

Hence, in speaking of someone who is "intellectually disabled," one could refer to any of the following scores:

- a standard score of 70
- a percentile score in the 2nd percentile
- 2 standard deviations below the mean

Each of those ways of referring to someone's scores is equivalent.

A point of caution, however, is in order. An advocate needs to be careful in reviewing and interpreting any test scores. Educational psychologists no longer believe it is accurate to describe someone's IQ as a single score. People have "multiple" IQs. The single-score IQ is a very crude measure of someone's abilities. It is not unusual for children to score quite differently on different IQ instruments. If possible, one would want a child who is on the borderline of qualifying as intellectually disabled to take more than one IQ test. Also, children's scores on IQ tests are considered more accurate during a one-on-one testing administration than in a group setting. Most states require a one-on-one administration of an IQ test to accurately determine that a child is two standard deviations below the mean and qualifies as intellectually impaired.

Further, the assessment score must be assessed with consideration of the "error of measurement." The "error of measurement" of the testing instrument is a way to reflect the imprecision of any measuring instrument. Examination scores are usually expressed within a confidence interval to reflect this problem. The standard error of measurement is used to estimate the range of scores that individual students might obtain on a test if they retook it repeatedly (and did not benefit from the repeated practice). An easy way to consider this concept is to consider the problem of guessing. If a student is lucky, he or she might provide correct guesses to every problem. By contrast, an unlucky student might miss each guessed response. The error of measurement takes into account these and other chance factors that raise or lower a student's score. Technical manuals published by test developers usually provide information about the standard error of measurement. When test scores are reported within a confidence interval, they are usually reported as plus or minus one standard error of measurement. Thus, if a student scores a 100 on an IQ test and the error of measurement is 5, then the score could be reported as between 95 and 105. In that case, we could also say we are 68 percent certain that the student's true IQ score is no lower than 95 and no higher than 105. If one wanted a confidence interval that reflected a 95 percent degree of certainty, then we would have to consider two standard errors of measurement. Thus, we could say, in the above example, that we are 95 percent certain that the student's true IQ score is between 90 and 110. An understanding of the standard error of measurement should allow us to see that there is room for much debate in the interpretation of test scores. Our certainty level would rise to 98% if we reported a band that takes into account three standard errors of measurement. Then, we would say that we are 98% confident that the actual IQ is no lower than 85 and no higher than 115. Those ways of reporting scores might make more sense if you look at the bell shaped curve above. You can see that 1 SD is 68%, 2 SD's is 95% and 3 SD's is 98% in a normal distribution. The typical way to report test scores is plus or minus one error of measurement. That way of reporting provides you with a confined band of results within a tolerable error of measurement.

The Ohio definition of "cognitive disability" takes into account the error of measurement in its definition. It states that: "Based on a standard error of measurement and clinical judgment, a child may be determined to have significant subaverage general intellectual functioning with an intelligence quotient not to exceed seventy-five." *See* Ohio Operating Standards, § 3301-51-01(B)(ii). In other words, it codifies a confidence ban of 70 to 75 when interpreting IQ results if that band is consistent with a clinical judgment irrespective of the error of measurement of the actual testing instrument.

B.   Subscores

When interpreting test results, it is important to consider subscores as well as the overall scores. An overall score for a section consists of various subtests. Sometimes, a child will have widely divergent scores on subtests, making an overall score appear to be in the normal range.

Examination of the subscores, though, can reflect areas of significant weakness. For example, a child with an IQ of 100 may have subscores of 70 and 130, which average out to 100. There is actually nothing "typical" about the child despite the overall score of 100. That is obviously an extreme example but nonetheless reflects the importance of looking at subscores. An IQ score of 100 may appear like the score of a typically developing child, but the subscores may reflect widely divergent aptitudes and give insight into possible impairments.

Consider the following fact pattern to see the importance of looking at subscores. The scores in this example are from an actual case and reflect that some children do have wide variation in their test scores. School district personnel often do not examine subscores and miss these signals of significant weakness in some areas.

In practice, you can expect to see test scores and evaluations containing a number of acronyms and technical terms. To assist with this exercise, here is a partial guide:

Age Score: SAS	standard age score
Age Score: PR	percentile within age group
Age Score: S	standard scale score for age (1 to 10 scale)
Grade Score: PR	percentile within current grade in school
Grade Score: S	standard scale score for grade (1 to 10 scale)
NPG	national percentile for grade in school
NPA	national percentile for age in school
NP	national percentile for grade in school
NS	national standard score for grade in school (1 to 10 scale)
GE	national grade equivalent

Jimmy Doe

Jimmy is an eight year old boy who is in first grade when the school district administers a battery of tests during the spring. His parents delayed his entry to first grade by a year so he is a year older than his peers. The school district administered an IQ test and an achievement test. These are Jimmy's scores on these tests:

Jimmy's First Grade IQ Test (Composite Score: 101)

Test	No. items	No. items attempted	Raw Score	Age Score: SAS	Age Score: PR	Age Score: S	Grade Score: PR	Grade Score: S
VERBAL APTITUDE	40	40	32	98	45	5	70	6
QUANTITATIVE APTITUDE	40	39	32	84	16	3	48	5
NONVERBAL APTITUDE	40	40	39	117	86	7	92	8
COMPOSITE APTITUDE				101	52	5	80	7

Jimmy's First Grade Achievement Tests

Scores Reported	Reading: Vocabulary	Reading: Comprehension	Reading: Total	Language: Listening	Language	Language: Total	Math Concepts	Math Problems	Math: Total	Reading, Language, Math Core: Total	Social Studies	Science	Word Analysis	Math Computation
Standard Score	74	71	72	52	61	56	41	72	56	61	63	67	53	45

In third grade, the school district administered another battery of aptitude and achievement tests. These are Jimmy's results:

Jimmy's Third Grade IQ Test (Composite Score: 98)

Scores	Nonverbal: Sequences	Nonverbal: Analogies	Total: Nonverbal	Memory	Verbal	Total
NPG	97	99*	99	17	6	65
NPA	88	90*	92	16	5	45

Jimmy's Third Grade Achievement Scores

Scores	Reading	Language	Math	Total Score	Science	Social Studies
NP	75	52	89	75	78	48
NS	6	5	7	6	7	5
GE	5.6	3.9	6.0	5.3	5.3	3.7

Are these the test scores of a typical child, or a child who qualifies as disabled under the IDEA? Try to arrive at your own answer before reading the analysis that follows.

---

* Perfect score on subtest

At first glance, these test scores are those of a typical child. Despite IQ scores around 100, Jimmy has been performing at or above grade level in all areas. And, standing alone, these test scores certainly do not suggest an immediate need for intervention. Nonetheless, close consideration of Jimmy's chronological age and subscores suggest that further testing may be appropriate.

When examining results for a child who is in school with peers who are a year younger (or a year older), one must separate out the age-based scores from the grade-based scores. Often, the test results are not clear in distinguishing between those two kinds of scores.

Jimmy's first grade scores reflect a stark discrepancy between quantitative and nonverbal aptitude. His 84 standard score placed him in the 16th percentile on quantitative aptitude and his 117 standard score placed him in the 86th percentile on nonverbal aptitude. Because Jimmy is being educated with children who are a year younger, his percentiles are much higher when compared with his grade. Then, his quantitative aptitude places him in the 48th percentile and his nonverbal aptitude places him in the 92nd percentile. When these scores are examined from a standard deviation perspective, one sees that Jimmy placed one standard deviation below the mean on quantitative aptitude and one standard deviation above the mean in nonverbal aptitude. When a discrepancy is two standard deviations, we say the discrepancy is "significant" in that factors other than chance most likely accounts for this difference in aptitude on these two parts of the exam. This seeming inconsistency in Jimmy's aptitude, however, did not translate into any significant deficits or inconsistencies in his performance in first grade.

Jimmy's third grade test scores reflect an even more marked discrepancy between his aptitudes. The school district reported his aptitude score as 98 in third grade, which would be average. But there is nothing average about Jimmy's test scores. He scored in the 92nd/99th percentile on the nonverbal aptitude section of the exam, receiving a perfect score on one of the two parts of that exam. On the memory component, he scored in the 17th/16th percentile and on the verbal component, he scored in the 6th/5th percentile. In other words, he scored about 2 standard deviations above the mean in nonverbal aptitude and scored more than 1 standard deviation below the mean in verbal aptitude and memory. Assuming that Jimmy understood the instructions and made an appropriate effort, those results suggest that Jimmy has a significant weakness along with tremendous strengths. One might wonder if there is an academic area that is lagging due to those significant weaknesses. One also must wonder if those aptitude subscores are valid because Jimmy scored no better in verbal aptitude than one would expect if he was engaging in random guessing. Yet his teachers report that he is a strong reader with a large vocabulary. On the state reading test administered in third grade, Jimmy scored in the "accelerated" range. It is odd that a child with a score in the 6th percentile on verbal aptitude could be reading above grade level. At a minimum, these kinds of scores should suggest an undetected problem.

Up to this point, the only evidence of Jimmy having any difficulty in school is related to his writing proficiency. In addition to the information above, Jimmy scored less than proficient on the state's writing examination in third grade. The school district conducted its own writing assessment in fourth grade and, again, he was in the less than proficient category. In light of these scores, the school district administered an achievement battery to Jimmy at the beginning of fourth grade. He performed at or above grade level in all subjects except for writing in which he performed about two grades below his current grade level. Thus, it appears that Jimmy's impairment seems to have an adverse impact on his written expression. Nonetheless, his reading scores continued to be quite high. He scored in the 99th percentile on some of the reading subtests. And he displayed no difficulty with spelling.

Based on these test scores, the school district indicated an inclination to label Jimmy as "learning disabled" so that he could get extra help with written expression. Jimmy's parents were happy for him to get extra help but were concerned that "learning disability" may not be the correct category for Jimmy. Why would a child be such a strong reader if his verbal aptitude were so low? And why would he have an enormous vocabulary? The verbal aptitude score seemed to be inaccurate given Jimmy's strong reading skills yet Jimmy clearly struggled in written expression.

Jimmy's parents asked the school district to administer a different IQ test to Jimmy. They had heard that the previous IQ test (which was administered in a group-based environment) had a strong oral component. Jimmy often had difficulty following oral instructions and they thought that the oral component may have dampened his test scores.

Jimmy Follow-Up

Based on the parents' request, the school district administered a different IQ test. Amazingly, Jimmy received a standard score of 124 on the verbal portion of the test! His overall IQ was measured at 120. By changing testing instruments, his verbal aptitude percentile went from nearly two standard deviations below the mean to nearly two standard deviations above the mean. Clearly, a factor other than chance must explain this difference.

How might one interpret these test scores? What further testing might be appropriate in light of this additional information?

Jimmy's parents tried to interpret these test scores in light of their own experience with Jimmy. He did not start talking in sentences until age three and had unusual speech patterns. Although he has a large vocabulary, he has trouble with basic syntax and speech patterns. He often misunderstands oral instructions and information. Ultimately, Jimmy's parents requested an audiological evaluation. They learned that Jimmy has a profound auditory processing impairment. Because of his high IQ (when administered a proper testing instrument), he was able to learn a lot of the material on his own without being able to hear classroom instruction. These problems would not have been apparent if one did not look at the subscores on the assessments because his overall numbers were typically in the average range. The scores, though, did not tell the whole story. The parents had to interpret those scores in light of their own experience with Jimmy.

III. CATEGORIES OF DISABILITIES

A. Statutory Definitions

1. Ages Three to Nine

In the opening section of this chapter, we saw the definition of disability that can be used to characterize any child as disabled who is covered by the IDEA. For children who are between the ages of 3 and 9, a special set of rules apply. The state has the discretion to cover children who are "(i) experiencing developmental delays, as defined by the State and as measured by appropriate diagnostic instruments and procedures, in 1 or more of the following areas: physical development; cognitive development; communication development; social or emotional development; or adaptive development; and (ii) who, by reason thereof, needs special education and related services." § 1401(3)(B). In other words, a state can cover a child who is experiencing developmental delays, and who is in need of special education and related services, but does not clearly fit one of the ten covered categories of disability. Typically, states exercise that authority by covering preschool children without a specific diagnosis of disability because of the strong benefits of early intervention and the difficulty of diagnosing the reason for a developmental delay in a young, often pre-verbal, child. For children between ages 3 and 9, a parent or advocate needs to check the state operating standards to see what rules apply for coverage. It is crucial to know how your state handles children between the ages of three and nine to know whether the more permissive standard applies.

California exercises that discretion for children between birth and 4 years 9 months of age. If a child is functioning at or below 50% of his or her chronological age level in one of five categories, or between 51% and 75% of his or her chronological age level in two of the five categories and needs intensive special education and services, then the child can qualify under IDEA without a diagnosis in one of the established categories. The five categories are: gross or fine motor development; receptive or expressive language development; social or emotional development; cognitive development; or visual development. *See* 5 C.C.R. § 3031. Because of the difficulty of testing children accurately at this age, especially if they are pre-verbal, these standards leave much room for interpretation.

New Jersey uses an approach similar to that of California but only requires a 33% delay in one area to qualify for services rather than a 50% delay. Alternatively, it permits a child to qualify with a 25% delay in two areas (which would be comparable to California). New Jersey also lists five categories but they are different categories. The New Jersey categories are: physical, including gross motor, fine motor and sensory (vision and hearing); cognitive; communication; social and emotional; and adaptive. *See* N.J.A.C. 6A:14-3.5. Hence, a child with a 33% delay in one area would qualify for special education services in New Jersey at age three but not in California. Further, California cuts off eligibility at age 4 years 9 months (without a diagnosis in one of the school-age categories), whereas New Jersey does not cut off eligibility until age 5. Both the California and New Jersey rules are consistent with the flexibility provided to states by Congress. When representing children who have moved from state to state, one therefore needs to be sensitive to these different standards for eligibility.

North Carolina exercises the discretion for children between the ages of three and seven with some nuances for ages three through five, as compared with five through seven. (North Carolina is unusual in extending that flexibility to age seven; most states extend it only to age five.) Its standards reflect the difficulty with diagnosis for young children. Hence, more flexibility is provided for ages three through five, than five through seven. But for all these children, there is more flexibility than for children older than age seven. It defines a developmental delay as follows:

(A) Between the ages of three through seven, whose development and/or behavior is so significantly delayed or atypical that special education and related services are required.

(B) Delayed/Atypical Development. A child may be defined as having delayed/ atypical patterns of development in one or more of the following five areas: physical development, cognitive development, communication development, social/emotional development or adaptive development.

a. The criteria for determining delayed development for ages three through seven are:

1. A 30 percent delay using assessment procedures that yield scores in months, or test performance of 2 standard deviations below the mean on standardized tests in one area of development; or

2. A 25 percent delay using assessment procedures that yield scores in months or test performance of 1.5 standard deviations below the mean on standardized tests in two areas of development.

b. Identification of these children will be based on informed educational/clinical opinion and appropriate assessment measures.

(C) Delayed/Atypical Behavior. A child with delayed or atypical behavior is characterized by behaviors that are so significantly inadequate or inappropriate that they interfere with the child's ability to learn and/or cope with normal environmental or situational demands. There must be evidence that the patterns of behavior occur in more than one setting over an extended period of time.

a. The criteria for determining delayed/atypical behavior for ages three through five must be documented in one or more of the following areas:

1. Delayed or abnormalities in achieving milestones and/or difficulties with issues, such as:

i. Attachment and/or interaction with other adults, peers, materials, and objects;

ii. Ability to communicate emotional needs;

iii. Ability to tolerate frustration and control behavior, or

iv. Ability to inhibit aggression.

2. Fearfulness, withdrawal, or other distress that does not respond to comforting or interventions;

3. Indiscriminate sociability, for example, excessive familiarity with relative strangers; or

4. Self-injurious or other aggressive behavior.

b. The criteria for determining delayed patterns of behavior and adaptive skills for ages six through seven must be exhibited in two or more of the following ways:

1. The inability to interact appropriately with adults and peers;

2. The inability to cope with normal environmental or situational demands;

3. The use of aggression or self-injurious behavior; or

4. The inability to make educational progress due to social/emotional deficits.

c. Identification of these children will be based on informed educational/clinical opinion and appropriate assessment measures.

See 64 NC 1503 — Evaluations, Eligibility Determinations, IEPs, and Educational Placements (available at:

http://www.nhcs.k12.nc.us/sped/MANUAL/RSE%20-%20Developmental%20Day.pdf).

The North Carolina rules, like many state rules, require a practitioner to understand the meaning of a "standard deviation" and the ability to interpret test results. A child needs to be below the norm by 2 standard deviations in one area or 1.5 standard deviations in two areas to qualify as a child with a disability. Ohio uses a similar approach. It identifies five areas of development (physical development, cognitive development, communication development, social or emotional development, and adaptive development) and requires a child to be below the norm by 2 standard deviations in one area or 1.5 standard deviations below the norm in two areas to qualify as a child with a disability. *See* OH ADC 3301-51-11.

Here is Jimmy's profile as a preschooler when he could qualify as disabled under the more flexible standard for children who are 3 to 9 (depending on the state's own rules). When Jimmy was three years old, his parents had him tested because he was generally delayed in speech and physical movement. Look at these test results and consider how you might argue that Jimmy is entitled to special education services in a state like North Carolina which provides that a child is disabled if he or she is two standard deviations below the mean on one measure, or 1.5 standard deviations below the mean in two measures.

Preschool Jimmy (3 years of age)

Educational Psychologist Report:

Developmental milestones were reportedly delayed. Jimmy walked without help at 18 months. He began using single words at approximately 24 months. Parents have been concerned about fine and gross motor skills and language development. He is not toilet trained.

Jimmy spoke primarily in short sentences with immature syntax. Speech was often tangential and answers to some questions were not closely related to the topic. Verbal material frequently needed to be repeated and he sometimes misinterpreted words (e.g., "snack" for "snap"). Eye contact was poor. He did not appear to be aware of success or failure. He displayed an awkward pencil grasp with his right hand and needed physical prompting to grasp pencil to draw a simple design.

The WPPSI-R was administered as a measure of cognitive ability. His overall score was 94, within the average range. An average score on the subtests was between 8 and 12. These are Jimmy's subscores:

Information:	11
Comprehension:	7
Arithmetic:	10
Vocabulary:	10
Similarities:	9
Object assembly:	9
Block design:	7
Mazes:	7
Picture completion:	14

Jimmy was also administered the Bracken Basic Concept Scale — Revised which is a measure of pre-academic skills. Jimmy achieved a standard score of 14 (average range 8-12) at the 91st percentile suggesting good kindergarten academic readiness.

Finally, Jimmy was administered the SIB-R Adaptive Behavior assessment. He received an overall score of 79 (8th percentile) with significant weakness in self-care (1st percentile) and social communication (6th percentile). Despite reports by his caregivers of significant problems in motor development, his motor skills were found to be in the 41st percentile.

Jimmy was also tested by a physical therapist. She provided the following results on the Peabody Developmental Motor Scale:

Balance:	2nd percentile
Nonlocomotor:	10th percentile
Locomotor:	2nd percentile
Receipt and Propulsion:	4th percentile
Total Score:	1st percentile

Using the North Carolina standards for qualifying for special education and related services as a three year old, what arguments would you make on Jimmy's behalf? Is he 2 standard deviations below the mean in one area, or 1.5 standard deviations below the mean in two or more areas? How would you deal with the seeming inconsistency between the gross motor test administered by the physical therapist and the motor skills assessment by the psychologist? What further testing might be indicated based on these preliminary results? Arrive at your own answers before reading below.

In thinking about these questions, remember that test scores are not the only accurate indicators of a child's level of development. Further, one often needs to know something about a test to assess its validity. The psychologist's assessment of motor skills appears to have been based on reports from parents and others — can Jimmy walk up a flight of stairs or run? The physical therapist directly measured his skill level using professionally designed instruments.

Jimmy's cognitive assessment reflected some significant variation. Again, it would be helpful to know more about the testing instruments. One theme is that tests that required Jimmy to use his fine motor skills were particularly weak. Both the blocks and maze were difficult for Jimmy due to his apparently weak fine motor skills. One suggestion might emerge from these test scores is that Jimmy's fine motor skills should also be measured. The Peabody has a fine motor instrument that was not administered. When that test was ultimately administered, Jimmy scored in the 2nd percentile on that test. The observations about his difficulty with pencil grasping suggested the need for that testing.

Finally, these test results suggest need for further speech/language evaluation. Jimmy's communication skills seem to have some significant areas of weakness even though his kindergarten readiness is very high. An audiological exam would also seem indicated given the problems reported with his comprehension.

These scores alone, though, should qualify Jimmy for special education services. His 1st percentile score in gross motor skills coupled with various subscores that are well below the mean suggest the need for a broad program of special education. When a full battery of tests were ultimately completed, Jimmy was found eligible for physical therapy, occupational therapy, adaptive physical education and speech/language therapy.

2.   School-Age Children

a.   General Considerations

Children who are not covered by the more permissive standard for children between the ages of three and nine must be found eligible by being found to be in one of the ten categories discussed below. These include:

1.   mental retardation (now called "intellectual disabilities")

2.   hearing impairments (including deafness)

3.   speech or language impairments

4.   visual impairments (including blindness)

5.   serious emotional disturbance

6.   orthopedic impairments

7.   autism

8.   traumatic brain injury

9.   other health impairments

10.   specific learning disabilities.

See 20 U.S.C. § 1401(3)(A)(i).

The regulations break these impairments into 13 categories. *See* 34 C.F.R. § 300.8.

The regulatory categories are (in alphabetical order):

1.   autism (listed seventh in statute)

2.   deaf-blindness (combining a subcategory of the second and forth statutory categories)

3.   deafness (a subset of the second statutory category)

4.   emotional disturbance (equivalent to what the statute calls "serious emotional disturbance")

5.   hearing impairment (a subset of the second category — defined not to include deafness)

6.   mental retardation (the first statutory category)

7.   multiple disabilities (not specifically listed in the statute)

8.   orthopedic impairment (the sixth statutory category)

9.   other health impairment (the ninth statutory category)

10.   specific learning disability (the tenth statutory category)

11.   speech or language impairment (the third statutory category)

12.   traumatic brain injury (not listed separately in the statute)

13.   visual impairment (fourth statutory category)

The different order between the statute and the regulations is due to the fact that the regulations list the categories in alphabetical order. Many states have their own list of covered disability categories and may have more than 13 categories. Some jurisdictions even have fewer than 13 categories. D.C. only has 12 categories, because it does not list orthopedic impairments in its regulations. *See* DCMR § 3003. Elsewhere in the D.C. code, it does state that any other disability described in the IDEA is an eligible category in D.C. *See* D.C. St. § 38-2561.01. So, D.C. would consider a child disabled solely on the basis of an orthopedic impairment if the child meets the federal definition. New Jersey has 13 categories plus the category "preschool child with a disability," but New Jersey often uses different terms for disabilities than the federal regulations. *See* N.J.A.C. § 6A:14-3.5. For example, New Jersey uses the term "social maladjustment" instead of "emotionally disturbed." Ohio has 13 categories including "developmental delay." It does not list "deafness" separately from hearing impairment. *See* OH ADC Ch. 3301-51.

If a child has one or more of those disabilities and "who, by reason thereof, needs special education and related services," then the child is covered by the IDEA. 20 U.S.C. § 1401(3)(A)(ii). In other words, the child's disability must be characterized as fitting into one of those ten categories (or thirteen categories) to be covered by the IDEA.

Each of the disability categories has its own distinctive definition, but there is also general information that must be collected for all children irrespective of the disability category. North Carolina uses the following form for all children who are possibly being identified as disabled.

ELIGIBILITY DETERMINATION

Check Purpose: ☐ **Initial Eligibility**   ☐ **Reevaluation**

Student: <u>Student Name</u>   **Grade: <u>Grade</u>**

School: <u>School Name</u>

The IEP Team has summarized all required screening and evaluation information including a discussion of the student's strengths and needs on attached evaluation/eligibility worksheet(s).

Based on information from a variety of sources that have been documented and carefully considered, the IEP Team has determined:

☐ **yes**   ☐ **no**   The student meets criteria for one or more of the fourteen disabling conditions consistent with the definitions described in *NC Policy 1500-2* (**must** *attach individual eligibility worksheets);*

☐ **yes**   ☐ **no**   The disability has an adverse effect on educational performance; and

☐ **yes**   ☐ **no**   The disability requires specially designed instruction.

All three **must** be yes in order for the student to be eligible for special education and related services if required to benefit from special education.

The IEP Team has also concluded:

☐ **yes**   ☐ **no**   The determination *is not* the result of lack of appropriate instruction in reading, including the essential components of reading instruction. The term "essential components of reading instruction" means explicit and systematic instruction in: phonemic awareness, phonics, vocabulary development, reading fluency (including oral reading skills), and reading comprehension strategies.

☐ **yes**   ☐ **no**   The determination *is not* the result of lack of appropriate instruction in math; and

☐ **yes**   ☐ **no**   The determination *is not* the result of Limited English proficiency of the student.

All three **must** be yes in order for the student to be eligible for special education and related services if required to benefit from special education.

Statement of Eligibility:

<u>Student Name</u>,

☐   **is eligible** for special education and related services if required to benefit from special education. He/she meets the eligibility criteria for **Primary Eligibility Category** (primary eligibility category) and **Secondary Eligibility Category** (secondary eligibility category(s), if applicable). *(Attach individual eligibility worksheets for all identified areas of eligibility.)*

☐   **is not eligible** for special education and related services.

IEP Team Signatures	Position	Date of Meeting	SLD Only*	
			☐ Agree	☐ Disagree
			☐ Agree	☐ Disagree
			☐ Agree	☐ Disagree
			☐ Agree	☐ Disagree
			☐ Agree	☐ Disagree
			☐ Agree	☐ Disagree
			☐ Agree	☐ Disagree
			☐ Agree	☐ Disagree

For SLD only. If an IEP Team member disagrees, he/she must submit a separate statement of their reason for disagreement.

Copy given/sent to parent(s) 00 / 00 / 2000

http://www.ncpublicschools.org/ec/policy/forms/statewide

Like many states, North Carolina takes the ten federal categories and breaks them into more than ten categories. The federal regulations use thirteen categories, North Carolina uses fourteen because it has a form especially for children who meet the more relaxed rules for children between the ages of 3 and 7, as discussed in the previous section.

The North Carolina form closely tracks the statutory disability requirements and, like most states, lists an additional requirement. The child needs to fit one of the statutory categories (which North Carolina subdivides into fourteen categories) and must need special education and related services. Additionally, North Carolina requires an "adverse educational effect."

The "adverse educational effect" rule is common to most states' practices but does not derive directly from the statutory language. The "adversely affect" language, though, can typically be found in the federal regulations. For example, the "deafness" definition says: "Deafness means a hearing impairment that is so severe that the child is impaired in processing linguistic information through hearing, with or without amplification that adversely affects a child's educational performance." 34 C.F.R. § 300.8(c)(3).

The final requirement on the North Carolina form is that the child needs "specialized instruction." That tracks the statutory language requiring the child to need "special education and related services."

The regulations emphasize the importance of both conditions (special education and related services) being met:

> (2)(i) Subject to paragraph (a)(2)(ii) of this section, if it is determined, through an appropriate evaluation under §§ 300.304 through 300.311, that a child has one of the disabilities identified in paragraph (a)(1) of this section, but only needs a related service and not special education, the child is not a child with a disability under this part.

> (ii) If, consistent with § 300.39(a)(2), the related service required by the child is considered special education rather than a related service under State standards, the child would be determined to be a child with a disability under paragraph (a)(1) of this section.

34 C.F.R. § 300.8. That rule, however, stands in some tension with the least restrictive environment rule in 34 C.F.R. § 300.114:

> Special classes, separate schooling, or other removal of children with disabilities from the regular educational environment occurs only if the nature or severity of the disability is such that education in regular classes with the use of supplementary aids and services cannot be achieved satisfactorily.

In other words, school districts should do their utmost to keep the child in the regular classroom especially if supplementary aids and services can make that possible. Yet, a child who *only* needs related services is not supposed to meet the definition of disability.

This tension becomes even more problematic when one realizes that child with a significant impairment who needs accommodations, but not special education, can receive those accommodations under Section 504 or the ADA. Thus, if a school district opposes a child as being qualified as disabled under the IDEA because the child only needs accommodations, then the parents can make the same request under Section 504 or the ADA. Unlike the IDEA, Section 504 and the ADA are not funding statutes. So the school district is often in a better financial position to secure the accommodation under the IDEA than under Section 504 or the ADA.

Consider the following hypothetical in light of those competing considerations:

Jamie Rodriquez

Jamie is an incoming first grader to the public schools. Her corrected vision is 20/100 in one eye and 20/80 in the other eye. She suffers eye strain if she tries to read regular size print but can learn to read with proper classroom magnification equipment. If a teacher types on a computer and projects the print in the classroom, then Jamie can also follow classroom "board work" at an individual computer monitor with magnification equipment. Jamie's IQ measures in the average range and her pre-reading and math skills are in the average range for an incoming first grader. She has a little trouble with navigation because her distance vision is so poor. She had an older sibling in the grade school, though, so she is pretty familiar with its layout. She is an independent and cheerful child who is looking forward to entering first grade. Her parents home schooled her for kindergarten, so she has not yet attended public school.

How would you argue that Jamie should be considered disabled under the IDEA? Are her average test scores problematic to demonstrate an "adverse educational impact" from her impairment? What about the fact that she does not necessarily need specialized instruction? Try to answer these questions before reading the explanation below.

With respect to adverse educational impact, the regulations state that a child does not have to be performing below grade level in order to qualify as disabled under the IDEA. For a five year old child, such as Jamie, this rule is particularly important. Because she has been home schooled and received one-on-one instruction at home, her visual impairment probably had little adverse effect on her education. It is easy to see that it is quite likely to have a profound effect on her performance in grade school given the kind of materials she would need to read as well as her need to travel around the building safely.

As for the rule that she should need specialized instruction, one could argue that she will need orientation and mobility instructions to navigate the building. Specialized instruction does not merely include academic instruction.

In addition, one can argue that providing her with specialized classroom equipment can avoid the need for specialized academic instruction outside the regular classroom. That policy would be consistent with the least restrictive environment rule.

It may also be true (depending on the school district) that they can access special education funds for her equipment if she is covered under the IDEA but will not have access to special funds if she is covered under Section 504/ADA.

Finally, one might argue that she is the kind of child who would benefit from the IDEA's procedural protections. Frequent meetings with the parents and school district may help Jamie successfully navigate her academic obligations. Because she is only entering first grade, there is significant room for difficulties ahead. It is too early to know if her visual impairment will impact her in math or science when spatial topics are under discussion. That observation will not guarantee her coverage under the IDEA but may help the school district understand the value of qualifying her as disabled under IDEA rather than Section 504/ADA.

B.   Ten Disability Categories for School-Age Children

The IDEA has its ten categories of disability, as discussed above, as well as more detailed definitions in the regulations. These ten categories are creatures of federal law. The American Psychiatric Association has its own manual entitled "The Diagnostic and Statistical Manual of Mental Disorders" which is considered to be the authoritative medical manual on various disabilities. The fourth edition was published in 1994 and it was updated in 2000. The fifth edition is scheduled for publication in 2012, but many of the updates can be found on the APA's website. *See* http://www.psych.org/mainmenu/research/dsmiv/dsmivtr.aspx. Advocates for children need to consult this manual to better understand various diagnoses.

1.   Intellectual Disabilities

a.   Basic Definition

Each state has its own procedures or forms to be used to determine if a child has one of the disabilities covered by the IDEA. North Carolina has one form for each of the ten categories.

The federal regulations provide the following definition: "significantly subaverage general intellectual functioning, existing concurrently with deficits in adaptive behavior and manifested during the developmental period, that adversely affects a child's educational performance." 34 C.F.R. § 300.8(c)(6). There are three components to this definition: significantly below average intellectual functioning, deficits in adaptive behavior, and adverse educational effects. For all disability categories, one has to demonstrate that the child needs special education and related services.

Hence, North Carolina, for example, has a form that tracks these various requirements. The local educational agency (rather than the parent) is required to conduct a "full and individual initial evaluation" of a child suspected of being disabled. 20 U.S.C. § 1414(a)(1). Federal regulations specify that a child should be evaluated in all areas related to the suspected disability "including, if appropriate, health, vision, hearing, social and emotional status, general intelligence, academic performance, communicative status, and motor abilities." 34 C.F.R. § 300.304(c)(4). The North Carolina form lists each of these areas, reflecting the expectation that a child would be assessed in each of those areas. Because it is difficult to determine the scope of a child's impairments until a full evaluation is completed, the North Carolina form reflects that the initial evaluation will measure each of those areas. Federal regulations reiterate that approach when they provide: "In evaluating each child with a disability under §§ 300.304 through 300.306, the evaluation is sufficiently comprehensive to identify all of the child's special education and related services needs, whether or not commonly linked to the disability category in which the child has been classified." 34 C.F.R. § 300.304(c)(6). Thus, a child's advocate needs to make sure that a sufficiently complete assessment has been conducted, including areas that might not be commonly linked to the child's suspected disability category.

The North Carolina form also reflects that it is not enough for a child to have an impairment in order to be covered under the IDEA. The child must also experience an adverse educational effect as a result of the impairment, and need special education and related services to make appropriate educational progress. Hence, the form requires documentation of those issues as well as the assessment of impairment.

This form also reflects that the 2004 Amendments to the IDEA emphasize the importance of what are called "scientific, research-based interventions" as part of the identification process. *See* 20 U.S.C. § 1414(b)(6)(B). The statute contains this rule specifically for the determination of a specific learning disability, but North Carolina refers to this rule for all categories of disability. The purpose of this rule is to avoid overdiagnosis of disability for children who simply need short-term interventions to address the fact that they may not be meeting grade-level expectations. Thus, North Carolina requires the school district to document two interventions that it attempted to help the child meet grade-level expectations without categorizing the child as "disabled" under the IDEA. Other states are less formal in documenting intervention attempts but do have such attempts as part of their identification process. Even though intervention attempts are embedded in the 2004 Amendments to the IDEA, such intervention attempts are also not supposed to be used to delay the identification of a child as disabled.

The heart of the North Carolina form for Intellectual Impairment is the requirement that there be sufficient evidence that the child has that specific impairment. North Carolina translates that rule into the requirement that the child's intellectual functioning be measured as falling at least "two standard deviations" below the mean plus or minus the standard error of measure.

The concepts of "two standard deviations" and "plus or minus the standard error of measure" are separate concepts that educational psychologists would suggest must be met in order to make an appropriate diagnosis. Those terms were defined above in Part I. Not all states rely heavily on IQ results to define intellectual disability. In California, that definition is governed by a consent decree which bans the use of nonvalidated IQ tests and agrees to plans to eliminate the disproportionate enrollment of African-American children in classes for the "educable mentally retarded." *See Larry P. v. Riles*, 793 F.2d 969, 972 (9th Cir. 1984). The California regulations state, "No single score or product of scores shall be used as the sole criterion for the decision of the individualized education program team as to the pupil's eligibility for special education." The definition of "intellectual disability" makes no reference to any particular test scores. It states: "A pupil has significantly below average general intellectual functioning existing concurrently with deficits in adaptive behavior and manifested during the developmental period, which adversely affect a pupil's educational performance." 5 CCR § 3030(h).

Although the *Larry P.* argument that African-American children are being overclassified as mentally retarded due to race-biased IQ scores has been made in other states, it has only been accepted by courts in California. The IDEA does require that assessments and other evaluation instruments must be "selected and administered so as not to be discriminatory on a racial or cultural basis." 20 U.S.C. § 1414(b)(3)(A)(ii). While school districts can use IQ scores, provided they are able to demonstrate that the test used is not racially or culturally biased, school districts typically use alternative testing methodologies to demonstrate cognitive functioning in California.

b.   Further Requirements in Assessing Intellectual Disabilities

The rules for defining an intellectual disability are not limited to an IQ test result. As the North Carolina form reflects, the test data must be accompanied by evidence of deficits in adaptive behavior. North Carolina requires evidence of "Adaptive behavior deficits at or below: a) two standard deviations below the mean in one domain or b) one and one-half standard deviations below the mean in two or more domains." *See* 64 NC 1503 — Evaluations, Eligibility Determinations, IEPs, and Educational Placements, available at http://www.nhcs.k12.nc.us/sped/MANUAL/RSE%20-%20Intellectual%20Disability.pdf.   Ohio requires "deficits in two or more applicable skill areas occurring within the context of the child's environments and typical of the child's chronological age peers." Ohio Administrative Code, § 3301-51-01(B)(10)(d)(ii)(b), available at http://codes.ohio.gov/oac/3301-51-01.

The term "adaptive behavior" refers to the skills that people need to function independently at home, school or in the community. Such skills include communication and social skills, independent living skills, personal care skills, employment/work skills and practical academics. Adaptive behavior skills are measured through surveys of the child's behavior and skills in a variety of settings including the classroom, school, home, neighborhood or community. Adaptive behavior scales have been developed to measure such behavior in various areas. The data can be collected through structured interviews or paper/pencil checklists of parents, teachers and others. Like IQ tests, this data is normed against a same-aged population sample. Obviously, one would expect a 14-year-old to have better self-help skills than a 3-year-old. Because a diagnosis of intellectual disability cannot be made without measurements of adaptive behavior, it is important for the appropriate people to cooperate in filling out checklists or being interviewed in order for this assessment to take place.

2.   Hearing Impairments (Including Deafness)

The IDEA regulations provide a definition for both "deafness" and "hearing impairment." "Deafness" means a "hearing impairment that is so severe that the child is impaired in processing linguistic information through hearing, with or without amplification, that adversely affects a child's educational performance." 34 C.F.R. § 300.8(c)(3). A "hearing impairment" means "an impairment in hearing, whether permanent or fluctuating, that adversely affects a child's educational performance but that is not included under the definition of deafness in this section." 34 C.F.R. § 300.8(c)(5). The federal standard would seem to include "auditory processing" impairments where a child can hear sounds but has difficulty processing these sounds into recognizable speech due to some kind of neurological disorder. State standards, however, rarely recognize auditory processing impairments as a kind of hearing impairment. For example, the New Jersey standards provide: "Auditorily impaired" means an inability to hear within normal limits due to physical impairment or dysfunction of auditory mechanisms . . . ." N.J. 6A:14.3.5.

For the audiological exam, North Carolina emphasizes the detection of "hearing loss" so an auditory processing impairment would not be covered under this state's definition. Other jurisdictions, like D.C. and Ohio, merely reprint the federal definition of "hearing impairment," which could be construed to cover an auditory processing impairment.

When children have auditory processing impairments, they usually get covered under another category of disability because they often have evidence of a learning disability due to a discrepancy between communication skills and verbal aptitude. Children with auditory processing disorders often have many of the distractibility characteristics of children with ADHD and can therefore be covered under "other health impairment."

The American Speech Language-Hearing Association counsels against using the term CAPD (Central Auditory Processing Disorder or APD interchangeably with other disorders that also can affect a person's ability to understand auditory information. In particular, the Association takes the position that children should not be misdiagnosed as having ADHD when they have CAPD. The ASHA website contains an excellent article on this subject by Dr. Teri James Bellis in which he notes:

> There are many disorders that can affect a person's ability to understand auditory information. For example, individuals with Attention Deficit/Hyperactivity Disorder (ADHD) may well be poor listeners and have difficulty understanding or remembering verbal information; however, their actual neural processing of auditory input in the [central nervous system] is intact. Instead, it is the attention deficit that is impeding their ability to access or use the auditory information that is coming in. Similarly, children with autism may have great difficulty with spoken language comprehension. However, it is the higher-order, global deficit known as autism that is the cause of their difficulties, not a specific auditory dysfunction. Finally, although the terms language processing and auditory processing sometimes are used interchangeably, it is critical to understand that they are not the same thing at all.

Teri James Bellis, *Understanding Auditory Processing Disorders in Children*, available at www.asha.org.

When advocating on behalf of a child with an auditory processing disorder, one may find reluctance on the part of the school district to classify the child as "hearing impaired." Instead, the school district may want to classify the child as learning disabled or ADHD. Unfortunately, that kind of "misclassification" may be necessary to get the child the services he or she needs. It is important that the record of auditory processing difficulties is documented on the disability evaluation document so that an individual educational program can be developed in response to evidence about how the child learns.

Children with hearing impairments who have no intellectual disability can face challenging coverage issues under the IDEA if they merely need accommodations but do not need special education services. Such children are clearly covered under Section 504 or the Americans with Disabilities Act because they have a "physical or mental impairment that substantially limits one or more major life activity" even if they are performing at or above grade level in school. Until recently, many courts have required parents to exhaust their IDEA remedies before pursuing a claim under Section 504 or the ADA so it was necessary to try to find coverage for these children under the IDEA. The Obama administration is apparently taking a different approach and accepting claims of discrimination under Section 504 for children who need accommodations but not special education.

3.   Speech or Language Impairments

The federal regulations define speech or language impairment as "a communication disorder, such as stuttering, impaired articulation, a language impairment, or a voice impairment, that adversely affects a child's educational performance." 34 C.F.R. § 300.8(c)(11).

The North Carolina form, reprinted below, recognizes these various categories of speech and language impairments.

DEC 3-SI (1 of 2)

SUMMARY OF EVALUATION/ELIGIBILITY WORKSHEET-SPEECH/LANGUAGE IMPAIRED

Student: <u>Student Name</u>   **DOB: 00 / 00 / 2000**

School: <u>School Name</u>   **Grade: <u>Grade</u>**

Date	Instrument	Summary of Required Screenings and Evaluations
00 / 00 / 2000	Hearing Screening:	☐ Pass ☐ Fail ____ dB (Intensity Level) _____ Hz (Frequencies) Method of Screening (if availability): _____
00 / 00 / 2000	Articulation Screening:	
00 / 00 / 2000	Fluency Screening:	
00 / 00 / 2000	Language Screening:	
00 / 00 / 2000	Voice/Resonance Screening:	
00 / 00 / 2000	Summary of conference(s) with parent(s) or documentation of attempts to conference:	
00 / 00 / 2000	Social/Developmental History:	
00 / 00 / 2000	Academic, Functional and Behavioral Observation across settings:	
00 / 00 / 2000	Educational Evaluation:	
00 / 00 / 2000	One of the following evaluations, based on screening results, individualized to address the specific area(s) of concern: • Articulation;	
00 / 00 / 2000	• Fluency;	
00 / 00 / 2000	• Language (including form, content, and function); or	
00 / 00 / 2000	• Voice/resonance;	
00 / 00 / 2000	Other:	

As a result of the required screenings, evaluations, and review of existing information, what do we now know about the student?

Strengths:
Needs:

Documentation of impairment in one or more of the following areas:

A.	Articulation-Two or more phonemic errors and/or phonological processes not expected at the child's age or developmental level;
B.	Fluency-Demonstration of non-fluent speech behavior;
C.	Language-Standard scores on an evaluation instrument suggest a language disorder and /or non-standardized/informal assessment indicates that the child has difficulty understanding and or expressing ideas and/or concepts (language); or
D.	Voice-Demonstration of consistent deviations in vocal production that are inappropriate for chronological/mental age, gender, and ability.

What is the adverse effect on educational performance?

What evidence exists that the student requires specially designed instruction?

AFTER COMPLETING WORKSHEET, IEP TEAM MUST DETERMINE ELIGIBILITY.
(See Eligibility Determination Form)
http://www.ncpublicschools.org/ec/policy/forms/statewide

An issue that can arise with respect to a speech and language impairment is: what is the standard considered "acceptable" for understandable speech? For example, April was diagnosed with a speech impediment when she entered grade school and received speech therapy several times a week for a half hour until fifth grade. When she was entering middle school, the school district argued that she no longer needed speech therapy because her speech was understandable 80 percent of the time. Is 80 percent understandability good enough for a child to no longer need speech therapy? Would one expect her speech to have no "adverse educational effects" if she is understandable 80 percent of the time?

An interesting exercise to conduct in order to understand what it means for someone to be understandable 80 percent of the time is to read a recipe out loud to a friend but omit every fifth word. Is the recipe still understandable? Now try reading a passage while omitting 1 of 10 words. Is it now understandable? What norms would you seek to use in the speech therapy context? The norming issue is quite complicated, because we would have different norms for a three-year-old than a thirteen-year-old. Further, people who know a child may find the child's speech understandable yet a stranger might not. Finally, one should remember that a disability assessment is supposed to be functional. Is the child's speech causing an adverse educational effect? If a child's speech cannot be understood by other students or causes the student embarrassment so the child is silent in the classroom, then those can be adverse educational effects. Hence, one would want to consider how speech impacts a child in the classroom irrespective of what norms might apply to the child's speech. The North Carolina form provides several different options for assessing speech and language impairments. Not all their options require norming information.

For a language disorder, California suggests that one should rely on standardized data. In a rather complicated regulation, it specifies that the "pupil scores at least 1.5 standard deviations below the mean, or below the 7th percentile" and "displays inappropriate or inadequate usage of expressive or receptive language as measured by a representative spontaneous or elicited language sample of a minimum of fifty utterances." *See* 5 C.C.R. § 3030(c)(4). There are various exceptions, and the rule only applies to "language" disorders, not articulation, abnormal voice or fluency disorders. New Jersey takes an approach similar to California. New Jersey requires that "the problem shall be demonstrated through functional assessment of language in other than a testing situation and performance below 1.5 standard deviations, or the 10th percentile on at least two standardized language tests, where such tests are appropriate, one of which shall be a comprehensive test of both receptive and expressive language." N.J.A.C. 6A:14-3.5. Notice that a child who scores in the 10th percentile might be disabled in New Jersey but not disabled in California.

4.   Visual Impairments (Including Blindness)

The federal regulations define visual impairment as "an impairment in vision that, even with correction, adversely affects a child's educational performance. The term includes both partial sight and blindness." 34 C.F.R. § 300.8(c)(13). As the North Carolina form indicates, uncorrected visual acuity of 20/200 is usually considered "blind," but any uncorrected vision of 20/70 or worse may have adverse educational effects. Also, visual impairments like strabismus ("cross-eyed") may have adverse educational effects because that condition affects depth perception and can cause eye strain. The North Carolina form recognizes the possibility of identification for those kinds of visual impairments. Nonetheless, its regulations state that a "visual impairment is the result of a diagnosed ocular or cortical pathology." N.C. 1500-2.4(14). Other states merely restate the federal definition and do not require an ocular or cortical pathology. North Carolina's form suggests more flexibility than the regulation itself.

5.   Serious Emotional Disturbance

Federal regulations define emotional disturbance as:

(4)(i) Emotional disturbance means a condition exhibiting one or more of the following characteristics over a long period of time and to a marked degree that adversely affects a child's educational performance:

A.   An inability to learn that cannot be explained by intellectual, sensory, or health factors.

B.   An inability to build or maintain satisfactory interpersonal relationships with peers and teachers.

C.   Inappropriate types of behavior or feelings under normal circumstances.

D.   A general pervasive mood of unhappiness or depression.

E.   A tendency to develop physical symptoms or fears associated with personal or school problems.

(ii) Emotional disturbance includes schizophrenia. That term does not apply to children who are socially maladjusted, unless it is determined that they have an emotional disturbance under paragraph (c)(4)(i) of this section.

34 C.F.R. § 300.8(c)

Some of the key elements of that definition are that the behavior should have occurred over a long period of time and cannot be explained by intellectual, sensory, or health factors. Hence, other explanations must be ruled out before an emotional disturbance classification can be made. Nearly every state uses the federal definition without modification in its own state regulations.

An issue that frequently arises with respect to the "emotional disturbance" label is that it can be used to describe a child who is merely frustrated because of other, possibly hidden, disabilities. Hence, states require that intellectual, health or sensory factors do *not* explain the child's behavior. In some jurisdictions, there have been lawsuits about the overdiagnosis of African-American boys in this category. Merely because children have behavioral problems in the classroom does not necessarily mean they have an emotional disturbance. The emotional disturbance label can also be a way to segregate children so that they do not participate in the regular classroom. This category requires special sensitivity and caution.

Consider the following hypothetical and determine whether you think the child should receive a classification as learning disabled, ADHD or serious emotional disturbance:

Julie

Julie is 15 years, nine months and enrolled in eleventh grade. This assessment was conducted during October of eleventh grade. She is under the supervision of a psychiatrist and takes medication for anxiety and depression. She has been diagnosed with ADHD-Inattentive type (two years ago) and was taking medication to assist with her concentration and attention skills. At the present time, her only medication is for anxiety and depression.

Julie did well during grade school and was in the gifted and talented class. In particular, she was a very strong reader. In middle school, she began to struggle in school especially with respect to her work habits. Although she received a B or C grade in all her academic classes, she received an unsatisfactory grade in most classes with respect to her work habits and cooperation. She frequently did not turn in assignments and appeared distracted during class.

Julie attended a regular high school for ninth and tenth grades. She failed about one-third of her classes and consistently received an unsatisfactory for work habits and cooperation. Her attendance was quite poor, especially for her first period class because she did not want to go to school and was frequently late. In the spring of tenth grade, she withdrew from the regular high school and enrolled in an Independent Studies program. In the alternative program, her grades improved to C's, B's and A's. Nonetheless, she still had tremendous difficulty meeting deadlines for assignments. When asked why she did not turn in assignments, she would report that she was not satisfied with the quality of her work. She did receive a psychiatric diagnosis of "obsessive compulsive disorder" and "depression" in eleventh grade. She saw a psychologist 60 minutes per week outside of school. The psychologist reported that Julie has considerable anxiety but that it has decreased in the Independent Studies program. The program, however, does not cause her to interact with other students and has therefore increased her social isolation.

Although Julie failed many of her high school classes, she performed well on various standardized tests that were administered. On the state standardized assessments, she scored advanced in English and Science, and proficient in History. Her cognitive abilities were measured in the high average range.

The school conducted a "functional behavior assessment." The primary result was that she engaged in "withdrawal" behavior when she was overwhelmed or anxious. Her general mood was feelings of helplessness and hopelessness.

Based on these results, would you recommend that Julie be classified as learning disabled, ADHD or emotionally disturbed? Her academic performance is not consistent with her cognitive ability. Is that sufficient evidence of LD? She does have a prior diagnosis of ADHD although she is currently not taking medication for the condition. Does ADHD appear to be negatively impacting her academic work? She has a diagnosis of depression and obsessive compulsive disorder. Are those conditions negatively affecting her academic performance? How should you handle both the ADHD and depression diagnoses?

6.   Orthopedic Impairments

Federal regulations define orthopedic impairment as "a severe orthopedic impairment that adversely affects a child's educational performance. The term includes impairments caused by a congenital anomaly, impairments caused by disease (e.g., poliomyelitis, bone tuberculosis), and impairments from other causes (e.g., cerebral palsy, amputations, and fractures or burns that cause contractures)." 34 C.F.R. § 300.8(c)(8). Most states use the federal regulatory language without modification. The existence of an orthopedic impairment is not usually in dispute. The harder question can be whether it causes an adverse educational effect and the child has a need for specially designed instruction.

7.   Autism

The federal regulations define autism as:

i.   Autism means a developmental disability significantly affecting verbal and nonverbal communication and social interaction, generally evident before age three, that adversely affects a child's educational performance. Other characteristics often associated with autism are engagement in repetitive activities and stereotyped movements, resistance to environmental change or change in daily routines, and unusual responses to sensory experiences.

ii.   Autism does not apply if a child's educational performance is adversely affected primarily because the child has an emotional disturbance, as defined in paragraph (c)(4) of this section.

iii. A child who manifests the characteristics of autism after age three could be identified as having autism if the criteria in paragraph (c)(1)(i) of this section are satisfied.

34 C.F.R. § 300.8(c)(1).

Checklists, like the Childhood Autism Rating Scale ("CARS") are often used to diagnose autism. Autism is usually considered to be a "spectrum" disorder. On the CARS scale, children are classified as nonaustistic, mildly-moderately autistic and severely autistic depending on where they fall on the rating scale. Another common inventory is the "Child Adaptive Behavior Inventory" which asks a teacher and parent to answer questions about the child's behavior such as: "Likes to meet new people," "Comes running to me with every little bump or scratch," "Is concerned about the feelings of others." Because the school setting is very important to a diagnosis for IDEA purposes, it is commonplace for a teacher's input to be considered crucial in completing these forms. Sometimes, parents and teachers have quite different experiences with children, so there should be evaluations in a number of settings. Further, special education teachers often have a different perspective than a regular classroom teacher. Why might that be true? (Possibly, special education teachers have a somewhat more lenient view of what is "normal" or "typical" behavior given their daily experiences.)

California takes a somewhat different approach to an autism diagnosis than many other states. It has a category called "autistic like behaviors." The list includes:

1)   An inability to use oral language for appropriate communication.

2)   A history of extreme withdrawal or relating to people inappropriately and continued impairment in social interaction from infancy through early childhood.

3)   An obsession to maintain sameness.

4)   Extreme preoccupation with objects or inappropriate use of objects or both.

5)   Extreme resistance to controls.

6)   Displays peculiar motoric mannerisms and motility patterns.

7)   Self-stimulating ritualistic behavior.

5 C.C.R. § 3030(g).

The list of autistic like behaviors from the California regulations can certainly be placed in the four categories listed in the federal regulations (and on the North Carolina form). The California list is more specific and may give parents and teachers a better sense of the kinds of behaviors that are typically associated with autism.

A recent area of controversy is children diagnosed as having "Asperger's Syndrome." The proposed revisions to the APA's Diagnostic Manual has removed Asperger's as a separate category due to what the APA considers to be an overdiagnosis and unclarity problem. *See* http://www.dsm5.org/ProposedRevisions/Pages/proposedrevision.aspx?rid=97#. The APA working group believes that many children currently classified as having "Asperger's" will fit the definition of "autism spectrum disorder" as reprinted below. The diagnostic criteria for Autism Spectrum Disorder are as follows. A person must meet criteria, 1, 2, and 3:

1. Clinically significant, persistent deficits in social communication and interactions, as manifest by all of the following:

a. Marked deficits in nonverbal and verbal communication used for social interaction

b. Lack of social reciprocity

c. Failure to develop and maintain peer relationships appropriate to developmental level

2. Restricted, repetitive patterns of behavior, interests, and activities, as manifested by at least TWO of the following:

a. Stereotyped motor or verbal behaviors, or unusual sensory behaviors

b. Excessive adherence to routines and ritualized patterns of behavior

c. Restricted, fixated interests

3. Symptoms must be present in early childhood (but may not become fully manifest until social demands exceed limited capacities).

See http://www.dsm5.org/ProposedRevisions/Pages/proposedrevision.aspx?rid=94. These are proposed revisions and could change before final publication in 2012. It is too early to know how states may respond to this new recommendation from the APA, but it could cause some states to be more restrictive in recognizing Asperger's as a diagnostic category for children to qualify for special education and related services. It is also important to notice that APA now refers to "autism spectrum" disorders rather than "autism." This change may cause some states to loosen their diagnostic criteria somewhat to recognize that children who are on the spectrum — but not at the extreme end — may still need special education and related services under the IDEA.

8.   Traumatic Brain Injury

Federal regulations define traumatic brain injury as follows:

Traumatic brain injury means an acquired injury to the brain caused by an external physical force, resulting in total or partial functional disability or psychosocial impairment, or both, that adversely affects a child's educational performance. Traumatic brain injury applies to open or closed head injuries resulting in impairments in one or more areas, such as cognition; language; memory; attention; reasoning; abstract thinking; judgment; problem-solving; sensory, perceptual, and motor abilities; psychosocial behavior; physical functions; information processing; and speech. Traumatic brain injury does not apply to brain injuries that are congenital or degenerative, or to brain injuries induced by birth trauma.

34 C.F.R. § 300.8(c)(12).

This category of disability is for children who have become disabled as a result of a trauma to the brain (but not during birth). Usually, the cause is an accident and the child was previously not disabled. Diagnosis is rarely an issue for these children; the harder question is creating an appropriate educational plan.

9.   Other Health Impairments

Federal regulations define "other health impairments" as follows:

Other health impairment means having limited strength, vitality, or alertness, including a heightened alertness to environmental stimuli, that results in limited alertness with respect to the educational environment that —

    i.   is due to chronic or acute health problems such as asthma, attention deficit disorder or attention deficit hyperactivity disorder, diabetes, epilepsy, a heart condition, hemophilia, lead poisoning, leukemia, nephritis, rheumatic fever, sickle cell anemia, and Tourette syndrome; and

    ii.   Adversely affects a child's educational performance.

34 C.F.R. § 300.8(c)(9).

This category is most typically used for children with ADHD. Again, the focus of the eligibility discussion is often the adverse impact on educational performance.

The 2004 IDEA amendments clarified that school districts cannot require children to be medicated as a condition of "attending school, receiving an evaluation . . . or receiving services." 34 C.F.R. § 300.174 (prohibition on mandatory medication). School districts often try to pressure parents to have their child use medication to control ADHD symptoms. That is a highly individualized decision that parents should make in consultation with a physician. School personnel are not qualified to make that decision for a child. If inquiries about medication arise during eligibility meetings, it is important to remind school districts of the prohibition on requiring medication.

A major issue for children who seek to qualify as disabled under "OHI" is demonstrating an adverse educational effect and need for specialized instruction. Consider the following fact pattern and consider whether the child should qualify for eligibility under OHI.

Jocelyn

Jocelyn was diagnosed with Type 1 diabetes on May 21, 2003, when she was three years old. She has recently completed kindergarten at Grandview Elementary School. Before entering kindergarten, she attended preschool at a Headstart program. An aide monitored her glucose level and diabetes symptoms during the entire school day and a nurse administered insulin injections at lunchtime.

When Jocelyn entered kindergarten, the school nurse worked with the classroom teacher to monitor Jocelyn's glucose level and administered insulin shots as needed. Jocelyn missed a significant amount of school due to doctor appointments and illnesses. She also frequently missed class time in order to have snacks or insulin injections as needed. When Jocelyn's sugar levels are too high or too low, it can interfere with her ability to concentrate. Jocelyn's diabetes care takes approximately 40 minutes out of her three hours and forty minutes of instructional time. Student has a "health care plan" in place to monitor her health care needs at school and that plan is working satisfactorily. She is a "fragile" diabetic who is very sensitive to insulin but, nonetheless, the health care plan appears to be working well.

Jocelyn's mother is concerned about the instructional time that Jocelyn misses due to her health care needs. She is also concerned that Jocelyn may miss valuable instruction during times of the day when her sugar levels are quite low.

The school district administered an educational evaluation of Jocelyn's academic performance during a time of day when her glucose levels were in the normal range. The test results suggested that Jocelyn was performing in the average or superior range in all subjects with her scores ranging from K.2 for math to 1.4 in oral language. Her nonverbal IQ was quite high with a score of 126. These tests were administered in the fifth month of kindergarten so an average score would be K.5.

Based on these scores, the school district argued that Jocelyn is not a child eligible for specialized instruction under the IDEA. Her health care needs can be met (and are being met) through a health care plan under Section 504. Jocelyn's mother believes that Jocelyn is performing at or above grade level because of her high IQ and her close work with Jocelyn at home. She thinks it is inevitable that Jocelyn will fall behind given the amount of instruction she misses each day due to her health care needs.

Jocelyn's mother appealed the lack of eligibility to a state hearing officer who ruled in favor of the school district with the following language:

> In light of the foregoing, the Hearing Officer finds that Jocelyn's diabetes does not adversely affect her educational performance at this time. On standardized testing, Jocelyn scored academically at grade level and above. Jocelyn performed at grade level in spite of having missed a month of school and then being absent 13 out of 33 days before the District's assessment. The Hearing Officer finds unpersuasive Mother's argument that any progress is due to Mother's providing the necessary curriculum at home. The Hearing Officer commends Mother for working so diligently with Jocelyn. However, all parents are expected to work with their children after school to reinforce the children's academic skills and support their progress in school. Further, there is no persuasive evidence that Jocelyn's above average academic achievement is attributable solely to the assistance provided to Jocelyn at home. Finally, the Hearing Officer finds to be without merit Mother's argument that Jocelyn's educational performance was adversely affected because she could have performed better academically if she had been provided more specialized instruction to address the missed instructional time. As noted in Board of Education v. Rowley, 458 U.S. 176 (1982), even a special-education-eligible child is not entitled to the best education available or instruction and services that maximize the child's abilities. A child is only entitled to a "basic floor of opportunity" consisting of access to specialized instruction and related services that are individually designed to provide educational benefit to the child. Id. at 201.

Do you agree with the Hearing Officer? Should Jocelyn have to fall behind in school before receiving individualized instruction to make up for the instructional time she misses each day? The *Rowley* decision is an important case involving whether a child has received an appropriate educational plan. Should it be cited as part of the eligibility decision? In any case, is *Rowley* good law in light of the 1997 and 2004 Amendments to the IDEA? [This case was taken from *Student v. La Habra City School District*, Case no. 1153 (California 2005), available at http://www3.scoe.net/speced/seho/seho_search/sehoSearchDetails.cfm?ID=2396.]

---

10. Specific Learning Disabilities

The federal regulations define "specific learning disability" as:

> a disorder in one or more of the basic psychological processes involved in understanding or in using language, spoken or written, that may manifest itself in the imperfect ability to listen, think, speak, read, write, spell, or to do mathematical calculations,

including conditions such as perceptual disabilities brain injury, minimal brain dysfunction, dyslexia, and developmental aphasia.

34 C.F.R. § 300.8(c)(10)(i). The regulation merely restates the statutory rule. *See* 20 U.S.C. § 1401(30).

The evaluation section of the IDEA contains more specific rules about assessing learning disabilities. It says:

A.   In general. Notwithstanding section 607(b), when determining whether a child has a specific learning disability as defined in section 602, a local educational agency shall not be required to take into consideration whether a child has a severe discrepancy between achievement and intellectual ability in oral expression, listening comprehension, written expression, basic reading skill, reading comprehension, mathematical calculation, or mathematical reasoning.

B.   Additional authority. In determining whether a child has a specific learning disability, a local educational agency may use a process that determines if the child responds to scientific, research-based intervention as part of the evaluation procedures described in paragraph (2) and (3).

20 U.S.C. § 1414(b)(6).

This statutory language typically provides school districts with two different methods to determine the existence of a learning disability: the discrepancy model or the response to intervention model. This language, which was added in 2004, is in response to arguments that the discrepancy model was problematic. Some argued that the discrepancy model overdiagnosed white, middle-class children as learning disabled because of its emphasis on IQ scores. Unless a child has a typical or above average IQ score, it is difficult to demonstrate a discrepancy between ability and achievement. Others argued that the discrepancy model was a "wait to fail" model because it was usually difficult to show a discrepancy until third grade when the child fell two years behind in school. The response to intervention model was also an attempt to align the IDEA with No Child Left Behind by emphasizing whether children could not meet state-mandated standards, even after receiving an appropriate group-based education rather than whether they were not meeting standards based on their inherent abilities. Finally, the response to intervention model was proposed as a way to save school districts money by allowing them not to administer costly, individual IQ tests.

States have responded to the flexibility provided in the 2004 Amendments with a wide variety of approaches. Colorado, Connecticut, Idaho, Indiana, Illinois, Iowa, New Mexico, New York and West Virginia have phased out the discrepancy model. Florida and Georgia appear to require students who are classified as learning disabled to satisfy *both* the discrepancy and response to intervention models. Most states that use the discrepancy model fail to identify how much discrepancy is needed to constitute a severe discrepancy. Fourteen states specify how much discrepancy constitutes a "severe discrepancy." The most typical rule is 1.5 standard deviations, but states range from 1 to 2 standard deviations.

Many states offer no guidance on the response to intervention model beyond what is already required in federal regulations. Connecticut, New Mexico and North Dakota are examples of states with extensive discussion of how one would establish a learning disability under the response to intervention model. The heart of the inquiry is whether the child is behind his or her same-grade or same-age peers and stays behind even after significant group-based intervention. North Dakota provides the following example of an acceptable approach under this model:

1. Organize the lowest 20% of students in the group (class, grade level, or school) to receive interventions.

2. Students in group interventions are monitored regularly.

3. Change interventions when 4 consecutive data points do not meet the student's goal line.

4. Move students to an individual intervention after two unsuccessful group interventions.

5. Students in individual interventions are monitored at least 1 time weekly.

6. Refer a student for special education after one unsuccessful individual intervention.

North Dakota Department of Public Instruction, Guidelines: Identification and Evaluation of Students with Specific Learning Disabilities, at 16, available at http://www.dpi.state.nd.us/speced/guide/SLDGuide07.pdf (last viewed on September 21, 2010).

One criticism of the response to intervention approach is that it can be quite time consuming and cause delay in the identification of students as disabled. If a state offers classification by either a response to intervention model or a discrepancy model, it is sometimes useful to insist on testing under the discrepancy model to speed up the disability classification. If a child does not tend to score well on aptitude tests, though, the response to intervention method may prove a better way to attain a disability classification and receive much-needed services.

Nonetheless, Congress did not want the flexibility provided in the 2004 Amendments to create an explosion in learning disability classifications. The following statutory language requires school districts to be somewhat cautious in classifying children as learning disabled:

(5) Special rule for eligibility determination.

In making a determination of eligibility under paragraph (4)(A), a child shall not be determined to be a child with a disability if the determinant factor for such determination is —

(A) a lack of appropriate instruction in reading, including in the essential components of reading instruction (as defined in section 1208(3) of the Elementary and Secondary Education Act of 1965);

(B) lack of instruction in math; or

(C) limited English proficiency

20 U.S.C. § 1414(b)(5).

In other words, school districts must rule out deficiencies in instruction or English before a learning disability diagnosis is made.

The North Carolina forms reflect these various requirements. North Carolina gives the school district the option of demonstrating disability with the discrepancy or with an alternative model. In the alternative model, an opportunity is provided to explain why the test scores do not appropriately reflect the existence of a learning disability. The school district records the child's response to intervention to make clear that a learning disability rather than a failure in instruction has caused the discrepancy between aptitude and achievement.

As with intellectual impairments, states differ on how they define learning disabilities under the discrepancy model. California requires a 1.5 standard deviation discrepancy between achievement and aptitude for a learning disability diagnosis to be made. *See* 5 C.C.R. § 3030(j). The California rule states:

> A computed difference which equals or exceeds this standard criterion [1.5 standard deviations], adjusted by one standard error of measurement, the adjustment not to exceed 4 common standard score points, indicates a severe discrepancy when such discrepancy is corroborated by other assessment data which may include other tests, scales, instruments, observations and work samples, as appropriate.

5 C.C.R. § 3030(j).

The California definition is fairly technical and requires an advocate to understand the concepts of standard deviation and error of measurement as well as standard scores. Applying the California rule, would a child be considered learning disabled who has an IQ of 100 and achievement scores of 85? Look at the testing bell curve we discussed earlier to answer this question. (One standard deviation is 15 standard score points.) What achievement score would be 1.5 standard deviations below 100 to constitute a "severe discrepancy"? What if the IQ score were 115? Would an 85 be a "severe discrepancy"? Other states, such as New Jersey, refer to the possibility of defining a learning disability based on a "severe discrepancy" but do not define that term in statistical terms. *See* N.J.A.C. 6A:14-3.5(12).

Consider the following fact pattern in determining whether a child meets the definition of "specific learning disability."

Simon

Simon's cognitive level has consistently tested in the average to high average range. Here are his cognitive aptitude results over the years:

1998: Wechsler Intelligence Scale for Children (WISC-III): full scale IQ of 95, verbal IQ of 97 and performance IQ of 94

2000: WISC III: full scale IQ of 109, verbal score of 98 and performance score of 121

2002: WISC III: full scale of 110, verbal of 103 and performance of 117

2004: Woodcock-Johnson Pyscho-Educational Test (WJ-III): full scale 105 within a range of 102-107

These are his various achievement test scores:

1998: average skill levels in reading and mathematics and low average skills levels in written language on Woodcock-Johnson Achievement Test (WJ-R)

2000: 17th percentile on reading comprehension and 3rd percentile in spelling on Peabody Individual Achievement Test

2002: 27th percentile on reading comprehension and written language; 32nd percentile on total reading on Peabody; 18th percentile in spelling on the WIAT-III; 34th percentile in oral reading, 25th percentile on passage score, and 5th percentile on reading rate on Gray Oral Reading Test.

2004: 12th percentile on broad reading on WJ-III with these subtests:

- letter-word identification at 41st percentile

- reading fluency at 2nd percentile

- passage completion at 60th percentile

  40th percentile in overall math cluster on WJ-III with these subtests:

- calculations at 59th percentile

- math fluency at 2nd percentile

- applied math ranking at 62nd percentile

  6th percentile in broad written language with these subtests:

- spelling in 19th percentile

- writing fluency at 2nd percentile

- writing sample at 44th percentile

  1st percentile in academic fluency

Additional test results: His auditory processing, conceptualization, short-term memory and working memory scores were over 100. His executive processing included concept formation ranking at the 94th percentile, planning at the 99th percentile, and pair cancellation below the 1st percentile. His processing speed was at the 3rd percentile.

The following information was provided about Simon's academic performance: In 1998, he was a middle school student receiving passing grades although he has Ds in science and an elective. He was found not to be eligible for assistance under the IDEA at that time but was provided with a Section 504 plan under which he received more time to complete tests, assistance with organizational skills, small group test administration and help with editing written assignments. His disability was listed as "ADHD." That program was in place until 2002 when he transferred to Washington Alternative High School's independent study program for eleventh grade. Prior to transferring, his accumulated GPA was 0.833. At Washington, his grades have been consistently in the A or B range with a C in biology. He took one or two classes per term at Washington. His mother said she tutored him at home up to sixty hours per week. She found his work habits to be "grindingly slow." He is currently 19 years old but, at this present rate of instruction, will take two years to finish his high school requirements.

What additional information would you like to know about Simon before determining whether he has a learning disability? How would you use the available information to argue he has a learning disability? Look at each of the required factors and marshal the evidence in favor of each of those factors.

Which learning disabled model would you use for this child: the discrepancy model or the alternative to the discrepancy model?

What is the evidence of a discrepancy between aptitude and achievement?

How would you deal with the child's improved performance in the new school with parental assistance?

Have any interventions been attempted and been unsuccessful?

Which basic psychological process appears to be disordered?

Is there evidence of a need for special education and related services?

Try to answer those questions before reading the material below. This example was taken from a 2004 California hearing officer decision. *See Student v. Colton Joint Unified School District*, Case No. 1457ZB (2004), available at http://www3.scoe.net/speced/seho/seho_search/sehoSearchDetails.cfm?ID=2245.

The hearing officer concluded that the evidence was sufficient to find a severe discrepancy between the student's cognitive abilities and academic achievement. The school district tried to argue that the student's achievement test scores should be considered as part of broad clusters. The student's expert argued that it was important to look at individual scores within the clusters. The hearing officer ruled in favor of the student on this issue concluding: "Although [the expert's] conclusions of a severe discrepancy between student's cognitive ability and achievement were based on individual scores that were part of a cluster, the Hearing Officer is persuaded that to do otherwise would effectively hide student's disabilities in recognized categories for special education." Specifically, the Hearing Officer found a severe discrepancy between the student's IQ and both reading fluency and math fluency. He has severe discrepancies in the qualifying categories of basic reading skills, mathematics calculation, and written expression because: "Being able to read fluently is a basic reading skill. Math fluency is also a significant part of mathematics calculation."

The Hearing Officer readily concluded that the student cannot be ameliorated within the regular education program. The grades within the alternative high school were not considered relevant to that consideration. It is not uncommon for school districts to try to classify children as ineligible for special education and related services because they are performing well with parental or other assistance. In an opinion letter issued in North Carolina, the state took the following position on that issue (relying on an older version of the current regulations):

> You also asked if the evaluation team should consider any tutoring that the child receives outside of the school day, or any modifications or compensatory strategies that are used with the child, and that the child needs in order to succeed academically, when determining whether the child is eligible for services under Part B. Although this specific issue is not addressed in the Part B regulations, a team may find that a child has a specific learning disability if the team determines that "[t]he child does not achieve commensurate with his or her age and ability levels in one or more of the areas listed in paragraph (a)(2) of this section when provided with learning experiences appropriate for the child's age and ability levels" [quoting former 34 C.F.R. § 300.541(a)(1)]. "Generally, it would be appropriate for the evaluation team to consider information about outside or extra learning support provided to the child in developing the written report required at [former 34 C.F.R. § 300.543], as such information may indicate what the child's achievement would be without such help. Such information may also have bearing on the evaluation team's conclusion, required by [former 34 C.F.R. § 300.543(b)(6)], on whether the child has "a severe discrepancy between achievement and ability that is not correctable without special education and related services."

Letter to Lillie/Felton, Office of Special Education Programs (April 5, 1995), 23 IDELR 714, 23 LRP 3420 (1995) (North Carolina).

The North Carolina opinion letter is based on the IDEA before the 1997 and 2004 amendments. The same concepts, however, are included in the current regulations. In the documentation section, the current regulations indicate that a child can qualify as learning disabled by exhibiting "a pattern of strengths and weaknesses in performance, achievement, or both, relative to age, State-approved grade level standards or intellectual development consistent with § 300.309(a)(2)(ii)." 34 C.F.R. § 300.311(a)(5)(ii)(B). Read 34 C.F.R. §§ 300.309 to 300.311 to get a full grasp of the requirements for identifying a child as having a learning disability. Section 300.309 makes reference to whether the child makes appropriate progress "when provided with learning experiences and instruction appropriate for the child's age or State-approved grade-level standards." Extensive parental or outside tutoring would go well beyond what one considers a regular educational environment.

11.   Multiple Disabilities

Often, children do not present with an obvious, single disability that explains their problems in the classroom. Examine the following profile and decide how you would approach a request that the child be identified as disabled.

Phillip

Philip resides with his natural parents and his two sisters. He was originally referred for evaluation as a preschooler due to behavioral difficulties. He was found eligible for special needs preschool based upon his behavior and attended a Franklin County Special Needs Preschool program for approximately one year. He was successful in his preschool program and met his behavioral objectives, as outlined in his IEP. Nonetheless, his mother continued to experience behavioral problems in the home setting. Phillip's special needs preschool teacher was concerned regarding his performance in the area of pre-reading skills. Consequently, a school-age evaluation was conducted in June to determine if Phillip was eligible for school-age special education services as a student with a learning disability. Phillip did not qualify for services as a result of that evaluation and he was placed in a regular Kindergarten program. Due to some concerns about his attention, he was placed in one of the full inclusion Kindergarten classrooms, which has a fulltime aide.

Phillip made good progress during the beginning of the Kindergarten year. His teacher was pleased with both his behavior and his academic skills. Phillip's mother continued to have behavioral difficulties with Phillip in the home setting, which resulted in Phillip being hospitalized at Ohio State University Hospitals during December and January due to psychiatric concerns. Phillip was subsequently diagnosed with Bipolar Disorder, Anxiety Disorder and ADHD. Consequently, this evaluation was conducted to determine Phillip's eligibility for special education services although his behavior in the school setting has continued to be appropriate.

These are the results of the various assessments that have been conducted since Phillip was 5 years old. He is now 7 years old:

Kauffman Assessment Battery for Children (age 5):

Subtest	Standard Score
Sequential Processing Scale	69
Simultaneous Processing Scale Score	103
Mental Processing Composite Score	85
Sequential Subtests	Scaled Score
Hand Movements	4
Number Recall	4
Word Order	6
Simultaneous Subtests	Scaled Score
Gestalt Closure	12
Triangles	10
Matrix Analogies	11
Spatial Memory	9

Woodcock-Johnson Test of Academic Achievement (age 5):

Subtests	Standard Scores	Percentile Rank
Letter-Word Identification	101	52
Passage Comprehension	93	31
Applied Problems	94	34
Writing Samples	100	50

Those two tests were administered when Phillip was entering kindergarten and were the basis for determining he was not eligible for special education and related services at that time. Notice how the "85" standard score is comprised of two quite divergent subtests. Also notice how scores may be reported in many different formats — as percentiles, scaled scores and standard scores. That can be very confusing to lay people who are trying to understand these scores.

If you were representing Phillip when he was entering kindergarten, how might you have argued he was eligible for special education and related services at that time?

Phillip was retested at age 7 (at the end of first grade). He was administered the Woodcock-Johnson Tests of Cognitive Abilities and Tests of Achievement. This test battery was developed to assess learning disabilities by reporting the discrepancy between achievement and aptitude. The Woodcock-Johnson form considers a discrepancy significant if it is at least 1.5 standard deviations below what one would expect based on aptitude. North Carolina form looks for a "15 point" difference. Fifteen standard scaled points is actually only 1 standard deviation. One would need to interpret the test results in light of that state's standards for defining learning disability.

Here are the various Woodcock-Johnson test scores:

Cluster/Test	Standard Score	90% Band
GIA (ext)	82	79-86
Verbal Ability (Ext)	91	85-97
Thinking Ability	88	84-93
COG Efficiency	77	72-83
Comp-Knowledge (Gc)	91	85-97
L-T Retrieval (Glc)	76	67-85
Vis-Spatial Think (Gv)	106	99-113
Auditory Process (Ga)	83	(76-90)
Fluid Reasoning (Gf)	94	(89-99)
Processing Speed (Gs)	87	(83-92)
Short-term Memory (Gsm)	73	(65-82)
Phonemic Aware	79	(71-87)
Working Memory	62	(50-74)
Broad Attention	64	(56-73)
Cognitive Fluency	56	(52-60)
Exec Processes	87	(82-92)
Oral Language (Ext)	84	(79-90)
Oral Expression	83	(75-91)
Listening Comp	90	(84-96)
Broad Math	82	(77-88)
Basic Reading Skills	72	(66-78)
Reading Comp	70	(64-76)
Math Calc Skills	80	(71-88)
Math Reasoning	78	(73-84)
Academic Skills	78	(74-82)
Academic Apps	76	(71-81)
Phon/Graph Know	76	(68-84)
Verbal Comprehension	88	(79-98)
Visual-Auditory Learning	80	(70-89)
Spatial Relations	101	(93-108)
Sound Blending	89	(82-97)
Concept Formation	98	(91-105)
Visual Matching	93	(89-98)
Numbers Reversed	74	(65-83)
Incomplete Words	80	(71-89)
Auditory Work Memory	0 raw score	
General Information	93	(84-102)
Retrieval Fluency	82	(72-93)
Picture Recognition	108	(100-117)
Auditory Attention	82	(74-89)
Analysis-Synthesis	90	(83-96)

Cluster/Test	Standard Score	90% Band
Decision Speed	83	(76-89)
Memory for Words	84	(75-94)
Rapid Picture Naming	58	(55-60)
Planning	87	(73-101)
Pair Cancellation	81	(76-85)

Form A of the following achievement tests was administered with the following results:

Test	Standard Score	90% Band
Letter-Word Identification	80	76-85
Story Recall	91	78-104
Understanding Directions	96	(90-101)
Calculation	96	(90-101)
Math Fluency	74	(61-87)
Spelling	84	(77-90)
Passage Comprehension	70	(63-77)
Applied Problems	87	(81-94)
Writing Samples	78	(64-91)
Story Recall-Delayed	—	—
Word Attack	64	(53-76)
Picture Vocabulary	84	(76-92)
Oral Comprehension	89	(82-97)
Reading Vocabulary	81	(73-89)
Quantitative Concepts	72	(65-80)
Spelling of Sounds	95	(89-102)

Based on these various tests, the test battery produced the following "discrepancy" results, first on "intra-cognitive" and then on "intellectual ability/achievement":

Discrepancies: Intra-Cognitive	Standard Scores: Actual	Standard Scores: Predicted	Difference	Discrepancy	Significant at + or − 1.5 SD
Comp-Knowledge	91	88	+ 3	+0.23	No
L-T Retrieval (Gc)	76	89	− 13	− 1.02	No
Vis-Spatial Think (Gv)	106	91	+ 15	+ 1.07	No
Auditory Process (Ga)	83	92	- 9	- 0.69	No
Fluid Reasoning (Gf)	94	87	+ 7	+ 0.55	No

Discrepancies: Intra-Cognitive	Standard Scores: Actual	Standard Scores: Predicted	Difference	Discrepancy	Significant at + or − 1.5 SD
Process Speed (Gs)	87	91	− 4	− 0.25	No
Short-Term Mem (Gsm)	73	92	-19	− 1.46	No
Phonemic Aware	79	92	-13	-0.87	No
Working Memory	62	92	-30	− 2.38	Yes
Discrepancies: Intellectual Ability/ Achievement Discrepancies[3]	Standard Scores: Actual	Standard Scores: Predicted	Difference	Discrepancy	Significant at + or − 1.5 SD
Basic Reading Skills	72	89	− 17	− 1.35	No
Reading Comp	70	90	− 20	− 1.79	Yes
Broad Math	82	89	− 7	− 0.60	No
Math Calc Skills	80	90	− 10	− 0.84	No
Math Reasoning	78	89	− 11	− 0.98	No
Oral Language (Ext)	84	85	− 1	− 0.07	No
Oral Expression	83	88	-5	− 0.40	No
Listening Comp	90	88	+ 2	+ 0.23	No

The first table reflects discrepancies within the child's various cognitive domains. Although the test designers used a 1.5 SD measure for significance, you would want to look at all the discrepancies, especially those more than 1.0 SD's. An educational psychologist would likely say that many of the areas of cognitive weakness are consistent with the ADHD diagnosis. The second table reflects the classic definition of learning disability under the discrepancy model. Again, look at each of these scores, including ones that do not quite meet the 1.5 SD threshold. And remember that learning disability is not the only basis upon which a child can be qualified as disabled and eligible for special education and related services. Is there evidence that this child's ADHD and psychological disorders may be impairing his academic performance?

Finally, look at his test results over time. You have test results from pre-kindergarten and then at the end of first grade. He received limited educational assistance during that time. He was in a full-inclusion classroom for kindergarten with a full-time aide, but that aide was not specifically assigned to assist Phillip. Are his test scores the same at age 5 and at age 7? What

---

[3] These discrepancies based on GIA (Ext) with ACH Broad, Basic, and Applied Clusters.

kinds of changes have occurred? How might those changes be used to suggest he needs special education and related services?

Which classification is most appropriate for Phillip? How should you respond if the school district suggests "severe emotional disturbance" as a classification given his record of hospitalization? What other classifications might be appropriate? Should the classification matter? Is it likely to matter?

IEP SIMULATION:
ELIGIBILITY DETERMINATION

The following IEP Simulation will give you an opportunity to test your understanding of the material covered in this chapter. The documents needed for the Simulation are:

1.   Directions for IEP Eligibility Meeting

2.   504 Plan dated August 25th

3.   Procedures for NC Testing

4.   Amended 504 Plan (dated December 18th)

5.   Homebound Services Procedures

6.   Letter from Nurse dated August 22nd

7.   Affidavit from Psychiatrist (Alicia Conlan)

8.   Psychological Evaluation

9.   Tables and Graphs Report

10. IEP form (see Section J in chapter 5, *infra*)

11. Eligibility Determination form.

DIRECTIONS FOR IEP ELIGIBILITY MEETING

In class, we will conduct a role play of an IEP eligibility meeting. This memorandum contains general instructions regarding how that role play will be conducted and the subject of the role play. Details regarding your individually assigned role will be e-mailed to you. Please keep the details of your individual role confidential and only reveal that information as appropriate (see discussion below).

In preparation for class, please read the materials on the syllabus and the information following this memorandum. Please also spend time thinking about your role and planning for the role play. The confidential information you will be sent about your character will give you only general parameters for your role. You are encouraged to develop your character as you see fit and supplement information as necessary, as long as your embellishments don't conflict with the information provided. Also, if your character would ordinarily speak with another character and share confidential information (e.g., a principal with a teacher, attorneys with their client, which in this case would be either the parent or the EC Director and principal, then you should do so in preparation for the meeting).

If you have questions about your role, please schedule a time to talk with your instructor to discuss your strategy or any questions you may have as you prepare for the meeting.

Role Play:

The setting for the meeting is an IEP eligibility meeting for Josephine Bass, a 14-year-old 8th grader at Constance Middle School in Grove County, North Carolina. The role play is based on an actual eligibility meeting, although all the names and identifying information have been changed to preserve client confidentiality. The purpose of the meeting is to determine whether Josephine qualifies as a disabled child in need of special education and related services under the IDEA.

Josephine's mother states that Josephine has been diagnosed with Fibromyalgia (or pain syndrome) and because of the pain and fatigue she experiences, she is no longer able to attend school and requires homebound instruction. Fibromyalgia is a recognized medical condition; however, it can be a fairly controversial diagnosis. The condition is characterized by widespread muscle pain (throughout the body, but especially in the back, legs and arms) and fatigue. Symptoms may also include tingling, numbness, dizziness, muscle spasms, insomnia, constipation and/or diarrhea as well as migraine headaches. It is diagnosed by a Rheumatologist, based on a patient's self-reporting of pain. There is no objective medical evidence (example Cat-scan, blood test, MRI, etc.) to substantiate the diagnosis. Rather, a diagnosis is made by checking 18 pain points in the body and if the patient complains of pain in at least 11 of them and the pain has been occurring for more than 3 months, then a diagnosis of Fibromyalgia is given. The patient is then treated with pain medication, anti-inflammatories and anti-depressants (depression is a common co-morbid condition with Fibromyalgia).

Fibromyalgia may clear up spontaneously or may last a lifetime. There is no known cure for Fibromyalgia, but it is not a fatal condition. A person with Fibromyalgia must learn to live with the condition as best as s/he can with pain medication, proper sleep and a physical therapy or exercise program.

In this case, Josephine's Fibromyalgia was diagnosed by Dr. Antoine Stackhouse, a rheumatologist. After his diagnosis, Josephine saw Brian Beckett, MSN, FNP (a nurse practitioner in Dr. Stackhouse's office) for pain management and follow up. Eventually, Dr. Stackhouse also referred Josephine to a psychiatrist, Dr. Alicia Conlan, for treatment of psychiatric issues related to her diagnosis of Fibromyalgia.

Brian Beckett, a family nurse practitioner treating Josephine, had early communication with the school (see letter from him attached) and based on this communication, a Section 504 plan was developed to help Josephine (the 504 plan is attached). Section 504 is a civil rights law designed to protect the rights of individuals with disabilities. A student may qualify for a 504 Plan if she has a disability that substantially limits a major life activity (e.g., such as walking, sitting or going to school). Plans generally provide for accommodations or modifications to the regular general education environment. 504 Plans do not provide specially designed instruction or related services as IEPs do.

In this case, Josephine's initial plan (providing accommodations in the regular learning environment) was only in place for a few months (from the start of school until November). In November, Ms. Bass decided to keep Josephine home from school under the Grove County homebound policy. Under the homebound policy, Josephine receives 2 hours a week of homebound instruction (see Grove County Homebound Service Procedures, also attached). Her 504 Plan was then amended to show that she was receiving homebound services under this policy in December.

Josephine's mother now has asked the school to find Josephine eligible for services under the IDEA rather than under Section 504. Ms. Bass would like Josephine's homebound services to continue (but be increased) and she would like the services to continue under an IEP rather than under the county's existing procedures and her 504 plan. Just before the meeting, Ms. Bass' attorney submitted the affidavit of Dr. Conlan (attached) supporting her request for homebound services.

If Josephine were to be found eligible for special education pursuant to the IDEA, it would most likely be under the category of disability known as "other health impaired." *NC Policies Governing Services for Children with Disabilities* states:

> To be determined eligible in the disability category of other health impairment, a child must have a chronic or acute health problem resulting in one or more of the following:
>
> (A) Limited strength;
>
> (B) Limited vitality;
>
> (C) Limited alertness, including heightened alertness to environmental stimuli that results in limited alertness with respect to the educational environment.

The disability must:

> (A) Have an adverse effect on educational performance, and
>
> (B) Require specially designed instruction.

The first task of the IEP team is to determine whether Josephine is a disabled child eligible for special education and related services under the IDEA. To do this, the team will need to determine first, whether Josephine's Fibromyalgia is a qualifying disability and second, whether, the disability has an "adverse effect on educational performance" requiring "specially designed instruction." To guide this discussion, the team should use the definition of "other health impaired" from above and the Summary of Evaluation/Eligibility Worksheet for Other Health Impairment (attached). Assume that all of the required screenings and evaluations listed on the form have been conducted and focus your discussion not on the results of those individual evaluations but on the following questions:

(1) Does Josephine have a disability? and, if so,

(2) Does Josephine's disability have an adverse effect on her educational performance and require specially designed instruction?[4]

Additional Information:

If the team determines that Josephine is <u>not</u> qualified for services under the IDEA, then it will need to inform the mother of her rights under the IDEA and will then need to turn its attention to whether or not Josephine's current Section 504 plan continues to be appropriate. If the team determines that she <u>is</u> eligible, then it will need to write an IEP (note that writing an IEP is an ambitious task and you may only have time to address the eligibility issue in the time allowed).

---

[4] In answering this second question, make sure you familiarize yourself with the definition of "special education" and "specially designed instruction" in the federal statute and corresponding regulations (20 U.S.C. § 1401(29); 34 C.F.R. § 300.39, which are consistent with the policies in North Carolina, where this meeting takes place).

Timeline:

1. It is early May.

2. Josephine was diagnosed with Fibromyalgia last spring.

3. The school year began August 25th and will end the first week of June.

4. A 504 plan was initially created for Josephine on August 25th.

5. Josephine's mother pulled her out of school over Thanksgiving break in November.

6. The 504 was amended on December 18th to include homebound education.

7. Josephine started homebound education on January 3rd.

8. Assume the psycho-educational evaluation by Hester Blackberry is valid and current (at the time this meeting occurred, the WISC-III was the current version of the Weschler Intelligence Scale for Children. The current version is WISC-IV, however, for the purposes of the role play, we will use these scores and assume they are current).

Instructions:

1. With the exception of the mother and school psychologist, each of you can use your real names during the IEP.

2. The EC Case Manager will start and control the pace of the meeting. It is the duty of the EC Case Manager to fill out all the IEP forms that the team uses at the meeting (this would include the eligibility form and an IEP, if necessary, both of which are attached).

3. The EC Director for the District will serve as the LEA Representative.

4. The 504 coordinator at the school is a certified special education teacher and therefore will be fulfilling both roles at this meeting.

5. No minutes will be taken at the meeting.

The members of the IEP team for the eligibility meeting are as follows:

- School Psychologist (Hester Blackberry)
- Principal
- Regular Education Teacher
- EC Director for District
- Attorney for Parent/Child
- School Attorney
- EC Case Manager
- Special Ed teacher/504 Coordinator
- Mother (Regina Bass)
- School Nurse

- **504-E**

GROVE COUNTY SCHOOLS
SECTION 504
INDIVIDUAL ACCOMODATION PLAN

1. **Name:** *Josephine Bass*   **Student ID#** *56823*

2. **School:** *Constance Middle School*   **Grade:** *8th*

3. **Type of Referral:** (√) **Initial:** ( ) **Reevaluation**

4. **Indicate handicapping condition**: *Josephine has fibromyalgia according to note from PT and FNP.*

5. **Basis for determination as a qualified individual:** *(See attached letter from Brian Beckett, MSN, FNP)*

6. **Major Life Activity:** *Sitting*   **Educational Impact:** *Learning*
   Josephine need not sit more than 30 minutes without a break. She is to sit through no more than 90 minutes of testing.

7. **Describe necessary accommodations:** *She needs a full back chair (no space in the lower back) in each room or a Lumbar pillow. (pillow purchased Aug. 26. Discussed with mother by telephone)*

8.

Committee Signature	Title	Date
Sylvania Klein	*Spanish Teacher*	*August 25th*
Patricia Hilton	FACS Teacher	8/25
Charles Turlington	Hlth/PeTeacher	Aug. 25th
F. Fitzpatrick	*Counselor*	*august 25th*
Regina Bass	*Mother*	*August 25th*

PROCEDURES FOR NORTH CAROLINA TESTING PROGRAMS

A.   Procedural Modifications Available

The following test modifications and administrative procedures should be implemented to assure that the student's needs are met:

_____Braille	_____Answers recorded by proctor
_____Large Print	_____Marking in test booklet
_____Magnification Aids	_____Use of a typewriter or Word Processor
_____Braillewriter/Cranmer Abacus	_____Testing in a separate room
_____Reading Test Aloud	___√____Extended time or multi-test sessions

B.   Recommendations For Modifications for NC Testing Programs:

END-OF-GRADE	MSDT	END-OF-COURSE	COMPETENCY
(√) Will use Modifications	( ) Will use Modifications	(√) Will use Modifications	( ) Will use Modifications
(√) End of Grade	( ) Reading	( ) specify course	( ) Reading
(√) Writing Essay	( ) Math	_____	( ) Math
	( ) Language	_____	( ) Writing Objective

SPECIFY MODIFICATION(S):

_____	_____	_____	_____
_____	_____	_____	_____
_____	_____	_____	_____
_____	_____	_____	_____
_____	_____	_____	_____

504-E
GROVE COUNTY SCHOOLS
SECTION 504 *(Amended)*
INDIVIDUAL ACCOMODATION PLAN

1. **Name:** *Josephine Bass*   **Student ID#** *56823*

2. **School:** *Constance Middle School*   **Grade:** *8th*

3. **Type of Referral:** (√) **Initial:** ( ) **Reevaluation**

4. **Indicate handicapping condition**: *Josephine has fibromyalgia according to note from PT and FNP.*

5. **Basis for determination as a qualified individual:** *(See attached letter from Brian Beckett, MSN, FNP)*

6. **Major Life Activity:** *Sitting*   **Educational Impact:** *Learning*
    Josephine need not sit more than 30 minutes without a break. She is to sit through no more than 90 minutes of testing.

7. **Describe necessary accommodations:** *She needs a full back chair (no space in the lower back) in each room or a Lumbar pillow. (pillow purchased Aug. 26. Discussed with mother by telephone)*

8.

Committee Signature	Title	Date
Sylvania Klein	Spanish Teacher	August 25th
Patricia Hilton	FACS Teacher	8/25
Charles Turlington	Hlth/PeTeacher	Aug. 25th
F. Fitzpatrick	Counselor	august 25
Regina Bass	Mother	August 25th

December 18th, 504 amended to homebound education.

Committee Signature	Title	Date
Patricia Hilton	FACS Teacher	12/18
Sylvania Klein	Spanish Teacher	December 18th
F. Fitzpatrick	Counselor	December 18
Charles Turlington	Hlth/PeTeacher	Dec. 18th
Regina Bass	Mother	December 18th

GROVE COUNTY SCHOOLS
HOMEBOUND SERVICE PROCEDURES

I. What are homebound services?

When a student is unable to attend school due to a medical condition or when the IEP calls for homebound services, a certified teacher serves the student in his or her home.

II. Who is eligible for homebound services?

    a. A student who is unable to attend school due to a medical condition for a period of at least 4 weeks. Documentation from a physician is required.

    b. A student whose IEP designates home placement.

III. How are homebound services obtained?

    a. When the school representative receives a request for homebound services, he or she checks the paperwork to make sure that the Homebound Form is complete with all necessary information and correct documentation attached (medical or IEP). A single school contact person must be named, clear directions to the student's home, and a current working phone number to reach the parent.

    b. The school representative sends the Homebound Request Form (along with appropriate documentation) to the Exceptional Education office at Support Services.

    c. When the request is received, the Director of Exceptional Education reviews and approves the request and the homebound teacher is contacted.

    d. The homebound teacher contacts the parent and arranges to meet with the student twice a week. The homebound teacher picks up assignments from the school contact (named on the request form). She does **NOT** go to the child's teacher. The homebound teacher goes to the home where:

- an adult is present with the student

- a quiet workspace is designated

- the child is ready to work

    If a session must be cancelled, the parent is responsible for calling the homebound teacher as soon as possible.

    e. The homebound teacher provides assignments, administers tests, collects completed work and returns it to the school contact to be given to the teacher(s) for grading. The homebound teacher does not grade assignments.

IV. How long does homebound continue?

School is the most desirable place for all students, so a homebound placement is reviewed after 30 calendar days. If there is updated medical documentation the service may continue with continuous review every 30 days. If the student's IEP places him or her on homebound it must be reviewed after 30 days and a plan must be made to return the student to school as soon as possible. Once the student returns to school homebound services cease.

The school contact may request a written or verbal report from the Homebound teacher about the student's compliance and/or performance in the homebound setting. This could provide valuable information to the school staff and the IEP team.

Grove County University
HEALTH CARE
Family Practice Center

August 22nd

Victoria Bentley @ 445-5621 x 554
Constance Middle School
8659 Stony Bridge Road
Grove City, NC 27278
Fax: 445-5623

Dear Ms. Bentley,

Thank you for speaking with me on the phone. I am writing this note for Josephine Bass. Josephine has been diagnosed with fibromyalgia and despite the fact that she is much more functional when on medication, she still has some restrictions that I hope we can ameliorate. I would appreciate if she:

1. sit in testing for no more than 30 minutes without a stretch break
2. sit through no more than 90 minutes of testing at a time

She is currently under my care and should be able to be a full participant in school activities. Physical exercise, as long as it's tolerated, is preferable. If she says she needs to sit out or get an ice pack on a muscle then I would appreciate if she could. I will assume you will speak with the athletics director.

Thank you once again for your assistance with her. If you need anything further please contact me.

Brian Beckett

Brian Beckett, MSN, FNP
Clinical Associate Professor

The University of Grove County at Grove County Family Practice Center, J.D. Haskins Family Medicine Building, 225 Evergreen Drive, Grove City, NC 45632-9856. Telephone: (323) 455-2114. Fax: (323) 455-2115.
www.fampraccent.ugc.edu

Clive Gibbons MD, MBA
Director, Clinical Services
Telephone: (323) 455-2116
Email: Clive_Gibbons@ugc.edu

Ramsey Silverback, MD, MBA
Director, Family Practice Center
Telephone: (323) 455-2117
Email: Ramsey_Silverback@ugc.edu

Weston Upton, MHSA
Practice Manager
Telephone: (323) 455-2118
Email:Weston_Upton@ugc.edu

NORTH CAROLINA	**AFFIDAVIT OF**
GROVE COUNTY	**ALICIA N. CONLAN, M.D.**

I, Alicia N. Conlan, do solemnly swear as follows:

1. I am a Psychiatrist at Grove County Mental Health Associates, 5656 Rolling Hwy, Suite 5, Grove City, NC 27279. In 1975, I received a BS in Biology with Summa cum Laude and was Phi Beta Kappa from Mount Vernon University. I received a MD degree from The School of Medicine, Mount Vernon University, in 1980. In 1984, I completed a Residency in Psychiatry at Mount Vernon University Hospitals. I became a licensed physician in North Carolina in 1981. In 1986, I became a Board-certified Diplomate by The American Board of Psychiatry and Neurology. From October 1981 until October of 1982 I worked at the Grove County Emergency Mental Health Services. In 1984, I was a Staff Psychiatrist at the Sunset Mental Health and Wellness Center where I had admitting privileges at Sunset County Hospital. In 1987, I began a private practice in psychiatry in both Glendale and Bridgeport. In Glendale, I worked the first of ten years in the office of Dr. Lilly Humphrey, Neurologist. In 1989, I co-founded Grove County Mental Health Associates, an independent practice association of mental health group practices in eastern and southern North Carolina. I have twelve and a half years of full-time experience as a psychiatrist evaluating and treating the full range of psychiatric problems in children, adolescents, adults, couples and the elderly. I have ten years of experience of being the primary treating physician for approximately fifty patients suffering from Fibromyalgia.

2. Josephine Bass was referred to me by Dr. Antoine Stackhouse, MD, MA, on February 11th for treatment of psychiatric issues related to her diagnosis of Fibromyalgia-like Syndrome. I examined Josephine on February 25th. I reviewed all the medical records brought by her mother. Nathaniel Lynch, RN, MSW, LCSW, CS, a clinical social worker and clinical psychiatric nurse specialist in our group practice at Grove County Mental Health Associates, has also been treating Josephine. Mr. Lynch and I have collaborated about Josephine's treatment.

3. Josephine's diagnosis of Fibromyalgia-like Syndrome has been well substantiated. Fibromyalgia-like Syndrome is a chronic autoimmune condition. Josephine's immune system is attacking her muscles and connective tissue, including the muscles and connective tissue of her joints. The resultant inflammatory process causes pain, weakness, fatigue, and decreased motor ability. After seven years of symptoms, her illness has progressed to the point of atrophy, which is muscle loss of her right quadriceps and her front thigh muscle. Josephine's symptoms also include migraine headaches, bladder spasms, and irritable bowel syndrome. All of her illnesses/disorders are exacerbated by stress, including psychosocial and physical stress. Treatment of Fibromyalgia includes the very gradual increase of physical activity without overdoing physical exertion that worsens the inflammatory process, leading to a setback. Treatment also involves medication to address the pain and other symptoms of the Fibromyalgia-like Syndrome, medication for her depression as well as her migraines and irritable bowel syndrome, and psychotherapy to decreases her psychosocial stress and to help her resolve her Adjustment Disorder with Depressed Mood.

4. Currently, Josephine's physical abilities are severely restricted because of her Fibromyalgia-like Syndrome. She can only undertake a few minutes of physical activity each day. Josephine is working on gradually increasing her daily physical activity. It is very important that she increase her activity in a gradual way. If she over extends herself one day, her progress will be set back significantly.

5. In addition to Fibromyalgia-like Syndrome, Josephine suffers from Adjustment Disorder with Depressed Mood. This means that Josephine experiences intermittent symptoms of depression each week that last for periods of hours or days at a time. The depression consists of decreased concentration, loss of interest in usual activities, sleep disturbance, decreased energy, decreased motivation, irritability, feelings of worthlessness, and social withdrawal.

6. Stress exacerbates the symptoms of both Fibromyalgia-like Syndrome and Adjustment Disorder. Josephine suffers from extraordinary psychological stress because of the stigma associated with having a disorder that is not detectable from her outward appearance. Josephine's peers have questioned her about her condition and she often feels like people do not believe that she is suffering. This reaction by others adds to the stress she experiences and exacerbates the symptoms of her disorders.

7. In my opinion, Josephine cannot attend school and should receive homebound instruction. Josephine has difficulty with activities of daily living. Preparing to leave the house in the morning in order to attend school requires most or all of her available strength and energy for the entire day, and thus limits how much she can learn that day.

8. In my opinion, Josephine cannot reasonably be expected to participate in a regular or adjusted school day. Because of her impaired concentration, she cannot focus on her schoolwork in the classroom setting, which has a higher degree of sensory input and pressure compared with the home setting. She cannot walk from one classroom to another and she cannot sit comfortably in a classroom chair for longer than 10 minutes at a time. Additionally, she cannot deal with the psychological stress associated with interacting with other students who question her about her limitations, such as using the elevator instead of the stairs.

9. In my opinion, it would be appropriate for Josephine to return to school for the regular school day when she is able to (1) walk comfortably at will as needed in the school setting, (2) sit comfortably in a classroom chair as required in the school setting, (3) exercise appropriately for at least 30 minutes 4 to 5 times a week, and participate in isotonic activity for at least 20 minutes 3 times a week, and (4) experience freedom from subjective symptoms and objective signs of depression for at least 3 months. In my opinion, she cannot achieve any of these benchmarks now. Because her Fibromyalgia-like Syndrome was just diagnosed in April of last year, Josephine's treatment plan is not yet fully implemented. She may achieve these benchmarks in six months to a year. If her illness has progressed too far in the last seven years for the inflammatory process to abate despite treatment, she may never attain these goals.

This is the 1st day of March.

Alicia N. Conlan, M.D.
Alicia N. Conlan, M.D.

GROVE COUNTY SCHOOL

PSYCHOLOGICAL EVALUATION
(CONFIDENTIAL)

NAME: Josephine Bass

DATE OF BIRTH: February

AGE: 14

SCHOOL: Constance Middle School

GRADE: 8th

EXAMINER: Hester Blackberry
                   School Psychologist

DATE OF EVALUATION: March 5th — March 8th

ASSESSMENT TECHNIQUES

Review of records
Behavioral Observation
Interview with student/parent/teachers
Wechsler Intelligence Scale for Children-Third Edition
Behavior Assessment Scale for Children (BASC) Structured Development History

Woodcock Johnson Psychoeducational Battery-III: March 1st

REASON FOR REFERRAL

This evaluation was requested by Josephine's mother to determine her need and eligibility to receive services from the Exceptional Children's Program. According to a letter from her doctor, Josephine suffers from Fibromyalgia-like Syndrome and Adjustment Disorder with Depressed Mood. She has been receiving homebound educational services since January 3rd.

BACKGROUND INFORMATION

Josephine is an 8th grader at Constance Middle School. She was enrolled in the normal school year program until October when she started receiving homebound services.

School records indicate that Josephine started kindergarten nine years ago. She attended Yellow Ray Elementary School. In second grade, she transferred to Springing Fountain Elementary School, the year round program in the Grove County Schools, where she completed up to the 5th grade. In sixth grade, Josephine attended Valley Charter School in Upper Eastside, NC. She transferred to Constance Middle School in January of last year while in the 7th grade.

Josephine's grades in elementary school were mostly A's, B's and C's. While at Valley Charter School, grades ranged within the 70's and 80's in most classes. Math grades had been one of her lowest grades. When she transferred to Constance in the 7th grade, Josephine had failing grades in math.

Josephine had a significant number of absences almost every year since she started school. Records show she was absent 26 days in Kindergarten, 10 days in 1st grade, 18 days in 2nd grade, 12 days in 3rd grade, 11 days in 4th grade, and 10 days in 5th grade. Absences were not recorded in her 6th grade report card, while enrolled at a Charter School. In 7th grade she had 14 absences at the Charter School and 14 absences at Constance Middle School during the last four months of school. In addition, Josephine had a significant number of tardy dates, which reached up to 95 days in the 5th grade.

Records show that Josephine earned passing scores on the reading End of Grade Testing in 3rd, 5th, 6th, and 7th grade. She scored below proficiency in math End of Grade Testing in the 3rd, 4th, and 5th grades. She was proficient in math (level 3) in the 6th grade. In her last testing in 7th grade, Josephine scored a level 2 (within one Standard Error of measurement) in math. That was considered a passing score.

Her 8th grade math and science teachers reported that Josephine was frequently absent at the beginning of this school year. When she was in school, she was very quiet and always did her work. Since she has been on homebound placement, she had been turning in her work on a regular basis. Her math work reflects some understanding of basic math concepts. However, it is very difficult for the teacher to judge her skill level, since Josephine is not in class to ask questions and participate in the daily instruction and discussions.

According to an affidavit signed by her attending psychiatrist, Josephine has been diagnosed with Fibromyalgia-like Syndrome. According to Dr. Conlan's letter, this is a chronic autoimmune condition (See letter in file).

Josephine passed a vision and hearing screening on September 2nd.

Social/Developmental History

Ms. Bass completed the BASC Structured Developmental History. She reported that Josephine lives with her and her father Daniel Bass. She has a nine-year old brother who attends Green Greyson Elementary School.

Josephine was born after a normal pregnancy and delivery. She was healthy at birth. Developmental milestones were reached within normal limits. Josephine's medical history is significant since age seven. She developed chronic pain and high blood pressure at age seven. She has muscle spasms and migraine headaches since age 12, and developed Chronic Fatigue and Irritable Bowel Syndrome at age 13. She is currently treated with different pain medications and antidepressant medication.

Josephine used to play soccer but had to discontinue it because of her illness. Ms. Bass said Josephine would like to spend more time with her friends and participate in activities, but due to her symptoms of pain, she cannot participate as well as she once could. She enjoys reading and drawing, and talking to her friends.

Ms. Bass reported that Josephine always enjoyed reading. Math has always been difficult for her, even in her early years.

Ms. Bass described Josephine as a very loving, outgoing, and respectful child. She is concerned about her physical symptoms that cause severe pain.

BEHAVIORAL OBSERVATIONS

Josephine's psychoeducational evaluation was scheduled on three different sessions. The first session lasted almost two hours. She was tested with the WJ III (educational testing) by Ms. Jennifer Humphrey, the educational diagnostician. The psychological testing was done in two one-hour sessions.

Josephine is an attractive child, who was neatly dressed and well groomed. She was cooperative and pleasant during the psychological evaluation. She appeared to be comfortable and did not complain of any discomfort during the sessions. Josephine was offered to take breaks between subtests, but she said she does not need them and opted to continue to work. She reported that due to her illness, there are days that she does not feel well. During the first session of the psychological testing, Josephine reported that the day before had been difficult for her, but she was starting to feel better. The second session she reported to be feeling good.

Josephine said she has been sick since the age of seven, but she "got worse" when she was in the 6th grade.

Josephine said that because of her illness, she has to stay home. She said she sees her friends sometimes when they come to her house, they go to a movie or they meet at the mall. She added that the meetings at the mall are not too long since she tires easily.

Josephine says she enjoys reading very much. She said math is difficult for her, and has been since she was in elementary school.

Josephine worked diligently throughout the testing. She showed good attention span and concentration. The present evaluation appears to be a fair estimate of her current functioning.

COGNITIVE EVALUATION

Verbal (VIQ)	82	Low Average
Performance (PIQ)	91	Average
Full Scale	85	Low Average

Interpretation of WISC-III Results

Josephine's general cognitive ability is within the low average range of intellectual functioning, as measured by the Wechsler Intelligence Scale for Children — Third Edition. Her overall thinking and reasoning abilities exceed those of approximately 16% of students her age (FSIQ = 85; 90% confidence interval = 81-90).

She performed slightly better on nonverbal than on verbal reasoning tasks, but there is no significant difference between Josephine's ability to reason with and without the use of words. Her verbal reasoning abilities are most appropriately characterized by her score on the Verbal Comprehension Index, which is low average and above those of approximately 21% of her peers (VCI = 88; 90% confidence interval = 83-94). Her nonverbal reasoning abilities are best described by her score on the Perceptual Organization Index, which is average and above that of approximately 42% of students Josephine's age (POI = 97; 90% confidence interval = 90-104).

Processing visual material quickly is an ability that Josephine performs poorly as compared to her nonverbal reasoning ability. Processing speed is an indication of the rapidity with which Josephine can mentally process simple or routine information without making errors.

Josephine's speed of information processing abilities are within the borderline range and better than those of approximately 3% of her age-mates (Processing Speed Index = 72; 90% confidence interval = 68-84).

Josephine performed significantly lower on the Arithmetic (Scaled Score = 3) subtest than on the Digit Span subtest (Scaled Score = 9). Both of these tasks require attention, concentration, and mental control, but the Arithmetic subtest also measures specific abilities in numerical operations and mathematics reasoning. Her lower score on the freedom of distractibility factor may have been affected by her weakness in math calculation rather than by her ability to pay attention.

Josephine's performance was significantly better on the Picture Completion subtest than her own mean score for all nonverbal reasoning tasks. Further, she performed better than most of her age-mates, thus demonstrating strong abilities on the Picture Completion subtest. The Picture Completion subtest required Josephine to identify the missing part in each of a series of common objects and scenes. An indication of her ability in visual discrimination, the Picture Completion subtest assesses the abilities to detect essential details in visually presented material and to differentiate them from nonessential details. Performance on this task also may be influenced by an individual's general level of alertness to the world around her and long-term visual memory (Picture Completion scaled score = 13).

Josephine achieved her best performance among the verbal reasoning tasks on the Similarities subtest and lowest score on the Comprehension subtest. Her performance across these areas differs significantly and suggests that these are the areas of most pronounced strength and weakness, respectively, in Josephine's profile of verbal reasoning abilities. Her weak performance on the Comprehension subtest was below that of most student's her age.

On the similarities subtest Josephine was required to respond orally to a series of word pairs by explaining how the words of each pair are alike. This subtest examines her ability to abstract meaningful concepts and relationships from verbally presented material (Similarities scaled score = 10).

The Comprehension subtest required Josephine to provide oral solutions to everyday problems and to explain the underlying reasons for certain social rules or concepts. This subtest provides a general measure of verbal reasoning. In particular, this subtest assesses her comprehension of social situations and social judgment as well as her knowledge of conventional standards of social behavior (Comprehension scaled score = 4).

(See additional scores report)

EDUCATIONAL EVALUATION

Woodcock Johnson Psychoeducational Battery — III

	SS	Discrepancy
Broad Reading	93	
Reading Comprehension	101	+16
Basic Reading	118	+33
Broad Math	77	
Math Calculation	74	-11

	SS	Discrepancy
Math Reasoning	80	−5
Broad Written Language	101	+16
Written Expression	93	+8

Josephine was quiet and reserved initially during testing. She said her best subject is Reading, and she finds Math a harder subject. Testing was administered from 10:00 a.m. until 11:50 a.m., with short pauses during and between subtests as needed. Josephine most often shifted positions in her chair, but got up and stretched during a few of these breaks. She sat in a cushioned chair. Josephine had good attention, persistence and appeared very motivated to do well. As testing progressed, Josephine became more relaxed and interactive, talking about her interests in drawing and the Japanese culture. She also said she reads in her spare time. She approached tasks in a serious, conscientious manner and was a pleasure to work with!

Reading was a strong area for Josephine on this test administration. She demonstrated skills in the High Average range when compared to other students her age on the Letter-Word Id., and Word Attack subtests with very good vocabulary recognition and decoding skills. She read many words quickly and used phonetic analysis effectively when decoding an unfamiliar word. Her scores on the Reading Vocabulary and Passage Comprehension subtests were Average for her age. She was able to use context clues effectively when asked to read passages and fill in a missing word to fit the context on the Passage Comprehension subtest. She was able to read vocabulary words and generate synonyms, antonyms, and complete analogies on the Reading Vocabulary subtest. Her weakest area was Reading Fluency. Josephine was asked to read brief statements and to circle yes/no answers within a three-minute timed period on this area. It was the only timed Reading area. She was slower than average, scoring in the Low range for her age, which is significantly weaker than her other reading skills.

Math is Josephine's weakest area on this test administration. She was much less confident in her skills in this subject and was not able to complete many items on the Calculation subtest. She scored in the Low Average range when compared to other students her age on the Calculation, Applied Problems, and Quantitative Concepts subtests, and in the Very Low range on the Math Fluency subtest. On the Calculation subtest, Josephine correctly calculated basic operations, addition and subtraction with regrouping. She made an error on multiplying a two-digit number by a one-digit number (i.e. $7 \times 13 = 141$), but was able to complete another similar problem ($6 \times 14 = 84$), so she appears to know the correct process. Josephine said she did not remember how to calculate any long division, fractions, negative numbers, or decimals. On the Math Fluency subtest, she had a high rate of errors, correctly calculating 50 basic math facts, with 10 errors within a three-minute timed period. She most often calculated the wrong operation, by not attending to operational signs, but was slow for her age. On the Applied Problems area, Josephine was asked to solve math word problems that were read aloud to her, presented in print and had picture cues present for some items in an un-timed format. She solved problems involving basic operations, and had good basic money skills. She wrote down her calculations and had good effort, but made minor errors in accuracy when making change from purchases. Josephine was able to solve a few measurement problems, but could not solve items involving mileage, distance, time, fractions, perimeter or percents. A few times she only completed the first step of a two step problem. She appeared to have difficulty determining the correct process and eliminating extraneous information on more difficult problems. On the Quantitative Concepts area, she was asked questions pertaining to Math concepts, symbols, terms, abbreviations, and also to complete series or patterns. Josephine identified basic math symbols and abbreviations, but could not round a number to the nearest hundredth, identify fractional parts, or answer geometry items. She was able to complete number series until they increased in difficulty.

Josephine had very strong writing skills, scoring in the High Average range for her age on the Spelling and the Writing Samples subtests. Her Writing Fluency was in the Average range, and was her strongest fluency subtest. On this area, Josephine was asked to compose brief sentences using given vocabulary and picture cues within a seven minute timed period. She said her arm was sore after this area. On the Spelling subtest, Josephine spelled many individually dictated words quickly without apparent struggle. She wrote in complete, on-topic sentences with good content and detail on the Writing Samples subtest. She appeared much more confident in her approach to Reading and Written Language subtests than she did on the Math areas. Josephine used capitalization and punctuation consistently, and attempted to self-edit her writing. She wrote right-handed in a manuscript writing style that was usually legible.

SUMMARY AND RECOMMENDATIONS

Josephine a 14-year-old, 8th grade student referred for a psycho-educational evaluation to determine her current needs. Josephine has been receiving homebound services since October as was recommended by a nurse practitioner treating her at the time.

According to an affidavit from her current physician, Dr. Alicia Conlan, Josephine has been diagnosed with Fibromyalgia-like Syndrome and Adjustment Disorder with Depressed Mood (See affidavit).

Josephine's cognitive skills were evaluated with the WISC III. Her general cognitive ability, as estimated by the WISC-III, is low average (FSIQ = 85). Josephine's general verbal abilities were in the low average range (VIQ = 82), and general nonverbal abilities were in the Average range (PIQ = 91).

An assessment of her educational functioning indicated that Josephine's reading and writing skills fell within the average to above average range. Math calculations skills were a significant weakness. Josephine also had difficulties with fluency tasks in math and reading. The writing fluency score fell within the average range.

In view of these findings:

1. The IEP Team should review this information along with documentation from her physician, to determine Josephine's need and eligibility to receive special education services or an accommodation plan under Section 504.

2. The overall test result did not show significant discrepancies between her estimated ability and educational achievement.

3. The overall data indicated that Josephine has the ability to participate in the standard course of study for her grade level. According to her teachers, she is able to successfully complete her assignments reflecting some understanding of basic math concepts.

4. According to the educational testing, Josephine's math calculation skills are a relative weakness. She may benefit from tutoring in this area to help her understand basic math facts.

5. Josephine may be allowed to use a calculator to solve math problems. This may help her focus on the reasoning aspect of a problem rather than on the calculation, which appears to be more difficult for her.

6. Josephine may benefit from extended time for tests and assignments, use of the

computer to type her written work, and abbreviated assignments as needed given her weakness in processing speed and fluency tasks.

7. According to a previous request from her nurse practitioner, she may benefit from the use of a lumbar pillow and special chair while seated in class. Other accommodations such as allowing her to take short breaks and stretches may be necessary to improve her physical comfort while in school.

8. If Josephine's physician can assist her in managing her symptoms, it is suggested that she attends school, at least for an abbreviated day. This will help her address her academic needs, avoid isolation from her peer group, and increase her social contacts. It may also help improve her symptoms of depression.

Hester Blackberry
Hester Blackberry, NCSP
School Psychologist

Tables and Graphs Report of WISC-III Testing
The Mental Health Group

NAME: Josephine Bass   REPORT DATE: March

AGE: 14 years   EXAMINER: Hester Blackberry

DATE OF BIRTH: February   TITLE: School Psychologist

GENDER: Female   LIC/CERT: NCSP

GRADE: 8th

TEST SITE: CMS

SCHOOL: Constance Middle School

Test Administered: WISC-III (04/08)

IQ SCORES SUMMARY

SCALE	IQ	90% CONFIDENCE INTERVAL	PR	CLASSIFICATION OF INTELLECTUAL FUNCTIONING
Verbal	82	78-88	12	Low Average
Performance	91	85-99	27	Average
Full Scale	85	81-90	16	Low Average

Difference Between VIQ and PIQ = 9 (p<.15, Freq = 49.3%)

INDEX SCORES SUMMARY

	INDEX	90% CONFIDENCE INTERVAL	PR
Verbal Comprehension	88	83-94	21
Perceptual Organization	97	90-104	42
Freedom from Distractibility	78	73-89	7
Processing Speed	72	68-84	3

SUBTEST SCORES SUMMARY

VERBAL SUBTESTS	RAW SCORE	SCALED SCORE	PR
Information (IN)	18	9	37
Similarities (SI)	22	10	50
Arithmetic (AR)	13	3	1
Vocabulary (VO)	33	8	25
Comprehension (CO)	18	4	2
(Digit Span DS)	15	9	37
PERFORMANCE SUBTESTS	RAW SCORE	SCALED SCORE	PR
Picture Completion (PC)	25	13	84
Coding (CD)	43	5	5

PERFORMANCE SUB-TESTS	RAW SCORE	SCALED SCORE	PR
Picture Arrangement (PA)	28	7	16
Block Design (BD)	48	9	37
Object Assembly (OA)	32	9	37
(Symbol Search SS)	18	4	2

DIFFERENCES BETWEEN SUBTEST SCORES AND MEAN OF SUBTEST SCORES

SUBTEST	SCALED SCORE	DIFF. FROM MEAN	SIGNIF. OF DIFF.	FREQ.	S/W
VERBAL					
Information (IN)	9	1.83	ns	>25%	
Similarities (SM)	10	2.83	.15	25%	
Arithmetic (AR)	3	-4.17	.05*	5%	W
Vocabulary (VO)	8	0.83	ns	>25%	
Comprehension (CO)	4	-3.17	.15	25%	
(Digit Span DS)	9	1.83	ns	>25%	

Mean of Six Verbal Subtest Scaled Scores = 7.17

Scatter = 7 (p<.05, Freq = 27.9%)

SUBTEST	SCALED SCORE	DIFF. FROM MEAN	SIGNIF. OF DIFF.	FREQ.	S/W
PERFORMANCE					
Picture Completion (PC)	13	5.17	.05	5%	S
Coding (CD)	5	-2.83	ns	>25%	
Picture Arrangement (PA)	7	-0.83	ns	>25%	
Block Design (BD)	9	1.17	ns	>25%	
Object Assembly (OA)	9	1.17	ns	>25%	
(Symbol Search SS)	4	-3.83	.05	10%	W

Mean of Six Performance Subtests Scales Scores = 7.83

Scatter = 9 (p<.05, Freq = 19.3%)

* significant at the.05 level

Eligibility Determination DEC 3

ELIGIBILITY DETERMINATION

Check Purpose: ( ) Initial Eligibility   ( ) Reevaluation

Student: _____ School: _____ Grade: _____

The IEP Team has summarized all required screening and evaluation information including a discussion of the student's strengths and needs on attached evaluation/eligibility worksheet(s).

Based on information from a variety of sources that have been documented and carefully considered, the IEP Team has determined:

> **Sources include information gathered during the referral process, reevaluation process, formal and informal assessments, records review, etc.**
> **At time of reevaluation, attach individual eligibility worksheets if additional data was collected in order to determine continued eligibility.**

☐ yes   ☐ no   The student meets criteria for one or more of the fourteen disabling conditions consistent with the definitions described in *NC Policies, section 1500-2 (**must** attach individual eligibility worksheets);*

> **Refer to the Summary of Evaluation/Eligibility Worksheet in responding to the following statements.**
> **At time of reevaluation if no additional data was collected, refer to the review of existing data documented on the DEC 7 in responding to the following questions.**

☐ yes   ☐ no   The disability has an adverse effect on educational performance; and

☐ yes   ☐ no   The disability requires specially designed instruction.

All three **must** be yes in order for the student to be eligible for special education and related services if required to benefit from special education.

The IEP Team has also concluded:

☐ yes   ☐ no   The determination *is not* the result of lack of appropriate instruction in reading, including the essential components of reading instruction. The term "essential components of reading instruction" means explicit and systematic instruction in: phonemic awareness, phonics, vocabulary development, reading fluency (including oral reading skills), and reading comprehension strategies.

☐ yes   ☐ no   The determination *is not* the result of lack of appropriate instruction in math; and

☐ yes   ☐ no   The determination *is not* the result of Limited English proficiency of the student.

All three **must** be yes in order for the student to be eligible for special education and related services if required to benefit from special education.

Statement of Eligibility:

☐ _____ (Student Name)

     is eligible for special education and related services if required to benefit from special education.
     He/she meets the eligibility criteria for _____ (primary eligibility category)
     and _____ (secondary eligibility category(s), if applicable).
     (Attach individual eligibility worksheets for all identified areas of eligibility.)

> **Eligibility determination must be made for the primary category of disability, and, as applicable, for the secondary category(s) of disability. Speech or language impaired is one of the fourteen disability categories. It is a related service when it is needed for a student to benefit from special education.**
> **Related services are not disability categories and do not have specified eligibility criteria. The need for related services must be based on data and determined by the IEP team. (Why is this service needed or not needed for this student to benefit from special education?)**
> **For a student who is already identified as a student with a disability, adding or discontinuing a related service will be done through the reevaluation process, which may or may not include formal assessment(s). The reevaluation process resets the date for the required reevaluation.**

☐   **is not eligible** for special education and related services.

> **IDEA requires signatures regarding the eligibility determination for students with specific learning disabilities. While signatures are not required for other areas of eligibility, participants in the eligibility meeting and their positions must be captured. LEAs are not prohibited from requiring signatures.**

IEP Team Signatures	Position	Date of Meeting	SLD Only Agree/Disagree*

For SLD only. If an IEP Team member disagrees, he/she must submit a separate statement of their reason for disagreement.

Copy given/sent to parent(s): ____/____/____   Directions 1-08

Chapter 5

THE IEP[1]

The basic promise of the Individuals with Disabilities Education Act is that each child with a disability will be provided a free, appropriate, public education in the least restrictive environment pursuant to an individualized education program. Each of those phrases — free, appropriate public education (FAPE), least restrictive environment (LRE), and individualized education program (IEP) — is reinterpreted millions of times a year across the country as teams of parents and school personnel sit around conference tables to consider the unique educational needs of children with disabilities and how they can be met. Because of the myriad variations in children and their needs, what is appropriate for one child is not appropriate for another; what is the least restrictive environment for one is not the least restrictive for another. As a result, the importance of an *individualized* education program cannot be overstated.

This chapter will explore the meaning of the terms, how they have been interpreted by courts, and how they are implemented through the IEP process. We start with the statutory definitions.

I. DEFINITIONS

The IDEA includes the following definitions:

The term "free appropriate public education" means special education and related services that —

(A) have been provided at public expense, under public supervision and direction, and without charge;

(B) meet the standards of the State educational agency;

(C) include an appropriate preschool, elementary, or secondary school education in the State involved; and

(D) are provided in conformity with the individualized education program required under [20 U.S.C. § 1414(d)].

20 U.S.C. § 1401(8).

The term "special education" means specially designed instruction, at no cost to parents, to meet the unique needs of a child with a disability including —

(A) instruction conducted in the classroom, in the home, in hospitals and institutions, and in other settings; and

---

[1] This chapter was authored by Jane R. Wettach and Brenda Berlin. Jane R. Wettach is a Clinical Professor of Law at Duke Law School and the Director of the Duke Children's Law Clinic. Brenda Berlin is a Senior Lecturing Fellow at Duke Law School and the Supervising Attorney of the Duke Children's Law Clinic.

(B)   instruction in physical education.

20 U.S.C. § 1401(25).

> The term "related services" means transportation, and such developmental, corrective, and other supportive services . . . as may be required to assist a child with a disability to benefit from special education . . . [examples omitted].

20 U.S.C. § 1401(26).

> The term "individualized education program" or "IEP" means a written statement for each child with a disability that is developed, reviewed, and revised in accordance with [20 U.S.C. § 1414(d)].

20 U.S.C. § 1401(9).

The IDEA does not include a definition of the "least restrictive environment" in the definitions section. Later in the Act, however, a provision sets out the policies and procedures that must be in place in states that accept federal special education dollars. States must have a policy to ensure that children are placed in the least restrictive environment, as follows:

> To the maximum extent appropriate, children with disabilities, including children in public or private institutions or other care facilities, are educated with children who are not disabled, and special classes, separate schooling, or other removal of children with disabilities from the regular educational environment occurs only when the nature or severity of the disability of a child is such that education in regular classes with the use of supplementary aids and services cannot be achieved satisfactorily.

20 U.S.C. § 1412(a)(5).

II. FAPE

Even with those definitions, many questions arise about what constitutes a free, appropriate public education in the least restrictive environment. The seminal case of *Board of Educ. v. Rowley*, 458 U.S. 176 (1982), addresses the FAPE question. In *Rowley*, the parents of Amy Rowley, a deaf child, challenged the school district's denial of a sign language interpreter, alleging that without one, their daughter could not get an appropriate education. Amy was a good lip reader and was provided an FM amplification system in her classroom. She was also provided a tutor for the deaf for one hour per day and speech therapy three hours each week. With this assistance, she performed better than the average child in her class and was advancing easily from grade to grade. Nevertheless, she was neither understanding nor learning as well as she could have with the aid of a sign language interpreter. In other words, she was not achieving her potential without a sign language interpreter.

The Court began its analysis by noting that the law contains no substantive standard prescribing the level of education to be accorded students with disabilities. In reviewing the history of the Act (then named the Education for All Handicapped Children Act of 1975, later renamed the Individuals with Disabilities Education Act), the Court focused on Congress's intention to make public education available to handicapped children, saying, "the Act imposes no clear obligation upon recipient States beyond the requirement that handicapped children receive some form of specialized education." 458 U.S. at 195. It continued, "Implicit in the Congressional purpose of providing access to a 'free appropriate public education' is the requirement that the education to which access is provided be sufficient to confer some educational benefit upon the handicapped child." *Id.* at 200. Stating that it would not attempt to establish any one test for determining the adequacy of educational benefits conferred on all children, it said that a free, appropriate public education was one including "personalized instruction with sufficient support services to permit the child to benefit educationally from that instruction." *Id.* at 203. It added the following descriptors: "Such instruction and services must be provided at public expense, must meet the State's educational standards, must approximate the grade levels used in the State's regular education, and must comport with the child's IEP. In addition, . . . if the child is being educated in the regular classrooms of the public education system, [the instruction] should be reasonably calculated to enable the child to achieve passing marks and advance from grade to grade." *Id.* at 203-04. The Court specifically rejected the lower court's determination that the educational services should be sufficient to maximize each handicapped child's potential. *Id.* at 198. Because Amy was performing at or above average level and passing from grade to grade without the sign language interpreter, the Court held that the school district had offered her a FAPE. *Id.* at 210.

The *Rowley* standard, while cited ubiquitously in nearly all special education cases, has proven problematic in several respects. First, its language "some educational benefit" indicated to some that even the most minimal of educational benefit would satisfy the FAPE requirement. Second, the case had limited applicability to cases in which the student was not at or even near grade level due to cognitive impairments not shared by Amy Rowley. Lower courts have grappled with those issues. In *Polk v. Cent. Susquehanna Intermediate Unit 16*, 853 F.2d 171 (3d Cir. 1988), *cert. denied*, 488 U.S. 1030 (1989), the plaintiff, Christopher, was a severely developmentally disabled child who at age 14 functioned like a toddler. The issue was whether weekly physical therapy was required to offer him a free, appropriate public education. The district court found that because Christopher derived "some educational benefit" from his program, despite the lack of physical therapy, the *Rowley* standard was met. The Court of Appeals for the Third Circuit reversed. Looking both at congressional intent and *Rowley*, the court said, "Just as Congress did not write a blank check, neither did it anticipate that states would engage in the idle gesture of providing special education designed to confer only trivial benefit. Put differently, and using *Rowley*'s own terminology, we hold that Congress intended to afford children with special needs an education that would confer meaningful benefit." *Id.* at 184. The court recognized the difficulty of determining how much benefit was meaningful as opposed to *de minimis*, and sent the case back to the lower court to resolve that question.

Courts around the country have generally embraced the "meaningful" educational benefit standard, though they continue to struggle with where to draw the line. The Court of Appeals for the Fifth Circuit approved a four-factor test articulated by the district court in *Cypress-Fairbanks Indep. Sch. Dist. v. Michael F.*, 118 F.3d 245 (5th Cir. 1997). In examining whether the student's IEP was reasonably calculated to provide a meaningful educational benefit under the IDEA, the court held that the test would be met if: (1) the program is individualized on the basis of the student's assessment and performance; (2) the program is administered in the least restrictive environment; (3) the services are provided in a coordinated and collaborative manner by the key "stakeholders"; and (4) positive academic and non-academic benefits are demonstrated. *Id.* at 253. Another court used a metaphorical approach to help lower courts and litigants understand the contours of a FAPE: "The Act requires that the Tullahoma schools provide the educational equivalent of a serviceable Chevrolet to every handicapped student. Appellant, however, demands that the Tullahoma school system provide a Cadillac solely for appellant's use. We suspect that the Chevrolet offered to appellant is in fact a much nicer model than that offered to the average Tullahoma student. Be that as it may, we hold that the Board is not required to provide a Cadillac, and that the proposed IEP is reasonably calculated to provide educational benefits to appellant, and is therefore in compliance with the requirements of the IDEA." *Doe v. Board of Educ. of Tullahoma City Sch.*, 9 F.3d 455, 459-60 (6th Cir. 2002). In line with this Chevrolet-Cadillac approach is the principle that educational services can meet the standards for IDEA even if they do not represent the best approach, so long as they offer appropriate services that allow the child to make educational progress.

The quantum of educational benefit that represents an appropriate education will vary depending on the potential of the child. *See, e.g., Lessard v. Wilton Lyndeborough Coop. Sch. Dist.*, 518 F.3d 18 (1st Cir. 2008) (holding that while the reported progress of the student was modest by most standards, it was reasonable in the context of the student's manifold disabilities and low IQ). Each case is intensely fact-specific and often a matter of opinion; there are no objective standards by which one can definitively conclude that a child's educational benefit is "enough" to satisfy the standard of FAPE, especially in cases in which the child is significantly impaired and functions well below grade level.

A number of courts have found that the vantage point from which to judge whether an IEP offers the child a FAPE is at its inception. The court in *Rowley* stated that a court's inquiry is whether the IEP was "reasonably calculated to enable the child to receive educational benefits." 458 U.S. at 207. Thus, the adequacy of the IEP and the issue of whether it provided a FAPE is not to be judged in hindsight, but rather, at the time of its implementation. *See, e.g., O'Toole ex rel. O'Toole v. Olathe Dist. Schs.*, 144 F.3d 692, 701-02 (10th Cir. 1998) ("[T]he measure and adequacy of an IEP can only be determined as of the time it is offered to the student. . . . Neither the statute nor reason countenance 'Monday Morning Quarterbacking' in evaluating the appropriateness of a child's placement."); *Fuhrmann v. East Hanover Bd. of Educ.*, 993 F.2d 1031, 1041 (3d Cir. 1993) ("[A]n individualized education program ('IEP') is a snapshot, not a retrospective. In striving for 'appropriateness,' an IEP must take into account what was, and was not, objectively reasonable when the snapshot was taken, that is, at the time the IEP was drafted."). Nevertheless, the history of the child's progress can inform whether an IEP was reasonably calculated to confer educational benefit. *See Richardson Indep. Sch. Dist. v. Michael Z.*, 580 F.3d 286 (5th Cir. 2009) (approving the district court's conclusion that the IEP did not offer a FAPE when the student had failed to progress and exhibited a stark pattern of regression under similar past IEPs.)

III. THE IEP PROCESS

The individualized education program, or IEP, has been described as the "centerpiece of the statute's education delivery system for disabled children." *Honig v. Doe*, 484 U.S. 305 (1988). The IEP is both a process and a document; it is the roadmap for the delivery of the education and services necessary to address the child's unique needs. Understanding the process for developing an IEP, the critical components of an IEP, and the vast array of legal requirements pertaining to the development and implementation of an IEP, are critical for the special education advocate to understand. If an IEP is never developed, is developed improperly, is not followed appropriately, or is inadequate to provide the child with a free appropriate education in the least restrictive environment, then the IDEA has been violated. The following sections detail the legal requirements for an IEP.

A.   The IEP Team

The IDEA requires that a child's IEP be developed at a meeting by an IEP team. 20 U.S.C. § 1414(d). This team must be convened by the school district within 30 days of the decision determining that a child is eligible to receive services under the IDEA. 34 C.F.R. § 300.323(c)(1). Federal law specifies the individuals who, at a minimum, must be in attendance at the meeting to constitute a lawful "IEP team." 20 U.S.C. § 1414(d)(1)(B). Persons in addition to those required by federal law may be required under various state laws and policies. For example, in New Jersey, in addition to the team members required by federal law, state law also requires the child's "case manager." N.J.S.A. 6A:14-2.3(k)(2)(v).

Under federal law, the required members of an IEP team are the following:

- the parent(s) of the child;

- at least one regular education teacher (if the child is or may be participating in the regular education environment);

- at least one special education teacher;

- a representative of the school district who "is qualified to provide or supervise the provision of specially designed instruction to meet the unique needs of children with disabilities; is knowledgeable about the general education curriculum; and is knowledgeable about the availability of resources of the local educational agency"; and

- an individual who "can interpret the instructional implications of evaluation results" (although this person can be one of the individuals described above, i.e., may also serve on the team as the regular or special education teacher, or as the school district representative).

In addition, other individuals may be invited to be members of a child's IEP team under certain circumstances. These are:

- the child, whenever appropriate; and

- at the parent's or school district's discretion, any other individuals who "have knowledge or special expertise regarding the child, including related services personnel as appropriate." 20 U.S.C. § 1414(d)(1)(B); 34 C.F.R. § 300.321(a).

Because of this last provision, parents may invite attorneys or other advocates to attend an IEP meeting with them.

B.   Parental Involvement in the IEP Process

The IDEA places a high value on the meaningful participation of parents in the development of their child's IEP. Indeed, the federal regulations impose specific requirements on schools regarding their efforts to seek out parental involvement in the IEP process. For instance, the federal regulations require that parents be notified of IEP meetings "early enough to ensure that they will have an opportunity to attend" and that the meetings be scheduled at a "mutually agreed on time and place." 34 C.F.R. § 300.322(a). Notice given to parents regarding IEP team meetings is also required to describe the purpose of the meeting and who has been invited to attend. 34 C.F.R. § 300.322(b)(i). In addition, the notice is required to inform the parents about the provisions of the law which allow individuals with special knowledge or expertise to be invited to the meeting; let the parents know if representatives from other agencies have been invited; and, for children for whom it would be appropriate, provide notice to the parents that the child has been invited to participate in the meeting. 34 C.F.R. § 300.322(b)(ii). Finally, ensuring meaningful parental involvement in the IEP process also includes arranging for interpreters for parents who are hearing impaired or for whom English is not their native language and providing a copy of the child's IEP to parents at no cost. 34 C.F.R. § 300.322(e) and (f).

If a child's parent is unable to attend an IEP meeting in person, the school must make efforts to allow the parent's participation in the meeting by alternative methods, such as by scheduling a conference call with the other assembled team members. *See* 34 C.F.R. §§ 300.322(c) and 300.328. As a last resort, schools may hold a meeting without parental participation, but only if, despite the school's good faith efforts to include the parent(s), the parent(s) remain unwilling to attend the meeting. In order to show their diligent attempts to include parents, school districts must keep detailed records documenting telephone calls made to the parent(s), correspondence sent to the parent(s), and visits made to the parents' home or place of employment. 34 C.F.R. § 300.322(d).

C. Definition of Parent

A parent is defined by the IDEA as:

- a child's biological, adoptive or foster parent;

- a child's legal guardian, so long as the child is not a ward of the State;

- an individual with whom the child lives who is acting in place of the child's parent (such as a grandparent, stepparent or other relative) or an individual who is legally responsible for the child's welfare; or

- a person appointed as the child's "surrogate parent."

20 U.S.C. § 1401(23) and 34 C.F.R. § 300.30(a).

Certain types of foster parents are prohibited by state law or by contract from acting as a parent in the IEP process. This includes individuals receiving a salary from the state for their foster parent services. For example, the *North Carolina Policies Governing Services for Children with Disabilities*, at § 1500.2.24(a)(2), specifically exclude "therapeutic foster parents" from the definition of "parents" because therapeutic foster parents get paid by the state for providing a therapeutic home to children who need more intensive care than their parents can provide.

In many situations, more than one adult in a child's life meets the definition of parent. Of course, adults sharing legal custody of a child are both "parents" of that child, but under the IDEA's definition, two or more adults who don't have a formal legal custody agreement but share in the child's care could be considered parents. Consider this case example and try to formulate an answer to the question it poses before reading the analysis below:

James

Mary is unmarried and has a son, James. She lives with James and her mother, Angela. There is no formal custody agreement between Mary and James' father, but James has always lived with his mother and grandmother and together they have provided all of his care and support. Mary's work often involves extensive out-of-town travel. For this reason, Angela, who does not work outside of the home, is primarily responsible for caring for James. In fact, the school personnel have never met Mary. It is Angela who attends school functions and parent-teacher conferences. The school wants to hold an IEP meeting to discuss some behavioral issues that James has been having. Unfortunately, Mary is out of town.

Can the school meet with Angela since she could be considered a "parent" under the definition provided by the IDEA?

Under the IDEA, although many individuals in a child's life may qualify as a "parent" under the law's definition, the biological or adoptive parent is presumed to be the parent authorized to make educational decisions for the child unless there is a judicial order giving another person that authority. 20 U.S.C. § 1401(23); 34 C.F.R. § 300.30(b). So, in the above example, the school district should make every effort to have Mary attend an IEP meeting to discuss James's behavior, as Mary is the parent with legal authority to make decisions about James's education. Angela would still be allowed to attend the IEP meeting at Mary's invitation as a person with "special knowledge or expertise" about James. *See* 34 C.F.R. § 300.321(a)(6).

If the district is under an obligation to hold the meeting within a certain time frame (i.e., within 30 days of the eligibility decision), it should attempt to use other means to involve Mary (such as to have her participate via conference call). If Mary wants Angela to make decisions regarding James in her absence, she should sign a release giving school personnel authority to share information about James with Angela and sign a document for the file giving Angela permission to make decisions in her place. She may want to consider signing a formal legal document (such as a Power of Attorney) granting Angela the right to make decisions regarding James' education in her absence.

Before undertaking a representation of a child, a special education attorney must understand the child's relationship with all adults in the child's life who exercise decision-making power regarding the child's education. When there is disagreement between two parents sharing legal authority to make decisions regarding their child's education, advocating for that child may be untenable. Moreover, in the above example, where the parent may have an informal arrangement with another adult in which the other adult is providing care and making decisions for the child in the parent's absence, it is still important to recognize that Mary is the "parent" authorized to make legal decisions regarding her child's education. If Mary wishes her attorney to take direction from another adult regarding her child's representation, then the specifics of that arrangement must be explained very clearly in the terms of the representation agreement.

D.   Surrogate Parents

If a child is a ward of the state, is an unaccompanied homeless child, or otherwise has no adult in his or her life who qualifies as a parent, a "surrogate parent" must be appointed by the school district. 20 U.S.C. § 1415(b)(2)(A)(ii); 34 C.F.R. § 300.519(a). The surrogate represents the child in all matters relating to the identification, evaluation, educational placement, and provision of special education services. 34 C.F.R. § 300.519(g). This includes entering into a representation agreement with an attorney to enforce the child's rights. The district must select someone who has the "knowledge and skills that ensure adequate representation of the child." 20 U.S.C. § 1415(b)(2)(A); 34 C.F.R. § 300.519(d). The person selected cannot be an employee of the state educational agency, the school district or any other agency that has responsibility for the child's education and must not have a personal or professional interest that conflicts with the interests of the child. The legal guardian of a ward of the state cannot be appointed, as the responsibilities of the guardian to the child could potentially conflict with the responsibilities of the guardian to the state. The guardian may be in a position to recommend someone who knows the child well and can function as a surrogate. If an attorney finds herself involved with a child who has no functioning parent, the attorney should immediately seek to have a surrogate appointed so that someone can direct the attorney and make binding decisions for the child.

E.   Transfer of Rights at Age of Majority

Unless a child has been deemed "incompetent" under state law, the IDEA allows for the transfer of all parental rights to the child when the child reaches the age of majority, as set by state law. 20 U.S.C. § 1415(m)(1); 34 C.F.R. § 520. In situations where a child has not yet been deemed incompetent, but still is unable to provide "informed consent" with respect to his or her educational program, the state must have procedures in place that provide for the appointment of a parent or other qualified adult to represent the educational interests of the child. 20 U.S.C. § 1415(m)(2); 34 C.F.R. § 520(b).

F.   Other IEP Team Members

As mentioned previously, the law requires at least one special education teacher and one regular education teacher (if the child may be participating in the regular education environment) to be members of the IEP team. 20 U.S.C. § 1414(d)(1)(B)(ii) and (iii); 34 C.F.R. § 300.321(a)(2) and (3). In addition, the team must include someone from the school district who is qualified to provide or supervise the provision of special education services, has knowledge of the regular education curriculum and "is knowledgeable about the availability of resources of the local educational agency." 20 U.S.C. § 1414(d)(1)(B)(iv)(III); 34 C.F.R. § 300.321(a)(4)(iii). This person is often referred to as the "LEA representative." LEA stands for "local educational agency" and, importantly, in this context, refers to the person at the meeting who has the authority to commit school district resources and ensure that whatever instruction or services are described in the IEP will be provided. *See* 71 Fed. Reg. 46670 (Aug. 14, 2006).

Finally, the IEP team must include an individual who can interpret and understand the evaluation results being presented at the meeting. This can be the individual that conducted the evaluation (such as the school psychologist), or a teacher or related service provider. 20 U.S.C. § 1414(d)(1)(B)(v); 34 C.F.R. § 300.321(a)(5). The law does not require that the actual evaluator be present at the meeting to interpret his or her test results. Moreover, the person serving in this role on the IEP team may concurrently be serving another role on the team (i.e., can be a regular or special education teacher).

Persons with "knowledge or special expertise regarding the child" may also be invited members of an IEP team. Unlike the team members identified above, these members are "optional," i.e., are not required by the law. Advocates, therapists, social workers or other professionals working with the child may be invited by parents to be a part of the team to share their professional and personal expertise about the child in the meeting. The parent's or child's attorney can be included on the IEP team as someone with "knowledge or special expertise regarding the child." However, many special education attorneys decline to participate as an IEP team member, but rather view themselves only as an observer and counselor to the parent. *See* 71 Fed. Reg. 46670-71 (Aug. 14, 2006).

Under certain circumstances, the child (before the age of majority) may be included as a member of the IEP team. In fact, a child must be invited to attend an IEP meeting if the child's postsecondary goals and the "transition services" will be discussed. 34 C.F.R. § 300.321(b)(1) (see discussion of transition services below). This must occur no later than the year in which the child turns 16. Children younger than 16 may also be invited to IEP team meetings at the discretion of the team. 20 U.S.C. § 1414(d)(1)(B)(vii); 34 C.F.R. § 300.321(a)(7). If a child does not attend an IEP meeting (either because she decides not to attend or the parent does not think her attendance is appropriate or necessary) then the school district must take other steps to ensure that the child's interests and preferences are considered by the IEP team. 34 C.F.R. § 300.321(b)(2). This could be accomplished by having someone at the school speak with the child prior to the meeting and then report to the team about the child's interests. 34 C.F.R. § 300.321(b)(2).

The invitation (or parental notice) regarding the meeting should list the individuals expected to attend. If an advocate believes that a particular person should be included in the meeting, i.e., the advocate has specific questions regarding the evaluations to be discussed at the meeting or believes certain special education or related services may be at issue at the meeting, then the advocate should endeavor to have that individual invited to attend the meeting.

G.   Excusal of IEP Team Members from Meetings

Required members of the IEP team, other than the parents, may be excused from attendance from an IEP meeting if certain conditions are met. First, a team member may be excused from attendance in whole or in part if the parent and school district agree, in writing, that the excused member's area of curriculum or related service will not be modified or discussed at the meeting. 20 U.S.C. § 1414(d)(1)(C)(i); 34 C.F.R. § 300.321(e)(1). Moreover, even if a team member's area of expertise will be discussed during an IEP team meeting, he or she may still be excused, so long as both of the following occur, in writing: (1) the team member submits his/her input to the team and (2) the parent and school agree to the excusal. 20 U.S.C. § 1414(d)(1)(C)(ii); 34 C.F.R. § 300.321(e)(2).

H.   The Team Process

The IDEA anticipates a collaborative process in which all members of the team are mutually engaged in the endeavor of discerning the child's educational needs and crafting a program of supports and services that will provide an appropriate education for the child. In *Deal v. Hamilton Co. Bd. of Educ.*, 392 F.3d 840 (6th Cir. 2004), the parent won a victory because the court determined that the school officials had predetermined the services that would be offered to the child prior to the IEP meeting. The court found that the predetermination effectively denied the parent of meaningful participation in the IEP process and therefore denied the child a FAPE. When the IEP team cannot come to a consensus, however, the representative of the school district must make a final decision about the services that will be offered. The representative must then provide the parents with "prior written notice" describing the decisions made and the proposals that were rejected. This notice triggers the parents' dispute resolution rights. (See Chapter Ten.)

The child can also be deprived of a FAPE if the team is not complete. The lack of appropriate school personnel at the meeting can result in an IEP that is not formulated with the necessary input. In *M.L. v. Federal Way Sch. Dist.*, 394 F.3d 634 (9th Cir. 2005), the court held that the omission of a regular education teacher from the IEP team, "fatally compromised the integrity of the IEP." Note, however, that most courts will engage in a "harmless error" analysis to determine whether the procedural violation resulted in the loss of educational opportunity for the child or seriously infringed on the parents' opportunity to participate in the IEP formation process. *See, e.g., R.B. v. Napa Valley Unified Sch. Dist.*, 496 F.3d 932 (9th Cir. 2007).

As the team works together to develop the child's IEP, it is required to consider the strengths of the child, the concerns of the parents for enhancing the education of their child, the evaluation results, and the academic, developmental, and functional needs of the child. 34 C.F.R. § 300.324(a)(1). In addition, it must consider a number of special factors, such as behavioral needs, language needs (for students with limited English proficiency), the special communication needs of a child who is deaf or hard of hearing, instruction in Braille for blind students, and the need for assistive technology or services. 34 C.F.R. § 300.324(a)(2). Students whose behavior impedes their own learning or the learning of others may need to have a behavior intervention plan developed as part of the IEP. (See Chapter Seven for a detailed description of behavior intervention plans.)

I.   When the IEP Must be in Effect

By the beginning of each school year, schools are required to have IEPs in effect for every child with a disability within their jurisdiction. 20 U.S.C. § 1414(d)(2)(A); 34 C.F.R. § 300.323(a). Some school districts write all of their students' IEPs so that the IEPs expire at the end of the academic year. In these districts, each child's IEP team must meet in the spring to develop the IEP for the following year. For larger districts, this can be unwieldy, and therefore IEPs are written to expire on the anniversary date of the child's initial IEP. Under this system, IEP annual review meetings occur throughout the academic year.

Eligible preschool-age children, ages 3-5 (or at the discretion of the state, age 2 if the child will turn 3 during the school year), must have either an IEP or an IFSP (Individual Family Services Plan) in effect. The IEP team must convene a meeting with the parents to review the child's IFSP and may decide to use the IFSP as the initial IEP of the child if using the IFSP is consistent with state policy and is acceptable to the school and to the parents. 20 U.S.C. § 1414(d)(2)(B); 34 C.F.R. § 300.323(b).

If a child moves into a school district from another school district in the state, the new school must continue to provide services comparable to those on the child's existing IEP until the new school either adopts the previous school district's IEP or develops a new IEP for the child. 20 U.S.C. § 1414(d)(2)(C)(i)(I); 34 C.F.R. § 300.323(e). If a child moves into a school from a school in another state, the new school is obligated to continue to provide services comparable to those in the child's out-of-state IEP until the new school can conduct its own evaluation (if the school feels a new evaluation is necessary) and develops and implements a new IEP. 20 U.S.C. § 1414(d)(2)(C)(i)(II); 34 C.F.R. § 300.323(f). To help facilitate the transition of students with disabilities, the federal law obligates schools to take reasonable steps to ensure that the child's IEP and accompanying documentation go with her to her new school. This includes requiring that the new school promptly request this documentation and that the old school promptly supply it. 20 U.S.C. § 1414(d)(2)(C)(ii); 34 C.F.R. § 300.323(g).

J.   The IEP Document

In order to comply with the provisions of IDEA, an IEP document must include certain elements. Although many state education departments design model forms, local jurisdictions are free to design their own. An IEP lasts for one year, although it can be amended during the year. The following components — each of which is discussed more fully following this list — are required in every IEP:

• A statement of the child's *present levels of academic achievement and functional performance*, including how the child's disability affects the child's involvement and progress in the general education curriculum;

• A statement of *measurable annual goals*, including both academic and functional goals designed to meet the educational needs resulting from the child's disability, including enabling the child to be involved in and make progress in the general education curriculum;

• A description of *how the child's progress toward meeting the annual goals will be measured*; and when reports on the child's progress toward meeting the annual goals will be provided;

• A statement of the *special education and related services and supplementary aids and services* (based on peer-reviewed research to the extent practicable), to be provided to the child; and a statement of any program modifications or supports necessary to allow the child to advance appropriately toward attaining his or her annual goals and participating with his or her peers in the general education curriculum, extracurricular and other nonacademic activities;

• An explanation of *the extent to which the child will not participate with nondisabled children*;

• A statement of any *appropriate accommodations necessary to measure the academic achievement and functional performance* of the child on state and district-wide assessments; and if the IEP Team determines that the child must take an alternate assessment instead of a particular regular state or district-wide assessment of student achievement, a statement of why the child cannot participate in the regular assessment, why the particular alternate assessment selected is appropriate for the child, and a description of benchmarks or short-term objectives for the child;

• The beginning date for providing the services and modifications under the IEP and the anticipated *frequency, location and duration* of those services and modifications; and

• In IEPs for children age 16 and older, *appropriate post-secondary goals and transition services.*

20 U.S.C. § 1414(d)(1)(A)(i); 34 CFR § 300.320(a), (b).

Here is an example of a blank IEP document:

Check Purpose:
- ☐ Initial
- ☐ Annual Review
- ☐ Reevaluation
- ☐ Addendum
- ☐ Transition Part C to B

INDIVIDUALIZED EDUCATION PROGRAM (IEP)

Duration of Special Education and Related Services: From: 00 / 00 / 2000   To: 00 / 00 / 2000

Student: Student Name   **DOB: 00 / 00 / 2000**

School: School Name   **Grade: _____**

Primary Area of Eligibility*   **Secondary Area(s) of Eligibility:** (if applicable)
(*Reported on Child Count)

Student Profile

Student's overall strengths:

Summarize assessment information (e.g. from early intervention providers, child outcome measures, curriculum based measures, state and district assessments results, etc.), and review of progress on current IEP/IFSP goals:

Parent's concerns, if any, for enhancing the student's education:

Parent's/Student's vision for student's future:

Consideration of Transitions

If a transition (e.g. new school, family circumstances, etc.) is anticipated during the life of this IEP/IFSP what information is known about the student that will assist in facilitating a smooth process?   ☐ N/A

The student is age 14 or older or will be during the duration of the IEP.   ☐ Yes   ☐ No

INDIVIDUALIZED EDUCATION PROGRAM (IEP)

Duration of Special Education and Related Services: From: 00 / 00 / 2000   To: 00 / 00 / 2000

Student: Student Name   **DOB: 00 / 00 / 2000**

School: School Name   **Grade: _____**

Consideration of Special Factors (Note: If you check yes, you must address in the IEP.)

Does the student have behavior(s) that impede his/her learning or that of others? ☐ Yes   ☐ No

Does the student have Limited English Proficiency? ☐ Yes   ☐ No

If the student is blind or partially sighted, will the instruction in or use of Braille be needed? ☐ Yes ☐ No ☐ N/A

Does the student have any special communication needs? ☐ Yes   ☐ No

Is the student deaf or hard of hearing? ☐ Yes   ☐ No
☐ The child's language and communication needs;
☐ Opportunities for direct communications with peers and professional personnel in the child's language and communication mode;
☐ Academic level;
☐ Full range of needs, including opportunities for direct instruction in the child's language; and
☐ Communication mode.
(Communication Plan Worksheet available at www.ncpublicschools.org/ec/policy/forms.)

Does the student require specially designed physical education? ☐ Yes   ☐ No

INDIVIDUALIZED EDUCATION PROGRAM (IEP)

Duration of Special Education and Related Services: **From: 00 / 00 / 2000   To: 00 / 00 / 2000**

Student: <u>Student Name</u>   **DOB: 00 / 00 / 2000**

School: <u>School Name</u>   **Grade: ____**

Present Level(s) of Academic and Functional Performance

Include specific descriptions of what the student can and cannot do in relationship to this area. Include current academic and functional performance, behaviors, social/emotional development, other relevant information, and how the student's disability affects his/her involvement and progress in the general curriculum.

Annual Goal

☐ Academic Goal   ☐ Functional Goal

Does the student require assistive technology devices and/or services?   ☐ Yes   ☐ No
If yes, describe needs:

(Address after determination of related services.) Is this goal integrated with related service(s)?   ☐ Yes*   ☐ No
*If yes, list the related service area(s) of integration:

INDIVIDUALIZED EDUCATION PROGRAM (IEP)

Duration of Special Education and Related Services: From: 00 / 00 / 2000   To: 00 / 00 / 2000

Student: Student Name   **DOB: 00 / 00 / 2000**

School: School Name   **Grade: _____**

Competency Goal

> **Required for areas (if any) where student participates in state assessments using modified achievement standards.**
> **Select Subject Area:** ☐ Language Arts   ☐ Mathematics   ☐ Science
> **List Competency Goal from the *NC Standard Course of Study*:**
> *(Standard must match the student's assigned grade.)*
>
>
> *Note: Selected Grade Standard Competency Goals listed are those identified for specially designed instruction. In addition to those listed, the student has access to grade level content standards through general education requirements.*

Benchmarks or Short Term Objectives (if applicable)
(Required for students participating in state alternate assessments aligned to alternate achievement standards)

>

Describe how progress toward the annual goal will be measured

>

IEP DEC 4 (5 of 10)

INDIVIDUALIZED EDUCATION PROGRAM (IEP)

Duration of Special Education and Related Services: From: 00 / 00 / 2000 To: 00 / 00 / 2000

Student: Student Name   **DOB: 00 / 00 / 2000**

School: School Name   **Grade: ____**

Least Restrictive Environment
I. General Education Program Participation

In the space provided, list the general education classes, nonacademic services, and activities (ex: lunch, recess, assemblies, media center, field trips, etc.) in which the student will participate and the supplemental aids, supports, modifications, and/or accommodations required (if applicable) to access the general curriculum and make progress toward meeting annual goals. Discussion and documentation must include any test accommodations required for state and/or district-wide assessment. If supplemental aids/services, modifications/ accommodations and/or assistive technology will be provided in special education classes include in the table below.

General Education/Special Education Nonacademic Services & Activities (If Applicable)	Supplemental Aids/Services Modifications/Accommodations Assistive Technology (If Applicable)	Implementation Specifications (Example: Who? What? When? Where?)

If the student is in preschool, describe how the student is involved in the general education program. ☐ N/A

Specify the technical assistance, if any, that will be provided to the general education teacher(s) and/or other school personnel for implementation of the IEP. ☐ None

Final 1-08

IEP DEC 4 (6 of 10)

INDIVIDUALIZED EDUCATION PROGRAM (IEP)

Student Name: Student Name   **Duration From: 00 / 00 / 2000 To: 00 / 00 / 2000**

II. North Carolina Assessment Program

Select the appropriate state assessment(s) that will allow the student to demonstrate his/her knowledge. Select testing accommodations that correlate to classroom accommodations used routinely throughout the academic year. Accommodations that are listed on the IEP must be used on a routine basis in classroom instruction. For specifics regarding accommodation use and availability for specific tests, refer to the Testing Students with Disabilities publication, available at *http://www.ncpublicschools.org/accountability/policies/tswd*

IEP Teams are instructed to select for each assessment, only those accommodations that do not invalidate the score.

☐ **Standard Test Administration with no Accommodations**

☐ **Student will participate in the Extend 1.**

NC Testing Program Approved Accommodations	End of Grade Tests (Grade 3 Pretest & Grades 3–8) Reading	Math	Science	NC Writing Test Grades 4, 7, and 10	NC Extend2 Grades 3–8 Reading	Math	Science	Writing 3-8 or OCS	English1 (Occupational Course of Study)	Math 1	Life Skills Science 1 & 2	EOC End of Course Test			High School Competency Test Reading	Math	Verbal	Test of Computer Skills – Begins Grade 8
Braille Edition	☐	☐	☐	☐	☐	☐	☐	☐	☐	☐	☐	☐			☐	☐	☐	☐
Computer Skills Portfolio	☐	☐	☐	☐	☐	☐	☐	☐	☐	☐	☐	☐			☐	☐	☐	☐
Large Print Edition	☐	☐	☐	☐	☐	☐	☐	☐	☐	☐	☐	☐			☐	☐	☐	☐
One Test Item Per Page	☐	☐	☐	■	☐	☐	☐	☐	☐	☐	☐	☐			☐	☐	☐	☐
Assistive Technology: Specify _____	☐	☐	☐	☐	☐	☐	☐	☐	☐	☐	☐	☐			☐	☐	☐	☐
Braille Writer/Slate and Stylus (and Braille Paper)	☐	☐	☐	☐	☐	☐	☐	☐	☐	☐	☐	☐			☐	☐	☐	☐
Cranmer Abacus	☐	☐	☐	☐	☐	☐	☐	☐	☐	☐	☐	☐			☐	☐	☐	☐
Dictation to scribe (For Writing assessment, will not receive valid conventions score)	☐	☐	☐	☐	☐	☐	☐	☐	☐	☐	☐	☐			☐	☐	☐	☐
Interpreter/ Transliterator Signs/Cues Test (Not for test of reading skills)	■	☐	☐	☐	☐	☐	☐	☐	■	☐	☐	☐			■	☐	☐	☐
Keyboarding Devices	☐	☐	☐	☐	☐	☐	☐	☐	☐	☐	☐	☐			☐	☐	☐	☐
Magnification Devices	☐	☐	☐	☐	☐	☐	☐	☐	☐	☐	☐	☐			☐	☐	☐	☐
Student Marks in Answers in Test Book	☐	☐	☐	☐	☐	☐	☐	☐	☐	☐	☐	☐			☐	☐	☐	☐
Student Reads Aloud to Self	☐	☐	☐	☐	☐	☐	☐	☐	☐	☐	☐	☐			☐	☐	☐	☐
Test Administrator Reads Test Aloud (Not for test of reading skills) ☐ Read Everything	■	☐	☐	■	☐	☐	☐	☐	■	☐	☐	☐			■	☐	☐	☐
☐ Read by Student Request	■	☐	☐	■	☐	☐	☐	☐	■	☐	☐	☐			■	☐	☐	☐
☐ Other	■	☐	☐	■	☐	☐	☐	☐	■	☐	☐	☐			■	☐	☐	☐
Hospital/Home Testing	☐	☐	☐	☐	☐	☐	☐	☐	☐	☐	☐	☐			☐	☐	☐	☐
Multiple Test Sessions ☐ More Frequent Breaks (Every ___ Min.)	☐	☐	☐	☐	☐	☐	☐	☐	☐	☐	☐	☐			☐	☐	☐	☐
☐ Over Multiple Days (Number of Days ___)	☐	☐	☐	☐	☐	☐	☐	☐	☐	☐	☐	☐			☐	☐	☐	☐
Scheduled Extended Time ☐ Approximately 30 minutes	☐	☐	☐	☐	☐	☐	☐	☐	☐	☐	☐	☐			☐	☐	☐	☐
☐ Approximately 1 Hour	☐	☐	☐	☐	☐	☐	☐	☐	☐	☐	☐	☐			☐	☐	☐	☐
☐ Other	☐	☐	☐	☐	☐	☐	☐	☐	☐	☐	☐	☐			☐	☐	☐	☐
Testing in Separate Room ☐ Small Group	☐	☐	☐	☐	☐	☐	☐	☐	☐	☐	☐	☐			☐	☐	☐	☐
☐ One-on-One	☐	☐	☐	☐	☐	☐	☐	☐	☐	☐	☐	☐			☐	☐	☐	☐
Computer/typewriter/word processor	☐	☐	☐	☐	☐	☐	☐	☐	☐	☐	☐	☐			☐	☐	☐	☐
☐ NCCLAS	☐	☐	☐	☐	■	■	■	■	■	■	■							

INDIVIDUALIZED EDUCATION PROGRAM (IEP)

Duration of Special Education and Related Services: From: 00 / 00 / 2000 To: 00 / 00 / 2000

Student: Student Name   **DOB: 00 / 00 / 2000**

School: School Name   **Grade: _____**

III. District-Wide Assessment Program

In the space provided, list the district-wide assessments, if any, and any accommodations or alternate assessments to be used by the student.

DISTRICT-WIDE ASSESSMENT(S) ACCOMMODATION(S) OR	ALTERNATE ASSESSMENT(S)	IMPLEMENTATION SPECIFICATIONS

IV. Alternate Assessment Justification

If the student is participating in *any* alternate assessment(s), explain *why* the regular testing program, with or without accommodations, is not appropriate and *why* the selected assessment is appropriate: ☐ N/A

V. Specially Designed Instruction, Related Services, and Nonacademic Services and Activities
A. Anticipated Frequency and Location of Specially Designed Instruction

Special Education:	Sessions Per: Week	Month	Reporting Period	Year	Session Length:	Location:
___	___	___	___	___	___	___
			1st Semester	___		
			2nd Semester	___		
___	___	___	___	___	___	___
			1st Semester	___		
			2nd Semester	___		
___	___	___	___	___	___	___
			1st Semester	___		
			2nd Semester	___		

INDIVIDUALIZED EDUCATION PROGRAM (IEP)

Duration of Special Education and Related Services: From: 00 / 00 / 2000 To: 00 / 00 / 2000

Student: Student Name   **DOB: 00 / 00 / 2000**

School: School Name   **Grade:** ____

B. Anticipated Frequency and Location of Related Services

☐ The IEP Team determined related services *are not required* to assist the student to benefit from special education.

☐ The IEP Team determined the following related services are required to assist the student to benefit from special education.

Related Service(s):	Sessions Per: Week Month Year	Reporting Period	Session Length:	Location:
____	__ __ ____	____	____ ☐ Support Description	____
____	__ __ ____	____	____ ☐ Support Description	____
____	__ __ ____	____	____ ☐ Support Description	____

☐ Transportation is required as related service. Describe special transportation services: ____

C. Nonacademic Services & Activities (*Refer to Section I: General Education Program Participation*)

List the nonacademic services and activities in which the student **will not** participate with nondisabled peers. This time must be factored into the determination of continuum of alternative educational placement below.

Nonacademic Services & Activities:	Sessions Per: Week Month Year	Reporting Period	Session Length:
____	__ __ ____	____	____
____	__ __ ____	____	____
____	__ __ ____	____	____
____	__ __ ____	____	____

VI. Continuum of Alternative Educational Placements

Indicate educational placement by checking only one box below:

(Educational placement is determined by calculating the amount of time the student is removed from nondisabled peers.)

School Age:
☐ Regular - 80% or more of the day with nondisabled peers
☐ Resource - 40% - 79% of the day with nondisabled peers
☐ Separate - 39% or less of the day with nondisabled peers
☐ Separate School
☐ Residential
☐ Home/Hospital

Preschool:
☐ Regular Early Childhood Program 80% of time
☐ Regular Early Childhood Program 40%-79% of time
☐ Regular Early Childhood Program less than 40% of time
☐ Separate Class
☐ Separate School
☐ Residential Facility
☐ Service Provider
☐ Home

INDIVIDUALIZED EDUCATION PROGRAM (IEP)

Duration of Special Education and Related Services: From: **00 / 00 / 2000** To: **00 / 00 / 2000**

Student: Student Name   **DOB: 00 / 00 / 2000**

School: School Name   **Grade:** _____

VII. Least Restrictive Environment Justification Statement
If the student will be removed from nondisabled peers for any part of the day (general education classroom, nonacademic services and activities), explain **why** the services cannot be delivered with nondisabled peers with the use of supplemental aids and services.

☐ N/A Student will not be removed from nondisabled peers.

VIII. Progress toward annual goals will be reported with the issuance of report cards unless otherwise specified below:

IX. Extended School Year Status (*ESY worksheet available at www.ncpublicschools.org/ec/policyforms.*)
☐ Is not eligible for extended school year
☐ Is eligible for extended school year
☐ Eligibility is under consideration and will be determined by **00 / 00 /2000**

X. Record of IEP Team Participation (*Note with an * any team member who used alternative means to participate.*)

A. IEP Team. The following were present and participated in the development and writing of the IEP.

Name	Position	Date
	LEA Representative	00 / 00 / 2000
	General Education Teacher	00 / 00 / 2000
	Special Education Teacher	00 / 00 / 2000
	Parent	00 / 00 / 2000
	Student	00 / 00 / 2000
		00 / 00 / 2000
		00 / 00 / 2000
		00 / 00 / 2000
		00 / 00 / 2000

Copy given/sent to parent(s): by _____ on **00 / 00 / 2000**.

Final 1-08

INDIVIDUALIZED EDUCATION PROGRAM (IEP) ADDENDUM

Duration of Special Education and Related Services: From: 00 / 00 / 2000   To: 00 / 00 / 2000

Student: __Student Name__   DOB: 00 / 00 / 2000

School: __School Name__   Grade: _____

X. Record of IEP Team Participation continued
(Note with an * any team member who used alternative means to participate.)

B.   **Reevaluation.** The IEP was reviewed at reevaluation and was found to be appropriate. An annual review of this IEP will be conducted on or before __00__ / __00__ / __2000__.

Name	Position	Date
	LEA Representative	00 / 00 / 2000
	General Education Teacher	00 / 00 / 2000
	Special Education Teacher	00 / 00 / 2000
	Parent	00 / 00 / 2000
	Student	00 / 00 / 2000
		00 / 00 / 2000
		00 / 00 / 2000
		00 / 00 / 2000
		00 / 00 / 2000

XI. Amending the IEP
The IEP was amended due to a disciplinary change in placement. ☐ yes ☐ no

A. IEP Addendum Team.
The following were present and participated in the development and writing of the addendum to the IEP.

Name	Position	Date
	LEA Representative	00 / 00 / 2000
	General Education Teacher	00 / 00 / 2000
	Special Education Teacher	00 / 00 / 2000
	Parent	00 / 00 / 2000
	Student	00 / 00 / 2000
		00 / 00 / 2000
		00 / 00 / 2000
		00 / 00 / 2000
		00 / 00 / 2000

B.   **Amending the IEP without holding a meeting after the annual IEP Team meeting for the school year.**

☐ The parent and LEA agreed that the IEP could be amended by   on **00 / 00 / 2000** without holding a meeting.

☐ Copies of the amendment were provided to individuals responsible for implementing changes to the IEP by   on **00 / 00 / 2000**

Indicate page(s) and section(s) where any amendment(s) were made:

☐ A revised copy of the IEP with amendments incorporated was provided to parent(s) on **00 / 00 / 2000** by

Final 1-08

1. Present Levels of Performance

This requirement pertains both to academic achievement (i.e., achievement in reading, writing, math, science, history, etc.) and functional performance (i.e., the child's social, communication, behavior, and daily living skills). The statement should be specific and objective, drawing upon data and, when appropriate, the results of standardized evaluation instruments. The statement of present levels must include a description of how the child's disability affects the child's involvement and progress in the general curriculum, or, for preschool children, how the child's disability affects the child's participation in appropriate activities. Some IEP forms are designed to allow for an extensive, global statement of the child's present levels of academic and functional performance including all areas of performance. Other IEP forms allow for separate statements of the present level for each of the areas for which goals will be articulated.

Consider these two examples of present level of performance, both in the area of reading for students in the sixth grade:

Example 1:

Dylan is a young man who loves to read when it is something of interest to him. He has difficulty understanding the main idea or topic of what he is reading at times. He also has difficulty drawing conclusions about what may happen in the story next. He can at times answer simple who, what, when, and where questions but has difficulty answering more complex questions. Dylan has a good grasp on basic sight vocabulary but does not often know that the words have multiple meanings. He needs to learn how to apply prefixes, suffixes, and roots to expand his vocabulary.

Example 2:

When given a list of basic sight words in April 2010, Tiquan correctly identified 60 out of 100. Tiquan can identify one-syllable words correctly. When given a 145-word passage from fifth-grade reading material in April 2010, Tiquan read only 60 words compared to an average of 139 words per minute by peers. Tiquan uses context clues to gain meaning. He does not independently use the decoding strategy of segmenting words into familiar patterns. This has implications for Tiquan's learning in other content areas. Sixth grade students are expected to monitor their own comprehension by adjusting speed to fit the purpose, or by skimming, scanning, reading on, looking back, note taking or summarizing what has been read so far in text. Tiquan's slow reading pace affects the amount of material he is able to read within an instructional period in all academic areas and affects his comprehension. He is able to complete work involving reading when the reading material is supported by visuals and when sixth-grade classroom material is read to him.

Can you tell, by reading the present level, what the child can and cannot do? Does the present level give you a starting place, a place from which the year's progress can be measured? Do you know how the child's disability affects his progress in the general curriculum? Can you use these statements to formulate specific and measurable goals for the next year?

2. Annual Goals

Annual goals are statements of what the IEP team believes the student can reasonably be expected to achieve over the duration of the IEP (i.e., one year). To be useful, annual goals must be specific, well-defined and objectively measurable. These goals will form the basis for determining whether a child is making appropriate progress under his or her IEP, whether the child's goals need to be revisited and revised and whether the child is receiving an appropriate education. The goals should be directly related to the present level of academic and functional performance in the goal area. For example, if the present level of academic performance in the area of math states that the child has not memorized the multiplication tables, the goal might be that the child will memorize the multiplication tables up to the 12's. If the child's present level of performance includes a Diagnostic Reading Assessment (DRA) score of 12, the goal should include a statement of what the DRA score should be at the end of the year.

Under the previous versions of the IDEA, IEPs were required to include "benchmarks and short term objectives" with each annual goal. The benchmarks set interim expectations and were helpful in breaking down the annual goal into more manageable objectives. In the 2004 revisions, however, the requirement for benchmarks was removed for all children except for the most cognitively impaired students who take alternate assessments aligned to alternate achievement standards. (See below for details on who takes alternate assessments.) Some jurisdictions, however, have maintained the use of benchmarks on their forms for all students.

Annual goals must be measurable. Writing measurable annual goals is more challenging in the absence of benchmarks and short-term objectives. Examples of immeasurable goals are statements like the following: "Julia will improve her study skills for academic success," or "Antonio will develop strategies and skills in reading comprehension." Contrast those with the following: "At least 85 percent of the time, Julia will demonstrate the following study skills when assigned a research task: skimming written material to locate the most important text, using reference materials, and taking notes on important points" and "After reading a fifth-grade level text, Antonio will demonstrate comprehension by a) identifying main events and supporting details, b) identifying main characters, and c) sequencing the main events, with 80 percent accuracy." The better annual goals are ones that identify observable behaviors or skills and provide some numeric standard that will allow for data collection and comparison.

IEP goals should be aligned with the state's academic standards. 20 U.S.C. § 1412(a)(15). Disabled children must be taught the same curriculum as non-disabled children, though it can be modified to meet a child's abilities and needs. The goals must meet the child's needs that result from the child's disability to enable the child to be involved in and make progress in the general education curriculum. 34 C.F.R. § 300.320(a)(1)(i); 34 C.F.R. § 200.1(f)(2). In other words, the goals should focus on the accomplishment of the same skills, whether academic or functional, that are accomplished by non-disabled children. Even students with the most significant cognitive disabilities should have goals that are aligned with the state's academic content standards and promote access to the general curriculum, although the academic standards can be altered in the judgment of the educators. 34 C.F.R. § 200.1(d).

The goals must represent reasonable progress. If the bar is set too low, then the child's progress will not be reasonable even if the goals are achieved. For example, in *Carter v. Florence County Sch. Dist. Four*, 950 F.2d 156 (4th Cir. 1991), *aff'd* 510 U.S. 7 (1993), the court agreed with the parents that reading goals proposing four months progress in reading over a year period of time were not reasonable for a 10th grade student who was reading at a 5th-6th grade level. Nevertheless, goals representing very modest progress may be appropriate for a child with significant cognitive impairments. *See, e.g., Thompson R-2 Sch. Dist. v. Luke P.*, 540 F.3d 1143 (10th Cir. 2008).

3.   Measurement of Progress

An IEP must include a description of how the child's progress toward meeting the annual goals will be measured. 34 C.F.R. § 300.320(a)(3). Implicit is the collateral requirement that progress must be measured. No particular method for measuring progress is required by the law. Generally, however, the most reliable measurement comes from the collection of objective data. While "teacher observation" may be valuable, it can often result in vague and unverifiable reports such as "Jamal is making progress." The use of data collection or the administration of standardized assessment instruments will typically produce more useful information.

The IEP must also state how often parents will receive progress reports on IEP goals. No distribution schedule, nor any particular report format, is mandated by federal law, though some state regulations require that IEP progress reports be distributed at least as often as regular report cards, which is typically quarterly. *See, e.g.*, N.J.A.C. 6A:14-3.7(c)(16); NC 1503-4.1(a)(3)(ii). Reports are typically in writing, but could potentially be provided by phone or electronically. Parents may ask for more frequent progress reports or reports in a particular format.

4.   Statement of Special Education and Related Services

The statement of special education and related services is at the heart of how the child's special education program will be implemented. This statement includes a description of supplementary aids and services to be provided to the child, program modifications to be made, and supports to school personnel who will be involved in the child's education. 34 C.F.R. § 300.320(a)(4). The regulations spell out that the special education services should enable the child to advance appropriately toward attaining the annual goals, be involved in the general curriculum and extracurricular and nonacademic activities, and be educated with both disabled and nondisabled students.

Special education can be delivered in a wide variety of ways and settings. Specially designed instruction from a special education teacher, which can be delivered either in a separate classroom or in the regular classroom, often forms the backbone of the student's program. Specially designed instruction is instruction that is modified in content, methodology, or delivery to address the unique needs of the child that result from the child's disability. Special education should be based on peer-reviewed research to the extent practicable. 34 C.F.R. § 300.320(a)(4).

A child's special education program might also include the use of assistive technology, which is any equipment or product used to increase, maintain, or improve a child's functional capacities. Examples of assistive technology are alternate keyboards, page turners, print enlargers, portable communication devices, and any of a variety of computer programs. (The definition does not include a surgically implanted medical device, such as a cochlear implant or a pacemaker, however.) Included with the use of technology can be services connected with its use, which could be training for both the student and the education professionals in the use of the device.

Classroom accommodations and modifications can also play a role in a student's special education program. Accommodations and modifications should help a student with disabilities access the curriculum more effectively when his disability interferes with his access. Examples of accommodations are: preferential seating in the classroom, repeated directions, an extra set of books for home, copies of teacher notes, enlarged print materials, and tests read aloud. Examples of modifications are: reduced length of assignments, multisensory teaching, simplified curriculum, and modified grading.

Supplementary aids and services are services and supports provided in the regular classroom and other educational settings (such as extracurricular and nonacademic settings) to enable children with disabilities to be educated with nondisabled students. 34 C.F.R. § 300.42. Often, supplementary aids and services come in the form of additional personnel: a health care aide, a one-on-one behavior specialist, a sign language interpreter, or an instructional aide, for example. Other supplementary services could be peer tutors, calculators, access to computer programs, and inclusion in a social skills group. The list is by no means limited, although school district personnel may be quick to remind a parent or advocate that it does not have to provide everything possible. Remember that Amy Rowley was denied a sign language interpreter because it was determined that such service was not necessary for her to receive a FAPE. *See Board of Educ. v. Rowley*, 458 U.S. 176 (1982). Nevertheless, the district is required to make use of supplementary aids and services in the regular classroom before it determines that a child must be removed to a more restrictive setting. *See Oberti v. Board of Educ.*, 995 F.2d 1204 (3d Cir. 1993) (school cannot place a child with disabilities outside of a regular classroom if education in the regular classroom with supplementary aids and support services can be achieved satisfactorily). (This concept is discussed more fully below in the subsection Participation with Non-Disabled Students.)

Related services are developmental, corrective, and other supportive services designed to assist a child with a disability to benefit from special education. 34 C.F.R. § 300.34. The regulations contain a nonexhaustive list, some of which overlap with supplementary aids and services. The following are examples of related services, each of which is defined in the federal regulations:

- Audiology
- Counseling services
- Early identification and assessment of disabilities in children
- Interpreting services
- Occupational therapy
- Orientation and mobility
- Medical services (for diagnostic/evaluation purposes only)
- Parent counseling and training
- Physical therapy
- Psychological services
- Recreation
- Rehabilitation counseling
- School health services and school nurse services

- Social work services

- Speech language services

- Transportation

The extent to which school districts are required to provide non-instructional services to children with disabilities has been the subject of considerable litigation. The first case to go to the U.S. Supreme Court on this topic was *Irving Independent Sch. Dist. v. Tatro*, 468 U.S. 883 (1984). *Tatro* involved a child with spina bifida who was unable to empty her bladder voluntarily. To protect her kidneys, she required a "clean, intermittent catheterization" process to be administered by a trained person every three to four hours. The Court held that the catheterization process was a related service under the IDEA that must be provided, free of charge, to the child. The Court distinguished the service from an excluded medical service, because it did not need to be performed by a physician. Even more extensive services were at issue in *Cedar Rapids Cmty. Sch. Dist. v. Garrett F.*, 526 U.S. 66 (1999). Garrett F. was a ventilator-dependent quadriplegic who needed full-time, one-on-one nursing services. Noting that Garrett could not attend school at all without the nursing service, the Court had no trouble categorizing the assistance as a supportive service designed to assist Garrett in benefiting from special education. It reaffirmed its previous distinction, holding that services that must be provided by a physician are excluded as non-diagnostic medical services, but that medically-related services that can be performed by a nurse or other trained personnel are "related services" under the IDEA and must be provided, free of charge, to a special education student.

5.   Amount, Duration, and Frequency

The IEP must state the amount, duration, and frequency of the special education services. A special education student might be with a special education teacher all day, part of the day, or only a few hours a week. Many of the accommodations and modifications can be offered in the regular classroom by the regular education teacher. Once the amount, duration, and frequency of the special education services are stated on the IEP, the IEP functions essentially as a contract as to those amounts. If the parent can prove that the child was not provided the amount of services described on the IEP, then the parent will have proved a violation of the IDEA. The remedy for such a violation is compensatory education to make up for the lost services. (See Chapter Ten for a more in-depth discussion of remedies.)

6.   Participation with Non-Disabled Students/Least Restrictive Environment

One of the most important decisions in the special education process concerns the setting in which the child will receive services. Every eligible child is entitled to be educated in the "least restrictive environment." 20 U.S.C. § 1412(a)(5). This means he or she is entitled to be educated with nondisabled peers to the greatest extent possible. Following the team's discussion of the child's needs, present levels of performance, and services needed, the team should then ask itself whether, with appropriate support, the child's needs can be met in a regular classroom. If they cannot, then the team should determine what is the least amount of time the child needs to be removed from the regular classroom.

The strong preference in the law for the inclusion of children with disabilities in the regular classroom comes directly from the law's initial goal, which was to end the practice of excluding children with disabilities from public education entirely. At the time the IDEA was first enacted in 1975 (known then as the Education for All Handicapped Act of 1975), Congress made the finding that a million children with disabilities in the U.S. were excluded entirely from the public school system. When it reauthorized the law in 2005, it recognized the success of the Act in opening the doors to public education to children with disabilities, but added the following finding: "Almost 30 years of research and experience has demonstrated that the education of children with disabilities can be made more effective by having high expectations for such children and ensuring their access to the general education curriculum in the regular classroom, to the maximum extent possible." 20 U.S.C. § 1400(c)(5). As of 2007, more than half of all students with disabilities were educated primarily in the regular classroom. *See* National Center for Education Statistics, Table 51, http://nces.ed.gov/programs/digest/d09/tables/dt09_051.asp.

The term used for the setting in which the student will be educated is "educational placement." "Educational placement" refers to the overall educational environment rather than the precise location in which the disabled child is educated. The "educational placement" is not a particular classroom in a particular school, but refers to how much of the day the student is being educated with typically-developing peers. *See A.W. ex rel Wilson v. Fairfax Co. Sch. Bd.*, 372 F.3d 674 (4th Cir. 2004). In some jurisdictions, various placements are categorized by the percentage of time the child is educated with typically developing peers. In North Carolina, for example, a child educated with nondisabled students at least 80 percent of the time is in a "regular placement;" from 40 to 79 percent, a "resource placement"; and less that 40 percent, in a "separate placement." Other terms of art connected with the least restrictive environment concept are "mainstreaming," and "inclusion," both of which refer to the integration of children with disabilities into regular schools and classrooms. In some places, a classroom called "the resource room" is a classroom in a regular school in which special education students are educated for part of the day. For example, a child with a reading disability might be in a regular classroom all day except for an hour, when he is "pulled out" for small group reading instruction in the resource room with a special education teacher.

The LEA is responsible for ensuring that a continuum of alternative placements is available to meet the varying needs of children with disabilities. 34 C.F.R. § 300.115(a). This continuum must include regular classes, special classes, special schools, home instruction, and instruction in hospitals and institutions. If the school district does not operate schools and instructional programs across the entire continuum, and cannot offer a child a FAPE in any of the schools and programs it operates, it must pay for a disabled child to attend an appropriate school elsewhere. *See, e.g., Cordero v. Penn. Dept. of Educ.*, 795 F. Supp. 1352 (M.D. Pa. 1992).

Under the IDEA, children should be removed from the regular education environment only if the nature or severity of the disability is such that education in regular classroom with the use of supplementary aids and services cannot be achieved satisfactorily. 20 U.S.C. § 1412(a)(5); 34 C.F.R. § 300.114. Unless the child's IEP requires some other arrangement, the child should be assigned to the school that he or she would attend if not disabled, and in any event as close as possible to the child's home. 34 C.F.R. § 300.116(b), (c). Children may not be removed from age-appropriate regular classrooms solely because of needed modifications in the general curriculum. Nevertheless, a child who cannot make progress in the general classroom or cannot receive the services that he or she needs in the general classroom should not be placed there.

The continuum of placements, from the least restrictive to the most restrictive, would generally include the following types of settings:

- General education classrooms, with needed supports & services offered in the classroom, staffed either by only a general educator or both a general educator and a special educator

- Resource classrooms, staffed by a special educator, where children can attend part-time with other disabled students to get special education services

- Special education classrooms, to which children are assigned most or all of the day, with appropriate opportunities to leave and mix with the nondisabled students

- Special education day schools, both public and private

- Special education residential schools, both public and private

- Instruction delivered in hospitals or at a child's home

34 C.F.R. § 300.115(b).

The team should always begin at the top of the list to determine if a child can be educated appropriately in that setting. The team then moves down the list to find the appropriate setting. If a child is removed from the general education classroom, he or she should be returned there as soon as it is appropriate.

As courts have considered the least restrictive environment mandate of the IDEA, they have recognized the inherent tension between the law's strong preference for integration of disabled children with nondisabled children and the law's requirement that each disabled child be provided an individualized program tailored to meet his or her specific needs. One of the early influential cases is *Roncker v. Walter*, 700 F.2d 1058 (6th Cir. 1983). The subject of that case was Neill Roncker, a severely mentally retarded child who was nine years old at the time the dispute arose. He was described as having the mental age of a two or three year old needing constant supervision because of his inability to recognize dangerous situations. The IEP team, over the parents' objection, placed him in a special education school exclusively for mentally retarded students, depriving him of all contact with nondisabled children. The court fashioned the following analysis: "In a case where the segregated facility is considered superior, the court should determine whether the services which make that placement superior could be feasibly provided in a non-segregated setting. If they can, the placement in a segregated school would be inappropriate under the Act." *Id.* at 1063. A decision to remove a child from the regular classroom must be justified by a finding that the benefits of mainstreaming are "far outweighed by the benefit gained from services which could not be feasibly provided in the nonsegregated setting." *Id.* The case was remanded for the district court to determine "whether Neill's educational, physical or emotional needs require some service which could not feasibly be provided in a class for handicapped children within a regular school." *Id.*

The later case of *Daniel R.R. v. State Bd. of Educ.*, 874 F.2d 1036 (5th Cir. 1989), rejected the *Roncker* approach as too intrusive and not sufficiently deferential to the school officials. Like *Roncker*, *Daniel R.R.* concerned a child with mental retardation. At the request of his parents, when he was six years old, he was placed for half a day in a mainstreamed setting. After a period of time, the mainstream teacher said that Daniel could not participate without constant, individual attention from the teacher, and failed to master any of the skills she was trying to teach the students. To reach him, she said, she would have to modify the curriculum beyond recognition. The court recognized that some disabled children may not be able to master as much of the regular curriculum as nondisabled children can. Nevertheless, the court concluded, there is educational benefit to mainstreaming beyond the strictly academic, such as the language and behavior models available from nondisabled children. The *Daniel R.R.* court devised a two-part test for determining compliance with the mainstreaming requirement of the Act: 1) Can education in the regular classroom, with the use of supplementary aids and services, be satisfactorily achieved; and 2) If placement outside the regular classroom is necessary for the child to benefit educationally, has the school mainstreamed the child to the maximum extent appropriate? In applying the test, the court said, no single factor would be dispositive; the inquiry involves examination of the nature and severity of the child's handicapping condition, his needs and abilities, and the school's response to the child's needs. *Id.* at 1048.

Certain factors can defeat the presumption of general education classroom placement. In *DeVries v. Fairfax Co. Sch. Bd.*, 882 F.2d 876 (4th Cir. 1989), the court identified three factors that support placement outside a general education classroom:

1) the child would not receive educational benefit from being placed in a general education classroom;

2) the marginal benefit of being educated in a general education classroom is outweighed by the benefits of a separate setting; or

3) the disabled child is a disruptive force in the general education classroom.

Id. at 879.

The "least restrictive environment" principle does not mean a child must be assigned to his or her neighborhood school or the school to which he or she would have been assigned if not disabled, although that is the preference. *See, e.g., Murray v. Montrose*, 51 F.3d 921, 929 (10th Cir. 1995) ("A disabled child should be educated in the school he or she would attend if not disabled (i.e., the neighborhood school), *unless* the child's IEP requires placement elsewhere. If the IEP requires placement elsewhere, then, in deciding where the appropriate placement is, geographical proximity to home is relevant, and the child should be placed as close to home as possible."). Courts are respectful of the practical concerns of school districts and their need to take efficiencies into account when placing children. *See, e.g., Flour Bluff Indep. Sch. Dist. v. Katherine M.*, 91 F.3d 689 (5th Cir. 1996) (assignment of deaf student to a regional day school rather than her neighborhood school approved as meeting the LRE principle, particularly given the scarcity of sign language interpreters available to the school district).

Advocates will soon learn that preferences about placement are subject to great variation in philosophic approach. Some parents strongly favor a mainstreamed environment for their child, valuing the benefits of inclusion with typical children and full exposure to the general education curriculum. Others favor a more restricted environment, which often offers a smaller classroom and more specialized services. The opinions of school personnel vary just as much; sometimes school personnel will support a mainstream environment and other times they will urge placement in a more restricted setting. Because the law itself favors a mainstreamed setting to the maximum extent appropriate, the starting place should always be whether the child can make progress in a general education classroom, with appropriate supports and services in place. Only if the child cannot make progress there can the child legally be placed in a more restrictive setting.

7.   Testing Accommodations and Alternate Assessments

All children with disabilities must be included in general state and districtwide assessments. 20 U.S.C. § 1412(a)(16). They may be tested with or without accommodations on the standard tests, or they may be tested using alternate assessments. *Id.* The IEP must itemize any accommodations that the team determines are appropriate for the child in order to accurately measure the academic and functional performance of the child on state and districtwide assessments. *See* 34 C.F.R. § 300.320(a)(6)(i). In addition, if the IEP team determines that a child must take an alternate assessment, the IEP must include a statement of why the child cannot participate in the regular assessment and why the particular alternate assessment selected is appropriate for the child. 34 C.F.R. § 300.320(a)(6)(ii).

State and districtwide assessments have two primary purposes. The first is to measure the progress of the individual student. From year to year, students and their parents can — at least theoretically — see if the child is making progress on objective educational standards. The second purpose is to provide overall accountability of the school and school district to the larger community as required by the No Child Left Behind Act (NCLB). 20 U.S.C. §§ 6311 *et seq.* NCLB requires that the scores of subgroups of children, including children with disabilities, be calculated and publicly reported to demonstrate whether a school as a whole is making "adequate yearly progress." Adequate yearly progress is measured by how many students within each subgroup of children, as well as the group as a whole, achieve a "proficient" score on the tests. Each state sets its own academic standards and scores that reflect proficiency. 20 U.S.C. § 6311(b)(1). While the IDEA requires only that students with disabilities participate in state and district-wide assessments, NCLB requires that the tests and scores meet certain standards if the students can be included in the NCLB calculations. Thus, state departments of education have developed testing options for students with disabilities that will allow compliance with both federal laws.

a.   Accommodations

Testing accommodations are adaptations of the testing environment, the presentation of the material, or the method of response. They are designed to minimize the impact of the child's impairments on the child's ability to demonstrate his or her knowledge on the test. Testing accommodations are individualized for each child and should be used on both the state and district-wide tests as well as classroom assessments. *See* 34 C.F.R. § 300.320(a)(6)(i). Common accommodations include the following:

- Testing in a separate room, either alone or with a small group

- Seating near the test administrator

- Extra time; extra breaks

- Modified test materials, such as in large print or Braille

- Having the test read aloud or interpreted by a sign language interpreter or cued speech transliterator

- The use of certain tools and equipment, such as a word processor, calculator, number line, voice recognition software, etc.

- Dictation of answers to a scribe

• Marking directly in test booklet, rather than on an answer sheet

Each state is required to develop guidelines for accommodations that may be offered. 20 U.S.C. § 1412(a)(16)(B). State departments of education typically publish guidance regarding accommodations that are allowable. *See, e.g.*, Accommodations and Modifications of Test Administration Procedures for Statewide Assessments, New Jersey Department of Education, http://www.state.nj.us/education/specialed/accom900.htm; Testing Variations, Accommodations, and Modifications, California Department of Education, http://www.cde.ca.gov/ta/tg/sa/documents/varmodac2010rev210.doc. Accommodations are not permitted when they will invalidate the score. For example, if the purpose of the test is to assess a child's reading level, the score will be considered invalid if the test was read orally to the student. If the purpose of the test is to assess a child's calculation skills, the use of a calculator will invalidate the score. On the other hand, if the purpose of the test is to assess the child's ability to reason through a word problem in math and use the correct strategy, the question can be read to the student and the student can use a calculator. These principles are found within the various state policies about allowable accommodations.

b.   Alternate Assessments

For some children with disabilities, the standard state and district assessments would not be appropriate. When a child's instructional level is well below his or her age peers, such that the child has not been exposed to the curriculum being tested, then the IEP team can decide that the child should be tested using an alternate assessment. 20 U.S.C. § 1412(a)(16). An alternate assessment may be in the form of a typical assessment (i.e., a standardized test) or it may be in a completely different form, such as a collection of data kept over time or a portfolio of work samples. *See, e.g.*, Ohio's Standards-Based Alternate Assessment for Students with Disabilities ("The alternate assessment is a collection of evidence that shows student performance of standards-based knowledge and skills within the context of classroom instruction.") *See*:

> http://education.ohio.gov/GD/Templates/Pages/ODE/
> ODEPrimary.aspx?page=2&TopicRelationID=229

In order to be counted in the calculation of "adequate yearly progress" for NCLB purposes, alternate assessments can be based on one of two levels, depending on the severity of the child's disability. For children with the most significant cognitive disabilities who cannot be expected to master grade-level content, even with the best instruction, alternate assessments are based on *alternate achievement standards*. *See* 71 Fed. Reg. 46666 (Aug. 14, 2006) (commenting on 34 C.F.R. § 300.320(a)(6)). Although they are at a significantly reduced academic level, the alternate achievement standards must still be challenging for the students, aligned with the state's content standards, and yield results separately in reading/language arts and mathematics. *See* 34 C.F.R. § 200.1; 34 C.F.R. § 200.6.

For children with less severe disabilities, though still severe enough that they cannot be expected to reach grade-level proficiency even with effective instruction, alternate assessments can be based on *modified achievement standards*. *See* 34 C.F.R. § 200.1. Modified achievement standards must be aligned with grade-level content, but can be less difficult than the regular standards. *See* 34 C.F.R. § 200.1(e). The assessments based on modified achievement standards differ in complexity from grade-level assessments. In North Carolina, for example, the test known as NCEXTEND2 is based on modified achievement standards. NCEXTEND2 offers students only three answer choices instead of four, has less sophisticated vocabulary, and does not require the same depth of knowledge as the regular statewide tests. Nevertheless, the NCEXTEND2 covers the same basic concepts that are on the regular tests. *See* North Carolina Testing Program Assessment Options, http://www.ncpublicschools.org/accountability/testing/.

The choice of the type of assessment has significant consequences for the child. A child who is not tested on the regular test (with or without accommodations) will not be taught standard grade-level concepts at the level of depth expected of typical children. Even if the child "passes" the tests, he or she will not be demonstrating mastery of grade-level material. This has increasing importance as the child enters high school and must meet certain standards to be awarded a diploma. On the other hand, if the level of the test is so far above the level of the child and the child will consistently fail, then the test results will not provide sufficient information about whether the child is making progress. Advocates should be aware of their own state's testing program and graduation requirements to be able to advise parents about the appropriateness of various tests.

The choice of assessment has consequences beyond the individual child as a result of NCLB. The Secretary of Education, when issuing regulations to implement NCLB, restricted the number of children that may be tested using alternate assessments and be counted for purposes of calculating "adequate yearly progress" (AYP). *See* 34 C.F.R. § 200.13(c)(2). In order to count for AYP purposes, the number of "proficient" or "advanced" scores of students with the most significant cognitive disabilities taking tests based on alternate assessments cannot exceed one percent of the total number of students assessed at any grade level. *See* 34 C.F.R. § 200.13(c)(2)(i). The number of "proficient" or "advanced" scores of students with disabilities taking tests based on modified achievement standards cannot exceed two percent of the total number of students assessed at any grade level. *See* 34 C.F.R. § 200.13(c)(2)(ii). Given that approximately 13 percent of all students are students with disabilities, these limits strongly encourage school officials to include as many students with disabilities as possible in the regular testing program. This has the corollary effect of encouraging the inclusion of students with disabilities in regular classrooms and exposing them to the regular grade-level curriculum.

8. Transition Services

Transition services are designed to help students with disabilities prepare for post-secondary education, activities and independent adult living. While transition services for students who plan to attend college or other post-secondary school are primarily academic, transition services for students who will not go on to additional education are more functional. Transition services can include specialized instruction and related services designed to focus on the development of employment skills, independent living skills, and self-advocacy skills. They can provide opportunities for the student to become connected with other public agencies, such as Vocational Rehabilitation or the Division of Mental Health/Mental Retardation.

Under federal law, beginning no later than the school year in which a student will turn 16, transition services must be included in the child's IEP, and thereafter, along with IEP goals, they must be updated annually. 34 C.F.R. § 300.320(b). However, transition services may (and should) be included in the IEP of students under the age of 16 as an IEP team determines appropriate or as state regulations require. Indeed, many state policies left in place a provision of the IDEA that was changed in 2004 and continue to require that transition services be considered no later than the IEP year in which a student will turn 14. *See, e.g., North Carolina*

Policies Governing Children with Disabilities, § 1503-4.1(b)(1); N.J.S.A. 6A:14-2.3(k)(5)(ii). In California, the state regulations do not set an earlier age for incorporating transition services, but rather state generally that "[p]lanning for transition from school to postsecondary environments should begin in the school system well before the student leaves the system." Cal. Educ. Code § 56460(e).

Transition services are defined very broadly as a "coordinated set of activities" for a student that "is designed to be within a results-oriented process, that is focused on improving the academic and functional achievement" of the student and facilitate that student's transition from "school to post-school activities, including post-secondary education, vocational education, integrated employment (including supported employment), continuing and adult education, adult services, independent living, or community participation." 20 U.S.C. § 1401(34)(A); 34 C.F.R. § 43(a)(1). Transition services for a student must be based on the child's individual needs, strengths, preferences and interests and may include individualized instruction, related services, community experiences, the development of objectives related to employment or other post-school living objectives and, in appropriate circumstances, may involve the acquisition of daily living skills and a functional vocational evaluation. 20 U.S.C. § 1401(34)(B)-(C); 34 C.F.R. § 300.43(a)(2); *see also, Yankton Sch. Dist. v. Schramm*, 93 F.3d 1369, 1374 (8th Cir. 1996) (finding that transition services could include driver's education, self-advocacy, and independent living skills such as cooking and cleaning).

In considering transition services appropriate to a child's disability, it is critical to involve the child, as much as practicable, in his or her own transition planning. Indeed, once transition services will be included in a child's IEP, the child must be invited to an IEP meeting if a purpose of the meeting will be the consideration of the child's post-secondary goals and the transition services necessary to reach those goals. 34 C.F.R. § 300.321(b)(1). If the child cannot attend the meeting, the school district must still take steps to ensure that the child's preferences and interests are fully considered by the team. 34 C.F.R. § 300.321(b)(2).

In evaluating transition services necessary for a child, the IEP team should consider what the student's goals are after high school graduation. Will the student continue her education in a four-year college or university? Will the student attend a community college or vocational/ trade school? Different post-secondary goals require different preparation; therefore it is important that a student's course selection in high school adequately prepares her for any post-secondary education options she may be considering. Once students with IEPs graduate from high school, special education is no longer an entitlement and they must meet the specific entry requirements of the schools they wish to attend. For example, most four-year colleges and universities have advanced math and foreign language requirements, so students who do not take these courses in high school may be precluding themselves, at least at graduation, from continuing immediately with their educations at a four-year college.

In cases where a student is planning to move directly from high school to paid employment, the IEP team should consider what the student's career interests are and ensure that there is an opportunity, while the student is still in school, for him or her to gain experience that will allow him or her to explore a desired career path. This likely will involve conducting a vocational assessment of the student and offering the student an opportunity to explore his or her career interest. In North Carolina, children with significant disabilities may qualify, through the IEP process, to participate in the "Occupational Course of Study." This course of study is for the small number of disabled students who require a greatly modified curriculum that focuses on post-school employment and independent living. It does not prepare students for post-secondary education, but focuses intensely on job preparation skills: basic math (to allow a student to calculate a pay check and understand a work schedule, for example); basic reading and writing (functional reading, oral and written communication skills, basic technology skills); life skills (safety and health procedures, nutrition, basic science) and job skills. In addition to taking classes, each student participates in 900 hours of vocational training during the four years of high school.

Finally, the federal law requires that when appropriate, and with the consent of a parent or the child (if the child has reached the age of majority), the school district *must invite* other public agencies that are likely to be responsible for providing or paying for a child's transitional services. 34 C.F.R. § 300.321(b)(3); *see also Letter to Caplan*, 50 IDELR 168 (OSEP 2008). For example, local state departments of human services and labor have divisions charged with assisting persons with disabilities prepare for and keep employment and live, as much as possible, independent lives. In most states, Vocational Rehabilitation Services provides services that enable individuals with disabilities to find jobs or keep their existing jobs. These services include job training, education, adaptive equipment and job placement.

Focusing the team on available and appropriate transition services is an important function of a special education advocate. If you are representing a student entering or already in high school, it is important that you understand well your client's goals after high school and advocate for transition services appropriate to help him or her achieve those goals.

9.   Extended School Year Services

While most special education students attend school only during the times that school is regularly in session, some are entitled to additional educational services. These are known as "extended school year services" (ESY). While the IDEA itself does not mention ESY services, the federal regulations require that each school district ensure that ESY services are available to any child who needs them in order to receive a FAPE. 34 C.F.R. § 300.106(a). The definition of ESY services is "special education and related services that are provided to a child with a disability beyond the normal school year in accordance with the child's IEP and free of charge." 34 C.F.R. § 300.106(b). Typically, ESY services are provided during the summer months, but they can also be provided during other school vacations and before and after school. *See* 71 Fed. Reg. 46582 (Aug. 14, 2006).

Each child's IEP team must determine if the child needs ESY services to be provided a FAPE. As no specific eligibility standards are set by the regulations, states and local jurisdictions have developed a variety of standards to provide guidance to IEP teams to help them determine which children should be provided ESY services. Following a number of cases on the issue of eligibility for ESY, most jurisdictions have adopted standards that incorporate the following themes:

- Regression/recoupment: If the child will suffer a significant regression of skills during the school break that cannot be recouped within a reasonable period of time, then he or she is entitled to ESY services.

- Emerging skills: If the child is at a critical stage of the development of an important skill, such that an interruption in the child's education would jeopardize the mastery of that skill or the progress made to date, then he or she is entitled to ESY services.

One particularly influential case on this point is *Johnson v. Indep. Sch. Dist.*, 921 F.2d 1022 (10th Cir. 1990). The court in that case held that no single criterion could be used to determine eligibility for ESY; factors to be considered by the team include the degree of the child's impairment, the rate of the child's progress, the ability of the child's parents to provide educational structure at home, the child's behavioral and physical problems, the availability of alternative resources, the ability of the child to interact with non-disabled children, and the child's vocational needs. *Id.* at 1027. Some cases use a narrower articulation, as follows: "If the child benefits meaningfully within his potential from instruction under a proper IEP over a regular school year, then ESY service may not be required under the Act unless the benefits accrued to the child during the regular school year will be significantly jeopardized if he is not provided an [ESY]." *Cordrey v. Euckert*, 917 F.2d 1460, 1473 (6th Cir. 1990). The nature and extent of ESY services is left to the IEP team. The school district may not unilaterally limit the type, amount or duration of extended year services or limit services to particular categories of eligibility. 34 C.F.R. § 300.106(a)(3).

IV. PLANNING FOR AN IEP MEETING

In most special education cases, the first time you will represent your client will not be in an adversarial setting, such as in mediation or at a due process hearing, but at an IEP meeting. In fact, a parent anticipating a challenging IEP meeting often chooses the week or two prior to the meeting to seek out legal assistance. In other cases, parents may come to you with concerns about their child's education and you may decide to call an IEP meeting on their behalf in an effort to resolve their issues.

Advance preparation for an IEP meeting is necessary to represent your client at the meeting in a professional manner. This section will focus on the steps involved for adequate preparation and suggest tips to get you ready for your first meeting.

PREPARING FOR AN IEP MEETING REQUIRES:

- Collecting and organizing the student's records

- Scheduling the IEP meeting and/or informing the school that the parent will have an attorney at the already scheduled meeting

- Setting an agenda for the meeting with your client or contacting the school to add items to the meeting agenda not covered by the notice

- Finding out who has been invited to the meeting and inviting any other individuals who support your client's goals

- Exchanging information with the school to be discussed at the meeting

- Making a plan with your client about the meeting

A.   Collecting and Organizing the Student's Records

Prior to an IEP meeting, you should obtain a complete copy of the student's educational record. This includes information found in every student's school file, such as the student's attendance, grades, discipline record and results on any state-wide or district assessments.

These records are generally referred to as the student's "cumulative file" and should follow a student from school to school and as the student advances from grade to grade throughout K-12 education.

In addition, you should have a complete copy of the student's IEP-related records. These records are generally referred to as the student's "confidential" file and may be kept in a separate location from the student's general education file, for example, with the student's case manager or, if the student is in a separate setting, with his or her special education teacher. The "confidential" file of a student includes all psycho-educational evaluations, behavior assessments and/or behavior intervention plans; and all other IEP or Section 504-related documents (which would include the student's IEP or 504 Plan; meeting minutes and all other documents related to the child's IEP or Section 504 plan).

Even if the parent believes that she has a complete record of her child's educational file, it is important to collect the records directly from the school. Doing so may reveal that the school has documents that were not shared with the parent, that the parent may have misplaced certain records, or even that the school does not have documents that it should. In organizing your documents, especially if you find discrepancies, note the source of any documents you have. You may even want to keep documents from different sources in separate files, especially if you anticipate that the matter might become adversarial.

The parents, and by extension you with a signed release from the parents, are entitled to inspect and review the student's school records under both the IDEA and the Family Education Privacy Rights Act (FERPA), 20 U.S.C. § 1232g. The federal regulations under both FERPA and IDEA allow schools to charge a reasonable fee for copying the records, so long as the charge does not effectively prevent parents from exercising their right to inspect and review their child's educational file. 34 C.F.R. § 613.

Because a child's educational file may be voluminous, especially for an older child, you should be systematic in organizing the records. Prepare a summary chart or index of the most significant documents. Many schools maintain duplicate files on children, have files which have transferred from school to school and use different filing systems and, in general, are kept by case managers and teachers who are serving many children and do not have adequate time to spend organizing the students' records. As a result, the file you receive may be lacking any organization.

Some practitioners have found 3-ring binders to be a useful organizational tool. This allows for the easy arrangement (and rearrangement) of documents, the ability to easily remove duplicates or insert documents that are later found, and a means of dividing the documents in a functional way. For example, you might organize a client binder with the following sections:

- Administrative or internal documents (this section could include all internal/privileged documents such as private information about the student and her family, educational or medical releases executed by the parent, case notes, the representation agreement and memoranda to the file about the case);

- Correspondence (this could include all correspondence between the parent and the school, you and the school, and privileged correspondence between you and the child's parents and other outside individuals);

- General education records (such as attendance, grades, statewide assessments and the child's discipline record, if any);

- Evaluations (including evaluations related to the student's initial eligibility for services, reevaluations and any functional behavior assessments);

- IEP-related records (the student's IEPs; minutes from IEP meetings, worksheets for special education and related service eligibility, extended school year services, or manifestation determination reviews. In addition, for certain students, you may also keep documents related to the child's educational needs prior to identification under the IDEA, such as a Section 504 plan or supplementary aids and services attempted in the regular education classroom);

- Research (any case-related research).

Additional sections may be required, and can easily be created with notebook dividers, such as a section for documents that the client may have provided you (but which are not in the school records) or, for some children, medical and/or mental health records that are not part of the school record.

Finally, it is very helpful if you create a detailed "document chart" for some of the more important sections of your notebook, such as the education records, IEP records, and evaluation sections, and that you tab the most important documents within each section. The document chart should contain sufficient detail so that you have ready access to the most important information in the document. For example, a description of an evaluation would include the date of the evaluation, the examiner, what evaluation tools were used, the student's scores (including percentile rank) and any useful observations the examiner made during the evaluation. Having a thorough chart or table of contents of your client's documents and having those documents filed in an orderly and consistent way is a crucial and necessary step toward effectively advocating for your client at an IEP meeting. Following is an example of how you might summarize an IEP as part of your document summary:

April 8, 2008	IEP 04-09-2009 to 04-08-2010 Annual Review	Strengths: sociable, good attendance, artistic, athletic pg 2: Annual Goal is set to improve his ability to make choices, benchmarks include follow classroom and school rules 9 out of 10 times and when frustrated Eric will speak to an adult privately
		Measurements of progress journals and teacher observation/recording
		pg 3: Annual Goal is to improve his reading skills. Eric isn't doing grade level work although his reading skills have improved. Benchmarks to reach 85% accuracy read appropriate text w/ fluency 9 out of 10 times and to self-monitor. Measured by pre and post tests, teacher observation/recording
		pg 4: Annual goal to improve his written language skills. Benchmarks include: 85% accuracy in vocabulary, 85% accuracy in spelling commonly used words, be able to compose 3-4 paragraphs on a given topic, be able to edit final product. Measured by pre and post assessments, written work and teacher observation/recording
		pg 5: Improve his organizational skills. Benchmarks include beginning on tasks on time 90%, ask for more time if he needs it 90%, ask for help 90% etc. Measured by teacher observation/recording and work samples.

pg 6: Classroom modifications: Eric gets extended time, student marks in book, study guides, multiple test session and testing in separate room.

Special Education services: 60 minutes of inclusion teaching in Language Arts every day of the week and 30 min. regular class instruction in organization once a week.

Pg 7: Least Restrictive Environment (Placement). Eric will be placed in a regular classroom

Reports of progress: his parents will be notified of his progress through written reports every 4 weeks.

B. Scheduling the Meeting

The initial IEP meeting allowing for the provision of services must be held within 30 days from the date that a student is found eligible for special education, and thereafter, once a year, at a minimum. IEP meetings may happen more than once a year, and *should* happen whenever the teachers or parents have concerns about the child's special education or related services or when there is new information or evaluations about the child to review. Parents may ask that an IEP team meeting be scheduled at any time, although the federal law does not set a timeline within which a school district must respond. A state may have specific policies or guidance regarding when IEP meetings are to be held, if requested by parents. (For example, California state law requires that an IEP team meeting be convened within 30 days of parental request, not counting school vacations of more than 5 days. Cal. Educ. Code § 56343.5.)

C. Providing Advance Notice to the School District

Before accompanying a parent to an IEP meeting, make sure the school personnel know that you will be attending. Generally, if a parent is going to be represented by an attorney, the school district will also want its attorney present. However, each individual school district will have its own policies about dealing with represented parents. Some districts may allow school district employees to speak and meet directly with attorneys for parents; others may forbid it. Some may allow communication on some matters or with certain individuals within the school district. Therefore, if you do not inform the school of your attendance at the meeting and then appear unannounced with your parent and/or student, you run the risk of having the meeting cancelled and rescheduled at a later date when the school's attorney can be in attendance.

In addition, before making an initial contact with an employee of a school district on behalf of your client, you must be very familiar with your state bar rules regarding dealing with represented and unrepresented individuals, as well as any limits on your role as a law student attorney.

D. Creating the IEP Meeting Agenda

If you, as the advocate for the student, wish to call an IEP meeting, be sure you have in mind a clear agenda or goal for the meeting and that the purpose of the meeting is shared with the school district in advance of the meeting, if at all possible. If the school district has called the meeting, contact the appropriate special education teacher or administrator to find out the purpose of the meeting. Although school personnel are not required to share an actual meeting agenda with the parent, the law requires that they provide parents prior written notice of the meeting, indicating, among other things, the purpose of the meeting. 34 C.F.R. § 300.322(b)(i). Therefore, if school personnel called the meeting, examine the notice given the parent and make sure you understand the issue(s) that will be discussed at the meeting. If it is not clear from the notice, or if the parent has issues she wants to raise at the meeting that are not included in the notice, let the school district know what those issues are.

E.   Inviting Participants to be a Part of The IEP Team

If the meeting was called by the school district, look to see who has been invited. Discuss the invitees with your client. Is there anyone who has been invited that you or your client do not recognize? If so, contact the school and find out who the person is and what role he or she will play at the meeting. Is anyone missing from the list of school attendees? For example, if your client has concerns about her child's speech therapy or progress in speech, has the child's speech therapist been invited to attend the meeting? If not, ask that she be invited.

In light of the proposed meeting attendees or your client's goals for the meeting, discuss with your client whether there are other outside individuals that you should invite. For example, if you are sharing an outside evaluation, is the evaluator willing and able to come to discuss his or her findings? If the evaluator cannot be present at the meeting, can he or she be available for a conference call during the meeting? If so, talk to the convener of the meeting about arranging that. If your outside evaluator cannot be available for the meeting, is there someone at the school who is qualified to interpret their results (e.g., school psychologist or related service provider, such as occupational or speech-language therapist)? If so, ask that the school invite that person to the meeting. Does the child have a therapist, mentor, case manager, or social worker that works with her that can be helpful to the team or is supportive of a position that the parent has? If so, that person should be invited by the parent to the meeting.

F.   Exchanging Information Prior to the Meeting

In preparing for the IEP meeting, think about what evaluations or evidence the parents have in support of their goals. For example, are the parents' goals for their child based on the opinion of an outside expert or on an evaluation done by that expert? If so, has this information been shared with the school? If the information or evaluation has not yet been shared with the school, you should share it with them, in advance of the meeting, if possible. Similarly, if the school has conducted evaluations or collected data on the child that you believe will be discussed at the meeting, you should request the information so that you have ample opportunity to review the information with your client prior to the meeting. If the evaluations or information from the school does not support your client's position, you may have to try to counter the report with information from an outside evaluator.

If the purpose of the IEP meeting is to discuss or draft IEP goals, you should request that the school send you any drafts of its proposed goals prior to the meeting so you can review them with your client. It is not unlawful to have a draft IEP before an IEP meeting, so long as it is clear that the document is a draft and can and should be revised by the team at the meeting. In commenting on new IDEA regulations, the U.S. Department of Education addressed a request that parents receive drafts of IEPs prior to the team meeting, as follows:

> With respect to a draft IEP, we encourage public agency staff to come to an IEP Team meeting prepared to discuss evaluation findings and preliminary recommendations.

Likewise, parents have the right to bring questions, concerns, and preliminary recommendations to the IEP Team meeting as part of a full discussion of the child's needs and the services to be provided to meet those needs. We do not encourage public agencies to prepare a draft IEP prior to the IEP Team meeting, particularly if doing so would inhibit a full discussion of the child's needs. However, if a public agency develops a draft IEP prior to the IEP Team meeting, the agency should make it clear to the parents at the outset of the meeting that the services proposed by the agency are preliminary recommendations for review and discussion with the parents. The public agency also should provide the parents with a copy of its draft proposals, if the agency has developed them, prior to the IEP Team meeting so as to give the parents an opportunity to review the recommendations of the public agency prior to the IEP Team meeting, and be better able to engage in a full discussion of the proposals for the IEP. It is not permissible for an agency to have the final IEP completed before an IEP Team meeting begins.

71 Fed. Reg. 46678 (Aug. 14 2006).

Although it is not illegal for a school district to have a draft IEP before an IEP meeting, it is illegal for a school district to "predetermine" a child's services or placement prior to the meeting. In *Deal v. Hamilton County Bd. of Educ.*, 392 F.3d 840 (6th Cir. 2004), the court found that the school district denied parents the opportunity to meaningfully participate in the IEP process when it "predetermined" the services that their autistic child would receive without considering his individual needs. Even though the parents were present at the IEP meetings, the court found that the school's "unofficial policy" of denying the type of services requested by the parents showed that they were not considering the parents' request with an open mind. *Id.* at 858. Note, however, that in a later case, the court found that "predetermination is not synonymous with preparation," finding that while federal law prohibits a completed IEP from being thrust upon parents, schools are permitted to come to IEP meetings with "pre-formed opinions" so long as they still are willing to listen to the parents and give parents the opportunity to make objections and suggestions. *Nack v. Orange City Sch. Dist.*, 454 F.3d 604, 610 (6th Cir. 2006).

G.   Making a Plan With Your Client

Finally, before the IEP meeting, discuss with the parents what their main objectives are and prioritize those objectives. In other words, what is most important to the parents? Are some objectives non-negotiable, and if so, what are they and why? Are other priorities more negotiable? If so, again, what are they and under what circumstances would the parent be willing to forego this objective?

Here are some questions that might help the parents articulate their concerns:

- What are the child's impairments? How are the symptoms manifested in the child?

- How does the child's impairment impede academic progress?

- Using the child's evaluations and educational history, how does the child's impairment specifically affect the child's ability to learn and make overall educational progress? Examples: Is the child paying attention? Processing? Remembering? Following through? Communicating? Conforming conduct to school rules and expectations?

- What can special education do to allow better academic progress?

- Can special education overcome the impairment?

    - Example: a child with a reading disability can be taught to read using a different teaching method; once the child learns to read, the impairment is overcome.

    - Example: a non-verbal autistic child can be taught to speak, which overcomes the impairment of being non-verbal

    - Example: a child with ADHD and organizational problems can be taught certain organizational techniques that help overcome the effects of ADHD

    - Example: a child with a behavioral problem can be taught to adjust behavior and overcome the behavioral issues.

- Can special education only accommodate the impairment?

    - Example: a child with severe anxiety cannot be taught not to be anxious. Special education must accommodate for the anxiety with appropriate placement and services.

    - Example: a child with limited cognitive skills cannot be taught to have higher cognitive skills. Special education must accommodate the child's slower learning pace.

    - Example: a child with chronic fatigue/pain cannot be taught to have no fatigue or pain. Special education must accommodate the needs for a shorter day/rest periods, etc.

- What does the current IEP provide for the child, and how is each aspect of it successful or unsuccessful in either overcoming or accommodating the impairment so that the child can make reasonable progress?

- What changes in the IEP are necessary for reasonable progress? Is it more time with a special education teacher — which would involve a new placement — or is it more time with a related services provider? Is it different classroom accommodations and modifications?

You should also endeavor to understand what the parents' relationship has been with the school up until this point. Is it amicable or contentious? Are there individuals at the school who support the parents' position? Are there individuals at the school who oppose it? How have IEP meetings gone in the past? What do the parents expect this IEP meeting will be like, and why? Decide with your clients who will speak at the meeting. If past meetings have been contentious, unproductive, or upsetting to the parents, or if the parent is intimidated by the individuals at the meeting, it may be better for you to be the parent's spokesperson.

Counsel the parents to try and remain calm. Attempting to reduce the level of emotion at the meeting, focusing instead on the needs of the child and the objective evidence supporting those needs, will help make the meeting much more productive. If, despite your planning, your clients become emotional at an IEP meeting, take a break to allow them to re-group, to discuss any upsetting issues and to revise, if necessary, your plan, so that you may complete the meeting and accomplish as many of the parents' objectives as possible.

H.   Deciding Whether to Record IEP Meetings

Some parents, especially those that feel overwhelmed and intimidated by IEP meetings, may want to video or audio record the IEP meeting. Both parents and the school district have the right to record IEP meetings, but the decision to record an IEP meeting should be considered carefully. For example, while a recording certainly will provide the most accurate record of what was said at the IEP meeting, it also likely will have a chilling effect on the school team members in attendance and it sends a strong signal that the parent distrusts the school. Rather than encouraging parents to record an IEP meeting (even if they have recorded them in the past), it may be more helpful to take accurate notes of the meeting, especially as it relates to the parents' primary objectives. However, in cases where you anticipate a dispute with the school or where a dispute already exists, the "chilling effect" of recording the meeting may be outweighed by the need to have an accurate record of the discussion.

Regardless of whether you choose to record the meeting or not, at the end of the meeting, you should review the minutes taken by school personnel to ensure that they accurately reflect the important points. At some meetings, the meeting minutes are read at the conclusion of the meeting; at others, they are simply passed around to be read by the participants. In either case, if you find important points missing or errors in the minutes, you should raise them before the meeting is adjourned and the minutes become a part of the client's confidential file.

I.   Signing the IEP

Neither the federal statute nor the federal regulations mention signatures on IEPs. Following the development of the initial IEP, a parent must consent to the provision of special education services to his or her child. 34 C.F.R. § 300.300(b). This consent can be obtained on the initial IEP itself, or on another document. The parent's signature is not required for implementation of subsequent IEPs, however, unless the state has added that requirement. In Ohio, for example, the state policy does not allow the IEP team to change the child's placement without consent from the parents. *See* Operating Standards for Ohio Educational Agencies Serving Children with Disabilities. Ohio Admin. Code § 3301-51-05(C)(4). In New Jersey, the IEP form asks for the parent's signature and states that the IEP will not be implemented for 15 days following the annual review unless the parent consents to a sooner start date. The North Carolina form has a space for the signatures of all members of the IEP team, including the parent, but this signature indicates only presence at the team meeting. A parent's refusal to sign the IEP form does not authorize the school district to cease offering special education to the child, though a parent may revoke consent for the provision of special education services for his or her child at any time, which requires the district to end the provision of services.

In light of what you have learned in this chapter, break into groups and participate in the following simulation involving the development of an IEP. The group information for each part is listed below. Confidential information can be found in the teacher's manual.

Group Instructions for IEP Meeting

Katie Smith is a ten-year-old student with athetoid cerebral palsy (CP). Cerebral palsy (CP) is a condition that results from damage to one of the parts of the brain that controls muscle tone. Muscle tone is what keeps an individual's body in a certain position, like sitting up in a chair. Changes in muscle tone allow individuals to move. Depending on what part of the brain is injured and how big the injury is, the muscle tone of a person with CP may be too tight, too loose, or a combination of too tight and too loose. Athetoid CP is a type of cerebral palsy in which the person experiences a combination of tightness and looseness in muscle tone. Children with this kind of cerebral palsy make involuntary movements because their muscles rapidly change from floppy to tense in a way they cannot control. Speech is nearly always affected to some degree because of difficulty in controlling the tongue, breathing, and vocal chords. Similarly there may be difficulties eating, and the individual may drool.

Katie lives at home with her mother Mary and her younger brother. Her mother works full time as a manager at a local store. Katie attends Crestview Elementary and is in the fourth grade. She uses an electric wheelchair to move around the school building. She has somewhat limited use of her arms, and struggles with fine motor activities. Katie requires assistance with daily living activities such as toileting. At lunch, Katie needs assistance with opening the containers such as a milk carton and packages of potato chips, crackers, and other foods wrapped or bagged in plastic. Her individualized education program (IEP) provides her with a personal aide who is with her throughout the school day to assist with these needs. The aide also assists in note taking by acting as a scribe during class.

Katie likes to be independent and gets annoyed when people treat her like she is incapable of doing things for herself. She wishes to be as independent as possible. She has an outgoing personality and is well liked by her peers.

In the last few months, Katie lost a considerable amount of weight and has missed school numerous times due to illness. Missing school is highly unusual for Katie: she has been known to hide symptoms of illness from her mom in order to go to school. Because Katie's mom must stay home from work to assist Katie on days she is sick, Katie's recent illnesses have taken a toll on the family physically, emotionally, and financially.

Katie's IEP for the current school year was written by the team in May of last year. Katie's mom Mary recently requested an IEP meeting to address some changes that have occurred since the last IEP meeting. Specifically, she requested an IEP meeting because of a recent change in Katie's needs related to eating. In December, Katie aspirated while eating dinner and had to be rushed to the hospital. Based on the incident leading to that visit to the hospital, Katie's treating physician ordered a video fluoroscopic swallow study (VFSS) examination of swallowing. Based on the results of those studies, he has recommended that Katie no longer be fed solid food. All food Katie eats will need to be pureed. Because Katie eats lunch at school, her mom requested an IEP meeting to address this issue.

The meeting was originally scheduled for last Monday. However, the school failed to invite Katie's aide to the meeting as requested by Katie's mother. The meeting was therefore postponed to today. The following people will be attending this meeting:

1. Parent — Mary Smith

2. Advocate

This is the first time that Ms. Smith has brought an advocate to one of these meetings.

3. Special Education Director

This person has authority to allocate resources on behalf of the district and can supervise the provision of special education supports and services.

4. Special Education Teacher (a/k/a intervention specialist)

The special education teacher taught Katie during first, second, and third grade. The special education teacher advocated for Katie to be moved to the regular education classroom during fourth grade because she felt that Katie could succeed in a regular education setting. The team agreed to provide Katie with a personal aide during fourth grade so that she could be in her current less restrictive setting.

5. Regular Education Teacher

The regular education teacher is Katie's fourth grade teacher. This is the first time she has taught a student with disabilities in her classroom. She has no prior training regarding students with disabilities.

6. Occupational Therapist (OT)

The occupational therapist has been involved with Katie since Katie began school at Crestview Elementary. The occupational therapist designs purposeful activities to help students with disabilities develop fine motor skills and become independent. OTs may recommend and provide training in adaptive equipment such as bathroom aids, seating and mobility systems, and adapted toys. They can advise on wheelchair accessibility issues at home or school.

7. School Principal

8. Personal aide (a/k/a paraprofessional)

The team scheduled today's meeting to discuss any changes that need to be made to the IEP to incorporate the recent report from Katie's physician ordering that all of Katie's food be pureed.

Chapter 6

EARLY INTERVENTION SERVICES[1]

Early intervention services are designed to enhance the developmental abilities of eligible infants and toddlers, ages birth to three, with disabilities or developmental delays, or diagnosed with a condition that has a "high probability of resulting in developmental delays." 20 U.S.C. § 1432(5)(A). In 1986, Congress expanded the federal law governing special education to include services for infants and toddlers with disabilities from birth to age three through the creation of the Early Intervention Program. This initially was passed as Part H (now Part C) of the Education of the Handicapped Act ("EHA"), P.L. 99-457 (predecessor to the Individuals with Disabilities Education Act). Prior to this time, the Act covered children between the ages of three and 21 only, with services optional for children between the ages of three and five. The 1986 amendments to the EHA mandated the provision of special education and related services to preschool-age children (ages three to five), in addition to creating the Early Intervention Program.

The Early Intervention Program was conceived in response to research findings that significant brain development occurs during the first three years of life and that timely services provided during this critical period can reduce and even prevent developmental delays in young children, thereby influencing lifelong development. H.R. Rep. 99-860 (1986) 2401, 2405-6. Congress recognized that providing services to children early in life would reduce the need for special education and related services during the school-age years and maximize children's potential to develop into independent, self-sufficient adults. 20 U.S.C. § 1471(a) (1988). Congress further acknowledged that providing early intervention services to eligible children as well as their families would improve the families' abilities to care for their children. 20 U.S.C. § 1471(a) (1988). This last congressional finding highlights one of the notable differences between the special education and early intervention systems: special education programming solely focuses on the needs of and programming for the individual child or student, whereas the Early Intervention Program aims to enhance not only the individual child's capacity but also the capacity of families of children with disabilities to address their young children's special needs. 20 U.S.C. § 1431(a)(1)-(5).

Because the Early Intervention Program was developed as an amendment to the EHA, the IDEA's predecessor, it too is Spending Clause legislation. As such, Congress provides states with financial incentives to run an Early Intervention Program, and states have the opportunity to opt out if they so choose. Unfortunately, federal financial incentives cover only a small percentage of the total program costs, thus the majority of funding for Early Intervention Programs comes from state budgets. Currently, every state, as well as the District of Columbia, operates an Early Intervention Program.

In exchange for federal funding, each state must designate a "lead agency" to administer the

---

[1] This chapter was written by Jennifer N. Rosen Valverde, Clinical Professor of Law, Special Education Clinic, Rutgers-Newark School of Law.

Early Intervention Program. 20 U.S.C. § 1435(a)(10). Responsibilities of the lead agency include identifying and coordinating available resources, coordinating evaluations and the provision of early intervention services, resolving disputes within the lead agency and between the lead and other agencies, and ensuring that the state abides by the mandates set forth in the Act and corresponding implementing regulations. 20 U.S.C. § 1435(a)(10). The lead agency may be a division of the educational agency that also oversees the special education programming for the state or territory, such as the District of Columbia's Office of the State Superintendent of Education, Department of Special Education, DC Early Intervention Program; or it may be another state agency such as the Department of Health and Senior Services in New Jersey, the California Department of Developmental Services, the Division of Public Health in North Carolina's Department of Health and Human Services or Ohio's Department of Health. In some ways, housing the Early Intervention Program in the state's department of health or developmental services improves service provision to infants and toddlers and their families because these agencies oversee other potentially relevant programs, such as Medicaid and Supplemental Security Income. However, placing the Early Intervention Program in a different agency from a state department of education may adversely affect a child's transition into special education at age three, because the existence of multiple agencies can increase the potential for children to fall through the cracks or for disputes between agencies to arise.

The early intervention process parallels the special education process in many ways, from the duty to abide by child find requirements to planning for transition when children exit the system. Each step in the early intervention process is discussed in more detail below.

I. CHILD FIND

The lead agency is responsible for putting in place a comprehensive system to locate, identify and evaluate all eligible infants and toddlers. 20 U.S.C. § 1435(a)(5); 34 C.F.R. § 303.321.[2] As part of its child find system, each state must coordinate with other major state agencies, including education, health and social service programs, to ensure that all eligible children are found, including children who are wards of the state and children who are homeless. 34 C.F.R. § 303.321(c). In addition, the lead agency must promote the participation of "primary referral sources" in the child find process. 20 U.S.C. § 1435(a)(5). "Primary referral sources" include hospitals, physicians, parents, day care programs, local educational agencies and other health care and social service providers. 34 C.F.R. § 303.321(d).

In conjunction with its child find duties, the lead agency must implement a public awareness campaign, which includes developing and disseminating information about early intervention across the state, including the referral and evaluation process, available services, and the rights of infants and toddlers and their families. 34 C.F.R. § 303.320. This information must be distributed to relevant state agencies as well as to all primary referral sources, including parents, so that they are aware of the system and knowledgeable about how to access it. 34 C.F.R. § 303.320; 34 C.F.R. § 303.321.

---

[2] In this chapter, we utilize the Federal Regulations adopted in 1999 since, to date, the proposed Part C regulations following IDEA 2004 have not been finalized. The 1999 regulations remain in effect unless they conflict with IDEA 2004.

Unfortunately, the quality of child find efforts and public awareness campaigns varies among states and even within states, resulting in a failure to identify, evaluate and provide services to many eligible infants and toddlers and their families who so desperately need them. For example, New Jersey falls below the nationwide average in identifying eligible infants between the ages of birth and one, having identified and served only 0.56% of all infants in this age group with the national average at just shy of 1.0%. *See* Sarah V. Mitchell & Jennifer M. Halper, *New Jersey's Early Intervention Program: The Need for Fiscal Reform and Long Term Financing*, New Jersey Protection & Advocacy (March 2008). The State of Illinois's failure to fully implement a comprehensive child find system was one of several issues addressed by the court in the case of *Marie O. v. Edgar*, 1996 U.S. Dist. LEXIS 1070 (N.D. Ill., Feb. 2, 1996), *aff'd*, 131 F.3d 610 (7th Cir. 1997).

MARIE O. v. EDGAR[3]
No. 94 C 1471, 1996 U.S. Dist. LEXIS 1070 (N.D. Ill., Feb. 2, 1996), *aff'd*, 131 F.3d 610 (7th Cir. 1997)

CHARLES P. KOCORAS, DISTRICT JUDGE:

This matter is before the court on the parties' cross motions for summary judgment. For the reasons set forth below, the plaintiffs' motion is granted. The defendants' motion is denied.

BACKGROUND

This action arises out of the state of Illinois' alleged failure to provide critical early intervention services to developmentally-delayed infants and toddlers. The plaintiffs purport to represent a class of infants and toddlers who are eligible for but not receiving the educational and developmental services needed to prevent or ameliorate their developmental-delay and other disabling conditions. Part H of the Individuals with Disabilities Education Act ("IDEA"), 20 U.S.C. § 1471 et seq. ("Part H") provides the statutory framework around which these services are to be structured. The present case involves roughly 26,000 eligible children whom the plaintiffs maintain are not presently receiving the early intervention services to which they are allegedly entitled under Part H. Part H is a federal program pursuant to which federal funds are granted to states developing and implementing coordinated systems for the provision of early intervention services to developmentally-delayed infants and toddlers. Congress enacted Part H for the purpose of addressing five "urgent and substantial" needs:

(1) to enhance the development of handicapped infants and toddlers and to minimize their potential for developmental delay,

(2) to reduce the educational costs to our society, including our Nation's schools, by minimizing the need for special education and related services after handicapped infants and toddlers reach school age,

---

[3] This version of the case has been edited.

(3) to minimize the likelihood of institutionalization of individuals with disabilities and maximize the potential for their independent living in society,

(4) to enhance the capacity of families to meet the special needs of their infants and toddlers with disabilities, and

(5) to enhance the capacity of State and local agencies and service providers to identify, evaluate, and meet the needs of historically unrepresented populations, particularly minority, low-income, innercity, and rural populations.

20 U.S.C. § 1471(a)(1)-(5).

In 1987, the State of Illinois opted to participate in the Part H program, and since that time, Illinois has received more than $34 million dollars in federal funds for use in planning and implementing a coordinated statewide system of service. Upon entering into its fifth year of participation in the program, Part H requires assurances in a state's application for federal funds that the state has in effect a statewide system providing early intervention services to all eligible infants and toddlers with disabilities and their families. 20 U.S.C. §§ 1475(c) and 1476(a). On September 23, 1991, the Illinois Early Intervention Services System Act, 325 ILCS 20/1 et seq. ("the Illinois Act"), became effective. On December 1, 1992, Illinois began its fifth year of participation in Part H, thus allegedly requiring Illinois under federal law to serve all eligible infants and toddlers.

The plaintiffs allege that Illinois has not complied with several components of Part H. Among other shortcomings, the plaintiffs allege that the state has failed "to develop policies and procedures for standards for training early intervention personnel, has not established a procedure securing timely reimbursement of funds used to provide services, and has not established a system for compiling data on the numbers of infants and toddlers with disabilities in need of services, the number served, and the types of services provided." See Class Action Complaint, ¶ 33. According to the plaintiffs, Illinois was required by federal law to have these policies, procedures, and services implemented at the beginning of Illinois' fifth year of participation in the Part H program. Instead, numerous eligible children have been placed on waiting lists for services. The plaintiffs allege that as a result of the state's noncompliance, the plaintiffs have been denied adequate early intervention services to which they are allegedly entitled under Part H.

The plaintiffs bring this action on their own behalf, and on behalf of all others similarly situated, seeking declaratory and injunctive relief. Plaintiffs seek a judgment declaring that the defendants' acts and omissions are in violation of the rights of the plaintiffs and other similarly situated Illinois children under both Part H and 42 U.S.C. § 1983. The plaintiffs further seek an injunction directing the defendants "to recognize Part H as an entitlement for all eligible children, begin providing early intervention services to all children entitled by law to those services, and bring the State of Illinois into compliance with the components of a statewide system of early intervention required under Part H." In addition, the plaintiffs seek an award of attorneys' fees and costs as allowed under 42 U.S.C. § 1988. Both parties have moved for summary judgment.

LEGAL STANDARD

[The court summarizes the summary judgment standard.]

It is in consideration of these principles that we examine the parties' motions.

DISCUSSION

The plaintiffs brought this action pursuant to 42 U.S.C. § 1983, alleging violations of Part H of the Individuals With Disabilities Education Act ("IDEA"), 20 U.S.C. § 1471 et seq. [Court quotes Section 1983.] 42 U.S.C. § 1983. [Court discusses why it concludes a cause of action exists under Section 1983.] Since Congress has expressed an intention for a private right of action to exist under § 1983 for violations of the IDEA and Part H is an unequivocal component of the IDEA, we reaffirm our previous conclusion that Part H of the IDEA may be enforceable under 42 U.S.C. § 1983.

As presented by the plaintiffs, the matter before the court is simple. Illinois has voluntarily chosen to participate in Part H. As a participant in the federal program, Illinois is required to provide certain services to all eligible children. Illinois' failure to adequately accomplish this renders the state liable. Although we agree with the defendants that the realities surrounding full compliance with the mandates of Part H are not quite as straightforward as the plaintiffs suggest, we are nonetheless obligated to follow the law, and the law on the issue ultimately favors the plaintiffs.

Part H defines two groups of infants and toddlers who must be served by a state's early intervention system and one group which a state may, at its discretion, choose to serve. 20 U.S.C. § 1472(1). The two groups which must be served by a state's early intervention system are defined as "infants and toddlers with disabilities" from birth to age 2, inclusive, who need early intervention services because they —

> (A) are experiencing developmental delays, as measured by appropriate diagnostic instruments and procedures in one or more of the following areas: cognitive development, physical development, language and speech development, psychosocial development, or self-help skills, or

> (B) have a diagnosed physical or mental condition which has a high probability of resulting in developmental delay.

20 U.S.C. § 1472. In addition, a state may, at its option, elect to serve "individuals from birth to age 2, inclusive, who are at risk of having substantial developmental delays if early intervention services are not provided." 20 U.S.C. § 1472(1). The Illinois Act provides that all three groups of children are eligible for early intervention services in Illinois. 325 ILCS § 20/3.

As specified by Part H, the "early intervention services" which a state is required to provide include family training, counseling, home visits, special instruction, speech pathology and audiology, occupational therapy, physical therapy, vision services, psychological services, case management services, diagnostic medical services, assistive technology, early identification and screening services, and transportation. 20 U.S.C. § 1472(2)(E). Moreover, these services are to be provided by specially qualified personnel and at no cost (except where federal or state law provides). 20 U.S.C. § 1472(2)(B) and (F).

Section 1476(2) of the federal statute sets forth the early intervention programs which a state is to have in effect by the beginning of its fifth year of participation in Part H. According to this section, a "statewide system of coordinated, comprehensive, multidisciplinary, inter-agency programs providing appropriate early intervention services to all infants and toddlers with disabilities and their families shall include, . . . at a minimum":

* * *

(2) timetables for ensuring that appropriate early intervention services will be available to all infants and toddlers with disabilities in the State . . . ,

(3) a timely, comprehensive, multidisciplinary evaluation of the functioning of each infant and toddler with a disability in the State and the needs of the families to appropriately assist in the development of the infant or toddler with a disability,

(4) for each infant and toddler with a disability in the State, an individualized family service plan . . . including case management services in accordance with such service plan,

(5) a comprehensive child find system, . . . including a system for making referrals to service providers that includes timelines and provides for participation by primary referral sources,

(6) a public awareness program . . . ,

(7) a central directory which includes early intervention services, resources, and experts available in the State and research and demonstration projects being conducted in the State,

(8) a comprehensive system of personnel development,

* * *

(11) a procedure for securing timely reimbursement of funds . . . ,

* * *

(12) procedural safeguards with respect to the programs under this subchapter . . . ,

* * *

(14) a system for compiling data on the numbers of infants and toddlers with disabilities and their families in the State in need of appropriate early intervention services. . . .

20 U.S.C. § 1476(b). As a prerequisite for continued federal funding under Part H (commencing the fifth year of participation and for each year thereafter), the state must file an application providing "information and assurances demonstrating to the satisfaction of the Secretary that the State has in effect the statewide system required by section 1476 of this title and a description of services to be provided . . . ." 20 U.S.C. § 1475(c). On December 1, 1992, Illinois began its fifth year of participation in Part H. Although the deficiencies in implementation to which the plaintiffs cite are necessarily detailed in the state's yearly application for funding, to

date, Illinois has not been denied federal funds.

The plaintiffs set forth some disturbing statistics as to the numbers of children who are purportedly not receiving the full range of services afforded them under Part H. According to the plaintiffs, at any one point in time, only about one-fourth of the eligible population of disabled youngsters is being serviced under Part H in Illinois. Hundreds and hundreds of Illinois children are routinely placed on waiting lists for Part H services. Moreover, the state has reportedly been delinquent in its efforts to identify and evaluate the needs of all of the state's eligible children. By allowing these circumstances to exist, the plaintiffs maintain that these children have been denied early intervention services at a time critical to their future development. Supported by statements of representatives in the United States Department of Education, the plaintiffs assert that Part H is an entitlement program and that at the start of a state's fifth year of participation in Part H, a state must have in place fully implemented program under which all eligible children are receiving services.[4] This, the plaintiffs maintain, the defendants have plainly failed to do.

In establishing a statewide system of service, Part H affords a considerable amount of discretion to the state. The state may, for example, elect whether to serve children in the "at risk" population, 20 U.S.C. § 1472(1), and state law may also impact who pays for the services under Part H. 20 U.S.C. § 1472(2)(B). The Illinois Act, which went into effect on September 23, 1991, in many ways mirrors Part H and establishes as a matter of state law the system requirements embodied in Part H. Section 20/7 of the Illinois Act, for example, incorporates many of the requirements set forth in 20 U.S.C. § 1476(b), explicitly referencing the federal laws and regulations. 325 ILCS 20/7. The Illinois Act, however, further provides:

> Within 60 days of the effective date of this Act, a five-fiscal-year implementation plan shall be submitted to the Governor by the lead agency with the concurrence of the Interagency Council on Early Intervention. The plan shall list specific activities to be accomplished each year, with cost estimates for each activity. . . .

325 ILCS 20/7. Having become effective in late 1991, the Illinois Act, by its own terms, does not contemplate full implementation until late 1996. The defendants note that this five-year time

---

[4] [1] A March, 1990 policy memorandum issued by Dr. Judy A. Schrag, former Director of the Office of Special Education Programs, United States Department of Education states:

> Part H is an entitlement program. This means that subject to specific provisions in the Act and regulations, each eligible child in a State and the child's family are entitled to receive the rights, procedural safeguards, and services that are authorized to be provided under a State's early intervention program.

> Each State must ensure that appropriate early intervention services will be available to all eligible children in the State no later than the beginning of the fifth year of a State's participation in Part H.

March 1990, Policy Memorandum by Judy A. Schrag, Ed.D, Director of Office of Special Education Programs, (1 Early Childhood Law and Policy Reporter ("ECLPR") P 10) (3/20/90).

In 1988, G. Thomas Bellamey, former Director of the Office of Special Education Programs for the United States Department of Education responded to an inquiry as follows:

> H is interpreted to be an entitlement program on behalf of each eligible child and Part the child's family, based on statutory provisions.

Response by G. Thomas Bellamey, Ph.D., Director, Office of Special Education Programs (1 ECLPR P 38) (12/20/88).

Finally, Dr. Thomas Hehir, the current Director of the Office of Special Education Programs of the United States Department of Education, stated the following:

> States in full implementation of the Part H early intervention program are required to provide appropriate early intervention services to all children who are eligible and their families.

Response by Thomas Hehir, Director, Office of Special Education Programs (2 ECLPR P 59) (11/30/93).

frame for implementation has never been raised by the United States Department of Education as being inconsistent with the state's federal obligations under Part H.

Consistent with the state's ongoing efforts at implementation, a new Central Billing Office ("CBO"), designed "to receive and dispense all relevant State and federal resources, as well as local government or independent resources available, for early intervention services," is presently being developed. 325 ILCS 20/13. Under the new system, individualized family service plans ("IFSP") will be standardized state-wide,[5] enabling the family to seek out services from any provider it chooses (whether under Part H or not). Moreover, a more equitable distribution of funds will ensue, because funds will be spent on a fee-for-service basis rather than to providers in lump sum grants. The CBO will also provide a means by which to fully utilize available Medicaid funds, significantly increasing the funds brought into the early intervention system. Although the CBO is not yet implemented, the defendants attest that the State Board is presently attempting to begin experimental operations of the CBO in certain regions of the state.

Section 1476 of Part H requires that a state have a statewide system in place to serve all eligible children. Although not yet fully implemented, the defendants attest that Illinois has a statewide system. As summarized in its Year 7 Annual Report, Illinois at present serves thousands of children in all parts of the state. Forty-five Local Interagency Councils exist throughout the state, and numerous committees are devoted to personnel standards, public awareness, and financial issues. An interagency staff team works on early intervention issues. Numerous state agency officials and departments participate in the statewide early intervention system, in addition to the over 100 providers of services (56 receiving Part H funds) throughout the state.

However, surveys conducted by the Illinois State Board of Education have indicated that the early intervention system needs more capacity. Children are routinely placed on waiting lists for services. The plaintiffs take issue with a portion of the Illinois Act which states that the Act shall be implemented "as appropriated funds become available." See 325 ILCS 20/14. However, as the defendants submit, financial considerations account for only part of the problem. It is not disputed that outside resources such as private insurance and Medicaid are tremendously under-utilized under the present system. Nevertheless, even if the federal and state funds devoted to early intervention services were greatly increased, a state and national shortage of professionally trained personnel still would remain. Moreover, even if there was sufficient personnel to accommodate the mandates of Part H, additional problems would emerge as to their proper distribution. Difficulties exist in attracting doctors to rural areas. A conspicuous

---

[5] Although the IDEA does not set forth any specific timelines under which a family must receive an IFSP, the Code of Federal Regulations do so provide. The plaintiffs moreover suggest that the state's failure to abide by the regulations in this regard constitutes a violation of § 1983. The Circuits are at present split on the issue of whether a violation of a federal regulation may be cognizable under § 1983 . . . . We do, however, take note of a dissenting opinion written by Justice O'Connor in *Wright v. Roanoke Redev. & Housing Authority*, 479 U.S. 418 (1987), which expresses concern over such a possibility:

> . . . it is necessary to ask whether administrative regulations *alone* could create such a right. This is a troubling issue not briefed by the parties, and I do not attempt to resolve it here. . . . I am concerned, however, that lurking behind the Court's analysis may be the view that, once it has been found that a statute creates some enforceable right, *any* regulation adopted within the purview of the statute creates rights enforceable in federal courts, regardless of whether Congress or the promulgating agency ever contemplated such a result. . . . Such a result, where determination of § 1983 "rights" has been unleashed from any connection to congressional intent, is troubling indeed.

Id. at 479 U.S. 437-38 (emphasis in original).

consequence of this is the dearth of professionals involved in early intervention services in parts of southern Illinois.

Section 1476 declares that a statewide system must serve "all" infants and toddlers with disabilities. *See* 20 U.S.C. § 1476. However, a strict reading of the term "all" cannot conform to present realities. In a report prepared by the National Early Childhood Technical Assistance System ("NECTAS") at the University of North Carolina, an agency providing technical assistance to the states on early intervention services, a 1995 briefing paper in a section entitled "Moving Part H into the 21st Century" stated:

> The promises and expectations of Part H of IDEA, although not fully realized, have become a reality, through the development of partnerships among families, governmental agencies, and public and private providers. Through continued needed resources, the intent of the law — a contract with American citizens to meet the needs of their infants and children with disabilities and families — will be fully realized in the next century.

As indicated by this report, the notion of serving "all" eligible children is understood to be a goal to be attained in the future. It is not — and indeed cannot be — a rigid legal standard activated on a state's first day of full participation in Part H. Given the breadth of the requirements set forth in Part H, it is doubtful if any state could ever meet such a standard as the plaintiffs suggest. By consistently approving the state's annual application for federal funding of its early intervention system, the federal government has not held Illinois to so rigid a standard. Given the practicalities of the situation, neither should we.

That is not to say, however, that the plaintiffs are not entitled to relief. Part H was enacted by Congress with the desire that, by encouraging states to develop and implement coordinated systems for the provision of early intervention services to developmentally-delayed infants and toddlers, the disabilities which these children ultimately experience might be lessened or suspended. In its efforts to relay the importance of these goals, Congress expressly chose to frame Part H in definite, explicit terms, declaring that, after five years, a state "shall" have in effect "at a minimum" certain programs serving "all" eligible children. Recognizing the value which such a system might provide, Illinois, in 1987, voluntarily elected to participate in Part H. Illinois subsequently set about creating a statewide system in accordance with the provisions of Part H. Illinois' efforts at implementation, however, have been far from perfect.

Section 1475 of the federal statute contemplates that, by the beginning of its fifth year of participation in Part H, a state must have in place the minimum components enumerated in 20 U.S.C. § 1476. However, as suggested above, rigid enforcement under such a timetable would render state participation in Part H a virtual impossibility. Still, the mandates of the statute must not be neglected. Meaningful compliance by the state, at the very least, should be required by the state's fifth year. Eight years into the Part H program, Illinois' efforts remain well below this standard.

The plaintiffs seek an injunction by this court, recognizing Part H as an entitlement to all eligible children and directing the state to begin providing early intervention services to all eligible children and to bring the state of Illinois into full compliance with the requirements of Part H. Although the practical impact of this court's intervention to achieve these goals remains unclear, we nevertheless are obligated under the law to honor the plaintiffs' request to become involved. The state's failure, for example, to adequately develop and implement programs which train early intervention personnel and seek out and inform eligible youngsters of available services must not be condoned. The regularity with which disabled children are placed on waiting lists for services and evaluations — some waiting for up to one year — should not be tolerated. The existence of waiting lists is especially tragic given that the time lost is so often critical to the future development of these disabled youngsters.

As the opinion above reflects, certain problems in implementation are inevitable. We remain ever mindful of this reality. However, after eight years of "dragging its feet" the state needs to do better. Critical to the future of Part H is the continued participation of the state, and we recognize that judicial intervention which might ultimately threaten this participation may not be a step forward. As the above cited NECTAS report indicates, the goal of Part H is to create an entitlement which will be fully realized in the next century. That is not to say, however, that the thousands of disabled infants and toddlers in Illinois *today* are not entitled to reap the benefits of Part H. The statutory language makes no mention of the next century. To the contrary, Part H bestows upon the state five years. After eight years without meaningful compliance, court intervention has thus become justified. Summary judgment will be entered in favor of the plaintiffs. The defendants' motion for summary judgment is denied.

CONCLUSION

For the reasons set forth above, the plaintiff's motion for summary judgment is granted. The defendants motion for summary judgment is denied.

In light of the court's decision in *Marie O*, and your understanding of the statutory requirements, consider the following hypothetical:

Jeanne Joseph

You are the advocate for Jean-Michel Joseph, the parent of an infant, Jeanne Joseph. Mr. Joseph emigrated from Haiti to the U.S. approximately three years ago — his primary language is Creole, and you communicate with him via an interpreter. Mrs. Joseph, Jeanne's mother, returned to Haiti to care for her ailing mother when Jeanne was three months old. She remains there today.

According to Mr. Joseph, Jeanne developed severe jaundice shortly after birth. He did not recognize this to be a problem, and as a result Jeanne did not receive light and other therapy for several days. Jeanne is now 14 months old and experiencing developmental delays in several areas. Mr. Joseph first had concerns about Jeanne's development when she was approximately six months old because she was unable to roll over, did not reach for objects and could not sit up. He described her as "floppy." Mr. Joseph states that he tried to ask about these issues during Jeanne's "brief" pediatrician visits but nothing ever came of it.

Recently, Mr. Joseph learned about the possibility of accessing services through the state's Early Intervention Program from another parent at the daycare center Jeanne attends. He tells you that Jeanne's pediatrician's office and daycare center have some pamphlets and informational brochures about dental hygiene, immunizations and a few other topics, but nothing on early intervention.

1. Is anyone responsible for Mr. Joseph's lack of information about the Early Intervention Program? Who? Why?

2. Who/what agency(ies) may be held responsible for the lack of information? How?

3. Following the court's reasoning in *Marie O.*, how far does a state's child find duty extend? Are there limitations? Explain.

4. Do you think the court make the wrong decision? Should full compliance be excused? If yes, to what degree? Should this be expressed in the law? How?

5. What remedy should be available for children who are not identified, evaluated and provided with Early Intervention services in a timely fashion? How would you go about quantifying the remedy?

II. REFERRAL

The state lead agency must have in place a referral process so that infants and toddlers identified as potentially eligible for early intervention are referred for an evaluation. 34 C.F.R. § 303.321(d). Anyone may refer a child to the Early Intervention Program for an evaluation if he or she has concerns about the development of a child between the ages of birth and three, because parental consent is not required for a referral; however, written parental consent is required for an early intervention evaluation to be conducted. 34 C.F.R. § 303.404(a)(1). Therefore, the discussion in Chapter Two on defining the "parent" for special education purposes applies herein as well.

DEVELOPMENTAL AGES AND STAGES FOR 0-3

(This is meant as a guide only)

Ages 0-5 months:

- Moves arms and legs
- Lifts head and raises chest
- Focuses/follows objects with eyes
- Smiles, laughs, coos
- Rolls over one way

Ages 6-11 months:

- Keeps head up when pulled up
- Bears some weight on legs
- Sits up without support
- Looks for dropped object
- Reaches for toy
- Feeds self cracker
- Pulls up from sitting to standing with support
- Plays peek-a-boo
- Understands "no"

Ages 12-17 months:

- Walks with support
- Claps hands
- Indicates wants/needs without crying
- Waves good-bye
- Uses "mama" and "dada" intentionally
- Follows one step verbal commands
- Imitates
- Scribbles
- Uses two words
- Drinks from a cup

For parents and others to know whether to refer a child, they must familiarize themselves with developmental ages and stages so that they can identify whether a child is developing at the proper pace. Without knowledge about child development, parents must rely on the expertise of others with whom their child comes into contact, including physicians, health care professionals, and day care providers to identify whether concerns exist and warrant a referral to the Early Intervention Program.

Federal regulations require that primary referral sources refer children to the Early Intervention Program "no more than two working days after a child has been identified" as potentially eligible. 34 C.F.R. § 300.321(d)(2)(ii). The stringent timeline is based on recognition that time is of the essence due to the rapid pace of physical and mental development for young children. Despite this recognition, primary referral sources commonly fail to adhere to the timeline, in large part because they are unaware of it; moreover, noncompliance typically goes unpunished. As a result, many children are not identified until concerns become significant and/or unmanageable, which, for some children, may not occur until years pass and, ultimately, may be too late for the child to regain much of what has been lost.

DEVELOPMENTAL AGES AND STAGES FOR 0-3 CONTINUED

(This is meant as a guide only)

Ages 18-24 months:

- Points to desired object
- Uses more and more words
- Uses fork and spoon
- Runs and walks up steps
- Builds towers with cubes
- Kicks a small ball forward
- Puts on and takes off some clothing
- Feeds a doll
- Identifies 2 items in a picture by pointing
- Points to body parts

Ages 2-3 years:

- Expanded vocabulary using combined words
- Identifies picture by naming it
- Jumps
- Brushes teeth
- Washes and dries hands
- Calls a friend by name
- Throws a ball overhand
- Converses in 2-3 word sentences and can be understood

In the 2004 version of the IDEA (called the "Individuals with Disabilities Education Improvement Act"), Congress, for the first time, specifically identified two populations of children under age three for whom early intervention referrals are now mandatory: children "involved in a substantiated case of child abuse or neglect" and children who are "identified as affected by illegal substance abuse, or withdrawal symptoms resulting from prenatal drug exposure." 20 U.S.C. § 1437(a)(6)(A)-(B). The state lead agency must have in place policies and procedures that require the referral of these two groups of children to the Early Intervention Program regardless of whether anyone suspects they have disabilities or developmental delays. A smooth referral process for children who fall into these two categories requires quality communication and collaboration between the early intervention and child welfare and health care systems, which in many states does not exist. Thus, cross-systems advocacy is essential for this population (see Chapter Eight for discussion on the overlap between the child welfare and special education systems as many of the same issues apply herein).

Each state has in place a referral process, which typically requires the referring individual to contact the lead agency administering the Early Intervention Program, relay to them the concerns he or she has about the child warranting a referral, and provide key information about the child, including name, birth date, and address. Unlike the special education system, which requires written referrals, early intervention referrals may be made by phone. However, good legal practice dictates that referrals be made in writing with a copy saved to evidence the date of referral and that the referral actually was made.

SAMPLE EI REFERRAL LETTER

Date _____

Early Intervention Program for the State of _____

To Whom It May Concern (address to lead agency referral coordinator for your state):

My name is (state name) and I am the (state relationship to child) of / for (state name of child), who was born on (state child's birth date). I am concerned about my child's development and request that s/he be evaluated by the Early Intervention program. I understand that you are required to conduct a full, multidisciplinary evaluation of my child within 45 calendar days of this referral. Please contact me at (state phone number) once you receive this letter so that we may discuss the evaluation process. Thank you for your prompt attention to and assistance with this matter.

  Sincerely,

Once the lead agency receives the referral, it assigns a service coordinator to help the family understand the Early Intervention Program, navigate the evaluation and eligibility process, and inform the family of their rights and the state's responsibilities with respect to the child. 34 C.F.R. § 303.23(a)-(b). The service coordinator serves as the family's liaison with the early intervention system. 34 C.F.R. § 303.23(a)(2)(ii).

Consider the following hypothetical:

Lucy

The head nurse of a pediatric neonatal intensive care unit (NICU) in a local area hospital contacts you, an advocate, about an infant named Lucy who was abandoned in the hospital NICU at birth. Lucy is now six months old, and the local child welfare agency is searching for a special needs foster home in which to place her. Physicians have diagnosed Lucy with fetal alcohol syndrome and developmental delays, but believe that Lucy is ready to leave the hospital. In the developmental pediatrician's opinion, Lucy will require early intervention services wherever she is placed.

1. Who is responsible for making the referral to the Early Intervention Program?

2. When should Lucy be/have been referred to the Early Intervention Program?

3. What information should be provided at the time of referral?

4. Once the referral is made, who may consent to an early intervention evaluation for Lucy? Who/what entity is responsible for identifying someone to consent to the evaluation?

5. Does your answer to Question 4 change if Lucy's mother or father resurfaces? How?

6. How does the situation change, if at all, if Lucy is placed in the home of her maternal grandmother? The home of a foster parent?

7. Does Lucy's mother or father have the right to refuse to consent to an early intervention evaluation? If Lucy's grandmother is caring for her, does she have a right to refuse to consent to an early intervention evaluation? What about a non-relative foster parent caring for Lucy?

III. EVALUATIONS

The IDEA requires that states ensure "a timely, comprehensive, multidisciplinary evaluation of the functioning of each infant or toddler with a disability in the State, and a family-directed identification of the needs of each family of such an infant or toddler, to assist appropriately in the development of the infant or toddler." 20 U.S.C. § 1435(a)(3). Federal regulations mandate that the lead agency complete a multidisciplinary evaluation of the child and family and hold a meeting to determine the child's eligibility for early intervention *within 45 days of receiving the referral*. 34 C.F.R. § 303.321(e). Significantly, the 45-day evaluation timeline for early intervention commences on the date the referral is received; in contrast, the 60-day evaluation timeline for special education commences on the date that written parental consent to evaluate is obtained. The shorter early intervention timeline again reflects Congress's recognition that timing is critical when addressing the special needs of young children. Only in the event of exceptional circumstances that make it impossible for the lead agency to adhere to this timeline (e.g., child too ill to be tested, parental noncompliance) may a state exceed the 45 days allotted for evaluation. 34 C.F.R. § 303.322(e)(2).

The multidisciplinary evaluation must include a review of the child's health and medical records and history, and an assessment of the child's unique strengths and needs in each of the five developmental domains: physical, cognitive, communication, social/emotional and adaptive behavior. 20 U.S.C. § 1436(a)(1); 34 C.F.R. § 303.322(c)(3). The Early Intervention Program also must offer to conduct a family-directed assessment of the "resources, priorities, and concerns of the family." 20 U.S.C. § 1436(a)(2). The purpose of the family-directed assessment is to determine the supports and services that the family needs to enhance its ability to care for the child and meet his/her developmental needs. 34 C.F.R. § 303.322(b)(2)(ii). The family assessment is voluntary, and parents may opt not to undergo the family assessment while still having their child evaluated for early intervention services. 34 C.F.R. § 303.322(d)(2).

Federal regulations require that qualified personnel conduct the evaluation and assessment, with professional qualifications set by the states. 34 C.F.R. § 303.361. In addition, evaluation and assessment must be based on informed clinical opinion. 34 C.F.R. § 303.322(c). Informed clinical opinion typically is defined as a judgment regarding the child's developmental status made by a qualified practitioner acting within his or her scope of practice, using methods and techniques that are well-recognized in the practitioner's discipline. States also must ensure that evaluation and assessment procedures are racially and culturally non-discriminatory, and are conducted in the child and family's native language or other mode of communication "unless it is clearly not feasible to do so." 34 C.F.R. § 303.323(a)-(b). The state may not rely on a single procedure or tool as the sole basis on which to determine a child's eligibility for early intervention, 34 C.F.R. § 303.323(c), as multidisciplinary is defined, for purposes of the Act, as "the involvement of two or more disciplines or professions in the provision of integrated and coordinated services, including evaluation and assessment activities . . . ." 34 C.F.R. § 303.17.

Unlike special education, the IDEA provides no right to parents to request independent evaluations for early intervention purposes at state expense. Parents may still seek out independent evaluations by paying for them out-of-pocket or using health insurance where available. The Early Intervention Program must consider any outside reports submitted by the family in determining a child's early intervention eligibility and programming; however, the Early Intervention Program need not adopt any findings or recommendations made by independent evaluators. Although the IDEA includes no provisions for independent evaluations at state expense in early intervention matters, in the event that a parent disagrees with either the quality of an early intervention evaluation or the findings and recommendations made in a report, the parent may challenge the report using one of three dispute resolution mechanisms in place (discussed in more detail below), and request that the state pay for an independent evaluation as the remedy.

Consider the following hypothetical:

Sandra Rivera

You have just conducted your first intake interview with Mr. Rivera, father of Sandra, who is two years old. Mr. Rivera recently referred Sandra for an early intervention evaluation and would like your assistance at the evaluation planning meeting so that the proper evaluations are performed in assessing her eligibility.

According to Mr. Rivera, Sandra's medical and developmental history is as follows:

During her mother's first prenatal ultrasound, at approximately 17 weeks, doctors detected two plexus cysts in Sandra's brain. According to Mr. Rivera, plexus cysts develop when air pockets exist in the brain. The doctors informed Mr. and Mrs. Rivera that Sandra might be born with Down's syndrome or have other side effects. However, by the time of her birth, the cysts had disappeared.

Sandra was born prematurely at approximately 33 weeks. She was a breach presentation, necessitating delivery by cesarean section, and weighed 6 lbs., 1 oz. at birth. Mr. and Mrs. Rivera had concerns about Sandra's development immediately after birth, as Sandra exhibited oral motor difficulties and was unable to breastfeed; she did not like to be held; she lacked expression (she never smiled); and she also was very lethargic.

Shortly after she was born, the Riveras had to take Sandra to the emergency room on two occasions because she had blood in her stool. Sandra did not maintain her birth weight, which resulted in her being placed on a special amino acid base formula that she still takes today. Sandra participated in a feeding clinic until she was one year old.

Since birth, Sandra has had pneumonia three times. Doctors have diagnosed her with asthma requiring the use of a nebulizer, digestive issues, and severe constipation. Mr. Rivera informs you that Sandra bangs her head on the wall and floor and bites herself at times.

Developmentally, Sandra did not roll over until she was 6 months old. She began babbling "mama" and "dada" at 8 months old, but stopped talking soon thereafter. She sat up independently at 11 months; however, she could not sit unattended until recently because she could not support her upper body for more than two to three minutes at a time. At 14 months, Sandra started trying to walk, but did not walk independently until recently. She knows how to use a spoon, but will not eat anything unless her father feeds it to her. The Riveras often puree Sandra's food to make it easier for her to swallow.

The Riveras speak to Sandra in both Spanish and English, with Spanish tending to be the more dominant language. According to Mr. Rivera, Sandra often appears not to understand what her parents say to her. The Riveras recently separated with Sandra living equal time at both homes. The shared custody is not a formal arrangement (i.e., court-ordered or settlement required). When you ask Mr. Rivera how Mrs. Rivera feels about getting Sandra evaluated for early intervention services, he dodges the question and you do not push him for a response.

1. Based on this information, what developmental areas are of concern and require assessment?

2. What types of evaluations would you request? Why?

3. What special factors, if any, should you consider in getting Sandra assessed?

4. What red flags, if any, are raised in the interview with respect to representation of Mr. Rivera on behalf of Sandra? How will you go about resolving them?

5. Can the lead agency require that Sandra be evaluated even if Mr. and Mrs. Rivera refuse to consent to same?

IV. ELIGIBILITY

Also within the 45-day evaluation timeline, the Early Intervention Program must hold a meeting to review the evaluation reports, determine the child's eligibility for services and, if eligible, develop an Individualized Family Service Plan ("IFSP") for the child and family.

The following individuals must participate in the initial eligibility meeting: The child's parent(s); other family members as requested by the parent(s) if feasible; an advocate if the parent so requests; the service coordinator assigned to the family; any person(s)/ professional(s) directly involved in conducting the evaluations and assessments; and person(s)/ professional(s) who will be providing services to the child and family as appropriate. 34 C.F.R. § 303.343(a)(1). If one or more of these individuals is unable to attend the meeting, arrangements must be made to include this person via either telephone conference call, having a knowledgeable authorized representative attend on the person's behalf, or making relevant records available at the meeting. 34 C.F.R. § 303.343(a)(2).

For an infant or toddler to be eligible to receive early intervention services, the child must be under three years of age and either have a developmental delay, based on measurements by appropriate diagnostic instruments and procedures (including informed clinical opinion) in one or more of the five developmental domains (cognitive, physical, communication, social-emotional, and adaptive behavior), or be diagnosed with a physical or mental condition that has a "high probability of resulting in developmental delay." 34 C.F.R. § 303.16(a). States have discretion to serve children at risk of having a substantial developmental delay if early intervention services are not provided. 34 C.F.R. § 303.16(b). Some states also have presumptive eligibility categories, whereby if a child is diagnosed with a particular condition, e.g., Fragile X syndrome, Down's Syndrome, Fetal Alcohol Syndrome, the child is automatically eligible to receive early intervention services. *See* N.J. Admin. Code 8:17-7.1(c)-(d).

The IDEA permits each state to define the term "developmental delay," resulting in significant differences among states regarding entitlement to receive services. For example, New Jersey defines "developmental delay" as having a 33% delay or falling 2.0 standard deviations below the mean in one developmental area, or a 25% delay or falling 1.5 standard deviations below the mean in two or more areas. N.J. Admin. Code 8:17-1.3; N.J. Admin. Code 8:17-7.1(b). New Jersey does not serve "at risk" children. North Carolina has a similar definition, with the exception that the developmental delay in one area need only be a 30% delay. *See* North Carolina Infant-Toddler Program Policy Bulletin #18, Eligibility Categories. Ohio defines developmental delay the most broadly of the five sample states/territories as having a delay of 1.5 standard deviations below the mean in one or more areas as measured by a developmental evaluation tool. Ohio Admin. Code 3701-8-03(C). In contrast, the District of Columbia defines the term most restrictively of the five sample states/territories as a delay of at least 50% or 3.0 standard deviations below the mean in one or more developmental areas. http://osse.dc.gov/seo/frames.asp?doc=/seo/lib/seo/special_education/finalcomprehensive_child _find_system_policy_3_22_2010.pdf. California defines developmental delay to include any child for whom there is a significant difference between expected and current levels of development as determined by a multidisciplinary team that includes parents, or as a child with atypical development based on informed clinical opinion. Cal. Gov't Code, Division 14, Chapter 4, 95014(a). California defines "significant difference" as a 33% delay in one developmental area for children under 24 months, and a delay of 50% in one area or 33% in two or more areas for children between 24-36 months of age. Cal. Gov't Code, Division 14, Chapter 4, 95014(a).

Consider the following hypothetical:

James

James, age two years, is evaluated for early intervention services. The multidisciplinary evaluation team finds that he is functioning like a 15-month-old in terms of physical development, as he is unable to walk without support, cannot stack blocks, nor can he feed himself finger foods or a bottle. It also finds that he functions like an 18-month-old in terms of language, saying just a few words.

1. Applying the eligibility definitions for each of the five states discussed above to the fact pattern, is James eligible for early intervention services? If yes, in which state(s)?

2. Should states be permitted to define early intervention eligibility? Why should this process differ from determining special education eligibility? Is it fair for a child and family to be eligible to receive services in one state but not in another?

3. Draft federal legislation defining eligibility for early intervention from both a parent and EI system perspective. How will you measure eligibility? Who will measure it? Will at-risk children be included in your definition? How will you define this term?

V. INDIVIDUALIZED FAMILY SERVICES PLAN (IFSP)

Once the IFSP team finds a child eligible for early intervention services, it develops an IFSP for the child and family. This plan serves as the roadmap for services the child and family will receive and acts as a contract between the state and family whereby the state is obligated to provide all of the services at the rates and frequencies specified therein unless the IFSP states otherwise. Notably, the parent is an equal member of the IFSP team and must have the opportunity to participate in the development of the IFSP. 20 U.S.C. § 1436(a)(3).

Federal law and regulations provide a lengthy list of the mandatory contents of an IFSP. 20 U.S.C. § 1436(d); 34 C.F.R. § 303.344. For example, the IFSP must include a statement of the child's present levels of development in the five developmental domains, information about the family's resources, priorities and concerns regarding enhancing the child's development (provided the family agrees with including this information), and a statement of the outcomes the child and family are expected to achieve. 34 C.F.R. § 303.344(a)-(c). The IFSP also must include a statement of the specific early intervention services, including transition services, that are needed to meet the child and family's unique needs so that the outcomes are achieved; the frequency, method and intensity of service delivery; and the location (e.g., natural environment) and payment arrangements for the services. 34 C.F.R. § 303.344(d). The anticipated service start date and service duration must be documented in the IFSP as well. 34 C.F.R. § 303.344(f).

Generally speaking, it is rare for a child and family to receive early intervention services without having an IFSP in place. However, a child and family may receive early intervention services prior to completion of the evaluation and IFSP development process provided the parent(s) consent and an interim IFSP, which includes the services determined to be needed immediately by the child and family, is developed. 34 C.F.R. § 303.345.

The lead agency must review a child's IFSP every six months to monitor the child and family's progress in achieving the outcomes set forth therein, and must reevaluate the child every year. 20 U.S.C. § 1436(b). Parental consent must be obtained for an initial IFSP to go into effect. 34 C.F.R. § 303.404(a)(2). If a parent refuses to consent to a particular service, the child and family still must receive the other services for which consent has been obtained. 20 U.S.C. § 1436(e).

Every state has its own IFSP form. Reprinted here is the form used in Ohio.

Ohio Department of Health

Ohio's Individualized Family Service Plan

Help Me Grow A program of family supports and services for expectant parents, newborns, infants and toddlers and their families.

Ohio's Vision To assure that newborns, infants and toddlers have the best possible start in life.

Our vision for _____ and our family while in Help Me Grow is

Child's name	Date of Birth
Child lives with (name)	(Relationship)

Interpreter needed? ☐ Yes ☐ No   Surrogate parent ☐ Yes ☐ No

HMG Service Coordinator	Agency	
Phone	FAX	E-mail

Family Support Specialist	Phone	E-mail

Section I: Family Information and Timelines
Primary Care Giver Contact Information

☐ Parent(s) ☐ Guardian ☐ Custodial parent ☐ Foster parent (identify one)				Home telephone
First Name: Last Name:				
Address *street*	*city*	state	zip	Cell telephone
Native Language and / or communication method used Interpreter needed? ☐ Yes ☐ No	E-mail address			Work telephone

☐ Parent ☐ Guardian ☐ Foster Parent (identify one)				Home telephone
First Name: Last Name:				
Address *street*	*city*	state	zip	Cell telephone
Native Language and / or communication method used Interpreter needed? ☐ Yes ☐ No	E-mail address			Work telephone

Surrogate Parent			Home telephone
Address *street*	City	state	zip

Help Me Grow Timelines

Date of referral to HMG for ongoing services	Date of suspected delay (when applicable)	Date of developmental screening (not applicable if there is a diagnosed physical or mental condition)	Date determined eligible for ongoing HMG services
Initial IFSP IFSP review	Annual review IFSP reviews	Annual review IFSP reviews	
School District / LEA	Initial Transition Plan date	Transition Planning Conference date	
Early Track ID numbers	BCMH number	Social Security number	Medicaid number
Healthy Start / CHIP number	Primary Insurance		

Section II: **Health and Medical Information**

Child's Medical home: The doctor's office, health center or other place, you regularly take your child for check-ups, shots, or illness.

Name			Phone
Mailing Address			FAX
City	State	Zip	E-mail

Child's General Health (physical, emotional, behavioral) including: significant family, prenatal, medical or birth history or hospitalizations:

Dates of child's last well child check up?	2.	3.	4.
Are Immunizations: ☐ up to date ☐ late up to date ☐ not up to date ☐ not medically recommended			
Are there any concerns about your child's dental health? ☐ Yes ☐ No *If Yes, specify*			
Are there any concerns about your child's sleep patterns? ☐Yes ☐ No *If Yes, specify*			
Has your child been tested for lead? ☐ Yes ☐ No *If Yes, specify*			
Does your child have allergies? ☐Yes ☐ No *If Yes, specify*			
Does your child take any medications? ☐ Yes ☐ No *If Yes, specify*			
Does your child see any medical specialists? ☐ Yes ☐ No *If Yes, specify*			
Does your child have a medical diagnosis? ☐ Yes ☐ No *If Yes, specify*			
Does your child have a BCMH managing doctor? ☐ Yes ☐ No ☐ Pending if so, who is it?			
Updated health information (e.g. ear infections, immunizations, hospitalizations):			

Section III: **Present Level of My Child's Development**
This section should include all screening, evaluation and assessment information.

Child's name	Date of birth	Age Chronological Age-Adjusted

Area of Development	Screening/evaluation/assessment tool or method, * by whom and date	Results	Describe the child's strengths / needs in each area.
Cognitive / problem solving			
Physical / Gross Motor			
Physical / Fine Motor			
Communication / Language			
Personal / Socialand Emotional			
Adaptive / self help			
Vision			
Hearing			
Nutrition			

*Method means Professional Observation or Parent Report.

Updated; August 2009
HEA 7720 (03/07)

Section IV: **Family Concerns and Priorities**
Please identify your concerns and your priorities related to enhancing the development of your child.
This will assist us in developing a child or family outcome with you.

Child's name	Date of Birth

Caregiver(s) have questions about or want help
for my child in the following areas:

☐ Assistive technology or other equipment/supplies

☐ Behavior (helping my child calm down, be comfortable, getting along with others, biting, expresses feelings)

☐ Eating and drinking (sucking, breastfeeding, taking a bottle, using a spoon)

☐ Helping my child learn to read

☐ Information about diagnosis or disability

☐ Information on whether my child's condition is hereditary

☐ Language (cooing, babbling, smiling, talking and listening)

☐ Learning new things

☐ Moving around (holding head up, rolling, sitting, crawling, standing, walking)

☐ Pain or discomfort

☐ Safety in our home and other places

☐ Self Help (diapering, toileting, dressing, sleeping, other daily routines)

☐ Special health care needs

☐ Other

☐ Vision and Hearing (responding to what they hear and see)

Caregivers want information about or help with:

☐ Budgeting

☐ Childcare

☐ Discussing emotional issues for myself and child(ren)

☐ Education for myself

☐ Family conflict

☐ Finding or working with doctors or other specialists

☐ Help with insurance

☐ Housing, clothing, jobs, food, telephone

☐ Ideas for siblings, friends, extended family members

☐ Improving my parenting skills

☐ Learning how different services work and how they could work better for my family

☐ Legal

☐ Linking with other parents

☐ Managing anger

☐ Meeting my child's special health care needs

☐ Money for extra costs relating to my child's special needs

☐ Obtaining respite care

☐ Planning for the future; what to expect

☐ Recreation

☐ Safety in our home (smoke alarms, first aid supplies)

☐ Spending time with family and friends, social interaction skills

☐ Transportation services for my child or family

Comments / Priorities:

Section V: **Everyday Routines, Activities and Places (ERAP)**
It is helpful for us to know where your child regularly spends time, because young children learn best through their routines
and in activities which interest them.

A. What is a typical day like for your child and family?

B. What does your child and family like to do together?

C. What does your child and family find challenging or difficult to do? (e.g. people, activities)

Updated; August 2009
HEA 7720 (03/07)

Section VI: **Outcome**

Number _____

Child's name	Date of birth	Date Outcome written

What do we want to happen in the next 6 months? (refer to Section IV: **Family Concerns and Priorities**)

What's happening now? (include a pre-literacy and language skills as developmentally appropriate)

What supports and resources do I/we have available to achieve this outcome?

Who will help us and what strategy will they use so we can achieve our outcome? These strategies are to occur during our child/family's daily activities and routines. (refer to Section V: **Everyday Routines, Activities and Places – ERAP**)

After reviewing our outcome, my family and IFSP team, have decided:

☐ My child and / or family met this outcome.   Date of IFSP Review:_____

☐ We have partially met this outcome. Why?

☐ The outcome was not met. Why?

Updated; August 2009
HEA 7720 (03/07)

Section VII: Help Me Grow Services and Supports
This section is for all children receiving ongoing services to meet an outcome / goal identified in Section VI.

Child's name										

Service Type	Service provider name and agency	Service location	Method C, I or G (Consultant, Individual or Group)	Frequency (e.g. # times per month)	Intensity (length of session)	ERAP (If 'No' explain below)	Duration: Projected start date and end date	Actual start date	Payment Source	Outcome Number
29. Service Coordination						☐ Yes / ☐ No				
						☐ Yes / ☐ No				
						☐ Yes / ☐ No				
						☐ Yes / ☐ No				
						☐ Yes / ☐ No				
						☐ Yes / ☐ No				
						☐ Yes / ☐ No				
						☐ Yes / ☐ No				

ERAP

Service type	If 'No', why?	Service type	If 'No', why?
Service type	If 'No', why?	Service type	If 'No', why?
Service type	If 'No', why?	Service type	If 'No', why?
Service type	If 'No', why?	Service type	If 'No', why?

Service types

1. Assistive Technology Services / Devices *
2. Audiological Services *
3. Child Care
4. Children's Protective Service
5. Clothing
6. Counseling
7. Dental / Orthodontic Care
8. Drug / Alcohol Counseling
9. Educational
10. Employment
11. Family Training
12. Financial Services
13. Genetic Counseling
14. Habilitative Services for Hearing Loss
15. Health Services *
16. Home visits
17. Housing
18. Legal
19. Medical (Diagnostic or Evaluation)
20. Nursing Services *
21. Nutrition Services *
22. Occupational Therapy *
23. Parenting Educational
24. Physical Therapy *
25. Psychological / Mental Health Services *
26. Recreation / Social
27. Rehabilitation
28. Respite Care
29. Service Coordination
30. Shelter (temporary)
31. Social Work Services *
32. Special Instruction *
33. Speech / Language Therapy *
34. Support / Self Help Group
35. Transportation
36. Vision Services *

Service locations

1. Child Care Center
2. Clinic
3. Community Center
4. Early Childhood Center
5. EI Center / Class for Children with Disabilities
6. Family Day Care
7. Grocery Store
8. Head Start
9. Home
10. Hospital
11. Library
12. Park
13. Preschool
14. Regular Nursery School
15. Residential facility
16. Restaurant

*Early intervention specialized services covered under the ODH / BEIS Early Intervention System of Payment.

Updated; August 2009

HEA 7720 (03/07)

Section VIII: **Transition at Age Three Outcome**

Child's name	Date of birth

A. What do we want to happen before _____ turns three and leaves Help Me Grow?
(e.g. preparing the child and family for change and identifying possible options)

What program are we interested in for _____ once he turns 3 ?

B. Who will help us and what strategy will they use so we can achieve our goal to ensure a smooth transition?

C. After reviewing our transition goal, my family and IFSP team (and the LEA, if applicable) have decided that at age three:

☐	My child and / or family met this outcome.
☐	We have partially met this outcome. Why?
☐	The outcome was not met. Why?

Updated; August 2009
HEA 7720 (03/07)

Section IX: **Transition Documentation Checklist**

Child's name	Date of birth

Italics = Child may quality for Part B Services

Between 6-9 months prior to child's third birthday Begin preparing for the Transition Planning Conference.	Projected Date	Actual Date	Service Coordinator's Initials
1. Discuss the transition process and develop outcome(s) and activities/strategies on the Individual Family Service Plan (IFSP).			
2. Review child's progress and identify any concerns.			
3. Identify possible program options (public preschool, Head Start, preschool special education, childcare, other)			
4. Identify participants for the Transition Planning Conference. *If the child is suspected of having a disability at age 3, the LEA representative, with parental permission, must be invited to attend the transition planning conference.*			
5. Obtain informed written parental consent to invite identified participants to the Transition Planning Conference (TPC).			
6. Obtain written parental consent for the release of information/records. (Specify what records are to be released and to whom).			
7. Determine mutually agreed upon time and date for Transition Planning Conference (90 days or up to 9 months before the child's third birthday).			
8. Send each identified individual / agency written notification of the Transition Planning Conference including the date, time and location.			

At least 90 days prior to the child's third birthday, conduct the Transition Planning Conference with invited participants.	Projected Date	Actual Date	Service Coordinator's Initials
1. Discuss transition process, review and update the Transition outcome to ensure a smooth transition by age three.			
2. *The LEA / School district representative will:*			
a. Inform family of the due process and procedural safeguards.			
b. Review child's records.			
c. Decide with family and other team members if there is a suspected disability, as defined by Part B.			
3. *If a disability is suspected, complete a Referral for Evaluation PR-04.*			
4. *Obtain written parental permission for a multi – factored evaluation (MFE) using the Parent Consent for Evaluation Form PR-05.*			
5. If a disability is not suspected the team explores other community and program options for the child at age 3.			

Section X: **IFSP Signatures and Consents**

Child's name	Date of birth

Please check all that apply:

☐ I participated fully in the development of this plan and give my consent to implement the IFSP.

☐ I have been given and understand my parental rights under Help Me Grow.

☐ I understand my child is eligible for additional rights under Part C of IDEA.

☐ I understand I can ask the team and anyone else to meet to make changes to this IFSP at any time.

☐ I consent to provide a copy of the following sections of my IFSP to _____.

　　　　☐ All sections　　☐ Only sections　　_____.

☐ I consent to provide a copy of this IFSP to my IFSP team

Parent/Guardian/Surrogate Parent signature	Date

To be noted prior to the Transition Process :

For Part C eligible children in HMG, notification that includes the names, address, birth date, parent(s) name(s), and telephone number, will be sent to the LEA/school district informing the district that the child may be eligible for Part B services at age 3 years. This notification is a requirement of Part C of the Individuals with Disabilities Education Act (IDEA) and is beneficial in preparing the school district of the child's possible eligibility for special education preschool services. *Opting out of this notification must be obtained at the IFSP meeting closest to the child becoming 18 months old or immediately upon entry into HMG if the child enters after 18 months of age.* Opting out of this notification must be recorded below with check box and parent signature.

　　☐　I have been informed of the notification requirement and choose **NOT** to have the above identified information sent to the LEA.
　　Parent Signature_____Date_____

For children who may be eligible for Part B pre-school services and supports, attendance by a representative from the school district at the Transition Planning Conference is essential to the transition process and preparation for the exit from HMG .

　　☐　I give consent to have a school district representative attend my child's Transition Planning Conference.
　　Parent Signature_____ Date_____

IFSP Team member's Approval of Plan:

We agree that the goals/outcomes selected reflect the family's priorities and concerns and the strategies selected support those goals. We agree to carry out the plan in a manner that supports the family's ability to help their child participate in and learn from their everyday routines and activities whenever possible.

Signature (or printed name if not in attendance)	Title / Role / Agency	Method of Participation	Date
	Service Coordinator	**Present**	

*Method includes present (P) Written (W) Conference Call (C)

Updated; August 2009
HEA 7720 (03/07)

Review each section of the sample IFSP form. Is the form parent-friendly? Why or why not? What suggestions do you have, if any, for improving the format of an IFSP? You are asked to assess the strength of a parent's claim that his/her child's IFSP is inappropriate — how will you approach this task? As an advocate, what is the most important section of an IFSP? Why? How do the sections of the IFSP work together?

IFSPs must be needs-driven, not diagnosis-driven. To illustrate, consider a child diagnosed with autism. If the child has social skills and language concerns, the lead agency should provide proper services to address these weaknesses. The IFSP should not, however, presume that the child has social skills and language concerns simply because he or she has been diagnosed with autism. Diagnosis-driven IFSPs result in "cookie cutter" plans for all children who are diagnosed with the same condition, as opposed to plans that are individually tailored to meet a child and family's unique needs, in accordance with 34 C.F.R. § 303.344(d)(10). For this reason, IFSP teams should focus their attention on the child and family's needs when developing an IFSP, and not the child's diagnosis.

Just as the legal standard requires IEPs be appropriate for classified school-age children, IFSPs, too, must be appropriate. The IFSP must provide services that are "likely to produce progress, not regression or trivial . . . advancement." *Polk v. Central Susquehanna Intermed. Unit 16*, 853 F.2d 171, 183 (3d Cir. 1988). Moreover, when more than one service is being provided, each developmental service must be likely to produce meaningful progress. *Id.; see also DeMora v. Dept. of Public Welfare*, 768 A.2d 904 (Pa. Commw. 2001).

Consider the following hypothetical:

Brandon Wilson

     Mr. and Mrs. Wilson attend the initial IFSP meeting for their 16-month-old son, Brandon. Brandon has some delays in walking, holding and manipulating objects, and interacting with others. He attends a local daycare, from 9-5, Monday through Friday, because both of his parents work. The IFSP team quickly finds Brandon eligible for early intervention services and then, at the same meeting, produces an IFSP that the lead agency has prepared for him. The IFSP provides that Brandon will receive occupational therapy twice per week for 30 minutes per session, physical therapy once per week for 30 minutes and family training once per week for 45 minutes with a social worker.

1.   As the parents' advocate, what questions/concerns, if any, do you have about the IFSP process?

2.   How will you go about addressing your questions/concerns?

ADVOCACY TIPS FOR IFSP MEETINGS:

√   Request copies of all evaluation reports and review prior to the meeting, seeking out assistance to understand them if needed.

√   Review the results of evaluations with your client prior to the meeting to prepare your client and eliminate surprises.

√   Request a copy of draft IFSP prior to the meeting if EIP intends to introduce one at the meeting; if you don't receive a copy in advance, but do receive one at the meeting, ask for the meeting to adjourn to a later time or date (with your client's consent) so that you are able to review the IFSP with your client prior to discussing it at the meeting.

√   Inform your client that he or she may bring a family member or friend to the meeting who knows the client and the client's family and who is able to provide the client with support and assistance during the course of the meeting should he or she need it.

√   Prepare for the meeting as if you are preparing for a hearing. Know what your client wants. Identify those areas in which you wish to question the evaluators and EIP professionals and set the type of questioning (i.e., open or closed questions) and the tone of questioning based on the tone of the meeting. Befriend those evaluators and EIP professionals who support your client.

√   Advise your client not to sign the IFSP unless he or she fully understands and agrees to it. Encourage your client to take time to think things over. Remind the client that he or she may consent to some services and reject others. Those services to which the client consents must be implemented.

VI. EARLY INTERVENTION SERVICES

Early intervention services are services designed to meet the developmental needs of eligible infants and toddlers as well as the needs of the family as they relate to improving the child's development. 34 C.F.R. § 303.12(a). Federal regulations provide a lengthy list of services available through the early intervention system, including: audiology, hearing and vision services; family training and counseling; health, medical and nursing services; nutrition services; occupational and physical therapies; speech and language therapy; psychological and social work services; service coordination; and transportation services to name a few. 34 C.F.R. § 303.12. It is important to note that this list is not exhaustive; if a child requires a service not on the list, he or she still must receive the service. All services must be provided by qualified personnel. 34 C.F.R. § 303.12(e).

The lead agency must ensure that early intervention services are provided, to the maximum extent appropriate, in "natural environments," defined as home and community settings in which children without disabilities participate. 34 C.F.R. § 303.12(a)(4). Early intervention services may be provided in settings other than the natural environment, "only if early intervention cannot be achieved satisfactorily for the infant or toddler in a natural environment." 34 C.F.R. § 303.167(b)(2).

If the IFSP team determines that a child should exit the early intervention system either because of age or other reason for ineligibility, it must develop a transition plan as part of the child's IFSP to support the child's transition to preschool, school, or other services. 20 U.S.C. § 1437(a)(9)(A); 34 C.F.R. § 303.344(h). Families must be included in the transition planning. 20 U.S.C. § 1437(a)(9)(A)(i). In the event that a child may be eligible for preschool special education services, with the family's approval, no fewer than 90 days and no more than nine months prior to the child's third birthday, the lead agency must convene a conference with the lead agency, the family and the local school district to assess the child for special education eligibility and plan for any services he or she may receive. 20 U.S.C. § 1437(a)(9)(A)(ii). Congress set this timeframe to ensure a seamless transition of children from the early intervention system into the school system; unfortunately, however, transition meetings often do not occur in a timely fashion or, in some cases, at all, resulting in gaps, large and small, in service provision for children with disabilities with detrimental results.

EARLY INTERVENTION TIMELINE

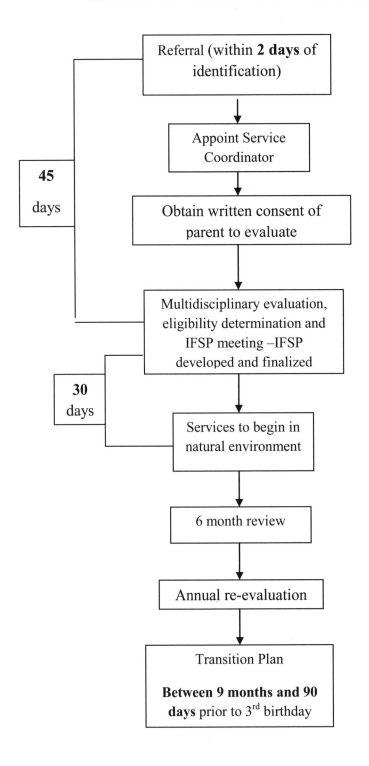

The IDEA allows states flexibility to continue to serve children from age three until their entrance into Kindergarten in the Early Intervention Program, instead of the special education system. 20 U.S.C. § 1435(c). Among other mandates, if a state elects to extend its Early Intervention Program to this older population, the child's program must include "an educational component that promotes school readiness and incorporates preliteracy, language, and numeracy skills." 20 U.S.C. § 1435(c)(2)(B).

Review the early intervention laws and regulations for your state. Has your state elected to extend its early intervention programming to children ages three to five? What are the benefits for states and families of extending the programming? What are the risks/consequences, if any? What effect would extending this programming have on the right of children between the ages of 3-21 to receive a FAPE?

Consider the following hypothetical:

Marie

It is February 15 and you have just conducted your first interview of a potential new client, Ms. Abrams, who is concerned about the transition of her child, Marie, from the Early Intervention Program into special education. Marie has been receiving early intervention services for the last 18 months. Her IFSP calls for speech and language therapy twice per week for 30-minute sessions, occupational therapy twice per week for 30-minute sessions, physical therapy once per week for 45 minutes, and family training once per week for 60 minutes.

Marie will turn three years old on March 15. According to Ms. Abrams, the family's EI service coordinator first spoke to her about transition four months earlier, during the preceding October. Shortly thereafter, a meeting was held with the EI service coordinator, Ms. Abrams, and the case manager from the local school district's preschool child study team. At this meeting, the school district's case manager gave Ms. Abrams a list of general education preschools to contact about possible programming for Marie once she turns three.

After the meeting, Ms. Abrams called each of the preschools on the list. All of the schools told her that they could not provide the services that her daughter currently is receiving. In the beginning of December, the school district's child study team met concerning Marie. At this meeting, they discussed the evaluations that needed to be performed, including physical therapy, occupational therapy, speech and language therapy and psychological assessments. The case manager also gave Ms. Abrams a list of special education preschools to contact.

Ms. Abrams called all of the schools on the new list. Each of the schools told her either that they could not provide the services that her daughter needed or that they were full.

The evaluations were completed in December and January and a follow-up meeting to discuss the results was held during the first week of February. At the meeting, the school district determined that Marie was eligible for special education and related services and classified her as preschool disabled. The case manager told Ms. Abrams that an IEP would be developed shortly for Marie and that, in the meantime, Ms. Abrams should contact three remaining possible schools. Ms. Abrams subsequently contacted the schools and learned that the first school was full and the second school has yet to implement its preschool disabilities program. Despite her repeated attempts to call the third school, she has not been able to speak to anyone.

1. As an advocate, what concerns, if any, do you have about the process and the end result?

2. What are the legal violations? Are they procedural or substantive? Does this matter?

3. In what order do you intend to address the issues? Why?

4. What additional information, if any, do you need to proceed on the issues?

VII.   PAYMENT FOR EARLY INTERVENTION SERVICES

The state must provide certain early intervention services for children and families free of charge, including child find, identification, evaluation and assessment, IFSP development and monitoring, service coordination services, and other administrative activities. 34 C.F.R. § 303.521(b). The lead agency pays for these components out of the state early intervention budget. Because the actual developmental services provided by the early intervention system are not free for families unless they meet the individual state's income guidelines, multiple sources exist to pay these costs. They include family cost-shares, Medicaid (for eligible children and families), private health insurance (in certain circumstances) and, after all other funding sources are exhausted or if there are disputes between agencies over payment resulting in a delay in service provision to a child and family, the early intervention system itself as the "payor of last resort." 34 C.F.R. § 303.527.

No family may be denied early intervention services based solely on their inability to pay for them. 34 C.F.R. § 303.520(b)(3)(ii). Typically, each state's sliding fee scale takes into consideration, at the very least, family income and size. Some states, like New Jersey, also consider the number of service hours a child and family are to receive (charging a progressive fee for each hour of early intervention services provided) in computing the family cost-share. N.J. Admin. Code 8:17-9.1(b)(4). Income guidelines are set by the states, and the factors considered in computing the same are not consistent across all of the states. Based on each individual state's factors, the lead agency determines whether a family is able to pay for early intervention services and, if so, how much. Typically, states choose a percentage of the federal poverty level whereby if a family's gross income falls below that level, they receive early intervention services at no cost. For example, the District of Columbia allows children and families to receive free services if their income falls below 200% of the federal poverty level. DCMR 22-B3028.7. New Jersey authorizes free services to any family falling below 350% of the federal poverty level. N.J. Admin. Code 8:17-9.2(b)(2).[6] Some states, like North Carolina, also cap the fees a family can pay at 5% of their total annual income to ensure that the cost of early intervention services is reasonable. *See* North Carolina Infant-Toddler Program Policy Bulletin #23, Fees, Billing, and Reimbursement.

Each state regulates the use of private insurance to pay for early intervention services. For example, North Carolina requires that parents provide informed, written consent to bill private insurance. *See* North Carolina Infant-Toddler Program Policy Bulletin #23, Fees, Billing, and Reimbursement. Prior to doing so, the parent must be fully informed of the impact of using private health insurance, including any effects on deductibles, monthly premiums or lifetime caps. *See id.* The lead agency also must offer parents the option to pay using a sliding fee scale instead of private health insurance. *See id.* Early intervention advocates should investigate their state's policy on the use of private health insurance for developmental services.

Some states succeed more than others in drawing down federal dollars to pay for early intervention services. For example, in FY 2004, New Jersey received $16 million in federal funds for early intervention, including Medicaid funding, forming approximately 25% of its total budget, whereas Pennsylvania received $29.7 million in federal funding including Medicaid, comprising 38.5% of its total early intervention budget. *Testimony of Lowell Arye, Executive Director of Alliance for the Betterment of Citizens with Disabilities, on Medicaid*

---

[6] At the time of this writing, there is a proposal to reduce the number of children and families eligible for free early interventions services to those who fall under 300% of the Federal Poverty Level.

Waiver Funding, available at http://www.abcdnj.org/publications/early-intervention-pubs/early-intervention-testimony-on-medicaid-waiver-funding/. It appears that states that draw down more federal dollars do so by better utilizing the federal Early and Periodic Screening, Diagnosis and Treatment (EPSDT) program as a source of evaluations and service provision for children eligible for early intervention to maximize all federal Medicaid revenue sources, and/or by receiving a federal Medicaid Home and Community Based Services Waiver for Early Intervention.

Much overlap exists between the Early and Periodic Screening, Diagnosis and Treatment and Early Intervention Programs, thus one would be remiss not to discuss the former when presenting the latter. Congress added the EPSDT program to the Medicaid Act in 1967 as Medicaid's child health component. *See generally* 42 U.S.C. § 1396d. It was developed to address the physical, emotional and developmental needs of children in low-income families by providing both preventive care as well as treatment. More specifically, and using the program's name as a guide, EPSDT aims to do the following: identify concerns *early*, beginning at birth; check children's health at *periodic* age-appropriate intervals and when problems are suspected; conduct *screening* tests to assess possible problems, including physical, mental, developmental, dental, vision, and hearing screens; perform evaluations when problems and risks are identified, so that *diagnosis* may occur; and provide *treatment* services to address the identified problems.

EPSDT benefits are available to all children under the age of 21 who are enrolled in Medicaid based on income eligibility requirements. Children also may qualify through Medicaid's "spend down" program for the medically needy, which allows some individuals to qualify for Medicaid even where they do not meet income eligibility requirements, provided that they either pay for or incur a certain amount of monthly medical expenses (the spend down) before receiving Medicaid coverage. Finally, children may qualify for EPSDT through home and community care waiver programs. Waiver programs, discussed in more detail below, are available to children at any income level who have serious disabilities that require an "institutional level of care" as defined by the state. 42 U.S.C. § 1915(c); 42 C.F.R. §§ 440.180 et seq.

At a minimum, screening services provided under EPSDT must include a comprehensive health and developmental history, an unclothed physical exam, recommended immunizations, laboratory tests and health education. 42 U.S.C. § 1905(r)(1). In addition, children are entitled to vision and hearing assessment, treatment and services (including eye glasses, hearing aids and speech therapy) as well as preventive, restorative and emergency dental services. 42 U.S.C. § 1905(r)(2)-(4). Children also must receive any and all needed health care diagnosis services, treatment and other medical assistance necessary to correct or improve conditions discovered by screening devices, no matter whether these services are covered under the individual state's medical assistance plan. Even if a service will not "cure" a condition, the child must receive it if it is medically necessary to ameliorate the child's general health. Some of the services available to children pursuant to the EPSDT program or through Medicaid itself include:

- Inpatient hospital services (other than services in an institution for mental illness)

- Outpatient hospital services

- Rural health clinic services (including home visits for homebound individuals)

- Federally-qualified health center services

- Laboratory and X-ray services

- Physician services (in office, recipient's home, hospital, nursing facility, or elsewhere)

- Home health care services (nursing services; home health aides; medical supplies, equipment, and appliances suitable for use in the home; physical therapy, occupation therapy, speech pathology, audiology services provided by a home health agency or by a facility licensed by the state to provide medical rehabilitation services)

- Private duty nursing services

- Clinic services (including services outside of clinic for eligible homeless individuals)

- Dental services (including surgical) and dentures

- Physical therapy, occupational therapy, and services for individuals with speech, hearing, and language disorders

- Prescribed drugs

- Prosthetic devices

- Eyeglasses and hearing aids

- Services in an intermediate care facility for the mentally retarded

- Medical care, or any other type of remedial care recognized under state law, furnished by licensed practitioners within the scope of their practice as defined by state law, specified by the Secretary (includes transportation)

- Other diagnostic, screening, preventive, and rehabilitative services, including any medical or remedial services (provided in a facility, a home, or other setting) recommended by a physician or other licensed practitioner of the healing arts within the scope of their practice under state law, for the maximum reduction of physical or mental disability and restoration of an individual to the best possible functional level

- Inpatient psychiatric hospital services for individuals under age 21

- Case-management services

- TB-related and other respiratory care services

- Services furnished by a certified pediatric nurse practitioner or certified family nurse practitioner, which the practitioner is legally authorized to perform under state law

- Personal care services (in a home or other location) furnished to an individual who is not an inpatient or resident of a hospital, nursing facility, intermediate care facility for the mentally retarded, or institution for mental disease

- Primary care case management services

42 U.S.C. § 1396d(a); 42 C.F.R. §§ 440.1-440.170.

Although EPSDT has great potential to improve vastly the health and well-being of children in this country, the program is significantly underutilized. For example, a 2001 GAO report which reviewed Medicaid screening rates for lead poisoning and dental care found, "only 19 percent of children on Medicaid ages 1 through 5 had blood lead levels tested, and only 21 percent of children on Medicaid ages 2 through 5 had a dental visit in the previous year."

http://www.kff.org/medicaid/upload/Early-and-Periodic-Screening-Diagnostic-and-Treatment-Services-Fact-Sheet.pdf.

States may access Medicaid Home and Community Based Services (HCBS) Waivers as another source of federal funding for early intervention services. Each state may apply for one or more Medicaid HCBS waivers to allow them flexibility in designing and implementing home and community based services for persons who otherwise would require institutionalization. These waivers permit states to provide services in children's homes and communities as long as the estimated cost of home or community services does not exceed the cost of institutional care and the child would have been Medicaid-eligible had s/he been placed in an institution. *See* http://aspe.hhs.gov/daltcp/reports/primer.htm#Chap2. States may develop waivers for various populations, such as persons with a specific diagnosis (e.g., AIDS) or persons with developmental disabilities. *See* http://aspe.hhs.gov/daltcp/reports/primer.htm#Chap9. The waiver program gives states much latitude in defining "institutional level of care," the definition of which may either vastly expand or limit the number of persons who qualify for the benefits of the waiver.

For example, California has been granted an HCBS waiver that applies to a number of infants and toddlers eligible for early intervention services. To qualify for services under the waiver, a child must: 1) be eligible for full scope Medi-Cal; 2) have a formal diagnosis of a developmental disability that begins before the age of 18, is expected to continue indefinitely, presents a substantial disability, and the disability is due to mental retardation, autism, cerebral palsy, epilepsy, and other closely related conditions as defined in the California Lanterman Developmental Disabilities Services Act, Welfare and Institutions Code, Section 4512 (a); 3) be a regional center consumer; and 4) require the level of care for an intermediate care facility for the developmentally disabled. If a child meets these qualifications, he or she may receive the following services, to name a few: Home health aide services, respite care, habilitation (residential or day), skilled nursing, transportation, family training, and behavior intervention. *See* http://www.dhcs.ca.gov/services/ltc/pages/dd.aspx.

The failure of states to access additional sources of federal funding to implement the early intervention system has adverse effects on state budgets which lose out on federal dollars that help to fund these programs. This, in turn, results in an increased burden on families as cost-shares rise and states restrict access to services by making eligibility definitions more restrictive, by including rate and frequency of service needed when computing cost-shares, and by implementing other methods of cost-cutting. Not only will these measures have harmful lifelong consequences for infants and toddlers with disabilities and their families, but also they will overburden society's already stressed social services framework for this population into adulthood.

Investigate your state's use of EPSDT services. Where does EPSDT overlap with your state's Early Intervention Program? Where are the gaps? Which program provides more entitlements and safeguards? How would you go advise a client who wants to know which program to pursue for an infant or toddler with a disability?

VIII. PROCEDURAL SAFEGUARDS AND DISPUTE RESOLUTION

Each early intervention lead agency must develop and ensure the implementation of procedural safeguards to protect the rights of infants and toddlers with disabilities and their families within the early intervention system. 20 U.S.C. § 1439(a); 34 C.F.R. § 303.400. These protections resemble, in many ways, those afforded to parents and children within the special education system. For example, the lead agency must obtain informed, written consent from the parent prior to evaluating a child for early intervention or initially providing a child with early intervention services (i.e., implementing a child's initial IFSP). 34 C.F.R. § 303.404. A parent has the right to provide informed written consent to some early intervention services while declining to accept others. 20 U.S.C. § 1439(a)(3); 34 C.F.R. § 303.405.

Many of the early intervention rights under the IDEA are vested in parents, just as in special education, thus the lead agency also must have procedures in place to appoint a surrogate parent for an eligible child in the event no parent for the child can be identified; the child's parent cannot, after reasonable efforts, be located; or the child is a ward of the state. 34 C.F.R. § 303.406. Parents also have the right to examine records, 34 C.F.R. § 303.402, and to have personally identifiable information kept confidential, 20 U.S.C. § 1439(a)(2). They have the right to written notice any time the public agency or service provider "proposes, or refuses, to initiate or change the identification, evaluation, or placement of the child, or the provision of appropriate early intervention services to the child and the child's family." 34 C.F.R. § 303.403(a). Such notice must be in the native language of the child's parent(s) unless it is "clearly not feasible to do so." 34 C.F.R. § 303.403(c). Parents also have the right to timely prior written notice of any meetings to ensure they are able to attend. 34 C.F.R. § 303.342(d). The initial eligibility and any subsequent IFSP meetings must be conducted in places and at times that are convenient for families as well. 34 C.F.R. § 303.342(d).

Additionally, each state must have in place procedures for timely resolution of complaints. Just as with special education, there are three primary mechanisms for resolving disputes regarding the early intervention system: complaint investigations, mediation, and due process hearings. The simplest method is the filing of a complaint with the lead agency, which the lead agency then investigates and issues a finding. 34 C.F.R. § 303.510; 20 U.S.C. § 1435(a)(10). In the event that the lead agency, in investigating a complaint, finds a failure to provide appropriate services to a child and family, the decision must set forth how the denial of services will be remediated, including the awarding of monetary reimbursement or other corrective action, and how proposed services will be provided in the future to infants and toddlers with disabilities and their families. 34 C.F.R. § 303.510(b). This may be the simplest method for resolving disputes; however, because the complaint investigation and findings are made by the very agency against which the complaint has been lodged, and which is responsible for implementing and monitoring the Early Intervention Program, many prefer to use the other two dispute resolution methods instead.

States must provide a mediation process for resolving early intervention disputes, at the very least, when a due process hearing is requested. 34 C.F.R. § 303.419(a). Similar to the mediation process in special education matters, the parties must participate voluntarily, and a qualified and impartial third party who is trained in mediation techniques and knowledgeable about relevant law and regulations must conduct the mediation. 34 C.F.R. § 303.419(b). Mediation discussions must remain confidential and cannot be used as evidence in court proceedings, and any agreement reached by the parties must be reduced to writing. 34 C.F.R. § 303.419(b).

Parents also have the right to an administrative hearing to resolve early intervention disputes. Again, as in special education due process hearings, parents have numerous rights specified in the law and regulations: the right to counsel or to be accompanied by persons with special knowledge or training regarding early intervention services; the right to present evidence and confront, and cross-examine witnesses and compel their attendance; the right to prohibit the introduction of any evidence that has not been disclosed to the parent at least five days before the hearing; the right to a written or electronic transcript of the proceedings; and the right to written findings of fact and decisions. 34 C.F.R. § 303.422(b). The lead agency must ensure that within 30 days of receiving a parent's due process complaint, the matter is heard and a written decision is issued to the parties, unless the state adopts the state's Part B due process procedures, in which case it has 45 days to conduct the hearing and issue a decision. *See* 34 C.F.R. § 303.423 and companion Note. In the event a party feels aggrieved by the findings or a decision rendered on an administrative complaint, that party has the right to bring a civil action in state or federal court regardless of the amount in controversy. 20 U.S.C. § 1439(a)(1).

Significantly, an infant or toddler with a disability must continue to receive appropriate early intervention services currently being provided or, if the dispute concerns the initial IFSP, the services not in dispute, during the pendency of any complaint proceedings, unless the parents and lead agency otherwise agree. 20 U.S.C. § 1439(b). This is comparable to the "stay put" provision in special education matters. However, the right to "stay put" for children transitioning from early intervention into special education programming applies only if a parent files for due process prior to the child's third birthday. *See* 34 C.F.R. § 300.518(c) ("If the complaint involves an application for initial services under this part from a child who is transitioning from Part C of the Act to Part B and is no longer eligible for Part C services because the child has turned three, the public agency is not required to provide the Part C services that the child had been receiving."); *see also Pardini v. Allegheny Intermediate Unit*, 420 F.3d 181 (3d Cir. 2005) (holding that where a dispute arises over the initial IEP for a child transitioning from the early intervention program to preschool at age three, the district, with the consent of the parent, must provide the child the program and services the child was receiving under the Individualized Family Service Plan until the dispute is resolved (Note: when dispute first arose, child was not yet three)); *but see D.P. ex rel. E.P. v. School Board of Broward County*, 483 F.3d 725 (11th Cir. 2007) (holding that the IDEA does not provide for continued services to students pursuant to their IFSPs after they turn three).

Unlike special education matters, the IDEA includes no provision for attorneys' fees for prevailing parties in early intervention matters. Despite this, a prevailing party may still be entitled to fees in limited circumstances under the Civil Rights Attorneys' Fees Act, 42 U.S.C. § 1988, provided that the plaintiff successfully advances a Section 1983 claim. While no such study has been undertaken, one may posit that the absence of prevailing party fee awards is the reason why few early intervention cases are litigated. One also might attribute the low number of cases to higher levels of satisfaction with the early intervention program, misinformation about the early intervention rights and entitlements of children and families, and/or the failure of parents to identify the effects of insufficient or problematic early intervention programming until several years later.

EARLY INTERVENTION PROCEDURAL SAFEGUARDS

Infants and toddlers with disabilities and their families have the right to:

- [ ] Participate in the Early Intervention process at all stages in the process

- [ ] Free, multi-disciplinary EI evaluation conducted by qualified professionals, and IFSP created, within 45 days of referral (provided written consent obtained)

- [ ] Notice, meetings, evaluations and assessment conducted in native language unless clearly not feasible to do so

- [ ] Give and withdraw consent for evaluations and services (may consent to some services and refuse to consent to others)

- [ ] Receive all EI services listed in the child's IFSP

- [ ] Have IFSP reviewed every six months and child reevaluated annually

- [ ] Continue receiving EI services during dispute resolution

- [ ] Review records

- [ ] Confidentiality / Privacy

- [ ] Timely complaint resolution procedures

Compare the procedural safeguards and dispute resolution rights of parents as set forth in Parts B and C of IDEA. How are they similar? Where do they differ? Does the law afford parents in Part C proceedings fewer rights than in Part B proceedings?

Chapter 7

SCHOOL DISCIPLINE AND STUDENTS WITH SPECIAL NEEDS[1]

Students with special needs are at a greater risk of school exclusion than those without disabilities, especially if they are students with emotional and behavioral disorders. *See* Russell Skiba et al., *Are Zero Tolerance Policies Effective in the Schools? An Evidentiary Review and Recommendations*, American Psychological Association Zero Tolerance Task Force (2006). Like all students, students with disabilities are guaranteed certain basic constitutional rights in the school discipline context. *See* Eileen L. Ordover & Joseph B. Tulman, *The Special Education Process: School Discipline and Students with Disabilities in Special Education Advocacy under the Individuals with Disabilities Education Act (IDEA) for Children in the Juvenile Delinquency System*, 4-6 (Joseph B. Tulman & Joyce A. McGee eds., 1998). Although students do not have a federal constitutional right to their education, the Supreme Court, in its *Goss v. Lopez* ruling, recognized that students do have a state property interest in their education that "may not be taken away for misconduct without adherence to the minimum procedures required by [the Due Process] Clause." 419 U.S. 565, 573 (1975). The Due Process Clause requires "at least . . . rudimentary precautions against unfair or mistaken findings of misconduct and arbitrary exclusion from school." *Id.* at 581.

In *Goss*, students brought a class action challenging suspensions of ten days or less that were imposed by their schools. The Court found that schools must provide students with notice of the charges against them and an opportunity to tell their side of the story or explain what happened, and commented that longer exclusions may require more formal procedures. *Id.* at 579, 584.

The type of notice and hearing that is required, including how formal the hearing must be, and the student's rights at the hearing, depend upon the seriousness of the charges and the severity of the possible penalty. *See* Ordover & Tulman, *supra* at 4-7, citing 419 U.S. at 578-80; *Mathews v. Eldridge*, 424 U.S. 319, 333-335 (1976) (finding that specific dictates of due process require consideration of the private interest at stake, the risk of erroneous deprivation of that interest through procedures used, the probable value of additional procedural safeguards, and the government's burden, including additional fiscal and administrative burdens).

There is little uniformity in how states and local school districts design procedures relating to school discipline, such as the timeframe for a hearing, the hearing process itself (whether students may present evidence, confront witnesses, etc.), or the length of school exclusion for various offenses. Some states, like California, have codified school discipline through state law while other states leave some or all of it to the discretion of the local school districts to adopt their own policies. *See* Cal. Educ. Code §§ 48900, et seq. (2009); *see also* N.C. Gen. Stat.

---

[1] This chapter was written by Julie K. Waterstone, Associate Clinical Professor of Law and Director of the Children's Rights Clinic, Southwestern Law School, and Jane Wettach, Clinical Professor of Law and Director of the Children's Law Clinic, Duke Law School.

§ 115C-391 (2009). When representing a student who is facing school exclusion, the student advocate must first determine the source for the school discipline laws (i.e., state law, local policy, or a combination of both).

There is also little uniformity in the terms used to describe school exclusion. In California, "suspension" refers to a short-term removal from school (up to ten days) and "expulsion" refers to exclusion from the school district for up to one year. *See* Cal. Educ. Code § 48925 (2009). In North Carolina, the term suspension is used for both short and long-term exclusions, whereas expulsion describes a permanent exclusion from the public schools. *See* N.C. Gen. Stat. § 115C-391 (2009). Throughout this chapter, we will use the term "school exclusion" to refer to a long-term removal from school (i.e., any exclusion in excess of ten days).

If a student with a disability violates school rules or acts in an inappropriate manner, administrators may remove that student for no more than ten school days without the protections of the IDEA being triggered. 34 C.F.R. § 300.530(a). In other words, students with a disability may be disciplined in the same manner as any other student for less than ten days. During that time period of less than ten days, students may be deprived of educational services if nondisabled students may likewise be deprived of educational services under state or local policy.

The IDEA provides critical due process protections for children with disabilities so that schools cannot unilaterally remove children with disabilities from classrooms for disciplinary purposes. These protections are necessary given the long history of schools excluding children who were found to be "difficult" to educate. *See Honig v. Doe*, 484 U.S. 305, 323 (1988) ("Congress very much meant to strip schools of the unilateral authority they had traditionally employed to exclude disabled students . . . from school"). When supporting students with challenging behaviors, it is essential for schools to adhere to the central purpose of the IDEA: "to ensure that all children with disabilities have available to them a free appropriate public education that emphasizes special education and related services designed to meet their unique needs and prepare them for further education, employment, and independent living," and "to ensure that the rights of children with disabilities and parents of such children are protected." 20 U.S.C. § 1400(d)(1)(A)–(B).

I. PROTECTIONS FOR DISCIPLINED STUDENTS

Three special protections are provided under IDEA for children with disabilities who are the subject of school discipline. First, they may not be excluded from school for more than ten days if their behavior was a symptom or manifestation of their disability. Second, even if their behavior was not a manifestation of their disability, they are entitled to continued educational services during any period of exclusion beyond ten school days. Third, in certain cases, they are entitled to specific services designed to help them avoid misbehavior in the future. These protections also extend to children who had not been, but should have been, identified as eligible for special education.

A. Manifestation Determination Review

The Manifestation Determination Review (MDR) is a process to be used by the child's IEP team to protect a child from being excluded from school (for more than ten days) if the child's conduct is a "manifestation" of his or her disability. 20 U.S.C. § 1415(k)(1)(E); 34 C.F.R. § 300.530(e). Shortly after a disciplinary event, the team must meet to determine the relationship between the child's disability and the misbehavior. The MDR process is designed to prevent school officials from punishing a child with a disability when the child has exhibited the symptoms of his or her disabilities. While children with disabilities are expected to follow school rules and conform their behavior to generally-applicable school standards, some of them are simply unable to do so as a result of the disability. For example, a child may have severe difficulties regulating his emotions due to a traumatic brain injury. If the child loses emotional control at school, using highly-charged or threatening language, that behavior would be a manifestation of his disability. The child should not be punished as a non-disabled child would be for the same behavior.

The MDR must occur within ten school days of any decision to exclude a child from school for more than ten days. The statute uses the term "change in placement" to trigger the requirement of a MDR. 20 U.S.C. § 1415(k)(1)(A), (C), (F). Though not defined in the statute, "change of placement" is defined in the federal regulations as a removal of a child with a disability from the child's current educational placement for more than ten consecutive school days *or* a series of removals that "constitute a pattern." 34 C.F.R. § 300.536. A "pattern" is evidenced when the child has been subjected to a series of removals totaling more than ten school days in a school year, the child's behavior is substantially similar in each incident, and "because of such additional factors as the length of each removal, the total amount of time the child has been removed, and the proximity of the removals to one another." 34 C.F.R § 300.536(a)(1). School officials have the authority to decide whether a "pattern" exists, though that decision is subject to review through due process. 34 C.F.R. § 300.536(b). A pattern would exist if the child was consistently disciplined for talking back to the teacher, for example, if each disciplinary removal was for only a few days but accumulated to more than ten days over a period of several months. On the other hand, a pattern would probably not exist if the child was disciplined for theft at the beginning of the year, a dress code violation mid-year, and a fight at the end of the year, even though the disciplinary removals for such events might add up to more than ten days.

The MDR must be conducted at a meeting of the parent, a representative of the school district, and "relevant members of the IEP Team (as determined by the parent and the local educational agency)." 20 U.S.C. § 1415(k)(1)(E). Neither the statute nor the regulations address further who are "relevant" members of the IEP team, so there is room for advocacy to get the right people in the room. Usually, the student will benefit from the presence of a professional — often a psychologist — who can help the team understand the nature of the disability and the kinds of actions that may be symptomatic of the disability. One or more of the student's general education or special education teachers may also be able to contribute to the discussion of how the student's disability manifests itself. While the parents do not have the authority to veto the presence of any individuals that are invited by the school district to participate in the meeting, they may invite persons they believe have relevant information to contribute. *See Fitzgerald v. Fairfax Co. Sch. Bd.*, 556 F. Supp. 2d 543 (E.D. Va. 2008) (holding that school personnel determine the school system's MDR members and the parents determine whom they wish to invite in addition to those designated by the school system). The parent may wish to bring the child's therapist, mental health case worker, a family friend or relative who understands the child well, or an advocate or attorney.

The team is required to review the relevant information in the child's file, the IEP, teacher observations, and any relevant information provided by the parent. Upon review of the information, the team is to answer the following questions:

- Was the conduct in question (i.e., the conduct leading to the discipline) caused by, or did it have a direct and substantial relationship to, the child's disability? *or*

- Was the conduct in question the direct result of the local educational agency's failure to implement the IEP?

If the answer to either of the questions is yes, then the conduct is determined to be a manifestation of the disability.

Consider the following fact pattern and whether the child's actions were a manifestation of his disability.

Michael

Michael is 16 years old and in the tenth grade. He was removed from his mother's care when he was two years old. He currently lives with his great-uncle, who functions as a parent and holds his educational rights. Michael has lived with his great-uncle only for the past five months. Prior to that, since the age of two, he has lived in sixteen different placements, including foster family homes, group homes and the homes of various relatives. Michael has a history of depression and psychosis. He has been hospitalized eight times for suicidal ideations and attempts. Michael qualifies for special education under the category of Emotional Disturbance. He attends regular public school, receiving academic instruction in Math and English in a special education class. He does not receive any other services.

One Tuesday morning, Michael was in his second period class with his cousin. They were talking and being disruptive in class. After the class period, another student told the school principal that Michael had a knife on campus and was threatening to kill her with it. Michael was taken to the principal's office and questioned about the presence of the knife. Michael admitted that he had a knife. He said that he did not threaten anyone with the knife; rather, the reason he brought the knife was that he was going to cut himself during fifth period in the bathroom. He also told the principal that he did not want to do it at home because he didn't want his cousins to see him bleeding. He decided that fifth period was the right time because he did not have any friends in that class so they would not miss him.

The student that accused him of threatening to kill her wrote a statement saying that he threatened to kill her with his knife during second period. There were no other students that were able to corroborate her statement. His cousin wrote a statement that said that Michael told him that he had a knife, but did not threaten anyone with it.

Michael was immediately suspended for having a dangerous weapon on campus. Several days later, a manifestation determination review was held. Present at the meeting were: Michael, the principal, his great-uncle, a special education teacher, a general education teacher, a school psychologist, and a therapist. The therapist had only met with Michael one time a few days before the incident occurred. The school psychologist had never met Michael.

At the beginning of the meeting, the school psychologist stated that the team had to answer two questions: (1) was Michael's possession of the knife caused by or related to his disability? or (2) was Michael's possession of the knife a result of the school's failure to implement his IEP? The group began to discuss Michael and his disability. The school psychologist asked Michael whether he knew that bringing a knife to campus was wrong. The conversation then focused on whether Michael knew right from wrong and whether he knew what he did was wrong. The principal never told anyone what Michael said in her office. The great-uncle was never asked about Michael's history or whether there was possibility that Michael may actually hurt himself. The therapist did not know Michael's prior medical history. The IEP team ultimately decided that Michael's action was not a manifestation of his disability.

How would you challenge the finding at the MDR? What arguments would you make to show that Michael's act was a manifestation of his disability? Were there any procedural violations that occurred? Try to answer these questions before continuing the reading.

In determining whether the conduct in question was caused by or had a direct and substantial relationship to the child's disability, the MDR team should be looking at the child's IEP records, psycho-educational evaluations, behavior assessments, assessments of other impairments such as speech and language deficits, and any other available data to identify the symptoms and conditions that form the basis of the child's disability. If the child's present level of performance notes particular behaviors, or if the IEP goals relate to the curbing of certain behaviors, then actions consistent with those noted behaviors should be considered manifestations of the disability. Attenuated connections between the behaviors in question and the disability — such as engaging in prohibited activities to gain attention from peers and counter the low self-esteem caused by being labeled disabled — are unlikely to be considered "having a direct and substantial relationship to the child's disability." Nevertheless, such factors as the inter-relatedness of a child's several disabilities and particular challenges facing an individual student must be taken into account.

Following is a factual summary from a Wisconsin due process hearing at which an administrative law judge considered a MDR. Read it and answer the questions that follow.

An eighth-grader was eligible for special education services in the category of serious emotional disability. He was diagnosed by a private therapist as having adjustment disorder with mixed disturbance of emotions and conduct, triggered by his brother's suicide and his father's death, with a serious to moderate level of impairment. At the time of his eligibility determination, during his seventh grade year, the IEP team acknowledged severe, chronic, and frequent behavior problems. The evaluation report noted two prior arrests, one for disorderly conduct and a weapons violation. He was described on his IEP as being a bright young man with very disruptive behavior who was receiving failing grades because he often didn't complete work. His IEP also noted that he tended to act defiantly at school toward teachers and authority figures, and appeared to misbehave to gain attention from peers and adults.

During the summer vacation prior to the start of his eighth grade year, the student was at home all day with friends and family at a get-together held for the one-year anniversary of his brother's death. He got a telephone call from a friend and two older boys inviting him to go throw eggs and toilet paper at a school administrator's house. Although he initially declined, he got in the car when they came to pick him up. The older boys drove him and his friend to the school principal's house. The student participated in the egging, toilet papering, and spray painting of the house. School officials learned of the vandalism in September and sent his parents a notice of expulsion.

The school convened an MDR meeting. The team reviewed the records in the student's file and discussed his behavior. In the evaluation was a report of teacher observations recorded on behavioral scales, indicating significant concerns regarding hyperactivity, aggression, conduct problems, attention problems, atypicality, adaptability, social skills, leadership, study skills, and functional communication. The student's private therapist participated by phone. The therapist told the team that he had diagnosed the student with post-traumatic stress disorder, which falls under the umbrella of an adjustment disorder. He offered the opinion, based on having met with the student ten times for an hour each time that the student's misbehavior at the principal's house was related to the reoccurrence of the trauma he was experiencing on the anniversary of his brother's death and that it came out through his acts of vandalism. As such, in his opinion, the vandalism was directly related to the student's post-traumatic stress syndrome. Therefore, in the opinion of the therapist, the vandalism was a manifestation of the student's disability.

The team, which in addition to the student's parent and therapist included several teachers and administrators but did not include a school psychologist, came to the following conclusions: The student displayed a pattern of behaviors during the previous school year which included defiance towards school staff and disruptive classroom behaviors. Although his behaviors appeared calculated to gain peer and adult attention, the student's behaviors were also influenced by his anger, depression, and family issues. The student does not have any documented instances of vandalism or revenge in his behavioral records. The student's act of vandalism toward a school employee's house was substantially different from the pattern of behaviors that he displayed at school. Past behaviors have been ones of defiance, not vandalism. Thus, despite the parent's and therapist's disagreement, the team concluded that the act of vandalism was not a manifestation of the student's disability.

At the due process hearing, school personnel testified that they did not believe that the student's vandalism was caused by and did not have a direct and substantial relationship to his disability because they viewed it as different than the misbehaviors he displayed at school and very different than the reasons that led them to identify him as having a serious emotional disability. They said they saw the student act as a leader who was seeking attention from peers and adults and who acted defiantly towards authority figures. They testified that the misbehavior at the principal's house was different because he did not initiate the vandalism and was a follower of the other boys and because the student was secretive about the incident and did not initially admit his involvement.

How should the administrative law judge rule? Did the team consider the connection between the student's disability, his individual circumstances, and the misbehavior at issue? How different can the behavior be from past behaviors and still be considered a manifestation of the disability? Does it matter that the team members did not know of the diagnosis of post-traumatic stress disorder until the therapist shared it at the MDR meeting?

In addition to determining whether there is a relationship between the conduct in question and the disability, the team must examine whether the conduct in question was the direct result of the school district's failure to implement the IEP. To answer this question, the team must focus on all the special education and related services that are included in the IEP. Any number of failures might have occurred. If the student already had behavioral services incorporated into his or her IEP, but no one was providing those services, there would be a good argument that the conduct resulted from the district's failure. An example would be a plan that required the student to be escorted between classes to prevent the student from engaging in aggressive behavior with other students. If the escort was not present, and the student became involved in a fight between classes, one could make the case that the conduct was the direct result of the failure to implement the IEP. Prior to the 2004 amendments to the IDEA, the team was required to consider whether the IEP was appropriate in addition to considering whether it was being implemented. This provided more opportunity for advocacy around the services the student should have been receiving, but wasn't. If you see that an IEP is inappropriate — for example, the evaluations verify an intermittent explosive disorder, but the IEP provides only academic and no behavioral services — it is still worth raising this point at the meeting and pointing out the inadequacy of the IEP. At the very least, you can get the team's agreement to revise the IEP going forward.

TIPS FOR PREPARING FOR THE MDR:

√ Before attending the MDR, the student advocate should review the child's school records, including the child's previous IEPs and the notes from those meetings, any prior assessments, all medical records and mental health records.

√ Discuss the process with the parent or guardian to ensure that they understand what information is important to discuss at the MDR. Explain the two questions that will be addressed by the team.

√ Do a thorough interview with the parent or guardian to fully understand the symptoms of the child's disability and his or her behavioral history. Find out whether the child has ever received any mental health services. If not, find out whether the parent or guardian is willing to have the child assessed for any mental health concerns.

√ Be sure to have someone who has ACTUAL knowledge about the child's disability at the MDR. Do not assume that the school psychologist is knowledgeable about your client's disability. You want someone who is qualified to discuss your client and behaviors that are unique to that child. Ask ahead of time who the school has selected to participate and ask that any preferred staff with knowledge of the child attend.

√ If the child is being or has been treated by a mental health professional, contact that professional to ascertain his or her opinion about the relationship between the child's disability and the behavior. If the response is helpful, ask that individual to participate in person or by phone in the MDR. If that person is unwilling or unable to do so, ask the professional to write a report or recommendation that can be considered at the MDR. That report or recommendation will then become part of the child's confidential school records. The professional may be willing to have you draft a statement for him or her memorializing your conversation and explicitly stating an opinion about the relationship between the disability and the behavior. You do a first draft, send it to the professional for review and revision, and then get it signed. You can then present the statement to the team.

√ Bring a copy of the Diagnostic Statistic Manual of Mental Disorders Fourth Edition ("DSM IV") and use it to discuss what typical symptoms of the child's disability look like. If a psychologist or other mental health professional is unable to attend, it is even more important to bring the DSM IV or other psychological literature that helps frame the discussion of the child's disability. (The DSM is being updated and the Fifth Edition is expected soon. Make sure you have the latest version.)

√ Ask the parent or guardian what other professionals could contribute to the MDR discussion or provide necessary information about the child's life, e.g., regional center case managers, therapists, social workers, paraprofessionals, big brother/sister or other mentor type figure, or other service providers. Invite all of those individuals with relevant information to the MDR.

The questions to be answered by the team at the MDR were changed in the 2004 reauthorization of the IDEA, so earlier interpretations should not be relied upon. The new questions are narrower and tend to result in fewer children being protected by the MDR process. As noted above, under previous law, one question was whether the child's IEP and placement were appropriate, opening the door to a wide-ranging discussion of whether the IEP was providing needed support. The current question assumes the appropriateness of the IEP and asks only if, as written, the IEP was implemented. The other previous questions focused on whether the child's disability impaired his or her ability to understand the impact and consequences of his or her behavior or to control the behavior. Likewise, these questions allowed for a broader inquiry into the effect of the child's disabilities on the child's overall abilities to conform his or her conduct to the rules. For some current interpretations of the MDR questions, see *B.D. v. Puyallup Sch. Dist.*, U.S. Dist. LEXIS 91743 (W.D. Wash. 2009); *Rodriguez v. San Mateo Union High Sch. Dist.*, U.S. Dist. LEXIS 111376 (N.D. Cal. 2008).

As with other IEP team decisions, the decision about whether behavior is a manifestation of the child's disability should be reached by consensus if at all possible. If consensus cannot be reached, however, the school personnel make the ultimate decision. *See Doe by Gonzales v. Maher*, 793 F.2d 1470, 1490 (9th Cir. 1986). When no consensus is reached, the parents must be provided with "prior written notice," describing the decision made and giving the parents notice of their procedural due process rights to challenge the decision. If the parents wish to challenge the decision of the team about the manifestation, they are entitled to an expedited due process hearing. 34 C.F.R. § 300.532(c). In an expedited hearing, all of the time frames are shortened, so that the hearing must occur within twenty school days of the request, and the decision made within ten school days of the hearing.

A particularly tricky situation arises in the MDR when the student denies the conduct for which he is accused. The assumption of the review is that the student engaged in certain prohibited behaviors, but typically, he or she will not yet have had an opportunity to challenge the accusation in a school discipline hearing. Thus, the parent or advocate has to decide how to engage in the meeting. One option is for the student to take the following position: "I deny engaging in the conduct of which I am accused. But if I did do it, then it was directly and substantially related to my disability." This is obviously an awkward position, and the student and advocate have to balance the pros and cons of proceeding this way. Sometimes, the student will admit some, but not all, of the accusations. In that case, it is a little easier for the student to say, "I don't admit to all of that. But I do admit to some of it, and the part I admit to was directly and substantially related to my disability." Finally, the student might choose either not to attend the MDR, or to take a consistent position: "I did not engage in the behavior I'm accused of, so there is no reason to consider whether it was a manifestation of my disability." The student's advocate can help the student process the alternatives and decide which is most advantageous in the particular circumstances.

TIPS FOR ADVOCATING AT THE MDR:

√ Do not allow the school personnel to engage in a discussion about whether a child knows right from wrong or whether that child knew that their actions were wrong. That is wholly inappropriate. Keep the conversation focused on the necessary questions: (1) Was the conduct in question caused by, or did it have a direct and substantial relationship to, the child's disability? or (2) Was the conduct in question the direct result of the local educational agency's failure to implement the IEP?

√ For children with ADHD, school district personnel should not engage in a discussion about whether the child is taking medication. The discussion should be limited to the characteristics of the child's disability and whether the conduct in question was caused by or had a substantial relationship to the disability.

√ Use this opportunity to review the current IEP to ensure that the child is receiving the right services and is correctly placed.

√ In jurisdictions where recording an IEP meeting is permissible, you should record the Manifestation Determination Review Meeting. Be sure to notify the school district of your intent to record at least twenty-four (24) hours prior to the MDR. *See* Cal. Educ. Code §§ 56341.1(g) and 56321.5.

---

1. Results of the Manifestation Determination Review

a. The Conduct is Found to be a Manifestation

If the team determines the conduct is a manifestation of the child's disability, then the child must be returned to the placement from which he or she was removed, unless the parent and the school personnel agree to a different placement, or unless one of the exceptions applies (see below). 20 U.S.C. § 1415(k)(1)(F). If the team concludes that the conduct was a manifestation on the grounds that the LEA had failed to implement the IEP, then the school district must take immediate steps to remedy the deficiencies. 34 C.F.R. § 300.530(e)(3). In addition, if the team concludes that the conduct was a manifestation for either possible reason, then the child's IEP team must either conduct a functional behavioral assessment and implement a behavior plan or review and modify, if necessary, a behavior plan already in place. (See section below for description of functional behavioral assessment and behavior intervention plans.) The federal regulations do not provide a time limit for conducting the functional behavior assessment, though some state rules do provide a time frame. Ohio, for example, requires that it be started within ten days of the manifestation determination review and completed as soon as practicable. *See* Ohio Operating Standards § 3301-51-05(K)(20)(f)(1).

The child must be returned to his or her usual placement following the decision of the IEP team that the behavior was a manifestation. However, if school district personnel believe that such a return is substantially likely to result in injury to the child or to others, they may initiate a due process hearing to obtain the authority to change the child's placement. The due process hearing must be expedited in these situations, with a hearing scheduled within twenty school days of the request and a decision made within ten school days of the hearing. If the hearing officer agrees that maintaining the current placement is substantially likely to result in injury to the child or to others, the hearing officer may order a change of placement to an interim alternative educational setting for not more than forty-five school days. Pending the decision of the hearing officer, the child must remain in an interim alternative educational setting. 34 C.F.R. § 300.533. Regardless of this change of setting, the child must continue to receive all the services contained in his IEP. (See below for discussion of "interim alternative educational setting.")

b.   Exceptions

Students who have engaged in certain dangerous conduct can be removed from their school placement even if their conduct is determined to be a manifestation of their disability. If the student possessed a weapon or illegal drugs at school or at a school function, or inflicted serious bodily injury on another person at school or at a school function, then the student can be removed for up to forty-five school days. In this context, a weapon is "a . . . device . . . that is used for, or is readily capable of, causing death or serious bodily injury, except that such term does not include a pocket knife with a blade of less than 2 1/2 inches in length." 18 U.S.C. § 930(g). Illegal drugs are controlled substances (defined in 21 U.S.C. § 812(c)), but do not include drugs legally prescribed to the possessor. "Serious bodily injury" means bodily injury which involves a substantial risk of death, extreme physical pain, protracted and obvious disfigurement, or protracted loss or impairment of the function of a body part or mental faculty. 18 U.S.C. § 1365(h)(3).

During the removal, the child must be placed in an "interim alternative educational setting" (IAES). 34 C.F.R. § 300.530(g). An IAES is a setting where the child can continue to have access to the general educational curriculum, progress toward meeting the goals in the child's IEP, and receive services and modifications designed to address the behavior violation so that it does not recur. An IAES can be in an alternative school or in alternative classes; it can involve the provision of instruction in alternative ways, such as using on-line resources or a home instruction program. Wherever it is, however, it must allow the student to continue with his or her educational program. *See A.W. ex rel Wilson v. Fairfax Co. Sch. Bd.*, 372 F.3d 674, 681 (4th Cir. 2004). The IEP team must determine the child's IAES for the period of removal from the child's regular placement. 34 C.F.R. § 300.531. The child's advocate should be vigilant to assure that the setting truly allows the child to have access to the general curriculum as well as to the services in the child's IEP. The longer the period of removal, the less likely the child can make reasonable progress in a non-school setting.

c.   The Conduct is Found Not to be a Manifestation

If the team determines that the conduct was not a manifestation of the child's disability, then the long-term exclusion may be imposed in the same manner as if the child were not disabled. Nevertheless, the child is entitled to continue to receive educational services so as to enable the child to participate in the general education curriculum, although in another setting. 34 C.F.R. §§ 300.101(a), 300.530(d). The child's educational services must allow the child to continue to make progress on the child's IEP goals. This means that the child is entitled to receive instruction from a qualified special education teacher and to receive his or her related services. The educational services may be provided in an "interim alternative educational setting," as described above. The IEP team must meet to determine what services will be provided during the period of exclusion from the child's regular placement. 34 C.F.R. § 300.530(d)(5). While the regulations are not explicit that the child must have exactly the same number of hours of instruction that the child received in school or that he or she have every opportunity he or she had in the previous placement, the level of services must be enough to allow the child to make reasonable progress. *See* 71 Fed. Reg. 46716 (August 14, 2006) (in commenting on the publication of 34 C.F.R. § 300.530(d), the U.S. Dept. of Education provided the following interpretation: "An LEA is not required to provide children suspended for more than 10 days in a school year for disciplinary reasons, exactly the same services in exactly the same settings as they were receiving prior to the imposition of discipline. However, the special education and related services the child does receive must enable the child to continue to participate in the general curriculum, and to progress toward meeting the goals set out in the child's IEP."). The presumption would seem to be that whatever services are included on the current IEP — which were previously determined by the IEP team to be necessary to allow the child to meet his or her goals — remain necessary to allow the child to get a FAPE. Certainly the child is entitled to get instruction, take required tests, and participate in assignments so that he or she can get credit for the work done. This is especially important in high school, where the student needs a certain number of credits and certain courses to get a high school diploma. See *Shelton v. Maya Angelou Pub. Charter Sch.*, 578 F. Supp. 2d 83 (D.D.C. 2008), for a good analysis of the services required to an excluded student whose behavior was not a manifestation of his disability.

In addition to continued educational services, the child is entitled "as appropriate" to receive a functional behavior assessment and behavioral intervention services and modifications that are designed to address the behavior violation so that it does not recur. 34 C.F.R. § 300.530(d)(1)(ii). (These services are described below.) Although no guidance is provided as to when behavior services are "appropriate," advocates should suggest their use whenever it appears that some type of behavior support could help the child refrain from misconduct in the future. This is particularly true when the child has had consistent difficulties conforming his conduct to the school rules.

Both the decision on the issue of manifestation and the decisions about the services that will be provided to the student during the period of suspension are appealable decisions. (See Chapter 10 for more detail about dispute resolution under the IDEA.) Due process hearings in this context are expedited, so that the hearing must occur within twenty school days of when the complaint was filed and the decision must be issued within ten school days after the hearing. States are given the option to establish different procedural rules for expedited hearings, although the requirements for due process hearings described in 34 C.F.R. §§ 300.510-514 must be met. During any appeal processes, the child must remain in the interim alternative educational setting with appropriate services and support until the suspension would otherwise expire or until a favorable decision by the hearing officer. 34 C.F.R § 300.533.

During an appeal of the MDR, it is possible that the child will be excluded from his or her current school for up to one year. In such a circumstance, it is important to check your state or local statutes to determine whether it is possible to appeal the decision to exclude the child from his or her current school. In California for example, if a student is determined to be excluded from school for up to one year, the California Education Code allows a student to appeal that decision based on whether, in that situation, long-term exclusion was warranted by the student's behavior. *See* Cal. Educ. Code §§ 48919-48924. In most jurisdictions, the appeal of the MDR can occur at the same time the student is taking advantage of his or her right to appeal the underlying exclusion.

TIPS FOR POST MDR:

√ If you receive the case after the MDR occurred, find out whether the parent or guardian understood what was supposed to be discussed at the MDR. Ask the parent or guardian whether anyone from the district explained the type of information that should be discussed.

√ Sometimes, you may be able to negotiate a "re-do" of the MDR when the parent was unrepresented and did not fully understand the nature of the inquiry. Some school personnel will prefer this to a due process appeal.

√ In determining whether to appeal a MDR, pay close attention to any issues relating to time limitations, such as whether the MDR was held within ten days of the decision to exclude and whether the parent was provided with prior written notice in a "timely" manner.

B.   Functional Behavioral Assessments and Behavior Intervention Plans

The IDEA requires the use of "functional behavioral assessments" and "behavior intervention plans" for children who have behavioral issues. These are tools designed to allow school personnel to better understand the child's conduct and intervene to prevent it from recurring. Although an IEP team could decide to use these tools whenever the members think they would be helpful, or when they are required by local policy, the federal law requires them following a determination that a child's conduct was a manifestation of his or her disability. They are also required "as appropriate" when the IEP team determines the conduct was not a manifestation of the disability.

1.   Functional Behavioral Assessment

A Functional Behavioral Assessment (FBA) is a process used to understand why a child is misbehaving. If done well, it should lead to strategies and interventions that will allow the student to avoid the undesirable conduct and replace the behaviors with more socially-acceptable behaviors that perform the same function for the child. Children may misbehave because they are embarrassed, bored, angry, overstimulated, overwhelmed, hungry, frustrated, disrespected, or depressed. They may need more attention, less attention, more challenging work, less difficult work, an escape, or an emotional outlet. They may lose control only in the morning, or in the cafeteria, or with a particular peer or teacher. The actual behavior may be the same regardless of the underlying function; without an understanding of the function, effective behavior strategies cannot be devised.

A good FBA will be a structured process, based on the collection of specific data and the formulation of a hypothesis. The IEP team typically begins by identifying the problem behaviors, and then, through observation and interviews, obtains data on aspects of the targeted behavior such as the setting in which it occurs, antecedent or triggering events, and previous consequences that have reinforced the behavior. For example, the identified behavior may be the use of profanity by a student in class. Through the collection of data, it may be discovered that the use of profanity occurs only in math and science class, typically when the class is engaged in group work, and results first in classmates laughing and then the offending student being removed from the classroom. The hypothesis might be that the student uses profanity when his lack of skill in math or science will be revealed to his classmates in the group work, that the laughter of his classmates gives him self-esteem, and the removal from the classroom provides an escape from the embarrassment that will occur when his classmates realize he cannot contribute to the group.

Multiple professionals should be involved in the FBA process. Many school districts have behavior specialists on staff who are trained in collecting and analyzing behavior data and developing interventions. The involvement of a behavior specialist who is not one of the child's teachers will often lend needed objectivity to the process. The team should consider the need for new evaluations and assessments to be conducted by educational psychologists or other professionals. The parent may wish to share information from the child's medical or mental health providers. When the IEP team agrees that it has gathered all relevant data, correctly identified the problem behaviors, and understands when and why it occurs, it can then develop effective and practical interventions to address the behaviors. For more resources about FBAs, *see* LDOnline, http://www.ldonline.org/article/Addressing_Student_Problem_Behavior and Center for Effective Collaboration and Practice, http://cecp.air.org/fba/.

2.   Behavior Intervention Plan

A Behavior Intervention Plan (BIP) is a plan of interventions to be put in place to reduce or eliminate the undesired behavior of the student. While neither the statute nor the regulations provide any substantive requirements for a behavior intervention plan, educational experts generally agree that behavior intervention plans should include positive strategies, instructional or curricular adjustments, modifications to the physical environment, or changes to the student's IEP to address the disruptive behaviors. A BIP also should contain strategies to teach the student "functionally equivalent" replacement behaviors (i.e., behaviors that serve the same purpose but are more acceptable). While consequences can be a part of a behavior plan, they should not be the focus of it. Unless agreed otherwise, the student will remain subject to the school's disciplinary code, so there is no reason to include those same disciplinary consequences in an individual BIP. The focus should be interventions put in place by school personnel that change the dynamic to lessen the triggers and teach the student better strategies for responding to challenging situations. A good BIP is as much about how the teachers and other school personnel will change their behavior as it is about how the student will change his or hers. *See, e.g.*, Center for Effective Collaboration and Practice, http://cecp.air.org/fba/; LD Online, http://www.ldonline.org/article/6031. California has a detailed regulatory scheme entitled Designated Positive Behavioral Interventions that incorporates many of the best practices for FBAs and BIPs. *See* 5 CCR § 3052.

Functional behavioral assessments and behavior intervention plans are not static; they must be reviewed and reconceptualized after some time has passed and an analysis can be done of what worked and what needs tweaking. The IDEA requires that an existing behavior intervention plan be reviewed each time the student is facing a change of placement of more than ten days. 20 U.S.C. § 1415(k)(1)(F).

ADVOCACY TIPS RELATED TO FBAs AND BIPs:

✓ If the disability is found to be related to the child's disability, use the Functional Behavioral Assessment, Behavior Intervention Plan, or other assessments to ensure that the child receives the appropriate supports and services in the future. The student advocate can also use these assessments to ensure the appropriate placement for the child.

✓ If an FBA from the school district was already conducted in the last year, request a reassessment or even an Independent Education Evaluation.

II.   UNIDENTIFIED CHILDREN

A child who has not been determined to be eligible for special education at the time he or she is facing exclusion of more than ten days may claim the protections of a child with a disability if the school district had knowledge that the child was a child with a disability prior to the behavior that lead to the exclusion. 34 C.F.R. § 300.534. A school district is deemed to have knowledge if, prior to the disciplinary event, the parent had expressed concern _in writing_ to either a teacher or administrator that the child needed special education, if the parent had requested an evaluation of the child, or if the child's teacher or other school personnel had expressed specific concerns about the child's pattern of behavior to the director of special education or other supervisory personnel. If the parent can establish that any of these conditions exist, then the child is entitled to a manifestation determination review prior to a disciplinary exclusion of more than ten days.

It is difficult for a team to engage in an MDR before a child has been identified, because the child typically will not have a file with assessments, psycho-educational evaluations, or an IEP. In that case, the advocate should demand that the child be returned to the classroom after the first ten days of the suspension, and that an evaluation proceed in an expedited manner. An MDR can be held as soon as the evaluation is complete and there is a determination of eligibility. The federal regulations do not explicitly require that the child be returned to the classroom, but they do explicitly say that the child may "assert any of the protections provided for." 34 C.F.R. § 300.534(a). The child would be unable to take advantage of those protections unless he is returned to the classroom pending the results of the evaluation.

If the parent cannot establish that the district had knowledge that the child was a child with a disability, the parent can still ask for an evaluation at the time of the suspension. Under those circumstances, the district must engage in an expedited evaluation. The student can be disciplined as any other child while the evaluation is proceeding, however. He would not be entitled to continued educational services unless all children are so entitled. The advocate for the child should consider whether a "child find" violation can be established in this circumstance. (See Chapter Three for more information about the child find obligation.)

In North Carolina, the circumstances of when the district will be considered to have known that the child was a child with a disability were expanded in state law. The school district will be charged with knowledge, even in the absence of a written request from the parent or an expression of concern by a teacher, "if, prior to the behavior that precipitated the disciplinary action, the behavior and performance of the child clearly and convincingly establishes the need for special education." N.C. Gen. Stat. § 115C-107.7. This standard is narrowed, however, with the following language: "Prior disciplinary infractions shall not, standing alone, constitute clear and convincing evidence." To date, there is no case law interpreting this standard.

TIPS FOR ADVOCATING FOR A CHILD WHO HAS NOT YET BEEN EVALUATED FOR SPECIAL EDUCATION AND IS INVOLVED WITH A DISCIPLINARY ISSUE:

√ Review the child's school records and medical records to find evidence of a disability (e.g., failing grades, numerous behavioral incidents, evaluation or referral by a doctor).

√ Interview the parent or guardian to find out whether a request for an evaluation has ever been made to the school.

√ Request, in writing, that the child be evaluated for special education. Also, request that the disciplinary proceedings be stayed while the child is being evaluated. If the school is not cooperative, you can suggest that the child be moved to an interim setting while the evaluation is taking place. (See Sample Letter Requesting Evaluation and Stay of Proceedings, below.)

Exclusion for 10 days or less

Student is treated like regular education student; no extra protections exist.

Exception: When exclusions add up to more than 10 days total and form a "pattern" (e.g., same type of conduct led to exclusion), school must treat it like an exclusion of more than 10 days.

Exclusion for more than 10 days

Student can be treated like regular education student for first 10 days of exclusion.

But, school must hold **Manifestation Determination Review (MDR)**, which is a specialized IEP team meeting, before student can be excluded for more than 10 days.

What Happens at the MDR?

IEP team, including parent, answers the following questions:

- Was the conduct caused by, or directly and substantially related to, the disability?
  - Example: If student gets in a fight and has only a learning disability in math, the conduct is probably not caused by the disability. But if that student has a conduct disorder, the conduct probably was caused by the disability.
- Was the conduct a direct result of the school's failure to implement the student's IEP?

If the team determines that the answer to either question is "yes," then the conduct was a "manifestation."

If conduct **is not a "manifestation"**:

- School can impose exclusion as it would for nondisabled child.
- Student can appeal finding that conduct was not a manifestation, but exclusion stands pending appeal.
- School must still provide a "free appropriate public education" to student during period of exclusion, though in another setting.
- School should perform functional behavioral assessment "as appropriate."
- School should establish a behavior intervention plan "as appropriate."

If conduct **is a "manifestation"**:

- Exclusion cannot be imposed beyond 10 days.
- IEP team can change services provided to student.
- IEP team can change student's placement.
- School must always perform "functional behavioral assessment."
- School must always establish "behavior intervention plan."
- Exception applies, allowing removal to an alternative education setting for 45 school days if the student possessed a weapon or illegal drugs or inflicted serious bodily injury.

Ronald

Ronald is a 17-year-old student who receives special education services under the category of Other Health Impaired. He is in his third year as a ninth grader because he has not accumulated enough credits to be considered a tenth grader. He has a diagnosis of Attention Deficit Hyperactivity Disorder. His most recent psycho-educational evaluation completed by a school psychologist noted in the "reason for referral" section of the report that when he was enrolled in a new school during 7th grade that his behavior deteriorated as he attempted to fit in with socially maladjusted classmates. The psychologist added, "He developed an attitude in which he swaggered down the halls, refused redirection and became annoying to both students and staff." Therefore, a decision was made to refer for a special education evaluation.

The psychologist included in her report that Ronald's mother produced a medical evaluation from Ronald's doctor confirming the diagnosis of ADHD and saying that Ronald was not taking medication because previous medication attempts were unsuccessful. The psychologist administered several formal instruments to assess cognitive potential, visual-motor integration, achievement tests, and behavior scales. She noted that Ronald resisted the academic tests at first and required consistent encouragement to complete the tests. The psychologist also noted significant attention problems during the testing. He needed breaks every 15-20 minutes, frequently asked how much longer he would need to be there, was very physically active — i.e., moving about in his chair, tipping it backwards, and was unable to maintain a high level of concentration on auditory or visual tasks for more than 90 seconds without needing redirection. As a result, the psychologist suggested that while the tests results likely provided a good picture of Ronald's "typical" performance, it is likely that they underestimate his "true" or potential abilities.

The psychologist administered the WISC-IV, but did not report a full scale IQ score. On the subscores, she reported the following:

Verbal comprehension — 77

Perceptual Reasoning — 63

Working Memory — 68

Processing Speed — 73

These scores are considered "extremely low" to "borderline." The psychologist also administered the Woodcock-Johnson III to measure his academic achievement. These scores showed that his academic achievement is in the average range:

Basic reading — 93

Reading comprehension — 84

Math Calculation — 97

Math Reasoning — 91

Written Expression — 88

The psychologist also administered the Achenback scales to three teachers to assess Ronald's emotional and social adjustment. These results show him presenting as having more "total problems" than 90 to 98% of boys his age. On social problems, he ranked in the 92nd - 97th percentiles; attention problems, 89th - 97th percentiles; hyperactivity-impulsivity 77th-

97th percentiles.

On the referral form for special education services, teachers noted his difficulties concentrating, frustration with routine tasks, difficulty following directions, careless and messy work, disorganization, and susceptibility to distractions.

On his IEP, he has an organizational goal and a behavior goal. His present level of performance regarding behavior is as follows: "Ronald's behavior is erratic. He is sociable with peers and adults at times. When reprimanded/redirected for relatively minor infractions, he becomes disrespectful and belligerent, uses profanity and refuses to comply. His responding behavior escalates and disrupts the normal routine and results in out-of-school suspension." His annual goal is, "Ronald will demonstrate appropriate behavior in the school setting."

In the recent past, Ronald has been suspended from school on several occasions. Here are the descriptions of behavior, as recorded by school administrators:

October 15 — 4-day suspension:

"A student reported that Ronald touched her on the butt. I asked Ronald to tell me his side of the story. He reacted by yelling, walking out of the cafeteria, and becoming very irate. He walked down the hallway yelling and punching doors with his fist. I continued to try to get his attention and directed him to the office, but he ignored my request. Ronald's behavior disrupted the lunch period, guidance department, office area and the overall school environment."

December 10 — 2-day suspension:

"Ronald was very disruptive in in-school suspension. He refused to stop talking and moving around the room. Ronald was told before serving ISS that he would be suspended if he did not follow the rules and was given two warnings while in ISS."

January 20 — 5-day suspension:

"A teacher reported that a tennis ball was thrown in her classroom and hit her in the head. The ball was thrown from the area Ronald was sitting. When questioned, Ronald said the ball did come from his area and he believed the person who threw the ball meant to hit another student, not the teacher. During an investigation, many witnesses stated they saw Ronald throw the ball."

The school has performed a functional behavioral assessment and put a behavior intervention plan in place. The behaviors targeted in the plan are: class disruption, profanity, disrespect to authority, out of area, assault on other student." The desired behaviors are "follow class rules, speak respectfully, remain in assigned area." The team felt he engaged in the undesirable behaviors to "gain attention from staff and peers, assert power/control, and escape from an activity or task." The behavior intervention plan includes support from the Behavior Support Teacher during each period, assistance from the Behavior Support Teacher with problem-solving and controlling temper, being accompanied by a Behavior Support Teacher when removed from class, and daily feedback sheets. In addition, Ronald is to process his actions by writing out what happened. Reinforcers are: positive phone calls home, preferential seating, "behavior tickets" which can lead to weekly rewards, and verbal positive reinforcement. Consequences for non-compliance include removal from classroom and suspension when behaviors violate the Code of Conduct.

Ronald is now facing an exclusion for the remainder of the school year. The facts, as described by the school administrator, are as follows:

> February 12 — Ronald was being disruptive in Dr. Watson's third period class. Ronald pushed papers off of a student's desk. He later walked out. He was seen outside the building and was redirected to room 518 by Mr. Robinson. Ronald came to room 518 and Mr. Robinson called Ronald's mother to tell her what happened. Ronald became upset that Mr. Robinson called his mother and began to use profanity. Mr. Robinson asked Ronald to utilize his behavior plan and write out what happened. Ronald refused and failed to comply. He balled the paper and threw it in the trash. Mr. Robinson asked him to get the paper out and give it back so Mr. Robinson could have it for his records. Ronald took the paper out of the trash can and tore it up. As Mr. Robinson was talking to Ronald, Ronald started to tell Mr. Robinson to "shut the f — up" and "don't f — ing talk to me." Mr. Robinson asked Ronald to sit in a chair. Ronald continued with the profanity, grabbed a chair, and charged at Mr. Robinson. Mr. Robinson said to Ronald, "You are not going to intimidate me." Ronald then threw the chair to the floor. The chair landed near the feet of Mr. Robinson. At that point, the school resource officer (from the local police department) entered the room and escorted Ronald to another room.

The school administration has scheduled a Manifestation Determination Review. Questions: How would you make the argument that the behavior is a manifestation of the disability? What kind of argument would you expect the school officials to make? What is the correct result of the review? What should happen to Ronald next?

SAMPLE LETTER REQUESTING EVALUATION AND STAY OF PROCEEDINGS

[DATE]

[PRINCIPAL]
[SCHOOL]
[SCHOOL ADDRESS]

Sent Via Facsimile [NUMBER] and U.S. Mail

RE: Request for Initial Assessment and I.E.P. Meeting
  [STUDENT], D.O.B. [DATE OF BIRTH]

Dear Sir or Madam:

Our Clinic represents [STUDENT NAME], a student currently being recommended for expulsion from [SCHOOL]. I am including our authorization to release information signed by [NAME OF STUDENT'S PARENT OR GUARDIAN].

We are writing to request a comprehensive Psycho-Educational Assessment for [STUDENT NAME]. In addition, we ask that the pending expulsion hearing be held in abeyance until his/her assessments are completed. [STUDENT] is in [INSERT GRADE LEVEL] and has been exhibiting behavioral problems and failing grades since the [INSERT GRADE LEVEL].

[INSERT DISCUSSION OF PROBLEM]

[AN EXAMPLE OF DESCRIPTION OF THE PROBLEM: In the expulsion packet provided to us, the school expressly admits that "during the past two years, STUDENT has been suspended five different times. Prior offenses include disruption of school activities, defiance to authority, physical confrontations, and possession/use of inhalants. Interventions for the mentioned violations included counseling, parent conferences, Saturday school detention, citations, behavior contracts, intervention transfers to another middle school and suspensions."

STUDENT'S school records show that she has had 22 different behavior disruptions or incidents within the last two years. With respect to these incidents, STUDENT has specifically been disciplined in the following manner: in the form of Saturday school 7 times, assigned detention 4 times, suspended from school 5 times, and conference/counseling 4 times. STUDENT'S behavior shows a pattern of disruptive conduct that is inhibiting her ability to learn. This 2009-2010 school year alone she has missed 15 days of school as a result of her behavior. Aside from the punitive measures taken by the school as noted above, the school has not attempted to use any other forms of intervention such as anger management classes, school counseling, or other restorative practices that would attempt to correct STUDENT'S negative behavior. The types of behaviors that STUDENT has exhibited are troublesome. These behaviors suggest that STUDENT may be experiencing other issues that are causing her to act out.]

Thus, we are requesting a multi-disciplinary team evaluation to determine whether [STUDENT NAME] is eligible for special education and related services under IDEA, 20 U.S.C. 1400 et seq. (including the IDEA "Other Health Impaired" category), Section 504 of the Rehabilitation Act of 1973, 29 U.S.C. Section 794, California Education Code Sections 56029 and 56302, and 5 CCR Section 3021.

In preparation for this meeting, we are requesting that comprehensive assessments be conducted in all areas of suspected disability including, but not limited to: [health and development, vision, including low vision, hearing, motor abilities, language function [speech/language], general intelligence, academic performance, communicative status, self-help, orientation and mobility skills, career and vocational abilities and interests, and social and emotional status. *See* Cal. Educ. Code Section 56320(f).

[**Option 1:** Because of [STUDENT NAME'S] low reading level, we also request that HE/
SHE][be assessed for a reading disorder by a neuropsychologist or a reading specialist trained to diagnose such disorders. *See*, e.g. Cal. Educ. Code Section 56320(f) (child must be assessed in all areas of "suspected disability"); Cal. Educ. Code Section 56337(a) (discussing identification of children with disabilities in the areas of "basic reading skills" and "reading comprehension"). If the district does not have such a specialist, we request that the district pay for an appropriately trained specialist to assess [STUDENT'S NAME].] Id.

[**Option 2:** [DESCRIBE PROBLEM] We are also requesting an assessment of the fine and gross motor skill deficits to determine whether occupational and physical therapy are appropriate related services. *See* Cal. Educ. Code Sections 56320(f); 56363(b)(6), and 2 CCR Section 60320.]

[**Option 3:** We are concerned that [STUDENT NAME] is having difficulty with basic visual functions, such as eye teaming. Thus, we are making a specific request a vision behavioral assessment to determine whether [STUDENT NAME] needs vision therapy. *See* Cal. Educ. Code Sections 56320(f) and 56363(b)(7); CCR Section 3051.75.]

[**Option 4**: We are also making a specific request for a speech/language assessment to determine whether [STUDENT NAME] is eligible for speech/language therapy. *See* Cal Educ. Code Sections 56320(f) and 56363(b)(1).]

[**Option 5:** As you know, [STUDENT'S NAME] is 16, and therefore old enough to begin receiving transitional services. We look forward to discussing the individual transitional plan ("ITP") with you at this meeting, which shall include "appropriate measurable postsecondary goals based upon age-appropriate transition assessments" and "needed transition services." *See* Cal. Educ. Code Section 56345.1; 56043(g)(1); 56345(a)(8). In order to create an effective plan, please invite the following agency representatives: [FOR EXAMPLE: (1) DEPARTMENT OF REHABILITATION; (2) WORKABILITY SPECIALIST; (3) DEPARTMENT OF CHILDREN AND FAMILY SERVICES INDEPENDENT LIVING PROGRAM CO-ORDINATOR, IF APPROPRIATE; (4) REGIONAL CENTER]

[**Option 6:** As you know, [STUDENT'S NAME] will be entering high school [or has just begun high school] and is in need of an appropriate transition plan. Please ensure that a copy of the student's transcript, and the appropriate transition personnel are available for the meeting. *See* Cal. Educ. Code Section 56043(e) and (h).]

[**Option 7:** At this time, we are also requesting a copy of all school records for [STUDENT NAME], including, but not limited to, the cumulative file and **ALL**:

- Individualized Education Programs ("IEPs");
- Disciplinary Records, including, but not limited to, suspension and expulsion notices and referrals to a counselor or other school official;
- Attendance Records;
- Standardized Test Scores;
- Reports;

- Assessments and protocols;
- Grades/Progress Reports;
- Notes by teachers or other staff members;
- Memoranda.

See IDEA, 20 U.S.C. Sections 1415(b)(1), 34 C.F.R. Section 300.562, FERPA, 20 U.S.C. 1232(g), and 34 C.F.R. Section 99.10. As you are aware, <u>the law mandates that our office receive such records within the next five days</u>. *See* Cal. Educ. Code Sections 56504 and 56043(n).]

[**Option 8:** We are requesting that a district representative who is knowledgeable about district programs and who has the authority to encumber funds be present at the IEP meeting. *See* Cal. Educ. Code Section 56341(b)(4). Please provide us with documentation that [NAME OF DISTRICT REPRESENTIVE] or designee has been contacted.]

[**Option 9:** We are also requesting that the following individuals be invited to the meeting: [FOR EXAMPLE, REGIONAL CENTER REPRESENTATIVE, DCFS REPRESENTATIVE, TEACHER W/ KNOWLEDGE OF CLIENT'S ABILITIES]

[**Option 10:** Because [NAME OF CLIENT]'s primary language is [LANGUAGE], please provide an individual trained in special education terminology who can provide contemporaneous translation services in [LANGUAGE]. *See* Cal. Educ. Code Sections 56341.5(i) and 56341(b)(5).]

[**Option 11:** A [MORNING/AFTERNOON] IEP meeting would be convenient for [NAME OF CLIENT]. As you know, all efforts should be made to schedule the IEP meeting at a mutually agreed upon time and place. *See* Cal. Educ. Code Sections 56341.5(c) and 56341.1(f).]

<u>I look forward to receiving a copy of the assessment plan sent to [CLIENT'S NAME] within 15 days</u>. Please be sure to attach a notice of parent's rights. *See* Cal. Educ. Code Section 56321(a).

[**Option 12:** Please ensure that the assessment plan is in the primary language of the parent or guardian. *See* Cal. Educ. Code Section 56321(b)(2). As you may know, [CLIENT'S NAME]'s primary language is [LANGUAGE].]

Please also:

1. Fax or send a copy of <u>any and all assessments, evaluations, and the protocols</u> to my attention within a reasonable time prior to the meeting, *See* Cal. Educ. Code Section 56329(a)(3);

2. Schedule at least three hours for the meeting; and

3. Ensure that all required members of the I.E.P. team may participate for the duration of the meeting.

<u>I look forward to receiving notice regarding the proposed date and time for the I.E.P. meeting</u>. Thank you in advance for your prompt action regarding these matters.

Sincerely,

[NAME]
[TITLE]

Enclosure

III.   MANIFESTATION DETERMINATION REVIEW SIMULATION

In light of what you have learned in this chapter, break into groups and participate in the following simulation involving a manifestation determination review meeting. The group information for each part is listed below. Confidential information can be found in the teacher's manual.

MEMORANDUM

To: Clinic Students
From: Clinic Professor
RE: Role Play Exercise —
           MDR
Date:

The following will give you the background you will need to participate in a role-play exercise of a Manifestation Determination Review. This is a meeting that must be held by relevant members of the IEP team before a disabled student is subject to long-term exclusion resulting in a "change in placement." The purpose of the meeting is to determine whether the behavior subject to discipline was a manifestation of the student's disability. If it was, then the student may not be suspended from school. The regulations regarding MDRs are found at 34 C.F.R. § 300.356; the statutory provisions are at 20 U.S.C. § 1415(k)(1)(A), (C), (F). Additional material is found in the Discipline chapter of your textbook.

The case involves a 17-year-old student, TK Connor. TK is in the 10th grade. He has been in special education throughout his time in school due to his low IQ. He was originally labeled as "Educable Mentally Disabled," but now is considered "Intellectually Disabled." This is only a matter of a change in terminology, not definition. TK participates in what is known as the "Occupational Course of Study." This is a high school course of study especially designed for students with cognitive impairments who cannot reasonably be expected to meet the requirements of a standard high school diploma. They can get an OCS diploma if they successfully complete the OCS. The OCS is a combination of classroom work and vocational work. Students must complete 900 hours of work during their high school years. These include in-school work hours (unpaid); community hours (unpaid) and paid work. The school provides a job coach who helps the students find work and understand the requirements of the job. The academic work is vocationally oriented as well.

In North Carolina, where this exercise is set, a principal has the power to suspend a student for misconduct for up to ten days, and may recommend to the Superintendent of the school district a "long-term suspension" (up through the end of the current academic year). Students have the right to a hearing to challenge the recommendation of long-term suspension, but when a student is disabled, the MDR occurs before the hearing. Thus, if the conduct is determined to be a manifestation of the disability, the principal is required to withdraw the recommendation for long-term suspension. If it is found not to be a manifestation, then the student may proceed with a hearing as would any non-disabled student.

In the MDR, two questions are asked of the team: 1) Was the conduct in question caused by, or did it have a direct and substantial relationship to the child's disability? 2) Was the conduct in question the direct result of the school district's failure to implement the student's IEP? You should assume, for purposes of this exercise, that there is no argument that the school district did not implement the IEP. The IEP was just about to have a behavior plan attached to it, as a result of the meeting held earlier in the day on the day of the suspension, but the incidents in question took place before this meeting. Thus, the behavior plan was not in place when the alleged behavior occurred. Thus, the focus should be on whether there is a direct and substantial relationship between the conduct and the disability.

The documents included for your use during the exercise are the following:

1.   TK's current IEP;

2. TK's most recent psychological evaluation;
3. Minutes from an IEP meeting conducted on the morning of the suspension;
4. The Notice of Suspension;
5. MDR Form.

Each of you will play a role at the meeting. Each of you should think about your role in the meeting, especially in relation to the questions that should be answered by the team at the meeting. You will receive some information about the role you are to play, but you should develop your own character and position (consistent with the information you are provided about your character). Think through what your goals would be, were you the person assigned, and how you would articulate them to the rest of the meeting participants. In preparation for the exercise, you should talk to the other persons that you would talk to in your role. For example, the parent and the parent's attorney would be in conversation; the teachers might talk together ahead of time; the school's attorney would likely consult with the Assistant Principal.

Roles:

Ms. Connor, parent

Attorney for parent

Ms. Spencer, assistant principal

Ms. Salls, school psychologist

Ms. Angell, special education facilitator

Ms. Yarborough, special education teacher

Mr. Foster, OCS job coordinator (optional role)

Attorney for school district

DURHAM PUBLIC SCHOOL
INDIVIDUALIZED EDUCATION PROGRAM (IEP)

Duration of Special Education and Related Services: From: <u>10/29/10</u> To: <u>10/28/11</u>

Student: <u>TK Connor</u>   DOB: <u>7/23/93</u>

School: <u>Northside High School</u>   Grade: <u>10th</u>

I. Area of Eligibility

( ) Autistic   ( ) Speech-Language Disabled

( ) Behaviorally-Emotionally Dis-   ($\checkmark$) Intellectually Disabled   ( ) Traumatic Brain Injured
abled

( ) Deaf-Blind   ( ) Orthopedically Impaired   ( ) Developmentally Delayed

( ) Hearing Impaired   ( ) Other Health Impaired   ( ) Visually Impaired

( ) Multihandicapped   ( ) Specific Learning Disabled

A. Additional Area(s) of Need: N/A

II. Consideration of Special Factors

A.	Student overalls strengths: TK has relative strength in math calculations. He will talk about things if he is feeling troubled.
B.	Parent's concerns, if any, for enhancing the student's education: None

C.	Special factors to be considered:
	Does the student have behavior(s) that impede his/her learning or that of others?
	( ) Yes ($\checkmark$) No
	Does the student have Limited English Proficiency?
	( ) Yes ($\checkmark$) No
	If the student is blind or partially sighted will the instruction in or use of Braille be needed?
	( ) Yes ($\checkmark$) No

Does the student have any special communication needs? If the student is deaf or hard of hearing, see directions.)

      ( ) Yes ($\checkmark$) No

Does the student require assistive technology devices and/or services

      ( ) Yes ($\checkmark$) No

D.	Other factors to be addressed: _____

Does the student require adapted physical education?

      ( ) Yes ($\checkmark$) No

Is the student's age 14 or older, or will the student turn 14 during the duration of the IEP?

      ($\checkmark$) Yes ( ) No

      If yes, transition services:

      $\checkmark$ component attached _____ stated in the IEP: n/a

Has the student been informed of his/her own rights, if age 17 or older?

( ) Yes ( ) No

Prime Exceptionality Intellectual Disability

Student's Name	Grade	School	DOB	IEP Begin Dt.	IEP End Dt.
Connor, TK	10th		07/23/93	10/29/10	10/28/11

Exceptionality/Rel. Service	**Teacher Provider**	**#Sessions**	**Mins. Per Session**
Intellectual Disability	EC Teacher	30 per week	56

Present Level of Performance (Include specific descriptions of strengths and needs that apply to academic performance, behaviors, social/emotional development, learning styles, physical limitations, and other relevant information).

TK will participate in reading activities. He will need to increase his vocabulary to become a better reader and to interpret and understand the information that he is reading.

Identified Area: **Communication Skills**   Skill Area: Levels 9-12

Annual Goal #: 1 The student will develop essential vocabulary.

Benchmarks or Short-Term Instructional Objectives	**Criteria for Mastery**	**How Progress will be measured**	**How and when Parents will be informed**	**Notes**
Defines new words encountered in reading selections	With 80% accuracy	Teacher Observation and recording	Progress Report and Report Card	
Uses dictionary to determine meanings of new words encountered in different reading selections	With 80% accuracy	Teacher Observation and recording	Progress Report and Report Card	

Identified Area: **02**   Skill Area: Levels 9-12

Annual Goal #: 2 The student will listen carefully and with discrimination in order to interpret information with understanding

Benchmarks or Short-Term Instructional Objectives	**Criteria for Mastery**	**How Progress will be measured**	**How and when Parents will be informed**	**Notes**
Listens interpretatively in order to infer purpose	With 80% accuracy	Teacher Observation and recording	Progress Report and Report Card	
Listens interpretatively in order to infer main ideas	With 80% accuracy	Teacher Observation and recording	Progress Report and Report Card	
Listens interpretatively in order to infer supporting details	With 80% accuracy	Teacher Observation and recording	Progress Report and Report Card	

Prime Exceptionality: Intellectual Disability

Student's Name	Grade	School	DOB	IEP Begin Dt.	IEP End Dt.
Connor, TK	10th		07/23/93	10/29/10	10/28/11

Exceptionality/Rel. Service	**Teacher Provider**	**#Sessions**	**Mins. Per Session**
ID	EC Teacher	30 per week	56

Present Level of Performance (Include specific descriptions of strengths and needs that apply to academic performance, behaviors, social/emotional development, learning styles, physical limitations, and other relevant information).

TK is working on campus. He knows the importance of coming to school, he will need assistance in developing skills to get him ready for working outside of school

Identified Area: **Work**   Skill Area: Prevocational

Annual Goal #: <u>3</u> The student will begin to develop good work habits through personal performance at school.

Benchmarks or Short-Term Instructional Objectives	Criteria for Mastery	How Progress will be measured	How and when Parents will be Informed	Notes
Comes to school regularly and on time	With 90% accuracy	Teacher Observation and recording	Progress Report and Report Card	
Accepts and carries out assigned responsibilities	With 90% accuracy	Teacher Observation and recording	Progress Report and Report Card	
Works independently for a given time	With 90% accuracy	Teacher Observation and recording	Progress Report and Report Card	

Identified Area: **Work** Skill Area: Prevocational

Annual Goal #: <u>4</u> The student will begin to develop good work habits through personal performance at school

Benchmarks or Short-Term Instructional Objectives	Criteria for Mastery	How Progress will be measured	How and when Parents will be Informed	Notes
Brings proper supplies to school	With 90% accuracy	Teacher Observation and recording	Progress Report and Report Card	
Identifies needs and ways to be less dependent on adults	With 90% accuracy	Teacher Observation and recording	Progress Report and Report Card	
Correlates school experiences with work experiences	With 90% accuracy	Teacher Observation and recording	Progress Report and Report Card	

Prime Exceptionality Intellectual Disability

Student's Name	Grade	School	DOB	IEP Begin Dt.	IEP End Dt.
Connor, TK	10th		07/23/93	10/29/10	10/28/11

Exceptionality/Rel. Service	Teacher Provider	#Sessions	Mins. Per Session
ID	EC Teacher	30 per Week	56

Present Level of Performance (Include specific descriptions of strengths and needs that apply to academic performance, behaviors, social/emotional development, learning styles, physical limitations, and other relevant information).

TK is able to compute whole numbers, he will need assistance with understanding decimals and how they can be related to everyday life.

Identified Area: **Math Skills**   Skill Area: Levels 6-8

Annual Goal #: 1 The student will demonstrate an understanding of decimals and their applications

Benchmarks or Short-Term Instructional Objectives	Criteria for Mastery	How Progress will be measured	How and when Parents will be Informed	Notes
Reads and writes decimals	With 80% accuracy	Teacher Observation and Recording	Progress Report and Report Card	
Reads and writes money values	With 80% accuracy	Teacher Observation and Recording	Progress Report and Report Card	
Compares any two decimals	With 80% accuracy	Teacher Observation and recording	Progress Report and Report Card	

Identified Area: **06**   Skill Area: Levels 6-8

Annual Goal #: 2 The student will demonstrate an understanding of decimals and their applications

Benchmarks or Short-Term Instructional Objectives	Criteria for Mastery	How Progress will be measured	How and when Parents will be Informed	Notes
Round decimals to a designated place	With 80% accuracy	Teacher Observation and recording	Progress Report and Report Card	
Adds, subtract, multiplies and divides decimals	With 80% accuracy	Teacher Observation and recording	Progress Report and Report Card	
Solves problems using decimals	With 80% accuracy	Teacher Observation and recording	Progress Report and Report Card	

Prime Exceptionality Intellectual Disability

Student's Name	Grade	School	DOB	IEP Begin Dt.	IEP End Dt.
Connor, TK	10th		07/23/93	10/29/	10/28/

Exceptionality/Rel. Service	Teacher Provider	#Sessions Per	Mins./ Session	Hours/Week
ID	EC Teacher	30 per Week	56	28.00

Present Level of Performance (Include specific descriptions of strengths and needs that apply to academic performance, behaviors, social/emotional development, learning styles, physical limitations, and other relevant information).

TK has a good understanding of the functions of a bank, he will need assistance in learning how to calculate his hours worked, reading and understanding his paycheck stub

Identified Area: **Math Skills**   Skill Area: Levels 6-8

Annual Goal #: 3 The student will solve problems related to banking

Benchmarks or Short-Term Instructional Objectives	Criteria for Mastery	How Progress will be measured	How and when Parents will be Informed	Notes
Completes deposit slips and checks	With 90% accuracy	Teacher Observation and Recording	Progress Report and Report Card	
Reconciles bank statements	With 90% accuracy	Teacher Observation and Recording	Progress Report and Report Card	
Uses table to find interest on a loan	With 90% accuracy	Teacher Observation and recording	Progress Report and Report Card	

Identified Area: **Math Skills**   Skill Area: Levels 6-8

Annual Goal #: <u>4</u> The student will solve problems related to income

Benchmarks or Short-Term Instructional Objectives	Criteria for Mastery	How Progress will be measured	How and when Parents will be Informed	Notes
Computes wages	With 90% accuracy	Teacher Observation and recording	Progress Report and Report Card	
Computes pay using hourly wage and overtime	With 90% accuracy	Teacher Observation and recording	Progress Report and Report Card	
Interprets paycheck	With 90% accuracy	Teacher Observation and recording	Progress Report and Report Card	

DURHAM PUBLIC SCHOOL
INDIVIDUALIZED EDUCATION PROGRAM (IEP)

Duration of Special Education and Related Services: From: 10/29/ 10   To: 10/28/11

Student: TK Connor _____ DOB: 7/23/93_____

School: ____Northside High_____ Grade: 10th_____

V. Least Restrictive Environment (Placement)

A. Appropriate supplementary aids, services, and modification(s)/accommodation for instruction and testing and/supports for school personnel, if any:

Tests get read aloud, except on reading tests; student gets 1.5 times the regular time for tests; student may mark answers in the test booklet; student may have multiple test sessions; student may be tested in a separate room.

1. Regular Program Participation: Circle the regular class(es) and activities in which the student is enrolled and list the letters for any modifications in the blank provided.

___Reading	___Library	___History	___Foreign Language	___Recess
___English	___Music/Art	___Science	___Physical Education	___Homeroom
___Spelling	___Economics	___Health	___Chapter 1	___Vocational
___Math	___Soc. Studies	___Writing	___Remediation	___Other
√ Lunch	√ Assemblies	___Lang. Arts	___Extracurricular Activities	

2. North Carolina Testing Program: List the letter(s) of any accommodations on the line provided.
   ( ) Regular Test Administration_____   _____
   (√) Test Administration with Accommodations read aloud, extended time, mark in book, multiple sessions, separate room
   ( ) N.C. Alternate Assessment Academic inventory_____
   ( ) N.C. Alternate Assessment Portfolio_____
   ( ) Computer Skills Test_____
   ( ) Computer Skills Portfolio_____

If a student is taking an alternate assessment, why is the regular testing not appropriate:
_____

Comments (if needed):_____

For preschool children, describe how the child is involved in a regular program:
_____

A.   Anticipated Frequency and Location:

Type of Service	Sessions Per: Week or Month or Reporting Period	Amount of Time Per Session	Location
Special Education *pullout*	30	56	EC Classroom
Related Services			
( ) Counseling Services	_____	_____	_____
( ) Occupational Therapy	_____	_____	_____
( ) Physical Therapy	_____	_____	_____
( ) Speech Language	_____	_____	_____
( )Other	_____	_____	_____
( )Transportation			
(√)None			

DURHAM PUBLIC SCHOOL
INDIVIDUALIZED EDUCATION PROGRAM (IEP)

Duration of Special Education and Related Services: From: 10/29/10   To: 10/28/11

Student: TK Connor _____   DOB: 7/23/93_____

School: __Northside High School_____   Grade: _10th_____

C. Continuum of Alternative Placements: Check placement selected by IEP Team:
School Age

( ) Regular- 80% or more of the day with non-disabled peers   ( ) Private Separate School
( ) Resource- 40%-79% of the day with non-disabled peers   ( ) Public Residential
(√) Separate-39% or less of the day with non-disabled peers   ( ) Private Residential
( ) Public Separate School   ( ) Home/Hospital

Preschool

( ) Early Childhood Setting   ( ) Residential Setting
( ) Part-Time Early Childhood/Part-Time Early Childhood Special Education   ( ) Home
( ) Early Childhood Special Education Setting   ( ) Itinerant Service Outside Home
( ) Separate Setting   ( ) Reverse Mainstream Setting

D. If the student will be removed from his/her non-disabled peers for any part of the day (regular class, extracurricular activities non-academic activities), explain why.
TK requires small setting for optimal academic success.

VI. Explain how and when parents will be informed of the student's progress toward annual goals:
    Through progress reports and report card.

VII.   Extended School Year Status
        (√) Is not eligible for extended school year
        ( ) Is eligible for extended school year
        ( ) Eligibility is under consideration and will be determined by ___/___/___

VIII. IEP Team.   The following were present and participated in the development and writing of the IEP.

Signature	Position	Date
Ms. Spencer	LEA Representative	
Mr. Carter	Regular Education Teacher	
Ms. Yarborough	Special Education Teacher	
Ms. Connor	Parent	
Ms. Angell	EC Facilitator	
Ms. Salls	School Psychologist	

IX. IEP Addendum Team. The following were present and participated in the development and writing of the IEP.

Signature	Position	Date
	LEA Representative	
	Regular Education Teacher	
	Special Education Teacher	
	Parent	

X. Reevaluation. The IEP was reviewed at reevaluation and was found to be appropriate. An annual review of this IEP will be conducted on or before ___/___/___.

Signature	Position	Date
	LEA Representative	
	Regular Education Teacher	
	Special Education Teacher	
	Parent	

DURHAM PUBLIC SCHOOLS

Confidential Psychological Report

Name: TK Connor
Date of Birth: 7/23/93
Dates of Evaluation: 9/3/09, 9/9/09
Chronological Age: 17-1
Gender: Male
Race: African-American
School: Northside High School
Grade: 10
Psychologist: Ms. Linda Salls

REASON FOR REFERRAL:

TK is currently being referred for a psychological evaluation as part of his required three year re-evaluation. He is currently identified as Intellectually Disabled (ID) and is in the Occupational Course of Study (OCS).

SOURCES OF INFORMATION:

Review of Records

Behavioral Observations

Student Interview

Wechsler Intelligence Scale for Children - Third Edition (WISC-III)

Behavior Assessment for Children (BASC) — Teach Rating Scales

BASC Parent Rating Scales

BASC Self-Report of Personality

Incomplete Sentences Blank — High School Form

BACKGROUND INFORMAION:

In reviewing TK's Exceptional Children's folder it was noted that he was originally evaluated in the fall of 1999 at the age of six. At the time he demonstrated mildly mentally impaired cognitive ability on the Wechsler Preschool Scale of Intelligence — Revised Edition (Verbal — 69, Performance — 66, Full Scale — 65). He had the following scores on the Vineland Adaptive Behavior Scales: Communication — 60, Daily Living Skills — 53, Socialization — 61, Adaptive Behavior Composite — 53. On the Woodcock-Johnson Tests of Achievement-Revised Edition (WJ-R — ACH) he demonstrated mildly mentally impaired math skills and low average reading and written language skills (Broad Reading — 82, Broad Math — 58, and Broad Written Language — 88). This evaluation resulted in TK being identified as Educable Mentally Handicapped (EMH). Occupational therapy was added as a related service in November of 1999.

TK was re-evaluated in the fall of 2002, at the age of nine. He demonstrated mildly mentally impaired ability on the Wechsler Intelligence Scale for Children — Third Edition (WISC-III) Verbal — 69, Performance — 69, and Full Scale — 66). On the WJ-R — ACH he demonstrated mildly mentally impaired written language skills, borderline math skills, and low average reading skills (Broad Reading — 82, Broad Math — 79, and Broad Written Language — 55). The following scores were reported on the Vineland Adaptive Behavior Scales: Communication — 64, Daily Living Skills — 64, Socialization — 60, and Adaptive Behavior Composite — 58. This re-evaluation resulted in TK continuing to be identified as EMH.

TK's most recent comprehensive evaluation occurred during the '04-'05 school year, when he was 11 years old. He continued to demonstrate mildly mentally impaired cognitive ability on the WISC-III (Verbal — 65, Performance — 72, Full Scale — 66). On the Vineland Adaptive Behavior Scale he received an Adaptive Behavior Composite of 76 on the Interview Edition and 78 on the Classroom Edition. He received the following scores on the WJ-R — ACH (Broad Reading — 73, Broad Math — 79, and Broad Written Language — 67). He received the following score on the Diagnostic Achievement Battery — Second Edition: Listening — 73, Speaking - <50, Reading — 58, Writing — 62, Math — 76. This re-evaluation resulted in TK being identified as Intellectually Disabled (which was not a substantive change; the law changed the terminology).

In October of 2004, no formalized testing was completed. However, it was determined that TK continued to have an Intellectual Disability (ID). He has had a history of behavioral problems and at one point in middle school was in a self-contained classroom for students who have a Behavioral Emotional Disability (BED). In December of 2009, when he was in 9th grade, TK was given a long term suspension for fighting and was sent to an alternative school for the remainder of the school year.

During the pre-re-evaluation meeting on 11/05/10 it was reported that TK was able to do modified work within the classroom. Reading continues to be an area of weakness. Concentration and impulsive behavior are problems for TK. His mother reported that he has not had a behavior evaluation. TK passed a hearing and vision screening on 11/17/10.

BEHAVIORAL OBSERVATIONS:

Ms. Salvendy, school psychologist observed TK on 9/9/10 in his self-contained Occupational Course of Study (OCS) class. He is considered a 10th grader. During the observation the class was working on consumer education. A total of five male students, two female students, a teaching assistant, and the teacher were present. Later, an additional male student entered the room. TK sat in the third seat from the front in the middle of the room. The lights were off with one blind open. TK was following in his book while the students took turns reading. He read aloud okay and knew where the class was when it was his turn to read. He read aloud several times, volunteering to read one of the times. He answered written questions and worked on his vocabulary independently (as did his classmates). The teacher walked around the room checking the student's work. TK needed some minor corrections.

TK approached the evaluation in a neutral manner with his arms crossed. However, rapport was established and maintained throughout the evaluation. TK was cooperative and maintained good attention and concentration. He was not willing to take a guess to questions that he wasn't sure he knew the answer. It is felt that the following results are a fairly accurate measure of his current ability level.

ASSESSMENT RESULTS AND INTERPRETATION:

Wechsler Intelligence Scale for Children — Third Edition

Verbal	Scaled Score	Performance	Scaled Score
Information	2	Picture Completion	5
Similarities	1	Coding	5
Arithmetic	5	Picture Arrangement	4
Vocabulary	1	Block Design	1
Comprehension	2	Object Assembly	3

	IQ	Percentile	95% Confidence Interval
Verbal	56	0.2	52-64
Performance	62	1	57-73
Full Scale	55	0.1	51-62

TK was administered the Wechsler Intelligence Scale for Children — Third Edition (WISC-III) in order to assess his current ability level and his learning strengths and weaknesses. The WISC-III is an individually administered intelligence test that yields subtest scores which range from a low of 1 to a high of 19, with an average score of 10. Scores between 8 and 12 are considered average. The WISC-III also generates 3 IQ scores, one for the Verbal domain (responding verbally to orally presented materials), one for the Performance domain (nonverbal, visual-motor-spatial tasks), and the Full Scale IQ score which is a composite of 10 of the subtests administered. The mean IQ for each domain is 100. It should be noted here that IQ scores are not fixed. When tested again some students demonstrate increases or decreases on individual subtests, and on one or more IQ scores, as a result of practice, motivation, testing conditions, or fatigue.

TK may experience great difficulty in keeping up with his peers in a wide variety of situations that require age-appropriate thinking and reasoning abilities. His general cognitive ability is within the mildly mentally impaired range of intellectual functioning, as measured by the Wechsler Intelligence Scale for Children — Third Edition. His overall reasoning abilities exceed those of approximately 1% of students his age (FSIQ = 55; 90% confidence interval = 59-72).

His ability to think with words is comparable to his ability to reason without the use of words. Both TK's verbal and nonverbal reasoning abilities also are in the mildly mentally impaired range. His verbal reasoning abilities are above those of approximately 1% of his peers (VIQ = 56; 90% confidence interval = 53-63). His nonverbal reasoning abilities are better than those of approximately 1% of students TK's age (PIQ = 62; 90% confidence interval = 59-72).

TK achieved his best performance among the verbal reasoning tasks on the Arithmetic subtest and lowest score on the Similarities and Vocabulary subtests. His performance across these areas differs significantly and suggests that these are the areas of most pronounced strength and weakness, respectively, in TK's profile of verbal reasoning abilities. Although better developed than his other verbal reasoning abilities, TK's ability on the Arithmetic subtest was below that of most students his age. His weak performance on the Similarities and Vocabulary subtests were far below that of most students his age.

TK was required to mentally solve a series of orally presented problems on the Arithmetic subtest. A direct measure of his numerical reasoning abilities, the subtest requires attention, concentration, short-term memory, and mental control (Arithmetic scaled score = 5).

On the Similarities subtest TK was required to respond orally to a series of word pairs by explaining how the words of each pair are alike. This subtest examines his ability to abstract meaningful concepts and relationships from verbally presented material (Similarities scaled score = 1). The Vocabulary subtest required TK to explain the meaning of words presented in isolation. As a direct assessment of word knowledge, the subtest is one indication of his overall verbal comprehension. Performance on this subtest also requires abilities to verbalize meaningful concepts as well as to retrieve information from long-term memory (Vocabulary scaled score = 1).

TK achieved his best performance among the nonverbal reasoning tasks on the Coding and Picture Completion subtest and lowest score on the Block Design subtest. His performance across these areas differs significantly, suggesting that these are the areas of most pronounced strength and weakness, respectively, in TK's profile of nonverbal reasoning abilities. Although better developed than his other nonverbal reasoning abilities, TK's performance on the Coding and Picture Completion subtests was still below that of most students his age. His weak performances on the Block Design subtest was far below that of most students his age.

The Coding subtest required TK to use a key to associate a series of symbols with a series of shapes and to use a pencil to draw the symbols next to the shapes. A direct test of speed and accuracy, the Coding subtest assesses ability in quickly and correctly scanning and sequencing simple visual information. Performance on this subtest also may be influenced by short-term visual memory, attention, or visual-motor coordination (Coding scaled score = 5). The Picture Completion subtest required TK to identify the missing part in each of a series of pictures of common objects and scenes. An indication of his ability in visual discrimination, the Picture Completion subtest assesses the abilities to detect essential details in visually presented material and to differentiate them from nonessential details. Performance on this task also may be influenced by an individual's general level of alertness to the world around him and long-term visual memory (Picture Completion scaled score = 5).

The Block Design subtest required TK to use two-color cubes to construct replicas of two-dimensional, geometric patterns. This subtest assesses ability to mentally organize visual information. More specifically, this subtest assesses his ability to analyze part-whole relationships when information is presented spatially. Performance on this task also may be influenced by visual-spatial perception and visual perception-fine motor coordination, as well as planning ability (Block Design scaled score = 1).

INTERVIEW

When discussing school, TK reported that TK liked being in the BED classroom better than his current class (OCS) and asked the examiner how he could get back to the BED class. He felt like he learned more in the BED class than he is learning in his current class.

TK takes the bus home from school where he lives with his mom, fourteen-year-old sister, two brothers (ages 17 and 19) his mom's boyfriend. When he gets home from school he plays basketball and goes to his uncle's/grandma's house. When he gets back home he takes a shower, watches T.V., and goes to sleep at 10:00 or 11:00.

When given three wishes and asked what he would wish for, TK could not think of a single wish.

SOCIAL/EMOTIONAL ASSESSMENT

TK was asked to complete the Sentence Completion Test to help assess his current level of social/emotional functioning. This test required him to complete sentence stems so as to create true sentences. It is meant to tap into emotional and sensitive information. TK chose to complete this in an interview format. TK had difficulty understanding how to complete this task. The following are examples to some of his responses. My mind "is all right." I am best when "I go home with my mom." The only trouble "when I walk the halls and people look at me." My greatest worry is "when somebody trying to fight me."

TK Completed the BASC Self-Report of Personality in order to help assess his perspective on his current level of social/emotional functioning. TK was required to respond to 186 True/False statements. TK chose to complete the rating scale independently. Based on his responses to these items an Emotional Symptom Index is computed along with three composite scores (school maladjustment, clinical maladjustment, and personal adjustment). Each composite consists of a number of scales. There are additional clinical scales that are not included in any composite. Any score in the Clinically Significant range suggests a high level of maladjustment, while scores in the At-Risk range identify either a significant problem that may not be severe enough to require formal treatment or a potential of developing a problem that needs careful monitoring.

The following items are considered to be a Critical Item because TK responded "True" to them: I can't seem to control what happens to me, I don't seem to do anything right, I hear voices in my head, I just don't care anymore, sometimes I want to hurt myself, nothing goes my way, I cannot control my thoughts, sometimes voices tell me to do bad things, I get into fights at school, and I cannot stop myself from doing bad things. The school psychologist and school counselor spoke with TK about some of his responses. It was determined that the voices he hears in his head are a sort of conscience. TK had only thought of hurting himself last spring when he got into a fight. He was unable to explain how he would hurt himself, but finally indicated he would bite his arm. He shared that he has never had any thoughts of killing himself.

TK rated himself in the Average range on the Emotional Symptom Index (total score). However, his Clinical Maladjustment composite and Personal Adjustment composite fell within the At-Risk range. Specifically, Atypicality, Somatization, Anxiety, and Interpersonal Relations fell within the At-Risk range. Self Reliance fell within the Clinically Significant range.

TK's mother completed the BASC Parent Rating Scales in order to help assess TK's current level of social/emotional functioning. The rating scale required her to respond to 126 statements as "Never", "Sometimes", "Often", or "Almost Always". Based on her responses, a Behavioral Symptom Index along with three composites (Externalizing Problems, Internalizing Problems, and Adaptive Skills) is computed. Every composite consists of several subscales. There are additional clinical scales that are not included on any composite. Her F Index fell within the Extreme Caution range. The F Index is a measure of the rater's tendency to be excessively negative in describing the child's behavior. The following items caused TK's F Index to fall within the Extreme Caution range: Begins conversations appropriately — Never; Volunteers to help with things — Never; Shows interest in others' ideas — Never; Smiles at others — Never. The following items are considered critical because they were endorsed: stutters, has muscle spasms, has seizures.

Based on her responses to the above-mentioned items, she placed his Behavioral Symptom Index (total score) within the Average range. However, his Adaptive Skills composite fell within the Clinically Significant range with Social Skills being Clinically Significant and Leadership being At-Risk.

TK's OSC teacher and teacher assistant completed the BASC Teacher Rating Scales in order to help assess his current level of social/emotional functioning. TK spends all day with this teacher and her assistant. The BASC required his teachers to respond to 138 statements as either "Never", "Sometimes", "Often", or "Almost Always". Any scores in the Clinically Significant range suggest a high level of maladjustment. Scores in the At-Risk range identify either a significant problem that may not be severe enough to require formal treatment or a potential of developing a problem that needs careful monitoring. The following items are considered critical because they were endorsed: is in trouble with police, uses foul language, has eye problems, threatens to hurt others, throws tantrums, uses medication, uses alcoholic beverages, says "I want to die" or "I wish I were dead", and says "I want to kill myself". It should be noted that the teacher assistant was the one that endorsed the comments about dying, but when questioned could not remember hearing the statements. Her Consistency Index was in the Caution range, indicating that many pairs of similar items received different responses. Her F Index was in the Caution range indicating that she may have been excessively negative in describing TK's behavior. The following items caused his F Index to be within the Caution range: Refuses to join group activities — Almost Always; Says, "please" and "thank you" — Never; Completes homework — Never; Avoids other children — Almost Always.

Both TK's teacher and teacher assistance placed his Behavioral Symptom Index in the Average range, Adaptive Skills composite in the At-Risk range, and Social Skills At-Risk. In addition, his teacher rated his Leadership and Study Skills as being At-Risk, while the teacher assistant rated Hyperactivity, Aggression, and Withdrawal as being At-Risk.

SUMMARY:

TK is currently being referred for a psychological evaluation as part of a comprehensive re-evaluation. He is presently identified as ID and is in the OCS program. He demonstrated mildly impaired intellectual ability. A current measure of adaptive behavior and achievement were not available at the time of this report. Teacher, parent, and self rating scales all placed TK's current level behavioral/emotional functioning within the Average range. Based on currently available information, TK appears to still function as an ID student and the OCS program best meets his needs. However, current adaptive behavior and achievement scores are needed to make this determination. It will be up to the IEP Committee to review all pertinent information in determining whether TK still qualifies for Exceptional Children's Services and the best way to meet his educational needs.

Linda Salls, M.A., N.C.S.P.
Nationally Certified School Psychologist

DURHAM PUBLIC SCHOOLS
Exceptional Children's Programs

IEP TEAM MEETING MINUTES

Name of Student: TK Connor   Meeting Date: 09/12/10
DOB: 7/23/   School: Northside

Present for meeting: TK Connor (student), Ms. Yarborough (teacher), Ms. Salls (school psychologist) Ms. Tiller (teacher), Ms. Angell (special education facilitator), Ms. Connor (student's mother), Ms. Spencer (assistant principal), Ms. Alden (guidance counselor), Mr. Foster (job coordinator for OCS program), Mr. Scott (TK's uncle).

Purpose of meeting: Discuss credits and behavior plan.

Parent received copy of *Parents' Rights Handbook* prior to meeting: Yes xx No ?

If no, explain

Presentation:

Ms. Logan wrote some information because she could not attend mtg. She reported that TK does his work in her class and is not a behavior problem. He comes late to 1st period. Ms. Yarborough said TK participates and does his work in class. He behaves in her class.

Ms. Alden shared the credits — he has seven — but did not pass English. Because he did not pass English he is technically still a 9th grader, but he has enough credits to be a 10th grader. He can finish in 2 more years past this yr. Can double up on the Eng. and go to summer school.

TK's mother, Ms. Connor, said she did not know that he failed English and didn't get credit.

Mr. Foster talked about TK's participation in the Occupational Course of Study. He needs in classroom credits as well as his work hours. He has to get 300 unpaid hours on school jobs; he has accumulated 162 hours to date. He is also working on getting him the community hours he needs. Mr. Foster said he talked to TK about community credits. TK was to start a job at the Y — but he was suspended right before it was to start. TK did very well at his interview. Previously, he had a job lined up at Wal-Mart, but TK was late and missed what he needed to start. It seems he just misses what he needs. He does well at interviews/in class but then when he's out of class, in the hall, etc., he gets in trouble. Mr. Foster states that he can find him a job. Mr. Foster thinks a lot of him, but he gets in trouble and gets suspended, which makes working with him to get his job hours difficult.

TK's uncle Mr. Scott states that TK always gets in trouble outside the classroom in the small span while he's out of the class. He always gets in trouble when he tries to be someone else, especially in front of his friends. Mr. Scott encouraged the team to come up with a plan to prevent him from being in a transitional situation where he gets in trouble.

Ms. Spencer has given TK directives to stay in certain areas during transitions, but he won't do as directed.

Ms. Connor said TK needs to be watched when going to class.

Ms. Spencer stated that the teachers can watch him going to class — if he doesn't abide by this, what would be the consequence?

Mr. Scott says he will not let him play basketball after school as a consequence.

But Ms. Spencer wants an in-school consequence. The team talked about in-school suspension, but with the number of students in ISS it would be impossible to provide specific one-on-one attention to him. Ms. Spencer stated that perhaps a more restrictive setting would be better.

Ms. Tiller stated that TK is not a behavior problem in her class. He does his work. He often comes late, though, and he's out a lot.

Ms. Angell agreed with TK being watched during transition, but said TK needs to take some responsibility. The team is especially concerned about lunchtime and him going to and from Ms. Tiller's class because it is a longer distance.

Ms. Spencer described an incident of TK not following her directive — he used profanity and "went off."

Ms. Connor reminded the team that TK has a disability and is not able to handle things like lunchtime and transitions.

Ms. Yarborough suggested TK having lunch with her in her room. TK states he gets in trouble in the A.M. in the common areas. So he will get his breakfast and go to Ms. Yarborough's class then Ms. Yarborough will walk him to Ms. Tiller's class.

Ms. Spencer stated that if there is a real serious infraction, this plan does not prevent him from being suspended. If he commits a board policy infraction, then a suspension will follow. Mother is to be made aware of any infractions — whoever sees it contacts her. TK is unhappy with this lunch restriction, so it may need to be on a day-to-day basis. If he behaves, then the restrictions can loosen up. The use of a behavior chart will be helpful. If he earns less restrictions — then we can let up on them.

Decision Recommendation: A behavior plan will be developed to prevent suspensions & infractions during transition time. This is in effect today — will be in writing by Mon. 9/22/10

Report Submitted By: Ms. Angell   Copy Given to Parent 9/16/10

Notice of Student Suspension from School

TO THE PARENT(S)/GUARDIAN: This notice is to officially inform you that your child has been suspended from school for the reason(s) explained below.

Student's Name: TK Connor _____ School: Northside High School   Grade: 10 _____

Date of Birth: __07/23/93 _____ Age: ___17 _____ Race: _AA _____ Sex _xx_M __ F

Parent/Guardian Name: Mary Connor _____ Home Telephone: _(919) 246-9753 _____

Address: __365 Smithville Ave. Durham NC _____ Work Telephone: _____

Type of Suspension		
☐**Short-term** *Short-term suspensions are not appealable. Parents are entitled to a conference with the principal or designee.*	☐**Short —term with...** XX Recommendation for long-term *Rest of Year* ☐Recommendation for 365 days* ☐Recommendation for expulsion*	**If you wish to appeal this recommendation, you and /or your child have 3 working days to contact the Hearing Officer at 560-2350**

Beginning Date: _9/12/10 _____ Ending Date: _6/13 _____ Number of school days suspended on this occasion: _10, with recommendation of rest of school year_ May return to school on: _first day of school next year, if recommendation followed_

Number of days out-of school suspension served this year prior to this suspension: __10_

This student is charged with violating School Board Policy (or Policies): Prohibition of gang-related activities on incident date 9/11/10 and 9/12/10

Describe the nature of the offense: On 9/11/10 TK and other students on buses 366 and 392 were engaged in "stacking" a common gang communication tool used to show loyalty and/or disrespect. This behavior continues to add to an ongoing disruption of the school day. On 9/12/10 TK and others surrounded an alleged member of the Bloods gangs. TK told him "I'm an O.G. and I'm going to get you."

PLEASE BE AWARE that any student under suspension from school is trespassing if he/she appears on the property of any school during the suspension period without the express permission of the principal.

Is this student currently identified under/referred to the Exceptional Children's Program or Section 504? ☐No xxYes ** Exceptionality: ☐In referral process** *(**Enclosed is a handbook of Parents' rights.)*	**Will proposed suspension result in a change in placement?** ☐ No xx Yes *If yes, an IEP or Section 504 committee meeting must be held to determine the Relationship between the incident and the student's disability. Enclosed is an Invitation to Conference.*

White Copy—Central/ Office   Parent refused to sign 9/12/03 10:20a,
Yellow Copy—School   in Mr. C's office

John L. Tharpe _____   9/12/10 _____

Signature of Principal   Date

Pink—Parent/Guardian

Worksheet 4 (Page 1 of 2)
MANIFESTATION DETERMINATION

Student's Name: _____ **Birth date: :** ____ / ____ / ____ **Date:** ____ / ____ / ____

School: _____ **Grade:** _____

Area of Disability: _____**Current Educational Setting (LRE):** _____
Data being considered (check each one):

____ IEP	Dates:_____
____ Assessment/evaluations	Dates: _____
____ Medical information, including diagnosis and medication	Dates: _____
____ Interviews conducted	Dates: _____
____ Direct observations	Dates:_____
____ Discipline reports for the current school year	Dates:_____
____ Functional Behavioral Assessment (attach)	Dates:_____
____ Behavioral Intervention Plan (attach)	Dates:_____
____ Other	Dates:_____

History of disciplinary actions during current school year:
    Number of incidents: _____ Dates:_____
    Number of administrative assignments of in-school suspension: _____, total # of actual days: _____
    Number of administrative assignments of out-of-school suspension: _____, total # of actual days: ____
    Longest # of consecutive days suspended: _____ days.

Current Disciplinary Incident: Was a weapon involved? _____ Were drugs involved? _____
    Did serious bodily injury occur? ____
    Summarize the administrative authority's written findings: _____
_____

Summarize the available information from persons who observed the violation of the student code of conduct when it occurred: _____

Implementation of IEP:
    Describe how the academic and behavioral goals on the child's IEP are being implemented: _____

_____

    Describe how the accommodations, modifications and supplementary services included in the child's IEP are being implemented: _____

    Describe how the related services included in the child's IEP are being implemented: _____

_____

Consider the following questions prior to reaching a decision about the behavior being a manifestation of the disability:
    Does the child have a behavior intervention plan (BIP) based on a functional behavioral assessment? Summarize the BIP.

    Explain how and when the interventions and/or plans were revised if they were not effective? List dates these occurred:

Worksheet 4 (Page 2 of 2)

Student's Name: _____   **Birth date: :** ___ / ___ / ___   **Date:** ___ / ___ / ___

School: _____   **Grade:** _____

Did behavior patterns change over time, e.g., increase in frequency, duration and/or intensity? If so, please explain.

Has this behavior or similar behaviors associated with the disability been exhibited in the past? If so, describe the pattern of behavior.

Describe the information that is being considered from evaluations and additional diagnostic procedures.

Describe the relevant information provided by the parents.

List and summarize other agency involvement with the child.

Assessment of Manifestation Determination:
1. Based on the above factors, was the conduct in question caused by the child's disability? ___ YES ___ NO

2. Based on the above factors, did the conduct in question have a direct or substantial relationship to the child's disability?
    ___ YES ___ NO

3. Was the conduct in question the direct result of the school district's failure to implement the IEP?
    ___ YES ___ NO

The violation of the student code of conduct is a manifestation of the student's disability.
    ___ YES ___ NO

If ALL the questions have an answer of "NO", the discipline procedures for students that do not have a disability can be used. If the student is removed from the school placement, the student must continue to receive education services to enable the student to continue to participate in the general education curriculum and to progress toward meeting the goals set out in the student's IEP. The IEP team determines the interim alternative educational setting for services. Parents shall be informed of their procedural safeguards.

If ANY of the questions has an answer of "YES", the manifestation team has decided that the behavior is a manifestation of the student's disability and the behavior did not have to do with weapons, drugs or serious bodily injury. The student must remain in the educational placement indicated on the IEP unless the parent and LEA agree to a change of placement at an IEP team meeting. The student may NOT be disciplined using procedures applicable to nondisabled students. The manifestation team should review the student's IEP for implementation, including the current placement and review the functional behavioral assessment and behavioral intervention/support plan. If no behavior intervention plan exists, the IEP team should be convened to conduct a functional behavioral assessment and create a behavior intervention plan.

COMMITTEE PARTICIPATION	Position	Date
	LEA Representative	
	Parent	
	Other Relevant Member	
	Other Relevant Member	

Chapter 8

CHILD WELFARE AND SPECIAL EDUCATION[1]

I. INTRODUCTION

Over the last two decades, increasing attention has been paid to the overlap between the special education and child welfare systems in both the research and, more recently, the advocacy arenas. Studies examining the educational experiences of children in foster care have exposed society's persistent failure to address their needs, leading to outcomes that are mediocre at best and dismal at worst. Since education is critical to future success, insufficient responses to this problem often result in lifelong consequences for children in foster care, increasing their risks of joblessness, poverty, homelessness, and criminal involvement. *See* Thom Reilly, *Transition from Care: Status and Outcomes of Youth Who Age Out of Foster Care*, 82 Child Welfare 727, 735-41 (2003); *see also* Jennifer Walter, *Averting Revictimization of Children*, 1 J. Center for Child. & Cts. 45 (1999).

The research findings are staggering. More than 75% of children in foster care perform below grade level and more than 50% have been retained at least one year in school. *See* Thomas Parrish, Education of Foster Group Home Children: Whose Responsibility Is It? Study of the Educational Placement of Children Residing in Group Homes (2001). Studies have found that mobile students score more poorly than non-mobile students on math and reading tests. Lisa M. Heinlein & Marybeth Shinn, *School Mobility and Student Achievement in an Urban Setting*, 37 Psychology in the Schools 349-355 (2000). To illustrate, statewide standardized tests administered in the third, sixth and ninth grades in Washington State revealed that children in foster care attending public schools scored 16-20% lower than children not in foster care. Mason Burley & Mina Halpern, Educational Attainment of Foster Youth: Achievement and Graduation Outcomes for Children in State Care (Washington State Inst. for Public Policy 2001.)

Significantly, children in foster care attend an average of nine different schools by the age of 18. *See* Kathleen Kelly, *The Education Crisis for Children in the California Juvenile Court System*, 27 Hastings Const. L.Q. 757, 759 (2000). School transfers often result in days missed due to delays in enrollment, lost school records and academic credits, and difficulties in grasping new and/or different material taught with different styles in new settings. *See* Steve Christian, National Conference of State Legislatures, Educating Children in Foster Care 1-2 (2003). Of even greater concern is that each time a child changes a foster family or placement that results in a change in schools, he or she loses up to four to six months of educational ground. *Testimony of Kathleen M. McNaught* on behalf of the American Bar Association before the Subcommittee on Income Security and Family Support Committee on Ways and

---

[1] This chapter was written by Jennifer N. Rosen Valverde, Clinical Professor of Law, Special Education Clinic, Rutgers-Newark School of Law, and Randi Mandelbaum, Clinical Professor of Law and Director of the Child Advocacy Clinic, Rutgers-Newark School of Law.

Means, United States House of Representatives (September 15, 2009).

School mobility affects graduation rates as well. Up to 50% of youth exit the foster care system without a high school diploma or GED. *See* Reilly, *supra*, at 735. A California study revealed that high school students who changed schools just once were less than half as likely to graduate as students who did not change schools at all. Russell W. Rumberger et al., The Educational Consequences of Mobility for California Students and Schools (1999). The converse has been found to be true as well: In a national study of 1,087 former foster care youth, children who experienced one fewer placement change per year were almost twice as likely to graduate from high school before leaving foster care. Peter J. Pecora et al., Assessing the Effects of Foster Care: Early Results from the Casey National Alumni Study (2003). With respect to post-secondary education, fewer than 2% of youth formerly in foster care complete a bachelor's degree before the age of 25, compared with 24% of the general population. *See* Peter J. Pecora et al., Improving Family Foster Care: Findings from the Northwest Foster Care Alumni Study (2005).

The outcomes are even worse when one takes into account the correlation between disability, special education and foster care. 50-60% of children in foster care have developmental disabilities or delays (including social-emotional development) compared to 10% of the general pediatric population. *See* Paula K. Jaudes & Linda Diamond Shapiro, *Child Abuse and Developmental Disabilities, in* Young Children in Foster Care (1999). Between 40-85% of children in foster care have mental health disorders, *see* Lisette Austin, *Mental Health Needs of Youth in Foster Care: Challenges and Strategies*, 20 The Connection 6 (2004), and 50-75% of children entering foster care suffer from severe behavior and emotional problems. *See* John Landsverk et al., *Mental Health Service for Children Reported to Child Protective Services*, in The APSAC Handbook on Child Maltreatment 487, 491-92 (2002).

Whether due to a higher disability incidence rate, poorer performance in school as a result of external factors (e.g., multiple transitions, trauma due to abuse and neglect and foster care placement), teacher bias, or some combination of these and other factors, children in foster care are three times more likely to be referred for special education services than their non-foster care peers, and as many as 40% receive special education and related services. *See* Elisabeth Yu et al., Child Welfare League of America, Improving Educational Outcomes for Youth in Care: Symposium Summary Report ix (2002). This population of children is both over-identified for special education eligibility, particularly in the behavioral and emotional disability classifications, and under-identified, particularly in the learning and language disability classifications, each with adverse consequences. *See* Cheryl Smithgall et al., *Chapin Hall Center for Children at the Univ. of Chi., Educational Experiences of Children, in* Out-of-Home Care 36, 57, 70 (2004). Moreover, despite their eligibility for special education, some children are not identified as having special education needs at all and thus go without the services to which they are entitled and which are essential to them if they are to learn effectively. *See* White House Task Force for Disadvantaged Youth, Final Report 110 (2003).

The link between abuse/neglect and disability must be noted as well. Higher prevalence rates of maltreatment have been found in children with disabilities, with one study noting that 31% of children with disabilities had experienced maltreatment compared to 9% of children without disabilities. Patricia M. Sullivan & John F. Knutson, *Maltreatment and Disabilities: A Population Based Epidemiological Study*, 24 Child Abuse & Neglect 1257-1273 (2000). Children who experience maltreatment are at higher risk of developing physical, emotional and behavioral disabilities that adversely affect their ability to learn. *See* Steve Christian, *supra*.

These reciprocal influences and their adverse effects have the potential to create an unending cycle.

Disability diagnosis and special education classification also affect foster care placement and permanency efforts. Children with developmental delays remain in care for greater lengths of time than their non-disabled peers, and once a child is classified as having an emotional disorder, s/he is less likely to exit foster care. *See* Cynthia Godsoe, *Caught Between Two Systems: How Exceptional Children in Out-of-Home Care Are Denied Equality in Education*, 19 Yale L. & Pol'y Rev. 81, 90-91 (2000). When advocates consider these findings alongside statistics concerning the adverse effects of foster care mobility on educational success, the need to address these issues becomes paramount.

To make matters worse, children in foster care often lack a knowledgeable, consistent educational advocate, who can be critical to obtaining appropriate special education programming and services. *See* Robert H. Ayasse, *Addressing the Needs of Foster Children: The Foster Youth Services Program*, Social Work in Education 17(4), 207-216 (1995). The IDEA is a parent-driven statute, as the rights guaranteed therein are vested in parents on behalf of children or adult children themselves. Without someone to serve as the parent and advocate educationally on behalf of children in foster care, home placement and permanency efforts can fail, leading to additional home and school transitions which further exacerbate already challenging situations. *See* Dennis Cichon, *Encouraging a Culture of Caring for Children with Disabilities*, 25 J. Legal Med. 39, 55 (2004).

Cross-systems collaboration and advocacy are essential to improving educational outcomes for children, particularly those with disabilities, in foster care. It is important to remember that there are several local and/or state agencies responsible for ensuring the well-being of children with disabilities, including: the child welfare agency, the state department of education (SEA), and the local school district. Some states also have agencies exclusively dedicated to providing services to children with developmental delays and/or emotional and behavioral concerns. For example, in New Jersey, there is a Division of Child Behavioral Health Services, which is part of New Jersey's Department of Children and Families, and a Division of Developmental Disabilities, which is part of New Jersey's Department of Human Services. Similarly, the California Department of Mental Health administers a number of programs for children and youth. The programs' services are directly provided at the local level by counties and their contract providers. California also has a Department of Developmental Services (DDS), which provides services to children and adults with developmental disabilities. Because California is such a large state, it has established regional centers, which serve as the single points of entry into the service system for persons with developmental disabilities. In fact, in 1985, the California Supreme Court determined that the DDS-regional center system is an entitlement program. *Association for Retarded Citizens — California v. Department of Developmental Services*, 38 Cal. 3d 384, 696 P.2d 150 (1985).

These state and local governmental entities often have overlapping responsibilities. In other words, child welfare agencies typically are charged with ensuring that children in the custody of the state receive an appropriate education. And conversely, school districts must act in the interest of the children it serves, and they are charged with, among other obligations, providing therapeutic services to children with mental health and developmental disabilities, where these disabilities affect the children's ability to be educated. For example, federal law requires that each state have "a plan for ensuring the educational stability of the child while in foster care, including assurances that the placement of the child in foster care takes into account the appropriateness of the current educational setting and the proximity to the school in which the child is enrolled at the time of placement." 45 U.S.C. § 675G(1)(i). At the state level, New Jersey's child welfare agency "has the obligation to make every reasonable effort to assure that every child in out-of-home placement receives an education appropriate to his or her abilities." N.J.A.C. § 10:122D-2.6. And in North Carolina, foster parents shall ensure that children of school age attend school, and residential child care facilities "ensure that each child of school age is provided an education in accordance with the public school laws or the nonpublic school laws in North Carolina." 10A N.C.A.C. §§ 70E.1101, 70I.0608.

In addition, children with disabilities in foster care may have several persons assigned to care for them and/or protect their interests. For example, a child, Sarah, who was removed from the care of her mother and placed in a foster home, may have her mother and perhaps a foster parent ready and able to make educational decisions on her behalf. In addition, the juvenile or family court may have appointed Sarah an attorney and/or a Court Appointed Special Advocate (CASA) to represent her in the child protection matter.[2] It also is possible that Sarah's mother or foster parent retained an attorney to assist in advocating for appropriate services for Sarah in school.

Because there may be numerous persons charged with ensuring the well-being of a particular child, coordination and collaboration among and between "parents," advocates and other professionals is essential. It also is incumbent upon everyone to gain an understanding of the benefits and limitations of each other's role and to become knowledgeable about relevant systems. Many of the services offered to children with disabilities through school districts also may be offered, for different, but related reasons, by the child welfare agency. By joining forces, collectively strategizing, and trying to maximize, through advocacy and the sharing of information, what each system of care has to offer, a child will be better served, and hopefully experience better outcomes.

II. DEFINING THE IDEA PARENT

All children need someone to make educational decisions on their behalves, preferably a parent or caregiver, who knows them well. For children in need of, or receiving, special education services, this takes on even greater significance because a parent, or someone standing in the place of a parent, is essential to ensuring that a child is receiving an appropriate and individualized education. Most state and federal special education laws and regulations, and the procedural safeguards included within them, are written from the perspective of the parent. In other words, it is the "parent" who has standing to enforce special education laws on behalf of a child until the child turns eighteen.

For example, a parent or someone acting in the place of the parent must consent to evaluations (20 U.S.C. § 1414(a)(1)(D)(i)(I); 34 C.F.R. § 300.300), agree to the initial provision of special education and related services (34 C.F.R. § 300.300(b)), and provide permission for the release of records. Moreover, only a parent can request an independent evaluation (20 U.S.C. § 1415(b)(1)) and file for a due process hearing and/or mediation (20 U.S.C.

---

[2] Pursuant to the Child Abuse Prevention and Treatment Act (CAPTA), all children who are brought before the court due to allegations of child abuse or neglect are to be appointed a representative, who can be an attorney or a lay advocate, such as a Court Appointed Special Advocate (CASA). 42 U.S.C. § 5106a(b)(2)(A)(xiii). Currently, in 37 American jurisdictions, attorneys are appointed. Jean Koh Peters, Representing Children in Child Protective Proceedings: Ethical & Practical Dimensions 59 (3rd ed. 2007).

§ 1415(b)(7)), when there are disputes. The parent also is a member of the IEP Team (20 U.S.C. § 1414(d)(1)(B)), is permitted to examine all records (20 U.S.C. § 1415(b)(1)), and is required to receive written notice of all requests to evaluate (34 C.F.R. § 300.304(a)), all IEP Team meetings (34 C.F.R. § 300.322(a)(1)), and all changes in placement (20 U.S.C. § 1415(b)(3)(A)).

A.   Parent Defined

Due to the parent-driven nature of the IDEA, every child who falls under the Act must have someone identified as the "parent," including children in foster care. The federal regulations define parent in the following ways: (1) a biological or adoptive parent, so long as parental rights have not been terminated, (2) a foster parent, unless State law, regulations, or contractual obligations preclude a foster parent from acting as a parent, (3) a guardian (but not the state if the child is a ward of the state), (4) an individual acting in the place of a biological or adoptive parent with whom the child lives or an individual who is legally responsible for the child's welfare (including a grandparent, step-parent, or other relative), or (5) a "surrogate parent." 34 C.F.R. § 300.30(a). Importantly, any court order designating someone as the "parent" takes precedence over the hierarchy outlined in the federal regulations. 34 C.F.R. § 300.30(b)(2). A family or juvenile court judge also can appoint someone solely for the purpose of consenting to an initial evaluation if, after reasonable, efforts the whereabouts of the parent cannot be discovered. 34 C.F.R. § 300.300(a)(2).

Most states follow the federal definition of parent, at times, with some amendments. Cal. Educ. Code § 56028; N.C.G.S.A. § 115C-106.3(14); N.J.A.C. § 6A:14-1.3; O.A.C. § 3301-51-01(B). For example, in North Carolina, foster parents are included in the first prong, along with natural and adoptive parents. N.C.G.S.A. § 115C-106.3(14)a. Yet, in Ohio, foster parents are explicitly excluded from the definition of parent. O.A.C. § 3301-51-01(B). Some jurisdictions, like New Jersey, include the adult student (over eighteen years of age) in the definition of parent, N.J.A.C. § 6A:14-1.3, while the federal regulations, and other states, provide a separate definition for the over eighteen-year-old student. 34 C.F.R. § 300.520; N.C.G.S.A. § 115C-109.2.

For children who are in foster care or residing with relative caregivers due to child abuse or neglect, defining who can act as "parent" for special education purposes, at times, can be difficult. However, it should not be assumed that the biological parents are unfit to continue in this role. In other words, the act of removing a child from the care of his or her parents, due to allegations of child abuse or neglect, does not in and of itself render the child's biological parents incapable of making educational decisions on behalf of the child. In fact, the converse is true — it is presumed that the biological parents are still the educational decision-makers so long as the biological or adoptive parent is "attempting to act as the parent." 34 C.F.R. § 300.30(b)(1).

Yet, determining when someone is "attempting to act as parent" also can be difficult. Are certain actions by the parent required? Is it sufficient for the parent to express interest in the child's education? What should be done when a parent's mental illness or substance abuse addiction causes the parent's participation to be inconsistent? Or consider the circumstances where a parent is not permitted to know, for safety reasons, where the child (who has been placed into foster care) is residing? Are there ways that a parent in this situation can still participate? These are all challenging questions to which there are no clear answers in statutes, regulations, or case law. To a large extent, the answers will depend on the factual circumstances of a given situation. At times, such uncertainty also can lead to tension between the statutorily protected rights of the biological or adoptive parents to participate in and make educational decisions on behalf of their child and the need to ensure that a child has someone in place who is ready, able, and willing to make educational decisions on the child's behalf.

How might you define the parent in the case of Jason?

Jason

Jason, an eight-year-old boy with autism, was placed into foster care one month ago, after being found alone in his mother's apartment. The apartment was in deplorable condition, with no food, utilities, or phone service. The whereabouts of Jason's father are and have been unknown. Jason's mother has a long-standing substance abuse addiction, which is what caused her to neglect Jason. Because no relatives were able or willing to care for Jason, he was placed in the foster home of Ms. Miller. The new school district wishes to make changes to Jason's IEP and has scheduled an IEP Team Meeting for next week. Jason's new teacher orally informed Ms. Miller about the meeting. A written notice of the meeting also was sent to Jason's mother at her last known address.

1. If both Jason's mother and Ms. Miller attend the meeting, who has the authority to sign and consent to the IEP?

2. If only Ms. Miller is in attendance, can she sign and consent to the IEP? Do you have any concerns about this?

3. Does your answer to question #2 change if you learn that Jason's mother recently entered an in-patient drug rehabilitation program and never received notice of the meeting?

4. If the school district knows that Jason's mother no longer resides at her last known address, what efforts, if any, does the school district need to make to locate and notify her of the meeting? What efforts should they make?

5. What if Jason was removed for reasons other than neglect, and it was found not to be safe for Jason's mother to know where he is living and attending school? Should Jason's mother still be able to participate in the IEP Team Meeting? If yes, how can this be achieved?

B.   Surrogate Parents

If there is no one available to make educational decisions on behalf of a child like Jason (in other words, no one meets the definition of "parent" as defined in numbers 1-4 above), then the school district has an obligation to appoint a "surrogate parent." 34 C.F.R. § 300.519. This appointment should take place within 30 days after the school district becomes aware that there is a need for the appointment of a surrogate parent. 34 C.F.R. § 300.519(h); 20 U.S.C. § 1415(b)(2). For foster children, defined as "wards of the state" under the IDEA (34 C.F.R. § 300.45), the judge overseeing the child protection proceeding also can appoint someone to act in the role of "surrogate parent." 34 C.F.R. § 300.519(c).

A "surrogate parent" has the authority to act in the capacity of "parent." 34 C.F.R. § 300.30. When such surrogate parents should be appointed will depend upon state law, but most states usually require such an appointment when the biological parent cannot be identified or located, and there is no one else available, such as a relative caregiver or foster parent, who meets the definition of parent. Cal. Gov. Code § 7579.5; N.C.G.S.A. § 115C-109.2(c); N.J.A.C. § 6A:14-2.2; O.A.C. § 3301-51-05(E). A surrogate parent may not be an employee of the local school district or the state department of education (SEA), and also may not be an employee of any state agency which is involved with the care or education of children, including the child welfare agency. 34 C.F.R. § 300.519(d)(2)(i). The person selected as surrogate parent also must not have any personal or professional interests which conflict with the interests of the child, and must have sufficient "knowledge and skills that ensure adequate representation of the child." 34 C.F.R. § 300.519(d)(2)(ii) and (iii). Typically, the recruiting and training of surrogate parents is the responsibility of the local school districts. 34 C.F.R. § 300.519(d)(2)(i).

Consider who may serve as the "parent" for Jessica in the following fact pattern:

Jessica

Jessica is a ten-year-old girl with severe emotional and psychological concerns who has been in foster care for the past six months due to allegations of sexual abuse on the part of her mother's paramour. Her mother no longer lives at the home from which Jessica was removed, and the child welfare agency has not been able to locate her mother. Jessica was recently placed by the child welfare agency into a residential treatment facility because of her emotional instability. Local school officials, concerned about her performance at school, also seek to evaluate Jessica for special education services.

1. At the moment, who can consent to these evaluations?

2. If the local school district seeks to find Jessica eligible for special education services and develop an IEP, who can consent to this initial IEP being implemented? Would your answer be different if Jessica was in a foster home?

In some jurisdictions, court reform efforts aimed at educating juvenile and family court judges about special education, generally, and the need to ensure that every child has a person appointed to make educational decisions, more specifically, has led to a decrease in the number of children who go without someone to make educational decisions and advocate on their behalf. *See, e.g.*, Casey Family Programs, Court-Based Education Efforts for Children in Foster Care: The Experience of the Pima County Juvenile Court (Arizona) (2007). Yet, many foster children still lack a parent or someone to stand in the place of a parent. Efforts to ensure that all foster children with disabilities have such a recognized person must continue.

One effort, which has helped some children, is to encourage juvenile and family court judges to appoint guardians for the limited purpose of making educational decisions. Not only do family and juvenile court judges have the authority to appoint surrogate parents,[3] but

---

[3] One drawback that has been noted is that when surrogate parents are appointed by a court, the training of the

these judges also are able to appoint guardians. In most jurisdictions, these guardians can be appointed to act in the role of "parent" generally, or for a special purpose, with limited authority. For example, in Maryland, a juvenile master, overseeing a child protection proceeding, can appoint someone with limited guardianship for educational purposes. Md. Code Ann. § 3819(c)(1)(ii). Modeled after the practice in Maryland, a special project taking place in a few counties in New Jersey permits family court judges to appoint limited guardians for special education or early intervention purposes. As guardians, these appointed persons fall under the definition of "parent," pursuant to 34 C.F.R. § 300.30(a).

III. GETTING THROUGH THE SCHOOL DOORS

While quality special education advocacy is critical for children with disabilities in foster care, these children often must clear several hurdles to enter the school doors. This section addresses some of the unnecessary obstacles created by schools that result in excluding children in foster care from the classroom. Typically, these obstacles surface at the outset of the child's transfer into a new school district, and fall into the areas of registration/enrollment/attendance, transfer of school records and residency. Each state/territory has its own general education statutes and regulations governing these areas, and references to relevant statues and regulations from a sampling of states/territories, specifically New Jersey, North Carolina, California, Ohio and Washington, D.C., will be provided throughout the discussion below. Only after these "entry level" issues are tackled can advocates begin to address the special education needs of these children.

A.   Registration, Enrollment and Attendance

Children typically are registered in the school district in which they are domiciled. In New Jersey, a child in foster care is domiciled in a school district for educational purposes if the child welfare agency, acting as guardian, places the child in the school district. N.J.A.C. § 6A:22-3.1; *see also* Ohio Rev. Code Ann. § 3313.64(B)(2); N.C. Gen. Stat. § 115C 366; Cal. Educ. Code § 48204(a); *but see* Cal. Educ. Code § 48853.5 (providing that children in foster care have a right to stay in their school of origin); D.C. Code Ann. § 38-307 (providing non-resident students can attend school in the D.C. district if they are "wards of the district"). The school district in which the child resides is responsible for *providing* an education to the child; however, depending on the state in which the child resides, that same district or a different one may be responsible for *paying* for the child's education — this issue will be discussed in more detail in the residency section below.

When registering a child for school, parents, including foster parents, generally must provide proof of their residence and the child's domicile in the school district. State requirements for registration vary, and different documents may serve as evidence of domicile or residence. Typical documents that establish domicile for a child in out-of-home placement are a letter from the state child welfare agency or other document (e.g., court order) indicating the child has been placed in a home (either foster home or group home, residential placement, etc.) by the child welfare agency. N.J.A.C. § 6A:22-3.4; N.C. Gen. Stat. § 115C-366(a6); Cal. Educ. Code § 48204(a)(1)(B). Documents verifying residence in a school district include the caregiver's lease, mortgage statement, utility bills, or an affidavit. N.J.A.C.

---

surrogate parent is not always ensured, despite federal requirements to the contrary.

§ 6A:22-3.4; N.C. Gen. Stat. § 115C-366(a3); Ohio Rev. Code § 3313.64(F); Cal. Educ. Code § 48204(a)(4); D.C. Code Ann. § 38-309.

Some states have timelines for school registration of children in out-of-home placements. These timelines may be statutory or regulatory based, or simply may be agency policy. For example, the District of Columbia gives the child welfare agency four days to obtain and provide educational documentation to the foster parent, who then has one day to register the child after receiving the documents. D.C. Mun. Regs. § 29-6021.1. New Jersey requires school-age children to be registered in school within 72 hours of out-of-home placement. This timeline is agency policy that arose out of the child welfare modified settlement agreement entered into by the state during its massive child welfare system overhaul back in the mid 2000s. *See* New Jersey Department of Children and Families, Field Operations Casework Policy and Procedures Manual 906 (4-5-2010).

It is important to note that requirements for registration differ from those for enrollment/attendance; just because the proper documents are submitted for a child to *register* in school does not mean that all necessary documentation has been provided such that the child may *attend* school. In addition to documents required for registration, states typically require that a child's immunization records be submitted, and that the child's birth certificate or other identification be produced in order for the child to be allowed to attend school. N.J.S.A. § 18A:36-25.1; N.J.A.C. § 8:57-4.2; Ohio Rev. Code §§ 3313.67, 3313.672; D.C. Code Ann. § 38-502; D.C. Mun. Regs. § 5-E2002.6. However, some states like California, waive the immunization records requirement for attendance for children in out-of-home care. Cal. Educ. Code § 48853.5(d)(4)(B). Additionally, while some states, like New Jersey, require production of the child's birth certificate or proof of identity within 30 days of enrollment, they also may provide that non-production of the birth certificate cannot be the sole basis for denying a child admission into school. N.J.A.C. §§ 18A:36-25.1, 8:57-4.2.

To ensure a smooth registration, enrollment and admissions process for a child living in an out-of-home placement, advocates must familiarize themselves with the roles and responsibilities of the various individuals and agencies involved in the child's life. For example, state statute, regulation, and/or internal agency policy delineate many of the responsibilities of school districts, child welfare agencies, and foster parents/caregiver agencies with respect to education of children in their care. In some areas, responsibility crosses system lines and is vested in more than one party; in others, responsibility is vested in one party only. In still others, responsibility is not specifically delineated anywhere. For this reason, advocates representing children involved in both the child welfare and special education systems must learn to ask the "right" questions to ensure children in foster care are permitted through the school doors.

Consider the issues of registration, attendance and enrollment and the delineation of responsibility in the following hypothetical scenario:

Keisha

Keisha is thirteen years old and in the seventh grade. She attended Shabazz Junior High School until approximately one month ago when allegations of abuse were made against her mother. After visiting Keisha's home, the state child welfare agency took temporary custody of her and placed her in a foster home two towns away. The closest middle school to her new home is Martin Luther King, Jr. Middle School, but she has yet to begin attending. Unsure of what to do, Keisha calls her attorney representative for help and the attorney representative contacts you, an education advocate.

1. Who are the relevant parties?

2. What are the responsibilities of the relevant parties (i.e., biological parent, foster parent, child welfare agency, school district) with respect to Keisha's education, particularly in the areas of registration, enrollment, and attendance (investigate your state's general education laws and regulations, child welfare laws and regulations, and education and child welfare agency policies)?

3. What advocacy strategies should be used where responsibilities set forth in the law and regulations are shared?

4. What advocacy strategies should be used where no responsibility has been assigned either by law or regulation?

5. What legislative or policy changes would you make in your state to fill any gaps and/or clarify current laws and regulations to ensure children in foster care are registered, enrolled and attending school in a timely fashion?

B.   School Records

When children in foster care move from one living arrangement to another, they often are forced to transfer schools as well. Each state's general education laws and/or regulations include provisions that address the transfer of a child's school records and timelines for the same. For example, Ohio requires requests for records from the receiving school be sent out within 24 hours of a child's enrollment, and the transferring school to send the records within 14 days of receiving the request, Ohio Rev. Code § 3313.672(A)(3); North Carolina law provides that the receiving school request a child's school records no more than 30 days after enrollment, N.C. Gen. Stat. § 115C-403; and in New Jersey, when a child transfers between school districts, the district into which the child transfers must request the child's school records from the former district within two weeks of the child enrolling, and the former district must forward the school records to the new district within ten days of receiving the request. N.J.S.A. § 18A:36-19a; N.J.A.C. § 6A:32-7.5. Obviously, these provisions rely on one critical assumption — that the new school district knows the name of the school district the child previously attended. Typically, written consent of the child's parent is not required as a condition of the records transfer, whereas written notice to the parent of the records transfer is required. *See* Cal. Ed. Code § 49068; D.C. Mun. Regs. § 5-E 2603.3; N.J.S.A. § 19A:36-19a.

California places great emphasis on the prompt transfer of student records for children in foster care, by requiring that new school districts request the student records within *two business days* of receiving an enrollment request and that prior school districts comply with requests for records within *two business days*. Cal. Educ. Code §§ 48853.5(d)(4)(C) & 49069.5(d)-(e). By not requiring parental consent or court orders to allow social workers access to student records, California ensures that social workers can quickly and efficiently compile a child's health and education records for school transfer purposes. Cal. Educ. Code § 49076(a)(11).

For children with disabilities, advocates must look beyond the general education laws and regulations pertaining to school records to federal and state special education law and regulations, as specific provisions address transfers of students with disabilities. Federal special education regulations require both the new and prior school districts to obtain and provide, respectively, the child's school records. 34 C.F.R. § 300.323. However, while the individual states typically set timelines as discussed above, the federal regulations merely require that "reasonable steps" be taken to obtain the child's records and that the prior school district take "reasonable steps" to respond to requests for the same. 34 C.F.R. § 300.323(g).

Responsibility for the transfer of school records for a child in foster care often crosses agency lines, with the local education agency, the child welfare agency, and, in some states, the foster parent or caregiver agency all having responsibility for this task. For example, in Ohio, in addition to state general and special education laws and regulations concerning the transfer of school records discussed above, the state child welfare agency must develop a "Child's Education and Health Information" form, which includes current educational information and records for the child in foster care, and provide the plan to the child's "substitute caregiver" (a.k.a. foster parent/caregiver agency) at the time of placement. Ohio Admin. Code Ann. § 5101:2-38-08; *see also* N.J.A.C. § 10:122D-2.6; Cal. Educ. Code § 49069.5(e); Cal. Wel. & Inst. Code § 16010(a); D.C. Mun. Regs. §§ 29-6224.2(x), 29-6021.1. In addition, the substitute caregiver must share necessary records with the school district to develop proper educational programming for the child as well as to monitor the child's progress. Ohio Admin. Code Ann. § 5101:2-42-90(E); N.J.A.C. § 10:122D-2.6 & 6.3; Cal Wel. & Inst. Code § 16010; D.C. Mun. Regs. §§ 29-6021.1, 29-6021.2.

C.   Residency

In some states, the school district in which a child resides is responsible for providing an education to the child, but may not always be responsible for paying for the child's education. The school district with financial responsibility for a child sometimes is referred to as the "district of residence," which is a term of art not to be confused with the district in which a child resides. *See* Ohio Rev. Code § 3313.64(C)(2); N.C. Gen. Stat. § 115C-366; N.J.S.A. § 40:4C-26(c). In certain circumstances, the state itself may be responsible for a foster child's education costs. These circumstances may include where a foster child's parents are deceased or reside out-of-state, parental rights have been terminated and the state has legal guardianship, or the parents' whereabouts are unknown and the state is unable to determine the parents' prior residence. Disputes between school districts over financial responsibility for children in foster care are all too common and can result in the wrongful exclusion of children from the classroom pending resolution. For this reason, advocates must be familiar with state laws and regulations concerning residency.

Using the educational residency laws of New Jersey, located at N.J.S.A. § 18A:7B-12, determine which school district(s) is responsible for educating and paying for the education of Taliah in the following situations:

Taliah

1. Taliah was removed from her mother's care in Trenton and placed in the home of her aunt in Camden. Which district is responsible for educating Taliah? Which district is responsible for paying for Taliah's education?

2. Taliah is then moved to a group home in Hamilton. Which district is responsible for educating Taliah? Which district is responsible for paying for Taliah's education?

3. Six months from the date Taliah was removed from her mother's care, Taliah's mother moves from Trenton to Atlantic City. Which district is responsible for educating Taliah? Which district is responsible for paying for Taliah's education?

4. Taliah returns to her mother's care while her mother resides in Atlantic City. She is removed again shortly thereafter and placed in a residential treatment facility in Cleveland, Ohio. Which district or state is responsible for educating Taliah? Which district or state is responsible for paying for Taliah's education?

IV. CONFIDENTIALITY AND INFORMATION-SHARING

When advocating for a child across multiple systems, issues related to confidentiality and information-sharing often arise. This holds true particularly for children in foster care. At least some information-sharing across systems is vital to improving educational outcomes for children in foster care. However, this must be done carefully in order to prevent any violation of applicable laws of confidentiality. The primary federal laws concerning confidentiality that affect the sharing of information between the child welfare and education systems are the Child Abuse Prevention and Treatment Act (hereinafter "CAPTA"), 42 U.S.C. §§ 5101 et seq., and the Federal Educational Rights and Privacy Act (hereinafter "FERPA"), 20 U.S.C. §§ 1232 et seq.

A. Confidentiality

CAPTA is the principal federal legislation that addresses prevention, assessment, treatment and reporting of child abuse and neglect. Under the Act, states must enact laws that, among other things, protect the confidentiality of a child's foster care records. 42 U.S.C. § 5106(a)(b)(2)(A)(viii)-(ix). CAPTA sets forth the limited circumstances in which a child's foster care records may be shared and with whom, including the subject of the abuse or neglect report; federal, state or local government entities that need the information to carry out their duty to protect children from abuse or neglect; a court or grand jury; and other entities or individuals as set forth in state law. 42 U.S.C. § 5106a(b)(2)(A)(viii); 45 C.F.R. § 1340.14(i).

Some states have enacted laws that permit the sharing of foster care records with the education system. *See* Cal. Wel. & Inst. Code § 18986.46 (consent needed); Ohio Admin. Code Ann. § 5101:2-42-90(E); D.C. Mun. Regs. § 29-6023.1(h) (sharing of records permitted if necessary for the provision of educational services). In the event that a state does not have such a statute, foster care records may be released only if it is established that the education system requires this information to protect the child from abuse and neglect. 42 U.S.C. § 5106a(b)(2)(A)(viii); 45 C.F.R. § 1340.14(i). The Federal Educational Rights and Privacy Act (hereinafter "FERPA"), 20 U.S.C. §§ 1232 et seq., governs access to a child's educational records. It sets forth the rights of parents and adult children to access their school records, as well as the confidentiality parameters concerning children's education records. 20 U.S.C. § 1232g(a)(1).

> The term "education records" means . . . records, files documents, and other materials which —
>
> (i)   contain information directly related to a student; and
>
> (ii)   are maintained by an educational agency or institution or by a person acting for such agency or institution.

20 U.S.C. § 1232g(a)(4). The term "education records" is defined broadly, and includes special education records as well as school health and immunization records. *See* 45 C.F.R. §§ 160 and 164.

Generally speaking, FERPA prohibits disclosure of personally identifiable information from education records without written parental consent (or consent of a student age 18 or over or a student who attends a postsecondary institution no matter what age). 34 C.F.R. § 99.30. Information or data that does not include any personally identifiable information may be disclosed without consent. 34 C.F.R. § 99.31. This includes information that does not directly relate to a student, for example anonymous data or statistical information, or "directory information," such as, "the student's name, address, telephone listing, date and place of birth, major field of study, participation in officially recognized activities and sports, weight and height of members of athletic teams, dates of attendance, degrees and awards received, and the most recent previous educational agency or institution attended by the student." 20 U.S.C. § 1232g(a)(5)(A).

FERPA applies to all educational agencies that receive federal funds under any program administered by the U.S. Department of Education. 34 C.F.R. § 99.1. This does not include private and religious schools where such schools receive no funding from a program administered by the U.S. DOE. "For example, if a school district places a student with a disability in a private school that is acting on behalf of the school district with regard to providing services to that student, the records of that student are subject to FERPA, but not the records of the other students in the private school." United States Department of Health and Human Services and United States Department of Education, Joint Guidance on the Application of the Family Educational Rights and Privacy Act (FERPA) and the Health Insurance Portability and Accountability Act of 1996 (HIPAA) to Student Health Records 1 (November 2008).

On a federal level, there are three different ways that a child's education records may be shared with a state child welfare agency. The easiest is to obtain written consent of the child's parent. Child welfare workers in some areas have developed a practice of gaining parental consent for this purpose by developing consent forms that are presented to parents either when the child is removed from care or at the first hearing date (temporary custody). Kathleen McNaught, *Solving the Data Puzzle: A How-To Guide on Collecting and Sharing Information to Improve Educational Outcomes for Children in Out-of-Home Care*, ABA Legal Center for Foster Care and Education and Casey Family Programs 12 (2008).

The second is to include the child welfare agency in the definition of parent. While the federal law itself provides no such definition, federal implementing regulations define parent under FERPA as, "a parent of a student and includes a natural parent, a guardian, or an individual acting as a parent in the absence of a parent or a guardian." 34 C.F.R. § 99.3. In developing state regulations, some states have overtly included the state child welfare agency within the definition of parent under FERPA. McNaught, *Solving the Data Puzzle, supra*, at 12. In states that have not included the child welfare agency within this definition, there may be room to argue that the definition itself encompasses the child welfare agency which acts in parens patriae where it has taken legal responsibility for children in out-of-home care.

Finally, although the state child welfare agency may not fall under the definition of parent under FERPA, a child's foster parent or relative caregiver is included within the definition as "an individual acting as a parent in the absence of a parent or a guardian." 34 C.F.R. § 99.3. However, while the foster parent, relative caregiver or state child welfare agency may be considered the parent under FERPA, the child's biological or adoptive parent continues to have the right to access the child's education records. The vesting of the right to make educational decisions for a child in a party other than the parent does not necessarily abrogate the parent's right to access the child's school records. *See* Kathleen McNaught, *Mythbusting: Breaking Down Confidentiality and Decision-Making Barriers to Meet the Education Needs of Children in Foster Care*, in ABA Center for Children and the Law and Casey Family Programs 26 (2005). The child's biological or adoptive parent will lose his or her right to access school records under FERPA only if parental rights are terminated or the court enters an order revoking the parents' right to same. 34 C.F.R. § 99.4. In the event of a court order, typically only those records designated in the order will be withheld. *See* Ohio Rev. Code §§ 3319.321(4), 3319.321(5); D.C. Mun. Regs. § 5-E2603.7.; Cal. Educ. Code § 49077; N.J.A.C. § 6A:7.6(a)(5). This is an important concern where no contact or limited contact orders have been entered against the parents and the child's school records include the child's new contact information.

Where consent of the parent cannot be obtained and the state refuses to accept the child welfare agency as the parent for this purpose, advocates must rely on the exceptions to parental consent set forth in the Act and implementing regulations in order for a child's education records to be shared with the state child welfare agency.

FERPA allows schools to disclose those records, without consent, to the following parties or under the following conditions (34 CFR § 99.31):

- School officials with legitimate educational interest;

- Schools to which a student is transferring;

- Specified officials for audit or evaluation purposes;

- Appropriate parties in connection with financial aid to a student;

- Organizations conducting certain studies for or on behalf of the school;

- Accrediting organizations;

- To comply with a judicial order or lawfully issued subpoena;

- Appropriate officials in cases of health and safety emergencies; and

- State and local authorities, within a juvenile justice system, pursuant to specific State law.

http://www2.ed.gov/policy/gen/guid/fpco/ferpa/index.html. The most germane exception herein for a child in foster care is for the child welfare agency to obtain the release of the child's education records in compliance with a judicial order or lawfully issued subpoena. McNaught, *Solving the Data Puzzle, supra,* at 12. Even in this instance, however, the parent still must receive notice of the educational agency's intent to release the records prior to their release. 20 U.S.C. § 1232g(b)(2)(B).

B.   Information-Sharing

Based on the above discussions of CAPTA and FERPA, in most states, it is far easier for the education system to release a child's school records to the state child welfare agency than vice versa. The Adoption Assistance and Child Welfare Act (hereinafter "AACWA") now requires child welfare agencies to keep a child's education records in his or her child welfare case plan, as appropriate. 42 U.S.C. § 675(1)(c). In addition, some states have made the transfer of education records from the education to the child welfare systems quite simple. For example, New Jersey education regulations authorize the state child welfare agency to gain access to the education records of a child in foster care within ten days of receiving a written request for same. N.J.A.C. §§ 6A:32-7.1, 7.5, 7.6; *see also* Cal. Educ. Code § 49069.3. These records also may be released pursuant to court order. N.J.A.C. § 6A:32-7.6; Ohio Rev. Code § 3319.321(C); Cal. Educ. Code § 49077; D.C. Mun. Regs § 5-E2605.4.

In contrast, the sharing of information in reverse is more difficult under relevant state law. New Jersey provides, in pertinent part, that the state child welfare agency may share information with other entities and professionals in accordance with the following, among other things: a court order; to a parent, foster parent, guardian or other person responsible for a child's welfare where the information relates to the provision of care, treatment, assessment or evaluation of the child and disclosure is in the child's best interests; to a child's legal counsel, parent or guardian when the information is needed to discuss the child's case with the state child welfare agency to make decisions relating to or concerning the child; or to members of a family team or other case planning group formed by the state child welfare agency to address the child's safety, permanency or well-being when provision of such information is in the child's best interests. N.J.S.A. § 9:6-8.10a; *see also* Ohio Admin. Code § 5101:2-5-10; Ohio Rev. Code § 5101.27; Chapter 8 DHSS Protective Services 1428-Interagency sharing of Information of Juveniles http://infOhiodhhs.state.nc.us/olm/manuals/dss/csm-60/man/CS1428-01.htm#P21_1894; N.C. Gen. Stat. §§ 108A-80, 7b-302(a), 7b-302(e); Cal. Wel. & Inst. Code § 18986.46; D.C. Mun. Regs. § 29-6023.1. States and territories restrict the sharing of information in this direction to avoid, in large part, unnecessary intrusions into child and family life, misuse of this information and the potential for stigma attached with the same.

Questions related to the sharing of information require attention in the hypothetical of Bethany.

Bethany

Bethany is undergoing an initial evaluation for special education and related services by the new school district in which she was placed by the child welfare agency. Since starting in the new school nearby her foster parent's house approximately six months ago, she has exhibited signs of depression and anxiety, such that she is now refusing to attend school. The state child welfare agency is conducting a psychiatric evaluation of Bethany at present. The purpose of this evaluation is to assess her mental state, determine whether she needs medication and to develop a plan for therapeutic support outside of school. The school district learned of the evaluation from her foster parent and has requested a copy of the psychiatrist's evaluation report.

1. Based on your state's laws and regulations, as well as federal law, can the psychiatric evaluation be shared?

2. If the school district conducted the psychiatric evaluation as opposed to the child welfare agency, can it be shared with the agency?

3. If the school district conducted the psychiatric evaluation, who else may be permitted to obtain a copy?

V. EVALUATIONS, PROGRAMS/PLACEMENTS AND SERVICES

Both the education and child welfare systems have a role to play when it comes to conducting evaluations, making placements, providing therapeutic services, and assisting youth transitioning into adulthood. Advocates should understand these shared responsibilities and use both systems to maximize evaluation, program/placement, and service options for children in foster care.

A. Evaluations

As discussed in Chapter 4, upon request, unless it is deemed unnecessary, local school districts must conduct an evaluation of a child to determine if the child is eligible for special education, and if eligible, what the educational needs of the child are. 34 C.F.R. § 300.301. In conducting evaluations, local school districts are required to "use a variety of assessment tools and strategies," and not use any "single measure or assessment." 34 C.F.R. § 300.304(b). Local school districts also must ensure that "the child is assessed in all areas related to the suspected disability, including if appropriate, health, vision, hearing, social and emotional status, general intelligence, academic performance, communicative status, and motor abilities." 34 C.F.R. § 300.304(c)(4). In other words, the local school districts have the obligation to assess comprehensively, both in terms of the types of evaluations it must conduct, as well as the manner in which it must conduct each evaluation. 34 C.F.R. § 300.304(c)(6).

Typical evaluations that the local school district must conduct are the following: psychological, educational, social work, speech and language, and, beginning at age sixteen, an assessment to determine postsecondary outcomes. Less typical, but still common, are psychiatric, neurological, neuropsychological, occupational therapy, and physical therapy evaluations.

Likewise, the child welfare agency on its own, or pursuant to a juvenile or family court order, which can be requested by the child's appointed representative, can secure any number of evaluations of a child in the custody of the state. Typical evaluations that a child welfare agency may secure are the following: psychological, psychiatric, medical, and beginning at age 14-16, most child welfare agencies also assess a youth's strengths and needs in order to begin to plan for the youth's transition into adulthood. However, a child welfare agency is not limited to these evaluations and can and must obtain whatever evaluations are necessary to ensure that the child's well-being and needs are being met.

Because both entities have the obligation to evaluate, parents, caregivers, and advocates, working together and on behalf of a child, should strategize to ensure that the child is appropriately assessed, that there is a clear understanding of what the child's needs are, and that there are detailed recommendations as to how those needs can best be addressed both in the school setting, and in the home (or out-of-home placement). For example, at times, it may be helpful to have an evaluation, separate from the school evaluation, in other words, a "second opinion," or what is referred to in federal regulations, as well as in many jurisdictions, as an "independent evaluation." 34 C.F.R. § 300.502. Any outside evaluation submitted to the local school district must be considered (although it does not need to be followed) by the IEP Team in making decisions regarding special education and related services. 34 C.F.R. § 300.502(c)(1).

Requesting that the juvenile or family court presiding over the child protection proceeding order such evaluations can achieve this objective. This is often the only way that low-income children and families can secure evaluations outside of the school setting.[4] At other times, it may be more appropriate to obtain a certain type of evaluation through the child welfare system, but some or all of the information obtained from the assessment may be helpful in planning for the child's education program.

Thus, when working with a child with disabilities in foster care, it is important to always ask whether it would be helpful to get outside evaluations, and if so, which ones? In other words, should you obtain outside evaluations in all areas that the school district is assessing, or just the most important, if that even can be discerned?

Questions of timing also will arise. Do you want to get the outside evaluations before making a referral for special education with the local school district? Or do you want to make the referral for special education and arrange for simultaneous outside evaluations? Another approach is to wait until after the local school district has performed its evaluations and then determine what if any outside evaluations are needed. Concerns about delay, strategy, the quality of evaluations conducted by a local school district and the age and needs of the child all play a role in answering these questions.

It is important to recognize that, while it can be incredibly beneficial to look to all of the relevant governmental entities involved with a child in order to properly evaluate a child, it

---

[4] *But see* Chapter Ten, *infra*, for information concerning the rights of parents to request that local school districts provide for independent evaluations when assessments performed by the local school district are not adequate. 34 C.F.R. § 300.502(b).

also can create some complications because evaluations arranged by agencies other than the local school district are not being administered solely (or even largely) for the purpose of identifying appropriate educational services for a child. Thus, the assessment may contain extensive information about the abuse and/or neglect the child suffered and/or the family history or current family circumstances. This may be information that the school district may not be permitted to know, pursuant to confidentiality statutes and regulations. Even if it is permissible to share the information, it may not be information that the child or family wants shared with the local school district. Concomitantly, school officials tend to resist recommendations in evaluations that they perceive address issues not directly related to the child's performance or functioning in school.

Think about what evaluations are needed for Joseph, a sixteen-year-old-boy who is failing all of his subjects at school.

Joseph

Joseph has never been identified for special education. Joseph's mother has a long-standing substance abuse addiction and was arrested on drug charges. She likely will be incarcerated for awhile. Joseph was placed by the child welfare agency with his maternal grandmother. Joseph's behavior is challenging. It is hard for the grandmother to control his behaviors and ensure his safety. She is not certain for how long she will be able to care for Joseph in her home.

1. Should a request be made to the local school district to evaluate Joseph for special education services?

2. If so, when? Do you want to obtain outside evaluations from the child welfare agency before making a referral for special education?

3. What outside evaluations would you want to get? Do some types of evaluations seem more important than others?

It is important for advocates to be familiar with regulations governing school transfers as they pertain to evaluations and IEPs. Where a student already is being evaluated for or has been classified as eligible for special education and that student changes school districts, additional regulations govern the transfer process. With respect to the evaluation process, 34 C.F.R. § 300.305(c)(5) provides that sending and receiving school districts must ensure that evaluations of children who change school districts during the school year are coordinated quickly so that the evaluations are completed in a prompt manner. Specifically, the new school district must complete the special education evaluation process commenced in a different district within the same 60-day timeline (or other deadline set by the state) unless the new district is making adequate progress to ensure prompt completion and that district and the child's parent agree to another specific deadline for completion. 34 C.F.R. § 300.301(d)(2) & (e).

Where a child already has an IEP, 34 C.F.R. § 300.323(e) requires that when a child with an IEP moves from one school district to another within the same state, the new district must provide the child with a comparable program until the new district either adopts the child's IEP from the prior school district or develops, adopts and implements a new IEP for the child. If a child with an IEP transfers from out-of-state, the new school district must provide the child with a FAPE while it conducts an evaluation of the child and develops, adopts and implements a new IEP, if needed. 34 C.F.R. § 323(f). States set reasonable timelines for IEP reviews and reevaluations in these situations, with 30 days being the norm. Cal. Educ. Code § 56325(a)(1); Ohio Admin. Code § 3301-51-07(K)(5); N.J.A.C. § 6A:14-4.1(g)(1).

Think about the rules and regulations regarding school transfers in the hypotheticals of Michael and Charles below, and the way in which you, as an advocate, would approach their situations.

Michael

Michael is removed from his home due to allegations of physical abuse committed by his mother. The state child welfare agency places him in the home of his grandmother in the same town. Michael is a student with a disability and has an IEP that provides he is to be educated in a self-contained classroom for students with learning and language disabilities and to receive speech and language therapy individually at a rate of two times per week.

1.   What should happen with Michael's educational programming once he is moved?

2.   If Michael's grandmother lives in a neighboring school district, as opposed to the same one as his parents, what should happen with Michael's educational programming once he is moved?

3.   Michael has not yet been found eligible for special education and related services, but his school district started the evaluation process to determine eligibility 40 days earlier. How many days does the new school district have to complete the evaluation process and determine his eligibility?

4.   Which agency, based on your state's education and child welfare laws and regulations, is responsible for ensuring that the transfer of school records has occurred? What is the timeline? How will you, as an advocate, proceed in the event that no school records are transferred?

Charles

Charles, age 10, is removed from his home in one school district and placed in a non-relative foster home in another town that is approximately 30 miles away. Charles has an IEP. The new school district informs the foster parent that she cannot register Charles in school until he undergoes a full reevaluation, even though the new district has obtained all of Charles' school records from the prior district. The foster parent asks the state child welfare agency to remove Charles from her care because she cannot continue to miss work to watch him.

1. What federal and state statutes and regulations apply?

2. What legal arguments will you make? In which forums? Why?

B.   Placements

In both the educational and foster care settings, placements need to be made. IEP teams determine types of classroom or school placements. For a child placed by the court in foster care, child welfare agencies must determine what type of out-of-home placement is needed, and which specific placement will be chosen. In both instances, these determinations are driven by the child's age, various needs, and experiences to date, and family situation, among other considerations, with different emphasis being given to these factors by the two different governmental entities.

Placement changes by one entity can influence, or even force, changes in placement by the other. The most obvious example is when a child needs to be placed in a foster home or moved from one foster care placement to another. Depending on where the foster placement is located and the reason for the move, as well as other concerns, the child may need to change schools. Such a decision implicates the school stability provisions of Fostering Connections, discussed in Section VI.B. below. The presumption is that it is in the child's interest to remain in his or her same school, and transportation should be provided to maintain this school placement. 45 U.S.C. § 675G(1)(ii).

For children with severe disabilities, there are additional considerations. At times, children with significant special needs must be placed in a congregate care treatment facility, at least temporarily. These facilities often have schools on site. It is often assumed, if not required by the facility, that the child, upon being placed at the facility, will attend the on-site school. However, the IDEA requires that a child's school placement be appropriate and consistent with the child's IEP. Likewise, though less often, children are placed by local school districts at particular schools, based upon their educational needs, which have residential facilities attached. At times, the child welfare agency, due to ease and convenience, will secure a bed for the child in the attached residence. However, while placement at the school may be necessary and appropriate, the child may not require such a restrictive placement for his or her out-of-home placement. Moreover, federal law requires that children be placed in the most "family-like" setting. 45 U.S.C. § 675(5)(A).

In sum, "parents" of and advocates for children in foster care with disabilities, especially severe disabilities, must be cognizant of and on guard for how school and home placements can influence one another. These "parents" and advocates must seek to ensure that children are appropriately placed in the least restrictive and most family-like setting.

Think back to the case of Joseph described above. Joseph is not able to be stabilized in the home of his grandmother. He, therefore, is placed by the child welfare agency in a residential treatment center for youth with severe emotional and behavioral concerns. If the center has a school that is part of the facility, it likely will be assumed that Joseph will go to this school. However, such an assumption should not be made unless the IEP team had determined that it is appropriate.

C. Services

Both local school districts and child welfare agencies provide services to children with disabilities. Services from the local school districts are determined by the IEP Team and are set forth in the child's IEP. In most instances, these are referred to as "related services." 34 C.F.R. § 300.34. Related services are defined as "transportation and such developmental, corrective, and other supportive services as are required to assist a child with a disability to benefit from special education." 34 C.F.R. § 300.34(a). As explained above, it is essential to be mindful of the scope of these services, how often they are provided, and the credentials and expertise of the provider. Typical related services include, but are not limited to: speech and language pathology, occupational and physical therapy, psychological and counseling services, nursing and medical services, recreational activities, social work services, and transportation. 34 C.F.R. § 300.34(c). Related services are broadly defined. Thus, if a service is determined to be needed to enable a child with a disability to benefit from his or her special education program, then the service must be provided. 34 C.F.R. § 300.34(a).

Similarly, child welfare agencies have the obligation to provide services to children who are in foster care in order to ensure that the children's needs are being met. In fact, federal law mandates a "case review system," which is a "procedure for assuring that each child has a case plan designed to achieve placement in a safe setting that is the least restrictive (most family like) and most appropriate setting available . . . consistent with the best interest and special needs of the child." 42 U.S.C. § 675(5)(A). *See also* N.J.S.A. § 30:4C-55. Moreover, the status of each child must be "reviewed periodically but no less frequently than once every six months by either a court or by administrative review . . . in order to determine the safety of the child, the continuing necessity for and appropriateness of the placement, the extent of compliance with the case plan . . . ." 42 U.S.C. § 675(5)(B). Common services provided by child welfare agencies include, but are not limited to: medical care, various mental health services, tutoring, mentoring, recreational activities, and summer camp. Like the related services provided by school districts, there are no limitations or restrictions on the scope of services available. If a particular service is required to meet a child's individual needs and to ensure his or her well-being, then it must be secured and offered.

A child's needs will be met optimally when "parents" and advocates maximize the services afforded by each governmental entity. However, it is important to remember that the purpose underlying the provision of therapeutic services is different for each agency. School districts provide related services to enable children with disabilities to benefit from their educational program. Child welfare agencies offer such services to help the child heal and overcome the trauma and/or family dysfunction, which brought the child into foster care in the first place.

For example, mental health services in the educational setting are primarily geared toward assisting a child with maladaptive behaviors and emotional instability that affect the child's learning. These services focus on helping the child to adapt at school so that the child can learn and progress, and do not seek to cure any underlying psychological disorders or deep-rooted emotional disturbance. On the other hand, child welfare agencies provide therapeutic services to children to help them overcome the impact of abuse and neglect as well as to meet any other mental health needs. Accordingly, for a child who has been the victim of physical or sexual abuse, she will need counseling at school to assist her in coping during the school day, but also certainly will require intensive therapy outside of the school setting to overcome the trauma of the abuse.

D. Transitional Planning and Services

In some jurisdictions, beginning at age fourteen, or younger if appropriate, the IEP Team should begin planning for a student's life after graduation or the age of 21. *See e.g.*, N.J.A.C. § 6A:14-3.7; O.A.C. § 3301-51-07(H)(2)(a). By age sixteen, the child's IEP must include "appropriate measurable postsecondary goals" and "the transition services (including courses of study) needed to assist the child in reaching those goals." 34 C.F.R. § 300.320(b); *see also* O.A.C. § 3301-51-07(H)(2)(a); Cal. Educ. Code § 56462. Federal law also mandates that other public agencies, which may have a role to play in providing or paying for services for the student as an adult (i.e., vocational rehabilitation, developmental disabilities, mental health), be invited to IEP Team Meetings. 34 C.F.R. § 300.321(b)(3).

Some jurisdictions are even more specific about what planning must be conducted and what services must be offered to youth age fourteen or older. For example, in New Jersey, beginning at age fourteen, a student's IEP should include: (1) a statement of the student's strengths, interests, and preferences; (2) the identification of a course of study and related strategies, consistent with strengths and interests, intended to assist in developing goals related to training, education, and employment; and (3) identification of needed interagency consults and linkages. N.J.A.C. § 6A:14-3.7(e)(11). At the age of sixteen, in New Jersey, the local school districts must provide a "coordinated set of activities . . . designed . . . to facilitate the student's movement from school to post-school activities." N.J.A.C. § 6A:14-3.7(e)(12). In addition to basic instruction and related services, the local school districts in New Jersey must provide postsecondary education, vocational education, integrated employment (including supported employment), continuing and adult education, independent living skills training, other community experiences, and daily living skills. N.J.A.C. § 6A:14-3.7(e)12i(1).

California's education code also provides a detailed explanation about the scope and variety of transitional services, which should be offered. Cal. Educ. Code § 56462. Specifically, in California, transition services must include, but not be limited to, the following: "the provision of work skills training, including those skills that are necessary in order to exhibit competence on the job; the provision of . . . a variety of vocational experiences; . . . coordination of the transition planning process, including development of necessary interagency agreements and procedures at both state and local levels; and the provision of instructional learning strategies that will assist pupils who find learning difficult in acquiring skills that will enable them to obtain diplomas, promote a positive attitude toward secondary and postsecondary education and training, and make a successful transition to postsecondary life." Cal. Educ. Code § 56462(b).

Similar obligations exist for child welfare agencies concerning youth who find themselves in foster care at the age of fourteen or beyond. In fact, there are two federal statutes focused exclusively on the needs of older youth. In 1999, the John H. Chafee Foster Care Independence Program was established, through the passage of the Foster Care Independence Act of 1999. In 2001, the Promoting Safe and Stable Families Amendments of 2001 were enacted, which created The Educational and Training Voucher Program. Both programs can be found as amendments to Title IV-E in Section 477 of the Social Security Act, and both programs provide federal funding for services and assistance for youth transitioning out of the foster care system. 42 U.S.C. § 677. In addition, there are specific provisions in the Fostering Connections to Success and Increasing Adoptions Act of 2008, which went into effect on October 1, 2010, concerning the needs of transitioning youth. 42 U.S.C. § 675(8). Specifically, these new statutory amendments allow states to seek additional federal funds to cover the cost of increased services and resources for foster youth ages 18-21, or for youth who were adopted or who went to live with a relative, through guardianship, after the age of sixteen. 42 U.S.C. § 675(8).

The array of transition services that is statutorily mandated to be available to older foster youth from state child welfare agencies is quite comprehensive. Yet, the scope and extent of services vary from state to state, depending on whether the youth's child welfare case remains open beyond the age of 18, and, if it does, at what age it terminates. Currently, in most states, foster care benefits end at the age of eighteen. Illinois, New Jersey, Vermont, and most recently California are among a handful of states that permit a youth's child welfare case to remain open beyond the age of eighteen. 20 I.L.C.S. § 505/5 (Illinois); N.J.S.A. § 30:4C-2.3 (New Jersey); 33 V.S.A. § 4904 (Vermont); CA AB 12 (California). This number may increase as more states take advantage of the new federal funding, which is available through Fostering Connections (see Section VI.B., below). 42 U.S.C. § 675(8).

Yet, all state child welfare agencies must provide services, including transition services, up to the age of eighteen, and all, pursuant to federal law, must develop a transition plan, prior to terminating the child welfare case, if not more frequently under state and local regulations and policies. 42 U.S.C. § 675(5)(H). Such a plan should be "personalized at the direction of the child," and must include "specific options on housing, health insurance, education, local opportunities for mentors and continuing support services, and work force supports and employment services." 42 U.S.C. § 675(5)(H).

Additionally, in many states, regardless of their foster care status, former or current foster youth may be able to maintain their Medicaid (publically provided health insurance) until at least their 21st birthday. 42 U.S.C. § 677(a)(5). Housing assistance, through the provision of financial assistance or actual housing programs, also will be available until at least the age of eighteen, if not beyond. 42 U.S.C. §§ 675(8), 677(a)(5). Through the federal Education and Training Voucher (ETV) program, financial assistance for college or post-secondary vocational programs is available to a youth who "ages out" of foster care, beyond what the youth might be entitled to receive through federal and state aid. 42 U.S.C. § 677(a)(6). Federal funding also makes some financial assistance available to help ease the transition into adulthood. 42 U.S.C. § 677(a)(5). For example, depending on state regulations, federal funding may be used for a first month's rent and security deposit, furniture, driving lessons, or even a used car. Finally, it is important to remember that while the youth's child welfare case continues to be open, the state remains obligated to ensure that the youth's needs are met. Thus, any necessary assistance must be provided, including therapy, mentoring, or tutoring.

The provision of services, by both local school districts and child welfare agencies, is critical in assisting older foster youth, especially youth with disabilities, in making a successful transition into adulthood. Not only do these youth face multiple challenges due to their disabilities, but many youth who age out of foster care are forced to make the transition into adulthood alone, without vital family support or a network of persons who will help guide and support them through these difficult and stressful years.

Many youth are ill-informed as to their rights and entitlement to services. For example, they are unaware that local school districts must meet with them, through the IEP Team process, to discuss their career and life objectives, and that the local school districts must provide services, such as vocational education and work experience opportunities, to help them accomplish their goals. Likewise, many youth do not know that the local child welfare agency must provide for their basic needs, so long as their child welfare case remains open, and, even if it closes, that they might still be entitled to Medicaid or financial assistance for college or vocational training or other necessities, simply because they were once in foster care.

Accordingly, it is essential that all of the public entities charged with aiding a youth, as well as all of the persons responsible for advocating on behalf of the youth, work together to ensure as smooth an adjustment as possible. Unfortunately, because many of these services share the goal of preparing the youth to be a self-sufficient adult, at times, it can appear as if there is a duplication of services. Thus, there can be significant confusion as to which governmental entity is responsible, often resulting in a situation where neither agency takes affirmative steps to aid the youth.

For example, the child welfare agency may assume that because the local school district is providing vocational training, the child welfare agency does not need to assist the youth in planning or arranging for a vocational program once the youth graduates from high school. Yet, the local school district is responsible for providing services until the youth turns 21 or graduates, whichever comes first. Likewise, the IEP Team may assume that because the child welfare agency is convening a transitional planning meeting to discuss the youth's long-term plans, the local school district, through the IEP Team, does not need to do any transitional planning or provide any transition services. Such an approach completely disregards the local school district's obligation to provide an array of transition services while the youth is in secondary school. An attorney or advocate who is representing the youth can ensure that both agencies are complying with their statutory obligations, maximizing their resources to ensure a smooth transition for the youth, and ensuring that the youth is receiving all of the assistance to which he or she is entitled. An advocate also can ensure that collaboration between the various governmental agencies takes place so that all of the necessary services are coordinated and complement one another.

Consider Tara who is seventeen years old and in foster care.

Tara

When Tara's mother died and there was no one to care for her, she was placed into foster care. After moving between foster care placements for several years, Tara moved into her current foster home, where she has resided for the past two years. Tara has been a special education student for as long as she can remember. Tara has been diagnosed with significant developmental delays, due to some complications at birth. She can read, but only at the fifth grade level, and she struggles with basic math skills. Since the fifth grade, Tara has been in special education classes for all of her academic subjects. Tara has no idea what she wants to do when she completes high school. She also does not know for how long she can stay in high school, or for how long she will be able to remain in her current foster home. Tara lives in a state where child welfare cases can remain open until the youth's 21st birthday and foster children are represented by attorneys.

1.   Who should be invited to participate in the IEP Team?

2.   For how long can Tara remain a student in the local school district?

3.   What type of transitional planning and services could or should the local school district offer to Tara?

4.   For how long can Tara remain in her current foster home? If the foster home no longer wishes to care for her, where can she go? Who is responsible for providing for her housing needs? Until when?

5.   What additional obligations does the child welfare agency have with respect to assisting Tara transition into adulthood?

6.   What if Tara still needs assistance after turning 21 years of age?

VI.   ACHIEVING SCHOOL STABILITY

The introduction to this chapter provides much statistical information to illustrate the link between school mobility and poor educational outcomes. Two federal laws enacted in the last decade support school stability for children facing instability in their home placements: The McKinney-Vento Homeless Assistance Act of 2002, 42 U.S.C. §§ 11431 et seq. (hereinafter "McKinney-Vento") and The Fostering Connections to Success and Increasing Adoptions Act of 2008, P.L. 110-351, 42 U.S.C. §§ 675 et seq. (hereinafter "Fostering Connections"). Successful implementation of these laws is critical to improving educational outcomes for children with disabilities in foster care.

A.   McKinney-Vento

The McKinney-Vento Act provides educational stability to "homeless children and youth" by granting them the right to remain in their school of origin, despite changes to their living situation, as long as it is in their best interest. 42 U.S.C. § 11432(g)(3)(A). The term, "homeless children and youth," is defined as those who have no "fixed, regular and adequate nighttime residence," and includes children living in the homes of others due to loss of housing or economic hardship, children living in emergency or transitional shelters, and children "awaiting foster care placement" as defined by the state. 42 U.S.C. § 11435(2)(A)-(B). "School of origin" is defined as the school the child last attended when in permanent housing or the school in which the child was last enrolled; a homeless child has the right to stay in the school of origin for as long as the child is homeless or, if the child becomes permanently housed during the course of an academic year, for the remainder of that year. 42 U.S.C. § 11432(g)(3)(A) & (G). McKinney-Vento requires that state and local educational agencies have in place policies and procedures to provide necessary transportation where a child remains in the school of origin, and to apportion responsibility for providing and paying for the transportation. 42 U.S.C. § 11432(g)(1)(J).

In the event that staying in the school of origin is determined not to be in a child's best interest, the child has the right to be enrolled immediately in the new school district in which the student is residing. 42 U.S.C. § 11432(g)(3)(A). Significantly, the typical obstacles to registration and enrollment discussed in detail above, such as non-production of immunization records, birth certificate, or proof of residency, cannot serve as a barrier to enrollment, defined to include attending classes and participating fully in school activities, for children who qualify under McKinney-Vento. 42 U.S.C. §§ 11432(g)(3)(C), 11435(1). Regardless of where the child attends school, he or she is entitled to receive services that are comparable to those offered to other students in the school, including transportation, vocational services, programs for gifted and talented students and programs for students with disabilities. 42 U.S.C. § 11432(g)(4). It is important to note that children with disabilities who are considered homeless have the same right to a FAPE as non-homeless children, and receive the same rights and protections as non-homeless children under the 2004 Amendments to the IDEA.

States define "children awaiting foster care placement" for McKinney-Vento purposes, with some casting a wide net to include as many children as possible, while others limit the eligible pool. The District of Columbia defines the term as children who have been removed from their home and not yet entered a permanent placement; once a child is legally adopted or placed in a permanent placement, she is no longer entitled to McKinney-Vento protections. *See* McKinney-Vento Homeless Assistance Act State Plan for Washington, D.C. (SY 2009). North Carolina broadly defines this term as children who are not domiciled in a district but living there as a result of abuse, neglect, abandonment or the death or incarceration of a parent. N.C. Session Laws, HB 1074, Chapter 5 (2006) effective July 1, 2006. New Jersey, in contrast, defines the term stringently as children who are in a temporary location awaiting a foster care placement. N.J.A.C. § 6A:17-2.3(a). Despite the notable variance in states' definitions of this term, the federal law is clear in that it does not require that the protections extend to ALL children in foster care. As a result, school instability remains a very real problem for foster children who are not considered to be "awaiting" placement.

As an education statute, McKinney-Vento applies to state and local educational agencies only. Each local educational agency, or school district, is required to have a homeless student liaison who is familiar with the respective rights and duties of students and school districts and helps the children and families understand and access the same. 42 U.S.C. § 11432(g)(6)(A). The local educational agency has responsibility for making the best interest determination with respect to the student's school placement. 42 U.S.C. § 11432(g)(3)(B). In making this determination, the local school district must keep the child in the school of origin to the extent feasible, unless doing so contradicts the parent's or guardian's wishes. 42 U.S.C.

§ 11432(g)(3)(B)(i). If the local school district decides to send the child to a school other than the school of origin or the school requested by the parent or guardian, it must provide an explanation, in writing, to the child's parent or guardian. 42 U.S.C. § 11432(g)(3)(B)(ii). If the child is an unaccompanied minor, then the local school district's homeless liaison helps to make the placement decision, and the wishes of the unaccompanied youth must be considered. 42 U.S.C. § 11432(g)(3)(B)(iii). States must have in place dispute resolution processes and inform the parties of their right to appeal the best interest decision in the event a parent or guardian, or an unaccompanied homeless youth, disagrees with the local educational agency's best interest determination. 42 U.S.C. § 11432(g)(3)(E). Pending resolution of the dispute, children remain in the parent/guardian's school of choice. 42 U.S.C. § 11432(g)(3)(E).

Consider the term "awaiting foster care placement" as you approach the hypothetical of Jane.

Jane

Jane, age 13, was removed from her mother's care due to allegations of sexual abuse against her mother's boyfriend. No relative or non-relative placements could be located for Jane, thus the state child welfare agency placed her in a children's shelter in a neighboring town.

1. What criteria should be considered in defining "awaiting foster care placement"?

2. Would your opinion of the criteria differ if you were a child representative, a parent representative, or a school representative?

3. Apply your criteria to the above situation. Is Jane a child "awaiting foster care placement" using your criteria? Why or why not?

4. After three weeks in the shelter, Jane is moved into a foster home in another neighboring town. However, the foster parent tells Jane that this is a short-term situation only. Jane learns that her caseworker begged the foster parent to "do her a favor" and keep Jane in her home until another placement could be located. The caseworker anticipates that this could take between 2 and 12 weeks. Is Jane a child "awaiting foster care placement" using your criteria? Why or why not?

5. Twelve weeks pass, and the school year has now ended. Jane is placed in a group home in the same town as the foster parent with whom she was living. It does not look likely that Jane will return to her mother's care in the near future, if ever. Is Jane a child "awaiting foster care placement" using your criteria? Why or why not?

6. Now apply your state's definition of "awaiting foster care placement" and re-answer the questions in this hypothetical.

B. Fostering Connections

Fostering Connections requires educational stability for all children in out-of-home placements unless maintaining school stability is found not to be in a child's best interest. 42 U.S.C. § 675(1)(G). The Act also mandates that states make assurances that each child in foster care who has reached the minimum age for mandatory school attendance pursuant to state law is attending school, with minimal exceptions. 42 U.S.C. § 671(a)(30).

Unlike McKinney-Vento, which is a federal education law with limited application to children in foster care, Fostering Connections is a federal child welfare law that applies to ALL children in out-of-home care, including those children considered "awaiting foster care placement." Thus, overlap between the two federal statutes exists. Despite the fact that Fostering Connections is a child welfare law, it requires state child welfare agencies to work with local educational agencies to ensure school stability for children in out-of-home care. 42 U.S.C. § 675(1)(G)(ii).

In changing a child's home placement, either when initially placed into foster care or when moving from one foster home to another, the child welfare agency must consider both the appropriateness of the current educational setting and the proximity of the new home placement to the school. 42 U.S.C. § 675(1)(G)(i). The child welfare agency then must coordinate with the local educational agency to ensure that the child remains in the same school in which the child was enrolled at the time of placement, unless doing so is not in the child's best interest. 42 U.S.C. § 675(1)(G)(i)-(ii). If it is in the child's best interest to stay in the same school, the state must provide "reasonable travel for the child to remain in the school" (i.e., pay for transportation costs). 42 U.S.C. § 675(4)(A). If it is determined that remaining in the same school is not in the child's best interests, states must ensure "immediate and appropriate enrollment" of the child in a new school, with all of the child's educational records provided to the new school. 42 U.S.C. § 675(1)(G)(ii)(II). Unlike McKinney-Vento, Fostering Connections does not define "enrollment," thus there is some question as to whether the term means registration only or both registration and attendance.

Fostering Connections further provides that foster care maintenance payments may be expanded to include reasonable travel expenses for children to remain in their same schools. 42 U.S.C. § 675(4)(A). However, this provision applies to Title IV-E eligible children only, and states must match these funds. 42 U.S.C. § 675(4)(A). A Title IV-E eligible child is defined, generally speaking, as a child who would have been Aid to Families of Dependent Children (AFDC)-eligible or is SSI-eligible upon his or her removal from the parent's or guardian's care. http://www.childwelfare.gov/pubs/f_subsid.cfm; http://www.nacac.org/adoptionsubsidy /definitions.html No federal money is available under Fostering Connections to pay for transportation costs for non-Title IV-E eligible children, leaving states to absorb these costs. Questions persist as to whether these costs are the responsibility of the state child welfare agency, the state and local educational agencies, or all of the above.

Thus far, state approaches to implementing Fostering Connections have differed greatly, with varying levels of success. This is, in part, due to the fact that federal implementing regulations have yet to be developed and little federal guidance on Fostering Connections has been issued. Additionally, many states have not yet enacted their own legislation and/or provided implementing regulations or guidance on school stability for children in foster care. As a result, at present, numerous states continue to fail to abide by federal mandates.

Below is a discussion of the approaches of the five sample states/territories to Fostering Connections implementation:

1. California

In 2004, several years before the passage of Fostering Connections, California took the lead in enacting legislation to promote the educational progress of children in out-of-home care. AB 490 requires educators, county placing agencies, care providers, advocates, and the juvenile court personnel to work together to ensure children in foster care have stable school placements, access to the same academic resources, services and extracurricular activities available to all students, and are placed in the least restrictive educational programs. *See* http://info.sen.ca.gov/pub/03-04/bill/asm/ab_0451-0500/ab_490_bill_20031012_chaptered.html; Cal. Educ. Code § 48850(a).

More recently, California has enacted several state laws to implement Fostering Connections. For example, CA SB 1353 requires that the child welfare agency, when making an out-of-home placement, take into consideration the proximity of the placement to the child's current school, the number of school transfers the child already has experienced, and the child's school matriculation schedule to promote school stability in conformity with Fostering Connections. CA SB 1353 (amending Cal. Wel. & Inst. Code § 16501.1(c)). Furthermore, the child's case plan must provide assurances that the placement agency has "coordinated with the person holding the right to make educational decisions for the child and appropriate local educational agencies" in making decisions regarding the child's schooling. CA SB 1353 (amending Cal. Wel. & Inst. Code § 16501.1(c)(8)(B)).

In the event a child's home placement changes, he or she has the right to stay in the same school for the duration of the court's jurisdiction unless it is not in the child's best interest to do so; if the court's jurisdiction terminates prior to the end of the school year, the child has the right to continue his/her education in the same school for the remainder of the school year. CA AB 1933 (amending Cal. Educ. Code § 48853.5(d)). If it is determined not to be in the child's best interest to stay in the same school, the child's lawyer must discuss any proposed school changes with both the child and the educational decision-maker for the child, as appropriate, and either the child's lawyer or the educational decision-maker may request a hearing on any proposed school change if they disagree with it. Cal. Rules of Court § 5.651(e)(2)(A)-(B). Pending the results of the hearing, the child has a right to stay in the same school. Cal. Rules of Court § 5.651(e)(2)-(4). This law applies to all pupils in foster care. Cal. Educ. Code § 49069.5.

California law imposes other mandates not required by Fostering Connections. For example, each local education agency must appoint an educational liaison for children in foster care, whose responsibilities include ensuring and assisting with timely and proper placements, enrollments and transfers. Cal. Educ. Code § 48853.5(b). Fostering Connections makes no mention of educational liaisons. California law also requires immediate enrollment and attendance of children in foster care, regardless of whether school, immunization or other records are missing. Cal. Educ. Code § 48853.5(d)(7)(B).

2. New Jersey

The New Jersey Senate and House approved legislation to implement Fostering Connections in late June 2010, which went into effect on September 13, 2010. N.J. Assembly Bill No. A2137 (3R) of 2010. This law provides that where the state places a child in a resource family home (resource family home includes both relative and non-relative caregivers), the child must remain in his or her current school unless it is found in the best interest of the child to change schools. Notably, New Jersey limits the definition of child in foster care to those children being placed in "resource family homes." In contrast, the federal law mandates school stability for *all* children in foster care, which would include children in foster homes, as well as children in residential programs, group homes and other congregate care facilities.

In New Jersey, the state child welfare agency has five days to make a best interest determination and, in doing so, must make reasonable efforts to consult with the child's parent or guardian, the child, the child's law guardian (the child's attorney representative), and representatives from the school the child attended at the time of removal and any new school under consideration. Once the state child welfare agency makes the preliminary best interest determination, it must provide written notice of the same to the child's parent or guardian and the child's attorney. If any party to the family court proceedings wishes to challenge the state agency's best interest decision, it must file an application for review with the court within five days from the date that notice is transmitted. Pending the time period allowed to seek court review and any subsequent court review, the child must continue to attend his or her current school. The state child welfare agency has the burden of proof by a preponderance of the evidence to establish that it is not in the child's best interest to remain in the current school. If no challenge is made, the preliminary best interest decision becomes conclusive after the five-day period.

The law lists several factors the state child welfare agency and the court must consider in making a best interest determination. These factors include, among others: safety concerns; the proximity of the resource family home to the child's current school; the needs and preference of the child; the child's special education programming, if any; the expected duration of the change in home placement; and the point of time in the school year.

Under the new law, the district in which the child's parent or guardian presently resides is the "district of residence," and thus has financial responsibility for educating the child. The state child welfare agency is responsible for providing transportation for the child to attend school during the time that a best interest decision is being made or a court is reviewing such a decision. The state child welfare agency must notify the "district of residence" of its conclusive best interest decision or the court's decision regarding the child's schooling. By no later than five days after receiving this notification, the "district of residence" assumes responsibility for providing and paying for the child's transportation to attend school.

3. North Carolina

In 2006, North Carolina enacted N.S. Session Laws, HB 1074 Chapter 5 to clarify the procedures for admitting children into public schools in the state. N.C. Gen. Stat. § 115C-366. This state law predates the enactment of Fostering Connections; however, with respect to children in foster care, it permits children who are not domiciled in a district, as a result of removal for abuse, neglect or abandonment, among other things, to continue to attend school in the original district. N.C. Gen. Stat. § 115C-366(a3). Neither this state law nor any others address the role of best interests in making placement decisions, transportation or any other of the school stability mandates under Fostering Connections.

4. Ohio

Ohio also has yet to enact legislation implementing Fostering Connections. However, the state revised code does address the right of children who are placed by the state child welfare agency outside of their school district but within the same county, and provides that the child may continue to attend the school he or she was attending at the end of the first full week of October of that year. Ohio Rev. Code Ann. § 3313.64(I). This applies for the balance of the school year only. Ohio Rev. Code Ann. § 3313.64(I)(1). Alternatively, if the placement is outside of the child's original county, the child also may continue to attend the same school for the remainder of that academic year if the child's parent provides written notice of this request and the superintendents of both school districts agree. Ohio Rev. Code Ann. § 3313.64(F)(12). In the event that the two districts agree to a transportation arrangement, this service will be provided; however, if no such agreement is reached, the child will receive transportation based on Ohio's inter-district open enrollment process. Ohio Rev. Code Ann. § 3313.64(F)(12)

From the above, it is clear that there is no presumption of school stability for children in foster care, nor is any best interest determination made under current law; thus, typically, when children are placed by the state child welfare agency in a home in another school district, the district in which the child resides is where the child will attend school. Ohio Rev. Code Ann. § 3313.64(B)(1)-(2). However, like some other states, Ohio has created a collaboration of government departments and agencies, community groups and parents called the Family and Children First Council (FCFC). Ohio Rev. Code Ann. § 121.37; http://www.ofcfca.org/index.htm. Members of the FCFC work with relevant agencies throughout the state to improve the well-being of children and families, including school success. http://www.ofcfca.org/mission.htm.

5. District of Columbia

The District of Columbia has no implementing legislation for Fostering Connections to date. However, in its Title IV-B Child and Family Services Plan for FY 2010-2014 (June 30, 2009), one of the primary goals listed is to "[i]mprove the assessment of educational needs and the achievement of positive outcomes for children involved in the child welfare system" (at 10-11). Objectives to achieve this goal include:

- Identify educational decision-maker for children in foster care

- Improve educational teaming, planning and decision-making between child welfare and the state and local education agencies (SEA & LEA)

- Conduct timely and thorough assessments of children's educational needs

- Improve educational stability for children in foster care

- Strengthen early intervention supports and services for children in foster care ages 0 to 5

D.C. Title IV-B Child and Family Services Plan FY 2010-2014 (June 30, 2009) at 11.

The District of Columbia Children and Families Services Agency (hereinafter "CFSA") has been working on implementation of Fostering Connections and amending their current policies so that they comply with the Act's mandates. *See* http://cfsa.dc.gov/DC/CFSA/Publication%20Files/CFSA%20PDF%20Files/Publications/Annual%20Report%202009.pdf. For example, in an effort to ensure children remain in their school of origin, DC has started to put in place procedures such as education assessments which must be conducted on a twice yearly basis, including within thirty days of entering care, to evaluate whether the child has an educational decision-maker and determine whether school stability mandates have been followed, as well as to assess the child's school attendance, academic performance, and social adjustment in school. *See* http://cfsa.dc.gov/. . ./CFSA%20PDF%20Files/Partners/ Referral%20Forms/education_assessment_(out_of_home).doc - 2010-06-16 - Text Version.

Following is the District of Columbia's education assessment for children in out-of-home care.

District of Columbia Child Welfare

Education/Vocation Assessment: Out of Home

*An Education Assessment must be completed twice a year for every school-aged child/youth (ages 5-18) **and** for all older youth (ages 18-21) involved with the CFSA. Approved assessments should be submitted no later than November 15th of each year or within 30 days of a child's/youth's entry into care. Approved updated assessments should be submitted no later than April 15th.*
SECTION 8 (EDUCATIONAL/VOCATIONAL SERVICES FOR OLDER YOUTH) <u>MUST</u> BE COMPLETED FOR BOTH THE NOVEMBER AND APRIL SUBMISSIONS.
FACES information must be updated each time an assessment is completed.

Section 1: Child/Youth Information

Name: **FACES Client ID #:**   **Date of birth:**

School year: 20   **- 20**   **Date assessment completed:**

Jurisdiction of enrollment: ☐ **DC** ☐ **MD** ☐ **VA** ☐ **Other:**

Section 2: Educational Decision-Makers

Do the parents/legal guardian(s) retain educational decision-making authority for the child/youth?
  ☐ Yes
       Name of Parent/Legal Guardian #1:
       Relationship: ☐ Mother   ☐ Father   ☐ Legal guardian
       Does this person actively participate in educational planning for the child/youth?
           ☐ Yes
           ☐ No. *See Tip Sheet for guidance on rights of parents as education decision-makers.*

       Name of Parent/Legal Guardian #2:
       Relationship: ☐ Mother   ☐ Father   ☐ Legal guardian
       Does this person actively participate in educational planning for the child/youth?
           ☐ Yes
           ☐ No. *See Tip Sheet for guidance on rights of parents as education decision-makers.*

  ☐ No
       Who has educational decision-making authority for the child/youth?
       (A foster parent, surrogate parent, guardian, person legally responsible for the child, or a person the child lives with who acts as the parent can be the IDEA Parent if any of the following conditions applies to the birth/adoptive parent(s)' parental rights have been terminated, no active involvement in educational planning for the child/youth, or otherwise unable to locate.)
       Name:
       Relationship: ☐ Foster parent   ☐ Relative   ☐ Surrogate parent
                     ☐ Education advocate ☐ Other:

See Tip Sheet for additional guidance on identifying educational decision-makers.

Section 3: Enrollment & Attendance

With limited exceptions, DC Code §38-202 mandates compulsory school attendance between the ages of five and eighteen. Discuss public, charter, private, and voucher school options with parent(s)/caregiver(s).

1. Enrollment
☐ **Yes**, child/youth enrolled
- Type of educational program:
  - ☐ School   ☐ Vocational program   ☐ Enrichment program   ☐ Other
- Name of school/program:
- Duration of enrollment in current school/program:

☐ No, **child/youth** **not** **enrolled**
- Last grade child/youth completed:
- How long not attending school:
- Briefly describe plan to enroll child/youth:
  If there is no enrollment plan, discuss with supervisor or a CFSA/private agency education specialist.
- Barriers to enrollment, if applicable *(check all that apply)*:
  - ☐ Immunizations   ☐ Transportation   ☐ Prior suspension/expulsion
  - ☐ Other *(specify)*:

2. Attendance
☐ **Yes**, child/youth is attending school or vocational or enrichment program as directed and expected by the child's team

☐ No, child/youth is not attending as directed and expected by the child's team
- Briefly describe attendance pattern:
- Briefly describe barriers to attendance:
- How many of the following has child/youth received this year:
  - Tardies: Unexcused absences: Excused absences:
- Briefly explain tardiness and/or absences:
- Have you discussed excessive tardiness/absences with caregiver(s)?
  - ☐ No. *Plan next steps with your supervisor.*
  - ☐ Yes. Describe steps of caregiver(s) to address issue(s):

3. Transportation to/from School/Program
☐ Caregiver   ☐ Walk   ☐ Metrobus/rail   ☐ School bus   ☐ Home schooled   ☐ Other *(specify)*:

Distance from home to school/program: miles OR   minutes

Section 4: School Stability

The Fostering Connections to Success and Increasing Adoptions Act sets forth an important requirement for child welfare agencies to improve educational stability for all children in foster care by coordinating with local schools to ensure that children remain in their schools of origin unless that would not be in their best interest.

How long has child/youth attended current school or vocational/enrichment program?

How many schools has child/youth attended since kindergarten? *If you are not sure, ask youth or parent(s)/caregiver(s) to give best answer.*
☐ Less than 2 schools   ☐ 2-5 schools   ☐ 6-9 schools   ☐ Ten or more schools

Within the current academic year, has child/youth changed schools as a result of entering or changing placements in out-of-home care?

☐ No   ☐ Yes. Number of changes:

Did child/youth miss any days of school as a result of entering or changing placements in out-of-home care?
☐ No
☐ Yes. Number of days missed:
     Reason(s) why child/youth missed school *(check all that apply)*:
     ☐ Transportation   ☐ Immunizations   ☐ Program refused to enroll   ☐ School records
     ☐ No one available to enroll   ☐ Other:

Is a change in school placement necessary now?
☐ No
☐ Yes
- Are efforts being made to plan the school transfer during a natural break (i.e., summer or other school vacations)?   ☐ Yes   ☐ No
- Were efforts made to maintain child/youth in his/her original school despite entry into or a placement change in out-of-home care?   ☐ Yes   ☐ No
- Have child/youth educational records been transferred to the new school?   ☐ Yes   ☐ No
- Does child/youth have appropriate clothing or the required uniform?   ☐ Yes   ☐ No

Has this child/youth changed schools since the last Education Assessment?
☐ No
☐ Yes
- Were efforts made to plan the school transfer during a natural break (i.e., summer or other school vacation)?   ☐ Yes   ☐ No
- Were efforts made to maintain child/youth in his/her original school despite entry into or a placement change in out-of-home care?   ☐ Yes   ☐ No

Section 5: Health & Well Being

1. Health
Is child/youth current on all immunizations?
☐ Yes
☐ No. *Discuss with caregiver(s) and, if necessary, see an OCP nurse.*

Is child/youth current on the following health exams?
☐ Physical (annual)   ☐ Vision (annual)   ☐ Hearing (annual)   ☐ Dental (twice a year)
If child/youth is not current on any exam above, discuss with parent(s)/caregiver(s). If necessary, see an OCP nurse.

Are there any concerns about child's/youth's physical health, vision, hearing, or dental health that are affecting ability to participate in the school, vocational program, or enrichment activity?
☐ No
☐ Yes. Identify concern(s):
     Has the caregiver shared these concerns with the school, vocational program, or enrichment activity to ensure they make accommodations?
     ☐ Yes   ☐ No. *Discuss with caregiver(s) how to share this information.*

2. Well Being
What does the child/youth say about experiences at school or at vocational/enrichment programs?

Is the child/youth involved in extracurricular activities?
☐ Yes. List activities:
☐ No.
     Is there a plan to involve the child/youth in extracurricular activities?
     ☐ Yes   ☐ No. *Discuss options with caregiver and take appropriate next steps.*

How does the child/youth interact with peers and others? *(Select all that apply.)*

☐ Outgoing   ☐ Withdrawn and/or isolated   ☐ Has/maintains friendships
☐ Fights with others   ☐ Gets along well with others   ☐ Bullies others
☐ Respectful of others   ☐ Picked on by others   ☐ Friendly
☐ Overly anxious   ☐ Quiet and/or reserved   ☐ Involved in gangs/crews
☐ Involved in school activities ☐ Substance abuse/involvement   ☐ Disrespectful of authority
☐ Other *(Please identify:)*

Where are the behaviors indicated above observed?
       ☐ Home   ☐ School   ☐ Both   ☐ Other:

Is the caregiver concerned about any behaviors?
       ☐ No
       ☐ Yes. Explain concerns and plan to address them:

Are you concerned about any behaviors?
       ☐ No
       ☐ Yes. Explain concerns and plan to address them:

Since the last Education Assessment, have there been any recent improvements in child's/youth's behavior?
       ☐ No
       ☐ Yes. Describe:

Has the school disciplined the child/youth for his/her behavior?
       ☐ No
       ☐ Yes. *If child/youth has an IEP, contact a CFSA/private agency education specialist to ensure statutory compliance.*
   • Has child/youth been suspended since the last Education Assessment?
          ☐ No
          ☐ Yes. For most recent suspension, indicate:
              Date suspended:
              Number of days suspended:
              Reason for suspension:
   • Has the child/youth been expelled since the last Education Assessment?
          ☐ No
          ☐ Yes. For most recent expulsion, indicate:
              Date expelled:
              Reason expelled:
   • Has the child/youth been involuntarily withdrawn/transferred since the last Education Assessment?
          ☐ No
          ☐ Yes. For most recent involuntary withdrawal/transfer, indicate:
              Date:
              Reason:
   • For a "yes" answer to any question regarding discipline above, describe efforts underway to ensure child/youth does not fall behind in school (i.e., alternative school arrangements, receiving homework assignments, etc.):

Section 6: Performance & Support Services

1. General
For youth, indicate graduation track: ☐ Diploma   ☐ Certificate of completion
                                          ☐ N/A   ☐ Other:

Is English the child's/youth's primary spoken language?

☐ Yes
☐ No. List primary language(s):
    Does child/youth require ESL classes or other language assistance?
        ☐ No
        ☐ Yes. *Ensure child is receiving appropriate assistance.*

2. Educational Progress
☐ **Yes**, child/youth is demonstrating progress. Describe briefly:

☐ **No**, child/youth is not demonstrating progress.
    Have you discussed lack of progress with caregiver(s)?
        ☐ No. *Discuss next steps with your supervisor.*
        ☐ Yes. Describe steps of caregiver to address issues:

3. Academic/Program Goal *(Check all that apply)*
☐ Promotion to next grade   ☐ HS graduation   ☐ GED   ☐ Vocational training
☐ College   ☐ Employment   ☐ Other *(specify)*:

4. Achievement
Child's/youth's current GPA *(if applicable)*: N/A   Cumulative GPA *(if applicable)*: N/A

In regard to program expectations, child/youth is:
☐ Above grade level/exceeding expectations.
    • In what areas is child/youth excelling?
    • Has child/youth been considered for advanced learning or enrichment?
        ☐ No. *Discuss this possibility with caregiver(s).*
        ☐ Yes. Briefly describe actions to pursue this possibility:
☐ At grade level/meeting expectations.
☐ Below grade level/not meeting expectations.
    • In what areas is the child/youth performing poorly?
    • Indicate which of the following support services have been discussed with and considered by the educational decision-maker. *(check all that apply)*:
        ☐ Tutoring   ☐ Summer school   ☐ Retention
        ☐ Evaluation/testing   ☐ Student Support/Evaluation Team
        ☐ Special education   ☐ 504 services
    • If any of the options above have been considered, what is the current status?

5. Special Needs
Is child/youth suspected of having a special need that affects learning but is not currently addressed in the general classroom?
☐ No
☐ Yes.
    If yes, has the caregiver contacted the school to discuss school-related services?
        ☐ Yes. What is the current status?
        ☐ No. *Discuss with caregiver(s) and contact CFSA/private agency education specialist.*

6. Improvement
If applicable, since the last review, has child/youth made progress in areas where s/he was not meeting expectations?
☐ Yes
☐ No. *Discuss with supervisor to develop an action plan.*

7. Other
Currently, does child/youth have any other unmet educational, vocational, or enrichment needs not discussed above?
☐ No

☐ Yes. Describe:

Section 7: Special Education

☐ **NOT APPLICABLE,** Skip to Section 8.

1. Individual Education Plan (IEP)
Does the child/youth require an IEP?
☐ No
☐ Yes
   Is the IEP current (within the past 12 months)?
      ☐ Yes
      ☐ No. *Consult Tip Sheet and/or supervisor and discuss options with parent(s)/caregiver(s).*

Which of the following special needs categories identified in the IEP qualify the child/youth for special education services? *(Check all that apply.)*

☐ Autism   ☐ Visual impairment/blindness   ☐ Deafness
☐ Deaf-blindness   ☐ Hearing impairment   ☐ Emotional disturbance
☐ Mental retardation   ☐ Orthopedic impairment   ☐ Other health impairment
☐ Speech/language impairment   ☐ Specific learning disability   ☐ Traumatic brain injury
☐ Multiple disabilities *(Please identify)*:

Which of the following services is the child/youth currently receiving? This list is not exhaustive and does not include all services a school district may be required to provide. *(Check all that apply.)*

☐ Speech-language   ☐ Audiology   ☐ Transportation
☐ Extended School Year (ESY)   ☐ Physical therapy   ☐ Occupational therapy
☐ Medical   ☐ Rehab counseling   ☐ Social work in school
☐ Counseling   ☐ Other:
Does the child/youth have unmet special learning needs?
☐ No
☐ Yes. Indicate: *Discuss with parent(s)/caregiver(s) and encourage her/him/them to speak with the school.*

For youth age 16 or older, what transition goals does the IEP indicate?

Section 8: Educational/Vocational Services for Older Youth – This section MUST be completed for ALL youth aged 18-21.

The Fostering Connections to Success and Increasing Adoptions Act *sets forth certain educational or employment conditions that must be met in order to ensure eligibility for IV-E reimbursement.*
Please complete the following section as thoroughly and accurately as possible.

Please verify that the youth is at least 18 years old <u>at the time</u> of this assessment

☐ Yes
☐ No – Please stop. You do not need to complete this section at this time.

Please verify that <u>at least one</u> of the following is occurring:

The youth is finishing high school or taking classes in preparation for a general equivalency diploma exam (GED).
☐ Yes
☐ No

The youth is enrolled full-time or part-time in a university or college **or** is enrolled in a vocational or trade school.

☐ Yes
☐ No

The youth is enrolled in a program or activity that is designed to promote, or remove barriers to, employment, e.g., Job Corps, classes on resume writing or interview skills.

☐ **Yes** - Please specify which program/activity:
☒ **No**

The youth is employment for at least 80 hours per month (either full-time or part-time, at one or more places of employment).
☐ **Yes** – Where is the youth employed?
☐ **No**

OR

The youth is incapable of doing any of the previously described educational or vocational activities due to a medical condition.
☐ **No**
☐ **Yes** - If the youth is in foster care in this circumstance, the agency must maintain information in the youth's case plan concerning the medical condition and the youth's incapability to participate in educational or vocational and provide regularly written or recorded updates.

> Is there current/updated information in the youth's case plan regarding the youth's medical condition and the youth's inability to participate in educational or vocational activities?
> ☐ Yes
> ☐ **No – Please note: This information must be updated immediately and approved by a supervisor prior to submission of this document.**

Section 9: Requested Actions

☐ **Educational needs are being met. No action required at this time.** *Skip to Section 10.*

☐ **Child/youth requires support/intervention in the area(s) of:**
☐ Educational Decision-Makers	☐ Enrollment/Attendance	☐ School Stability
☐ Health & Well Being	☐ Performance & Support Services	☐ Specialized Learning Needs
☐ Other:		

Discuss plan of action:

Additional comments:

Review the Tip Sheet for guidance and consult with your supervisor. If necessary, also consult with a CFSA/private agency education specialist to determine appropriate school and community-based services to support this child/youth. When consulting an education specialist, bring a copy of this assessment.

Section 10: Verification & Signatures

1. Social Worker

> *Update all FACES education screens <u>before</u> completing this section.*

Name: CFSA Administration or Private Agency:

Save the completed assessment as a Word document, and e-mail as an attachment to your supervisor. Sign a printed copy below <u>*after*</u> *your supervisor has reviewed the assessment and discussed it with you.*

_____   _____

Signature   *Date*

2. Supervisor

> *Verify that all FACES education screens are up to date* <u>*before*</u> *completing this*

I,   , verify that the social worker named above has:

- Updated all background educational information in FACES. (*(Insert initials)*

- Developed clear plans of action to address concerns in this assessment. ()

I will continue to monitor, through supervision, provision of indicated services and interventions and completion of action plans.

Comments:

After discussing this assessment with the social worker, place the hard copy that includes both signatures in the case file. Save the completed assessment as a Word document, and e-mail as an attachment to cfsa.EdAssess@dc.gov.

_____   _____

Signature   *Date*

Finally, in the CSFA Annual Public Report on Implementing the Adoption and Safe Families Amendment Act of 2000 in the District of Columbia for FY 2009 and with plans for FY 2010, the CFSA has expressed an intent to push through legislation in the coming year to implement the educational and school stability mandates of Fostering Connections, among other things. *See* http://cfsa.dc.gov/DC/CFSA/Publication%20Files/CFSA%20PDF%20Files/ Publications/Annual%20Report%202009.pdf (at 38).

Consider the school stability laws that might impact Xavier.

Xavier

Xavier is 12 years old and in the seventh grade, and is classified as having a communication impairment for which he receives extensive supports and services in his local public school. The state child welfare agency removed Xavier from his parents' care due to allegations of educational neglect, as he was cutting school frequently and his parents failed to appear in court on three occasions to address truancy claims. He is placed in the care of his aunt and uncle who reside two towns away (in a different school district) and the question of where he should attend school arises.

1. Which federal law(s) applies? Explain.

2. What factors should be considered in making the best interest determination under Fostering Connections?

3. Who makes the decision regarding school stability?

4. From whom should input be sought to make this decision?

5. Who has education decision-making rights for Xavier?

6. Is Xavier eligible for transportation? Who is responsible for providing transportation? Paying for it?

Compare the implementation of Fostering Connections in the above described states with your own. Which state provides the most protections to children in foster care? Which provides the least? Do gaps remain that you would like to see addressed? How does your opinion change, if at all, as an advocate for a child in care, an advocate for the state child welfare agency or an advocate for the local department of education? Where, if any, should compromises be made to address the interests and concerns of all affected?

Draft your own legislation implementing Fostering Connections. Make sure to define all key terms and address all mandates set forth in the federal law as well as any additional ones you would like to see in the law.

VII. STANDARDS FOR EDUCATING CHILDREN IN OUT-OF-HOME CARE

In a handful of states, seven as of the writing of this text, legislatures have sought to ensure that children in foster care, or other out-of-home placements, have their needs met by statutorily creating rights to certain services and resources. Arkansas (A.C.A. § 9-28-1003(b)); Arizona (A.R.S. § 8-529); California (CA Welf. & Inst. Code § 16001.9(a)); Connecticut (C.G.S.A. § 17a-16); Hawaii (H.R.S. § 587-3); New Jersey (N.J.S.A. § 9:6B-4); Rhode Island (RI Gen. Laws § 42-72-15). An eighth state — Florida — has a similar statute, but it sets forth goals for children in foster care, rather than establish entitlements or rights that the children possess. F.S.A. § 39.4085. All of the statutes, with the exception of those from Connecticut and Rhode Island, contain language establishing a right for foster children to attend school and have their educational needs met. For example, Arkansas' statute provides that a child in foster care is entitled "to receive free appropriate education, training, and career guidance to prepare him or her for a useful and satisfying life." A.C.A. § 9:28-1003(b)(13). In California and Hawaii, the child welfare agency must ensure that foster children "have the right to attend school" and "participate in extracurricular activities." CA Welf. & Inst. Code § 16001.9(a)(7); H.R.S. § 587-3(a)(7).

To a large extent, these statutory provisions merely reinforce rights that all children have to receive an education and to participate in extracurricular activities, which will nurture and enrich their lives and prepare them to be self-sufficient and successful adults. Yet, the fact that the legislature elected to enact these "Bills of Rights" and to include a focus on education elevates this need and reinforces for everyone involved with the child that education is an important part of a child's general well-being. The statutes place an obligation on the child welfare agencies to ensure that the child is attending school and having his or her educational needs met. It sends a message to the child's appointed representative (attorney, Court Appointed Special Advocate (CASA), or someone else) that the educational needs of the child are one of the many interests about which the representative needs to advocate. And finally, the presence of education among the enumerated rights of foster children alerts the juvenile and family court judges that this is an issue about which they need to be concerned.

Two states — Arizona and New Jersey — go even further and provide special rights to foster children in the educational setting. In Arizona, a child in foster care has the right "to go to school and receive an education that fits the child's age and individual needs." A.R.S. § 8-529(A)(7). In New Jersey, a child "placed outside his home" has the right to "receive an educational program which will maximize the child's potential." N.J.S.A. § 9:6B-4(m). These two statutes appear to provide for a higher educational standard for foster children, as compared to other children in the respective state.

For example, in Arizona, foster children have the right to an education based upon the foster child's individual needs. In most jurisdictions, such explicit individualization is reserved for children who have been found eligible for special education through the development of an Individual Education Plan (IEP). Likewise, by mandating that foster children should be able to receive an education that enables the child to maximize his or her potential, New Jersey's Bill of Rights arguably offers a higher standard to foster children than the "some educational benefit" standard set forth in *Board of Educ. of the Hendrick Hudson Central Sch. Dist. v. Rowley*, 458 U.S. 176 (1982), and the even higher standard of "significant learning" and "meaningful benefit" set forth in the Third Circuit's decision in *Polk v. Central Susquehanna Intermed. Unit 16*, 853 F.2d 171 (3d Cir. 1988). In other words, while a child with disabilities is entitled only to reasonably benefit from his or her education, a foster child in New Jersey, regardless of disability status, has the right to maximum benefit. Moreover, a child has been found to have a right to bring a lawsuit pursuant to New Jersey's Child Placement Bill of Rights. *See K.J. v. Department of Youth and Family Servs.*, 363 F. Supp. 2d 728 (N.J. 2005) (finding a private right of action under New Jersey's Child Placement Bill of Rights).

VIII. CONCLUSION: CROSS-SYSTEMS ADVOCACY — HOW DOES IT WORK?

Now that the myriad challenges facing children with disabilities in foster care have been addressed, one question remains: How does cross-systems advocacy work? No rules exist for cross-systems advocacy outside of ensuring that advocates abide by state laws and regulations in place, agency policies, and the rules of professional conduct that guide the discipline with which the advocate is affiliated. Cross-systems advocacy is not restricted to attorneys. To the contrary, anyone, be it a parent/guardian, foster parent/caregiver, caregiver agency, school personnel, child welfare agency personnel, attorney for the parent, attorney for the child, attorney for the state, or even a judge for that matter can engage in advocacy across systems.

Cross-systems advocacy also can take many forms. It may involve a child welfare agency worker attending an IEP meeting alongside the child's educational decision-maker (as long as the worker does not make the educational decisions for the child or sign consents for evaluations or IEP implementation). The worker may provide valuable information to the IEP team that affects the child's educational programming, for example, plans to place the child in a residential or group home or to return the child home. The worker also may gain invaluable information by attending the meeting; for example, learning which areas of need are not considered educational and therefore are not being addressed by the school district and must be addressed elsewhere. Such information would enable the worker to go back to the agency or into court to put those services in place. Or perhaps school personnel will advocate for the child by providing testimony regarding the child's performance at school after weekly traumatic visits with a relative. Or a special education attorney on behalf of the educational decision-maker will report to the family court judge on efforts made to stabilize the school programming in hopes of thus stabilizing the home situation as well. The possibilities for cross-systems advocacy are endless, provided that advocates pay heed to laws and regulations governing the multiple systems, including information sharing and confidentiality, as well as any ethical rules that may govern.

Think creatively about how you would approach cross-systems advocacy as you review the following case of Nate.

Nate

Nate is an eight-year-old boy with severe learning, language and behavioral problems. He experienced extreme physical and sexual abuse at a very young age. At school, he is educated in a self-contained program for students with emotional and behavioral issues, but has made little progress. His expressive language is assessed at a two-year-old level, with his receptive language slightly higher at a three-year-old level. When upset, angry or frustrated, he reacts by hiding under the desk, kicking and lashing out at the teacher, and by hoarding and later throwing his feces at teachers and students.

Nate's foster mother, with whom he has lived for the past three years, comes to you for assistance with his educational programming. Nate's foster mother expresses that while Nate does exhibit behavioral problems at home, she is able to handle his outbursts on most occasions. She then informs you that termination of parental rights is likely going to occur in the next few months; however, despite this, the agency continues to allow Nate's mother to visit him on a bi-weekly basis. After each visit, Nate's negative behaviors escalate significantly, both at home and at school.

Nate's foster mother also states that while she wants to adopt Nate, the child welfare agency is threatening to remove him from her care and place him residentially because of his severe needs. She feels that this would cause him irreparable harm.

As the foster mother's advocate for Nate's special education needs, how might you engage in cross-systems advocacy to address the many issues posed by this case?

Chapter 9

THE DUE PROCESS COMPLAINT[1]

I. FILING THE DUE PROCESS COMPLAINT

The IDEA provides many procedural safeguards to protect the rights of parents and their children with disabilities. 20 U.S.C. § 1415(b). These protections include the right to file a due process complaint. *Id.* A due process complaint may be brought by a parent, adult student, a public agency or local school district, or their respective legal representatives. 34 C.F.R. §§ 300.507(a), 300.508(a). The subject matter of the complaint may relate to any matter pertaining to the "identification, evaluation, or educational placement of the child, or the provision of a free and appropriate public education of the child." 34 C.F.R. §§ 300.503(a), 300.507(a).

Every State Educational Agency (SEA) is required to adopt written procedures for resolving complaints, which includes, among other things, where to file the complaint. 34 C.F.R. §§ 300.151, 300.511. In California for example, the SEA has entered into an agreement with the Office of Administrative Hearings to conduct mediation and hear complaints. *See* Cal. Educ. Code § 56504.5(a). Accordingly, in California, a complaint must be filed with the Office of Administrative Hearings, Special Education Division, in Sacramento. *See* http://www.documents.dgs.ca.gov/oah/SE/SE%20Guide%20to%20understanding%20DPH.pdf. In New Jersey, a request for a due process hearing is filed with the State Director of the Office of Special Education Programs. *See* N.J. Admin. Code § 6A:14-2.7(c). In North Carolina, a due process complaint is filed with the Office of Administrative Hearings and with the Superintendent or the Director of Special Education (Exceptional Children Director) of the LEA or public agency. *See* NC § 1504-1.9(a).

II. CONTENTS OF THE DUE PROCESS COMPLAINT

All due process complaints and proceedings are confidential. 34 C.F.R. § 300.508(a). At a minimum, the complaint must include the following information to meet the sufficiency standard under IDEA:

1) The name of the child;

2) The address of the residence of the child;

3) The name of the school the child is attending;

4) Available contact information and the name of the school the child is attending where a child is homeless;

---

[1] This chapter was written by Esther Canty-Barnes, Clinical Professor of Law and Director, Special Education Clinic, Rutgers-Newark School of Law.

5) A description of the nature of the problem, including facts relating to the problem; and

6) A proposed resolution to the problem.

20 U.S.C. § 1415(b)(7); 34 C.F.R. § 300.508(a)-(b). If the complaint fails to meet the minimum requirements, it stands the risk of being challenged on sufficiency grounds and may be dismissed. 20 U.S.C. § 1415(c)(2)(A). A complaint notice must be served upon the opposing party and the State Educational Agency. 20 U.S.C. § 1415(b)(7)(A)(i). The party filing the due process complaint must indicate that the appropriate parties were served.

In addition to the minimum requirements, the due process complaint must set forth a violation that occurred within two years "before the date the parent or public agency knew or should have known" of the issues raised in the complaint, unless the state has a different statute of limitations. 20 U.S.C. § 1415(b)(6)(B); *see also* 34 C.F.R. § 507(a)(2). There are some exceptions to the two year statute of limitations where the parent was prevented from requesting a hearing 1) "due to specific misrepresentations" by the school district that it had "resolved the problem" that is the "basis of the complaint," or 2) the school district withheld information that was required to be provided to the parent. 20 U.S.C. § 1415(f)(3)(D); *see also* 34 C.F.R. § 300.511(f). Some states have shorter statutes of limitations; therefore, it is important to review the applicable state statute to determine when the statute of limitation runs.

The party bringing the complaint may not raise issues that were not contained in the due process complaint unless the other party agrees. 34 C.F.R. § 300.511(d). Once a due process complaint is filed, it may only be amended with the written consent of the opposing party or with the permission of the hearing officer at least five days prior to the hearing. 20 U.S.C. § 1415(c)(2)(E). In either case, the specific timelines set forth in the Act for resolving the complaint begin anew with the filing of the amended complaint. 34 C.F.R. § 300.508(d)(4). If the complaint is dismissed on insufficiency grounds and the statute of limitations has run, unless there is an exception, the parent may be precluded from refiling the complaint.

Other issues often arise after a due process complaint has been filed. In these situations, a party may file a separate due process complaint. 20 U.S.C. § 1415(o); *see also* 34 C.F.R. § 300.513(c). The subsequent complaint is also subject to the mandatory meeting and time requirements. Each state is required to develop and publish forms to assist parents in filing complaints. 20 U.S.C. § 1415(b)(7)(B). Sample due process complaints may be found on the website of each State Department of Education or Agency responsible for monitoring compliance under IDEA. A sample Complaint is included below as a reference.

Julie K. Waterstone, SBN 211888
Jenny Rodriguez-Fee, SBN 262592
Children's Rights Clinic
Southwestern Law School
3050 Wilshire Blvd.
Los Angeles, Calif. 90010
O: (213) 738-6621
F: (213) 738-5751

Attorneys for Petitioner
LISA JONES

BEFORE THE CALIFORNIA OFFICE OF ADMINISTRATIVE HEARINGS
DIVISION OF SPECIAL EDUCATION

L. J. O/B/O M. J.	CASE NO. *Unassigned*
Petitioner,	PETITIONER'S REQUEST FOR DUE
v.	PROCESS
LA NEW SCHOOL DISTRICT	
Respondent.	

COME NOW, Lisa Jones, Petitioner, (Hereinafter L.J.) on behalf of Mary Jones

(Hereinafter M.J.), a minor child, alleges and complains as follows:

I.   STUDENT BACKGROUND

    1.   M.J. was born on August 25, 2003.

    2.   M.J. resides with her mother, L J., at 554 Westmoreland Ave., Los Angeles, CA

90005 located in the local educational area served by LA New School District (Hereinafter,

"District"). She currently attends New School Academy.

    3.   M.J. has maintained special education eligibility since September 10, 2006. She

1 is eligible to receive special education and related services as a student who has multiple

2 disabilities. M. J. was born with numerous medical problems that affect her heart, liver, lung,

3 respiratory and immune systems. She is developmentally and cognitively delayed in all areas, is

4 fed primarily via a nasal-gastric tube and requires one-to-one assistance from a Registered

5 Nurse throughout the entire school day.

6

7   4.   The District's current offer of FAPE includes placement in a public school

8 program not yet developed, and one-to-one assistance from either a 'Registered Nurse or

9 Licensed Practical Nurse."

10   5.   L.J. contends that the District has failed to offer a free and appropriate public

11 education in an appropriate educational placement for the 2010-2011 school year and hereby

12 files for due process.

13

14

15 II.   ISSUES FOR HEARING

16   A. THE DISTRICT FAILED TO PROVIDE ADEQUATE PLACEMENT FOR THE
    2010-2011 SCHOOL YEAR AND THEREFORE HAS DENIED FAPE.

17

18   1. The District's Current Offer of Placement Cannot Adequately Meet M.J.'s
    Unique Medical and Educational Needs

19

20 Pursuant to California Education Code §56001(g), individuals with exceptional needs

21 must be offered special assistance programs that promote maximum interaction with the general

22 school population in a manner which is appropriate to the needs of both. In determining

23 whether a student is being educated to the maximum extent appropriate with her nondisabled

24 peers, the court in Sacramento City Unified School District v. Holland provided several factors

25 critical in analyzing whether a district is complying with the LRE mandate. 14 F.3d 1398 (9th

26 Cir. 1994). These factors include:

27

28   1. Educational benefits available to the student with a disability in a regular
    classroom, supplemented with appropriate aids and services, as compared with

-2-

Petitioner's Request for Due Process

educational benefits of a special education classroom;

2. Nonacademic benefits of interaction with children who are not disabled;
3. Effect on the teacher and the other children in the classroom of the presence of the student with disabilities in terms of disruptive behavior and/or undue consumption of the teacher's time;
4. Cost of mainstreaming a student with disabilities in a regular education classroom as compared to the cost of placement of the student in a special education classroom.

14 F.3d 1398 (9th Cir. 1994).

Although the law requires that to the maximum extent appropriate, children with disabilities should be educated with their nondisabled peers, the IDEA allows separate schooling where "the nature or severity of the disability is such that education in regular classes with the use of supplementary aides and services cannot be achieved satisfactorily." See 34 C.F.R. § 300.114(a)(2).

In this case, M.J's medical problems impact her ability to access her education to such an extent that a regular public school program is inadequate to meet all of her complex medical needs. According to the last agreed upon IEP, M.J's current placement at New School Academy is in a program that specializes in educating medically-fragile students. While at the New School, M.J has steadily progressed and has succeeded in meeting most of her 2009-2010 academic and social goals. Additionally, the current placement has properly addressed M.J's significant medical and educational needs while providing her with a safe environment to learn.

Despite her progress however, the District now seeks to remove her from her current placement and enroll her in a public school program. The District's current offer of FAPE provides that M.J's one-to-one medical assistance will be provided by either a Registered Nurse (RN) (as is currently required) or a licensed practical nurse (LPN). As is discussed further below, a LPN generally has significantly less education, training and experience than a Registered Nurse. Therefore, for the 2010-2011 school year, the District has significantly

-3-

Petitioner's Request for Due Process

1   decreased the amount of support that M. J. is to receive and will continue to need according to

2   medical professionals. Not only does this reduction of individual support fail to address M.J.'s

3   unique educational needs, it also and places her at significant risk of harm.

4

5   2. The District's Current Offer of Placement Fails to Offer M.J. a Research Based
        Program As Required By State and Federal Law.

6   School districts receiving federal funds under IDEA are required under 20 U.S.C. §

7   1414(d)(1)(A)(i) to establish an IEP for each child with a disability that includes: (1) a

8   statement regarding the child's then-present levels of academic achievement and functional

9   performance; (2) measurable annual goals, including academic and functional goals designed to

10 meet the child's educational needs and enable the child to make progress; (3) a description of

11 how the child's progress will be measured; (4) a statement of the special education and related

12 or supplementary aids and services, based on peer-reviewed research to the extent practicable,

13 to be provided to the child; (5) a statement of the program modifications or supports that will be

14 provided; (6) an explanation of the extent to which the child will not participate with

15 nondisabled children in the regular class; and (7) other required information, including the

16 anticipated frequency, location, and duration of the services. (*See also*, Cal. Ed. Code, § 56345,

17 subd. (a).)

18 The IDEA does not mandate that a district use a particular methodology, however, the

19 District's proposed instructional method must meet the student's needs such that the student is

20 able to make meaningful educational progress against her goals and objectives.

21 The District's proposed placement is not tailored to M.J's unique needs. M.J requires an

22 educational environment that utilizes specific instructional methodologies tailored to her

23 significant cognitive and developmental delays. Additionally, her program must be capable of

24 addressing her severe medical needs. Until the most recent IEP meeting, M.J's program and

25

26

27

28

-4-

Petitioner's Request for Due Process

placement appropriately addressed all of her academic and medical needs. However, at the most recent IEP meeting, the District proposed to remove M.J from her current school and place her in a public school program that has yet to be developed. While the District argues that M.J. will receive all necessary supports through this new program, it has failed to inform L.J. of specific instructional methodologies because the program has yet to be formed. Without this critical information the District's placement offer is wholly inappropriate and deprives the parent of her right to obtain all relevant information prior to the IEP meeting.

      B. THE DISTRICT FAILED TO PROVIDE ADEQUATE RELATED SERVICES FOR THE 2010-2011 SCHOOL YEAR AND THEREFORE HAS DENIED FAPE.

         1. The District Denied M.J. a Qualified Medical Assistant for the 2010-2011 School Year, Resulting in a Denial of FAPE.

FAPE requires that a child make meaningful educational progress. While the selection and retention of an aide to assist a student with special needs is an administrative function of the District and not subject to review under the IDEA, however, the District's selection must meet the student's needs and provide meaningful educational progress toward her goals and objectives. Freeport Sch. Dist. 145, 34 IDELR 104 (SEA Illinois 2000). A school district's proposed program is not designed to meet a child's unique needs if the staff designated in the IEP to provide services is not adequately trained and qualified to do so. See Rowley, 458 U.S. at 207-208; see also, Student v. Long Beach Unified Sch. Dist., 29 IDELR 541. Any required training or qualifications should be written into the IEP, and include the frequency, location, amount and type of services the aide will provide. See 34 CFR §300.550 and 300.551.

In this case, M.J. is assigned a Registered Professional Nurse due to the complexity of her medical needs. During the school day, the RN is required to change M.J's nasal-gastric feeding tube, monitor oxygen saturation levels, and to generally assess whether additional

1   medical treatment and oxygen would be needed. M.J's pediatrician, cardiologist and

2   pulmonologist all indicate the need for a RN to be assigned to monitor her condition throughout

3   her school day and attested to this need at the most recent IEP meeting. Moreover, the RN from

4   M.J's current school, who is a member of the IEP team, also indicated that an RN is required to

5   attend to M.J's needs throughout the day.

6

7   Despite all of these testaments as to M.J.'s level of need, the District discontinued its

8   offer of a RN and instead offered a "RN or a Licensed Practical Nurse (LPN)" to assist M.J.

9   while at school. The differences between the licenses of a RN and an LPN are quite substantial.

10 The type of care provided, based on training, differs significantly. While LPNs are generally

11 responsible for giving medication, taking patients' vital signs and maintaining patient records,

12 RNs are responsible for delivering, planning and managing the care for patients in specialty

13 areas, as well as supervising LPNs and other medical assistants. Allied Health World LPN v.

14 RN, http://www.alliedhealthworld.com/lpn-vs-rn.html (last visited October 25, 2010).

15

16   M.J's unique set of needs requires the specialty training of a RN to assist her throughout

17 her school day. The District's failure to recognize and assist M.J's level of need not only denies

18 her FAPE, but actually puts her health and well-being at great risk.

19

20   2. Based on the District's Failure to Assess in the Area of Occupational Therapy,
                with a Focus on Feeding Therapy, It Denied Student a Necessary Related
21   Service.

22   Both the IDEA 2004 and the 2006 IDEA Part B regulations compel IEP teams to

23 consider the following when developing a child's IEP:

24
        - The strengths of the child;
25   - The concerns of parents for enhancing the education of their child;
        - The results of the initial or most recent evaluation of the child; and
26   - The academic, developmental, and functional needs of the child.
        20 U.S.C. 1414(d)(3)(B); 34 CFR 300.324(a)(1).
27

28

-6-

Petitioner's Request for Due Process

1   The related services provided in a child's IEP includes such developmental, corrective,

2 and other supportive services as are required to assist a child with a disability to benefit from

3 special education, and includes speech-language pathology and audiology services, interpreting

4

5 services, psychological services, physical and occupational therapy, recreation, early

6 identification and assessment of disabilities in children, counseling services, including

7 rehabilitation counseling, orientation and mobility services, and medical services for diagnostic

8 or evaluation purposes. 34 CFR 300.34(a). In looking particularly at the service of occupational

9 therapy, help with activities of daily living, including *feeding*, dressing, and toileting, must be

10 incorporated in related services if called for by a child's unique needs. See Guidelines for

11

12 Occupational Therapy and Physical Therapy in California Public Schools, Cal. Dept. of

13 Education (1996) (Emphasis added).

14   M.J.'s feeding history is marred with challenges and difficulties. While she currently

15 takes medication and nutrition through a nasal-gastric tube, feeding therapy would allow her to

16 gradually increase the type and amount of food and liquid ingested orally. To date, the District

17 has failed to attempt this necessary related service.

18

19   C. ERRORS IN THE IEP PROCESS DEPRIVED STUDENT OF EDUCATIONAL
        BENEFITS, IMPEDED PARENTAL INVOLVEMENT, AND DENIED FAPE.

20

21   1. The District Impeded The Parents' Rights To Participate In The IEP Process.

22   Full and effective parental participation is an integral part of the IEP process. As the

23 U.S. Supreme Court explained in Schaffer v. Weast, IDEA requires school districts to develop

24 an IEP for each child with a disability with parents playing "a significant role" in this process,

25 546 U.S. 49, 53, 126 S. Ct. 528, 163 L. Ed. 2d 387 (2005). Parents serve as members of the

26 team that develops the IEP. 20 U.S. C. § 1414(d)(1)(B). Moreover, the "concerns" and input of

27 parents "for enhancing the education of their child" must be considered by the team. 20 U.S.C.

28

§ 1414(d)(3)(A)(ii). IDEA accords parents additional protections that apply throughout the IEP process. See, e.g., 20 U.S.C. § 1414(d)(4)(A) (requiring the IEP Team to revise the IEP when appropriate to address certain information provided by the parents); 20 U.S.C. § 1414(e) (requiring States to "ensure that the parents of [a child with a disability] are members of any group that makes decisions on the educational placement of their child").

Without any supporting data or testimony from other IEP team members, the District unilaterally determined that M.J.'s placement should change from her current private school to a public school program that has yet to be developed. Offering a program that parents, cannot visit and observe to determine whether it is appropriate for their child, denies them the opportunity to participate as equal members of the IEP team and ultimately, denies the student FAPE.

     2.   The District Failed To Consider The Reports of Outside Experts and Assessors.

If parents initiate an outside evaluation that meets agency criteria, the results of that evaluation must be "considered" by the district in any decision made with respect to the provision of FAPE to the student. 34 CFR 300.502(a), (c); T.S. ex re. S.S. v. Board of Educ. of the Town of Ridgefield, 20 IDELR 889 (2d Cir. 1993). Similarly, if parents request the participation of a particular expert at the IEP meeting, who can provide critical information about a student's unique needs, the information and recommendations from the expert must also be considered by the district. See Id.

The district must document its consideration at the IEP meeting, including:

-   How the report or information was made available to IEP team members;
-   The forum in which the information was reviewed and discussed by the IEP team;
-   To the extent the district disagrees with the independent information, the reasons why the findings and recommendations of the IEE are not accepted.

Ibid.

In this case, L. J. provided reports from her daughter's pediatrician, cardiologist, pulmonologist and the RN at M.J.'s current school. Each of these professionals indicated that M.J.'s multiple medical problems required the services of a RN. L.J. and the doctors provided detailed information and reasoning to support this recommendation. However, the District refused to consider these opinions. Moreover, the District provided little to no explanation as to the reasons for its denial. The District's unilateral action denies L.J. her procedural rights under the IDEA and denies M.J. her substantive rights to receive a free and appropriate public education.

III.   PETITIONER'S RIGHT TO AMEND

There has been a pervasive failure on the part of the District to comply with its obligations under the IDEA and state law. For this reason, Petitioner reserves the right to amend the above stated issues on discovery of new issues in advance of hearing as allowed by law.

IV.   PROPOSED RESOLUTION

Petitioner requests the following resolution:

1. The District shall provide continued placement at M.J's current school, New School Academy, the private school specializing in educating medically-fragile children, for the 2010-2011 school year;

2. The District shall provide a Registered Nurse to assist M.J. throughout the entire school day, including transportation;

3. The District shall fund an independent and complete occupational therapy assessment, focusing on M.J.'s potential need for feeding therapy, by a qualified, mutually agreed upon independent assessor;

4. The District shall provide supportive services in the areas of occupational therapy and/or feeding therapy as indicated by the independent assessment, if substantiated;

5. An appropriate IEP shall be developed and include all necessary IEP team

Petitioner's Request for Due Process

members;

6. The Petitioner reserves the right to seek attorney's fees and costs incurred; and

7. Such other and further relied as the Court may deem just and proper.

DATED:

CHILDREN'S RIGHTS CLINIC

By: _____
            Jenny Rodriguez-Fee
            Attorney for Petitioner

Petitioner's Request for Due Process

III. ANSWERING THE DUE PROCESS COMPLAINT

Generally, any party who receives a due process complaint must respond to the complaint within ten days and address the issues raised. 34 C.F.R. § 300.508(f). If the school district is the receiving party of a due process complaint, and has not previously sent a prior written notice regarding the subject matter contained in the parent's complaint, its answer must include:

(i) an explanation of why the agency proposed or refused to take the action raised in the due process complaint;

(ii) a description of other options that the IEP Team considered and the reasons why those options were rejected;

(iii) a description of each evaluation procedure, assessment, record, or report the agency used as the basis for the proposed or refused action; and

(iv) a description of the other factors that are relevant to the agency's proposed or refused action.

34 C.F.R. § 300.508(e)(i)-(iv). The school district's response to the due process complaint does not preclude it from challenging the complaint on sufficiency grounds. 34 C.F.R. § 300.508(e)(2).

IV. SUFFICIENCY CHALLENGE

Subsequent to receiving a due process complaint notice, there are several timelines that apply. A due process complaint is deemed sufficient unless the receiving party "notifies the hearing officer and the other party in writing, within fifteen days," that the due process complaint is deficient. 34 C.F.R.§ 300.508(d). If there is a sufficiency challenge, "within five days of receipt of notification," the hearing officer must determine "on the face of the due process complaint" whether it meets the statutory requirements and notify the parties of the determination. 34 C.F.R. § 300.508(d). If the hearing officer determines that the complaint is deficient, it may be dismissed. If the hearing officer determines that the complaint is sufficient, the case will proceed within the specified time frames.

V. RESOLUTION MEETING AND 30 DAY WAITING PERIOD

After a complaint is deemed sufficient but before a due process hearing can begin, the school district must convene a resolution meeting with the parent to attempt to resolve the issues that were raised in the due process complaint within fifteen days of receiving notice of the due process complaint. 34 C.F.R. §§ 510(a)(1), (2). The meeting must include relevant members of the IEP team and representatives from the agency who have decision-making authority. 34 C.F.R. § 510(a)(1)(i). An attorney for the school district is not permitted to attend unless the parent is accompanied by an attorney. 34 C.F.R § 300.510(a)(1)(ii). The resolution meeting is not required if the parties agree in writing to waive the 15 day resolution meeting or agree to hold mediation in lieu of a resolution meeting. 34 C.F.R. § 300.510(a)(3). If the LEA has not resolved the issues that were raised in the parent's due process complaint to the satisfaction of the parents within thirty days, the due process hearing may proceed and all applicable timelines concerning the hearing will begin. 34 C.F.R § 300.510(b)(1), (2). The public agency must ensure that a final decision is reached not later than 45 days after the expiration of the 30 day resolution period. 34 C.F.R. § 300.515(a).

Except in those circumstances where the parties have agreed to waive the resolution meeting or to proceed to mediation, the parent's failure to participate in the resolution meeting will delay the timelines for the due process hearing until the resolution meeting is held. 34 C.F.R. § 300.510(b)(3). Additionally, if the LEA is unable to obtain the parent's participation in the resolution meeting after reasonable efforts, the LEA may, "at the conclusion of the 30 day period," request that the parent's due process complaint be dismissed. 34 C.F.R. § 300.510(b)(4). On the other hand, if the LEA fails to hold or participate in the meeting within the prescribed fifteen day period, the parent may seek the intervention of a hearing officer to begin the due process timeline. 34 C.F.R. § 300.510(b)(5).

If, however, there is an agreement reached at the resolution meeting, the parties must execute a legally binding agreement that is "signed by both the parent and a representative of the agency who has authority to bind the agency." 34 C.F.R. § 300.510(d)(1). Either party may void the agreement within three business days. After three days, the agreement becomes a binding and enforceable agreement in any state or federal district court of competent jurisdiction or by the SEA if the state has procedures for parties to seek enforcement of resolution agreements. 34 C.F.R. § 300.510(d)(2)-(e).

Consider the following hypothetical and determine how you would respond to the school district's treatment of this situation.

Jane

Jane is an eleven-year-old, non-verbal student who uses a wheelchair. She has been diagnosed with Joubert Syndrome, shunted hydrocephalus, global developmental delay, and a history of neonatal seizures. She is unable to speak, walk, toilet, or feed herself independently. To address her multiple disabilities, Jane was placed in an out-of-district placement at a private school specializing in educating children with multiple disabilities. Several months ago, the District advised its parents whose children attended the private school that it would be seeking to place their children in an in-district program the following September. An IEP meeting was scheduled. Jane's parents attended the scheduled meeting and participated in the development of the IEP. The IEP team recommended that placement be continued at the private school. The IEP Team consisted mainly of personnel from the private school as well as the appropriate school district representatives. Despite the recommendations of the IEP Team, the District advised the parents that it would be returning Jane to the in-district program. Jane's mother filed a due process complaint.

Within 15 days of receiving the due process complaint notice, a resolution meeting was held. During that resolution meeting, the District again proposed an in-district program that was described as appropriate for meeting Jane's special needs. On the basis of the District's representations, and without viewing the program, Jane's parents orally consented to consider a change in placement for their daughter, pending review of the program. The District amended the IEP based upon the parents' oral consent. The only document Jane's parents signed was the attendance sheet that showed the names and titles of the persons who were present at the meeting. The IEP revision indicated that the new placement was the in-district program effective September of the new school year. The amended IEP was never implemented.

One week after the resolution meeting, Jane's parents visited the proposed program and determined that it was inappropriate. Jane's wheelchair could not fit in the bathroom, the classroom was not handicap accessible and the staff was insufficiently trained to handle the number of children in the classroom. Jane's parents immediately sent a letter to the District revoking their oral consent. Since the case was not satisfactorily resolved, it proceeded to a hearing officer after 30 days. During this period, the District failed to answer the parent's complaint. The matter is being heard before an administrative law judge where the District asserts that the parents consented to the change in placement and that the parents were bound by the oral agreement made at the resolution meeting.

What arguments would you make in opposition to the District's assertions? What relief would you seek if the student had been out of school and the District refused to provide transportation? (See Chapter 10 for more on remedies.) Would you file any motions? If so, please explain.

VI. PROCEDURAL PROTECTIONS IN DUE PROCESS

A.   The Hearing Officer's Responsibilities

A parent has a right to an impartial due process hearing that is "conducted by the SEA or the public agency directly responsible for the education of the child." 34 C.F.R. § 300.511(b). In order to ensure that the parent obtains an impartial hearing, there must be an impartial hearing officer. 34 C.F.R. § 300.511(c). A hearing officer is not deemed to be disqualified from conducting a hearing "solely because he or she is paid by the agency to serve" in that capacity. 34 C.F.R. § 300.511(c)(2). However, the hearing officer must not be an "employee of the SEA or the LEA that is involved in the education or care of the child" or have a "personal or professional interest that conflicts" with his or her objectivity. 34 C.F.R. § 300.511(c)(1)(i)(A),(B). Additionally, the individual must possess knowledge of the IDEA, federal and state regulations, and federal and state court interpretations of the Act; and must have "special knowledge and ability" to conduct hearings and "render and write decisions" in compliance with "appropriate, standard legal practice." 34 C.F.R. § 300.511(c)(1)(ii)-(iii). Thus, the hearing officer must also be capable of conducting pre-hearing conferences, ruling on motions, calling witnesses, ordering impartial assessments if necessary, restricting witnesses and evidence, as well as developing an appropriate record. District of Columbia Public Schools, The Special Education Student Hearing Office, Due Process Hearing Standard Operating Procedures § 600.1 (2006).

In some states, such as Ohio, hearing officers are appointed from a list of attorneys, while they are administrative law judges in others such as the State of New Jersey. State Board of Education of Ohio, Operational Standards for Ohio Educational Agencies Serving Children with Disabilities, 3301-51-05(K)(8)(d) (2008); N.J. Admin. Code § 6A:14-2.7(a).

B.   Hearing Rights

A parent has a right to a fair hearing as well as other rights specified by the Act. 34 C.F.R. § 300.511(a). These rights include the right to be "accompanied and advised" by legal counsel and "individuals with specialized knowledge" or "training" regarding children with disabilities.

34 C.F.R. § 300.512(a)(1). An individual accompanying or advising a parent at a due process hearing need not be an attorney unless required under state law. *See, e.g.*, 34 C.F.R. § 300.512(a)(1); N.J. Admin. Code § 1:6A-5.1(b). *But see In re Arons*, 756 A.2d 867 (Del. 2000) (finding that the IDEA does not authorize representation by non-attorneys in due process hearings).

Representing a parent in a due process proceeding is not a simple matter. There are many complex rules, statutes, timelines and proofs that the parent's representative must understand and adhere to. In many cases, although the proceedings are informal, the process can be overwhelming and the documents can be voluminous.

The right to be represented by an attorney is vital in many cases, since the process involves complex procedural and substantive issues. The attorney's legal responsibilities include reviewing and interpreting numerous documents, evaluations and reports; determining whether procedural and/or substantive rights have been violated; developing and planning strategies for representation; determining the appropriate relief and remedies; drafting documents, correspondence, and motions; filing appeals within the statutory timelines; adhering to appropriate timelines and statute of limitations; presenting the case before a hearing officer; marshalling witnesses and evidence; obtaining, consulting with and preparing experts and lay witnesses; and counseling the parent throughout the process. The attorney is also expected to present opening and closing remarks, conduct direct and cross-examination of witnesses, and be able to admit or exclude evidence.

The parent also has a right to present evidence and confront, cross-examine, and compel the attendance of witnesses. 34 C.F.R. § 300.512(a)(2). Presenting evidence in a due process case requires the skill of an attorney or person with specialized skills in special education matters. The student's records normally contain many documents such as evaluations, IEPs for every school year, annual reviews, and disciplinary records. Despite the complexity of the information, the attorney must be able to present the evidence in a logical, understandable and persuasive manner.

Moreover, the parent must have witnesses to substantiate the claims alleged in the due process complaint and to counter any witnesses the school district intends to call. In most cases, it is important for the parent to obtain expert witnesses in anticipation of filing a due process complaint. These experts may be available from the student's treating or health care professions, through independent evaluations obtained by the parent from the school district, or experts secured with the assistance of the parent's attorney. If the IEP team evaluations and school personnel are sufficient to substantiate the parent's claims, it will be necessary to call or subpoena the appropriate persons from the school district.

A parent may compel the attendance of potential witnesses by having subpoenas issued. 34 C.F.R. § 300.512(a)(2). In some states, the hearing officer is responsible for issuing subpoenas; however, the parent bears the expense. State Board of Education of Ohio, Operational Standards for Ohio Educational Agencies Serving Children with Disabilities, 3301-51-05(K)(12), (16) (2008). In other states, the parent or the parent's representative is responsible for issuing subpoenas. N.J. Admin. Code § 1:1.11.1(a). Subpoenas may also be used to compel witnesses to provide documentary evidence that is in the possession or control of the witness.

The parent also has a right to confidentiality in the hearing process, however, the hearing may be open to the public if the parent chooses this option. 34 C.F.R. § 300.512 (c)(2). In the event the parent seeks to have the child present at the hearing, the parent has a right to do so. 34 C.F.R. § 300.512(c)(1).

Moreover, a parent has the right to "obtain a written or electronic record of the hearing" and "written or electronic findings of fact and decisions." 34 C.F.R. § 300.512(a)(4)-(5). The written or electronic record and decisions must be provided at no costs to the parent. 34 C.F.R. § 300.512(c)(3). In the event that the parent receives an unfavorable decision at the administrative level, a request should always be made to obtain a copy of the verbatim record.

C.   Discovery

The parent has a right to obtain discovery in a due process proceeding. 34 C.F.R. § 300.511(a)(3), (b). The process, however, is informal. The limited time frame for completing a final decision makes it difficult to impose lengthy discovery timelines that are available in civil litigation. Thus, the use of depositions and interrogatories are not normally permitted. N.J. Admin. Code § 1:6A-10.1(d). Parties have an affirmative obligation to disclose all evidence they intend to use at least five business days before the due process hearing. 34 C.F.R. § 300.512(a)(3). Attorneys should freely exchange information and make discovery requests and disclosures to the opposing party. The parties must disclose "all evaluations completed" and "recommendations based upon the offering party's evaluations" that the party intends to use. 34 C.F.R. § 300.512(b)(1).

Typically, each party is required to provide a list of witnesses to be called and a description of the nature and extent of their testimony as a part of the informal discovery process. If a party fails to disclose evidence, a hearing officer may bar the evidence not disclosed within the time frame. 34 C.F.R. § 300.512(a)(3), (b). In some cases, even if a party fails to provide the evidence five days prior to the hearing, the hearing officer may, in his or her discretion, determine whether the evidence should be admitted. District of Columbia Public Schools, The Special Education Student Hearing Office, Due Process Hearing Standard Operating Procedures, § 500(A)(2) (2006).

An integral part of the right to cross-examine witnesses and to present a case is the parent's right to obtain all student records or the records, evidence and information concerning the disabled student that is in the possession of the school district. In addition to the discovery obligation, there is an independent obligation to provide access to student records that are "collected, maintained or used" by the LEA. 34 C.F.R. § 300.613(a). Upon request, an LEA must provide access to school records prior to any meetings regarding a child's IEP, or any hearing regarding a due process complaint, resolution session, discipline proceeding, and appeal regarding discipline matters. *Id.* The LEA must allow access without any unnecessary delay, and no longer than forty-five days after the request is made. *Id.* This right includes the right to inspect, review and obtain copies of student records by the parent or the parent's legal representative. 34 C.F.R. § 300.613(b); *see also* 20 U.S.C. § 1232(g).

In some instances, LEAs fail to provide parents copies of records in a timely manner. If the LEA fails to provide records that the parent or legal representative has requested, a party may file an appropriate motion to compel disclosure or request that the hearing officer issue an order to compel compliance with the IDEA or discovery rules.

D. Right to "Stay-Put"

Among the procedural protections during the pendency of a due process complaint is the right of a parent to have her disabled child remain in the current placement. The IDEA provides that "during the pendency of any [such] proceedings . . . , unless the State or local educational agency and the parents otherwise agree, the child shall remain in the then-current educational placement of such child . . . ." 20 U.S.C. § 1415(j). The federal regulations have interpreted this provision to encompass complaints pending in "any administrative or judicial proceeding." 34 C.F.R. § 300.518. The "then current placement" is that placement where the child was attending at the time the complaint was filed. *Honig v. Doe*, 484 U.S. 305, 325 (1988). If the complaint involves the admission to public school of a student with a disability, the child, with the consent of the parent, is to be placed in public school until the proceedings are completed. 34 C.F.R. § 300.518(b).

Usually, the "stay-put" provision of IDEA acts as an "automatic" mechanism to maintain the status quo. There are some exceptions to the "stay-put" provision of IDEA. If a hearing officer or a state review officer on appeal of an administrative appeal, "agrees with the parent that a change in placement is appropriate," the placement is treated as an agreement between the state and the parent for purposes of the "stay-put" provision. 34 C.F.R. § 300.518(d). In some disciplinary matters, the "stay-put" provision does not apply. A LEA may place a student with a disability in an interim alternative placement for forty-five school days in cases where a student: 1) "carries or possesses a weapon to or at school, on school premises, or at a school function"; 2) "knowingly possesses, uses illegal drugs, or sells or solicits the sale of a controlled substance while at school, on school premises, or at a school function"; or 3) "inflicted serious bodily injury upon another person while at school, on school premises, or at a school function." 20 U.S.C. § 1415(k)(1)(G). The "stay-put" placement during these instances is the "interim alternative" educational placement as determined by the IEP team. 20 U.S.C. § 1415(k)(2). Moreover, where a suspension exceeds more than ten days and the behavior that gives rise to the suspension is not deemed a manifestation of the student's disability, the "stay-put" placement is not the current placement. The "stay-put" placement is determined by the IEP team. 20 U.S.C. § 1415(k)(1)(C). If the IEP team determines that an alternative placement is appropriate, and the parent appeals this decision, the "stay-put" placement is the interim alternative placement. 20 U.S.C. § 1415(k)(4)(A).

VII. BURDEN OF PROOF

The IDEA does not indicate which party bears the burden of proof at impartial due process hearings. Prior to the decision of *Schaffer v. Weast*, 546 U.S. 49 (2005), federal courts were split on the issue of which party bore the burden of proof in these matters. Some states placed the burden of proof on the parent, while others placed the burden of proof on school districts. Joanne Karger, *A New Perspective on Schaffer v. Weast: Using a Social-Relations Approach to Determine the Allocation of the Burden of Proof in Special Education Due Process Hearings*, 12 U.C. Davis J. Juv. L. & Pol'y 136, 163-171 (2008) (discussing the burden of proof in states prior to and after *Schaffer v. Weast*).

The burden of proof encompasses two distinct burdens: the burden of persuasion, "which party loses if the evidence is closely balanced," and the burden of production, "which party bears the obligation to come forward with the evidence at different points in the proceeding." *Schaffer*, 546 U.S. at 56. The Court in *Schaffer* ruled that the burden of persuasion in impartial due process proceedings where the appropriateness of the IEP is at issue is on the party bringing the action. *Id.* at 61. Although the Court recognized that school districts have a "natural advantage" over parents in "expertise and information," it reasoned that the protections provided by Congress were adequate to safeguard the parent's rights. *Id.* at 60. The Court did not decide the allocation of the burden of production, or set the standard in cases where states have specific laws concerning the burden of proof. *Id.* at 61. In response to *Schaffer*, some states have enacted laws pertaining to the burden of proof. Some place the burden on the party seeking relief, while others place the burden on the school district. *See* Karger, *supra*, at 210-215. New Jersey was one state that enacted legislation to overturn *Schaffer*, returning the state to its longstanding practice of placing the burden of persuasion and production on school districts. *Lascari v. Board of Educ.*, 116 N.J. 30 (1989). A copy of the Burden of Proof Legislation Enacted by the State of New Jersey is indicated below:

NEW JERSEY SENATE, No. 2604
S. 2604, 212th Leg. Reg. Sess. (N.J. 2007)

Places the burden of proof and burden of production on school districts in due process hearings conducted to resolve special education issues.

AN ACT concerning special education and supplementing chapter 46 of Title 18A of the New Jersey Statutes.

BE IT ENACTED *by the Senate and General Assembly of the State of New Jersey:*

1. Whenever a due process hearing is held pursuant to the provisions of the "Individuals with Disabilities Education Act," 20 U.S.C. s.1400 et seq., chapter 46 of Title 18A of the New Jersey Statutes, or regulations promulgated thereto, regarding the identification, evaluation, reevaluation, classification, educational placement, the provision of a free, appropriate public education, or disciplinary action, of a child with a disability, the school district shall have the burden of proof and the burden of production.

2. This act shall take effect immediately and shall apply to due process hearings requested in writing after the effective date of this act.

STATEMENT

This bill places the burden of proof on the school district in due process hearings conducted for the purpose of resolving issues related to special education. In *Schaffer v. Weast*, 126 S.Ct. 528 (2006), the United States Supreme Court held that the burden of proof in such a due process hearing is properly placed upon the party seeking relief. However, the Supreme Court in *Schaffer* declined to address the issue of whether a state could override this rule. Prior to the decision in *Schaffer*, New Jersey placed the burden of proof on the school district, pursuant to the holding of the New Jersey Supreme Court in *Lascari v. Bd. of Educ.*, 116 N.J. 30 (1989). This bill will return the burden of proof to the school district, as was the case in New Jersey prior to the holding in *Schaffer*. The bill also places the burden of production on the school district. The Supreme Court in *Schaffer* noted at the outset of its opinion that the case concerned only the burden of proof. The burden of production, prior to the *Schaffer* decision, was generally placed on the school district. This bill codifies that practice.

Should other states adopt New Jersey's approach? Do you think the New Jersey rule is likely to lead to more favorable outcomes for parents? Why or why not?

VIII.   EXPEDITED DUE PROCESS COMPLAINTS

An expedited due process complaint may be filed by the parent or a LEA. Often times, expedited due process complaints involve matters concerning disciplinary matters. These types of complaints may be filed in cases where 1) the parent disagrees with a decision of an LEA in a disciplinary action involving placement or a manifestation determination, or 2) by an LEA if it believes that maintaining a child in the current placement is "substantially likely to result in injury to the child or others." 34 C.F.R. § 300.532(a).

The hearing officer hears the case and makes a determination whether to 1) return the child to his placement if there is a determination that the removal was a violation of the disciplinary provisions of IDEA or the behavior was a manifestation of the child's disability; or 2) order a change of placement to an "interim alternative educational setting" for no longer than "45 school days," if there is a determination that "maintaining the current placement . . . is substantially likely to result in injury to the child and others." 34 C.F.R. § 300.532(b)(2).

The parties are entitled to an impartial due process hearing in these cases, except that the matter is heard on an expedited basis with a different timeframe than a regular due process complaint. 34 C.F.R. § 300.532(c)(2), (4). The SEA or LEA is responsible for arranging the hearing within "20 school days" of the date the complaint was filed. 34 C.F.R. § 300.532(c)(2). The hearing officer is required to render a final decision within "10 school days" after the hearing. 34 C.F.R. § 300.532(c)(2). Prior to the hearing, a resolution meeting must "occur within 7 days" of receiving notice of the due process complaint, unless the parties agree to waive the resolution meeting or agree to mediation. 34. C.F.R. § 300.532(c)(3)(i). If the matter is not resolved to the parties' satisfaction within fifteen days of receipt of the due process complaint, the due process hearing may proceed. 34. C.F.R. § 300.532(c)(3)(ii).

States may establish different "State-imposed procedural rules" to resolve expedited proceedings. In New Jersey, the state has established rules for determining when a due process complaint is heard on an expedited basis on "emergent relief." These issues include 1) break in the delivery of services; 2) disciplinary actions, including manifestation determinations and determinations of interim alternative placements; 3) placements pending outcome of due process proceedings; and 4) issues involving participation in graduation ceremonies. N.J. Admin. Code § 6A:14-2.7(r)(1). In the event that states establish rules, the procedural rules must be consistent with the standards set forth in the IDEA and ensure that the due process rights of the parties are not violated. 34 C.F.R. § 300.532(c)(4).

Consider the following hypothetical in which a request for an expedited hearing might be helpful:

Johnny

Johnny is a 6-year-old student who attends the ABC Public Charter School in Green Acres. He has been suspended four times during the school year for explosive behavior, striking other students, and destruction of school property. Early in the year, the ABC Public Charter School personnel became concerned that Johnny was unable to sit, attend, follow instruction, or engage in any of the academic work that the teacher provided. When Johnny's behavior worsened, his mother requested a child study team evaluation that included a psychological, educational, physical therapy, occupational therapy, speech and language, functional behavioral assessment, and neurodevelopmental evaluations. The Charter School agreed to complete all evaluations. Soon thereafter, Johnny's behavior deteriorated further. Ultimately, he punched and scratched his kindergarten teacher, who required medical treatment. The Charter School immediately issued a suspension notice to the parent for 10 days. When the parent sought to return the student to school the next school year, the Charter School refused to admit him and offered home instruction pending completion of the IEP. The Charter School believes that the only appropriate placement is a private school for the handicapped. The Charter School agreed to classify Johnny as "Other Health Impaired" and has developed an IEP for an out-of-district placement. The parent disagrees with the Charter School and seeks to file an expedited complaint for due process.

Can the Charter School seek relief? If so, what will it allege? What jurisdiction does the hearing officer have in this case? Can the parent file a request for an expedited due process hearing? If so, what can the parent allege? What are the parent's defenses against the Charter School?

IX. APPEAL OF DUE PROCESS DECISION

The IDEA recognizes that some states have one-tiered complaint systems, while others have two-tiered systems. In a one-tiered system, once an impartial due process hearing has been held and a decision rendered, the decision of the hearing officer becomes final. 20 U.S.C. § 300.514(a). In a two-tiered system, if a hearing is conducted by the LEA, an aggrieved party may request an appeal to the SEA where a subsequent "independent" and "impartial review" may be conducted. 20 U.S.C. § 1415(g)(1)-(2). During this process, the official reviewing the hearing officer's decision is required to 1) examine the entire hearing record; 2) ensure that due process requirements were followed at the hearing; 3) receive additional evidence if necessary; 4) allow the parties an opportunity to present oral and/or written arguments at the discretion of the official; and 5) make an independent decision at the conclusion of the review. 34 C.F.R. § 300.514(b)(6). The decision of the reviewing officer is final for purposes of appeal. 34 C.F.R. § 300.514(d).

X. TIMELINES FOR COMPLETION OF HEARING AND APPEAL REVIEW

In addition to the thirty day waiting period prior to the transmittal of the complaint to a hearing officer, IDEA mandates other time frames in which special education cases must be completed. A public agency "must ensure" that a final decision is rendered and a copy of the decision mailed to the parties within forty-five days after the expiration of the thirty day waiting period or the adjusted period agreed to by the parties. 34 C.F.R. § 300.515(a). In two-tiered systems, there is an additional period of time to complete the administrative review. In addition to the forty-five day period, the SEA must within thirty days of receipt of a request for a review, render a final decision and mail a copy of the decision to the parties. 34 C.F.R. § 300.515(b).

Either party in the due process proceeding may request an extension of time beyond the time mandated to complete the hearing and review. 34 C.F.R. § 300.515(c). Unfortunately, due to heavy dockets, in some cases, and the unavailability of the parties, witnesses, or their representatives, these timelines may not always be complied with. To ensure that the rights of parties are protected, the District of Columbia has established additional protections in its Due Process Standard Operating Procedure to address these problems. It requires a showing of "good cause" in cases where extensions are requested and creates a "rebuttable presumption that good cause does not exist for a continuance" in a number of circumstances which include the "unavailability . . . of witnesses or counsel" or a "judge." District of Columbia Public Schools, The Special Education Student Hearing Office, Due Process Hearing Standard Operating Procedures, § 402(A)(1)-(2) (2006).

XI. APPEAL OF ADMINISTRATIVE DECISION

Any party who has exhausted administrative remedies and is "aggrieved" with the outcome of the administrative hearing or review, may appeal the decision to the United States District Court or any "State court of competent jurisdiction." 34 C.F.R. § 300.516(a). Depending upon the applicable state laws and regulations, the party bringing the complaint must appeal the administrative decision no later than 1) ninety days from the date of the decision of the hearing officer or state review official or 2) the time limitation explicitly set forth by state law. 34 C.F.R. § 300.516(b). If the matter is appealed in federal court, jurisdiction is brought "without regard to the amount in controversy." 34 C.F.R. § 300.516(b).

An aggrieved party must first exhaust administrative remedies before filing an action under IDEA in federal or state court. 20 U.S.C. § 1415(l); *see also* 34 C.F.R. § 300.516(e). Exceptions to the exhaustion requirement have been recognized where the relief sought would be futile or inadequate. *Honig*, 484 U.S. 305, 327 (1988). Where a complaint alleges claims under the Rehabilitation Act of 1973, the Americans with Disabilities Act or other federal and civil rights statutes that are "also available" under IDEA, the party must also exhaust administrative remedies to the same extent as an IDEA matter. 34 C.F.R. § 300.516(e).

When a due process case is appealed to federal or state court, the court 1) receives the records of the administrative proceedings, 2) hears additional evidence at the request of a party, and 3) makes a decision based on the preponderance of evidence. 20 U.S.C. § 1415(i)(2)(C). The burden of proof on appeal of an administrative decision, "is on the party who seeks to overturn the findings and decision of the agency." *Town of Burlington v. Dep't of Educ. for Com. of Mass.*, 736 F.2d 773, 794 (1st Cir. 1984), *aff'd*, 471 U.S. 359 (1985). The role of the reviewing court is to determine 1) whether the State has "complied with the procedures" set forth in the IDEA; and 2) whether the IEP developed is reasonably calculated to enable the child to receive an educational benefit. *Board of Educ. v. Rowley*, 458 U.S. 176, 206-07 (1982). A reviewing court must grant "due weight" to the underlying administrative proceedings. *Id.* at 206. Some courts have described the "due weight" standard of review as "modified de novo." *S.H. v. State-Operated Sch. Dist. of the City of Newark*, 336 F.3d 260, 270 (3d Cir. 2003). Due weight, however, does not mean that a reviewing court must accept the administrative findings. *Id.* Where the reviewing court rejects the administrative findings, it must provide some basis in the record for the decision or explain why it has not accepted the administrative findings. *Id.* at 271.

XII.   DUE PROCESS COMPLAINT EXERCISES

After you read the chapter on Remedies, return to this section and draft a due process complaint using the following facts. Consider what relief you would request and how you would like each case to be resolved.

Mary

Mary is a multiply disabled 7-year-old child who was born with multiple medical problems that affected her heart, liver, lung, respiratory and immune systems. She was developmentally and cognitively delayed in all areas and had been placed in a private school that specialized in educating medically-fragile children. She is under the care of approximately nine medical specialists, is fed primarily via a nasal-gastric tube and is accompanied to school by a registered nurse because of the multiple medical diagnoses. Mary's doctors consistently prescribe nursing by a Registered Professional Nurse (RN) due to the complexity of her medical needs. A RN was recommended to change Mary's nasal-gastric feeding tube, to monitor oxygen saturation levels, and to generally assess whether additional medical treatment and oxygen would be needed. Moreover, the RN from the private school, who is a member of the IEP team, has indicated that a RN is required to attend to Mary's needs throughout the day. The current IEP provides for the services of a RN as a related service to accompany Mary on the school bus and throughout the school day.

In order to save money, the School District offered an IEP for the current school year which included a "Registered Nurse or a Licensed Practical Nurse." The parent objects to the changes in the IEP since Mary's pediatrician, cardiologist and pulmonologist all indicated that her multiple medical problems require the services of a Registered Nurse. The district refuses to include the services of a Registered Nurse in Mary's IEP. In addition to the changes to the related services, the District is seeking to return the student to a public school program that is yet to be developed. Although the parent and Mary's doctors have provided detailed information concerning her needs, the District refused to consider these opinions.

In drafting your complaint, consider the following questions:

- What facts should the parent include in the due process petition?

- What relief should the parent request?

- How would you want the hearing officer to resolve the case?

- What procedural violations would you allege?

- What substantive violations would you allege?

- At what point would you file a complaint for due process?

In preparation for the hearing, develop a witness list of potential witnesses you would want to call and the nature and extent of their testimony.

Prepare an opening and closing statement on behalf of the Parent or the School District.

Sam

Sam is 13-year-old student who is classified as Emotionally Disturbed and has been diagnosed as suffering from hemophilia, bi-polar disorder, attention deficit and hyperactivity disorder, combined type learning disorder, oppositional defiant disorder, intermittent explosive disorder, mood disorder, and sleep apnea. Medical and psychiatric evaluations suggest that he may also suffer from obsessive-compulsive disorder, conduct disorder, post traumatic stress disorder, attachment disorder, and Tourette's syndrome.

Sam's recurrent acts of violence have resulted in regular visits to the emergency rooms of local hospitals for psychiatric treatment. He has had eight psychiatric hospitalizations for suicidal ideation, aggression, and violence. He has a history of uncontrollable outbursts of violence toward his parents, siblings, school age children, and involvement with the police. Sam has been hospitalized for throwing hot pasta in his mother's face and attempting to assault his father. Moreover, he has spent several days in juvenile detention when he could not be restrained by local police who were called to the parents' home.

Sam receives outpatient treatment at a local Adolescent Psychiatric Services Program. He has undergone extensive trials of numerous potent medications including Ritalin, Klonopine, Tegretol, Dexedrine, Elavil, Clonodine, Mellaril, Buspar, Depakote, and Zoloft. Sam's mother reports that the drugs have not had a sufficiently beneficial effect on her son.

Sam has attended several schools in three counties during his time in elementary school. He was expelled from pre-school after four months "due to disruptive behavior." When he began middle school in September, he received in-class support in the core curriculum. By December of that year, he was placed on home instruction, due to disruptive behavior. Since Sam's entry into the current school district, he has had numerous detentions, as well as in-school and out-of-school suspensions. He has repeatedly been reported as a threat to other students, has been cited for truancy, vandalism to school property, threatening and attacking other children, disobedience, and engaging in inappropriate behavior that distracts and endangers his classmates. In September of his first year in high school, Sam's parents requested a re-evaluation to determine if his current placement was appropriate. In December of the ninth grade, a psychiatric evaluation was conducted to determine whether a change in school placement was appropriate. The psychiatrist identified Sam as being in a regular state of rage, having a desire to violate the boundaries of other people, an affinity for sociopathic behavior, and incapable of tolerating stress. She further opined that Sam was incapable of accepting responsibility for his behavior, and could not solve any problems without violence or threats. Due to Sam's psychiatric instability, the psychiatrist indicated that he was an extreme threat to other children and recommended that he be precluded from returning to a regular classroom setting. Furthermore, she recommended that Sam be placed in a highly restrictive program, with extremely strong boundaries, and full time, 24-hour monitoring and supervision. Sam's personal therapist agreed with the psychiatrist's recommendations and recommended that he be placed in a residential placement.

The District, however, believed that Sam could be educated in its alternative school and provided an IEP for the alternative school. The only health care professional on staff in the district's alternative school was a school social worker. There was no time out room or health professional to address his psychiatric needs.

Sam was considered by numerous private schools. Only one school agreed to consider him for placement on a trial basis. After attending the private school for a few months, Sam was suspended several times and failed to meet the behavioral requirements. Ultimately, the District was advised that the private school could not meet Sam's needs.

Sam's parents contacted several agencies in the community for treatment. Although Sam was receiving treatment at a psychiatric counseling facility, he refused to attend counseling on a regular basis. His parents were subsequently able to obtain services at a partial hospital treatment facility that provided medication management and psychiatric counseling. The treating therapists at both programs agreed that the appropriate placement for Sam was a residential program.

Sam's parents have approached you and requested that you draft a due process complaint in which you argue that Sam should be placed in a residential facility. Please draft this complaint.

Assume that the district responded to your complaint by alleging that it could provide an in-district alternative placement for Sam. At the hearing, the District presented members of its Child Study team who conducted evaluations. During the hearing, the District asserted that Sam could attend its in-district alternative school. It offered no testimony that the program was appropriate. The parents offered testimony from experts and community officials that Sam could only benefit from placement at the private facility selected by the parents. The ALJ ruled in Sam's favor and ordered placement at the residential program recommended by the parent. The ALJ rendered a written decision and relied upon the testimony of the parents' witnesses and documents from various agencies that provided treatment and services. The District appealed the decision of the ALJ to the U.S. District Court. The parents answered the complaint and filed a counterclaim.

What do you think the District would allege in its appeal? What might the parents allege in their counterclaim? Please outline the basis for the parents' motions setting forth the standard of review. Are there grounds to file a request for attorneys' fees? If so, please draft a complaint for attorneys' fees and costs.

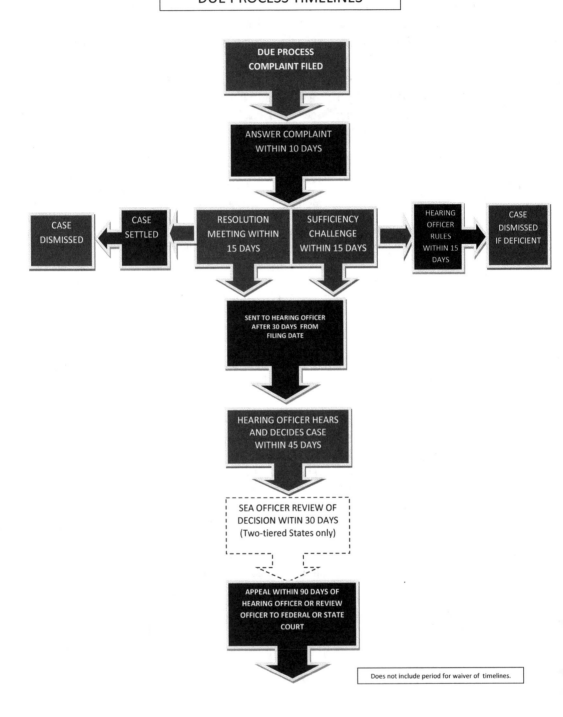

DUE PROCESS TIMELINES

DUE PROCESS COMPLAINT FILED

ANSWER COMPLAINT WITHIN 10 DAYS

CASE DISMISSED

CASE SETTLED

RESOLUTION MEETING WITHIN 15 DAYS

SUFFICIENCY CHALLENGE WITHIN 15 DAYS

HEARING OFFICER RULES WITHIN 15 DAYS

CASE DISMISSED IF DEFICIENT

SENT TO HEARING OFFICER AFTER 30 DAYS FROM FILING DATE

HEARING OFFICER HEARS AND DECIDES CASE WITHIN 45 DAYS

SEA OFFICER REVIEW OF DECISION WITIN 30 DAYS (Two-tiered States only)

APPEAL WITHIN 90 DAYS OF HEARING OFFICER OR REVIEW OFFICER TO FEDERAL OR STATE COURT

Does not include period for waiver of timelines.

Chapter 10

REMEDIES[1]

I. REMEDIAL AUTHORITY OF DUE PROCESS HEARING OFFICERS

As discussed in Chapter Nine, the IDEA provides for administrative due process hearings as the impartial adjudication system for disputes under the statute. An attorney who represents a family in a special education matter should research and consider various remedies prior to filing a due process complaint and counsel his or her client appropriately on the varied forms of relief that the client could seek through a complaint. A due process complaint must include a proposed resolution of the problem to the extent known and available to the party at the time. 20 U.S.C. § 1415(b)(7)(A)(ii)(IV). Specificity in a complaint as to the proposed resolution could assist in earlier resolution of the issue, through a dispute resolution session or settlement agreement, if the education agency is willing to agree to the specific remedies requested. However, because a complaint only requires relief to the extent known and available at the time, attorneys may be able to develop the requested remedy in further detail between the time of the filing of the complaint and the hearing. For example, a complaint may include a request for compensatory education, as discussed below, to make up for the time in which a child was denied a free and appropriate public education ("FAPE"), but the parent and attorney may still be working with an expert psychologist to develop the exact form and amount of compensatory education services they wish to request. These details must, of course, be fleshed out, with supporting evidence, in time for the hearing. Hearing officers in different jurisdictions may vary in terms of the lack of detail they will tolerate in a complaint, and a local educational agency (LEA) can try to allege that a complaint is insufficient if it does not include the necessary information. 20 U.S.C. § 1415(c)(2)(B)(i)(II). Counsel should always try to investigate the policies and practices in a particular jurisdiction or of a particular hearing officer or hearing office before filing a complaint.

In determining the remedy or remedies to request, it is important for counsel to remember that the IDEA provides the opportunity to present a complaint on an extremely broad array of issues related to the rights outlined in the statute. Specifically, a due process hearing can be initiated through a complaint with respect to any matter relating to the identification, evaluation, or educational placement of a child, or the provision of a free appropriate public education to a child. 20 U.S.C. § 1415(b)(6). Because a complaint can be brought for a due process hearing about issues as wide in scope as the provision of a free appropriate public education to a child, which essentially encompasses the full range of the substantive rights

---

[1] This chapter was written by Yael Zakai Cannon, Practitioner in Residence at the Washington College of Law at American University. The author would like to gratefully acknowledge the invaluable feedback and guidance provided by Robert D. Dinerstein, Professor of Law and Director of Clinical Programs at the Washington College of Law at American University, and the thorough and thoughtful research assistance of Bridget Koza and Melanie Bennett.

outlined in the IDEA, it follows that hearing officers can issue the relief necessary to ensure that a child receives a free appropriate public education. Moreover, because a hearing can cover any issues related to the identification, evaluation or educational placement of a child, a hearing officer can order related remedies, such as a change in disability classification (which relates to identification) and a new school for a child (which relates to educational placement).

The IDEA and its accompanying regulations also explicitly provide for the availability of certain remedies through a due process hearing. For example, hearing officers are specifically provided with the authority to order reimbursement to parents for the cost of enrollment in a private school if the hearing officer finds that the public agency did not make a FAPE available to the child in a timely manner prior to that enrollment. 20 U.S.C. § 1412(a)(10)(C)(ii); 34 C.F.R. § 300.148(b). The IDEA also vests hearing officers with the authority to override lack of parental consent for evaluations of a child, except where prohibited by state law. 20 U.S.C. § 1414(a)(1)(D)(ii)(I). Additionally, hearing officers have the power to determine whether a school district's evaluation is appropriate and to order independent educational evaluations as part of a due process hearing. 34 C.F.R. § 300.502(b), (d). For a discussion of a hearing officer's power to order relief, see Perry A. Zirkel, *The Remedial Authority of Hearing and Review Officers Under the Individuals with Disabilities Education Act*, 58 Admin. L. Rev. 401 (Spring 2006).

Litigation under the IDEA largely focuses on the authority of courts, rather than administrative hearing officers, to order relief based on civil actions that have been brought through the IDEA. Attorneys should look to the remedies and limitations on remedies discussed by courts in the relevant case law to understand the scope of the remedial authority of hearing officers, which is often treated as derived from and largely commensurate with the remedial authority of the courts.

Attorneys should also look to their state and local laws, regulations, and rules, including those that discuss special education and those that cover administrative hearings, if applicable to the special education due process system in that state, for any further guidance as to the remedial authority of hearing officers in their jurisdictions. Some states use administrative law judges who have responsibility for subject areas other than special education, some of whom may feel that their authority is delineated in state administrative law or regulations. Of course, if any interpretation of the remedial authority of a hearing officer varies from the authority provided for in the IDEA or set out by a controlling court's interpretation, the remedial authority provided for by the IDEA or controlling court applies. Even due process hearing officers and state administrative review officers who are specifically charged with special education matters do not always accurately interpret the scope of the hearing officer's remedial authority. If necessary, in order to justify the remedy he or she is requesting, an attorney should be prepared to provide supporting legal authority to demonstrate the broad discretion of a hearing officer in awarding that form of relief. Regardless of the jurisdiction, there is a strong argument that the remedial authority of a hearing officer is as broad as that of a court. Several courts and the Department of Education's Office of Special Education Programs have affirmed that hearing officers and state review officers have the same broad authority to grant appropriate remedial relief as courts.

In determining the available remedies in a particular case, it is important to identify which party has the burden of persuasion. In *Schaffer v. Weast*, 546 U.S. 49 (2005), the Supreme Court held that the burden of persuasion in a special education due process hearing is placed on the party seeking relief, whether that party is the parent of a child with a disability or the school district, unless a state provides otherwise. Although the Court acknowledged that school districts have a "natural advantage" in information and expertise, the Court concluded that Congress provided protections to counteract this advantage by requiring schools to safeguard the procedural rights of parents and to share information with them. *Id.* at 60. Because special education cases are usually brought by parents and their children with disabilities, they will most often bear the burden of persuasion. An attorney litigating an IDEA case before an administrative hearing officer in which his or her client bears the burden of persuasion should prepare to marshal the evidence effectively so as to meet this burden in arguing for the desired remedy.

A.   Statutory Limitations on Hearing Officer's Remedial Authority

Despite the broad remedial authority of hearing officers, they are explicitly limited in their decision-making by several specific provisions of the IDEA.

1.   Substantive Violations Required, Except Where Procedural Violations Meet Statutory Exceptions

A decision by a hearing officer must be made on substantive grounds based on a determination of whether the child received a free appropriate public education, not on procedural grounds. 20 U.S.C. § 1415(f)(3)(E)(i). However, hearing officers can find that a child did not receive a free appropriate public education based on procedural violations where those procedural inadequacies impeded the child's right to a free appropriate public education, significantly impeded the parent's opportunity to participate in the decision-making process regarding the provision of a free appropriate public education to the child, or caused a deprivation of educational benefits. 20 U.S.C. § 1415(f)(3)(E)(ii).

For example, the IDEA requires that parents be provided with written notice of their procedural safeguards upon initial referral of a child for special education services or a request for evaluation. 20 U.S.C. § 1415(d)(1)(A). If a parent refers her child for special education and is not provided with this information, she might not be aware of her right to participate in the IEP process and might not participate as a result. Consequently, she could argue that the school district's failure to provide her with notice of her procedural safeguards impeded her participation in the decision-making process and that the procedural violation amounted to a denial of a free appropriate public education upon which the hearing officer can base his decision and provide a remedy.

Likewise, if a school does not provide a parent with an opportunity to examine her child's educational records as required by the IDEA, the parent might miss an opportunity to identify inaccuracies or discrepancies in the record, which could result in the deprivation of educational benefits or impede the right to a free appropriate public education for the child. 20 U.S.C. § 1415(b)(1). For example, assume a child's records erroneously showed that the child has an intellectual disability and the school was educating the child in an inappropriately restrictive classroom specifically designed for children with intellectual disabilities in which the child was being deprived of educational benefit. If the parent of that child is denied an opportunity to examine the child's records and identify and correct the mistake, the denial of the parent's right to examine the records — a procedural violation — can be linked to an impediment of the child's right to a free appropriate public education and a deprivation of educational benefit. Consequently, a hearing officer could link the procedural violation with a denial of the child's right to a free appropriate public education and issue remedies to redress this denial.

Attorneys can similarly try to connect the failure to provide a parent with prior written notice of the school's initiation of a change or refusal to initiate a change related to the child's special education with one or more of the statutory exceptions. 20 U.S.C. § 1415(b)(3). For example, without being provided notice in advance of a proposed change in her child's speech/language services, a parent will not be able to participate in the decision-making related to that service. Without prior written notice, the change may happen without her even knowing. Even if she is provided with some notice, if that notice does not include the basis for and reasons behind a school district's decision not to provide a particular special education service and the other options that the school district considered, as required by the IDEA, she can argue that her participation in the decision-making process was significantly impeded without this critical information. 20 U.S.C. § 1415(c)(1). If the hearing officer agrees that the failure to provide a legally compliant prior written notice significantly impeded her participation in the decision-making process, he can find that this procedural violation amounts to a denial of a free appropriate public education and order an appropriate remedy.

Despite limitations on a hearing officer's ability to determine that procedural violations rose to the level of a denial of a free appropriate public education, hearing officers may nevertheless order an LEA to comply with procedural requirements in the future, as discussed further below. 20 U.S.C. § 1415(f)(3)(E)(iii).

Consider the following hypothetical:

Bobby

Bobby has an IEP based on his special education disability classifications of speech/language impairment and traumatic brain injury. Without the consent or knowledge of Bobby's mother, the school conducted an updated speech/language evaluation of Bobby. His mother was not provided with a copy of the evaluation report. Bobby's IEP team convened an IEP meeting without informing Bobby's mother, reviewed the evaluation, and determined that Bobby no longer qualifies as having a speech/language impairment. The team also decided that Bobby's hours of specialized instruction should be reduced from ten hours per week to five hours per week. The school did not provide Bobby's mother with any advance notice of the meeting or any prior written notice of its decision to change Bobby's disability classification or reduce his hours of specialized instruction. Instead, after the IEP team had convened and after the changes to Bobby's schedule had already been implemented, the school staff sent her a copy of the new IEP, reflecting Bobby's sole disability category of traumatic brain injury, and only five hours of specialized instruction.

During Bobby's due process hearing, Bobby's mother alleged violations of her right to consent to evaluations, participate in legally compliant IEP meetings, and receive prior written notice of changes the school district makes in her child's education. In response, the attorney for the school district argues that the hearing officer cannot find a violation of FAPE in this instance and is therefore powerless to issue any remedy for Bobby because the only violations alleged by Bobby's mother are procedural. What arguments should Bobby's mother's attorney make in response?

2.   Statute of Limitations

The scope of the hearing officer's determination and any remedy issued are also limited by a two year statute of limitations, in that a complaint can only set forth an alleged violation that occurred no more than two years before the parent or public agency knew or should have known about the alleged violation that forms the basis of the complaint, unless a state provides for a different time limitation. 20 U.S.C. § 1415(b)(6)(B), (f)(3)(C). However, this rule is not absolute, and the IDEA provides for exceptions to the statute of limitations if a parent was prevented from requesting a hearing due to specific misrepresentations by the LEA that it had resolved the problem forming the basis of the complaint or due to the LEA's withholding of information from the parent that was required by § 1415 of the IDEA to be provided to the parent. 20 U.S.C. § 1415(f)(3)(D). Attorneys can try to argue common law exceptions to the statute of limitations, such as the continuing violation doctrine and the doctrine of equitable tolling, but should research whether such doctrines apply to IDEA claims in the jurisdiction at issue, given the split among courts on this issue. *Compare, e.g., Bell v. Board of Educ. of the Albuquerque Pub. Schs.*, 2008 U.S. Dist. LEXIS 69087, at *39-48, *50-53 (D.N.M. Mar. 26, 2008); *Vandenberg v. Appleton Area Sch. Dist.*, 252 F. Supp. 2d 786, 789-93 (E.D. Wis. 2003), *with Hammond v. District of Columbia*, 2001 U.S. Dist. LEXIS 25846, at *15, *19 n.8 (D.D.C. Mar. 1, 2001); *Weyrick v. New Albany-Floyd County Consol. Sch. Corp.*, 2004 U.S. Dist. LEXIS 26435, at *41-44 (S.D. Ind. Dec. 23, 2004).

3.   Lack of Parental Consent to Initial Provision of Services

A hearing officer is also limited in that he or she may not override a lack of parental consent to the initial provision of special education and related services to a child. The IDEA specifically prohibits LEAs from pursuing due process hearing procedures to challenge a parent's refusal to provide consent to the agency to allow the LEA to provide a child with special education services for the first time. 20 U.S.C. § 1414(a)(1)(D)(ii)(II).

B.   Case Law Discussing the Broad Remedial Authority of Hearing Officers

Neither the IDEA nor the implementing regulations explicitly discuss the full range of remedies a hearing officer can award or the full scope of the hearing officer's remedial authority. Courts, in contrast, are explicitly empowered by the IDEA to grant such relief as they determine appropriate. 20 U.S.C. § 1415(i)(2)(C)(iii). Despite the IDEA's silence regarding the remedial power of a hearing officer, courts have reasoned that a hearing officer also has broad authority, coextensive with that of a court's, to award remedial relief that is necessary to address IDEA violations, especially given that the impartial due process hearing is the cornerstone of the safeguards that the IDEA creates for parents. *B.B. v. Perry Township Sch. Corp.*, 2008 U.S. Dist. LEXIS 53246, at 32 (S.D. Ind. July 11, 2008). Indeed, "it is logical to infer that a hearing officer should have the same equitable discretion as the district court." *Ivan P. v. Westport Bd. of Educ.*, 865 F. Supp. 74, 80 (D. Conn. 1994). Various courts have concluded that hearing officers should be able to order all necessary and appropriate remedies. *See, e.g., S-1 by and Through P-1 v. Spangler*, 650 F. Supp. 1427, 1432 (M.D.N.C. 1986), *vacated as moot*, 832 F.2d 294 (4th Cir. 1987); *Cocores v. Portsmouth, N.H. Sch. Dist.*, 779 F. Supp. 203, 205 (D.N.H. 1991) (quoting *Spangler*, 650 F. Supp. at 1431).

C. Broad Remedial Authority of Hearing Officer as Discussed by OSEP

The Department of Education's Office of Special Education Programs (OSEP) also concluded that hearing officers have the same broad authority as courts to award appropriate relief in IDEA cases. *Letter to Kohn*, 17 EHLR 522 (OSEP Feb. 13, 1991). Indeed, OSEP's position is that "although the Part B regulations do not comprehensively list all of the specific remedies available to a hearing officer if he or she finds the child has been denied FAPE, we have stated that an impartial hearing officer has the authority to grant any relief he or she deems necessary, inclusive of compensatory education, to ensure that a child receives the FAPE to which he or she is entitled." *Letter to Riffel*, OSEP List of Correspondence July 1, 2000 through Sept. 30, 2000, Federal Register: March 9, 2001, Volume 66, Number 47, Notices, pages 14291-14293, 14292 (OSEP Aug. 22, 2000), *available at* http://www2.ed.gov/policy/speced/guid/idea/letters/2000-3/riffel82200fapesec.pdf (citing *Letter to Kohn*). The IDEA "intends an impartial hearing officer to exercise his/her authority in a manner which ensures the right to a due process hearing is a meaningful mechanism for resolving disputes." *Letter to Kohn*. The D.C. District Court reasoned in *Harris v. District of Columbia* that it was appropriate to look to the OSEP *Letter to Kohn* to understand a hearing officer's remedial authority because the Supreme Court established in *Honig v. Doe*, 484 U.S. 305 (1988), that a policy letter could be given great deference in construing an ambiguous statute, and the phrase "appropriate relief" in the IDEA creates just such an ambiguity. *Harris v. District of Columbia*, 1992 U.S. Dist. LEXIS 11831, at *13 (D.D.C. Aug. 17, 1992).

In light of these rules and decisions, consider the following hypothetical:

Jane

Jane has struggled in school since first grade, but received no special education services from the school district. At her mother's request, she was finally evaluated by the school district at age eleven as a sixth grade student. The evaluating psychologist determined that Jane has a significant learning disability, affecting both her reading and writing. Jane is reading and writing at a third grade level. As Jane's mother's attorney, you file a due process complaint and request that the hearing officer order that Jane be placed by the school district in a full-time special education private school focused on serving children with learning disabilities and that Jane receive after-school tutoring as compensatory education services. You have documentary and testimonial evidence to support that the school placement is necessary for Jane to make educational progress and that the compensatory education will help her make up for the time she lost when she was receiving no special education services whatsoever. The hearing officer responds that he does not have the authority to prospectively order a school placement or to order that Jane be provided with compensatory education services.

What arguments would you make to the hearing officer that he has the authority to order the requested remedies?

II. REMEDIES IN CIVIL ACTIONS

States can choose a one-tiered system with an impartial due process hearing mechanism or a two-tiered system, which includes both an impartial due process hearing at the local educational agency level and an additional administrative officer review by the state educational agency. 20 U.S.C. § 1415(g); 34 C.F.R. § 300.514. If a party is aggrieved by the finding of a due process hearing officer or state administrative review officer, the party may bring a civil action in federal court, but the administrative options in that jurisdiction — whether a due process hearing or due process hearing followed by a state administrative review process — must be exhausted first. 20 U.S.C. § 1415(l); 34 C.F.R. § 300.516(e). When the administrative remedies are exhausted, the aggrieved party can appeal through the filing of a civil action within ninety days of the date of the hearing officer's decision, or such time as the state allows if the state provides for an explicit time limitation. The action can be filed in any state court of competent jurisdiction or a federal court, without regard to the amount in controversy, within ninety days of the decision of the hearing officer, unless the state has a different time limitation. 20 U.S.C. § 1415(i)(2).

However, parents may bypass the administrative process in IDEA cases and file a civil action directly in a state court of competent jurisdiction or a federal court where exhaustion would be futile or inadequate. *Honig v. Doe*, 484 U.S. 305, 326-27 (1988) (partially superseded by statute at 20 U.S.C. § 1415(k)(1)(G); *see also Massey v. District of Columbia*, 400 F. Supp. 2d 66, 69-70 (D.D.C. 2005)). In some circumstances, the rationale of the exhaustion requirement — to prevent "premature interruption of the administrative process" — is not served by the requirement of exhaustion. *Massey*, 400 F. Supp. 2d at 71, *quoting Randolph-Sheppard Vendors of Am. v. Weinberger*, 795 F.2d 90, 104 (D.C. Cir. 1986).

If a parent obtains a favorable hearing officer decision in the final administrative remedy stage, but the orders are not implemented, a parent's recourse to enforce those orders may depend on the case law in that jurisdiction. Some courts have found that the parent may bring a civil action in federal court where a final hearing officer decision has not been implemented by the education agency. *See, e.g., Porter v. Board of Trs. of Manhattan Beach Unified Sch. Dist.*, 307 F.3d 1064, 1069 (9th Cir. 2002); *Robinson v. Pinderhughes*, 810 F.2d 1270, 1274 (4th Cir. 1987); *Jeremy H. v. Mount Lebanon Sch. Dist.*, 95 F.3d 272, 279 n.13 (3d Cir. 1996). A parent could also argue that he or she is in fact a "party aggrieved" even by a favorable hearing officer decision, and therefore entitled to bring a civil action, arguing, for example, that the decision did not include enforcement mechanisms. *See, e.g., James S. v. School Dist.*, 559 F. Supp. 2d 600, 615 (E.D. Pa. 2008) (leaving open the possibility that a party could seek judicial enforcement of a favorable due process hearing order as a "party aggrieved").

In some courts, actions pursuant to 42 U.S.C. § 1983 (§ 1983), a statute that allows for enforcement suits in conjunction with the Constitution and other laws, may provide an opportunity for judicial review where a hearing officer decision has not been implemented, but in other courts, civil actions under § 1983 are specifically foreclosed in this situation. *See A.W. v. Jersey City Pub. Sch.*, 486 F.3d 791 (3d Cir. 2007) (holding that § 1983 actions are not available for IDEA violations, and discussing the views of various courts as to the availability of § 1983 claims in IDEA cases); *Chavez v. Board of Educ.*, 614 F. Supp. 2d 1184, 1213 (D.N.M. 2008) (not foreclosing the possibility of such an enforcement action under 42 U.S.C. § 1983). For a more comprehensive discussion of § 1983 remedies in special education cases, see the discussion of the availability of monetary damages in IDEA cases below.

A parent could also try to bring a separate due process complaint alleging the implementation failure. *See, e.g., Chavez.*, 614 F. Supp. 2d at 1213. Sometimes, where there is a question of whether the orders in a hearing officer decision will actually be implemented by the LEA, a hearing officer can maintain jurisdiction over a case by issuing an interim order, rather than a final order, and then later issue a final order when he or she is assured of implementation.

When a civil action is filed under the IDEA, the court must receive the records of the administrative proceedings, hear additional evidence at the request of a party, base its decision on the preponderance of the evidence, and grant such relief as the court determines is appropriate. 20 U.S.C. § 1415(i)(2)(C). The IDEA does not, by its plain language, require that a court defer to the decision of the impartial hearing officer at the due process hearing or the state review officer. However, in *Board of Educ. v. Rowley*, the Supreme Court underscored that the requirement that courts receive the administrative record implies that "due weight" should be given to those proceedings. *Board of Educ. v. Rowley*, 458 U.S. 176, 206 (1982).

Courts have defined this standard differently. The United States Court of Appeals for the Third Circuit, for example, refers to this standard as "modified *de novo*," explaining that reviewing courts are "required to defer to the . . . [hearing officer's] factual findings unless . . . [they] can point to contrary nontestimonial extrinsic evidence on the record" or "unless the record read in its entirety would compel a contrary conclusion." *Bucks Cnty. Dep't of Mental Health/Mental Retardation v. Commonwealth of Pa., Dep't. of Pub. Welfare*, 379 F.3d 61, 65 (3d Cir. 2004) (quoting *Carlisle Area Sch. Dist. v. Scott P.*, 62 F.3d 520, 529 (3d Cir. 1995)). The Eighth Circuit described its standard of review in IDEA cases differently, noting that less deference is required to state administrative hearings than is required "under the substantial evidence test commonly applied in federal administrative law cases, but consideration should be given to the fact that the state hearing panel has had the opportunity to observe the demeanor of the witnesses." *Fort Zumwalt Sch. Dist. v. Clynes*, 119 F.3d 607, 610 (8th Cir. 1997) (quoting *Independent Sch. Dist. No. 283 v. S.D.*, 88 F.3d 556, 561 (8th Cir. 1996)). Courts should not "substitute their own notions of sound educational policy for those of the school authorities which they review." *Id.* (quoting *Rowley*, 458 U.S. at 206).

The D.C. Circuit, in contrast, has held that reviews of determinations by administrative hearing officers in IDEA cases is more rigorous than in "typical agency cases," as the "IDEA plainly suggest[s] less deference than is conventional in administrative proceedings." *See, e.g., Reid v. District of Columbia*, 401 F.3d 516, 521 (D.C. Cir. 2005). Accordingly, a hearing officer decision "without reasoned and specific findings deserves little deference." *Id.*

When the state has two administrative review tiers, some courts have deferred to the final reviewing tiers, while others have deferred to the initial due process hearing determination in the first tier. *Compare Heather S. v. Wisconsin*, 125 F.3d 1045, 1053 (7th Cir. 1997), *with Clynes*, 119 F.3d at 610 (giving the court the opportunity to defer to an initial hearing panel's findings "based on observation of the witnesses and reject the reviewing officer's analysis if it does not appear to give sufficient weight to the views of the professional educators").

Despite the deference accorded to the decisions reached at the state administrative hearing level, a court enjoys "broad discretion" in fashioning appropriate relief under the IDEA. *Florence Cnty. Sch. Dist. Four v. Carter*, 510 U.S. 7, 16 (1993). In looking at the requirement that the court grant "appropriate" relief, the Supreme Court explained in *School Comm. of Burlington v. Department of Educ.* that "the only possible interpretation is that the relief is to be 'appropriate' in light of the purpose of the Act." 471 U.S. 359, 369 (1985). Equitable considerations should be taken into account, in light of the purpose of the Act. *Id.* at 374. A court is not limited to the remedies considered by the hearing officer; instead, a district court can fashion appropriate relief, regardless of the options considered by the administrative hearing officer. *See, e.g., Draper v. Atlanta Indep. Sch. Syst.*, 518 F.3d 1275 (11th Cir. 2008). This chapter will detail the varied forms of relief that have been approved by courts in IDEA cases.

An attorney litigating an IDEA case in federal court should take note that the IDEA specifically abrogates state sovereign immunity, providing that a state is not immune under the Eleventh Amendment to suit in federal court for a violation of the IDEA, and remedies at both law and in equity are available to the same extent as those available for a violation against any other public entity. 20 U.S.C. § 1403; *see Pace v. Bogalusa City Sch. Bd.*, 403 F.3d 272, 280 (5th Cir. 2005) (discussing this provision of the IDEA and the conditioning of a state's receipt of federal funds under the Act on consent to suit).

III.   STATE COMPLAINTS

Pursuant to its authority to create rules and regulations to govern the programs it administers, the Department of Education requires that state education agencies have a state complaint procedure, sometimes known as a complaint resolution procedure, in order to receive federal funds under the IDEA. 20 U.S.C. § 1221e-3; 34 C.F.R. § 300.151. A complaint must include a statement of the violations by the public agency, the related facts, and a signature and contact information for the complainant. 34 C.F.R. § 300.153(b)(1)-(3). If the complaint relates to a specific child, more detail is required, such as a description of the nature of the problem, and a proposed solution to the extent available to the party at the time the complaint is filed. 34 C.F.R. § 300.153(b)(4). The violation alleged must have occurred within one year prior to the filing of the complaint, making the statute of limitations for state complaints shorter than the two year statute of limitations for due process complaints. *Compare* 34 C.F.R. § 300.153(c) *with* 20 U.S.C. § 1415(f)(3)(C). While the IDEA includes exceptions to the statute of limitations for due process hearings, no such exceptions are explicitly provided for in the state complaint procedures. 20 U.S.C. § 1415(f)(3)(D).

Within sixty days of the filing of a complaint, the SEA must carry out an independent, on-site investigation if it determines such an investigation is necessary, give the complainant the opportunity to submit additional information verbally or in writing, and provide the public agency an opportunity to respond to the complaint, including an opportunity to resolve the complaint through a proposal or through mediation. 34 C.F.R. § 300.152(a). The sixty day deadline can be extended under certain circumstances, such as an agreement between the parties to extend the time in order to mediate. 34 C.F.R. § 300.152(b)(1). The SEA must also review all relevant information and make an independent determination as to whether the IDEA or the applicable regulations were violated and issue a written decision with findings of fact, conclusions, and reasoning in support of the decision. 34 C.F.R. § 300.152(b). In resolving a complaint, if the SEA determines that there has been a failure to provide appropriate services, the SEA should order corrective action where appropriate to address the needs of the child, such as compensatory services and monetary reimbursement, and should take steps to ensure the appropriate provision of services for all children with disabilities. 34 C.F.R. § 300.151(b). Implementation of the final decision can include technical assistance activities, negotiations, and corrective actions to achieve compliance. 34 C.F.R. § 300.152(b)(2). If issues raised in a state complaint were also included in a due process complaint, the SEA must set aside that part of the state complaint until the conclusion of the due process hearing. 34 C.F.R.

§ 300.152(c)(1). Any issue in a state complaint that is not included in a due process complaint must be resolved under the state complaint timeline. *Id.* If an issue is raised in a state complaint that was already resolved in a due process hearing determination, the hearing officer's determination is binding. 34 C.F.R. § 300.152(c)(2). However, an SEA should resolve a complaint alleging an educational agency's failure to implement a due process hearing decision. 34 C.F.R. § 300.152(c)(3).

Unlike due process hearing procedures, courts have generally found that state complaint procedures are elective and need not be exhausted prior to judicial review. *See, e.g., Porter v. Board of Trs. of Manhattan Beach Unified Sch. Dist.*, 307 F.3d 1064, 1071 (9th Cir. 2002). Similarly, the use of state complaint procedures does not satisfy the exhaustion requirement under the IDEA, which applies specifically to due process hearings, as well as state administrative reviews of due process hearing decisions in states that have two administrative tiers. *Weber v. Cranston Sch. Comm.*, 212 F.3d 41, 53 (1st Cir. 2000); *but see Christopher S. v. Stanislaus Cnty. Office of Educ.*, 384 F.3d 1205, 1219-1220 (9th Cir. 2004) (noting that state complaint was sufficient and due process procedure was not required, prior to judicial review, where exhaustion of due process remedies would not further the purposes of the exhaustion requirement in the IDEA). There remains some controversy as to whether final state complaint decisions are reviewable in court. *Compare Christopher S.*, 384 F.3d 1205 (finding that state complaint decisions are subject to judicial review), *with Virginia Office of Prot. and Advocacy v. Virginia Dep't of Educ.*, 262 F. Supp. 2d 648 (E.D. Va. 2003) (concluding that there is no private right of action for review of state complaint decisions).

IV.   ELIGIBILITY AND DISABILITY CLASSIFICATION

Due process complaints can be brought on any matter relating to the identification of a child as a special education student. 20 U.S.C. § 1415(b)(6); 34 C.F.R. § 300.507(a)(1). Consequently, a hearing officer can issue declaratory relief in the form of an order that a student is covered under one or more of the eligibility classifications of the IDEA. Federal courts have also provided orders of eligibility for special education as part of their remedial authority. *See, e.g., Muller v. Comm. on Special Educ.*, 145 F.3d 95, 103-104 (2d Cir. 1998); *Yankton Sch. Dist. v. Schramm*, 93 F.3d 1369 (8th Cir. 1996). Courts have varying views on eligibility requirements, and some courts have read these requirements more narrowly than others. *See* Mark Weber, *The IDEA Eligibility Mess*, 57 Buffalo L. Rev. 83 (2009) (discussing sources of confusion in IDEA eligibility and calling for renewed attention by courts and educational policy makers to the actual terms of the statute and its underlying purposes). For a detailed discussion of eligibility requirements under the IDEA, see Chapter Four.

V.   INDEPENDENT EVALUATIONS

A due process hearing complaint can also be brought on any issue related to the evaluation of a child for special education purposes. 20 U.S.C. § 1415(b)(6); 34 C.F.R. § 300.507(a)(1). Where a child requires an evaluation for special education and one has not been provided, a hearing officer or court can order that the school district conduct an evaluation or fund an independent evaluation, especially given the affirmative Child Find responsibility that Congress has placed on school districts. 20 U.S.C. § 1412(a)(3); 34 C.F.R. § 300.502(d). When an education agency has already conducted an evaluation with which the parent disagrees, hearing officers can resolve a conflict between the parent and the agency about the need for an independent evaluation. When a parent requests funding for an independent evaluation based on a disagreement with the education agency's evaluation, the agency can file for a due process hearing in response to challenge the parent's disagreement and show that its evaluation was appropriate and that funding for an independent evaluation is unwarranted. If the hearing officer finds that the agency's evaluation is in fact appropriate, he or she can issue a declaratory order to that effect, thereby denying the parent public funding for an independent evaluation. 34 C.F.R. § 300.502(b). A hearing officer or court can also determine whether an evaluation meets the requirements of the IDEA, regardless of whether the evaluation was conducted by the school district or an independent evaluator. 20 U.S.C. § 1414(b)-(c); 34 C.F.R. § 300.502(e). Additionally, a hearing officer has the power to order independent educational evaluations at public expense as part of a due process hearing. 34 C.F.R. § 300.502(d).

Where parents fund their own evaluations, they may be able to get reimbursement if they can show that they disagreed with the school district's evaluation and that it was inappropriate. *Holmes v. Millcreek Twp. Sch. Dist.*, 205 F.3d 583, 590-91 (3d Cir. 2000). While parents should not, of course, expressly *agree* with an agency evaluation if they want reimbursement for an independent evaluation, some courts have held that express disagreement with a school district's evaluation is not required at any point in order for a parent to seek reimbursement for an independent evaluation. Other courts have found that parents need not notify the school district of their disagreement with its evaluation *prior* to initiating the independent evaluation. *See e.g., Lauren W. v. DeFlaminis*, 480 F.3d 259, 274-75 (3d Cir. 2007); *Hudson v. Wilson*, 828 F.2d 1059, 1065 (4th Cir. 1987).

The IDEA additionally vests hearing officers with the authority to override lack of parental consent for evaluations of a child, except where prohibited by state law. 20 U.S.C. § 1414(a)(1)(D)(ii)(I).

VI.   CHANGES TO AN IEP AND IMPLEMENTATION OF AN IEP

A parent can also request that a hearing officer or court order changes to an IEP. For example, if a child requires a related service that is not being provided by the school district, the hearing officer or court can order that the service be provided as part of the child's IEP. *See, e.g., Cedar Rapids Cmty. Sch. Dist. v. Garret F.*, 526 U.S. 66 (1999). In addition to an order for the provision of a specific related service, remedies could also include other changes to an IEP such as changes in the number of hours of specialized instruction or of a particular related service or an order that an appropriate IEP actually be implemented where the school district has failed to carry out the services and/or accommodations in the IEP.

VII.   COMPLIANCE WITH PROCEDURAL REQUIREMENTS

Notwithstanding that procedural violations need to meet the statutorily required standard in order to rise to the level of a denial of FAPE, a hearing officer can order that a school district comply with the procedural requirements of the IDEA. 20 U.S.C. § 1415(g)(3)(E)(ii)-(iii). For example, a hearing officer can order that the school district provide the parent with an opportunity to examine her child's educational records or that the school provide the parent with a prior written notice of its decision to initiate or refuse to initiate a change with respect to the child's IEP, with all of the information required by the statute included therein. 20 U.S.C. §§ 1415(b)(1), (b)(3), (c)(1).

VIII. SCHOOL PLACEMENT

A student can be placed in an appropriate special education school through his or her IEP based on a decision by the IEP team, or through prior written notice issued by the school district notifying the parent of the placement. When there is no appropriate public school available for the child, the least restrictive environment may be a private school funded at public expense. Generally, special education students can be placed at private schools at public expense when "such children are placed in, or referred to, such schools or facilities by the State or appropriate local education agency as a means of carrying out the requirements of [the IDEA]." 20 U.S.C. § 1412(a)(10)(B). A parent has two options if she disagrees with the placement proposed by the other members of the IEP team or by the school district and cannot negotiate an acceptable agreement. The parent can file a complaint seeking a due process hearing officer's order to prospectively place the child in an appropriate placement, whether that placement is a different public school or a private school. Or, if the parent seeks a private placement and can afford to pay for the placement up front, the parent can personally fund the child in a private school and seek reimbursement later. 20 U.S.C. § 1412(a)(1)(C)(ii). Public funding for a special education student to attend private schools at public expense is also available when the local education agency failed to make a "free appropriate public education available to the child." 20 U.S.C. § 1412(a)(10)(B)-(C).

A.   Inappropriateness of the Current Placement

A parent contesting the appropriateness of the school district's proposed school, and requesting a prospective order for a new placement or reimbursement for tuition at a private school placement must specifically allege that the school district's placement is inappropriate and provide specific evidence to support that contention. *See Hessler v. State Bd. of Educ. of Md.*, 700 F.2d 134 (4th Cir. 1983). Education agencies are required to make available a continuum of alternative placements to meet the individualized needs of a child, including instruction in regular classes, special classes, special schools, home instruction, and instruction in hospitals and institutions. 34 C.F.R. § 300.115; *see, e.g., Straube v. Florida Union Free Sch. Dist.*, 801 F. Supp. 1164, 1173 (S.D.N.Y. 1992). A failure to provide a continuum of alternative placements can serve as a basis for a claim for relief, and potentially allow a parent to secure prospective placement at a private (or "nonpublic") school as a remedy. However, the parent must be able to demonstrate that the student would not benefit educationally at the school district's proposed placement in order to secure a nonpublic placement instead. *See, e.g., Knight v. District of Columbia*, 877 F.2d 1025 (D.C. Cir. 1989) (noting that there was simply no evidence to support the proposition that the student would be unable to obtain educational benefits in the school district's proposed placement). Consider the following hypothetical:

Jamie

A psychologist evaluates Jamie, a fifteen year old student, and determines that he has a severe reading disorder and that he requires a full-time special education school specializing in addressing learning disabilities. The psychologist specifies in his evaluation that a separate classroom within a regular public school will not suffice for Jamie. An IEP is agreed upon by the team incorporating the psychologist's placement recommendation. The school district does not have such a separate school available within its public school offerings, and instead proposes a separate classroom within a regular public school. The parent objects to the proposed placement and identifies a private school that meets the criteria outlined by the psychologist.

Does the parent have a basis for seeking the private school placement at public expense?

B.   The Supreme Court's Key Reimbursement Cases

In *School Comm. of Burlington v. Department of Educ.*, 471 U.S. 359 (1985), Robert Panico, the father of Michael Panico, a first grader with specific learning disabilities, rejected the town of Burlington's proposed placement at a public school and sought review by a hearing officer with the Massachusetts Department of Education's Bureau of Special Education Appeals. While he awaited the review, Mr. Panico enrolled Michael in a private special education school at his own expense. The hearing officer ordered that the town pay for Michael's tuition and reimburse Mr. Panico for the tuition expenses that he had already put forth. The town refused to reimburse Mr. Panico and sought judicial review. On review, the Supreme Court held that the grant of authority to a reviewing court under the IDEA includes the power to order school authorities to reimburse parents for their expenditures on private special education schools if the court ultimately determines that such placement, rather than the placement in the proposed IEP, is appropriate. *Id.* at 370. The opinion was unanimous and delivered by Chief Justice Rehnquist, evidencing that even a court viewed by some as conservative on many issues accepted, without great controversy, private school tuition reimbursement as a remedy for special education students.

The Court established a standard for reimbursement for private special education tuition under the IDEA. If a court concludes (1) that the child's IEP is inappropriate and (2) that the private school placement desired by the parent is proper under the IDEA, then a prospective injunction can be ordered directing school officials to develop and implement an IEP placing the child at a private school. *Id.* at 370. A parent who places the child at the private school without public consent in this situation is entitled to retroactive tuition reimbursement. *Id.*

Eight years later, in *Florence Cnty. Sch. Dist. Four v. Carter*, 510 U.S. 7 (1993), the Court examined whether a court may order reimbursement for parents who unilaterally withdraw their child from a public school that provides an inappropriate education and put the child in a private school that does not meet all of the requirements for a FAPE outlined in the IDEA, particularly the requirement that a private school meet the standards of the state education agency. Rejecting the school district's proposed IEP, the parents of Shannon Carter, a student with learning disabilities, placed her in a private special education school at their own expense. The Court concluded that, where tuition reimbursement would be appropriate under the standard outlined in *Burlington*, parents are not barred from reimbursement simply because the private school did not meet the IDEA's definition of a "free appropriate public education." *Id.* at 18. The version of the IDEA being reviewed by the Court stated within 20 U.S.C. § 1401(a) that special education be provided at public expense, under public supervision and direction and that IEPs must be designed by a representative of the LEA and established, revised and reviewed by the agency. The Court reasoned that these requirements "do not make sense in the context of a parental placement" and that to apply these requirements to parental placements would effectively eliminate the right of unilateral withdrawal recognized by *Burlington*. *Id.* at 13. Specifically, it would not make sense to require that the private school be under the supervision and direction of the public school district that generated the very IEP rejected by the parent or to require that the school meet the standards of the state educational agency, "where the school lacks the stamp of approval of the same public school system that failed to meet the child's needs in the first place." *Id.* at 13-14, quoting *Carter v. Florence Cnty. Sch. Dist. Four*, 950 F.2d 156, 164 (4th Cir. 1991). The Court also noted that courts fashioning equitable relief under the IDEA must consider all relevant factors, including the appropriate and reasonable level of reimbursement and that total reimbursement will not be appropriate if the court determines that the cost of the private education was unreasonable. *Carter*, 579 U.S. at 16.

Most recently, in *Forest Grove v. T.A.*, 129 S. Ct. 2484 (2009), the Court grappled with the question of whether the IDEA categorically prohibits reimbursement for private special education costs if a child has not previously received special education services under the authority of a public agency. After struggling in public schools since kindergarten without being found eligible for special education or receiving any special education services, during his junior year of high school, T.A. was finally diagnosed by a private specialist with Attention Deficit Hyperactivity Disorder and a number of disabilities related to learning and memory. Upon the advice of the independent specialist, T.A.'s parents enrolled him in a private special education school. After T.A.'s parents provided the school district with written notice of the private placement and requested an administrative hearing in regards to his eligibility for special education services, the District convened a multi-disciplinary meeting, in which it determined that T.A. was not eligible for special education services and declined to provide T.A. with an IEP. His parents kept him in the private school, and a hearing officer ultimately ordered the school district to reimburse them for tuition costs, given the district's failure to offer T.A. a free appropriate public education and the determination by the hearing officer that the private school was appropriate.

The school district pointed to a provision in the IDEA added as part of the 1997 Amendments to the Act, which provides that a court or hearing officer may require tuition reimbursement where the public agency has not made a free appropriate public education available and the child has previously received special education and related services under the authority of the agency. 20 U.S.C. § 1412(a)(10)(C)(ii). The district argued that because this section only discussed "reimbursement for children who have previously received special education services through the public school, IDEA only authorizes reimbursement in that circumstance." *Forest Grove*, 129 S. Ct. at 2492.

To the contrary, the Court concluded that the 1997 Amendments do not expressly prohibit reimbursement under the circumstances of T.A.'s case. The Court reasoned that the only explicit bar on reimbursement in the statute occurs in situations where the school district made a free appropriate public education available by correctly identifying the child and proposing an adequate IEP. *Id.* at 2493. The Court read the clause in 20 U.S.C § 1412(a)(10)(C)(ii) as "elucidative rather than exhaustive" as a result of the wording that hearing officers "may" order reimbursement in circumstances where a school district had provided a child with some special education services and the parents believe those services to be inadequate. *Id.* Furthermore, the Court concluded that the interpretation of the statute argued by the school district would mean that Congress intended to silently abrogate the decisions in *Burlington* and *Carter*, which authorized reimbursement when a school district fails to provide a free appropriate public education and a child's private school placement is appropriate, without regard to the child's prior receipt of services. *Id.* at 2493-94. The Court underscored that "it would be particularly strange for the Act to provide a remedy, as all agree it does, when a school district offers a child inadequate special-education services but to leave parents without relief in the more egregious situation in which the school district unreasonably denies a child access to such services altogether." *Id.* at 2495. The Court ultimately concluded that the IDEA authorizes reimbursement for the cost of a private special education placement when a school district fails to provide a free appropriate public education and the private placement is appropriate, regardless of whether the child previously received special education services through the public school. *Id.* at 2496.

C.   Codification of Tuition Reimbursement as a Remedy in the IDEA

At the time *Burlington* was decided by the Supreme Court, the IDEA did not specifically reference the possibility of private school tuition reimbursement. Since then, the amendments to the IDEA have codified the opportunity to seek tuition reimbursement as a remedy and placed limitations on this form of relief. 20 U.S.C. § 1412(a)(10)(C).

The IDEA provides for a free appropriate public education, defined by the statute as special education and related services that have been provided at public expense under public supervision, meet the standards of the state educational agency, include an appropriate preschool, elementary school, or secondary school education in the state involved, and are provided in conformity with an IEP that meets the standards in the statute. 20 U.S.C. § 1401(9). This mandate requires school districts to fund a child's education at a private school where the school district cannot or has not offered an appropriate public school placement that can implement an appropriate IEP for the child. While the statute generally requires that special education students be educated in the least restrictive environment with children who are not disabled, this requirement only applies to the maximum extent appropriate and allows for children to be educated in separate special education schools, including private institutions, when the nature or disability of the child is such that education in regular classes with the use of supplementary aids and services cannot be achieved satisfactorily. 20 U.S.C. § 1412(a)(5)(A). If the parents of a child with a disability who previously received special education services under the authority of the public agency enroll the child in a private school without the consent of or referral by the public agency, a court or a hearing officer can require the agency to reimburse the parents for the cost of tuition if the court or hearing officer determine that the agency did not make a free appropriate public education available to the child in a timely manner prior to enrollment. 20 U.S.C. § 1412(a)(10)(C)(ii).

However, the statute does place limitations on the payment for education of children enrolled in private schools without the consent of or referral by the public agency. Generally, local educational agencies are not required to pay for the cost of special education services of a child with a disability at a private school if that agency made a free appropriate public education available to the child and the parents chose instead to place the child in the private school. 20 U.S.C. § 1412(a)(10)(C)(i).

If reimbursement for tuition at a private school is awarded by a court or hearing officer, the cost of reimbursement can be reduced if the parents did not inform the IEP team that they were rejecting the placement proposed by the public education agency at the most recent IEP meeting, including stating their concerns and their intent to enroll their child in a private school at public expense. 20 U.S.C. § 1412(a)(10)(C)(iii)(I)(aa). Reimbursement can also be reduced if the parents did not give the public educational agency notice that they were removing the child from the public school ten business days prior to the removal. 20 U.S.C. § 1412(a)(10)(C)(iii)(I)(bb). Additionally, the amount of reimbursement can also be reduced if, prior to the parents' removal of the child, the public agency informed the parents through the notice requirements in section 20 U.S.C. § 1415(b)(3) of its intent to evaluate the child, including a statement of the purpose of the evaluation that was appropriate and reasonable, but the parent did not make the child available for such evaluation. 20 U.S.C. § 1412(a)(10)(C)(iii)(II). Alternatively, the cost of reimbursement can be reduced upon a judicial finding of unreasonableness with respect to actions taken by parents. 20 U.S.C. § 1412(a)(10)(C)(iii)(III).

Despite the requirement that parents provide notice to the educational agency of their intent to remove their child and place him or her in a private special education school, the cost of reimbursement should not be reduced if the school prevented the parent from providing the required notice, the parents had not been informed of this notice requirement pursuant to the statute's requirement that parents be provided with information about their procedural rights, or compliance with the notice requirement would likely result in physical harm to the child. 20 U.S.C. § 1412(a)(10)(C)(iv)(I). Nor should the amount of reimbursement be reduced or denied for failure of the parent to provide the required notice if, in the discretion of a court or a hearing officer, the parent is illiterate or cannot write in English or compliance with the notice requirement would likely result in emotional harm to the child. 20 U.S.C. § 1412(a)(10)(C)(iv)(II).

Once a child is placed in a private special education placement at public expense, the state educational agency is responsible for ensuring that the educational program is under the general supervision of individuals in the state who are responsible for educational programs for children with disabilities. The state educational agency is also responsible for ensuring that the educational program meets the agency's educational standards, although other agencies may be responsible for providing or paying for the costs of the child's education. 20 U.S.C. § 1412(a)(11)(A). At the private school, the child must also be provided with special education and related services in accordance with his or her IEP, and the state educational agency has the responsibility of ensuring that such schools meet standards that apply to state and local educational agencies and that a child so served has all of the rights that he or she would have if served by those agencies directly. 20 U.S.C. § 1412(a)(10)(C).

D. The Right to "Stay Put"

During the pendency of any due process proceedings, the student remains in his or her then-current educational placement, unless the state or local educational agency and the parents agree otherwise. 20 U.S.C. § 1415(j). This provision is often referred to as the "stay put" or "pendent placement" provision. In *Honig v. Doe*, 484 U.S. 305 (1988), the Supreme Court explained that the purpose of the stay put provision is to prohibit "state or local school authorities from unilaterally excluding disabled children from the classroom . . . during the pendency of review proceedings." The Court emphasized that Congress intended special education law to address the problem of arbitrary exclusion from school. Additionally, the Supreme Court noted in *Burlington* that at least one purpose of the stay put provision was "to prevent school officials from removing a child from the regular public school classroom over the parents' objection pending completion of the review proceedings." *Burlington*, 471 U.S. at 373. Some courts have further provided that a parent can invoke the stay put provision anytime that the school system proposes "a fundamental change in, or elimination of, a basic element of the [then-current education placement]." *See, e.g., Laster v. District of Columbia*, 394 F. Supp. 2d 60, 64 (D.D.C. 2005); *Lunceford v. District of Columbia Bd. of Educ.*, 745 F.2d 1577, 1582 (D.C. Cir. 1984).

The IDEA does not define the term "then-current educational placement," but the meaning "falls somewhere between the physical school attended by a child and the abstract goals of a child's IEP." *Board of Educ. of Cmty. High Sch. Dist. No. 218 v. Illinois State Bd. of Educ.*, 103 F.3d 545, 548 (7th Cir. 1996). If a child's then-current educational placement is not available, the school system must provide the student with placement in a similar program during the pendency of administrative and judicial proceedings. *See, e.g., Knight v. District of Columbia*, 877 F.2d 1025, 1029 (D.C. Cir. 1989); *McKenzie v. Smith*, 771 F.2d 1527, 1533 (D.C. Cir. 1985); *Block v. District of Columbia*, 748 F. Supp. 891, 898 n.9 (D.D.C. 1990).

However, if a due process hearing results from a parent's disagreement with a school district's change in placement based on disciplinary reasons or from a local educational agency's belief that maintaining the current school placement is substantially likely to result in injury to the child or others, the stay put provision does not apply pending the resolution of the litigation. Instead, the child remains in the interim alternative educational setting in which he or she has been placed as a result of the disciplinary measures pending the decision of the hearing officer or until the expiration of the disciplinary period instituted after a child's behavior has been found not to be a manifestation of his or her disability, pursuant to 20 U.S.C. § 1415(k)(1)(C), whichever comes first. 20 U.S.C. §§ 1415(j), (k)(4)(A); 34 C.F.R. § 300.518(a). Nonetheless, the parent and the state or local educational agency may agree otherwise. 20 U.S.C. § 1415(k)(4)(A). A child can be removed regardless of the stay put provision to an interim alternative educational setting for up to forty-five school days without regard to whether the behavior is determined to be a manifestation of the child's disability if the child carried or possessed a weapon; knowingly possessed, used or sold a controlled substance; or has inflicted serious bodily injury upon another person at school. 20 U.S.C. § 1415(k)(1)(G); 34 C.F.R. § 300.530(g).

Apart from school discipline, there are special provisions for defining the then-current education placement if the stay put issue arises when a child is applying for initial admission to a public school. In that situation, with the consent of the parents, the child is placed in the public school program until the proceedings have been completed. 20 U.S.C. § 1415(j); 34 C.F.R. § 300.518(b).

Sometimes, there is a dispute as to whether a particular placement is in fact the then-current educational placement. Usually, for purposes of the stay put provision, the dispositive factor in deciding a child's then-current educational placement is the IEP. *See, e.g., Drinker v. Colonial Sch. Dist.*, 78 F.3d 859, 867 (3d Cir. 1996); *Board of Educ. of Montgomery Cnty. v. Brett Y.*, 959 F. Supp. 705, 709 (D. Md. 1997). If a placement is ordered by a hearing officer determination, that placement becomes the current educational placement for these purposes because an administrative decision in favor of the parents' position in a due process hearing constitutes an "agreement" between the state and the parents to change the current educational placement. 34 C.F.R. § 300.518(d). Specifically, where a hearing officer or a state reviewing official agree with the parent that a change in placement is appropriate, that placement is treated as an agreement between the state and parent, and therefore becomes the current placement pursuant to the provision allowing for the educational agency and the parent to agree on an alternate placement. *Id.*

Therefore, if a parent seeks a prospective order for a private placement or tuition reimbursement for a unilateral placement at the administrative due process hearing level and the hearing officer agrees with the parent and grants the requested relief, the private placement becomes the then-current placement if the dispute and litigation continue. Because the stay put provision can mean that a child remains in an inappropriate school placement for a lengthy period of time, parents who can afford to do so often remove their children from their current placements and enroll them in private schools and then seek reimbursement. *See* Russo & Osborne, Essential Concepts and School-Based Cases in Special Education Law 233 (Corwin Press 2008).

Alexis

Alexis, a special education student with learning disabilities and an emotional disturbance, was not receiving appropriate instruction for her learning disabilities or the counseling services required by her IEP at her public school, King Elementary School. Her mother, Ms. Sanchez, sought placement for her at the Roberts Private Day School, a private special education school that specializes in serving children with both learning disabilities and an emotional disturbance. When the hearing date arrived, Alexis had already completed the school year at King Elementary School and had failed all of her classes. At a due process hearing, the hearing officer agreed that King Elementary School was inappropriate, and ordered that Alexis be placed at the Roberts Private Day School immediately. At this point, it was the beginning of the summer, and Alexis began attending the Roberts Private Day School for Extended School Year (ESY), which lasted for several months during the summer. She began to make progress immediately at the Roberts Private Day School. As the summer came to a close, the school district sent Alexis' mother a notice informing her that Alexis was being placed back at King Elementary School. Ms. Sanchez filed for a due process hearing to dispute the school district's decision and invoked Alexis' right to "stay put" at Roberts Private Day School as the new school year was beginning, pending the outcome of the litigation. The school district argued that Alexis should attend King Elementary School until the litigation concludes pursuant to the stay put provision.

What are the school district's arguments in favor of King Elementary School serving this role? What arguments should Ms. Sanchez make in favor of Roberts Private Day School serving as her then-current educational placement? Which is the appropriate placement for Alexis pursuant to the stay put provision and why?

E.   Prospective Placement Order as a Remedy

Most case law discusses the school system's obligation to reimburse parents who have paid for private school placements and are seeking reimbursement. However, the Supreme Court confirmed that "it seems clear beyond cavil that 'appropriate' relief would include a prospective injunction directing the school officials to develop and implement at public expense an IEP placing the child in a private school." *Burlington*, 471 U.S. at 370. *See also Draper*, 518 F.3d 1275. Many parents will not have the financial capacity to pay up front for private school tuition and seek reimbursement. Consequently, an attorney can seek as a remedy an order from a hearing officer or judge prospectively requiring a school system to place a child in an appropriate private school if the school district has failed to provide the child with an appropriate IEP and school placement. If the parents ultimately prevail in demonstrating that the school district's placement is inappropriate, the hearing officer or court can order a new placement and compensatory education to make up for the time the student spent in the inappropriate placement.

F. Factors to Consider in Identifying an Appropriate Placement

Once an attorney identifies a current placement as inappropriate, the attorney can assist the parent in identifying an appropriate school placement to pursue for the child, regardless of whether the parent can pay prospectively for a private placement or whether the parent will be seeking an administrative or judicial order prospectively requiring the school district to place and fund the child at an appropriate placement. If the desired placement is a private placement, the private school will need to meet the *Burlington* standard of being an appropriate school for the student under the equitable standards identified by the Supreme Court. *Burlington*, 471 U.S. at 369-370. Specific to placement decisions, "courts have identified a set of considerations 'relevant' to determining whether a particular placement is appropriate for a particular student, including the nature and severity of the student's disability, the student's specialized educational needs, the link between those needs and the services offered by the private school, the placement's cost, and the extent to which the placement represents the least restrictive educational environment." *Branham v. District of Columbia*, 427 F.3d 7, 12 (D.C. Cir. 2005).

Despite the IDEA's least restrictive environment mandate, parents seeking reimbursement for tuition at a private placement or prospective placement by a hearing officer can argue that the desired placement need not be the child's least restrictive environment where the school district violated the child's right to a free appropriate public education by failing to provide an appropriate IEP. For example, the Sixth Circuit has noted that reimbursement for a parental placement at a school for children with disabilities was appropriate because: "It will commonly be the case that parents who have not been treated properly under the IDEA, and who exercise the right of parental placement, will place their child in a school that specializes in teaching children with disabilities and thus will not satisfy the mainstreaming requirement. Adopting such a limitation on parental placements would therefore effectively vitiate the remedy." *Cleveland Heights-Univ. Heights City Sch. Dist. v. Boss*, 144 F.3d 391, 400 n.7 (6th Cir. 1998).

Some private schools may in fact provide students some interaction with non-disabled peers or utilize the state or local curricula, both of which may allow for an easier transition back to a public school at some point. Furthermore, state and local curricula are often viewed as having inherent credibility, thereby potentially strengthening a parent's argument in support of a particular public school that utilizes the state or local criteria.. If applicable, a lawyer may want to provide evidence of these factors to a judge or hearing officer in support of a particular nonpublic school placement. For a discussion of these and other issues related to the selection of a proper private school, see Lewis M. Wasserman, *Delineating Administrative Exhaustion Requirements and Establishing Federal Courts' Jurisdiction Under the Individuals with Disabilities Education Act: Lessons from the Case Law and Proposals for Congressional Action*, 29 J. Nat'l Ass'n L. Jud. 349 (2009) . In addition, although *Carter*, 510 U.S. 7, discussed earlier, clarified that a private school selected by parents need not be approved by the state in order for the parent to be provided reimbursement, a parent's case that the private school is appropriate may be strengthened if the school is in fact approved by the state or the staff at the private school (particularly the staff who will interact with the child) are appropriately credentialed in the relevant areas. An attorney assisting a parent or caregiver with seeking an appropriate private placement as a remedy for a child should keep these various factors in mind in identifying the placement to pursue and in building the case in support of the appropriateness of the placement.

Most importantly, the proposed school placement must be able to provide the services and accommodations the child requires and meet the child's needs. If the school does not have a particular service that the child requires, the school can contract with another provider in order to ensure the child receives the service, or the service can be supplemented outside of the school day, if appropriate. If the child already has an appropriate IEP, but the school district's proposed placement cannot implement the IEP, the parent's attorney will need to demonstrate that the parent's proposed school placement can in fact implement the child's IEP. If the school district has proposed an inappropriate IEP, an attorney may choose to try to collaborate with the school district to come to an agreement on an appropriate IEP for the child while he or she works to identify a different school placement that could implement that IEP. If the parent is alleging the inappropriateness of both the IEP and the school district's proposed placement, and seeking a new placement as a remedy, the parent can request that a hearing officer or judge order changes to the IEP as part of the remedy. In the alternative, a parent could instead seek an order that the school district place the child at the sought-after school and then convene an IEP meeting with the multi-disciplinary team at the new school to develop an appropriate IEP once the child begins attending the new school.

The parent may also have identified an appropriate public school placement for the student, but find that the school district refuses to place a child in that particular public school. For example, the school district may maintain that it can serve the child's needs in his or neighborhood school, but the child may require a program at a different public school, such as a separate full-time special education public school or a school that offers a specialized classroom or cluster program that can meet the student's needs.

Conversely, the school district may be proposing to place the child at a different public school or at a private school, or may have already placed the child at such a school, but the parent feels that his or her child can be served appropriately in the neighborhood school. If the latter situation applies, an attorney should also keep in mind the requirement that students be served in the least restrictive environment and related arguments that could bolster his or her advocacy. *See* 20 U.S.C. § 1413(a)(5). Disputes among public school options can sometimes be resolved through informal negotiations, but, at times, litigation may be required to seek prospective placement at an appropriate public school.

For some students, public charter schools or other school choice options in that jurisdiction might provide alternative placement choices. Some jurisdictions, like the District of Columbia, have embraced public charter schools to a greater extent than others. Parents must generally apply directly to a charter school for admission. Charter schools range widely in the special education services that they provide. Therefore, each individual charter school should be investigated to determine whether it is appropriate. Additionally, public school districts that serve as local educational agencies may or may not have a role to play in the charter school's provision of special education services, or the charter school may have elected to serve as its own local educational agency. *See, e.g.,* Cal. Educ. Code § 47641. Attorneys should check the statutes, regulations, and local policies in their jurisdiction to determine the means through which special education services in charter schools are provided and monitored, and which entities are accountable for the various responsibilities under special education law. *See, e.g.,* 5 D.C.M.R. § E-3019.

Regardless of whether the parent ultimately wants to pursue a public school or private school placement, if a parent is looking for a different school placement for his or her child, the attorney needs to think carefully about the student's needs and work with the parent to identify an appropriate placement to attempt to secure for the child.

G. The Process of Identifying an Appropriate Placement to Pursue as a Remedy

There are a number of ways to begin the process of identifying an appropriate school. To explore public school options, the school district may have information available on the Internet or in hard copy materials describing the special education options available within the public school system. Some school districts do not make this information as readily available, but the special education division of the school district's central administration offices may be willing to provide a parent or attorney with information verbally. The attorney should be strategic in how much information he or she provides to any school official with whom he or she might be inquiring, or the attorney may decide simply to ask more general questions rather than providing specific identifying information for the student, depending on the posture of the case.

The exploration of options for private special education schools, often termed "nonpublic schools," will involve a different approach. The parent may already have schools in mind to explore, but an attorney may be starting the search for an appropriate nonpublic school with little or no information about the options available. Some nonpublic schools belong to associations of private special education schools that maintain lists of their member schools or could provide a parent or attorney with contact information for possible school placements. For example, many of the private special education schools in the state of Maryland belong to an association called the Maryland Association of Nonpublic Special Education Facilities, or MANSEF. *See* www.mansef.org. MANSEF maintains a list of private special education schools, which it organizes by disability classification and by county.

Pediatricians and other health and mental health providers outside of the school system, such as psychologists, psychiatrists, and social workers, as well as educational consultants, can often serve as useful resources in identifying private school options. Other special education attorneys practicing in the attorney's jurisdiction, or law school clinics that provide special education representation, might also be able to provide the attorney with suggestions for private school options or resources through which information can be found.

The attorney may want to work with the parent to identify necessary characteristics of an appropriate placement for the child based on his or her evaluations and IEP, or the services, goals, and accommodations that an appropriate IEP would include if the child had one. The parent and attorney can also seek recommendations as to necessary characteristics of an appropriate school from educational consultants, pediatricians and other health and mental health providers who might know the child. It is critical that the attorney talk through with the parent and/or the child, if the child is able to have such a conversation, any suggestions that they have for characteristics they would like to see in the child's school. After taking these steps, an attorney should consider generating a comprehensive list of necessary characteristics for a school placement and review the list with the parent. For example, this list could include such requirements for the school as small class sizes, an adaptive physical education program, or a full-time speech/language therapist.

Based on the necessary placement characteristics that are identified, the attorney and parent can generate a list of questions to ask potential schools. As this list is generated, the attorney should consider what questions a hearing officer might ask to determine whether the school placement being sought is appropriate for the student. Keeping an eye toward litigation in this way helps an attorney make sure that there is legal justification to pursue the placement as a remedy. It is helpful to keep litigation in mind, even if there is a possibility of resolving the matter with the school district, so that the attorney is prepared in case the issue does result in a due process hearing and/or civil action. In addition, the attorney can anticipate criticisms that opposing counsel from an educational agency could generate to attack a placement proposed by the parent as a remedy. Anticipating questions or concerns that might arise in a hearing can help to get all of the information needed to assess whether a school placement might be appropriate to seek as a remedy and help the attorney to prove the appropriateness of that school in the course of litigation.

Consider the following hypothetical concerning an appropriate school placement:

Andrea

Andrea is fourteen years old. Her IEP calls for full-time special education instruction in a separate special education school targeted at addressing the needs of students with emotional disturbances and attention deficit hyperactivity disorder (ADHD). She requires thirty hours of specialized instruction a week. There are no related services listed on her IEP. Despite the fact that her IEP calls for a full-time special education school, the school district has not proposed any school that meets the criteria, and Andrea remains in her neighborhood public school with only fifteen hours per week of specialized instruction. Andrea has outbursts when she gets frustrated and sometimes needs to leave the classroom to cool off. Ideally, she would have a quiet place to go in her school to unwind, where she is well-supervised, when she does need to leave the classroom. Andrea's therapist from her community-based mental health agency also believes Andrea needs counseling services in school and has documented this recommendation in an evaluation. Andrea's mother agreed with the therapist's recommendation and shared the evaluation with her IEP team, but the other members refused to add counseling as a related service to Andrea's IEP.

Andrea's mother has asked you to help her look for an appropriate school placement for Andrea.

Consider this problem within your local jurisdiction. Based on the information you have, make a list of characteristics you think might be necessary in an appropriate school for Andrea. What sources would you consult to generate that list? Using that list, what questions would you ask the school to learn whether they can meet Andrea's needs? How would you find out the answers to your questions?

H.   Visiting a Potential School Placement

Prior to visiting a school or beginning the admissions process, an attorney can try to get as many of the questions he or she generated answered in advance over the telephone and by researching the school through other means such as the Internet. A telephone conversation with the admissions director, school director, principal, special education coordinator, or a teacher, can often provide much of the information needed to determine whether the placement might be appropriate for the student.

Once an attorney has identified schools to explore more seriously, he or she can assist the parent in initiating applications to those schools and setting up visits. A public school placement may or may not offer the opportunity for a parent of a prospective student for whom the school district has not yet offered placement to come to the school to visit, although the attorney may be able to argue that the public school must provide the parent with an opportunity to visit that school if it is strategically advantageous to make such arguments. For private school placements, typically a letter from the attorney or the parent to the admissions director or a senior administration official such as the educational director or principal, accompanied by the child's current IEP, recent evaluations, school records, and any other records that might be useful, can suffice to get the admissions process started. Usually, the school will review the submitted documents and let the attorney and/or the parent know based on a preliminary assessment of the records whether the student appears to be an appropriate candidate for the school. If the school believes the student might be an appropriate candidate and has space available for the student, the next step is usually a tour of the school, in which the parent and student can determine whether the school is a good fit for them and the school in turn can determine whether the student is appropriate for admission. It can be helpful and sometimes critical for the attorney to accompany the parent on the school visit. The attorney has spent time thinking about the student's needs and the factors that will be critical in a possible dispute resolution proceeding, and will have prepared for the visit and will know what questions to ask. The attorney can assist the parent in identifying any possible red flags that might make the school inappropriate. Additionally, the visit can provide an opportunity for the attorney to develop relationships with staff at the school, which can prove useful during the course of the admissions process and during the course of a future IEP meeting or any possible litigation. The opportunity for the attorney to see the potential school placement with his or her own eyes can also assist tremendously in the preparation of an attorney's arguments at an IEP meeting or in litigation. Even a savvy parent might benefit from being accompanied by an attorney on a visit to a potential school placement. Before accompanying a parent on a school visit, the attorney should consider any risks. For example, a school district that is aware that placement is an issue for the child may insist on having the school district's lawyer accompany the parent and his or her lawyer to the school visit, especially if the parent's lawyer intends to participate in the visit. If the school district's lawyer attends as well, he or she may try to limit the questions posed by the parent or parent's lawyer, or the answers provided by the prospective school.

It may also be advantageous to have someone other than the parent's lawyer, such as a non-attorney advocate, an investigator, or a paralegal, accompany the parent on the school visit, in addition to or in lieu of the lawyer visiting. This person can testify to his or her observations from the school visit at a due process hearing, whereas a lawyer would not be able to provide testimony. Having a non-lawyer visit the school can also serve to limit the demands on the lawyer, and possible additional costs to the parent for the expense of the lawyer's time. If the attorney is working with an expert, such as a psychologist, the expert can also visit the potential school placement. The expert can then advise the parent on whether the school placement is appropriate, and if selected by the parent, testify at the hearing about the reasons why that placement is appropriate for the child. Such expert testimony can greatly strengthen a case, especially where a placement is strongly contested.

The school visit can be used to obtain responses to any unanswered questions, and to take thorough notes that can be helpful in preparation for advocacy to secure the placement. The attorney and parent should see as much of the school as possible, including spaces like a resource room in which the child might spend time during the school day, and observe a classroom in session. If it is possible to visit and observe the classroom in which the student would likely be placed, that observation can yield information useful in determining whether the school placement is appropriate. Conversations with the student's likely teachers, aides, related service providers, and other school staff who would be interacting with the student can provide helpful insight into the appropriateness of the school.

Sometimes the school will want to interview the parent and student. The attorney should prepare the parent or student for this possibility, and consider discussing with them in advance questions they might be asked in such an interview. Some schools will also provide the opportunity for a potential student to attend the school for part of a school day in order to determine whether the school can meet the student's needs. Indeed, some schools will even require a student to attend the school for several days prior to formally admitting the student. An opportunity for the student to participate fully in the school's programming for any period of time can often be helpful in determining whether the school truly can meet the student's needs.

If the parent identifies a private school that he or she wants to seek from a hearing officer as a prospective private school placement when the parent cannot afford to unilaterally fund the child and then seek reimbursement, there are two different ways that an attorney can help the client strategically. First, a private school may agree to accept and enroll a student, and allow that student to begin attending prior to receiving any tuition funding, while the attorney seeks prior notice of placement from the school district or an order from a hearing officer in a due process hearing or a judge in a civil action for the child to be placed and funded by the school district at that school. The acceptance would then be contingent on the attorney seeking reimbursement for expenditures incurred by the school at the due process hearing. This strategy has the advantage of allowing the child to be placed in an appropriate school quickly, without delaying this opportunity for the child to receive an appropriate education while the attorney seeks the necessary relief to effectuate the funding. It also allows the school staff to get to know the student and for the student to begin benefitting from the education provided by the school, which will strengthen the testimony of a representative from that school. Placement in advance will also fortify the testimony of the parent or any experts on the appropriateness of the school and the academic benefit the child is receiving as a result of attending there. However, private schools are often unwilling to allow a student to begin attending their school without prior notice of placement from an educational agency or an order from a hearing officer or judge because such an arrangement poses a financial risk for the school, in that the school may not get reimbursed if the parent does not prevail in seeking the school placement as a remedy. *See* Mary G. Hynes & Joseph B. Tulman, *The Special Education Process: Remedies, in* Special Education Advocacy under the Individuals with Disabilities Education Act (IDEA) for Children in the Juvenile Delinquency System, 13-2 to 13-3 (Joseph B. Tulman & Joyce A. McGee eds., 1998).

If the school placement sought by the parent will not allow the student to begin attending without the appropriate documentation from the school district or order from a hearing officer or court requiring the school district to fund the placement, the attorney can file for a due process hearing and seek an order from a hearing officer requiring the school district to place and prospectively fund the child at this placement. This strategy will result in some delay, because the child will remain in the current placement, to which the parent objects, as the parent and attorney navigate the dispute resolution proceedings until the needed resolution, settlement, hearing officer determination, or court order is obtained. Depending on any applicable regulations or rules in that jurisdiction, an attorney may be able to seek an expedited hearing in order to secure the placement more quickly, for example, if the child is in crisis or his or her safety is at risk in the current school placement and he or she urgently requires the new placement. *See, e.g.*, Dist. of Columbia Special Education Student Hearing Office Due Process Hearing Standard Operating Procedures § 1008(B) (section providing for expedited hearings revised Aug. 21, 2008, detailing that requests for expedited hearings can be granted where the physical or emotional health or safety of the student or others would be endangered by the delay in the conduct of the hearing or there is other substantial justification for expediting the hearing).

This strategy does not provide the proposed school placement staff with the same opportunities to observe the child in the setting and for the child to begin benefitting from the instruction and programming provided at the school as would be afforded if the child had actually started attending the school. However, there are a number of ways for the prospective school placement staff to become knowledgeable about the student so that a representative or representatives of the school placement can testify effectively in a due process hearing. For example, the school staff can review the child's educational records and other documentation, interview the parent and child, and possibly observe the child for part of the school day or several school days in the proposed school setting or the child's current school setting. The staff can also talk with other professionals familiar with the child. The more knowledgeable a representative from the prospective school placement is about the child and his or her needs, the more effective that representative will be as a witness testifying in a due process hearing. The attorney for the family can help to ensure that such a witness has all of the information he or she needs to be effective and persuasive during testimony. For a helpful discussion of strategic considerations in seeking school placements and private related services, see Hynes & Tulman, *supra*, at 13-2 to 13-11.

IX.   REIMBURSEMENT FOR OTHER SERVICES

Along with awarding reimbursement to parents for unilateral placements at private schools where appropriate, courts have awarded reimbursement for other expenses related to the child's attendance at the private school, such as transportation costs. *See, e.g., Kantor v. District of Columbia*, 1991 U.S. Dist. LEXIS 1158 (D.D.C. Jan. 31, 1991); *David P. v. Lower Merion Sch. Dist.*, 1998 U.S. Dist. LEXIS 15160, at *18-19 (E.D. Pa. Sept. 18, 1998); *Hurry v. Jones*, 734 F.2d 879 (1st Cir. 1984). A court has even ordered reimbursement for residential and caretaking costs for a child who lived with his grandparents in order to obtain the special education services he required from a residential school far from his parents' home, which did not have a room available for him. *Ojai Unified Sch. Dist. v. Jackson*, 4 F.3d 1467, 1478-1479 (9th Cir. 1993). When seeking reimbursement on behalf of a parent for tuition for a private school, an attorney should think broadly about the other related expenses for which reimbursement might be sought. Moreover, when seeking a prospective private school placement as a remedy, an attorney should consider whether there are related needs, such as the provision of transportation, that should be requested as part of the remedy.

Courts have also awarded reimbursement for related services and other services that were parentally funded and privately provided, where the school district denied the child a free appropriate public education, and the services met the child's needs, such as speech therapy (*see Johnson v. Lancaster-Lebanon Intermediate Unit 13*, 757 F. Supp. 606, 620-23 (E.D. Pa.

1991)); psychotherapy (*see Max M. v. Illinois State Bd. of Educ.*, 629 F. Supp. 1504, 1519-1520 (N.D. Ill. 1986)); and occupational therapy (*see Rapid City Sch. Dist. 51-4 v. Vahle*, 733. F. Supp. 1364, 1370-71 (D.S.D. 1990)). Additionally, courts have awarded reimbursement for parentally-funded private tutoring services, when the school district failed to provide a child with a free appropriate public education. *See, e.g., W.G. v. Target Range Sch. Dist.*, 960 F.2d 1479, 1486-87 (9th Cir. 1992).

X. COMPENSATORY EDUCATION

If there has been a violation of a child's right to a free appropriate public education, a hearing officer or court can award appropriate compensatory education services (sometimes referred to as "comp ed"), which can best be described as supplemental services, over and above whatever the school must already provide, as appropriate to remediate educational damage. Where families cannot afford to place a child in a private school and seek tuition reimbursement later, compensatory education services provide a remedy for the time during which the child was not provided an appropriate education. In providing compensatory education services as relief for the time in which a child languished without a free appropriate public education, courts have emphasized that "Congress did not intend the child's entitlement to free education to turn upon her parent's ability to 'front' its costs." *M.C. v. Central Reg'l. Sch. Dist.*, 81 F.3d 389, 395 (3d Cir. 1996) (citing *Miener v. Missouri*, 800 F.2d 749, 753 (8th Cir. 1986)).

In fact, compensatory relief is similar to tuition reimbursement in that both awards are necessary to preserve the right to a free appropriate public education. "Like retroactive reimbursement, compensatory education required school districts to 'belatedly pay expenses that [they] should have paid all along.' " *Id.* Without compensatory education services, some parents would not have any form of relief available, and courts have explained that they "do not believe Congress intended to provide a right without a remedy." *See, e.g., Jefferson Cnty. Bd. of Educ. v. Breen*, 853 F.2d 853, 857-58 (11th Cir. 1988). This remedy is not only useful for parents who could not afford to pay for private services or a private school placement up front, it is also useful for parents who do not wish to seek private educational services, or more likely, were not even aware of the violation at the time it was occurring. *See* Russo & Osborne, *supra*, at 242; Hynes & Tulman, *supra*, at 13-11. Compensatory education also can serve as a deterrent against school districts unnecessarily prolonging litigation in order to decrease their potential liability. *Breen*, 853 F.2d at 858.

Compensatory education services give the child back the years lost languishing in an inappropriate placement. *Brown v. Wilson Cnty. Sch. Bd.*, 747 F. Supp. 436 (M.D. Tenn. 1990). However, this remedy is available not only when a placement is found to be inappropriate, but as a result of an inappropriate IEP or an unimplemented IEP, or when a child received no services whatsoever due to a failure to identify the child as in need of special education or a refusal to provide services. Essentially, compensatory education can be a remedy when there is evidence of a denial of a free appropriate public education, subject to limitations that may be imposed within a particular federal Circuit, as described below. Furthermore, because compensatory education services may be necessary relief in response to a violation a parent did not even know existed, courts have generally concluded that the failure of the parent to object to the school district's provision of special education as inappropriate or to protest the lack thereof does not bar a claim for compensatory education for years that child was denied a free appropriate public education. *See, e.g., G. ex rel. R.G. v. Fort Bragg Dependent Schs.*, 343 F.3d

295, 309 (4th Cir. 2003); *Ridgewood Bd. of Educ. v. N.E.*, 172 F.3d 238, 250 (3d Cir. 1999).

Compensatory education is not just a remedy available in a civil action in court. The U.S. Department of Education has explicitly determined that the authority to order compensatory education services is within the broad remedial power of a hearing officer. *Letter to Kohn*, 17 EHLR 522 (OSEP 1991). Courts also have established that hearing officers have the authority to order compensatory education under the IDEA. *See, e.g., Diatta v. District of Columbia*, 319 F. Supp. 2d 57, 65 (D.D.C. 2004). Additionally, parents initiating a state complaint, pursuant to the procedure established in the regulations accompanying the IDEA, can seek corrective action appropriate to address the needs of the child, which explicitly includes compensatory education. 34 C.F.R. § 300.152.

A.   Varying Approaches of the Federal Courts of Appeals

Most of the federal courts of appeals have explicitly recognized compensatory education as a form of relief, and a few courts of appeals have additionally provided specific guidance as to how to calculate a compensatory education award. The United States Courts of Appeals for the First, Second, Fourth, Fifth, Seventh and Eighth Circuits have specifically provided for compensatory education as an available remedy, but have not articulated standards for formulating the type or duration of compensatory education awards. Only the Tenth Circuit has not explicitly addressed the availability of compensatory education as a remedy but, in one recent case, the Tenth Circuit did imply that compensatory education services could be appropriate relief if substantive violations of a free appropriate public education were found. *Garcia v. Bd. of Educ. of Albuquerque Pub. Schs.*, 520 F.3d 1116 (10th Cir. 2008) (noting that the IDEA may provide plaintiffs with the remedy of compensatory education services when they have been denied a free appropriate public education).

While the Eighth Circuit declined to provide a specific formula for calculating compensatory education and instead left that task to the discretion of the lower courts, a district court in Minnesota used its discretion to impose a formula using a one-to-one ratio. In applying this standard, that court ordered six years of compensatory education services for the six years the student was denied a free appropriate public education. *Westendorp v. Indep. Sch. Dist.*, 35 F. Supp. 2d 1134, 1137 (D. Minn. 1998).

The Third Circuit has also provided for a one-to-one approach for determining the amount of compensatory education due. In the Third Circuit, a child is entitled to compensatory education for a period equal to the period of the deprivation, but excluding the time reasonably required for the school district to rectify the problem. *M.C. v. Central Reg'l Sch. Dist.*, 81 F.3d 389, 397 (3d Cir. 1996). Moreover, the Third Circuit rejected a requirement of bad faith on the part of a school district for compensatory education to be an appropriate award, reasoning that "a child's entitlement to special education should not depend upon the vigilance of the parent (who may not be sufficiently sophisticated to comprehend the problem) nor be abridged because the district's behavior did not rise to the level of slothfulness or bad faith." *M.C.*, 81 F.3d at 397.

In contrast, the D.C. Circuit refused to adopt the cookie cutter approach of an hour per hour standard to calculate compensatory education awards, reasoning that such an approach treats the remedy as a form of damages and counters the broad discretion afforded by the IDEA's remedial standard. *Reid v. District of Columbia*, 401 F.3d 516, 523 (D.C. Cir. 2005). The D.C. Circuit set out in *Reid* its standard for formulating compensatory education services through a fact-specific inquiry. The award must be "reasonably calculated to provide the educational benefits that likely would have accrued from special education services the school district should have supplied in the first place." *Id.* at 524. The Sixth Circuit and Eleventh Circuit have adopted similarly flexible approaches, citing to the D.C. Circuit's decision in *Reid*. *See Board of Educ. of Fayette Cnty. v. L.M.*, 478 F.3d 307, 316-17 (6th Cir. 2007); *Draper*, 518 F.3d at 1289-90.

The Ninth Circuit has a similarly flexible approach, but does not utilize the *Reid* formulation. According to the Ninth Circuit, compensatory education is an equitable remedy, not contractual, so "there is no obligation to provide a day-for-day compensation" for the period of the violation. *Park v. Anaheim Union High Sch Dist.*, 464 F.3d 1025, 1033 (9th Cir. 2006); *Parents of Student W. v. Puyallup Sch.*, 31 F.3d 1489, 1497 (9th Cir. 1994).

Some federal courts of appeals have limited the circumstances under which any compensatory education award is appropriate. The Second Circuit has required a gross violation of a child's free appropriate public education before compensatory education can be awarded as relief. *Garro v. Connecticut*, 23 F.3d 734, 737 (2d Cir. 1994) (requiring "gross procedural violation"); *Mrs. C. v. Wheaton*, 916 F.2d 69, 75 (2d Cir. 1990) (requiring "gross violation," defined as coercion of disabled child into terminating his right to further education). No other federal courts of appeals have required a "gross violation," and the Third Circuit explicitly rejected the Second Circuit's gross violation requirement because "in addition to being imprecise, it is not anchored in the structure or text of the IDEA." *M.C.*, 81 F.3d at 396.

The Seventh Circuit has limited compensatory education awards to exceptional circumstances in concluding that this remedy is "indeed exceptional and nowhere expressly authorized by the statute." *Board of Educ. of Oak Park & River Forest High Sch. Dist. 200 v. Todd A.*, 79 F.3d 654, 657 (7th Cir. 1996). That Court of Appeals also emphasized the broad authority of the district court to award — or deny — compensatory education services, explaining that such relief can be ordered if necessary to cure a violation, and that awarding compensatory education is a decision that rests in the sound discretion of the district court. *Brown v. Bartholomew Consol. Sch. Corp.*, 442 F.3d 588, 597 (7th Cir. 2006).

Some courts have denied compensatory education services where the allegations included only procedural violations of the IDEA. *See, e.g., Erickson v. Albuquerque Public Schs.*, 199 F.3d 1116, 1122 (10th Cir. 1999). However, the IDEA has since been amended to reflect that a procedural violation can amount to a denial of a free appropriate public education where that violation impeded the child's right to a free appropriate public education, significantly impeded the parents' opportunity to participate in decision-making around the provision of a free appropriate public education, or caused a deprivation of educational benefit. 20 U.S.C. § 1415(f)(3)(E)(ii). As a result, an attorney can cite to this provision if applicable when advocating for compensatory educational services as a form of relief based on procedural inadequacies.

Moreover, some courts have protected the integrity of compensatory education services in the implementation stage, specifically stating that neither a hearing officer nor a state reviewer may delegate to a child's IEP team the power to reduce or terminate a compensatory education award. *Board of Educ. of Fayette Cnty., Ky. v. L.M.*, 478 F.3d 307, 317 (6th Cir. 2007); *Reid*, 401 F.3d at 526-27. These courts reasoned that a due process hearing may not be conducted by an employee of the local education agency. An IEP team, in contrast, must include a representative of the local educational agency. If the IEP team were to have the authority to reduce or terminate a compensatory education award, that team would in effect be exercising the power of a hearing officer, which would violate the statute, given that it explicitly bars local educational agency employees from performing the functions of a hearing officer. *Board of Educ. of Fayette Cnty., Ky.*, 478 F.3d at 317 (*citing* 20 U.S.C. §§ 1415(f)(3), 1414(d)(1)(B)(iv)); *Reid*, 401 F.3d at 526-27. Moreover, such a grant of authority to the IEP team would run afoul of the provision that hearing awards are final unless modified through administrative appeal or judicial action. *Reid*, 401 F.3d at 527.

B.   Crafting a Request for a Compensatory Education Award

Attorneys crafting a compensatory education award need to be creative and strategic in devising the duration of the entitlement and the actual form and duration of the services requested. Tulman & Hynes, *supra*, at 13-12. A school district might agree to provide a compensatory education plan for a child without a due process hearing, if the school district is willing to admit the denial of a free appropriate public education and agree to the need for such compensatory relief. A compensatory education plan can be negotiated with a school district at an IEP meeting or through a settlement agreement. Regardless of whether counsel is preparing for a negotiation or litigation, the necessary evidence should be marshalled to support the need for compensatory education services, and both documentary and testimonial evidence of the denial of a free appropriate public education should be considered.

One important factor is the length of time over which the denial of a free appropriate public education occurred. The IDEA has a two year statute of limitations, limiting due process complaints to two years from the date the parent knew or should have known about the violation, but there are exceptions that may apply when compensatory education is at issue. 20 U.S.C. § 1415(f)(3)(C)-(D). For example, if the school district refused to provide necessary occupational therapy services for the past five years, but failed to provide the parent with the required prior written notice of its refusal, the parent may be able to argue that the statute of limitations does not apply because the LEA withheld information from the parent that is required under the IDEA. 20 U.S.C. § 1415(f)(3)(D). In considering the duration of the denial, the attorney can seek compensatory education for every year a child had no IEP or an inappropriate IEP and failed to make academic progress. Alternately, the duration may constitute the school years during which a school district failed to implement an IEP. If a child has been unlawfully excluded, suspended or expelled from school, the time period during which he was denied the special education services and accommodations he required might amount to the duration of the alleged violation. For a child who has not yet been identified and provided an IEP or who should have been identified earlier, the attorney can point to the period of time from which there is initial evidence of poor academic performance up through the time the child was identified and provided appropriate services. In short, an attorney can help a family seek relief for the entire time that the child was denied a free appropriate public education, if the evidence supports such an allegation and an exception to the statute of limitations can be argued, if necessary.

The attorney should also gather evidence to support the specific form of relief, taking into account any guidance from courts in that circuit as to the standard for compensatory education in that jurisdiction. For example, depending on the jurisdiction, the attorney may need to show that the requested compensatory education services are "reasonably calculated to provide the educational benefits that likely would have accrued from special education services the school district should have supplied in the first place." *Reid*, 401 F.3d at 524. While this standard requires speculation, the argument for compensatory education is likely to be more persuasive if the speculation comes from a qualified professional in the field. For example, if a child was denied necessary occupational therapy services for five years, an occupational therapist may provide a written report or testify at a hearing in order to provide the necessary supporting evidence for the parent's request for three hundred hours of occupational therapy services, for example, to provide the educational benefits that likely would have accrued for the child if the school district had provided the required services all along. Where the violation was a complete denial of any special education services or a failure to provide an appropriate IEP or placement more generally, to the child's detriment, an expert could be particularly useful in demonstrating the need for a particular tutoring service, summer program, or even a new placement as compensatory education. A compensatory education claim can often be strengthened by the testimony of a professional who is effectively qualified as an expert in the relevant field.

Compensatory education can take a wide variety of different forms and should be individually tailored to a child's needs. Hearing officers and courts can award special education services beyond the age of eligibility expiration, which is twenty-one in most jurisdictions. *See, e.g., W.B. v. Matula*, 67 F.3d 484, 494-95 (3d Cir. 1995); *Pihl v. Massachusetts Dep't of Educ.*, 9 F.3d 184, 188 n.8 (1st Cir. 1993); *Todd A.*,79 F.3d at 660; *Breen*, 853 F.2d at 857. Unlike in *Honig v. Doe*, where the Supreme Court declined to extend protections of the IDEA to a twenty-four year old who had passed the age of eligibility, courts have found that compensatory education services, in contrast, are not a request for school districts to comply with the IDEA in the future, but instead constitute relief to compensate a student for rights that were denied to a student in the past. *See, e.g., Pihl*, 9F.3d at 189; *Lester H. v. Gilhool*, 916 F.2d 865, 872 (3d Cir. 1990). In awarding compensatory education services past the age of eligibility, some courts have directed the parties to take into account the student's educational status and needs at the time the award would go into effect. *Pihl*, 9 F.3d at 188 n.8; *Straube*, 801 F. Supp. at 1181.

Courts have also awarded compensatory education services for a child after he has graduated high school. *Frazier v. Fairhaven Sch. Comm.*, 276 F.3d 52, 63 (1st Cir. 2002). The Department of Education explained that a student's decision to graduate with a regular high school diploma does not automatically relieve a school district of its responsibility to provide compensatory education services awarded to the student, given that the purpose of the award is to remedy the failure to provide services that the student should have received during the enrollment in high school when the child was entitled to a free appropriate public education. *Letter to Riffel, in* OSEP List of Correspondence July 1, 2000 through Sept. 30, 2000, Federal Register: March 9, 2001, Volume 66, Number 47, Notices, pages 14291-14293, 14292 (OSEP Aug. 22, 2000), *available at*:

    http://www2.ed.gov/policy/speced/guid/idea/letters/2000-3/riffel82200fapesec.pdf

A compensatory education award can include a full-time paraprofessional aide to assist the child in school. *Westendorp v. Indep. Sch. Dist.*, 35 F. Supp. 2d 1134, 1138 (D. Minn. 1998). If requesting an aide for the student as compensatory education, an attorney should specify as much detail as possible, such as any qualifications or training the aide might require, tasks in which the aide should assist the child, and/or the parts of the school day for which the aide is needed.

Summer school is another form of possible compensatory education. *Johnson v. Bismarck Pub. Sch. Dist.*, 949 F.2d 1000, 1002 (8th Cir. 1991). Summer school can include traditional summer school or Extended School Year services, or can incorporate recreational, therapeutic, or vocational services. A summer program awarded as compensatory education could even take place at a camp.

Assistive technology, including computers, can be provided as part of a compensatory education award. In the District of Columbia, attorneys representing a class of children whose rights under the IDEA were violated negotiated an agreement with the state educational agency to offer class members computers, computer software, and other forms of assistive technology, as options for compensatory education. *Agreement Regarding Blackman/Jones Compensatory Education, Blackman et. al. v. District of Columbia*, No. 97-1629 (D.D.C. December 10, 2007).

The relief could also include tutoring. *Pihl*, 9 F.3d at 188 n.8. If possible, counsel should specify in a request for compensatory education whether the tutor needs any specific qualifications or training, the number of hours of tutoring requested, any specific methodologies of tutoring services the student may need, the location of the tutoring, whether any transportation is required for the student to access the tutoring, and any other details that can be provided. Effective tutoring can provide immediate relief for a student who is having difficulty accessing the curriculum during the school day or struggling with homework assignments.

In addition to or in lieu of direct services to the child, compensatory education could include training for teachers, paraprofessional aides or related service providers. For example, the Ninth Circuit approved a compensatory education award that included weekly training for teachers to address the implementation of the self-help goals and objectives on the child's IEP. *Park*, 464 F.3d at 1034.

Compensatory education relief can also take the form of a private placement itself. *Draper*, 518 F.3d at 1286. Where a private school placement is the only way to remediate the educational damage caused by the failure to provide a child with an appropriate education, an attorney may want to consider requesting a private placement as compensatory relief. If strategically appropriate, an attorney may choose to argue first that a prospective private school placement is necessary for a child to receive academic benefit and appropriate under the *Burlington* standard, and then argue in the alternative that the hearing officer could instead order the placement as compensatory education if he or she thought the placement was not necessary as future relief, but appropriate to compensate the child for past denials.

In sum, compensatory education can take many forms, and may even be most helpful as a blend of a number of forms of relief, such as academic tutoring and speech/language services or summer school in addition to specialized instruction beyond the age of twenty-one. Compensatory education is an important remedy approved by the courts that can be sought as a sole form of relief, or as a supplement to other remedies, including as an addition to a request for an order for prospective private placement.

Consider this hypothetical regarding a potential request for compensatory education.

Jenny

Jenny is nine years old and is repeating the third grade due to poor academic performance. In first and second grades, her report cards were poor as well, and her teachers noted that she was not developing reading skills at an appropriate rate. In fact, at nine years old, she can't read at all. For the past two years, she has exhibited extreme behavioral problems, often bursting into tears and throwing a tantrum in the middle of class for no apparent reason. Jenny's parents take her to a private psychologist, who diagnoses her with a severe reading disorder and informs her parents that Jenny's self-esteem is extremely low and her tantrums in class are related to her frustration with her inability to read. The psychologist reviews her academic records and explains that Jenny should have been identified as having a learning disability back in kindergarten when she was five years old, and she should have received specialized instruction to address her reading disorder since that time.

Jenny's mother hires you as her attorney to assist her in securing appropriate special education services for Jenny. You begin to draft a due process complaint, and need to identify the relief you are requesting. Do you include compensatory education as a requested remedy? What evidence would you offer to support the need for compensatory education? What compensatory education services would you request and in what amount? What evidence would you offer to support your contention that these services are appropriate? Suppose you are in the Second Circuit, which requires a gross violation of the IDEA in order for compensatory education services to be provided. What arguments could you make to show that gross violations occurred in this instance?

XI.   ATTORNEYS' FEES

In most situations, the IDEA allows courts to award reasonable attorneys' fees to a parent who is a prevailing party. 20 U.S.C. § 1415(i)(3)(B)(i)(I); 34 C.F.R. § 300.517(a)(1)(i). A prevailing SEA or LEA can also be awarded reasonable attorneys' fees against the attorney of a parent who files a complaint or subsequent cause of action that is frivolous, unreasonable, or without foundation, or against the attorney of a parent who continued to litigate after the litigation clearly became frivolous, unreasonable, or without foundation. 20 U.S.C. § 1415(i)(3)(B)(i)(II); 34 C.F.R. § 300.517(a)(1)(ii). In addition, a prevailing SEA or LEA can be awarded attorneys' fees against the attorney of a parent or a parent himself or herself if the parent's complaint or subsequent cause of action was presented for an improper purpose, such as to harass, cause unnecessary delay or needlessly increase the cost of litigation. 20 U.S.C. § 1415(i)(3)(B)(i)(III); 34 C.F.R. § 300.517(a)(1)(iii). As the legislative history emphasizes, the standard for awarding attorneys' fees to school districts is purposely much stricter than the standard for parents to receive such awards, a distinction made in other civil rights contexts as well. 150 Cong. Rec. 11547 (daily ed. Nov. 19, 2004) (statement of Sen. Thomas Harkin). In such contexts, plaintiffs might be discouraged from pursuing legitimate claims if they had to fear paying defendant agencies attorneys' fees simply because they did not prevail. *Id.* Instead,

Congress provided a more stringent standard for the award of attorneys' fees to prevailing school districts, cautioning that awards on these grounds should only be pursued in the most "egregious cases." *Id.* Fees are based on rates prevailing in the community in which the action or proceeding arose for the kind and quality of services provided, and no bonus or multiplier can be used in calculating the fees awarded. 20 U.S.C. § 1415(i)(3)(C); 34 C.F.R. § 300.517(c)(1).

A. Defining "Prevailing Party"

The Education of the Handicapped Act ("EHA") did not originally include a provision for attorneys' fees. In 1984, the Supreme Court found that plaintiffs under the EHA did not retain the option of either § 1983 or § 504 remedies, such as attorneys' fees. Rehabilitation Act of 1973 § 504, 29 U.S.C. § 794; 42 U.S.C. § 1983; *Smith v. Robinson*, 468 U.S. 992, 1009-20 (1984).

In response to this case, Congress amended the EHA in 1986 to specify that a prevailing party could be awarded attorneys' fees. Congress changed the attorneys' fees provisions further when it amended the IDEA in 1997 and 2004. For two decades, the federal courts of appeals split on which test to use, the catalyst test or the merits test, to determine whether a plaintiff was a prevailing party entitled to attorneys' fees. *See, e.g., Nadeau v. Helgemoe*, 581 F.2d 275 (1st Cir. 1978), *overruled in part by Richardson v. Miller*, 279 F.3d 1 (1st Cir. 2002). Most federal courts of appeals favored the catalyst test. This theory defined a prevailing party eligible for attorneys' fees as a party whose suit "acted as a 'catalyst' for the change they sought, even if they did not obtain a judgment or consent decree." *Buckhannon Bd. & Care Home Inc. v. West Va. Dep't of Health & Human Res.*, 532 U.S. 598, 626 (2001).

In 2001, *Buckhannon* explicitly overruled those cases that utilized the catalyst theory. *Id.* at 610. The Court instead established the merits test analysis as the standard for determining the prevailing party, stating that parties are entitled to fees when they prevail on the merits of their claims by receiving "at least some relief" which includes "even an award of nominal damages." *Id.* at 603-04 (quoting *Hewitt v. Helms*, 482 U.S. 755, 760 (1987)); *Farrar v. Hobby*, 506 U.S. 103 (1992). Parties may also receive fees when a settlement agreement is enforced through a consent decree, whether or not it includes an admission of liability. *Buckhannon*, 532 U.S. at 603-04 (citing *Maher v. Gagne*, 448 U.S. 122 (1980)). However, plaintiffs who prevail through a private settlement without a consent decree are no longer considered prevailing parties and are therefore not entitled to attorneys' fees. *Id.* at 605.

Although *Buckhannon* was decided in relation to the Fair Housing Amendments Act and Americans with Disabilities Act and not the IDEA, most federal courts of appeals have held that it does apply to the attorneys' fees provisions in the IDEA. In the near decade since the Court's decision in *Buckhannon*, only the Eighth and Tenth Circuits of the United States Courts of Appeals have yet to explicitly address this issue. Although the federal courts of appeals have established tests with moderately different wording, the central tenets remain the same. For example, the United States Court of Appeals, District of Columbia Circuit, interpreted the merits test in early 2010 utilizing the following three-part test: "(1) there must be a 'court ordered change in the legal relationship' of the parties; (2) the judgment must be in favor of the party seeking the fees; and (3) the judicial pronouncement must be accompanied by judicial relief." *District of Columbia v. Straus*, 590 F.3d 898, 901 (D.C. Cir. 2010).

Because the merits test now controls, attorneys must take care to inform their clients of the risk that any settlement agreement created without judicial imprimatur may result in a denial of attorneys' fees. *See* Stefan R. Hanson, Note, *Buckhannon, Special Education Disputes, and Attorneys' Fees: Time for a Congressional Response Again*, 2003 B.Y.U. Educ. & L.J. 519, 544-47. An attorney should be explicit about any fee arrangements with his or her client from the beginning, and ensure that both the attorney and client are clear on the fee arrangement that will result from any settlement agreement. Depending on the jurisdiction, the rules of professional responsibility may require that the fee agreement be in writing. Some administrative hearing officers may allow a settlement to be read into the record, and then will issue a decision encapsulating the settlement agreement, thereby arguably giving the agreement the necessary imprimatur. Parents also retain the option of including attorneys' fees explicitly within the settlement agreement if the school district agrees to such a provision. *Id.* at 546.

B.   Limitations on Attorneys' Fees

The IDEA also limits the recovery of attorneys' fees for certain services. Attorneys' fees cannot be awarded and related costs cannot be reimbursed for services performed subsequent to the time of a written offer of settlement to a parent if the offer is made within the time prescribed by Rule 68 of the Federal Rules of Civil Procedure or, in the case of an administrative proceeding, at any time more than ten days before the start of the proceeding; if the offer is not accepted within ten days; and if the court or administrative hearing officer finds that the relief finally obtained by the parents is not more favorable to the parents than the offer of settlement. 20 U.S.C. § 1415(i)(3)(D)(i); 34 C.F.R. § 300.517(c)(2)(i). However, the prohibition on recovery of attorneys' fees for these services does not apply if the parent is the prevailing party and was substantially justified in rejecting the settlement offer. 20 U.S.C. § 1415(i)(3)(E); 34 C.F.R. § 300.517(c)(3).

Attorneys' fees may not be awarded for time spent by an attorney in an IEP meeting unless the meeting is convened as a result of an administrative proceeding or judicial action, or, at the discretion of the state, for a mediation. 20 U.S.C. § 1415(i)(3)(D)(ii); 34 C.F.R. § 300.517(c)(2)(ii). A dispute resolution session is not considered an administrative hearing or judicial action, or a meeting convened as a result of either proceeding, and therefore attorneys' fees may not be awarded for time spent in such a meeting. 20 U.S.C. § 1415(i)(3)(D)(iii); 34 C.F.R. § 300.517(c)(2)(iii).

The amount of attorneys' fees awarded is reduced if the court finds that the parent or the parent's attorney unreasonably protracted the final resolution of the controversy during the action or proceeding. 20 U.S.C. § 1415(i)(3)(F)(i); 34 C.F.R. § 300.517(c)(4)(i). The amount authorized to be awarded also will be reduced if it unreasonably exceeds the hourly rate prevailing in the community for similar services by attorneys of reasonably comparable skill, reputation, and experience. 20 U.S.C. § 1415(i)(3)(F)(ii); 34 C.F.R. § 300.517(c)(4)(ii). The amount will also be reduced if the time spent and legal services furnished were excessive considering the nature of the action or proceeding. 20 U.S.C. § 1415(i)(3)(F)(iii); 34 C.F.R. § 300.517(c)(4)(iii). Similarly, the amount of attorneys' fees will be reduced if the attorney representing the parent did not provide to the local educational agency the appropriate information in the notice of the due process complaint. 20 U.S.C. § 1415(i)(3)(F)(iv); 34 C.F.R. § 300.517(c)(4)(iv). However, none of these reductions in attorneys' fees applies in any action or proceeding if the court finds that the SEA or LEA unreasonably protracted the final resolution of the action or proceeding or violated the attorneys' fees section of the IDEA. 20 U.S.C. § 1415(i)(3)(G); 34 C.F.R. § 300.517(c)(5).

Counsel should keep detailed records of time spent on each portion of the case to provide to both the school district and the courts, in addition to the client, which can serve as appropriate documentation to ensure that the attorney receives the full amount owed for the work that was completed. Lynn M. Daggett, *Special Education Attorney's Fees: Of Buckhannon, the IDEA Reauthorization Bills, and the IDEA as Civil Rights Statute*, 8 U.C. Davis J. Juv. L. & Pol'y 1, 16-17 (2004). Timekeeping documents should show the exact actions of the attorneys, the time spent on that action, and the price placed on that action. *Id.* The fees available to an attorney for the prevailing party through the IDEA are not restricted based on the anticipated payment by a parent. Therefore, even attorneys providing parents with free legal representation should keep detailed time sheets, as they can collect attorneys' fees if the relevant requirements are satisfied. *Id.* at 16.

XII. EXPERT FEES

Prior to 2006, the federal courts of appeals split on whether expert fees were recoverable in IDEA actions. In 2006, the Supreme Court examined this issue and found the IDEA text to be unambiguous in this regard, ruling that expert fees are not recoverable in IDEA cases. 20 U.S.C. § 1415(i)(3)(B); *Arlington Cent. Sch. Dist. v. Murphy*, 548 U.S. 291, 304 (2006). After the lower courts found that the respondents in that case prevailed in their IDEA claim for their son's private school tuition, the respondents sought expert fees for an educational consultant who participated in the proceedings. However, the Court, looking to both precedent and the text of the statute, concluded that expert fees may not be recovered in IDEA cases. 548 U.S. at 297-98, 304 ("[The IDEA] language simply adds reasonable attorney's fees incurred by prevailing parents to the list of costs that prevailing parents are otherwise entitled to recover. This list of otherwise recoverable costs is obviously the list set out in 28 U.S.C. § 1920, the general statute governing the taxation of costs in federal court, and the recovery of witness fees under § 1920 is strictly limited by § 1821, which authorizes travel reimbursement and a $40 per diem. Thus, the text of 20 U.S.C. § 1415(i)(3)(B) does not authorize an award of any additional expert fees, and it certainly fails to provide the clear notice that is required under the Spending Clause."). A dissent from Justice Breyer, who was joined by Justice Souter and Stevens, pointed to a House of Representatives Conference Report showing that Congress intended to award reasonable expenses and fees of expert witnesses and underscored that the awarding of expert fees would further the purposes of the IDEA. *Id.* at 309. However, the majority declined to give the same weight to this legislative history. *Id.* at 304.

XIII. MONETARY DAMAGES

A.   Availability of Damages Under the IDEA Itself

Most of the federal courts of appeals have examined whether the IDEA alone provides for monetary damages, and have found that the statute does not provide for this remedy. *See, e.g.*, *Payne v. Peninsula Sch. Dist.*, 598 F.3d 1123, 1128 (9th Cir. 2010); *Chambers v. Sch. Dist. of Phil. Bd. of Educ.*, 587 F.3d 176, 184 (3d Cir. 2009). The federal courts of appeals that have not explicitly ruled on this issue are likely to follow their sister circuits in concluding that monetary damages are not available through IDEA claims.

B.   Availability of Damages in IDEA Cases Through § 1983

Several federal courts of appeals have also examined whether 42 U.S.C. § 1983 ("§ 1983") may ever be used in conjunction with the IDEA to seek monetary damages and if so, whether the IDEA administrative proceedings can ever be waived in seeking this relief. Monetary damages for special education complaints are often sought under the IDEA in conjunction with complaints brought under § 1983, a civil rights statute which does not in itself create any right under federal law, but provides remedies for violations of federal rights where a "federal statute creates an individually enforceable right in the class of beneficiaries to which [plaintiff] belongs." *City of Rancho Palos Verdes v. Abrams*, 544 U.S. 113, 120 (2005).

In 1984, the Supreme Court found that plaintiffs under the EHA did not retain the option of pursuing remedies available through either § 1983 or § 504 of the Rehabilitation Act. *Smith*, 468 U.S. at 1009-20. In response to this case, Congress enacted amendments in 1986 specifying that the statute should not be construed to restrict or limit the rights, procedures, and remedies available under the Constitution or federal statutes. 20 U.S.C. § 1415(l).

In 2005, in considering a case brought under the Telecommunications Act of 1996, the Supreme Court concluded that § 1983 remedies were not available to plaintiffs enforcing a statute in which Congress expressly included a means of separate redress and provided no indication that it intended to allow for other remedies beyond those enumerated in the statute. 42 U.S. § 1983; *see City of Rancho Palos Verdes*, 544 U.S. at 127. The Court noted that "[t]he provision of an express, private means of redress in [a] statute itself is ordinarily an indication that Congress did not intend to leave open a more expansive remedy under § 1983." *Id.* at 121. This implication can "be overcome by textual indication, express or implicit, that the remedy is to complement, rather than supplant, § 1983." *Id.* at 122. Following the Supreme Court's decision in *City of Rancho Palos Verdes*, all of the federal courts that have considered the issue have applied this ruling to the IDEA and concluded that § 1983 remedies are not available in IDEA actions. *See, e.g., A.W. v. Jersey City Pub. Sch.*, 486 F.3d 791, 803 (3d Cir. 2007); *Blanchard v. Morton Sch. Dist.*, 509 F.3d 934, 936 (9th Cir. 2007); *Long v. Dawson Springs Indep. Sch. Dist.*, 197 Fed. App'x. 427, 432 (6th Cir. 2006).

XIV.   SECURING SERVICES AND ACCOMMODATIONS THROUGH ALTERNATIVE ENTITLEMENTS

A.   Vocational Rehabilitation Services

Transition plans must be included in IEPs for students who are sixteen and older to prepare them for life after they complete school. Transition plans include the postsecondary goals for the student, such as "training, education, employment, and, where appropriate, independent living skills," and the means for reaching these goals. 20 U.S.C. § 1414(d)(1)(A)(i)(VIII). Vocational rehabilitation services can serve as a key component of a student's transition plan. A state's vocational rehabilitation services agency can take part in an IEP meeting in which a transition plan is developed and serve as a resource.

If a state opts to receive federal funding for vocational rehabilitation services, these services constitute a separate entitlement administered through a vocational rehabilitation services agency separate from the educational agency. 34 C.F.R. § 385.1(b). Vocational rehabilitation services are therefore also available to students who do not qualify for special education, provided the appropriate eligibility requirements are satisfied. Moreover, vocational rehabilitation services are available for students who have aged out of special education, and can provide critical support for these young adults. Vocational rehabilitation services agencies can work with school districts to provide a seamless transition of services once the student leaves the school and can remain available to the individual, without age restriction, as long as he or she meets the relevant eligibility criteria. An individual is eligible if he or she has "a physical or mental impairment, which for that individual constitutes or results in a substantial impediment to employment" so long as the individual can benefit from the rehabilitation services. 34 C.F.R. § 385.4(b) (definition of an individual with a disability).

Vocational rehabilitation services include "any services described in an individualized plan for employment necessary to assist an individual with a disability in preparing for, securing, retaining, or regaining an employment outcome that is consistent with" their goals. 29 U.S.C. § 723(a). The available services include counseling, job search assistance, vocational training, and rehabilitation technology. 29 U.S.C. § 723(a).

B. § 504 of the Rehabilitation Act of 1973 and the Americans with Disabilities Act

Because the IDEA only provides remedies for students who qualify to receive special education, attorneys often turn to the Rehabilitation Act ("RA") and the Americans with Disabilities Act ("ADA") to mitigate other barriers for students with disabilities. The RA and the ADA provide a means of resolution for denials of accommodations that fall outside of the IDEA, such as inaccessible school facilities. The statutes and regulations for both the RA and the ADA are now explicit as to who qualifies as a person with a disability and what constitutes discrimination against that person.

The RA provides that schools that receive federal financial assistance may not discriminate against a student with disabilities on the basis of his or her disability. 29 U.S.C. § 794(a)-(b)(2)(B). The Code of Federal Regulations defines discrimination under the RA to include the denial of equal benefits or services provided to others, the provision of separate benefits or services students for students with disabilities when the separation is not necessary to provide equally effective benefits or services, the aid or perpetuation of discrimination against students with disabilities, and any other limitation to a person with a disability in the enjoyment of opportunities given to students without disabilities. 34 C.F.R. § 104.4(b)(1).

The ADA provides that "no qualified individual with a disability shall, by reason of such disability, be excluded from participation in or be denied the benefits of the services, programs, or activities of a public entity, or be subjected to discrimination by any such entity." 42 U.S.C. § 12132. Furthermore, "no individual shall be discriminated against on the basis of disability in the full and equal enjoyment of the goods, services, facilities, privileges, advantages, or accommodations of any place of public accommodation by any person who owns, leases (or leases to), or operates a place of public accommodation." 42 U.S.C. § 12182(a). The definitions section for this part of the code clarifies that "places of public accommodation" includes private schools. 42 U.S.C. § 12181(7)(J). The 2008 amendments clarified the definition of the word "disability" in both the RA and the ADA:

As used in this Act:

(1) DISABILITY. — The term "disability" means, with respect to an individual —

(A) a physical or mental impairment that substantially limits one or more major life activities of such individual;

(B) a record of such an impairment; or

(C) being regarded as having such an impairment (as described in paragraph (3)).

(2) MAJOR LIFE ACTIVITIES. —

(A) IN GENERAL. — For purposes of paragraph (1), major life activities include, but are not limited to, caring for oneself, performing manual tasks, seeing, hearing, eating, sleeping, walking, standing, lifting, bending, speaking, breathing, learning, reading, concentrating, thinking, communicating, and working.

(B) MAJOR BODILY FUNCTIONS. — For purposes of paragraph (1), a major life activity also includes the operation of a major bodily function, including but not limited to, functions of the immune system, normal cell growth, digestive, bowel, bladder, neurological, brain, respiratory, circulatory, endocrine, and reproductive functions.

ADA Amendments Act of 2008, Pub. L. No. 110-325, 122 Stat. 3555 (2008) (codified as amended at 42 U.S.C. § 12102(1)-(2)).. Congress purposely made this definition more inclusive than its prior version, stating explicitly in committee reports that the purpose of the bill was to overturn the Supreme Court's restrictive and narrow interpretation of the definition of "disability" and restore protection for a broader range of individuals with disabilities. H.R. Rep. No. 110-730, at 6-7 (2008).

The RA and the ADA cover many students who are eligible for special education services, as well as many students with disabilities who are not found eligible for special education under the IDEA. In general, students are covered by the RA and the ADA if they face discrimination on the basis of an actual or perceived physical or mental disability that substantially limits a person's major life activities. 42 U.S.C. § 12102. Both the RA and the ADA cover discrimination in both public and private schools. 29 U.S.C. § 794 (RA); 42 U.S.C. § 12181(7) (ADA for private schools); 42 U.S.C. § 12132 (ADA for public schools).

The IDEA now explicitly provides that remedies available under the ADA and RA, as well as the Constitution, are not restricted or limited by the IDEA, so long as administrative due process procedures under the IDEA are exhausted before a civil action is brought if the relief sought can be obtained through an IDEA action. 20 U.S.C. § 1415(l). Both the RA and the ADA require that schools provide reasonable accommodations for children with disabilities to protect them from discrimination, unless it would fundamentally alter the services being offered. 42 U.S.C. § 12182(b)(2)(A)(ii) (ADA); 34 C.F.R. § 104.12 (RA). However, the ADA does not require reasonable accommodations for children who are discriminated against only because they are regarded as having a disability that they do not in fact have. 42 U.S.C. § 12201(h).

Both statutes also require that school facilities be made accessible to people with disabilities. 42 U.S.C. § 12182(b)(2)(A)(iv) (ADA); 34 C.F.R. § 104.22 (RA). As part of this requirement, schools must also ensure that any new facilities constructed are accessible to people with disabilities. 42 U.S.C. § 12182(b)(2)(A)(iv) (ADA); 34 C.F.R. § 104.23 (RA). These requirements are not included as part of the IDEA.

Forms of relief that may be available under the RA and the ADA include monetary damages (compensatory and punitive), injunctions, attorneys' fees, and costs. Laura Rothstein & Scott F. Johnson, Special Education Law 296 (4th ed. 2010). Schools can meet the needs of students with disabilities under the RA by creating a Section 504 plan that states why the student is eligible for accommodation and what accommodations will be provided.

Attorneys should consider seeking a Section 504 plan for a student with disabilities who does not qualify for special education, but needs accommodations or even services in school. If an attorney is preparing to file a civil action, he or she should consider whether there are claims under the ADA or RA that might be brought in addition to any IDEA claims.

Furthermore, the Department of Education Office for Civil Rights regulates the RA as it applies to schools and the ADA as it applies to public schools. 34 C.F.R. § 104.6 (RA); 28 C.F.R. §§ 35.101 *et seq.* (ADA). Though the Office for Civil Rights does not enforce the Individuals with Disabilities Education Act, many complaints related to systemic failures under the IDEA may be brought to the Office for Civil Rights under the RA. When there is a violation, a complaint may be filed with the Office for Civil Rights on the website www.ed.gov/ocr, but it must be filed within 180 days of the violation. The complaint may be filed by anyone with knowledge of the violation. There is no sanction for submitting a complaint to the Office for Civil Rights over which it does not have jurisdiction. The correct regional office will then investigate the complaint to determine whether a violation has occurred. At the conclusion of the investigation, the Office for Civil Rights will inform both parties of any violations. As a result of any infractions, the school could be stripped of its federal funding if it does not correct any violations, but this rarely happens. The Office for Civil Rights may also refer the case to the Department of Justice for investigation. www.ed.gov/ocr.

C.   Medicaid and EPSDT

The Early and Periodic Screening, Diagnosis and Treatment (EPSDT) mandate may provide an alternative source for securing services and equipment that a child requires. Children who are under twenty-one years old and who meet the income requirements for Medicaid are entitled to EPSDT services. These children are entitled to any medically "necessary health care, diagnostic services, treatment, and other measures . . . to correct or ameliorate defects and physical and mental illnesses and conditions discovered by the screening services." 42 U.S.C. § 1396d(r)(5). Courts have interpreted "medically necessary" very broadly, as prescribed by the EPSDT section of the code, to include everything listed in the Medicaid definition of "medical assistance," 42 U.S.C. § 1396d(a), which includes most care prescribed by a physician or medical professional. *Id.*

The EPSDT directive is limited to Medicaid recipients under the age of twenty-one. 42 U.S.C. § 1396d(4)(B). States may further limit this age maximum to twenty, nineteen, or eighteen. 42 U.S.C. § 1396d(a)(i). In general, only U.S. citizens are entitled to EPSDT benefits. 8 U.S.C. § 161. However there are some exceptions for qualified aliens. 8 U.S.C. §§ 1612(a)(2)(A)-(B), 1611(b)(1)(A)-(C).

Each state's plan creates the income eligibility requirements, but they must meet minimum federal standards. U.S. Department of Health and Human Services Centers for Medicare and Medicaid Services, *Medicaid Eligibility: Overview*, available at https://www.cms.gov/MedicaidEligibility/. For children ages one to five years old, the statute requires states to cover individuals whose family "income level . . . is equal to 133 percent of the income poverty level . . . applicable to a family of the size involved." 42 U.S.C. § 1396a(l)(2)(B). For children ages six to eighteen years old, the statute requires states to cover individuals whose family "income level . . . is equal to 100 percent of the income poverty level . . . applicable to a family of the size involved." 42 U.S.C. § 1396a(l)(2)(C). The Office of Management and Budget revises the income poverty level annually. 42 U.S.C. § 1396a(l)(2)(A)(i). Note that as a result of the major healthcare reform legislation passed in March 2010, as of 2014, Medicaid eligibility will be expanded to all individuals, regardless of age, whose income does not exceed 133 percent of the poverty line, meaning that more children ages six to eighteen will become eligible for EPSDT services at that time. Patient Protection and Affordable Care Act, Pub. L. No. 111-148, 124 Stat. 271, 271 (2010) (amending 42 U.S.C. § 1396a(a)(10)(A)(ii)(VII)).

Medicaid provides for "payment of part or all of the cost of the . . . care and services." 42 U.S.C. § 1396d(a). Services covered under EPSDT include screening, vision, dental, hearing, and other necessary medical assistance. 42 U.S.C. § 1396d(r). This coverage is specifically available for medically "necessary health care, diagnostic services, treatment, and other measures . . . to correct or ameliorate the defects and physical and mental illnesses and conditions discovered by the screening services." 42 U.S.C. § 1396d(r)(5). As a result of this language, the EPSDT mandate is known in shorthand as coverage of those services that are "medically necessary."

States must provide EPSDT recipients with regularly scheduled examinations and evaluations of the general physical and mental health, growth, development, and nutritional status of infants, children, and youth upon request by the recipient. 42 C.F.R. § 441.56(b). These screenings, provided at regular intervals determined by the state and whenever medically necessary, include:

(i) a comprehensive health and developmental history (including assessment of both physical and mental health development),

(ii) a comprehensive unclothed physical exam,

(iii) appropriate immunizations . . . according to age and health history,

(iv) laboratory tests (including lead blood level assessment appropriate for age and risk factors), and

(v) health education (including anticipatory guidance).

42 U.S.C. § 1396d(r)(1)(B). The results of an EPSDT screening can provide information that can be useful not only in securing diagnostic and treatment services and equipment through Medicaid or managed care organizations with which a Medicaid state agency contracts to carry out its EPSDT mandate, but also in securing special education services from a school. An attorney handling a special education matter may want to request all medical records from a child's physician and other health care providers, including any physicals or other screening exams that were carried out pursuant to EPSDT requirements. These records might provide diagnoses or treatment recommendations and therefore could serve as useful advocacy tools in the special education process.

The Code of Federal Regulations is specific in requiring diagnosis of and treatment for defects in vision and hearing, including eyeglasses and hearing aids, dental care needed for relief of pain and infections, restoration of teeth and maintenance of dental care, and appropriate immunizations. 42 C.F.R. § 441.56(c). However, both the U.S. Code and Code of

Federal Regulations are much less explicit on all other issues requiring care. The U.S. Code provides that the services covered by EPSDT include "[s]uch other necessary health care, diagnostic services, treatment, and other measures . . . to correct or ameliorate defects and physical and mental illnesses and conditions discovered by the screening services, whether or not such services are covered under the State plan." 42 U.S.C. § 1396d(r)(5). Courts have interpreted "medically necessary" very broadly, as prescribed by the EPSDT section of the code, to include everything listed in the Medicaid definition of "Medical assistance," which includes most physician or medical professional prescribed care. 42 U.S.C. § 1396d(a); *see, e.g., Collins v. Hamilton*, 349 F.3d 371, 374 (7th Cir. 2003); *Pittman by Pope v. Sec'y, Fla. Dep't of Health & Rehab. Servs.*, 998 F.2d 887, 891-92 (11th Cir. 1993) ("The language of § 1396d(r)(5) expressly requires Medicaid participating states to provide necessary treatment 'to correct or ameliorate defects and physical . . . illnesses and conditions discovered by the screening services, *whether or not such services are covered under the State plan.*' "); *Pediatric Specialty Care, Inc. v. Ark. Dep't of Human Services*, 293 F.3d 472, 480 (8th Cir. 2002) ("The State Plan, however, must pay part or all of the cost of treatments to ameliorate conditions discovered by the screening process when those treatments meet the definitions set forth in § 1396a.").

The services relevant to children include services furnished directly by a physician, inpatient hospital services, inpatient psychiatric hospital services, services in an intermediate care facility for individuals with intellectual disabilities, outpatient hospital services, laboratory and X-ray services, family planning services and supplies, dental services including medical and surgical services furnished by a dentist, home health care services, private duty nursing services, clinic services furnished by or under the direction of a physician, physical therapy and related services, prescribed drugs, dentures, prosthetic devices, eyeglasses, services furnished by a nurse-midwife, hospice care, case management services, TB-related services, respiratory care services, services furnished by a certified pediatric nurse practitioner or certified nurse practitioner, community supported living arrangements, personal care services that are authorized by a physician as part of a treatment plan (or, if required by the state, a plan authorized by the state) and performed by a non-family member in a non-medical location such as the individual's home, medical care, or any other type of remedial care by licensed practitioners, as well as other diagnostic, screening, preventative and rehabilitative services. This includes any medical or remedial services (provided in a facility, a home, or other setting) recommended by a physician or other licensed practitioner of the healing arts within the scope of their practice under state law, for the maximum reduction of physical or mental disability and restoration of an individual to the best possible functional level, and any other medical care recognized under state law. 42 U.S.C. § 1396d(a); *see Parents' League for Effective Autism Serv. v. Jones-Kelley*, 339 Fed. App'x 542, 549 (6th Cir. 2009) ("It is true that this provision can be read to mandate only services recommended by a physician that provide *both* a 'maximum reduction of physical or mental disability and restoration of an individual to the best possible functional level.' However, this provision can also be read to mandate *both* services recommended by a physician 'for the maximum reduction of physical or mental disability,' and services recommended by a physician for the 'restoration of an individual to the best possible functional level.' "). The Department of Health and Human Services Centers for Medicaid and Medicare Services' State Medicaid Manual more explicitly describes the services provided through EPSDT. Medicaid State Manual, http://www.hrsa.gov/epsdt/overview.htm#1 (follow "Medicaid State Manual Part 5 EPSDT" hyperlink).

The provision of "home health care services," which can greatly assist some children with disabilities, can potentially include medical supplies for the home. *See S.D. v. Hood*, 391 F.3d

581, 595 (5th Cir. 2004) ("[T]he agency's interpretation of 'home health care services' as referenced at § 1396d(a)(7), including 'medical supplies,' when used under the circumstances specified in its regulation, is clearly a permissible statutory construction."), *aff'g* No. 02-2164, 2002 U.S. Dist. LEXIS 23535 (E.D. La. 2002). One U.S. District Court found that EPSDT's mandate that "home health care services" be made available means that states must offer service alternatives to those provided by the educational agency for any services that overlap both special education requirements and EPSDT requirements. *Chisholm v. Hood*, 110 F. Supp. 2d 499, 506 (E.D. La. 2000), *aff'd*, 133 F. Supp. 2d 894 (E.D. La. 2001). When the state agency provides EPSDT services only through school districts, it violates EPSDT by not providing a home service option for those who need it and by failing to provide a requisite variety in service providers to give consumers a choice. *Chisholm*, 110 F. Supp. 2d at 506, *findings of fact/conclusions of law at* 133 F. Supp. 2d 894 (E.D. La. 2001).

Recently, a class action entitled *Rosie D. v. Romney* was brought against Massachusetts officials and agencies by all Medicaid-eligible children in the state with a serious emotional disturbance not receiving their entitled "intensive home-based services." *Rosie D. v. Romney*, 410 F. Supp. 2d 18, 22 (D. Mass. 2006), *rev'g* 256 F. Supp. 2d 115 (D. Mass. 2003), *rev'd*, 474 F. Supp. 2d 238 (D. Mass. 2007). The Plaintiffs claimed that Massachusetts violated EPSDT by not providing services to children suffering from "serious emotional disturbances such as autism, bi-polar disorder, or post-traumatic stress disorder." *Id.* The District Court found the State's Medicaid plan out of compliance with EPSDT. *Id.* at 23.

The court found that the state did not provide the proper assessments or services for children with emotional disturbances. *Id.* Both of these problems stemmed from the lack of any single state entity authorized to oversee the program. The court found this authority necessary to "(a) identify promptly a child suffering from a serious emotional disturbance, (b) assess comprehensively the nature of the child's disability, (c) develop an overarching treatment plan for the child, and (d) oversee implementation of this plan . . . ." *Id.* Without an entity to take these steps, the court found that the state could not meet the EPSDT requirement that children with serious emotional disturbance be provided with "reasonably comprehensive medical assessments and ongoing clinical oversight of the services being provided." *Id.*

The court also found that the state did not provide appropriate in-home behavioral services for children with emotional disturbances. *Id.* By failing to provide these services, the state forced many of these children to live in residential treatment facilities, which are known to exacerbate these symptoms. *Id.* at 23-24. The court found in-home services options medically necessary in addition to residential treatment services for children with serious emotional disturbances. The lack of this medically necessary option violates EPSDT. As a result of this decision, the court created a remedial plan. *Rosie D. v. Romney*, 474 F. Supp. 2d 238 (D. Mass. 2007). The *Rosie D.* case highlights the fact that states are not always in compliance with EPSDT requirements, and serves as a reminder of the strong entitlements that EPSDT provides to eligible children.

With its broad mandate that Medicaid-eligible children be provided with any "medically necessary" services, EPSDT can be a useful tool for attorneys who represent families with children with disabilities. If a qualified physician or other health practitioner asserts that a service or type of equipment is medically necessary for a child, pursuant to EPSDT, the Medicaid agency must ensure that the service or equipment is provided. EPSDT services can supplement special education services received during the school day in providing appropriate screening, diagnosis and treatment outside of school. Additionally, diagnosis information and treatment recommendations provided by health and mental health care providers pursuant to EPSDT can be useful for an attorney or parent in advocating for special education services. For children who do not qualify for special education services, EPSDT provides an alternative opportunity for Medicaid-eligible children to secure needed services.

D. Supplemental Security Income

Supplemental Security Income ("SSI") can provide extra money each month to a parent of a child with a disability to assist in the care of that child, and can be used, if a parent chooses, to purchase services or equipment the child needs for which the parent cannot secure funding elsewhere. SSI is available to eligible U.S. citizens of any age who are "disabled" under the relevant definition and have limited income and resources. 42 U.S.C. § 1382. The Social Security Act defines a person with a disability differently for individuals under eighteen. 20 C.F.R. § 416.924. The disability determination for a child is based on an evaluation of each individual disability to medically determine if any are severe. If the disability is not deemed severe, then it is not covered under SSI. *Id.* The considerations in determining whether a child is disabled under SSI include: 1) all relevant information from medical and nonmedical sources and 2) factors to determine the effects of the impairment on functioning such as the symptoms from the impairment, the effects of the impairment on activities other children can accomplish at that age, the multiplied effects from all of the child's impairments, and the effect of the impairment on the child's ability to "initiate, sustain, and complete an activity." 20 C.F.R. § 416.924a. A Listing of Impairments in the Code indicates the impairments that are considered severe, and those not on the list can still be deemed medically equal to those on the list and therefore severe under the Code. 20 C.F.R. § 416.925(a). The child's receipt of special education or lack thereof does not determine whether the child's disability is covered under SSI. 20 C.F.R. § 416.924a(b)(7)(iv).

The list includes impairments in a child's growth, musculoskeletal system, special senses and speech, respiratory system, cardiovascular system, and digestive system, as well as genitourinary impairments, hematological disorders, skin disorders, endocrine system, impairments that affect multiple body systems, neurological disorders, mental disorders, malignant neoplastic diseases, and immune system disorders. List of Impairments — Childhood Listing (Part B), available at

http://www.ssa.gov/disability/professionals/bluebook/ChildhoodListings.htm

Within each of these broad categories are specific impairments that are covered by SSI.

Children determined to have a disability under SSI are eligible for the benefit so long as they earn no more income than $1,752. 42 U.S.C. § 1382(b)(1). The Code of Federal Regulations specifies that the child's income is determined by subtracting from the parents' monthly income deductions for other children and for the parents. The leftover income is deemed to be the child's monthly income and is subtracted from the federal benefit rate to determine the benefit of that child. 20 C.F.R. § 416.1165. The child's total income and resources, along with the parents' holdings, can either disqualify the child from receiving SSI or decrease the benefit received under SSI. Social Security Administration, *SSI Eligibility Requirements*, available at http://www.ssa.gov/ssi/text-eligibility-ussi.htm. For more information on the calculation of benefits, see § 42 U.S.C. §§ 1382b(a)(1), (2), (6)–(10), (12)-(15), 1382(a)(3)(B); 20 C.F.R. §§ 416.1165(i)(3), 416.415, 416.1207.

Children found to have a disability under SSI may receive benefits from the state in addition to those provided by the federal government. 20 C.F.R. § 416.2001. The government does not monitor how the child spends the benefits, but investigations are conducted periodically to determine whether the child is still eligible for the benefit. 20 C.F.R. § 416.110(c). If the child is no longer following the prescribed treatment to improve the impairment, the child will no longer be eligible for the SSI payments. 20 C.F.R. § 416.994a(f)(4).

Most of the time, payments for children will go to a representative payee, who is usually a parent. 20 C.F.R. § 416.610(b). If the child should have received benefits from an earlier date, past-due benefits might be owed by the Social Security Administration (SSA) to the child. If the child is entitled to past-due benefits that exceed six times the benefit rate, these benefits must be paid into a dedicated account specifically for these funds. 20 C.F.R. § 416.546. Dedicated account funds may only go to medical treatment, personal needs assistance, special equipment, housing modification, therapy, rehabilitation, and other items and services related to the child's impairment and determined appropriate by the government. 20 C.F.R. § 416.640(e)(2). These funds may also go toward education or job skills training. *Id.* The representative payee must submit written records and receipts accounting for the benefits if requested by the government. 20 C.F.R. § 416.635(e). The benefits must be used by the representative payee for the costs of current maintenance of the beneficiary child, which includes food, shelter, clothing, medical care, and personal comfort. 20 C.F.R. § 416.640(a).

The child's qualifying status as "disabled" will be reevaluated periodically to determine whether the payments are still appropriate. 20 C.F.R. § 416.994a(a). At the time of this review, the representative payee must provide proof that the child received the medically necessary and available treatment as prescribed. 20 C.F.R. § 416.994a(i).

An attorney representing a parent or child in a special education matter can assist in helping the child apply for SSI benefits. A strong SSI application will include documentation of the child's disability, some of which might be found in a child's special education records. For example, a psychological evaluation completed through the special education process or an IEP might provide the information that the SSA needs in order to determine that a child does in fact meet the criteria as "disabled." The attorney may also decide to include a letter to the Social Security Administration with the application asserting that the child meets the criteria for SSI with supporting information, and explaining the documentation included in the application. An attorney may also choose to assist a family in appealing a denial, reduction, or termination of a child's SSI benefits.

The documentation provided through the SSI process can also, in turn, be useful in the special education process. Sometimes SSA requires that a child be evaluated by a doctor affiliated with SSA prior to the agency making a determination about eligibility. The report produced by the evaluating doctor may provide information that would be useful to an attorney in his or her special education advocacy, and could be submitted to an IEP team for consideration or submitted as evidence in a due process hearing.

The various programs and entitlements described above provide an avenue for a child with disabilities who does not qualify for special education to receive services, supports, additional income, accommodations, and equipment. For children who are eligible for special education, they also provide additional resources to supplement a child's IEP and provide services outside of the school day. Claims for relief related to these other areas of law may be brought through separate administrative actions or, where, applicable, as additional claims in federal court for attorneys filing a civil action pursuant to the IDEA.

Consider the following hypothetical regarding a child who is eligible for Medicaid:

Calvin

Calvin was injured in an accident, which resulted in him becoming paraplegic. He is dependent on a wheelchair for his mobility. Calvin is successful in school, but he has expressed frustration to his parents because his locker is located too high for him to reach and he does not have a way to carry his books around school. He has to ask another student for help to get things in and out of his locker, and for help carrying his books from class to class. His wheelchair is broken and his pediatrician determined that he requires a new wheelchair. Calvin's Medicaid managed care health insurance provider received the pediatrician's recommendation, but has not provided Calvin with a new wheelchair.

Calvin's mother comes to you for your legal assistance. What are your options for helping Calvin?

XV. ASSISTING CLIENTS AFTER THE REMEDY IS ORDERED

The IDEA, regulations, and interpreting case law provide for a wide breadth of remedies to protect and enforce a child's right to a free appropriate public education. A special education attorney can play a key role in helping a parent and child to think creatively about available remedies and in zealously pursuing the remedies chosen by the client. An attorney can also help a family explore supplementary programs and entitlements for a child receiving special education services, or help a child for whom special education is not an option pursue other sources to secure services, supports, accommodations, and equipment.

After an attorney helps a client secure a desired remedy, the attorney's job is not complete. Remedies ordered by a hearing officer or court, or negotiated at an IEP meeting or through a settlement agreement, may not be implemented with the necessary speed or may not be implemented at all. An attorney's diligence in making certain that a remedy is in fact implemented can make all of the difference in ensuring that the relief is actually provided to the parent and child.

Moreover, a parent's job in advocating for his or her child does not end when the case is over. The parent will have another annual IEP meeting the following year and each year that the child remains eligible for special education, and other concerns about the appropriateness of the child's education may arise. Counsel can help prepare the parent and child to become stronger self-advocates in the future, and make sure that they are armed with the necessary information. For example, if the attorney has engaged the parent throughout the case, walking the parent through the steps of the special education process and counseling her extensively on her rights under the IDEA, that parent will be better prepared for future self-advocacy. Moreover, at the time that the client and attorney are closing the case, the attorney can take the time to discuss any red flags for which the parent should vigilantly watch and ensure that the parent understands what to do if he or she disagrees with any changes proposed by the school. Certain situations may be resolvable by the parent herself, while, at other times, the parent may decide to refuse to sign an IEP or express explicit disagreement with a school district's action and call the attorney again for assistance. If the child is able to benefit from similar engagement and counseling, the attorney should also help prepare the child for improved self-advocacy throughout the case and at the time of case closure.

An effective attorney will work collaboratively with a parent and child throughout the life of a case to make sure that they have the information they need to protect their rights in the future. Before the attorney-client relationship formally ends, an effective attorney will ensure that the parent and child are empowered to advocate for themselves as successfully as possible going forward.

Chapter 11

SPECIAL EDUCATION ADVOCACY FOR YOUTH IN THE DELINQUENCY SYSTEM[1]

The principal objective of a young person facing delinquency charges is almost always, obviously, to avoid prosecution, to defeat the charges, or otherwise to elude punitive measures like pre-trial detention and post-adjudication incarceration. In representing clients in delinquency cases, lawyers and law students may be able to use special education services to shield clients from incarceration or other punitive delinquency sanctions. More broadly, lawyers and law students often can use special education rights to delay or derail delinquency adjudication, or use special education rights to extricate clients from the delinquency system altogether. Further, special education rights, and disability rights generally, may provide opportunities to develop delinquency defenses and procedural arguments that would otherwise not be available. This Chapter explores how to recognize and develop these legal arguments and problem-solving opportunities.

The Chapter starts, in Section I, with a critique of the delinquency system. This critique contains reasons for lawyers and law students representing delinquency clients to circumvent the delinquency system and to rely instead upon the special education system. Section II analyzes connections between the delinquency and special education systems and compares the two systems. The partial overlap of delinquency and special education suggests two major strategies. The first major strategy is substituting the individualized and comprehensive services available through the special education system for the limited and often counterproductive sanctions in the delinquency system. The second major strategy is identifying improper unilateral exclusions from school of children with disabilities and using delinquency intake procedures to stop improper and unnecessary delinquency referrals. Section III presents the stages of a delinquency case, highlighting some ways that the delinquency defense attorney or law student can use special education rights to advance the delinquency client's objectives.

I. A CRITIQUE OF THE DELINQUENCY SYSTEM

Since the creation of the first juvenile court in 1899, the delinquency system's premise has been that children are different and less culpable than adults, and the promise has been that children will have access to treatment. *E.g., In re Gault*, 387 U.S. 1, 14-18 (1967). The Supreme Court recognized in *Gault*, however, that the reality of the juvenile court did not comport with the promise. Juvenile courts historically delivered "the worst of both worlds" — a lack of procedural protections for the child and little, if any, treatment in return. *Id.* at 17-27. Accordingly, the Court in *Gault* required that children facing delinquency charges receive the basic array of due process and criminal procedural protections. The Court reasoned that

---

[1] This chapter was written by Joseph B. Tulman, Professor of Law, D.C. Law School, and Director of the Took Crowell Institute for At-Risk Youth. Professor Tulman directs the law school's Juvenile and Special Education Law Clinic.

providing procedural protections is consistent with maintaining confidentiality regarding a child's delinquency involvement and with other efforts to protect the child. *Id.* After *Gault*, the Court ruled that delinquency adjudications require proof beyond a reasonable doubt, *In re Winship*, 397 U.S. 358 (1970), and that children do not have a right to a trial by jury, *McKeiver v. Pennsylvania*, 403 U.S. 528 (1971).

The Court in *Gault* rejected the rationale that, rather than a liberty interest, a child has a right to be in the custody either of a parent or of the state, both of which are, in a sense, interchangeable and benevolent. *Id.* at 17-18. Ironically, however, a less-enlightened majority of the Court, seventeen years later, significantly backtracked, reasoning that a "juvenile's countervailing interest in freedom from institutional restraints, even for the brief time involved here, is undoubtedly substantial as well. But that interest must be qualified by the recognition that juveniles, unlike adults, are always in some form of custody." *Schall v. Martin*, 467 U.S. 253, 265 (1984) (internal citations omitted).

Children in America, and particularly children from low-income families, generally receive inadequate legal representation when facing delinquency charges. In some jurisdictions, children commonly waive their right to counsel. Court-appointed defense attorneys typically have unmanageably large caseloads. Defense attorneys in many jurisdictions handle four hundred or more delinquency cases each year. Defense attorneys lack sufficient training, and often they do not have access to investigators, social workers, and expert witnesses (including experts to conduct evaluations of the children facing charges). *See generally* A Call for Justice: An Assessment of Access to Counsel and Quality of Representation in Delinquency Proceedings 3-12, 19-27 (A.B.A. Juvenile Justice Center 1995); *see also* National Juvenile Defender Center Web site, http://www.njdc.info/assessments.php (NJDC state-by-state assessments of quantity and quality of indigent juvenile defense).

In a delinquency system that has too many children and too few defense attorneys, the result is a devaluing and diminution of procedural and substantive rights. In many jurisdictions, the delinquency court lacks true indicia of an adversarial system. Rather, defense attorneys do little or no investigation, do not conduct research, do not file pre-trial motions, and do not prepare for trial or disposition. Shockingly, in some jurisdictions, defense attorneys for children from low-income and indigent families routinely fail to interview their clients until the day of trial. Further, in many jurisdictions, defense attorneys do not engage proactively in post-disposition advocacy. Although an attorney may be assigned to represent an indigent child who is facing probation or parole (aftercare) revocation, typically no one is helping children to challenge problems like the lack of meaningful probation services or the squalid conditions at a juvenile incarceration facility. Correspondingly, probation officers, prosecutors, and judges function as administrators of an over-burdened bureaucracy rather than as professionals applying legal standards and exercising discretion in regard to well-developed and well-presented factual-legal disputes. Delinquency courts in many jurisdictions function essentially as conveyor belts for moving plea bargains rather than as deliberative adjudicatory bodies. *See generally, e.g.,* A Call for Justice, *supra; cf. generally, e.g.,* Amy Bach, Ordinary Injustice: How America Holds Court (2009); Steve Bogira, Courtroom 302: A Year Behind the Scenes in an American Criminal Courthouse (2005) (books by journalists documenting the mass production model of injustice that is typical for low-income defendants in America's criminal courts).

In this environment, defense attorneys rarely develop legal challenges based upon claims of racial or class-based discrimination. The courts are hostile to such claims. *See, e.g., McCleskey v. Kemp*, 481 U.S. 279 (1987) (study showing Georgia juries more likely to impose death penalty on black defendant who murders white victim than on white defendant who murders black victim does not establish discriminatory result with regard to the particular jury for purposes of equal protection challenge).

From the perspective of an individual child facing delinquency charges, the system is likely to appear non-responsive or hostile. For a child who has endured abuse and neglect, a series of truncated encounters with probation officers, prosecutors, and judges may fit a familiar pattern. Adult authority figures are threatening and abusive. Consider, for example, a scene in which a delinquency judge proposes to use incarceration as a consequence if the child fails to comply with conditions of release. The child may interpret that proposed consequence as a threat or a challenge. In essence, the judge's entreaties to behave "or else" (i.e., the judge's threat of impending incarceration) may feel to the child like emotional abuse and may seem to the child to be a precursor to physical abuse.

A child diagnosed with oppositional defiant disorder is likely to experience this kind of interaction with a judge — who is literally sitting above the child in the courtroom — as a contest of wills and as a familiar invitation to fight with the often-abusive and unpredictable authority figure. A child with a detachment disorder might liken the judge to threatening and abusive adult authority figures with whom the child has interacted over a period of years. The result will be an inability of the child to trust the judge and to interpret accurately and productively the judge's intended message. Similarly, a child who has experienced significant trauma and who may have a diagnosis of post-traumatic stress disorder likely will not effectively process the judge's message. More typically, children with these and similar problems will withdraw altogether from the interaction with the judge.

Indeed, in review, one may accurately describe communication from the judge to the child as sporadic, authoritarian, insensitive, and, literally, threatening. *Cf., e.g., In re Gault*, 387 U.S. 1, 27 (1967) (citing a study by sociologists, concluding that "when the procedural laxness of the 'parens patriae' attitude is followed by stern disciplining, the contrast may have an adverse effect upon the child, who feels that he has been deceived or enticed"). A hyper-vigilant child will likely react instinctively with a "fight-or-flight" response. A child with the kinds of vulnerabilities described above typically requires consistent and predictable relationships with nurturing adults. In special education terms, the child may need behavioral supports, behavioral management, counseling (including family counseling), parent training (for the child's parents), therapeutic recreation, and other related services.

A child in the delinquency system will likely encounter the opposite of consistent and predictable relationships with nurturing adults. In many jurisdictions, for example, the work of the juvenile probation office is organized into three separate functions: intake; diagnostic; and supervision. A different probation officer is responsible for each of the three functions. An intake probation officer handles a number of intake investigations each day and moves to another set of intakes the next day. For each child arrested and "booked" by the police, the intake worker does a brief investigation regarding the prior delinquency record (if any) of the child, the nature and circumstances of the pending charge, the child's adjustment at school and in the community, and the family's ability to control and care for the child. Based upon this review, the intake worker assesses the child's dangerousness and the risk that, if released, the child will not appear for future court hearings.

As part of the intake process, the intake probation officer interviews the child. The intake probation officer typically seeks to gain the child's trust and to convince the child to discuss his or her adjustment at home, in school, with friends, and in the community generally. The child might then discover that the intake probation officer has used sensitive information — e.g., my mother is often out late at night and she drinks alcohol — to support a recommendation to remove the child from the home pending trial. Thus, from the child's perspective, a brief interaction with an adult has resulted in a misuse of sensitive information. It is a betrayal of trust.

If the child subsequently pleads guilty or is found guilty in a trial, a different probation officer — a diagnostic probation officer — spends a period of perhaps one to six weeks doing a more exacting investigation regarding the child's circumstances. In many jurisdictions, the parties waive preparation of a diagnostic, pre-disposition report and go immediately to disposition. This waiving of the report is particularly likely with regard to non-serious and non-violent offenses in circumstances in which the prosecutor is not seeking incarceration.

In preparing a pre-disposition report for the judge to consider, this probation officer reviews evaluations and other documents concerning the child. The diagnostic probation officer also interviews the child, the parents, and other people who are involved with the child. The scenario from intake repeats: The diagnostic probation officer encourages the child to reveal and discuss sensitive information. That information then appears in the pre-disposition report to the judge, sometimes as part of a justification for committing the child for out-of-home placement or even secure custody. Thus, the child may experience another betrayal of trust.

A disposition order of probation is the usual result for a non-serious or non-violent offense, at least for the first two or three such adjudications. When the judge orders probation, a third probation officer — the supervision probation officer — enters the child's life. In many jurisdictions, supervision probation officers are responsible for scores of probationers, or even as many as 100 children apiece. This mass-production approach necessarily results in less one-on-one time between the probation officer and a particular probationer and arguably restricts the capacity of the probation officer to provide individualized, supportive services. The probation officer primarily tracks who arrives for an appointment and whose urine tests clean. For the children who do not follow directions, the probation officer files for revocation. The child experiences, with another adult authority figure, a relationship that is episodic, insensitive, and punitive.

II.   CONNECTIONS BETWEEN THE DELINQUENCY SYSTEM AND THE SPECIAL EDUCATION SYSTEM[2]

A.   A Strategy for Obtaining Treatment: Substituting the Individualized Services Available Through the Special Education System for the Limited and Often Counterproductive Sanctions in the Delinquency System

Children with education-related disabilities are dramatically over-represented in the delinquency system. *See generally*, *e.g.*, Joseph B. Tulman & Douglas M. Weck, *Shutting Off the School-to-Prison Pipeline for Status Offenders with Education-Related Disabilities*, 54 N.Y.L. Sch. L. Rev. 875, 876 n.1 (2010); Special Education and Disability Rights, Module 3

---

[2] Some of the material in this Section is adapted, with permission of the A.B.A., from Joseph B. Tulman, *Using Special Education Advocacy to Avoid or Resolve Status Offense Charges*, Chapter Six in Representing Juvenile Status Offenders (A.B.A. Children and the Law 2010).

MacArthur Foundation Models for Change Juvenile Court Training Curriculum, pp. 1-2 (2010). School personnel frequently fail to identify IDEA-eligible students and fail also to transfer special education evaluations, individualized education programs (IEPs), and other documents to delinquency system personnel. Consequently, rates of special education students in the juvenile system and in juvenile facilities are probably under-reported. *Id.* at 2.

Over-representation of children with disabilities in the delinquency system is a result, in part, of the failure by school personnel to serve these children appropriately. *See* Tulman & Weck, *supra*, at 884-85. Compounding the problem, school administrators historically have misused school discipline, disproportionately and improperly expelling students with disabilities. *Id.* Through a wave of "zero tolerance" laws and policies, legislators and school administrators have increasingly criminalized misbehavior in school. *Id.* Discrimination based upon both race and disability leads to a remarkable concentration of children of color with disabilities in the delinquency system and in juvenile incarceration facilities. *See* MacArthur Module 3, *supra*, at 6-8. Indeed, the delinquency system is populated overwhelmingly (and, in some jurisdictions, virtually exclusively) with minority children with unmet special education needs who come from low-income and indigent families. *See, e.g.*, Arthur L. Burnett, Sr., *Race and National Origin as Influential Factors in Juvenile Detention*, 3 D.C. L. Rev. 355, 370-71 (1995).

The IDEA applies in every school district, in every public school, and in every publicly-funded charter school in the United States. As detailed in other chapters of this book, children with education-related disabilities are entitled pursuant to the IDEA to an array of individualized services. Ordinarily, services through the school that are required pursuant to the IDEA should be available to address relatively minor behaviors that often trigger referrals to the delinquency court. Yet, as noted above, school officials have increasingly referred children (particularly children with education-related disabilities) to courts for truancy, for unruliness or disruptiveness at school, and for a range of minor delinquent behaviors (e.g., fighting, disorderly conduct, making threats, destruction of property, and drug possession).

Often, school personnel have failed to provide appropriate services prior to referring the child to the delinquency court. When school officials refer IDEA-eligible children to court, therefore, attorneys and law students defending those children should investigate what IDEA services school personnel should have been providing to the child, as well as what additional services might be appropriate. By identifying appropriate IDEA services to address the child's alleged delinquent behavior, the defenders might be able to forestall a prosecution for an alleged status offense or an alleged minor delinquency offense. Indeed, a child who is receiving appropriate individualized instruction and related services — including such common services as individual or group counseling, speech language therapy, therapeutic recreation services — is getting as much or more than what a juvenile court typically would be able to provide or require from executive branch agencies to address behaviors categorized as status offenses or minor delinquency charges.

ADVANTAGES OF USING THE SPECIAL EDUCATION SYSTEM RATHER THAN THE DELINQUENCY SYSTEM

Decision making in the delinquency system tends to be hierarchical; in contrast, special education decision making is designed to be collaborative. *Schaffer v. Weast*, 546 U.S. 49, 53 (2005) ("The core of the [IDEA] is the cooperative process that it establishes between parents and schools."). In delinquency matters, the parent typically has no formal role. In a status offense matter in which the government alleges "ungovernability" (i.e., that the child habitually disobeys the lawful and reasonable commands of the parent), the parent would likely be the complainant. Similarly, the parent could be the complainant if the delinquency charge is that the child allegedly assaulted the parent.

In a special education matter, the parent and child (at the parent's discretion) are members of the IEP Team. Special education law requires evaluations, free of charge to the parent, in any area of suspected disability; the focus of the evaluations is what instruction and services are required so that the child can become educated and successfully integrated into the mainstream. Evaluations produced through the delinquency system often include a diagnosis like "conduct disorder" and tend to address how to constrain the child. Delinquency system services tend to be undifferentiated; special education services are individualized. The delinquency judge's role in determining treatment for a child is limited typically, as a matter of double jeopardy, to a one-time disposition hearing (although revocation of probation can lead to a second disposition hearing). In special education matters, the team develops a new IEP at least once a year. At any time, the parent or school system representatives can request that the team reconvene to review and modify the child's program. The IEP Team can act, therefore, whenever the student requires different or additional services. Remedies in the special education system include access to a wide array of individualized services (including access to a private school and private services at no charge to the parent), compensatory education services for children previously denied appropriate services, and an award of attorney's fees at market rates for parents who prevail against the school system.

The disability "emotional disturbance" (ED) illustrates the problems and opportunities for attorneys representing children in delinquency cases. Because the IDEA requires developing an individualized program, a child's disability category does not limit what particular services are appropriate. So, for example, a child may need positive behavioral interventions and supports or psychological counseling even though the child is not identified as "emotionally disturbed."

EMOTIONAL DISTURBANCE

34 C.F.R. § 300.8(c)

(4)(i) Emotional disturbance means a condition exhibiting one or more of the following characteristics over a long period of time and to a marked degree that adversely affects a child's educational performance:

(A) An inability to learn that cannot be explained by intellectual, sensory, or health factors.

(B) An inability to build or maintain satisfactory interpersonal relationships with peers and teachers.

(C) Inappropriate types of behavior or feelings under normal circumstances.

(D) A general pervasive mood of unhappiness or depression.

(E) A tendency to develop physical symptoms or fears associated with personal or school problems.

(ii) Emotional disturbance includes schizophrenia. The term does not apply to children who are socially maladjusted, unless it is determined that they have an emotional disturbance under paragraph (c)(4)(i) of this section.

The definition of ED is a functional definition that requires chronic and intense emotional problems manifesting in one or more of five characteristics that affect educational performance. Excluded from the definition of ED, however, is a child who is "socially maladjusted" but who does not manifest one or more of the five characteristics. School administrators tend to over-identify minority and poor children as requiring special education, particularly unfairly and inaccurately labeling them as emotionally disturbed or mentally retarded. Joseph B. Tulman, *Disability and Delinquency: How Failures to Identify, Accommodate, and Serve Youth with Education-Related Disabilities Leads to Their Disproportionate Representation in the Delinquency System*, 3 Whittier J. Child & Fam. Advoc. 3, 31, n.140 (2003) (herafter "*Disability and Delinquency*") (citing authorities). On the other hand, children with unmet special education needs are dramatically overrepresented in the juvenile system. *Id.* The strategic choices include using the ED label as a way of avoiding the delinquency label and getting special education services. However, the ED label often covers another trap. A child who has an unaddressed learning disability, hearing impairment, or other education-related disability might develop over time a tendency to act out in school, as well as at home. If teachers and school administrators convince parents to label the child as emotionally disturbed *without identifying and addressing the underlying learning problems*, they might be condemning the child to a downward spiral.

The Downward Spiral of IDEA Violations and Delinquency Involvement

- The child acts out because the educational programming is inappropriate and because the child is making little or no academic progress.

- School personnel address only the child's acting out behaviors without identifying or addressing the child's underlying educational needs.

- The child continues to act out both in reaction to frustration or embarrassment concerning the lack of educational progress and also in reaction to the unfair and unsupportive behavioral constraints.

- School personnel segregate the child in a class or a school for ED students, or school personnel separate the child from school through suspensions or expulsion.

- The child is "hanging out" with other "misbehaving children" (either in the segregated ED program or on the streets).

- Recognizing both academic failure (no legitimate opportunities for academic and vocational progress) and the developmental imperative to require competence and to become self-sufficient, the child seeks affirmation, acceptance, and mentoring from unofficial mentors on the street (e.g., drug dealers, car thieves, gang members).

If the child's disabilities and behavioral issues affect relationships and performance at home and at school, the IEP should include such services as family counseling and parent training and the myriad other services contemplated under "counseling services," "parent counseling and training," "psychological services," "social work services." and "therapeutic recreation." 34 C.F.R. § 300.34(c). In addition, the IEP Team can order a functional behavioral assessment (FBA), leading to the design and implementation of a behavioral intervention plan (BIP). *See* 20 U.S.C. § 1414(d)(3)(B)(i); 34 C.F.R. § 300.324(a)(2)(i) (IEP Team shall consider positive behavioral interventions and supports); *see also* 20 U.S.C. § 1415(k)(1)(D)(ii) (FBA and behavioral intervention services for child removed to interim alternative educational setting); *see generally id.* 1400(c)(5)(F) (whole-school approaches, including positive behavioral interventions and supports, improves effectiveness of education for children with disabilities).

A PARTIAL CHECKLIST OF IDEA SERVICES

√   EVALUATIONS (in any area of suspected disability)

√   RELATED SERVICES

- Parent training

- Social work services

- Counseling

- Recreation and therapeutic recreation

- Other related services

√   FBA/BIP

√   VOCATIONAL TRAINING

√   ASSISTIVE TECHNOLOGY

√   TRANSITION SERVICES

√   CONTINUUM OF PLACEMENTS (including "wraparound services")

√   PRIVATE PLACEMENTS AND SERVICES (*"Burlington"* Remedy)

√   COMPENSATORY EDUCATION

If done correctly, the BIP should cover the child's behavior at home and at school, and teachers, school counselors, and parents should coordinate how they implement and evolve their behavioral interventions. If appropriate, the IEP can include training the parent to implement the BIP during non-school hours. The team can prescribe one-on-one services for the child. Transition services should also be in place to address the student's needs to prepare for the work world, post-secondary education, and living independently. 34 C.F.R. § 300.43; *see also id.* § 300.320(b) (transition services required in IEP in effect when child turns sixteen, or younger if appropriate).

In addition, each local education agency must have available a continuum of placements, keeping a special education student in the least restrictive environment that facilitates the student's learning. Although, if the child is not progressing academically and socially, the parents, school teachers and administrators, and other members of the IEP Team can place the child in a more intensive and more segregated setting, including, in extreme cases, placement in residential treatment facilities or mental hospitals. Under the principle of placing the child in the least restrictive environment, the IEP Team can prescribe wraparound services — like Multisystemic Therapy and Functional Family Therapy — to avoid placing the child in a residential treatment facility or mental hospital. Moreover, the IEP Team can bring in service providers from other agencies (e.g., mental health, vocational rehabilitation).

Based on a past denial of a FAPE, a parent can secure additional services for the child through a compensatory education agreement or hearing officer's order. *See, e.g., Reid v. District of Columbia*, 401 F.3d 516 (D.C. Cir. 2005). Remarkably, if the child is not receiving appropriate services in the public school, the parent is entitled to services in an appropriate private school at public expense. If, in such circumstances, the IEP Team members refuse the parent's request for private services or for placement in a private school, the parent can go to an administrative hearing to seek a hearing officer's determination that a private placement at public expense is required. *See* 34 C.F.R. § 300.148(c); *see also Burlington School Committee v. Massachusetts Department of Education*, 471 U.S. 359 (1985).

Alternatively, the parent can notify school administrators and then unilaterally place the child in a private school (or in private services) and then seek reimbursement through a due process hearing. *Id.* Considering this array of special education rights, one might credibly conclude that the only placement not available through special education is incarceration and that the only "service" not available through special education is the threat of incarceration.

Teenagers from across the socio-economic spectrum and from all races engage in deviant conduct. Illegal drug use, for example, occurs with approximately the same frequency among majority and minority group children. A primary factor that keeps children from higher income, white families out of the delinquency system is the perception by school personnel, police officers, intake probation officers, prosecutors, and judges that the parents are able to address their children's deviant conduct. That perception, in turn, is based partially on the corresponding access of those "empowered" parents to appropriate services outside of the delinquency system. Those services may be from public schools or private schools that are relatively high performing. In addition, parents with access to private health insurance often can obtain therapeutic services for children who are allegedly acting out.

By obtaining appropriate services through the special education system, low-income and minority parents — like wealthier, majority-group parents — should be able to keep their children out of the delinquency system. By definition, IDEA services are part of a "free appropriate public education" and are free of charge to the parent. By helping parents obtain these free IDEA services for their children who are facing delinquency charges, defense attorneys and law students should be able to keep those children out of the delinquency system. Using this strategy, lawyers and law students can help balance the scales of justice for low-income, minority children with unmet special education needs.

B.   A Strategy for Successfully Challenging Unfair Prosecutions: Identifying Improper Unilateral Exclusion from School of Children with Disabilities and Using Delinquency Intake Procedures to Stop Improper and Unnecessary Delinquency Referrals

Before going to court to enforce special education rights, a parent typically must exhaust administrative remedies. *See* 20 U.S.C. § 1415(l); 34 C.F.R. § 300.516(e). In other words, the parent must have an administrative hearing, called an "impartial due process hearing," before going to court. *See* 20 U.S.C. §§ 1415(f) & (g). An aggrieved party — that is, a party that loses a special education administrative hearing — can institute a lawsuit in either federal or state court. *See* 34 C.F.R. §§ 300.516(a), (b) & (d). Ordinarily, therefore, a parent who has not pressed a special education claim in an administrative hearing cannot intervene in a delinquency proceeding to ask a juvenile judge to adjudicate a special education claim. Generally speaking, neither a state court, including a juvenile court judge, nor a federal court has jurisdiction over a special education matter until the parties have exhausted administrative remedies. Through the federal special education law, Congress sought to ensure that children with disabilities received appropriate services. Congress also intended, remarkably, to stop public school administrators from using allegations of disruptive or even dangerous conduct to exclude children with disabilities. Interpreting these provisions, the Supreme Court noted in *Honig v. Doe* that "Congress very much meant to strip schools of the unilateral authority they had traditionally employed to exclude disabled students, particularly emotionally disturbed students, from school." 484 U.S. 305, 323 (1988). The intent of Congress to stop school administrators from unilaterally excluding children with disabilities provides an important framework for lawyers and law students who are defending children whom school administrators have referred to juvenile courts.

In some states, a juvenile court judge can grant a motion to dismiss in the interest of justice and in the best interest of the child, assuming that the judge finds that the dismissal does not jeopardize the safety of the community. *See, e.g., In re Robert T. Doe*, 753 N.Y.S.2d 656, 660 (N.Y. Fam. Ct. 2002) (relying upon juvenile court's inherent authority to dismiss status offense matter in the interest of justice). *Cf. In re Trent M.*, 569 N.W.2d 719, 725-26 (Wis. Ct. App. 1997) (recognizing in dictum that trial court could have dismissed the petition in the best interest of the child but holding that trial court ruled on legal grounds instead). Prevailing on such a motion is more likely, of course, if the child is relatively young and if the child has no prior record with the juvenile court. *See, e.g., In re Ruffel P.*, 582 N.Y.S.2d 631, 632 (N.Y. Fam. Ct. 1992) (dismissing status offense matter in the interest of justice, emphasizing that the child was eight and a half at the time of petitioning). A motion to dismiss in the interest of justice is also stronger if the defense can show that school administrators violated the IDEA's "child find" requirement, particularly if school administrators ignored requests by the parents to evaluate the child for special education eligibility.

In a small number of reported cases, attorneys have argued that school personnel used delinquency or status offense charges to circumvent or "end run" IDEA obligations to serve the child. *See, e.g., In re Trent M.*, 569 N.W.2d at 724. Because of the IDEA's exhaustion requirement, however, the juvenile court ordinarily is not a proper forum for establishing IDEA eligibility, for litigating a denial of FAPE, or for challenging school suspensions or expulsions. Accordingly, an attorney or law student is well-advised to establish special education rights through an impartial due process hearing. One such case is *Morgan v. Chris L.*, 927 F. Supp. 267 (E.D. Tenn. 1994), *aff'd*, 106 F.3d 401 (6th Cir. 1997) (unpublished opinion), *cert. denied*, 520 U.S. 1271 (1997).[3] In that case, the District Court upheld an administrative law judge's ruling that school administrators violated the IDEA by failing to identify and serve Chris L. and by attempting to change his educational placement by petitioning a delinquency matter for behavior that was a manifestation of Chris L.'s disability.

As Congress clarified in the 1997 IDEA amendments, the Act does not prohibit school administrators from referring alleged criminal activity by a child with a disability to the police

---

[3] A distinguishing feature of *Morgan v. Chris L.* is that Tennessee's statutes, at the time of that case, authorized school-initiated petitions in the juvenile court. *See In re Trent M.*, 569 N.W.2d at 725. *Accord Commonwealth v. Nathaniel N.*, 764 N.E.2d 883, 886-87 (Mass. App. Ct. 2002). In most states, school officials must rely upon juvenile court personnel to file a petition.

and to courts:

> Nothing in this subchapter shall be construed to prohibit an agency from reporting a crime committed by a child with a disability to appropriate authorities or to prevent State law enforcement and judicial authorities from exercising their responsibilities with regard to the application of Federal and State law to crimes committed by a child with a disability.

20 U.S.C. § 1415(k)(6)(A) (2005) (originally codified, following the 1997 amendments, at 1415(k)(9)(A)).[4]

A small number of courts and commentators have interpreted § 1415(k)(6)(A) as overturning *Morgan v. Chris L.* and similar cases. *See, e.g., Commonwealth v. Nathaniel N.*, 764 N.E.2d at 887. Clearly, however, "[t]he Act does not address whether school officials may press charges against a child with a disability when they have reported a crime by that student [and] school districts should take care not to exercise their responsibilities in a discriminatory manner." 64 Fed. Reg. 12631 (March 12, 1999). Section 1415(k)(6)(A) "does not authorize school districts to circumvent any of their responsibilities under the Act." *Id.* A fair interpretation of the section is that a special education hearing officer cannot prohibit a school from referring a child to the juvenile court, but the hearing officer may be authorized to order school officials not to press charges. For an expanded treatment of these issues, see Tulman & Weck, *supra* at 890-94.

During the intake stage of a delinquency case, those responsible for handling the delinquency referral should investigate whether the case is an attempt by school administrators to "end run" a child's IDEA rights. At that stage of the juvenile court process, decisions are made regarding "whether the case belongs in the juvenile system in the first instance . . . ." *In re Trent M.*, 569 N.W.2d at 724. One should not assume that intake probation officers and prosecutors will rubber stamp a faulty referral by school authorities; if they do, the court can correct the error. *Id.*

An intake probation officer typically is empowered by statute to investigate and to examine complaints to consider whether to commence a proceeding against a child. *See generally* Model Juv. Ct. Act § 6 (1968); *see, e.g.*, D.C. Code § 16-2305 (role of intake in recommending petitioning). Perhaps in recognition of this delinquency intake function, Congress provided in the IDEA that agencies referring children to the juvenile court should transmit special education and disciplinary records. 20 U.S.C. § 1415(k)(6)(B). Thus, state intake laws requiring court personnel to screen out inappropriate cases mesh with the congressional mandate that school authorities referring criminal (i.e., delinquency) allegations also provide relevant school records.

If an intake officer fails to investigate properly and fails to recognize the significance of special education violations by school personnel, the defense attorney can provide school records and explain to the intake officer — and subsequently, if necessary, to the prosecutor — that the case is really an unfair attempt by school officials to transform a failure to evaluate and to provide special education services into a dispute in the juvenile court. Furthermore, an intake probation officer who is fully informed of special education entitlements should only sparingly recommend petitioning a minor delinquency case against a child who is eligible for

---

[4] Congress addressed "crimes" but failed to mention "delinquent acts" and "status offenses" in subsection 1415(k)(6)(A). The significance of that omission is a matter left, for present purposes, to the judgment of the individual attorney or law student.

special education. Nevertheless, the defense attorney must be prepared to challenge the decision-making of, or failure to exercise discretion by, the intake officer. *See generally* Joseph B. Tulman, *The Role of the Probation Officer in Intake: Stories from Before During and After the Delinquency Initial Hearing*, 3 D.C. L. Rev. 235, 235-50 (1995) (discussing responsibilities of an intake officer). The attorney can file a motion to dismiss the petition based on violations of the statutory intake process.

With no grand jury in juvenile court to check a prosecutor's charging decisions, the delinquency court's intake process serves an important gate-keeping function. Generally, the court's intake officers should keep out unworthy cases and screen out children who, even if involved with delinquent conduct, do not require delinquency court intervention. That gate-keeping function tends to work well for children from upper-income, white families. In contrast, when the intake process does not work properly for low-income, minority children who have special education needs, those children get the worst of both worlds. School administrators fail to provide appropriate special education services and then, with impunity, refer the same children to the delinquency court.

III. SPECIAL EDUCATION, DISABILITY RIGHTS, AND THE STAGES OF A DELINQUENCY CASE

Special education rights, and disability rights generally, may provide opportunities to develop delinquency defenses and procedural arguments that would otherwise not be available. *See, e.g.*, Special Education Advocacy Under the Individuals with Disabilities Education Act (IDEA) for Children in the Juvenile Delinquency System chapters 1, 2, 3, 4, & 5 (Tulman & McGee, eds. 1998) (hereafter "Special Education-Delinquency Manual"), at:

https://udc.site-ym.com/resource/resmgr/facultydocs/tulman_special_ed_manual.pdf

In exploring ways to use special education rights to advance a delinquency client's objectives, strategic problems relating to timing are immediately apparent. Typically, prior to the initiation of a delinquency case against a child, the child's parent has not been aware of, and has not fully enforced, the special education rights. Indeed, that lack of awareness and enforcement may be, as suggested above, one of the reasons that the child is facing delinquency charges. To investigate and enforce the special education rights and to get appropriate IDEA services in place typically will take several months. (The special education advocacy process will probably require a longer period of time if the child was not previously identified as eligible for special education.) The attorney or law student must obtain school records, investigate the child's school history, and develop the special education case. Pursuant to the IDEA, the time period from the filing of a special education complaint to issuance of a hearing officer's order is seventy-five days. *See* 34 C.F.R. § 300.515(a). Assuming that the parent prevails in a special education hearing, implementing the order — getting the appropriate services for the child — will likely take additional time. The delinquency case, meanwhile, is likely to proceed at its own pace. In many jurisdictions, delinquency cases go from initial hearing (arraignment) to disposition (sentencing) in a matter of weeks.

An intake probation officer, prosecutor, or judge connected with the delinquency case will not necessarily rely upon an assertion by the delinquency defense team that school administrators have violated the child's IDEA rights or that the failure to provide appropriate IDEA services is directly relevant to the delinquency proceeding. The attorney or law student defending a child must also be mindful of the special education exhaustion requirement.

Without a special education hearing officer's order in hand, the defense lawyer is often, therefore, relying upon an intake probation officer, prosecutor, or judge to exercise discretion wisely and fairly. Furthermore, one is rarely successful in challenging on appeal an exercise of discretion in the context of a delinquency case.

This timing problem is also apparent with a challenge to the intake of delinquency cases. The defense attorney or law student typically is appointed to represent the child *after* the filing of a delinquency petition. To negotiate a dismissal of the petition or to effectively challenge the intake process, the attorney must rapidly uncover the facts and legal claims that are germane to the delinquency or status offense matter and to the parallel special education case. As noted above, however, the special education advocacy process often will require several months. For this reason, the defense attorney is not usually in a position early in the defense of a delinquency case to present to the juvenile court a hearing officer's determination establishing the denial of IDEA rights.

In light of these timing considerations, a practical strategy is to negotiate diversion of the delinquency case or negotiate an agreement to continue the delinquency case until the parent, with assistance from the attorney, can line up appropriate IDEA services for the child and for the family. From a broader perspective, a proper defense of a child who is enmeshed in the delinquency system may require sticking with the child and with the family through more than one delinquency case and through a prolonged period of special education advocacy. *See, e.g.,* Special Education-Delinquency Manual, *supra*, at 2.20-2.27 (two case studies of extended special education and delinquency representation). In excavating and interpreting the child's school history, a defense attorney or law student advocate will almost invariably find that the problems in school are longstanding. Usually, the educational problems pre-dated by a matter of years the child's school-attendance problems, the child's illegal drug use, and the child's other emerging delinquent conduct. Reversing that pattern of educational neglect by the school staff and reversing the child's downward-spiraling behavior often takes time.

Mindful of these timing and exhaustion considerations, one can contemplate the stages of a delinquency case and identify specific legal theories and problem-solving strategies that use special education as a basis for advancing the interests of a child who is a client in a delinquency case. *See generally* Special Education and Disability Rights 39-50 (MacArthur Juvenile Court Training Curriculum, Module 3, 2009).

A SAMPLING OF IDEA-RELATED, PROBLEM-SOLVING STRATEGIES FOR DELINQUENCY CASES

(1) Obtain agreement from the child and the parent to investigate and to enforce their special education rights. [Note that if the attorney or law student represents the child in a delinquency matter, then whether to pursue special education strategies and remedies is a decision that the child must make. If the child agrees to pursue the strategy, then the attorney or law student can offer to represent the child and parent jointly with regard to enforcement of special education rights. *See* Chapter Two for a more in-depth discussion of this issue.]

(2) Enforce rights for the child to receive appropriate IDEA services. Consider obtaining private services for the child, at public expense, if public school officials refuse to provide appropriate services. Seek compensatory education services for past violations of the IDEA.

(3) Use availability of special education services as a basis for demonstrating that a delinquency case is not needed.

(4) Move to dismiss the delinquency or status offense case "in the interest of justice" or "for social reasons."

(5) Move to dismiss the delinquency or status offense case based on a violation of the intake process and a failure to exercise discretion by the intake officer.

(6) In a special education case, argue that the delinquency or status offense petition was an "end run" around special education responsibilities and was intended to "change the educational placement" without due process; move for an order that school administrators seek withdrawal of the petition and discontinue their role in advancing the court matter.

(7) Use special education services to demonstrate that pre-trial (or pre-disposition) detention is not necessary.

(8) Use special education evaluations and other records to develop procedural arguments to exclude statements and to develop defenses.

(9) At disposition, demonstrate that the court should close the delinquency case because the availability of special education and related services means that "treatment" through the juvenile court is not needed and that imposing a delinquency order of probation or commitment would not be a fair result, particularly in light of previous violations of the IDEA by school personnel.

(10) As a protective measure, write into the IEP that school personnel will not refer the child to the juvenile or criminal court for relatively minor behavior that is a manifestation of the child's disability.

(11) Stick with the special education advocacy until the child is making appropriate academic and emotional progress.

A.   The Delinquency Intake Stage

As outlined in section II(B), above, the intake stage of a delinquency case serves a critical gate-keeping function. The court personnel should screen out cases if doing so is consistent with community safety and the best interest of the child. A central consideration in the screening process is whether a parent has access to services for the child and whether the parent apparently is able to control the child without assistance from the delinquency system. For a child who does not "need" the additional intervention of the delinquency system, involvement in the delinquency system is itself needlessly stigmatizing and can be counter-productive.

A defense attorney or law student typically commences representation of the child in the delinquency matter after court intake personnel and prosecutors have decided that the case should proceed. The defense counsel's approach, therefore, should include determining whether the court intake personnel actually conducted a reasonable investigation prior to recommending or approving petitioning of the delinquency case. Court intake personnel and prosecutors are generally not aware of IDEA rights and the relationship between special education and delinquency. Defense counsel should assume, therefore, that court intake personnel and prosecutors did not consider, for example, whether a school-based delinquency referral by school administrators was an "end run" around IDEA rights. Defense counsel should also assume, likewise, that school personnel did not attempt to send school records to the court, as contemplated by 20 U.S.C. § 1415(k)(6)(B).

Defense counsel can interview the court intake personnel to determine the extent to which they considered whether special education violations render the delinquency referral unfair and whether the availability of special education services makes the delinquency referral unnecessary. On some occasions, defense counsel can convince court intake personnel and prosecutors to drop, divert, or delay the prosecution. If that approach proves fruitless, then, in an appropriate case, defense counsel should file a written motion to dismiss. Defense counsel should base the motion upon a violation of the delinquency intake provisions in the state law and in the corresponding delinquency court rules.

B.   Initial Hearings and Detention Decisions

If the child qualifies (based on the family's income level) for appointed counsel, that attorney should enter an appearance prior to the initial hearing and should be representing the child at the initial hearing. At the initial hearing in a delinquency case, the child is entitled to receive notice of the charges. Among the issues addressed at an initial hearing is whether to release or to detain the child for the time period between the initial hearing and the trial. The standard for detention is essentially whether the child poses an unacceptable risk to the community or whether the child is likely, if released, not to appear at future court hearings.

In determining dangerousness and ruling on the child's liberty interest, the court should examine, as a matter of due process, only information that is relevant and probative. A history of previous adjudications for violent offenses, for example, would almost certainly be relevant to a determination of likely future dangerousness. On the other hand, social factors like the child's school attendance are not relevant to whether the child poses a danger or presents a risk of non-appearance. Nevertheless, notwithstanding the presumption of innocence and the constitutional limits on the use of pre-trial detention, judges sometimes consider such social factors and use detention improperly to address the child's alleged non-conforming behavior.

Defense counsel should attempt to keep the detention determination focused on the proper legal standard (dangerousness and risk of non-appearance). If the court improperly detains a child, defense counsel should pursue, in an appropriate case, an interlocutory appeal of the detention order.

In some circumstances, defense counsel may decide, with the client's permission, to present the child's needs for, and rights to, appropriate special education services. Counsel can assure the court that IDEA services must be available from the school system and that counsel will assist the parent to obtain those services. These assurances can often be persuasive in helping a judge to feel more comfortable with releasing the child pending trial. Even though social factors generally are not relevant to the determination of the child's dangerousness or risk of non-appearance, the availability of services is relevant to whether the court can and should release an otherwise-detainable child. Defense counsel might consider — again, with the concurrence of the client — having a special education coordinator, teacher, or counselor appear in person or by phone to confirm that the child is entitled to IDEA services and that school personnel will provide appropriate services.

Another problem that arises with some regularity at initial hearings is the imposition of school attendance as a condition of release. In theory, this condition on a release order should not present a problem. After all, school attendance is ordinarily, as a matter of law, mandatory for children. On the other hand, a child with special education needs who has not been properly evaluated, identified, and served in school, is likely to experience significant difficulty with school attendance. Moreover, a child with unmet special education needs is likely to be the subject of multiple, improper suspension orders. Thus, an order to attend school can be unfair if school personnel are failing to honor the child's IDEA rights.

Defense counsel can educate the court regarding this problem and, in so doing, might be successful in insulating the child from an unfair school-attendance order. In addition, defense counsel can help the parent enforce the parent and the child's right to protection from illegal disciplinary exclusions and can enforce the parent and child's "stay put" rights. If the court seeks to revoke the child's release based upon the child's alleged failure to comply with a school-attendance order, defense counsel can use IDEA rights as a defense to that effort to revoke release. Indeed, if the parent has a hearing pending against the school system regarding an illegal suspension or the failure of school personnel to provide special education services, an effort by a prosecutor or *sua sponte* by the delinquency court to adjudicate the child's attendance arguably would violate the IDEA's exhaustion requirement.

C.   Pre-Trial Motions

Special education information and rights may be useful as a basis for developing and pursuing pre-trial motions in a delinquency case. The most likely, as discussed previously, is a motion to dismiss in the interest of justice and the best interest of the child. Even assuming that the child is involved in the alleged delinquent conduct, the availability of IDEA services may render the delinquency case unnecessary. The failure of school personnel to have provided appropriate services may make the delinquency adjudication unfair, particularly if the events giving rise to the delinquency allegations arose in school and the child's alleged behavior is a manifestation of the child's disability.

Another fertile ground for using special education information is a motion to suppress statements that the child reportedly made to police officers. In a typical case, a prosecutor introduces police testimony that the child read and waived the *Miranda* rights (or that the officer read the rights to the child and that the child then waived the rights). Defense attorneys typically fail to obtain and review relevant school records regarding the child's reading comprehension level and auditory comprehension level. Assume, for example, that a psycho-educational evaluation of the child demonstrates that the child reads at the third-grade level and understands oral communication (auditory comprehension) also at the third-grade level. If the *Miranda* warnings are written at a seventh-grade level, then the child most likely was not able to knowingly, intelligently, and voluntarily waive the *Miranda* rights. In such a case, defense counsel should consider using the psychologist who conducted the psycho-educational evaluation as a witness. Further, the defense counsel would have to establish at what level the *Miranda* warnings are written. In addition, defense counsel should investigate carefully the circumstances of the interrogation and purported waiver in order to determine, among other things, whether the police officer provided any additional explanation of the *Miranda* rights in order to obtain the child's waiver.

Regarding a child who has a moderate or severe receptive and expressive language disorder, defense counsel may be able to demonstrate that — without regard to the validity of a *Miranda* waiver — the police officer was not aware of the child's language-based disability. Further, defense counsel might be able to demonstrate — again, with the use of expert testimony from a special education evaluator (and perhaps with the testimony of a special education teacher, as well) — that the child most likely could not and did not understand the police officer's questions and, indeed, that, due to the child's communications disorder, the child could not and did not formulate meaningful or reliable responses. This evidence would be analogous to proving the invalidity of a confession in English by a person who speaks almost no English.

The question of competency to stand trial raises difficult ethical questions. A defense attorney who has concerns about the client's competency must, nonetheless, engage the client in regard to whether to raise the competency issue. Assuming that the attorney is raising competency or that the court has, on its own motion, referred the child for a pre-trial competency evaluation, the child's special education evaluators may be able to provide information that is relevant. By carefully reviewing special education evaluations and interviewing the special education evaluators, defense counsel may become aware of information that is relevant to the competency evaluation. For example, a psychologist who has evaluated the child for special education purposes may have done more extensive testing of the child than a court-appointed psychologist who examines the child only on the question of competency. Special education evaluators, for example, may be able to testify that the child has post-traumatic stress disorder and a severe speech-language impairment. Thus, even though the court's psychologist has concluded that the child is competent, the special education evaluators may be in a position to demonstrate that the child, in fact, does not meet the standard.

In most jurisdictions, a prosecutor can move, in certain circumstances, to transfer a child for prosecution from the juvenile court to the adult criminal court. Typically, the standard that a judge must apply in ruling upon the transfer motion is whether the child is amenable to treatment through the juvenile system and, if so, whether the child likely can be rehabilitated during the time that the juvenile system would have jurisdiction or custody of the child. For a child who is not amenable to treatment, the judge presumably — depending, of course, on the seriousness of the alleged offense and other variables — would transfer the child for adult prosecution. A transfer motion is another opportunity for defense counsel to use special education rights in advocating for the client.

In defending against a transfer motion, defense counsel, representing the parent of the child, should secure a finding through an impartial due process hearing that school administrators have denied the child a free appropriate public education. Often, particularly with regard to children from marginalized neighborhoods that have under-performing public schools, one can establish that school personnel failed for years to provide appropriate special education services to the child. Defense counsel must ensure that the hearing officer's order provides for appropriate, intensive services for the child, including compensatory services to make up for the services that the child did not receive previously.

Defense counsel can enter the hearing officer's findings and order into evidence in the transfer hearing, and defense counsel can present testimony, explicating and amplifying the hearing officer's findings and order. This testimony should demonstrate that the government — through the school system — failed consistently to provide services to the child. Using this approach, defense counsel can argue that the government has "unclean hands" and is estopped from claiming that the child is not amenable to services. Alternatively, one can argue that fundamental fairness weighs on the side of denying the motion for transfer. Further, special education evaluators and service providers can testify regarding the intensive and comprehensive services that, pursuant to the hearing officer's order, will be available to the child. These witnesses can help to establish that the child will likely be rehabilitated in the relevant period of time that the juvenile system would retain jurisdiction.

Unless the child obtains a high school diploma earlier, the child will be eligible to receive special education services at least until the child turns twenty-two. 34 C.F.R. § 300.101(a). (In some states, the age of IDEA eligibility is older than twenty-two.) In addition, with compensatory education, the child may have extended eligibility past the ordinary IDEA age limit. The IDEA requires states to provide special education and related services to eligible persons in adult prisons. *See* 34 C.F.R. § 300.101(a). Defense counsel can argue, however, that the child is not likely to receive appropriate IDEA services if the court transfers the child to the adult criminal court and if the child is incarcerated ultimately in an adult prison.

D.   Factfinding Hearing (Trial)

In some instances, special education information and rights may be relevant to the trial of a delinquency or status offense charge. A charge of truancy provides a rather straightforward example. Consider a child who has a disability that leads to the child's avoiding people and, thus, results in the child's absences from school. If school personnel have failed to identify or address that disability, the child's absences would not likely support a charge of truancy. In addition, a referral of such a case to the delinquency court may be an example of an "end run" — a case that court intake personnel should refuse to petition. Moreover, the government's attempt to prosecute that case in delinquency court arguably would violate the administrative exhaustion requirement (i.e., the requirement that special education matters proceed through an administrative hearing prior to court).

In some jurisdictions, a child can be charged in a separate delinquency petition or contempt show-cause order for failing to appear in court or failing to follow a court order. Typically, a courtroom clerk or the judge may have read the order to the child in court. In regard to a child with auditory processing problems, low reading comprehension levels, an executive function disorder, or even attention deficit hyperactivity disorder, defense counsel might be able to use special education information and expert evaluators to establish that the child likely was not able to comprehend the orders.

An offense that allegedly involved more than one perpetrator provides another example. Assume that the government is alleging a robbery by force and violence in which a first perpetrator stopped the victim and took the victim's wallet from his pocket. Assume, in addition, that the government is alleging that a second perpetrator accompanied the first perpetrator and intended to help intimidate the victim. The government presents evidence that, before taking the wallet, the first alleged perpetrator said to the second alleged perpetrator, "Come on; let's show him we mean business." Ordinarily, evidence of that communication would allow the factfinder to infer that the second alleged perpetrator, through his presence, was aiding and abetting the first perpetrator. If, however, defense counsel established that the second alleged perpetrator is deaf, evidence of that disability obviously would be relevant to the question of that second alleged perpetrator's *mens rea* and would diminish or defeat the inference regarding the import of the communication from the first alleged perpetrator. Similarly, evidence that the second alleged perpetrator has mild cognitive impairment or a severe receptive language disorder would be relevant in this factual scenario. Defense counsel could introduce expert testimony regarding the degree and significance of the disabilities. Such testimony would be relevant to the criminal intent of the second alleged perpetrator and to the probativity of the communication from the first alleged perpetrator as to whether the second alleged perpetrator was, in fact, aiding and abetting in the robbery.

E.   Disposition (Sentencing)

A delinquency judge is required, in most jurisdictions, to determine whether a child — even if involved in a delinquent act — is "in need of treatment or rehabilitation." *See, e.g.*, D.C. Code § 16-2301(8) (definition of "delinquent child" includes element that the child is in need of care and rehabilitation); *cf., generally*, Model Juv. Ct. Act § 2(4)(iv) (1968) (definition of "unruly child" — like the definition of "delinquent child" — requires both the deviant conduct and a separate finding of a "need for treatment and rehabilitation."). Proof at trial or through a guilty plea that the child committed an offense ordinarily creates a presumption that the child requires care and rehabilitation. *E.g., In re M.C.F.*, 293 A.2d 874, 877 (D.C. 1972). By assisting the parent and the child to secure appropriate IDEA services, defense counsel may have a basis for rebutting the presumption that the child requires care and rehabilitation through the delinquency system. In those circumstances, defense counsel should ask the judge simply to dismiss or to close the case. Such a ruling would end the court's jurisdiction over the child.

The basic strategy, as discussed earlier in this chapter, is to use special education placements and services as a substitute for treatment through the delinquency system.[5] As part of this strategy, defense counsel can work with the parent and the child in an effort to increase the services in the special education system to a level necessary to satisfy the delinquency judge. Defense counsel ordinarily should also, prior to disposition, communicate with the court's diagnostic probation officer and with the prosecutor to seek agreement that the services identified through the special education system satisfy everyone's concerns.

---

[5] The reader should also review the previous discussion regarding how to defend against a transfer motion, in Section III[C], *supra*. Much of that material is relevant to disposition preparation and advocacy.

In preparing the special education case for an impartial due process hearing, one must (as discussed previously) excavate and re-construct the child's school history and demonstrate that school personnel failed for a period of years to serve the child appropriately. At the delinquency disposition hearing, in an appropriate case, defense counsel can present to the judge the special education hearing officer's findings of fact, conclusions of law, and order for appropriate IDEA services and compensatory services. In addition, defense counsel should chart the child's school history and use that chart as demonstrative evidence at the delinquency disposition hearing. In essence, the defense counsel should be able to show that the child's truancy and deviant (delinquent) behavior developed only after the child endured a period of years during which school personnel illegally denied services to the child.

If the order at disposition is for probation supervision, defense counsel should be prepared to demonstrate — based upon the child's special education evaluations — what reasonable accommodations the child requires on probation. Defense counsel can request that the accommodations be prescribed as part of the probation order. In the alternative, defense counsel can write a letter, on behalf of the child, to the appropriate probation officials and request appropriate accommodations. So, for example, if the child has a language-based learning disability, the assigned probation officer should be one who has the requisite training and experience to communicate effectively with the child. If, as one might predict, probation officers fail to provide reasonable accommodations, defense counsel likely will have a ready defense to a motion to revoke probation based upon the child's alleged failure to comply with probation conditions.

Defense counsel can also use the child's right to reasonable accommodations to insist that the court place the child into programs, services, and activities that otherwise might exclude the child. *See Pennsylvania Dep't of Corrections v. Yeskey*, 524 U.S. 206 (1998). In some jurisdictions, the courts can order a "blended sentence" or "youth act" treatment that affords a child convicted as an adult an opportunity to serve time in a juvenile facility, to have the length of sentence shortened, and possibly to have the conviction set aside if the child ultimately responds well to treatment. Defense counsel can use the child's right to special education services (and the corresponding history of denial of FAPE) to argue for a favorable sentencing option.

The special education system must have available a "continuum of alternative placements." *See* 34 C.F.R. § 300.115. This continuum includes residential treatment, if that level of service is required to provide "educational benefit" to the IDEA-eligible child. In extreme cases, when a child is facing long-term incarceration based upon involvement in a serious and violent offense, defense counsel can explore with the child and the parent whether placement in a residential treatment center through the special education system is a viable and preferred alternative.

In assisting a child to avoid placement in a juvenile prison or in an otherwise undesirable setting, defense counsel should investigate whether appropriate IDEA services (including related services and transition services) are available in that juvenile prison or other setting. If appropriate IDEA services are not available, defense counsel should craft and advance an argument that the judge is prohibited as a matter of law from so placing the child (or transferring custody of the child to an executive branch agency that would place the child in that inappropriate setting). The legal basis for the argument is the treatment mandate of the delinquency statute, as well as the IDEA. Furthermore, by knowingly placing the child in a facility that cannot provide state- and federally-mandated IDEA services, the judge, in effect, would be depriving the child of services to which the child is entitled. Such a deprivation arguably constitutes disability discrimination that is prohibited by Title II of the Americans with Disabilities Act. *See generally* Tulman, *Disability and Delinquency, supra* n. 9 at 15-19 and *id.* at 17-18 notes 80 & 81 and accompanying text (regarding applicability of the ADA to decisions by state and local judges).

F.   Post-Disposition Advocacy

On behalf of a child who is the legal custody of the state and who is placed by virtue of a delinquency disposition order into a juvenile prison or other undesirable setting, defense counsel can continue to assert and enforce special education rights. As discussed in Chapters Three and Eight, the "child find" obligation applies to children who are wards of the state. 20 U.S.C. § 1412(a)(3)(A). Defense counsel should consider, in particular, filing a special education complaint and requesting an impartial due process hearing to challenge the failure of administrators at the juvenile institution to provide appropriate special education services. Obviously, the preferred remedy would be to remove the child from the prison. Alternatively, in light of the IDEA's right to "appropriate relief," 20 U.S.C. § 1415(i)(2)(C)(iii), one can identify private tutors, counselors, and other providers to serve the child and ask the special education hearing officer to order that the school system pay for those private services. *See generally Burlington v. Dept. of Educ.*, 471 U.S. 359, 369-70 (1985).

As discussed above, by requesting appropriate accommodations for a child on probation, defense counsel can attempt to ensure that probationary supervision is effective. If, on the other hand, the probation office fails to accommodate the child and then seeks to revoke probation based upon the child's alleged failure to comply with conditions of probation, defense counsel can argue that the probation revocation motion is improper and unfair. The same approach applies, naturally, for accommodations for a child released into the community on parole (or "aftercare").

IV.   CONCLUSION

Most children who are in the delinquency system have experienced significant frustration and failure in school. The vast majority of those children have unmet — and often undiagnosed — education-related disabilities. America's vast school-to-prison pipeline is, in large part, a testament to the abject failure of school administrators to identify children with education-related disabilities and to provide those children with appropriate special education services. Indeed, although Congress created the special education law in part to strip schools of the power to unilaterally exclude children with disabilities, the practice of discriminatory exclusion continues and appears to be increasing. In recent years, policies requiring zero tolerance for misconduct in schools have proliferated. Jurisdictions around the country are placing more police or "school resource" officers in schools. These policies increase the volume of throwaway children in the school-to-prison pipeline.

The steps to ensuring that a child succeeds in school and in life are not a mystery. Academic success is critical. Finding a path to competency and self-sufficiency is also critical. The Individuals with Disabilities Education Act requires individualized services for children with education-related disabilities. With specialized instruction, appropriate supportive, related services, and a program of transition services, IDEA-eligible children successfully integrate into the economy and into the community. Absent appropriate services, however, these children drop out — or, more accurately, are pushed out — of school. Ironically, virtually all children find mentors. When *adults* behave properly, they ensure that children receive legitimate supports and work opportunities. When adults ignore IDEA obligations, marginalized and underserved children find illicit mentors on the street.

A juvenile defense attorney who also provides special education representation can obtain appropriate services for clients and often extricate those clients from the juvenile delinquency system. In addition, defense counsel often can use special education rights to inform and strengthen the defense of a delinquency case. Academic and behavioral problems that developed over a period of years will not dissolve and disappear immediately. The attorney should maintain the special education representation until the child is adjusting effectively in school and in the community.

INDIVIDUALS WITH DISABILITIES EDUCATION ACT, TITLE 20[1]

Part A

§ 1400. Short title; findings; purposes

(a) Short title

This chapter may be cited as the "Individuals with Disabilities Education Act".

(b) Omitted

(c) Findings

Congress finds the following:

(1) Disability is a natural part of the human experience and in no way diminishes the right of individuals to participate in or contribute to society. Improving educational results for children with disabilities is an essential element of our national policy of ensuring equality of opportunity, full participation, independent living, and economic self-sufficiency for individuals with disabilities.

(2) Before the date of enactment of the Education for All Handicapped Children Act of 1975 (Public Law 94-142), the educational needs of millions of children with disabilities were not being fully met because —

(A) the children did not receive appropriate educational services;

(B) the children were excluded entirely from the public school system and from being educated with their peers;

(C) undiagnosed disabilities prevented the children from having a successful educational experience; or

(D) a lack of adequate resources within the public school system forced families to find services outside the public school system.

(3) Since the enactment and implementation of the Education for All Handicapped Children Act of 1975, this chapter has been successful in ensuring children with disabilities and the families of such children access to a free appropriate public education and in improving educational results for children with disabilities.

(4) However, the implementation of this chapter has been impeded by low expectations, and an insufficient focus on applying replicable research on proven methods of teaching and learning for children with disabilities.

(5) Almost 30 years of research and experience has demonstrated that the education of children with disabilities can be made more effective by —

---

[1] This is an edited version of the IDEA that emphasizes its substantive and procedural requirements. The funding formulas have been omitted.

(A) having high expectations for such children and ensuring their access to the general education curriculum in the regular classroom, to the maximum extent possible, in order to —

(i) meet developmental goals and, to the maximum extent possible, the challenging expectations that have been established for all children; and

(ii) be prepared to lead productive and independent adult lives, to the maximum extent possible;

(B) strengthening the role and responsibility of parents and ensuring that families of such children have meaningful opportunities to participate in the education of their children at school and at home;

(C) coordinating this chapter with other local, educational service agency, State, and Federal school improvement efforts, including improvement efforts under the Elementary and Secondary Education Act of 1965 [20 U.S.C.A. § 6301 et seq.], in order to ensure that such children benefit from such efforts and that special education can become a service for such children rather than a place where such children are sent;

(D) providing appropriate special education and related services, and aids and supports in the regular classroom, to such children, whenever appropriate;

(E) supporting high-quality, intensive preservice preparation and professional development for all personnel who work with children with disabilities in order to ensure that such personnel have the skills and knowledge necessary to improve the academic achievement and functional performance of children with disabilities, including the use of scientifically based instructional practices, to the maximum extent possible;

(F) providing incentives for whole-school approaches, scientifically based early reading programs, positive behavioral interventions and supports, and early intervening services to reduce the need to label children as disabled in order to address the learning and behavioral needs of such children;

(G) focusing resources on teaching and learning while reducing paperwork and requirements that do not assist in improving educational results; and

(H) supporting the development and use of technology, including assistive technology devices and assistive technology services, to maximize accessibility for children with disabilities.

(6) While States, local educational agencies, and educational service agencies are primarily responsible for providing an education for all children with disabilities, it is in the national interest that the Federal Government have a supporting role in assisting State and local efforts to educate children with disabilities in order to improve results for such children and to ensure equal protection of the law.

(7) A more equitable allocation of resources is essential for the Federal Government to meet its responsibility to provide an equal educational opportunity for all individuals.

(8) Parents and schools should be given expanded opportunities to resolve their disagreements in positive and constructive ways.

(9) Teachers, schools, local educational agencies, and States should be relieved of irrelevant and unnecessary paperwork burdens that do not lead to improved educational

outcomes.

(10) (A) The Federal Government must be responsive to the growing needs of an increasingly diverse society.

(B) America's ethnic profile is rapidly changing. In 2000, 1 of every 3 persons in the United States was a member of a minority group or was limited English proficient.

(C) Minority children comprise an increasing percentage of public school students.

(D) With such changing demographics, recruitment efforts for special education personnel should focus on increasing the participation of minorities in the teaching profession in order to provide appropriate role models with sufficient knowledge to address the special education needs of these students.

(11) (A) The limited English proficient population is the fastest growing in our Nation, and the growth is occurring in many parts of our Nation.

(B) Studies have documented apparent discrepancies in the levels of referral and placement of limited English proficient children in special education.

(C) Such discrepancies pose a special challenge for special education in the referral of, assessment of, and provision of services for, our Nation's students from non-English language backgrounds.

(12) (A) Greater efforts are needed to prevent the intensification of problems connected with mislabeling and high dropout rates among minority children with disabilities.

(B) More minority children continue to be served in special education than would be expected from the percentage of minority students in the general school population.

(C) African-American children are identified as having mental retardation and emotional disturbance at rates greater than their White counterparts.

(D) In the 1998-1999 school year, African-American children represented just 14.8 percent of the population aged 6 through 21, but comprised 20.2 percent of all children with disabilities.

(E) Studies have found that schools with predominately White students and teachers have placed disproportionately high numbers of their minority students into special education.

(13) (A) As the number of minority students in special education increases, the number of minority teachers and related services personnel produced in colleges and universities continues to decrease.

(B) The opportunity for full participation by minority individuals, minority organizations, and Historically Black Colleges and Universities in awards for grants and contracts, boards of organizations receiving assistance under this chapter, peer review panels, and training of professionals in the area of special education is essential to obtain greater success in the education of minority children with disabilities.

(14) As the graduation rates for children with disabilities continue to climb, providing effective transition services to promote successful post-school employment or education is an important measure of accountability for children with disabilities.

(d) Purposes

The purposes of this chapter are —

(1) (A) to ensure that all children with disabilities have available to them a free appropriate public education that emphasizes special education and related services designed to meet their unique needs and prepare them for further education, employment, and independent living;

(B) to ensure that the rights of children with disabilities and parents of such children are protected; and

(C) to assist States, localities, educational service agencies, and Federal agencies to provide for the education of all children with disabilities;

(2) to assist States in the implementation of a statewide, comprehensive, coordinated, multidisciplinary, interagency system of early intervention services for infants and toddlers with disabilities and their families;

(3) to ensure that educators and parents have the necessary tools to improve educational results for children with disabilities by supporting system improvement activities; coordinated research and personnel preparation; coordinated technical assistance, dissemination, and support; and technology development and media services; and

(4) to assess, and ensure the effectiveness of, efforts to educate children with disabilities.

§ 1401. Definitions

Except as otherwise provided, in this chapter:

(1) Assistive technology device

(A) In general

The term "assistive technology device" means any item, piece of equipment, or product system, whether acquired commercially off the shelf, modified, or customized, that is used to increase, maintain, or improve functional capabilities of a child with a disability.

(B) Exception

The term does not include a medical device that is surgically implanted, or the replacement o such device.

(2) Assistive technology service

The term "assistive technology service" means any service that directly assists a child with a disability in the selection, acquisition, or use of an assistive technology device. Such term includes —

(A) the evaluation of the needs of such child, including a functional evaluation of the child in the child's customary environment;

(B) purchasing, leasing, or otherwise providing for the acquisition of assistive technology devices by such child;

(C) selecting, designing, fitting, customizing, adapting, applying, maintaining, repairing, or replacing assistive technology devices;

(D) coordinating and using other therapies, interventions, or services with assistive technology devices, such as those associated with existing education and rehabilitation plans and programs;

(E) training or technical assistance for such child, or, where appropriate, the family of such child; and

(F) training or technical assistance for professionals (including individuals providing education and rehabilitation services), employers, or other individuals who provide services to, employ, or are otherwise substantially involved in the major life functions of such child.

(3) Child with a disability

(A) In general

The term "child with a disability" means a child —

(i) with mental retardation, hearing impairments (including deafness), speech or language impairments, visual impairments (including blindness), serious emotional disturbance (referred to in this chapter as "emotional disturbance"), orthopedic impairments, autism, traumatic brain injury, other health impairments, or specific learning disabilities; and

(ii) who, by reason thereof, needs special education and related services.

(B) Child aged 3 through 9

The term "child with a disability" for a child aged 3 through 9 (or any subset of that age range, including ages 3 through 5), may, at the discretion of the State and the local educational agency, include a child —

(i) experiencing developmental delays, as defined by the State and as measured by appropriate diagnostic instruments and procedures, in 1 or more of the following areas: physical development; cognitive development; communication development; social or emotional development; or adaptive development; and

(ii) who, by reason thereof, needs special education and related services.

* * *

(9) Free appropriate public education

The term "free appropriate public education" means special education and related services that-

(A) have been provided at public expense, under public supervision and direction, and without charge;

(B) meet the standards of the State educational agency;

(C) include an appropriate preschool, elementary school, or secondary school education in the State involved; and

(D) are provided in conformity with the individualized education program required under section 1414(d) of this title.

* * *

(11) Homeless children

The term "homeless children" has the meaning given the term "homeless children and youths" in section 11434a of Title 42.

* * *

(14) Individualized education program; IEP

The term "individualized education program" or "IEP" means a written statement for each child with a disability that is developed, reviewed, and revised in accordance with section 1414(d) of this title.

(15) Individualized family service plan

The term "individualized family service plan" has the meaning given the term in section 1436 of this title.

(16) Infant or toddler with a disability

The term "infant or toddler with a disability" has the meaning given the term in section 1432 of this title.

* * *

(18) Limited English proficient

The term "limited English proficient" has the meaning given the term in section 9101 of the Elementary and Secondary Education Act of 1965 [20 U.S.C.A. § 7801].

(19) Local educational agency

    (A) In general

The term "local educational agency" means a public board of education or other public authority legally constituted within a State for either administrative control or direction of, or to perform a service function for, public elementary schools or secondary schools in a city, county, township, school district, or other political subdivision of a State, or for such combination of school districts or counties as are recognized in a State as an administrative agency for its public elementary schools or secondary schools.

    (B) Educational service agencies and other public institutions or agencies

The term includes —

        (i) an educational service agency; and

        (ii) any other public institution or agency having administrative control and direction of a public elementary school or secondary school.

* * *

(20) Native language

The term "native language", when used with respect to an individual who is limited English proficient, means the language normally used by the individual or, in the case of a child, the language normally used by the parents of the child.

* * *

(23) Parent

The term "parent" means —

(A) a natural, adoptive, or foster parent of a child (unless a foster parent is prohibited by State law from serving as a parent);

(B) a guardian (but not the State if the child is a ward of the State);

(C) an individual acting in the place of a natural or adoptive parent (including a grandparent, stepparent, or other relative) with whom the child lives, or an individual who is legally responsible for the child's welfare; or

(D) except as used in sections 1415(b)(2) and 1439(a)(5) of this title, an individual assigned under either of those sections to be a surrogate parent.

* * *

(26) Related services

(A) In general

The term "related services" means transportation, and such developmental, corrective, and other supportive services (including speech-language pathology and audiology services, interpreting services, psychological services, physical and occupational therapy, recreation, including therapeutic recreation, social work services, school nurse services designed to enable a child with a disability to receive a free appropriate public education as described in the individualized education program of the child, counseling services, including rehabilitation counseling, orientation and mobility services, and medical services, except that such medical services shall be for diagnostic and evaluation purposes only) as may be required to assist a child with a disability to benefit from special education, and includes the early identification and assessment of disabling conditions in children.

(B) Exception

The term does not include a medical device that is surgically implanted, or the replacement of such device.

* * *

(29) Special education

The term "special education" means specially designed instruction, at no cost to parents, to meet the unique needs of a child with a disability, including —

(A) instruction conducted in the classroom, in the home, in hospitals and institutions, and in other settings; and

(B) instruction in physical education.

(30) Specific learning disability

(A) In general

The term "specific learning disability" means a disorder in 1 or more of the basic psychological processes involved in understanding or in using language, spoken or written, which disorder may manifest itself in the imperfect ability to listen, think, speak, read, write, spell, or do mathematical calculations.

(B)   Disorders included

Such term includes such conditions as perceptual disabilities, brain injury, minimal brain dysfunction, dyslexia, and developmental aphasia.

(C)   Disorders not included

Such term does not include a learning problem that is primarily the result of visual, hearing, or motor disabilities, of mental retardation, of emotional disturbance, or of environmental, cultural, or economic disadvantage.

(31)   State

The term "State" means each of the 50 States, the District of Columbia, the Commonwealth of Puerto Rico, and each of the outlying areas.

(32)   State educational agency

The term "State educational agency" means the State board of education or other agency or officer primarily responsible for the State supervision of public elementary schools and secondary schools, or, if there is no such officer or agency, an officer or agency designated by the Governor or by State law.

(33)   Supplementary aids and services

The term "supplementary aids and services" means aids, services, and other supports that are provided in regular education classes or other education-related settings to enable children with disabilities to be educated with nondisabled children to the maximum extent appropriate in accordance with section 1412(a)(5) of this title.

(34)   Transition services

The term "transition services" means a coordinated set of activities for a child with a disability that —

(A) is designed to be within a results-oriented process, that is focused on improving the academic and functional achievement of the child with a disability to facilitate the child's movement from school to post-school activities, including post-secondary education, vocational education, integrated employment (including supported employment), continuing and adult education, adult services, independent living, or community participation;

(B) is based on the individual child's needs, taking into account the child's strengths, preferences, and interests; and

(C) includes instruction, related services, community experiences, the development of employment and other post-school adult living objectives, and, when appropriate, acquisition of daily living skills and functional vocational evaluation.

(35)   Universal design

The term "universal design" has the meaning given the term in section 3002 of Title 29.

(36)   Ward of the State

(A) In general

The term "ward of the State" means a child who, as determined by the State where the child resides, is a foster child, is a ward of the State, or is in the custody of a public child welfare agency.

(B) Exception

The term does not include a foster child who has a foster parent who meets the definition of a parent in paragraph (23).

* * *

§ 1403. Abrogation of State sovereign immunity

(a) In general

A State shall not be immune under the 11th amendment to the Constitution of the United States from suit in Federal court for a violation of this chapter.

(b) Remedies

In a suit against a State for a violation of this chapter, remedies (including remedies both at law and in equity) are available for such a violation to the same extent as those remedies are available for such a violation in the suit against any public entity other than a State.

(c) Effective date

Subsections (a) and (b) apply with respect to violations that occur in whole or part after October 30, 1990.

* * *

Part B

§ 1412. State eligibility

(a) In general

A State is eligible for assistance under this subchapter for a fiscal year if the State submits a plan that provides assurances to the Secretary that the State has in effect policies and procedures to ensure that the State meets each of the following conditions:

(1) Free appropriate public education

(A) In general

A free appropriate public education is available to all children with disabilities residing in the State between the ages of 3 and 21, inclusive, including children with disabilities who have been suspended or expelled from school.

(B) Limitation

The obligation to make a free appropriate public education available to all children with disabilities does not apply with respect to children —

(i) aged 3 through 5 and 18 through 21 in a State to the extent that its application to thos children would be inconsistent with State law or practice, or the order of any court, respecting the provision of public education to children in those age ranges; and

(ii) aged 18 through 21 to the extent that State law does not require that special education and related services under this subchapter be provided to children with disabilities who, in the educational placement prior to their incarceration in an adult correctional facility —

(I) were not actually identified as being a child with a disability under section 1401 of this title; or

(II) did not have an individualized education program under this subchapter.

(C) State flexibility

A State that provides early intervention services in accordance with subchapter III to a child who is eligible for services under section 1419 of this title, is not required to provide such child with a free appropriate public education.

(2) Full educational opportunity goal

The State has established a goal of providing full educational opportunity to all children with disabilities and a detailed timetable for accomplishing that goal.

(3) Child find

(A) In general

All children with disabilities residing in the State, including children with disabilities who are homeless children or are wards of the State and children with disabilities attending private schools, regardless of the severity of their disabilities, and who are in need of special education and related services, are identified, located, and evaluated and a practical method is developed and implemented to determine which children with disabilities are currently receiving needed special education and related services.

(B) Construction

Nothing in this chapter requires that children be classified by their disability so long as each child who has a disability listed in section 1401 of this title and who, by reason of that disability, needs special education and related services is regarded as a child with a disability under this subchapter.

(4) Individualized education program

An individualized education program, or an individualized family service plan that meets the requirements of section 1436(d) of this title, is developed, reviewed, and revised for each child with a disability in accordance with section 1414(d) of this title.

(5) Least restrictive environment

(A) In general

To the maximum extent appropriate, children with disabilities, including children in public or private institutions or other care facilities, are educated with children who are not disabled, and special classes, separate schooling, or other removal of children with disabilities from the regular educational environment occurs only when the nature or severity of the disability of a child is such that education in regular classes with the use of supplementary aids and services cannot be achieved satisfactorily.

(B) Additional requirement

(i)   In general

A State funding mechanism shall not result in placements that violate the requirements of subparagraph (A), and a State shall not use a funding mechanism by which the State distributes funds on the basis of the type of setting in which a child is served that will result in the failure to provide a child with a disability a free appropriate public education according to the unique needs of the child as described in the child's IEP.

(ii)   Assurance

If the State does not have policies and procedures to ensure compliance with clause (i), the State shall provide the Secretary an assurance that the State will revise the funding mechanism as soon as feasible to ensure that such mechanism does not result in such placements.

(6)   Procedural safeguards

(A)   In general

Children with disabilities and their parents are afforded the procedural safeguards required by section 1415 of this title.

(B)   Additional procedural safeguards

Procedures to ensure that testing and evaluation materials and procedures utilized for the purposes of evaluation and placement of children with disabilities for services under this chapter will be selected and administered so as not to be racially or culturally discriminatory. Such materials or procedures shall be provided and administered in the child's native language or mode of communication, unless it clearly is not feasible to do so, and no single procedure shall be the sole criterion for determining an appropriate educational program for a child.

(7)   Evaluation

Children with disabilities are evaluated in accordance with subsections (a) through (c) of section 1414 of this title.

(8)   Confidentiality

Agencies in the State comply with section 1417(c) of this title (relating to the confidentiality of records and information).

(9)   Transition from subchapter III to preschool programs

Children participating in early intervention programs assisted under subchapter III, and who will participate in preschool programs assisted under this subchapter, experience a smooth and effective transition to those preschool programs in a manner consistent with section 1437(a)(9) of this title. By the third birthday of such a child, an individualized education program or, if consistent with sections 1414(d)(2)(B) and 1436(d) of this title, an individualized family service plan, has been developed and is being implemented for the child. The local educational agency will participate in transition planning conferences arranged by the designated lead agency under section 1435(a)(10) of this title.

(10)   Children in private schools

(A) Children enrolled in private schools by their parents (omitted)

(B) Children placed in, or referred to, private schools by public agencies

(i) In general

Children with disabilities in private schools and facilities are provided special education and related services, in accordance with an individualized education program, at no cost to their parents, if such children are placed in, or referred to, such schools or facilities by the State or appropriate local educational agency as the means of carrying out the requirements of this subchapter or any other applicable law requiring the provision of special education and related services to all children with disabilities within such State.

(ii) Standards

In all cases described in clause (i), the State educational agency shall determine whether such schools and facilities meet standards that apply to State educational agencies and local educational agencies and that children so served have all the rights the children would have if served by such agencies.

(C) Payment for education of children enrolled in private schools without consent of or referral by the public agency

(i) In general

Subject to subparagraph (A), this subchapter does not require a local educational agency to pay for the cost of education, including special education and related services, of a child with a disability at a private school or facility if that agency made a free appropriate public education available to the child and the parents elected to place the child in such private school or facility.

(ii) Reimbursement for private school placement

If the parents of a child with a disability, who previously received special education and related services under the authority of a public agency, enroll the child in a private elementary school or secondary school without the consent of or referral by the public agency, a court or a hearing officer may require the agency to reimburse the parents for the cost of that enrollment if the court or hearing officer finds that the agency had not made a free appropriate public education available to the child in a timely manner prior to that enrollment.

(iii) Limitation on reimbursement

The cost of reimbursement described in clause (ii) may be reduced or denied —

(I) if —

(aa) at the most recent IEP meeting that the parents attended prior to removal of the child from the public school, the parents did not inform the IEP Team that they were rejecting the placement proposed by the public agency to provide a free appropriate public education to their child, including stating their concerns and their intent to enroll their child in a private school at public expense; or

(bb) 10 business days (including any holidays that occur on a business day) prior to the removal of the child from the public school, the parents did not give written notice to the public agency of the information described in item (aa);

(II) if, prior to the parents' removal of the child from the public school, the public agency informed the parents, through the notice requirements described in section 1415(b)(3) of this title, of its intent to evaluate the child (including a statement of the purpose of the evaluation that was appropriate and reasonable), but the parents did not make the child available for such evaluation; or

(III) upon a judicial finding of unreasonableness with respect to actions taken by the parents.

(iv) Exception

Notwithstanding the notice requirement in clause (iii)(I), the cost of reimbursement —

(I) shall not be reduced or denied for failure to provide such notice if —

(aa) the school prevented the parent from providing such notice;

(bb) the parents had not received notice, pursuant to section 1415 of this title, of the notice requirement in clause (iii)(I); or

(cc) compliance with clause (iii)(I) would likely result in physical harm to the child; and

(II) may, in the discretion of a court or a hearing officer, not be reduced or denied for failure to provide such notice if —

(aa) the parent is illiterate or cannot write in English; or

(bb) compliance with clause (iii)(I) would likely result in serious emotional harm to the child.

(16) Participation in assessments

(A) In general

All children with disabilities are included in all general State and districtwide assessment programs, including assessments described under section 6311 of this title, with appropriate accommodations and alternate assessments where necessary and as indicated in their respective individualized education programs.

(B) Accommodation guidelines

The State (or, in the case of a districtwide assessment, the local educational agency) has developed guidelines for the provision of appropriate accommodations.

(C) Alternate assessments

(i) In general

The State (or, in the case of a districtwide assessment, the local educational agency) has developed and implemented guidelines for the participation of children with disabilities in alternate assessments for those children who cannot participate in regular assessments under subparagraph (A) with accommodations as indicated in their respective individualized education programs.

(ii) Requirements for alternate assessments

The guidelines under clause (i) shall provide for alternate assessments that —

(I) are aligned with the State's challenging academic content standards and challenging student academic achievement standards; and

(II) if the State has adopted alternate academic achievement standards permitted under the regulations promulgated to carry out section 6311(b)(1) of this title, measure the achievement of children with disabilities against those standards.

(iii)   Conduct of alternate assessments

The State conducts the alternate assessments described in this subparagraph.

* * *

(22)   Suspension and expulsion rates

(A)   In general

The State educational agency examines data, including data disaggregated by race and ethnicity, to determine if significant discrepancies are occurring in the rate of long-term suspensions and expulsions of children with disabilities —

(i) among local educational agencies in the State; or

(ii) compared to such rates for nondisabled children within such agencies.

(B)   Review and revision of policies

If such discrepancies are occurring, the State educational agency reviews and, if appropriate, revises (or requires the affected State or local educational agency to revise) its policies, procedures, and practices relating to the development and implementation of IEPs, the use of positive behavioral interventions and supports, and procedural safeguards, to ensure that such policies, procedures, and practices comply with this chapter.

(23) Access to instructional materials (omitted)

(24)   Overidentification and disproportionality

The State has in effect, consistent with the purposes of this chapter and with section 1418(d) of this title, policies and procedures designed to prevent the inappropriate overidentification or disproportionate representation by race and ethnicity of children as children with disabilities, including children with disabilities with a particular impairment described in section 1401 of this title.

(25)   Prohibition on mandatory medication

(A)   In general

The State educational agency shall prohibit State and local educational agency personnel from requiring a child to obtain a prescription for a substance covered by the Controlled Substances Act (21 U.S.C. 801 et seq.) as a condition of attending school, receiving an evaluation under subsection (a) or (c) of section 1414 of this title, or receiving services under this chapter.

(B)   Rule of construction

Nothing in subparagraph (A) shall be construed to create a Federal prohibition against teachers and other school personnel consulting or sharing classroom-based observations with parents or guardians regarding a student's academic and functional performance, or behavior in the classroom or school, or regarding the need for evaluation for special education or related services under paragraph (3).

* * *

§ 1413. Local educational agency eligibility (omitted)

§ 1414. Evaluations, eligibility determinations, individualized education programs, and educational placements

(a) Evaluations, parental consent, and reevaluations

  (1) Initial evaluations

    (A) In general

A State educational agency, other State agency, or local educational agency shall conduct a full and individual initial evaluation in accordance with this paragraph and subsection (b), before the initial provision of special education and related services to a child with a disability under this subchapter.

    (B) Request for initial evaluation

Consistent with subparagraph (D), either a parent of a child, or a State educational agency, other State agency, or local educational agency may initiate a request for an initial evaluation to determine if the child is a child with a disability.

    (C) Procedures

      (i) In general

Such initial evaluation shall consist of procedures —

        (I) to determine whether a child is a child with a disability (as defined in section 1401 of this title) within 60 days of receiving parental consent for the evaluation, or, if the State establishes a timeframe within which the evaluation must be conducted, within such timeframe; and

        (II) to determine the educational needs of such child.

      (ii) Exception

The relevant timeframe in clause (i)(I) shall not apply to a local educational agency if —

        (I) a child enrolls in a school served by the local educational agency after the relevant timeframe in clause (i)(I) has begun and prior to a determination by the child's previous local educational agency as to whether the child is a child with a disability (as defined in section 1401 of this title), but only if the subsequent local educational agency is making sufficient progress to ensure a prompt completion of the evaluation, and the parent and subsequent local educational agency agree to a specific time when the evaluation will be completed; or

        (II) the parent of a child repeatedly fails or refuses to produce the child for the evaluation.

    (D) Parental consent

      (i) In general

        (I) Consent for initial evaluation

The agency proposing to conduct an initial evaluation to determine if the child qualifies as a child with a disability as defined in section 1401 of this title shall obtain informed consent from the parent of such child before conducting the evaluation. Parental consent for evaluation shall not be construed as consent for placement for receipt of special education and related services.

(II) Consent for services

An agency that is responsible for making a free appropriate public education available to a child with a disability under this subchapter shall seek to obtain informed consent from the parent of such child before providing special education and related services to the child.

(ii) Absence of consent

(I) For initial evaluation

If the parent of such child does not provide consent for an initial evaluation under clause (i)(I), or the parent fails to respond to a request to provide the consent, the local educational agency may pursue the initial evaluation of the child by utilizing the procedures described in section 1415 of this title, except to the extent inconsistent with State law relating to such parental consent.

(II) For services

If the parent of such child refuses to consent to services under clause (i)(II), the local educational agency shall not provide special education and related services to the child by utilizing the procedures described in section 1415 of this title.

(III) Effect on agency obligations

If the parent of such child refuses to consent to the receipt of special education and related services, or the parent fails to respond to a request to provide such consent —

(aa) the local educational agency shall not be considered to be in violation of the requirement to make available a free appropriate public education to the child for the failure to provide such child with the special education and related services for which the local educational agency requests such consent; and

(bb) the local educational agency shall not be required to convene an IEP meeting or develop an IEP under this section for the child for the special education and related services for which the local educational agency requests such consent.

(iii) Consent for wards of the State

(I) In general

If the child is a ward of the State and is not residing with the child's parent, the agency shall make reasonable efforts to obtain the informed consent from the parent (as defined in section 1401 of this title) of the child for an initial evaluation to determine whether the child is a child with a disability.

(II) Exception

The agency shall not be required to obtain informed consent from the parent of a child for an initial evaluation to determine whether the child is a child with a disability if —

(aa) despite reasonable efforts to do so, the agency cannot discover the whereabouts of the parent of the child;

(bb) the rights of the parents of the child have been terminated in accordance with State law; or

(cc) the rights of the parent to make educational decisions have been subrogated by a judge in accordance with State law and consent for an initial evaluation has been given by an individual appointed by the judge to represent the child.

(E)   Rule of construction

The screening of a student by a teacher or specialist to determine appropriate instructional strategies for curriculum implementation shall not be considered to be an evaluation for eligibility for special education and related services.

(2)   Reevaluations

(A)   In general

A local educational agency shall ensure that a reevaluation of each child with a disability is conducted in accordance with subsections (b) and (c) —

(i) if the local educational agency determines that the educational or related services needs, including improved academic achievement and functional performance, of the child warrant a reevaluation; or

(ii) if the child's parents or teacher requests a reevaluation.

(B)   Limitation

A reevaluation conducted under subparagraph (A) shall occur —

(i) not more frequently than once a year, unless the parent and the local educational agency agree otherwise; and

(ii) at least once every 3 years, unless the parent and the local educational agency agree that a reevaluation is unnecessary.

(b)   Evaluation procedures

(1)   Notice

The local educational agency shall provide notice to the parents of a child with a disability, in accordance with subsections (b)(3), (b)(4), and (c) of section 1415 of this title, that describes any evaluation procedures such agency proposes to conduct.

(2)   Conduct of evaluation

In conducting the evaluation, the local educational agency shall —

(A) use a variety of assessment tools and strategies to gather relevant functional, developmental, and academic information, including information provided by the parent, that may assist in determining —

(i) whether the child is a child with a disability; and

(ii) the content of the child's individualized education program, including information related to enabling the child to be involved in and progress in the general education curriculum, or, for preschool children, to participate in appropriate activities;

(B) not use any single measure or assessment as the sole criterion for determining whether a child is a child with a disability or determining an appropriate educational program for the child; and

(C) use technically sound instruments that may assess the relative contribution of cognitive and behavioral factors, in addition to physical or developmental factors.

(3)   Additional requirements

Each local educational agency shall ensure that —

(A) assessments and other evaluation materials used to assess a child under this section —

(i) are selected and administered so as not to be discriminatory on a racial or cultural basis;

(ii) are provided and administered in the language and form most likely to yield accurate information on what the child knows and can do academically, developmentally, and functionally, unless it is not feasible to so provide or administer;

(iii) are used for purposes for which the assessments or measures are valid and reliable;

(iv) are administered by trained and knowledgeable personnel; and

(v) are administered in accordance with any instructions provided by the producer of such assessments;

(B) the child is assessed in all areas of suspected disability;

(C) assessment tools and strategies that provide relevant information that directly assists persons in determining the educational needs of the child are provided; and

(D) assessments of children with disabilities who transfer from 1 school district to another school district in the same academic year are coordinated with such children's prior and subsequent schools, as necessary and as expeditiously as possible, to ensure prompt completion of full evaluations.

(4)   Determination of eligibility and educational need

Upon completion of the administration of assessments and other evaluation measures —

(A) the determination of whether the child is a child with a disability as defined in section 1401(3) of this title and the educational needs of the child shall be made by a team of qualified professionals and the parent of the child in accordance with paragraph (5); and

(B) a copy of the evaluation report and the documentation of determination of eligibility shall be given to the parent.

(5)   Special rule for eligibility determination

In making a determination of eligibility under paragraph (4)(A), a child shall not be determined to be a child with a disability if the determinant factor for such determination is —

(A) lack of appropriate instruction in reading, including in the essential components of reading instruction (as defined in section 6368(3) of this title);

(B) lack of instruction in math; or

(C) limited English proficiency.

(6)   Specific learning disabilities

   (A)   In general

   Notwithstanding section 1406(b) of this title, when determining whether a child has a specific learning disability as defined in section 1401 of this title, a local educational agency shall not be required to take into consideration whether a child has a severe discrepancy between achievement and intellectual ability in oral expression, listening comprehension, written expression, basic reading skill, reading comprehension, mathematical calculation, or mathematical reasoning.

   (B)   Additional authority

   In determining whether a child has a specific learning disability, a local educational agency may use a process that determines if the child responds to scientific, research-based intervention as a part of the evaluation procedures described in paragraphs (2) and (3).

(c)   Additional requirements for evaluation and reevaluations

(1)   Review of existing evaluation data

As part of an initial evaluation (if appropriate) and as part of any reevaluation under this section, the IEP Team and other qualified professionals, as appropriate, shall —

   (A) review existing evaluation data on the child, including —

      (i) evaluations and information provided by the parents of the child;

      (ii) current classroom-based, local, or State assessments, and classroom-based observations; and

      (iii) observations by teachers and related services providers; and

   (B) on the basis of that review, and input from the child's parents, identify what additional data, if any, are needed to determine —

      (i) whether the child is a child with a disability as defined in section 1401(3) of this title, and the educational needs of the child, or, in case of a reevaluation of a child, whether the child continues to have such a disability and such educational needs;

      (ii) the present levels of academic achievement and related developmental needs of the child;

      (iii) whether the child needs special education and related services, or in the case of a reevaluation of a child, whether the child continues to need special education and related services; and

      (iv) whether any additions or modifications to the special education and related services are needed to enable the child to meet the measurable annual goals set out in the individualized education program of the child and to participate, as appropriate, in the general education curriculum.

(2)   Source of data

The local educational agency shall administer such assessments and other evaluation measures as may be needed to produce the data identified by the IEP Team under paragraph (1)(B).

(3)   Parental consent

Each local educational agency shall obtain informed parental consent, in accordance with subsection (a)(1)(D), prior to conducting any reevaluation of a child with a disability, except that such informed parental consent need not be obtained if the local educational agency can demonstrate that it had taken reasonable measures to obtain such consent and the child's parent has failed to respond.

(4)   Requirements if additional data are not needed

If the IEP Team and other qualified professionals, as appropriate, determine that no additional data are needed to determine whether the child continues to be a child with a disability and to determine the child's educational needs, the local educational agency —

(A) shall notify the child's parents of —

(i) that determination and the reasons for the determination; and

(ii) the right of such parents to request an assessment to determine whether the child continues to be a child with a disability and to determine the child's educational needs; and

(B) shall not be required to conduct such an assessment unless requested to by the child's parents.

(5)   Evaluations before change in eligibility

(A)   In general

Except as provided in subparagraph (B), a local educational agency shall evaluate a child with a disability in accordance with this section before determining that the child is no longer a child with a disability.

(B)   Exception

(i)   In general

The evaluation described in subparagraph (A) shall not be required before the termination of a child's eligibility under this subchapter due to graduation from secondary school with a regular diploma, or due to exceeding the age eligibility for a free appropriate public education under State law.

(ii)   Summary of performance

For a child whose eligibility under this subchapter terminates under circumstances described in clause (i), a local educational agency shall provide the child with a summary of the child's academic achievement and functional performance, which shall include recommendations on how to assist the child in meeting the child's postsecondary goals.

(d)   Individualized education programs

(1) Definitions

In this chapter:

  (A) Individualized education program

  (i) In general

The term "individualized education program" or "IEP" means a written statement for each child with a disability that is developed, reviewed, and revised in accordance with this section and that includes —

  (I) a statement of the child's present levels of academic achievement and functional performance, including —

    (aa) how the child's disability affects the child's involvement and progress in the general education curriculum;

    (bb) for preschool children, as appropriate, how the disability affects the child's participation in appropriate activities; and

    (cc) for children with disabilities who take alternate assessments aligned to alternate achievement standards, a description of benchmarks or short-term objectives;

  (II) a statement of measurable annual goals, including academic and functional goals, designed to —

    (aa) meet the child's needs that result from the child's disability to enable the child to be involved in and make progress in the general education curriculum; and

    (bb) meet each of the child's other educational needs that result from the child's disability;

  (III) a description of how the child's progress toward meeting the annual goals described in subclause (II) will be measured and when periodic reports on the progress the child is making toward meeting the annual goals (such as through the use of quarterly or other periodic reports, concurrent with the issuance of report cards) will be provided;

  (IV) a statement of the special education and related services and supplementary aids and services, based on peer-reviewed research to the extent practicable, to be provided to the child, or on behalf of the child, and a statement of the program modifications or supports for school personnel that will be provided for the child —

    (aa) to advance appropriately toward attaining the annual goals;

    (bb) to be involved in and make progress in the general education curriculum in accordance with subclause (I) and to participate in extracurricular and other nonacademic activities; and

    (cc) to be educated and participate with other children with disabilities and nondisabled children in the activities described in this subparagraph;

  (V) an explanation of the extent, if any, to which the child will not participate with nondisabled children in the regular class and in the activities described in subclause (IV)(cc);

(VI) (aa) a statement of any individual appropriate accommodations that are necessary to measure the academic achievement and functional performance of the child on State and districtwide assessments consistent with section 1412(a)(16)(A) of this title; and

(bb) if the IEP Team determines that the child shall take an alternate assessment on a particular State or districtwide assessment of student achievement, a statement of why —

(AA) the child cannot participate in the regular assessment; and

(BB) the particular alternate assessment selected is appropriate for the child;

(VII) the projected date for the beginning of the services and modifications described in subclause (IV), and the anticipated frequency, location, and duration of those services and modifications; and

(VIII) beginning not later than the first IEP to be in effect when the child is 16, and updated annually thereafter —

(aa) appropriate measurable postsecondary goals based upon age appropriate transition assessments related to training, education, employment, and, where appropriate, independent living skills;

(bb) the transition services (including courses of study) needed to assist the child in reaching those goals; and

(cc) beginning not later than 1 year before the child reaches the age of majority under State law, a statement that the child has been informed of the child's rights under this chapter, if any, that will transfer to the child on reaching the age of majority under section 1415(m) of this title.

(ii) Rule of construction

Nothing in this section shall be construed to require —

(I) that additional information be included in a child's IEP beyond what is explicitly required in this section; and

(II) the IEP Team to include information under 1 component of a child's IEP that is already contained under another component of such IEP.

(B) Individualized education program team

The term "individualized education program team" or "IEP Team" means a group of individuals composed of —

(i) the parents of a child with a disability;

(ii) not less than 1 regular education teacher of such child (if the child is, or may be, participating in the regular education environment);

(iii) not less than 1 special education teacher, or where appropriate, not less than 1 special education provider of such child;

(iv) a representative of the local educational agency who —

(I) is qualified to provide, or supervise the provision of, specially designed instruction to meet the unique needs of children with disabilities;

(II) is knowledgeable about the general education curriculum; and

(III) is knowledgeable about the availability of resources of the local educational agency;

(v) an individual who can interpret the instructional implications of evaluation results, who may be a member of the team described in clauses (ii) through (vi);

(vi) at the discretion of the parent or the agency, other individuals who have knowledge or special expertise regarding the child, including related services personnel as appropriate; and

(vii) whenever appropriate, the child with a disability.

(C)   IEP Team attendance

(i)   Attendance not necessary

A member of the IEP Team shall not be required to attend an IEP meeting, in whole or in part, if the parent of a child with a disability and the local educational agency agree that the attendance of such member is not necessary because the member's area of the curriculum or related services is not being modified or discussed in the meeting.

(ii)   Excusal

A member of the IEP Team may be excused from attending an IEP meeting, in whole or in part, when the meeting involves a modification to or discussion of the member's area of the curriculum or related services, if —

(I) the parent and the local educational agency consent to the excusal; and

(II) the member submits, in writing to the parent and the IEP Team, input into the development of the IEP prior to the meeting.

(iii)   Written agreement and consent required

A parent's agreement under clause (i) and consent under clause (ii) shall be in writing.

(D)   IEP Team transition

In the case of a child who was previously served under subchapter III, an invitation to the initial IEP meeting shall, at the request of the parent, be sent to the subchapter III service coordinator or other representatives of the subchapter III system to assist with the smooth transition of services.

(2)   Requirement that program be in effect

(A)   In general

At the beginning of each school year, each local educational agency, State educational agency, or other State agency, as the case may be, shall have in effect, for each child with a disability in the agency's jurisdiction, an individualized education program, as defined in paragraph (1)(A).

(B)   Program for child aged 3 through 5

In the case of a child with a disability aged 3 through 5 (or, at the discretion of the State educational agency, a 2-year-old child with a disability who will turn age 3 during the school year), the IEP Team shall consider the individualized family service plan that contains the material described in section 1436 of this title, and that is developed in accordance with this section, and the individualized family service plan may serve as the IEP of the child if using that plan as the IEP is —

(i) consistent with State policy; and

(ii) agreed to by the agency and the child's parents.

(C)   Program for children who transfer school districts

(i)   In general

(I)   Transfer within the same State

In the case of a child with a disability who transfers school districts within the same academic year, who enrolls in a new school, and who had an IEP that was in effect in the same State, the local educational agency shall provide such child with a free appropriate public education, including services comparable to those described in the previously held IEP, in consultation with the parents until such time as the local educational agency adopts the previously held IEP or develops, adopts, and implements a new IEP that is consistent with Federal and State law.

(II)   Transfer outside State

In the case of a child with a disability who transfers school districts within the same academic year, who enrolls in a new school, and who had an IEP that was in effect in another State, the local educational agency shall provide such child with a free appropriate public education, including services comparable to those described in the previously held IEP, in consultation with the parents until such time as the local educational agency conducts an evaluation pursuant to subsection (a)(1), if determined to be necessary by such agency, and develops a new IEP, if appropriate, that is consistent with Federal and State law.

(ii)   Transmittal of records

To facilitate the transition for a child described in clause (i) —

(I) the new school in which the child enrolls shall take reasonable steps to promptly obtain the child's records, including the IEP and supporting documents and any other records relating to the provision of special education or related services to the child, from the previous school in which the child was enrolled, pursuant to section 99.31(a)(2) of title 34, Code of Federal Regulations; and

(II) the previous school in which the child was enrolled shall take reasonable steps to promptly respond to such request from the new school.

(3)   Development of IEP

(A)   In general

In developing each child's IEP, the IEP Team, subject to subparagraph (C), shall consider —

(i) the strengths of the child;

(ii) the concerns of the parents for enhancing the education of their child;

(iii) the results of the initial evaluation or most recent evaluation of the child; and

(iv) the academic, developmental, and functional needs of the child.

(B) Consideration of special factors

The IEP Team shall —

(i) in the case of a child whose behavior impedes the child's learning or that of others, consider the use of positive behavioral interventions and supports, and other strategies, to address that behavior;

(ii) in the case of a child with limited English proficiency, consider the language needs of the child as such needs relate to the child's IEP;

(iii) in the case of a child who is blind or visually impaired, provide for instruction in Braille and the use of Braille unless the IEP Team determines, after an evaluation of the child's reading and writing skills, needs, and appropriate reading and writing media (including an evaluation of the child's future needs for instruction in Braille or the use of Braille), that instruction in Braille or the use of Braille is not appropriate for the child;

(iv) consider the communication needs of the child, and in the case of a child who is deaf or hard of hearing, consider the child's language and communication needs, opportunities for direct communications with peers and professional personnel in the child's language and communication mode, academic level, and full range of needs, including opportunities for direct instruction in the child's language and communication mode; and

(v) consider whether the child needs assistive technology devices and services.

(C) Requirement with respect to regular education teacher

A regular education teacher of the child, as a member of the IEP Team, shall, to the extent appropriate, participate in the development of the IEP of the child, including the determination of appropriate positive behavioral interventions and supports, and other strategies, and the determination of supplementary aids and services, program modifications, and support for school personnel consistent with paragraph (1)(A)(i)(IV).

(D) Agreement

In making changes to a child's IEP after the annual IEP meeting for a school year, the parent of a child with a disability and the local educational agency may agree not to convene an IEP meeting for the purposes of making such changes, and instead may develop a written document to amend or modify the child's current IEP.

(E) Consolidation of IEP Team meetings

To the extent possible, the local educational agency shall encourage the consolidation of reevaluation meetings for the child and other IEP Team meetings for the child.

(F) Amendments

Changes to the IEP may be made either by the entire IEP Team or, as provided in subparagraph (D), by amending the IEP rather than by redrafting the entire IEP. Upon request, a parent shall be provided with a revised copy of the IEP with the amendments incorporated.

(4) Review and revision of IEP

(A) In general

The local educational agency shall ensure that, subject to subparagraph (B), the IEP Team —

(i) reviews the child's IEP periodically, but not less frequently than annually, to determine whether the annual goals for the child are being achieved; and

(ii) revises the IEP as appropriate to address —

(I) any lack of expected progress toward the annual goals and in the general education curriculum, where appropriate;

(II) the results of any reevaluation conducted under this section;

(III) information about the child provided to, or by, the parents, as described in subsection (c)(1)(B);

(IV) the child's anticipated needs; or

(V) other matters.

(B) Requirement with respect to regular education teacher

A regular education teacher of the child, as a member of the IEP Team, shall, consistent with paragraph (1)(C), participate in the review and revision of the IEP of the child.

(5) Multi-year IEP demonstration

(A) Pilot program

(i) Purpose

The purpose of this paragraph is to provide an opportunity for States to allow parents and local educational agencies the opportunity for long-term planning by offering the option of developing a comprehensive multi-year IEP, not to exceed 3 years, that is designed to coincide with the natural transition points for the child.

(ii) Authorization

In order to carry out the purpose of this paragraph, the Secretary is authorized to approve not more than 15 proposals from States to carry out the activity described in clause (i).

(iii) Proposal

(I) In general

A State desiring to participate in the program under this paragraph shall submit a proposal to the Secretary at such time and in such manner as the Secretary may reasonably require.

(II) Content

The proposal shall include —

(aa) assurances that the development of a multi-year IEP under this paragraph is optional for parents;

(bb) assurances that the parent is required to provide informed consent before a comprehensive multi-year IEP is developed;

(cc) a list of required elements for each multi-year IEP, including —

(AA) measurable goals pursuant to paragraph (1)(A)(i)(II), coinciding with natural transition points for the child, that will enable the child to be involved in and make progress in the general education curriculum and that will meet the child's other needs that result from the child's disability; and

(BB) measurable annual goals for determining progress toward meeting the goals described in subitem (AA); and

(dd) a description of the process for the review and revision of each multi-year IEP, including —

(AA) a review by the IEP Team of the child's multi-year IEP at each of the child's natural transition points;

(BB) in years other than a child's natural transition points, an annual review of the child's IEP to determine the child's current levels of progress and whether the annual goals for the child are being achieved, and a requirement to amend the IEP, as appropriate, to enable the child to continue to meet the measurable goals set out in the IEP;

(CC) if the IEP Team determines on the basis of a review that the child is not making sufficient progress toward the goals described in the multi-year IEP, a requirement that the local educational agency shall ensure that the IEP Team carries out a more thorough review of the IEP in accordance with paragraph (4) within 30 calendar days; and

(DD) at the request of the parent, a requirement that the IEP Team shall conduct a review of the child's multi-year IEP rather than or subsequent to an annual review.

* * *

(7) Children with disabilities in adult prisons

(A) In general

The following requirements shall not apply to children with disabilities who are convicted as adults under State law and incarcerated in adult prisons:

(i) The requirements contained in section 1412(a)(16) of this title and paragraph (1)(A)(i)(VI) (relating to participation of children with disabilities in general assessments).

(ii) The requirements of items (aa) and (bb) of paragraph (1)(A)(i)(VIII) (relating to transition planning and transition services), do not apply with respect to such children whose eligibility under this subchapter will end, because of such children's age, before such children will be released from prison.

(B) Additional requirement

If a child with a disability is convicted as an adult under State law and incarcerated in an adult prison, the child's IEP Team may modify the child's IEP or placement notwithstanding the requirements of sections 1412(a)(5)(A) of this title and paragraph (1)(A) if the State has demonstrated a bona fide security or compelling penological interest that cannot otherwise be accommodated.

(e) Educational placements

Each local educational agency or State educational agency shall ensure that the parents of each child with a disability are members of any group that makes decisions on the educational placement of their child.

(f) Alternative means of meeting participation

When conducting IEP team meetings and placement meetings pursuant to this section, section 1415(e) of this title, and section 1415(f)(1)(B) of this title, and carrying out administrative matters under section 1415 of this title (such as scheduling, exchange of witness lists, and status conferences), the parent of a child with a disability and a local educational agency may agree to use alternative means of meeting participation, such as video conferences and conference calls.

§ 1414a. Omitted

§ 1415. Procedural safeguards

(a) Establishment of procedures

Any State educational agency, State agency, or local educational agency that receives assistance under this subchapter shall establish and maintain procedures in accordance with this section to ensure that children with disabilities and their parents are guaranteed procedural safeguards with respect to the provision of a free appropriate public education by such agencies.

(b) Types of procedures

The procedures required by this section shall include the following:

(1) An opportunity for the parents of a child with a disability to examine all records relating to such child and to participate in meetings with respect to the identification, evaluation, and educational placement of the child, and the provision of a free appropriate public education to such child, and to obtain an independent educational evaluation of the child.

(2) (A) Procedures to protect the rights of the child whenever the parents of the child are not known, the agency cannot, after reasonable efforts, locate the parents, or the child is a ward of the State, including the assignment of an individual to act as a surrogate for the parents, which surrogate shall not be an employee of the State educational agency, the local educational agency, or any other agency that is involved in the education or care of the child. In the case of —

(i) a child who is a ward of the State, such surrogate may alternatively be appointed by the judge overseeing the child's care provided that the surrogate meets the requirements of this paragraph; and

(ii) an unaccompanied homeless youth as defined in section 11434a(6) of Title 42, the local educational agency shall appoint a surrogate in accordance with this paragraph.

(B) The State shall make reasonable efforts to ensure the assignment of a surrogate not more than 30 days after there is a determination by the agency that the child needs a surrogate.

(3) Written prior notice to the parents of the child, in accordance with subsection (c)(1), whenever the local educational agency —

(A) proposes to initiate or change; or

(B) refuses to initiate or change, the identification, evaluation, or educational placement of the child, or the provision of a free appropriate public education to the child.

(4) Procedures designed to ensure that the notice required by paragraph (3) is in the native language of the parents, unless it clearly is not feasible to do so.

(5) An opportunity for mediation, in accordance with subsection (e).

(6) An opportunity for any party to present a complaint —

(A) with respect to any matter relating to the identification, evaluation, or educational placement of the child, or the provision of a free appropriate public education to such child; and

(B) which sets forth an alleged violation that occurred not more than 2 years before the date the parent or public agency knew or should have known about the alleged action that forms the basis of the complaint, or, if the State has an explicit time limitation for presenting such a complaint under this subchapter, in such time as the State law allows, except that the exceptions to the timeline described in subsection (f)(3)(D) shall apply to the timeline described in this subparagraph.

(7) (A) Procedures that require either party, or the attorney representing a party, to provide due process complaint notice in accordance with subsection (c)(2) (which shall remain confidential) —

(i) to the other party, in the complaint filed under paragraph (6), and forward a copy of such notice to the State educational agency; and

(ii) that shall include —

(I) the name of the child, the address of the residence of the child (or available contact information in the case of a homeless child), and the name of the school the child is attending;

(II) in the case of a homeless child or youth (within the meaning of section 11434a(2) of Title 42, available contact information for the child and the name of the school the child is attending;

(III) a description of the nature of the problem of the child relating to such proposed initiation or change, including facts relating to such problem; and

(IV) a proposed resolution of the problem to the extent known and available to the party at the time.

(B) A requirement that a party may not have a due process hearing until the party, or the attorney representing the party, files a notice that meets the requirements of subparagraph (A)(ii).

(8) Procedures that require the State educational agency to develop a model form to assist parents in filing a complaint and due process complaint notice in accordance with paragraphs (6) and (7), respectively.

(c) Notification requirements

(1) Content of prior written notice

The notice required by subsection (b)(3) shall include —

(A) a description of the action proposed or refused by the agency;

(B) an explanation of why the agency proposes or refuses to take the action and a description of each evaluation procedure, assessment, record, or report the agency used as a basis for the proposed or refused action;

(C) a statement that the parents of a child with a disability have protection under the procedural safeguards of this subchapter and, if this notice is not an initial referral for evaluation, the means by which a copy of a description of the procedural safeguards can be obtained;

(D) sources for parents to contact to obtain assistance in understanding the provisions of this subchapter;

(E) a description of other options considered by the IEP Team and the reason why those options were rejected; and

(F) a description of the factors that are relevant to the agency's proposal or refusal.

(2) Due process complaint notice

(A) Complaint

The due process complaint notice required under subsection (b)(7)(A) shall be deemed to be sufficient unless the party receiving the notice notifies the hearing officer and the other party in writing that the receiving party believes the notice has not met the requirements of subsection (b)(7)(A).

(B) Response to complaint

(i) Local educational agency response

(I) In general

If the local educational agency has not sent a prior written notice to the parent regarding the subject matter contained in the parent's due process complaint notice, such local educational agency shall, within 10 days of receiving the complaint, send to the parent a response that shall include —

(aa) an explanation of why the agency proposed or refused to take the action raised in the complaint;

(bb) a description of other options that the IEP Team considered and the reasons why those options were rejected;

(cc) a description of each evaluation procedure, assessment, record, or report the agency used as the basis for the proposed or refused action; and

(dd) a description of the factors that are relevant to the agency's proposal or refusal.

(II)   Sufficiency

A response filed by a local educational agency pursuant to subclause (I) shall not be construed to preclude such local educational agency from asserting that the parent's due process complaint notice was insufficient where appropriate.

(ii)   Other party response

Except as provided in clause (i), the non- complaining party shall, within 10 days of receiving the complaint, send to the complaint a response that specifically addresses the issues raised in the complaint.

(C)   Timing

The party providing a hearing officer notification under subparagraph (A) shall provide the notification within 15 days of receiving the complaint.

(D)   Determination

Within 5 days of receipt of the notification provided under subparagraph (C), the hearing officer shall make a determination on the face of the notice of whether the notification meets the requirements of subsection (b)(7)(A), and shall immediately notify the parties in writing of such determination.

(E)   Amended complaint notice

(i)   In general

A party may amend its due process complaint notice only if —

(I) the other party consents in writing to such amendment and is given the opportunity to resolve the complaint through a meeting held pursuant to subsection (f)(1)(B); or

(II) the hearing officer grants permission, except that the hearing officer may only grant such permission at any time not later than 5 days before a due process hearing occurs.

(ii)   Applicable timeline

The applicable timeline for a due process hearing under this subchapter shall recommence at the time the party files an amended notice, including the timeline under subsection (f)(1)(B).

(d)   Procedural safeguards notice

(1)   In general

(A)   Copy to parents

A copy of the procedural safeguards available to the parents of a child with a disability shall be given to the parents only 1 time a year, except that a copy also shall be given to the parents —

(i) upon initial referral or parental request for evaluation;

(ii) upon the first occurrence of the filing of a complaint under subsection (b)(6); and

(iii) upon request by a parent.

(B) Internet website

A local educational agency may place a current copy of the procedural safeguards notice on its Internet website if such website exists.

(2) Contents

The procedural safeguards notice shall include a full explanation of the procedural safeguards, written in the native language of the parents (unless it clearly is not feasible to do so) and written in an easily understandable manner, available under this section and under regulations promulgated by the Secretary relating to —

(A) independent educational evaluation;

(B) prior written notice;

(C) parental consent;

(D) access to educational records;

(E) the opportunity to present and resolve complaints, including —

(i) the time period in which to make a complaint;

(ii) the opportunity for the agency to resolve the complaint; and

(iii) the availability of mediation;

(F) the child's placement during pendency of due process proceedings;

(G) procedures for students who are subject to placement in an interim alternative educational setting;

(H) requirements for unilateral placement by parents of children in private schools at public expense;

(I) due process hearings, including requirements for disclosure of evaluation results and recommendations;

(J) State-level appeals (if applicable in that State);

(K) civil actions, including the time period in which to file such actions; and

(L) attorneys' fees.

(e) Mediation

(1) In general

Any State educational agency or local educational agency that receives assistance under this subchapter shall ensure that procedures are established and implemented to allow parties to disputes involving any matter, including matters arising prior to the filing of a complaint pursuant to subsection (b)(6), to resolve such disputes through a mediation process.

(2) Requirements

Such procedures shall meet the following requirements:

(A) The procedures shall ensure that the mediation process —

(i) is voluntary on the part of the parties;

(ii) is not used to deny or delay a parent's right to a due process hearing under subsection (f), or to deny any other rights afforded under this subchapter; and

(iii) is conducted by a qualified and impartial mediator who is trained in effective mediation techniques.

(B) Opportunity to meet with a disinterested party

A local educational agency or a State agency may establish procedures to offer to parents and schools that choose not to use the mediation process, an opportunity to meet, at a time and location convenient to the parents, with a disinterested party who is under contract with —

(i) a parent training and information center or community parent resource center in the State established under section 1471 or 1472 of this title; or

(ii) an appropriate alternative dispute resolution entity, to encourage the use, and explain the benefits, of the mediation process to the parents.

(C) List of qualified mediators

The State shall maintain a list of individuals who are qualified mediators and knowledgeable in laws and regulations relating to the provision of special education and related services.

(D) Costs

The State shall bear the cost of the mediation process, including the costs of meetings described in subparagraph (B).

(E) Scheduling and location

Each session in the mediation process shall be scheduled in a timely manner and shall be held in a location that is convenient to the parties to the dispute.

(F) Written agreement

In the case that a resolution is reached to resolve the complaint through the mediation process, the parties shall execute a legally binding agreement that sets forth such resolution and that —

(i) states that all discussions that occurred during the mediation process shall be confidential and may not be used as evidence in any subsequent due process hearing or civil proceeding;

(ii) is signed by both the parent and a representative of the agency who has the authority to bind such agency; and

(iii) is enforceable in any State court of competent jurisdiction or in a district court of the United States.

(G) Mediation discussions

Discussions that occur during the mediation process shall be confidential and may not be used as evidence in any subsequent due process hearing or civil proceeding.

(f) Impartial due process hearing

(1) In general

(A) Hearing

Whenever a complaint has been received under subsection (b)(6) or (k), the parents or the local educational agency involved in such complaint shall have an opportunity for an impartial due process hearing, which shall be conducted by the State educational agency or by the local educational agency, as determined by State law or by the State educational agency.

(B) Resolution session

(i) Preliminary meeting

Prior to the opportunity for an impartial due process hearing under subparagraph (A), the local educational agency shall convene a meeting with the parents and the relevant member or members of the IEP Team who have specific knowledge of the facts identified in the complaint —

(I) within 15 days of receiving notice of the parents' complaint;

(II) which shall include a representative of the agency who has decisionmaking authority on behalf of such agency;

(III) which may not include an attorney of the local educational agency unless the parent is accompanied by an attorney; and

(IV) where the parents of the child discuss their complaint, and the facts that form the basis of the complaint, and the local educational agency is provided the opportunity to resolve the complaint, unless the parents and the local educational agency agree in writing to waive such meeting, or agree to use the mediation process described in subsection (e).

(ii) Hearing

If the local educational agency has not resolved the complaint to the satisfaction of the parents within 30 days of the receipt of the complaint, the due process hearing may occur, and all of the applicable timelines for a due process hearing under this subchapter shall commence.

(iii) Written settlement agreement

In the case that a resolution is reached to resolve the complaint at a meeting described in clause (i), the parties shall execute a legally binding agreement that is —

(I) signed by both the parent and a representative of the agency who has the authority to bind such agency; and

(II) enforceable in any State court of competent jurisdiction or in a district court of the United States.

(iv)   Review period

If the parties execute an agreement pursuant to clause (iii), a party may void such agreement within 3 business days of the agreement's execution.

(2)   Disclosure of evaluations and recommendations

(A)   In general

Not less than 5 business days prior to a hearing conducted pursuant to paragraph (1), each party shall disclose to all other parties all evaluations completed by that date, and recommendations based on the offering party's evaluations, that the party intends to use at the hearing.

(B)   Failure to disclose

A hearing officer may bar any party that fails to comply with subparagraph (A) from introducing the relevant evaluation or recommendation at the hearing without the consent of the other party.

(3)   Limitations on hearing

(A)   Person conducting hearing

A hearing officer conducting a hearing pursuant to paragraph (1)(A) shall, at a minimum —

(i) not be —

(I) an employee of the State educational agency or the local educational agency involved in the education or care of the child; or

(II) a person having a personal or professional interest that conflicts with the person's objectivity in the hearing;

(ii) possess knowledge of, and the ability to understand, the provisions of this chapter, Federal and State regulations pertaining to this chapter, and legal interpretations of this chapter by Federal and State courts;

(iii) possess the knowledge and ability to conduct hearings in accordance with appropriate, standard legal practice; and

(iv) possess the knowledge and ability to render and write decisions in accordance with appropriate, standard legal practice.

(B)   Subject matter of hearing

The party requesting the due process hearing shall not be allowed to raise issues at the due process hearing that were not raised in the notice filed under subsection (b)(7), unless the other party agrees otherwise.

(C)   Timeline for requesting hearing

A parent or agency shall request an impartial due process hearing within 2 years of the date the parent or agency knew or should have known about the alleged action that forms the basis of the complaint, or, if the State has an explicit time limitation for requesting such a hearing under this subchapter, in such time as the State law allows.

(D)   Exceptions to the timeline

The timeline described in subparagraph (C) shall not apply to a parent if the parent was prevented from requesting the hearing due to —

(i) specific misrepresentations by the local educational agency that it had resolved the problem forming the basis of the complaint; or

(ii) the local educational agency's withholding of information from the parent that was required under this subchapter to be provided to the parent.

(E)   Decision of hearing officer

(i)   In general

Subject to clause (ii), a decision made by a hearing officer shall be made on substantive grounds based on a determination of whether the child received a free appropriate public education.

(ii)   Procedural issues

In matters alleging a procedural violation, a hearing officer may find that a child did not receive a free appropriate public education only if the procedural inadequacies —

(I) impeded the child's right to a free appropriate public education;

(II) significantly impeded the parents' opportunity to participate in the decision-making process regarding the provision of a free appropriate public education to the parents' child; or

(III) caused a deprivation of educational benefits.

(iii)   Rule of construction

Nothing in this subparagraph shall be construed to preclude a hearing officer from ordering a local educational agency to comply with procedural requirements under this section.

(F)   Rule of construction

Nothing in this paragraph shall be construed to affect the right of a parent to file a complaint with the State educational agency.

(g)   Appeal

(1)   In general

If the hearing required by subsection (f) is conducted by a local educational agency, any party aggrieved by the findings and decision rendered in such a hearing may appeal such findings and decision to the State educational agency.

(2)   Impartial review and independent decision

The State educational agency shall conduct an impartial review of the findings and decision appealed under paragraph (1). The officer conducting such review shall make an independent decision upon completion of such review.

(h)   Safeguards

Any party to a hearing conducted pursuant to subsection (f) or (k), or an appeal conducted pursuant to subsection (g), shall be accorded —

(1) the right to be accompanied and advised by counsel and by individuals with special knoledge or training with respect to the problems of children with disabilities;

(2) the right to present evidence and confront, cross-examine, and compel the attendance of witnesses;

(3) the right to a written, or, at the option of the parents, electronic verbatim record of such hearing; and

(4) the right to written, or, at the option of the parents, electronic findings of fact and decisions, which findings and decisions —

(A) shall be made available to the public consistent with the requirements of section 1417(b) of this title (relating to the confidentiality of data, information, and records); and

(B) shall be transmitted to the advisory panel established pursuant to section 1412(a)(21) of this title.

(i) Administrative procedures

(1) In general

(A) Decision made in hearing

A decision made in a hearing conducted pursuant to subsection (f) or (k) shall be final, except that any party involved in such hearing may appeal such decision under the provisions of subsection (g) and paragraph (2).

(B) Decision made at appeal

A decision made under subsection (g) shall be final, except that any party may bring an action under paragraph (2).

(2) Right to bring civil action

(A) In general

Any party aggrieved by the findings and decision made under subsection (f) or (k) who does not have the right to an appeal under subsection (g), and any party aggrieved by the findings and decision made under this subsection, shall have the right to bring a civil action with respect to the complaint presented pursuant to this section, which action may be brought in any State court of competent jurisdiction or in a district court of the United States, without regard to the amount in controversy.

(B) Limitation

The party bringing the action shall have 90 days from the date of the decision of the hearing officer to bring such an action, or, if the State has an explicit time limitation for bringing such action under this subchapter, in such time as the State law allows.

(C) Additional requirements

In any action brought under this paragraph, the court —

(i) shall receive the records of the administrative proceedings;

(ii) shall hear additional evidence at the request of a party; and

(iii) basing its decision on the preponderance of the evidence, shall grant such relief as the court determines is appropriate.

(3)   Jurisdiction of district courts; attorneys' fees

(A)   In general

The district courts of the United States shall have jurisdiction of actions brought under this section without regard to the amount in controversy.

(B)   Award of attorneys' fees

(i)   In general

In any action or proceeding brought under this section, the court, in its discretion, may award reasonable attorneys' fees as part of the costs —

(I) to a prevailing party who is the parent of a child with a disability;

(II) to a prevailing party who is a State educational agency or local educational agency against the attorney of a parent who files a complaint or subsequent cause of action that is frivolous, unreasonable, or without foundation, or against the attorney of a parent who continued to litigate after the litigation clearly became frivolous, unreasonable, or without foundation; or

(III) to a prevailing State educational agency or local educational agency against the attorney of a parent, or against the parent, if the parent's complaint or subsequent cause of action was presented for any improper purpose, such as to harass, to cause unnecessary delay, or to needlessly increase the cost of litigation.

(ii)   Rule of construction

Nothing in this subparagraph shall be construed to affect section 327 of the District of Columbia Appropriations Act, 2005.

(C)   Determination of amount of attorneys' fees

Fees awarded under this paragraph shall be based on rates prevailing in the community in which the action or proceeding arose for the kind and quality of services furnished. No bonus or multiplier may be used in calculating the fees awarded under this subsection.

(D) Prohibition of attorneys' fees and related costs for certain services

(i)   In general

Attorneys' fees may not be awarded and related costs may not be reimbursed in any action or proceeding under this section for services performed subsequent to the time of a written offer of settlement to a parent if —

(I) the offer is made within the time prescribed by Rule 68 of the Federal Rules of Civil Procedure or, in the case of an administrative proceeding, at any time more than 10 days before the proceeding begins;

(II) the offer is not accepted within 10 days; and

(III) the court or administrative hearing officer finds that the relief finally obtained by the parents is not more favorable to the parents than the offer of settlement.

(ii)   IEP Team meetings

Attorneys' fees may not be awarded relating to any meeting of the IEP Team unless such meeting is convened as a result of an administrative proceeding or judicial action, or, at the discretion of the State, for a mediation described in subsection (e).

(iii)   Opportunity to resolve complaints

A meeting conducted pursuant to subsection (f)(1)(B)(i) shall not be considered —

(I) a meeting convened as a result of an administrative hearing or judicial action; or

(II) an administrative hearing or judicial action for purposes of this paragraph.

(E) Exception to prohibition on attorneys' fees and related costs

Notwithstanding subparagraph (D), an award of attorneys' fees and related costs may be made to a parent who is the prevailing party and who was substantially justified in rejecting the settlement offer.

(F)   Reduction in amount of attorneys' fees

Except as provided in subparagraph (G), whenever the court finds that —

(i) the parent, or the parent's attorney, during the course of the action or proceeding, unreasonably protracted the final resolution of the controversy;

(ii) the amount of the attorneys' fees otherwise authorized to be awarded unreasonably exceeds the hourly rate prevailing in the community for similar services by attorneys of reasonably comparable skill, reputation, and experience;

(iii) the time spent and legal services furnished were excessive considering the nature of the action or proceeding; or

(iv) the attorney representing the parent did not provide to the local educational agency the appropriate information in the notice of the complaint described in subsection (b)(7)(A), the court shall reduce, accordingly, the amount of the attorneys' fees awarded under this section.

(G)   Exception to reduction in amount of attorneys' fees

The provisions of subparagraph (F) shall not apply in any action or proceeding if the court finds that the State or local educational agency unreasonably protracted the final resolution of the action or proceeding or there was a violation of this section.

(j)   Maintenance of current educational placement

Except as provided in subsection (k)(4), during the pendency of any proceedings conducted pursuant to this section, unless the State or local educational agency and the parents otherwise agree, the child shall remain in the then-current educational placement of the child, or, if applying for initial admission to a public school, shall, with the consent of the parents, be placed in the public school program until all such proceedings have been completed.

(k)   Placement in alternative educational setting

(1)   Authority of school personnel

(A)   Case-by-case determination

School personnel may consider any unique circumstances on a case-by-case basis when determining whether to order a change in placement for a child with a disability who violates a code of student conduct.

(B) Authority

School personnel under this subsection may remove a child with a disability who violates a code of student conduct from their current placement to an appropriate interim alternative educational setting, another setting, or suspension, for not more than 10 school days (to the extent such alternatives are applied to children without disabilities).

(C) Additional authority

If school personnel seek to order a change in placement that would exceed 10 school days and the behavior that gave rise to the violation of the school code is determined not to be a manifestation of the child's disability pursuant to subparagraph (E), the relevant disciplinary procedures applicable to children without disabilities may be applied to the child in the same manner and for the same duration in which the procedures would be applied to children without disabilities, except as provided in section 1412(a)(1) of this title although it may be provided in an interim alternative educational setting.

(D) Services

A child with a disability who is removed from the child's current placement under subparagraph (G) (irrespective of whether the behavior is determined to be a manifestation of the child's disability) or subparagraph (C) shall —

(i) continue to receive educational services, as provided in section 1412(a)(1) of this title, so as to enable the child to continue to participate in the general education curriculum, although in another setting, and to progress toward meeting the goals set out in the child's IEP; and

(ii) receive, as appropriate, a functional behavioral assessment, behavioral intervention services and modifications, that are designed to address the behavior violation so that it does not recur.

(E) Manifestation determination

(i) In general

Except as provided in subparagraph (B), within 10 school days of any decision to change the placement of a child with a disability because of a violation of a code of student conduct, the local educational agency, the parent, and relevant members of the IEP Team (as determined by the parent and the local educational agency) shall review all relevant information in the student's file, including the child' s IEP, any teacher observations, and any relevant information provided by the parents to determine —

(I) if the conduct in question was caused by, or had a direct and substantial relationship to, the child's disability; or

(II) if the conduct in question was the direct result of the local educational agency's failure to implement the IEP.

(ii) Manifestation

If the local educational agency, the parent, and relevant members of the IEP Team determine that either subclause (I) or (II) of clause (i) is applicable for the child, the conduct shall be determined to be a manifestation of the child's disability.

(F) Determination that behavior was a manifestation

If the local educational agency, the parent, and relevant members of the IEP Team make the determination that the conduct was a manifestation of the child's disability, the IEP Team shall —

(i) conduct a functional behavioral assessment, and implement a behavioral intervention plan for such child, provided that the local educational agency had not conducted such assessment prior to such determination before the behavior that resulted in a change in placement described in subparagraph (C) or (G);

(ii) in the situation where a behavioral intervention plan has been developed, review the behavioral intervention plan if the child already has such a behavioral intervention plan, and modify it, as necessary, to address the behavior; and

(iii) except as provided in subparagraph (G), return the child to the placement from which the child was removed, unless the parent and the local educational agency agree to a change of placement as part of the modification of the behavioral intervention plan.

(G) Special circumstances

School personnel may remove a student to an interim alternative educational setting for not more than 45 school days without regard to whether the behavior is determined to be a manifestation of the child's disability, in cases where a child —

(i) carries or possesses a weapon to or at school, on school premises, or to or at a school function under the jurisdiction of a State or local educational agency;

(ii) knowingly possesses or uses illegal drugs, or sells or solicits the sale of a controlled substance, while at school, on school premises, or at a school function under the jurisdiction of a State or local educational agency; or

(iii) has inflicted serious bodily injury upon another person while at school, on school premises, or at a school function under the jurisdiction of a State or local educational agency.

(H) Notification

Not later than the date on which the decision to take disciplinary action is made, the local educational agency shall notify the parents of that decision, and of all procedural safeguards accorded under this section.

(2) Determination of setting

The interim alternative educational setting in subparagraphs (C) and (G) of paragraph (1) shall be determined by the IEP Team.

(3) Appeal

(A) In general

The parent of a child with a disability who disagrees with any decision regarding placement, or the manifestation determination under this subsection, or a local educational agency that believes that maintaining the current placement of the child is substantially likely to result in injury to the child or to others, may request a hearing.

(B) Authority of hearing officer

(i) In general

A hearing officer shall hear, and make a determination regarding, an appeal requested under subparagraph (A).

(ii) Change of placement order

In making the determination under clause (i), the hearing officer may order a change in placement of a child with a disability. In such situations, the hearing officer may —

(I) return a child with a disability to the placement from which the child was removed; or

(II) order a change in placement of a child with a disability to an appropriate interim alternative educational setting for not more than 45 school days if the hearing officer determines that maintaining the current placement of such child is substantially likely to result in injury to the child or to others.

(4) Placement during appeals

When an appeal under paragraph (3) has been requested by either the parent or the local educational agency —

(A) the child shall remain in the interim alternative educational setting pending the decision of the hearing officer or until the expiration of the time period provided for in paragraph (1)(C), whichever occurs first, unless the parent and the State or local educational agency agree otherwise; and

(B) the State or local educational agency shall arrange for an expedited hearing, which shall occur within 20 school days of the date the hearing is requested and shall result in a determination within 10 school days after the hearing.

(5) Protections for children not yet eligible for special education and related services

(A) In general

A child who has not been determined to be eligible for special education and related services under this subchapter and who has engaged in behavior that violates a code of student conduct, may assert any of the protections provided for in this subchapter if the local educational agency had knowledge (as determined in accordance with this paragraph) that the child was a child with a disability before the behavior that precipitated the disciplinary action occurred.

(B) Basis of knowledge

A local educational agency shall be deemed to have knowledge that a child is a child with a disability if, before the behavior that precipitated the disciplinary action occurred —

(i) the parent of the child has expressed concern in writing to supervisory or administrative personnel of the appropriate educational agency, or a teacher of the child, that the child is in need of special education and related services;

(ii) the parent of the child has requested an evaluation of the child pursuant to section 1414(a)(1)(B) of this title; or

(iii) the teacher of the child, or other personnel of the local educational agency, has expressed specific concerns about a pattern of behavior demonstrated by the child, directly to the director of special education of such agency or to other supervisory personnel of the agency.

(C)   Exception

A local educational agency shall not be deemed to have knowledge that the child is a child with a disability if the parent of the child has not allowed an evaluation of the child pursuant to section 1414 of this title or has refused services under this subchapter or the child has been evaluated and it was determined that the child was not a child with a disability under this subchapter.

(D)   Conditions that apply if no basis of knowledge

(i)   In general

If a local educational agency does not have knowledge that a child is a child with a disability (in accordance with subparagraph (B) or (C)) prior to taking disciplinary measures against the child, the child may be subjected to disciplinary measures applied to children without disabilities who engaged in comparable behaviors consistent with clause (ii).

(ii)   Limitations

If a request is made for an evaluation of a child during the time period in which the child is subjected to disciplinary measures under this subsection, the evaluation shall be conducted in an expedited manner. If the child is determined to be a child with a disability, taking into consideration information from the evaluation conducted by the agency and information provided by the parents, the agency shall provide special education and related services in accordance with this subchapter, except that, pending the results of the evaluation, the child shall remain in the educational placement determined by school authorities.

(6) Referral to and action by law enforcement and judicial authorities

(A)   Rule of construction

Nothing in this subchapter shall be construed to prohibit an agency from reporting a crime committed by a child with a disability to appropriate authorities or to prevent State law enforcement and judicial authorities from exercising their responsibilities with regard to the application of Federal and State law to crimes committed by a child with a disability.

(B)   Transmittal of records

An agency reporting a crime committed by a child with a disability shall ensure that copies of the special education and disciplinary records of the child are transmitted for consideration by the appropriate authorities to whom the agency reports the crime.

(7)   Definitions

In this subsection:

(A)   Controlled substance

The term "controlled substance" means a drug or other substance identified under schedule I, II, III, IV, or V in section 202(c) of the Controlled Substances Act (21 U.S.C. 812(c)).

(B) Illegal drug

The term "illegal drug" means a controlled substance but does not include a controlled substance that is legally possessed or used under the supervision of a licensed health-care professional or that is legally possessed or used under any other authority under that Act [21 U.S.C.A. § 801 et seq.] or under any other provision of Federal law.

(C) Weapon

The term "weapon" has the meaning given the term "dangerous weapon" under section 930(g)(2) of Title 18.

(D) Serious bodily injury

The term "serious bodily injury" has the meaning given the term "serious bodily injury" under paragraph (3) of subsection (h) of section 1365 of Title 18.

(l) Rule of construction

Nothing in this chapter shall be construed to restrict or limit the rights, procedures, and remedies available under the Constitution, the Americans with Disabilities Act of 1990 [42 U.S.C.A. § 12101 et seq.], title V of the Rehabilitation Act of 1973 [29 U.S.C.A. § 791 et seq.], or other Federal laws protecting the rights of children with disabilities, except that before the filing of a civil action under such laws seeking relief that is also available under this subchapter, the procedures under subsections (f) and (g) shall be exhausted to the same extent as would be required had the action been brought under this subchapter.

(m) Transfer of parental rights at age of majority

(1) In general

A State that receives amounts from a grant under this subchapter may provide that, when a child with a disability reaches the age of majority under State law (except for a child with a disability who has been determined to be incompetent under State law) —

(A) the agency shall provide any notice required by this section to both the individual and the parents;

(B) all other rights accorded to parents under this subchapter transfer to the child;

(C) the agency shall notify the individual and the parents of the transfer of rights; and

(D) all rights accorded to parents under this subchapter transfer to children who are incarcerated in an adult or juvenile Federal, State, or local correctional institution.

(2) Special rule

If, under State law, a child with a disability who has reached the age of majority under State law, who has not been determined to be incompetent, but who is determined not to have the ability to provide informed consent with respect to the educational program of the child, the State shall establish procedures for appointing the parent of the child, or if the parent is not available, another appropriate individual, to represent the educational interests of the child throughout the period of eligibility of the child under this subchapter.

(n) Electronic mail

A parent of a child with a disability may elect to receive notices required under this section by an electronic mail (e-mail) communication, if the agency makes such option available.

(o) Separate complaint

Nothing in this section shall be construed to preclude a parent from filing a separate due process complaint on an issue separate from a due process complaint already filed.

* * *

Part C

§ 1431. Findings and policy

(a) Findings

Congress finds that there is an urgent and substantial need —

(1) to enhance the development of infants and toddlers with disabilities, to minimize their potential for developmental delay, and to recognize the significant brain development that occurs during a child's first 3 years of life;

(2) to reduce the educational costs to our society, including our Nation's schools, by minimizing the need for special education and related services after infants and toddlers with disabilities reach school age;

(3) to maximize the potential for individuals with disabilities to live independently in society;

(4) to enhance the capacity of families to meet the special needs of their infants and toddlers with disabilities; and

(5) to enhance the capacity of State and local agencies and service providers to identify, evaluate, and meet the needs of all children, particularly minority, low-income, inner city, and rural children, and infants and toddlers in foster care.

(b) Policy

It is the policy of the United States to provide financial assistance to States —

(1) to develop and implement a statewide, comprehensive, coordinated, multidisciplinary, interagency system that provides early intervention services for infants and toddlers with disabilities and their families;

(2) to facilitate the coordination of payment for early intervention services from Federal, State, local, and private sources (including public and private insurance coverage);

(3) to enhance State capacity to provide quality early intervention services and expand and improve existing early intervention services being provided to infants and toddlers with disabilities and their families; and

(4) to encourage States to expand opportunities for children under 3 years of age who would be at risk of having substantial developmental delay if they did not receive early intervention services.

§ 1432. Definitions

In this subchapter:

(1)   At-risk infant or toddler

The term "at-risk infant or toddler" means an individual under 3 years of age who would be at risk of experiencing a substantial developmental delay if early intervention services were not provided to the individual.

(3)   Developmental delay

The term "developmental delay", when used with respect to an individual residing in a State, has the meaning given such term by the State under section 1435(a)(1) of this title.

(4)   Early intervention services

The term "early intervention services" means developmental services that —

(A) are provided under public supervision;

(B) are provided at no cost except where Federal or State law provides for a system of payments by families, including a schedule of sliding fees;

(C) are designed to meet the developmental needs of an infant or toddler with a disability, as identified by the individualized family service plan team, in any 1 or more of the following areas:

(i) physical development;

(ii) cognitive development;

(iii) communication development;

(iv) social or emotional development; or

(v) adaptive development;

(D) meet the standards of the State in which the services are provided, including the requirements of this subchapter;

(E) include —

(i) family training, counseling, and home visits;

(ii) special instruction;

(iii) speech-language pathology and audiology services, and sign language and cued language services;

(iv) occupational therapy;

(v) physical therapy;

(vi) psychological services;

(vii) service coordination services;

(viii) medical services only for diagnostic or evaluation purposes;

(ix) early identification, screening, and assessment services;

(x) health services necessary to enable the infant or toddler to benefit from the other early intervention services;

(xi) social work services;

(xii) vision services;

(xiii) assistive technology devices and assistive technology services; and

(xiv) transportation and related costs that are necessary to enable an infant or toddler and the infant's or toddler's family to receive another service described in this paragraph;

(F) are provided by qualified personnel, including —

(i) special educators;

(ii) speech-language pathologists and audiologists;

(iii) occupational therapists;

(iv) physical therapists;

(v) psychologists;

(vi) social workers;

(vii) nurses;

(viii) registered dietitians;

(ix) family therapists;

(x) vision specialists, including ophthalmologists and optometrists;

(xi) orientation and mobility specialists; and

(xii) pediatricians and other physicians;

(G) to the maximum extent appropriate, are provided in natural environments, including the home, and community settings in which children without disabilities participate; and

(H) are provided in conformity with an individualized family service plan adopted in accordance with section 1436 of this title.

(5) Infant or toddler with a disability

The term "infant or toddler with a disability" —

(A) means an individual under 3 years of age who needs early intervention services because the individual —

(i) is experiencing developmental delays, as measured by appropriate diagnostic instruments and procedures in 1 or more of the areas of cognitive development, physical development, communication development, social or emotional development, and adaptive development; or

(ii) has a diagnosed physical or mental condition that has a high probability of resulting in developmental delay; and

(B) may also include, at a State's discretion —

(i) at-risk infants and toddlers; and

(ii) children with disabilities who are eligible for services under section 1419 of this title and who previously received services under this subchapter until such children enter, or are eligible under State law to enter, kindergarten or elementary school, as appropriate, provided that any programs under this subchapter serving such children shall include —

(I) an educational component that promotes school readiness and incorporates pre-literacy, language, and numeracy skills; and

(II) a written notification to parents of their rights and responsibilities in determining whether their child will continue to receive services under this subchapter or participate in preschool programs under section 1419 of this title.

§ 1435. Requirements for statewide system

(a) In general

A statewide system described in section 1433 of this title shall include, at a minimum, the following components:

(1) A rigorous definition of the term "developmental delay" that will be used by the State in carrying out programs under this subchapter in order to appropriately identify infants and toddlers with disabilities that are in need of services under this subchapter.

(2) A State policy that is in effect and that ensures that appropriate early intervention services based on scientifically based research, to the extent practicable, are available to all infants and toddlers with disabilities and their families, including Indian infants and toddlers with disabilities and their families residing on a reservation geographically located in the State and infants and toddlers with disabilities who are homeless children and their families.

(3) A timely, comprehensive, multidisciplinary evaluation of the functioning of each infant or toddler with a disability in the State, and a family-directed identification of the needs of each family of such an infant or toddler, to assist appropriately in the development of the infant or toddler.

(4) For each infant or toddler with a disability in the State, an individualized family service plan in accordance with section 1436 of this title, including service coordination services in accordance with such service plan.

(5) A comprehensive child find system, consistent with subchapter II, including a system for making referrals to service providers that includes timelines and provides for participation by primary referral sources and that ensures rigorous standards for appropriately identifying infants and toddlers with disabilities for services under this subchapter that will reduce the need for future services.

(6) A public awareness program focusing on early identification of infants and toddlers with disabilities, including the preparation and dissemination by the lead agency designated or established under paragraph (10) to all primary referral sources, especially hospitals and physicians, of information to be given to parents, especially to inform parents with premature infants, or infants with other physical risk factors associated with learning or developmental complications, on the availability of early intervention services under this subchapter and of services under section 1419 of this title, and procedures for assisting such sources in disseminating such information to parents of infants and toddlers with disabilities.

(7) A central directory that includes information on early intervention services, resources, and experts available in the State and research and demonstration projects being conducted in the State.

(8) A comprehensive system of personnel development, including the training of paraprofessionals and the training of primary referral sources with respect to the basic components of early intervention services available in the State that —

(A) shall include —

(i) implementing innovative strategies and activities for the recruitment and retention of early education service providers;

(ii) promoting the preparation of early intervention providers who are fully and appropriately qualified to provide early intervention services under this subchapter; and

(iii) training personnel to coordinate transition services for infants and toddlers served under this subchapter from a program providing early intervention services under this subchapter and under subchapter II (other than section 1419 of this title), to a preschool program receiving funds under section 1419 of this title, or another appropriate program; and

(B) may include —

(i) training personnel to work in rural and inner-city areas; and

(ii) training personnel in the emotional and social development of young children.

(9) Policies and procedures relating to the establishment and maintenance of qualifications to ensure that personnel necessary to carry out this subchapter are appropriately and adequately prepared and trained, including the establishment and maintenance of qualifications that are consistent with any State-approved or recognized certification, licensing, registration, or other comparable requirements that apply to the area in which such personnel are providing early intervention services, except that nothing in this subchapter (including this paragraph) shall be construed to prohibit the use of paraprofessionals and assistants who are appropriately trained and supervised in accordance with State law, regulation, or written policy, to assist in the provision of early intervention services under this subchapter to infants and toddlers with disabilities.

(10) A single line of responsibility in a lead agency designated or established by the Governor for carrying out —

(A) the general administration and supervision of programs and activities receiving assistance under section 1433 of this title, and the monitoring of programs and activities used by the State to carry out this subchapter, whether or not such programs or activities are receiving assistance made available under section 1433 of this title, to ensure that the State complies with this subchapter;

(B) the identification and coordination of all available resources within the State from Federal, State, local, and private sources;

(C) the assignment of financial responsibility in accordance with section 1437(a)(2) of this title to the appropriate agencies;

(D) the development of procedures to ensure that services are provided to infants and toddlers with disabilities and their families under this subchapter in a timely manner pending the resolution of any disputes among public agencies or service providers;

(E) the resolution of intra- and interagency disputes; and

(F) the entry into formal interagency agreements that define the financial responsibility of each agency for paying for early intervention services (consistent with State law) and procedures for resolving disputes and that include all additional components necessary to ensure meaningful cooperation and coordination.

(11) A policy pertaining to the contracting or making of other arrangements with service providers to provide early intervention services in the State, consistent with the provisions of this subchapter, including the contents of the application used and the conditions of the contract or other arrangements.

(12) A procedure for securing timely reimbursements of funds used under this subchapter in accordance with section 1440(a) of this title.

(13) Procedural safeguards with respect to programs under this subchapter, as required by section 1439 of this title.

(14) A system for compiling data requested by the Secretary under section 1418 of this title that relates to this subchapter.

(15) A State interagency coordinating council that meets the requirements of section 1441 of this title.

(16) Policies and procedures to ensure that, consistent with section 1436(d)(5) of this title —

(A) to the maximum extent appropriate, early intervention services are provided in natural environments; and

(B) the provision of early intervention services for any infant or toddler with a disability occurs in a setting other than a natural environment that is most appropriate, as determined by the parent and the individualized family service plan team, only when early intervention cannot be achieved satisfactorily for the infant or toddler in a natural environment.

(b)   Policy

In implementing subsection (a)(9), a State may adopt a policy that includes making ongoing good-faith efforts to recruit and hire appropriately and adequately trained personnel to provide early intervention services to infants and toddlers with disabilities, including, in a geographic area of the State where there is a shortage of such personnel, the most qualified individuals available who are making satisfactory progress toward completing applicable course work necessary to meet the standards described in subsection (a)(9).

(c)   Flexibility to serve children 3 years of age until entrance into elementary school

(1)   In general

A statewide system described in section 1433 of this title may include a State policy, developed and implemented jointly by the lead agency and the State educational agency, under which parents of children with disabilities who are eligible for services under section

1419 of this title and previously received services under this subchapter, may choose the continuation of early intervention services (which shall include an educational component that promotes school readiness and incorporates preliteracy, language, and numeracy skills) for such children under this subchapter until such children enter, or are eligible under State law to enter, kindergarten.

(2)   Requirements

If a statewide system includes a State policy described in paragraph (1), the statewide system shall ensure that —

(A) parents of children with disabilities served pursuant to this subsection are provided annual notice that contains —

(i) a description of the rights of such parents to elect to receive services pursuant to this subsection or under subchapter II; and

(ii) an explanation of the differences between services provided pursuant to this subsection and services provided under subchapter II, including —

(I) types of services and the locations at which the services are provided;

(II) applicable procedural safeguards; and

(III) possible costs (including any fees to be charged to families as described in section 1432(4)(B) of this title), if any, to parents of infants or toddlers with disabilities;

(B) services provided pursuant to this subsection include an educational component that promotes school readiness and incorporates preliteracy, language, and numeracy skills;

(C) the State policy will not affect the right of any child served pursuant to this subsection to instead receive a free appropriate public education under subchapter II;

(D) all early intervention services outlined in the child's individualized family service plan under section 1436 of this title are continued while any eligibility determination is being made for services under this subsection;

(E) the parents of infants or toddlers with disabilities (as defined in section 1432(5)(A) of this title) provide informed written consent to the State, before such infants or toddlers reach 3 years of age, as to whether such parents intend to choose the continuation of early intervention services pursuant to this subsection for such infants or toddlers;

(F) the requirements under section 1437(a)(9) of this title shall not apply with respect to a child who is receiving services in accordance with this subsection until not less than 90 days (and at the discretion of the parties to the conference, not more than 9 months) before the time the child will no longer receive those services; and

(G) there will be a referral for evaluation for early intervention services of a child who experiences a substantiated case of trauma due to exposure to family violence (as defined in section 10421 of Title 42).

(5)   Rules of construction

(A) Services under subchapter II

If a statewide system includes a State policy described in paragraph (1), a State that provides services in accordance with this subsection to a child with a disability who is eligible for services under section 1419 of this title shall not be required to provide the child with a free appropriate public education under subchapter II for the period of time in which the child is receiving services under this subchapter.

(B) Services under this subchapter

Nothing in this subsection shall be construed to require a provider of services under this subchapter to provide a child served under this subchapter with a free appropriate public education.

§ 1436. Individualized family service plan

(a) Assessment and program development

A statewide system described in section 1433 of this title shall provide, at a minimum, for each infant or toddler with a disability, and the infant's or toddler's family, to receive —

(1) a multidisciplinary assessment of the unique strengths and needs of the infant or toddler and the identification of services appropriate to meet such needs;

(2) a family-directed assessment of the resources, priorities, and concerns of the family and the identification of the supports and services necessary to enhance the family's capacity to meet the developmental needs of the infant or toddler; and

(3) a written individualized family service plan developed by a multidisciplinary team, including the parents, as required by subsection (e), including a description of the appropriate transition services for the infant or toddler.

(b) Periodic review

The individualized family service plan shall be evaluated once a year and the family shall be provided a review of the plan at 6-month intervals (or more often where appropriate based on infant or toddler and family needs).

(c) Promptness after assessment

The individualized family service plan shall be developed within a reasonable time after the assessment required by subsection (a)(1) is completed. With the parents' consent, early intervention services may commence prior to the completion of the assessment.

(d) Content of plan

The individualized family service plan shall be in writing and contain —

(1) a statement of the infant's or toddler's present levels of physical development, cognitive development, communication development, social or emotional development, and adaptive development, based on objective criteria;

(2) a statement of the family's resources, priorities, and concerns relating to enhancing the development of the family's infant or toddler with a disability;

(3) a statement of the measurable results or outcomes expected to be achieved for the infant or toddler and the family, including pre-literacy and language skills, as developmentally appropriate for the child, and the criteria, procedures, and timelines used to determine

the degree to which progress toward achieving the results or outcomes is being made and whether modifications or revisions of the results or outcomes or services are necessary;

(4) a statement of specific early intervention services based on peer-reviewed research, to the extent practicable, necessary to meet the unique needs of the infant or toddler and the family, including the frequency, intensity, and method of delivering services;

(5) a statement of the natural environments in which early intervention services will appropriately be provided, including a justification of the extent, if any, to which the services will not be provided in a natural environment;

(6) the projected dates for initiation of services and the anticipated length, duration, and frequency of the services;

(7) the identification of the service coordinator from the profession most immediately relevant to the infant's or toddler's or family's needs (or who is otherwise qualified to carry out all applicable responsibilities under this subchapter) who will be responsible for the implementation of the plan and coordination with other agencies and persons, including transition services; and

(8) the steps to be taken to support the transition of the toddler with a disability to preschool or other appropriate services.

(e) Parental consent

The contents of the individualized family service plan shall be fully explained to the parents and informed written consent from the parents shall be obtained prior to the provision of early intervention services described in such plan. If the parents do not provide consent with respect to a particular early intervention service, then only the early intervention services to which consent is obtained shall be provided.

* * *

§ 1439. Procedural safeguards

(a) Minimum procedures

The procedural safeguards required to be included in a statewide system under section 1435(a)(13) of this title shall provide, at a minimum, the following:

(1) The timely administrative resolution of complaints by parents. Any party aggrieved by the findings and decision regarding an administrative complaint shall have the right to bring a civil action with respect to the complaint in any State court of competent jurisdiction or in a district court of the United States without regard to the amount in controversy. In any action brought under this paragraph, the court shall receive the records of the administrative proceedings, shall hear additional evidence at the request of a party, and, basing its decision on the preponderance of the evidence, shall grant such relief as the court determines is appropriate.

(2) The right to confidentiality of personally identifiable information, including the right of parents to written notice of and written consent to the exchange of such information among agencies consistent with Federal and State law.

(3) The right of the parents to determine whether they, their infant or toddler, or other family members will accept or decline any early intervention service under this subchapter

in accordance with State law without jeopardizing other early intervention services under this subchapter.

(4) The opportunity for parents to examine records relating to assessment, screening, eligibility determinations, and the development and implementation of the individualized family service plan.

(5) Procedures to protect the rights of the infant or toddler whenever the parents of the infant or toddler are not known or cannot be found or the infant or toddler is a ward of the State, including the assignment of an individual (who shall not be an employee of the State lead agency, or other State agency, and who shall not be any person, or any employee of a person, providing early intervention services to the infant or toddler or any family member of the infant or toddler) to act as a surrogate for the parents.

(6) Written prior notice to the parents of the infant or toddler with a disability whenever the State agency or service provider proposes to initiate or change, or refuses to initiate or change, the identification, evaluation, or placement of the infant or toddler with a disability, or the provision of appropriate early intervention services to the infant or toddler.

(7) Procedures designed to ensure that the notice required by paragraph (6) fully informs the parents, in the parents' native language, unless it clearly is not feasible to do so, of all procedures available pursuant to this section.

(8) The right of parents to use mediation in accordance with section 1415 of this title, except that —

(A) any reference in the section to a State educational agency shall be considered to be a reference to a State's lead agency established or designated under section 1435(a)(10) of this title;

(B) any reference in the section to a local educational agency shall be considered to be a reference to a local service provider or the State's lead agency under this subchapter, as the case may be; and

(C) any reference in the section to the provision of a free appropriate public education to children with disabilities shall be considered to be a reference to the provision of appropriate early intervention services to infants and toddlers with disabilities.

(b)   Services during pendency of proceedings

During the pendency of any proceeding or action involving a complaint by the parents of an infant or toddler with a disability, unless the State agency and the parents otherwise agree, the infant or toddler shall continue to receive the appropriate early intervention services currently being provided or, if applying for initial services, shall receive the services not in dispute.

* * *

§ 1450. Findings

Congress finds the following:

(1) The Federal Government has an ongoing obligation to support activities that contribute to positive results for children with disabilities, enabling those children to lead productive and independent adult lives.

(2) Systemic change benefiting all students, including children with disabilities, requires the involvement of States, local educational agencies, parents, individuals with disabilities and their families, teachers and other service providers, and other interested individuals and organizations to develop and implement comprehensive strategies that improve educational results for children with disabilities.

(3) State educational agencies, in partnership with local educational agencies, parents of children with disabilities, and other individuals and organizations, are in the best position to improve education for children with disabilities and to address their special needs.

(4) An effective educational system serving students with disabilities should —

(A) maintain high academic achievement standards and clear performance goals for children with disabilities, consistent with the standards and expectations for all students in the educational system, and provide for appropriate and effective strategies and methods to ensure that all children with disabilities have the opportunity to achieve those standards and goals;

(B) clearly define, in objective, measurable terms, the school and post-school results that children with disabilities are expected to achieve; and

(C) promote transition services and coordinate State and local education, social, health, mental health, and other services, in addressing the full range of student needs, particularly the needs of children with disabilities who need significant levels of support to participate and learn in school and the community.

(5) The availability of an adequate number of qualified personnel is critical —

(A) to serve effectively children with disabilities;

(B) to assume leadership positions in administration and direct services;

(C) to provide teacher training; and

(D) to conduct high quality research to improve special education.

(6) High quality, comprehensive professional development programs are essential to ensure that the persons responsible for the education or transition of children with disabilities possess the skills and knowledge necessary to address the educational and related needs of those children.

(7) Models of professional development should be scientifically based and reflect successful practices, including strategies for recruiting, preparing, and retaining personnel.

(8) Continued support is essential for the development and maintenance of a coordinated and high quality program of research to inform successful teaching practices and model curricula for educating children with disabilities.

(9) Training, technical assistance, support, and dissemination activities are necessary to ensure that subchapters II and III are fully implemented and achieve high quality early intervention, educational, and transitional results for children with disabilities and their families.

(10) Parents, teachers, administrators, and related services personnel need technical assistance and information in a timely, coordinated, and accessible manner in order to improve early intervention, educational, and transitional services and results at the State

and local levels for children with disabilities and their families.

(11) Parent training and information activities assist parents of a child with a disability in dealing with the multiple pressures of parenting such a child and are of particular importance in —

(A) playing a vital role in creating and preserving constructive relationships between parents of children with disabilities and schools by facilitating open communication between the parents and schools; encouraging dispute resolution at the earliest possible point in time; and discouraging the escalation of an adversarial process between the parents and schools;

(B) ensuring the involvement of parents in planning and decisionmaking with respect to early intervention, educational, and transitional services;

(C) achieving high quality early intervention, educational, and transitional results for children with disabilities;

(D) providing such parents information on their rights, protections, and responsibilities under this chapter to ensure improved early intervention, educational, and transitional results for children with disabilities;

(E) assisting such parents in the development of skills to participate effectively in the education and development of their children and in the transitions described in section 1473(b)(6) of this title;

(F) supporting the roles of such parents as participants within partnerships seeking to improve early intervention, educational, and transitional services and results for children with disabilities and their families; and

(G) supporting such parents who may have limited access to services and supports, due to economic, cultural, or linguistic barriers.

(12) Support is needed to improve technological resources and integrate technology, including universally designed technologies, into the lives of children with disabilities, parents of children with disabilities, school personnel, and others through curricula, services, and assistive technologies.

* * *

§ 1461.　Purpose; definition of eligible entity

(a)　Purpose

The purpose of this part is —

(1) to provide Federal funding for personnel preparation, technical assistance, model demonstration projects, information dissemination, and studies and evaluations, in order to improve early intervention, educational, and transitional results for children with disabilities; and

(2) to assist State educational agencies and local educational agencies in improving their education systems for children with disabilities.

(b)　Definition of eligible entity

(1)   In general

In this part, the term "eligible entity" means —

(A) a State educational agency;

(B) a local educational agency;

(C) a public charter school that is a local educational agency under State law;

(D) an institution of higher education;

(E) a public agency not described in subparagraphs (A) through (D);

(F) a private nonprofit organization;

(G) an outlying area;

(H) an Indian tribe or a tribal organization (as defined under section 450b of Title 25); or

(I) a for-profit organization, if the Secretary finds it appropriate in light of the purposes of a particular competition for a grant, contract, or cooperative agreement under this part.

(2)   Special rule

The Secretary may limit which eligible entities described in paragraph (1) are eligible for a grant, contract, or cooperative agreement under this part to 1 or more of the categories of eligible entities described in paragraph (1).

* * *

§ 1470.   Purposes

The purposes of this part are to ensure that —

(1) children with disabilities and their parents receive training and information designed to assist the children in meeting developmental and functional goals and challenging academic achievement goals, and in preparing to lead productive independent adult lives;

(2) children with disabilities and their parents receive training and information on their rights, responsibilities, and protections under this chapter, in order to develop the skills necessary to cooperatively and effectively participate in planning and decision making relating to early intervention, educational, and transitional services;

(3) parents, teachers, administrators, early intervention personnel, related services personnel, and transition personnel receive coordinated and accessible technical assistance and information to assist such personnel in improving early intervention, educational, and transitional services and results for children with disabilities and their families; and

(4) appropriate technology and media are researched, developed, and demonstrated, to improve and implement early intervention, educational, and transitional services and results for children with disabilities and their families.

Department of Education Regulations

United States Department of Education Individuals with Disabilities Education Act Regulations (Selected Provisions)

Subpart A   General

Purposes and Applicability

34 C.F.R. Sec. 300.1   Purposes.

The purposes of this part are —

(a) To ensure that all children with disabilities have available to them a free appropriate public education that emphasizes special education and related services designed to meet their unique needs and prepare them for further education, employment, and independent living;

(b) To ensure that the rights of children with disabilities and their parents are protected;

(c) To assist States, localities, educational service agencies, and Federal agencies to provide for the education of all children with disabilities; and

(d) To assess and ensure the effectiveness of efforts to educate children with disabilities.

Definitions Used in This Part

Sec. 300.4   Act.

Act means the Individuals with Disabilities Education Act, as amended.

Sec. 300.5   Assistive technology device.

Assistive technology device means any item, piece of equipment, or product system, whether acquired commercially off the shelf, modified, or customized, that is used to increase, maintain, or improve the functional capabilities of a child with a disability. The term does not include a medical device that is surgically implanted, or the replacement of such device.

Sec. 300.6   Assistive technology service.

Assistive technology service means any service that directly assists a child with a disability in the selection, acquisition, or use of an assistive technology device. The term includes —

(a) The evaluation of the needs of a child with a disability, including a functional evaluation of the child in the child's customary environment;

(b) Purchasing, leasing, or otherwise providing for the acquisition of assistive technology devices by children with disabilities;

(c) Selecting, designing, fitting, customizing, adapting, applying, maintaining, repairing, or replacing assistive technology devices;

(d) Coordinating and using other therapies, interventions, or services with assistive technology devices, such as those associated with existing education and rehabilitation plans and programs;

(e) Training or technical assistance for a child with a disability or, if appropriate, that child's family; and

(f) Training or technical assistance for professionals (including individuals providing education or rehabilitation services), employers, or other individuals who provide services to, employ, or are otherwise substantially involved in the major life functions of that child.

Sec. 300.8 Child with a disability.

(a) General.

(1) Child with a disability means a child evaluated in accordance with Sec. Sec. 300.304 through 300.311 as having mental retardation, a hearing impairment (including deafness), a speech or language impairment, a visual impairment (including blindness), a serious emotional disturbance (referred to in this part as "emotional disturbance"), an orthopedic impairment, autism, traumatic brain injury, an other health impairment, a specific learning disability, deaf-blindness, or multiple disabilities, and who, by reason thereof, needs special education and related services.

(2) (i) Subject to paragraph (a)(2)(ii) of this section, if it is determined, through an appropriate evaluation under Sec. Sec. 300.304 through 300.311, that a child has one of the disabilities identified in paragraph (a)(1) of this section, but only needs a related service and not special education, the child is not a child with a disability under this part.

(ii) If, consistent with Sec. 300.39(a)(2), the related service required by the child is considered special education rather than a related service under State standards, the child would be determined to be a child with a disability under paragraph (a)(1) of this section.

(b) Children aged three through nine experiencing developmental delays. Child with a disability for children aged three through nine (or any subset of that age range, including ages three through five), may, subject to the conditions described in Sec. 300.111(b), include a child —

(1) Who is experiencing developmental delays, as defined by the State and as measured by appropriate diagnostic instruments and procedures, in one or more of the following areas: Physical development, cognitive development, communication development, social or emotional development, or adaptive development; and

(2) Who, by reason thereof, needs special education and related services.

(c) Definitions of disability terms. The terms used in this definition of a child with a disability are defined as follows:

(1) (i) Autism means a developmental disability significantly affecting verbal and nonverbal communication and social interaction, generally evident before age three, that adversely affects a child's educational performance. Other characteristics often associated with autism are engagement in repetitive activities and stereotyped movements, resistance to environmental change or change in daily routines, and unusual responses to sensory experiences.

(ii) Autism does not apply if a child's educational performance is adversely affected primarily because the child has an emotional disturbance, as defined in paragraph (c)(4) of this section.

(iii) A child who manifests the characteristics of autism after age three could be identified as having autism if the criteria in paragraph (c)(1)(i) of this section are satisfied.

(2) Deaf-blindness means concomitant hearing and visual impairments, the combination of which causes such severe communication and other developmental and educational needs that they cannot be accommodated in special education programs solely for children with deafness or children with blindness.

(3) Deafness means a hearing impairment that is so severe that the child is impaired in processing linguistic information through hearing, with or without amplification, that adversely affects a child's educational performance.

(4) (i) Emotional disturbance means a condition exhibiting one or more of the following characteristics over a long period of time and to a marked degree that adversely affects a child's educational performance:

(A) An inability to learn that cannot be explained by intellectual, sensory, or health factors.

(B) An inability to build or maintain satisfactory interpersonal relationships with peers and teachers.

(C) Inappropriate types of behavior or feelings under normal circumstances.

(D) A general pervasive mood of unhappiness or depression.

(E) A tendency to develop physical symptoms or fears associated with personal or school problems.

(ii) Emotional disturbance includes schizophrenia. The term does not apply to children who are socially maladjusted, unless it is determined that they have an emotional disturbance under paragraph (c)(4)(i) of this section.

(5) Hearing impairment means an impairment in hearing, whether permanent or fluctuating, that adversely affects a child's educational performance but that is not included under the definition of deafness in this section.

(6) Mental retardation means significantly subaverage general intellectual functioning, existing concurrently with deficits in adaptive behavior and manifested during the developmental period, that adversely affects a child's educational performance.

(7) Multiple disabilities means concomitant impairments (such as mental retardation-blindness or mental retardation-orthopedic impairment), the combination of which causes such severe educational needs that they cannot be accommodated in special education programs solely for one of the impairments. Multiple disabilities does not include deaf-blindness.

(8) Orthopedic impairment means a severe orthopedic impairment that adversely affects a child's educational performance. The term includes impairments caused by a congenital anomaly, impairments caused by disease (e.g., poliomyelitis, bone tuberculosis), and impairments from other causes (e.g., cerebral palsy, amputations, and fractures or burns

that cause contractures).

(9) Other health impairment means having limited strength, vitality, or alertness, including a heightened alertness to environmental stimuli, that results in limited alertness with respect to the educational environment, that —

(i) Is due to chronic or acute health problems such as asthma, attention deficit disorder or attention deficit hyperactivity disorder, diabetes, epilepsy, a heart condition, hemophilia, lead poisoning, leukemia, nephritis, rheumatic fever, sickle cell anemia, and Tourette syndrome; and

(ii) Adversely affects a child's educational performance.

(10) Specific learning disability —

(i) General. Specific learning disability means a disorder in one or more of the basic psychological processes involved in understanding or in using language, spoken or written, that may manifest itself in the imperfect ability to listen, think, speak, read, write, spell, or to do mathematical calculations, including conditions such as perceptual disabilities, brain injury, minimal brain dysfunction, dyslexia, and developmental aphasia.

(ii) Disorders not included. Specific learning disability does not include learning problems that are primarily the result of visual, hearing, or motor disabilities, of mental retardation, of emotional disturbance, or of environmental, cultural, or economic disadvantage.

(11) Speech or language impairment means a communication disorder, such as stuttering, impaired articulation, a language impairment, or a voice impairment, that adversely affects a child's educational performance.

(12) Traumatic brain injury means an acquired injury to the brain caused by an external physical force, resulting in total or partial functional disability or psychosocial impairment, or both, that adversely affects a child's educational performance. Traumatic brain injury applies to open or closed head injuries resulting in impairments in one or more areas, such as cognition; language; memory; attention; reasoning; abstract thinking; judgment; problem-solving; sensory, perceptual, and motor abilities; psychosocial behavior; physical functions; information processing; and speech. Traumatic brain injury does not apply to brain injuries that are congenital or degenerative, or to brain injuries induced by birth trauma.

(13) Visual impairment including blindness means an impairment in vision that, even with correction, adversely affects a child's educational performance. The term includes both partial sight and blindness.

Sec. 300.9 Consent.

Consent means that —

(a) The parent has been fully informed of all information relevant to the activity for which consent is sought, in his or her native language, or through another mode of communication;

(b) The parent understands and agrees in writing to the carrying out of the activity for which his or her consent is sought, and the consent describes that activity and lists the records (if any) that will be released and to whom; and

(c) (1) The parent understands that the granting of consent is voluntary on the part of the parent and may be revoked at any time.

(2) If a parent revokes consent, that revocation is not retroactive (i.e., it does not negate an action that has occurred after the consent was given and before the consent was revoked).

(3) If the parent revokes consent in writing for their child's receipt of special education services after the child is initially provided special education and related services, the public agency is not required to amend the child's education records to remove any references to the child's receipt of special education and related services because of the revocation of consent.

Sec. 300.17   Free appropriate public education.

Free appropriate public education or FAPE means special education and related services that —

(a) Are provided at public expense, under public supervision and direction, and without charge;

(b) Meet the standards of the SEA, including the requirements of this part;

(c) Include an appropriate preschool, elementary school, or secondary school education in the State involved; and

(d) Are provided in conformity with an individualized education §§ 300.320 through 300.324.

Sec. 300.19   Homeless children.

Homeless children has the meaning given the term homeless children and youths in section 725 (42 U.S.C. 11434a) of the McKinney-Vento Homeless Assistance Act, as amended, 42 U.S.C. 11431 et seq.

Sec. 300.22   Individualized education program.

Individualized education program or IEP means a written statement for a child with a disability that is developed, reviewed, and revised in accordance with §§ 300.320 through 300.324.

Sec. 300.24   Individualized family service plan.

Individualized family service plan or IFSP has the meaning given the term in section 636 of the Act.

Sec. 300.25   Infant or toddler with a disability.

Infant or toddler with a disability —

(a) Means an individual under three years of age who needs early intervention services because the individual —

(1) Is experiencing developmental delays, as measured by appropriate diagnostic instruments and procedures in one or more of the areas of cognitive development, physical development, communication development, social or emotional development, and adaptive development; or

(2) Has a diagnosed physical or mental condition that has a high probability of resulting in developmental delay; and

(b) May also include, at a State's discretion —

(1) At-risk infants and toddlers; and

(2) Children with disabilities who are eligible for services under section 619 and who previously received services under Part C of the Act until such children enter, or are eligible under State law to enter, kindergarten or elementary school, as appropriate, provided that any programs under Part C of the Act serving such children shall include —

(i) An educational component that promotes school readiness and incorporates pre-literacy, language, and numeracy skills; and

(ii) A written notification to parents of their rights and responsibilities in determining whether their child will continue to receive services under Part C of the Act or participate in preschool programs under section 619.

Sec. 300.27 Limited English proficient.

Limited English proficient has the meaning given the term in section 9101(25) of the ESEA.

Sec. 300.28 Local educational agency.

(a) General. Local educational agency or LEA means a public board of education or other public authority legally constituted within a State for either administrative control or direction of, or to perform a service function for, public elementary or secondary schools in a city, county, township, school district, or other political subdivision of a State, or for a combination of school districts or counties as are recognized in a State as an administrative agency for its public elementary schools or secondary schools.

(b) Educational service agencies and other public institutions or agencies. The term includes —

(1) An educational service agency, as defined in § 300.12; and

(2) Any other public institution or agency having administrative control and direction of a public elementary school or secondary school, including a public nonprofit charter school that is established as an LEA under State law.

(c) BIA funded schools. The term includes an elementary school or secondary school funded by the Bureau of Indian Affairs, and not subject to the jurisdiction of any SEA other than the Bureau of Indian Affairs, but only to the extent that the inclusion makes the school eligible for programs for which specific eligibility is not provided to the school in another provision of law and the school does not have a student population that is smaller than the student population of the LEA receiving assistance under the Act with the smallest student population.

Sec. 300.29 Native language.

(a) Native language, when used with respect to an individual who is limited English proficient, means the following:

(1) The language normally used by that individual, or, in the case of a child, the language

normally used by the parents of the child, except as provided in paragraph (a)(2) of this section.

(2) In all direct contact with a child (including evaluation of the child), the language normally used by the child in the home or learning environment.

(b) For an individual with deafness or blindness, or for an individual with no written language, the mode of communication is that normally used by the individual (such as sign language, Braille, or oral communication).

Sec. 300.30 Parent.

(a) Parent means —

(1) A biological or adoptive parent of a child;

(2) A foster parent, unless State law, regulations, or contractual obligations with a State or local entity prohibit a foster parent from acting as a parent;

(3) A guardian generally authorized to act as the child's parent, or authorized to make educational decisions for the child (but not the State if the child is a ward of the State);

(4) An individual acting in the place of a biological or adoptive parent (including a grandparent, stepparent, or other relative) with whom the child lives, or an individual who is legally responsible for the child's welfare; or

(5) A surrogate parent who has been appointed in accordance with § 300.519 or section 639(a)(5) of the Act.

(b) (1) Except as provided in paragraph (b)(2) of this section, the biological or adoptive parent, when attempting to act as the parent under this part and when more than one party is qualified under paragraph (a) of this section to act as a parent, must be presumed to be the parent for purposes of this section unless the biological or adoptive parent does not have legal authority to make educational decisions for the child.

(2) If a judicial decree or order identifies a specific person or persons under paragraphs (a)(1) through (4) of this section to act as the "parent" of a child or to make educational decisions on behalf of a child, then such person or persons shall be determined to be the "parent" for purposes of this section.

Sec. 300.32 Personally identifiable.

Personally identifiable means information that contains —

(a) The name of the child, the child's parent, or other family member;

(b) The address of the child;

(c) A personal identifier, such as the child's social security number or student number; or

(d) A list of personal characteristics or other information that would make it possible to identify the child with reasonable certainty.

Sec. 300.33 Public agency.

Public agency includes the SEA, LEAs, ESAs, nonprofit public charter schools that are not otherwise included as LEAs or ESAs and are not a school of an LEA or ESA, and any other political subdivisions of the State that are responsible for providing education to children with disabilities.

Sec. 300.34 Related services.

(a) General. Related services means transportation and such developmental, corrective, and other supportive services as are required to assist a child with a disability to benefit from special education, and includes speech-language pathology and audiology services, interpreting services, psychological services, physical and occupational therapy, recreation, including therapeutic recreation, early identification and assessment of disabilities in children, counseling services, including rehabilitation counseling, orientation and mobility services, and medical services for diagnostic or evaluation purposes. Related services also include school health services and school nurse services, social work services in schools, and parent counseling and training.

(b) Exception; services that apply to children with surgically implanted devices, including cochlear implants.

(1) Related services do not include a medical device that is surgically implanted, the optimization of that device's functioning (e.g., mapping), maintenance of that device, or the replacement of that device.

(2) Nothing in paragraph (b)(1) of this section —

(i) Limits the right of a child with a surgically implanted device (e.g., cochlear implant) to receive related services (as listed in paragraph (a) of this section) that are determined by the IEP Team to be necessary for the child to receive FAPE.

(ii) Limits the responsibility of a public agency to appropriately monitor and maintain medical devices that are needed to maintain the health and safety of the child, including breathing, nutrition, or operation of other bodily functions, while the child is transported to and from school or is at school; or

(iii) Prevents the routine checking of an external component of a surgically implanted device to make sure it is functioning properly, as required in § 300.113(b).

(c) Individual related services terms defined. The terms used in this definition are defined as follows:

(1) Audiology includes —

(i) Identification of children with hearing loss;

(ii) Determination of the range, nature, and degree of hearing loss, including referral for medical or other professional attention for the habilitation of hearing;

(iii) Provision of habilitative activities, such as language habilitation, auditory training, speech reading (lip-reading), hearing evaluation, and speech conservation;

(iv) Creation and administration of programs for prevention of hearing loss;

(v) Counseling and guidance of children, parents, and teachers regarding hearing loss; and

(vi) Determination of children's needs for group and individual amplification, selecting and fitting an appropriate aid, and evaluating the effectiveness of amplification.

(2) Counseling services means services provided by qualified social workers, psychologists, guidance counselors, or other qualified personnel.

(3) Early identification and assessment of disabilities in children means the implementation of a formal plan for identifying a disability as early as possible in a child's life.

(4) Interpreting services includes —

(i) The following, when used with respect to children who are deaf or hard of hearing: Oral transliteration services, cued language transliteration services, sign language transliteration and interpreting services, and transcription services, such as communication access real-time translation (CART), C-Print, and TypeWell; and

(ii) Special interpreting services for children who are deaf-blind.

(5) Medical services means services provided by a licensed physician to determine a child's medically related disability that results in the child's need for special education and related services.

(6) Occupational therapy —

(i) Means services provided by a qualified occupational therapist; and

(ii) Includes —

(A) Improving, developing, or restoring functions impaired or lost through illness, injury, or deprivation;

(B) Improving ability to perform tasks for independent functioning if functions are impaired or lost; and

(C) Preventing, through early intervention, initial or further impairment or loss of function.

(7) Orientation and mobility services —

(i) Means services provided to blind or visually impaired children by qualified personnel to enable those students to attain systematic orientation to and safe movement within their environments in school, home, and community; and

(ii) Includes teaching children the following, as appropriate:

(A) Spatial and environmental concepts and use of information received by the senses (such as sound, temperature and vibrations) to establish, maintain, or regain orientation and line of travel (e.g., using sound at a traffic light to cross the street);

(B) To use the long cane or a service animal to supplement visual travel skills or as a tool for safely negotiating the environment for children with no available travel vision;

(C) To understand and use remaining vision and distance low vision aids; and

(D) Other concepts, techniques, and tools.

(8) (i) Parent counseling and training means assisting parents in understanding the special needs of their child;

(ii) Providing parents with information about child development; and

(iii) Helping parents to acquire the necessary skills that will allow them to support the implementation of their child's IEP or IFSP.

(9) Physical therapy means services provided by a qualified physical therapist.

(10) Psychological services includes —

(i) Administering psychological and educational tests, and other assessment procedures;

(ii) Interpreting assessment results;

(iii) Obtaining, integrating, and interpreting information about child behavior and conditions relating to learning;

(iv) Consulting with other staff members in planning school programs to meet the special educational needs of children as indicated by psychological tests, interviews, direct observation, and behavioral evaluations;

(v) Planning and managing a program of psychological services, including psychological counseling for children and parents; and

(vi) Assisting in developing positive behavioral intervention strategies.

(11) Recreation includes —

(i) Assessment of leisure function;

(ii) Therapeutic recreation services;

(iii) Recreation programs in schools and community agencies; and

(iv) Leisure education.

(12) Rehabilitation counseling services means services provided by qualified personnel in individual or group sessions that focus specifically on career development, employment preparation, achieving independence, and integration in the workplace and community of a student with a disability. The term also includes vocational rehabilitation services provided to a student with a disability by vocational rehabilitation programs funded under the Rehabilitation Act of 1973, as amended, 29 U.S.C. 701 et seq.

(13) School health services and school nurse services means health services that are designed to enable a child with a disability to receive FAPE as described in the child's IEP. School nurse services are services provided by a qualified school nurse. School health services are services that may be provided by either a qualified school nurse or other qualified person.

(14) Social work services in schools includes —

(i) Preparing a social or developmental history on a child with a disability;

(ii) Group and individual counseling with the child and family;

(iii) Working in partnership with parents and others on those problems in a child's living situation (home, school, and community) that affect the child's adjustment in school;

(iv) Mobilizing school and community resources to enable the child to learn as effectively as possible in his or her educational program; and

(v) Assisting in developing positive behavioral intervention strategies.

(15) Speech-language pathology services includes —

(i) Identification of children with speech or language impairments;

(ii) Diagnosis and appraisal of specific speech or language impairments;

(iii) Referral for medical or other professional attention necessary for the habilitation of speech or language impairments;

(iv) Provision of speech and language services for the habilitation or prevention of communicative impairments; and

(v) Counseling and guidance of parents, children, and teachers regarding speech and language impairments.

(16) Transportation includes —

(i) Travel to and from school and between schools;

(ii) Travel in and around school buildings; and

(iii) Specialized equipment (such as special or adapted buses, lifts, and ramps), if required to provide special transportation for a child with a disability.

Sec. 300.35 Scientifically based research.

Scientifically based research has the meaning given the term in section 9101(37) of the ESEA.

Sec. 300.37 Services plan.

Services plan means a written statement that describes the special education and related services the LEA will provide to a parentally-placed child with a disability enrolled in a private school who has been designated to receive services, including the location of the services and any transportation necessary, consistent with § 300.132, and is developed and implemented in accordance with §§ 300.137 through 300.139.

Sec. 300.39 Special education.

(a) General.

(1) Special education means specially designed instruction, at no cost to the parents, to meet the unique needs of a child with a disability, including —

(i) Instruction conducted in the classroom, in the home, in hospitals and institutions, and in other settings; and

(ii) Instruction in physical education.

(2) Special education includes each of the following, if the services otherwise meet the requirements of paragraph (a)(1) of this section —

(i) Speech-language pathology services, or any other related service, if the service is considered special education rather than a related service under State standards;

(ii) Travel training; and

(iii) Vocational education.

(b)   Individual special education terms defined. The terms in this definition are defined as follows:

(1) At no cost means that all specially-designed instruction is provided without charge, but does not preclude incidental fees that are normally charged to nondisabled students or their parents as a part of the regular education program.

(2) Physical education means —

(i) The development of —

(A) Physical and motor fitness;

(B) Fundamental motor skills and patterns; and

(C) Skills in aquatics, dance, and individual and group games and sports (including intramural and lifetime sports); and

(ii) Includes special physical education, adapted physical education, movement education, and motor development.

(3) Specially designed instruction means adapting, as appropriate to the needs of an eligible child under this part, the content, methodology, or delivery of instruction —

(i) To address the unique needs of the child that result from the child's disability; and

(ii) To ensure access of the child to the general curriculum, so that the child can meet the educational standards within the jurisdiction of the public agency that apply to all children.

(4) Travel training means providing instruction, as appropriate, to children with significant cognitive disabilities, and any other children with disabilities who require this instruction, to enable them to —

(i) Develop an awareness of the environment in which they live; and

(ii) Learn the skills necessary to move effectively and safely from place to place within that environment (e.g., in school, in the home, at work, and in the community).

(5) Vocational education means organized educational programs that are directly related to the preparation of individuals for paid or unpaid employment, or for additional preparation for a career not requiring a baccalaureate or advanced degree.

Sec. 300.41   State educational agency.

State educational agency or SEA means the State board of education or other agency or officer primarily responsible for the State supervision of public elementary schools and secondary schools, or, if there is no such officer or agency, an officer or agency designated by the Governor or by State law.

Sec. 300.42   Supplementary aids and services.

Supplementary aids and services means aids, services, and other supports that are provided in regular education classes, other education-related settings, and in extracurricular and nonacademic settings, to enable children with disabilities to be educated with nondisabled children to the maximum extent appropriate in accordance with §§ 300.114 through 300.116.

Sec. 300.43 Transition services.

(a) Transition services means a coordinated set of activities for a child with a disability that —

(1) Is designed to be within a results-oriented process, that is focused on improving the academic and functional achievement of the child with a disability to facilitate the child's movement from school to post-school activities, including postsecondary education, vocational education, integrated employment (including supported employment), continuing and adult education, adult services, independent living, or community participation;

(2) Is based on the individual child's needs, taking into account the child's strengths, preferences, and interests; and includes —

(i) Instruction;

(ii) Related services;

(iii) Community experiences;

(iv) The development of employment and other post-school adult living objectives; and

(v) If appropriate, acquisition of daily living skills and provision of a functional vocational evaluation.

(b) Transition services for children with disabilities may be special education, if provided as specially designed instruction, or a related service, if required to assist a child with a disability to benefit from special education.

Sec. 300.45 Ward of the State.

(a) General. Subject to paragraph (b) of this section, ward of the State means a child who, as determined by the State where the child resides, is —

(1) A foster child;

(2) A ward of the State; or

(3) In the custody of a public child welfare agency.

(b) Exception. Ward of the State does not include a foster child who has a foster parent who meets the definition of a parent in § 300.30.

Subpart B State Eligibility

General

Sec. 300.100 Eligibility for assistance.

A State is eligible for assistance under Part B of the Act for a fiscal year if the State submits a plan that provides assurances to the Secretary that the State has in effect policies and procedures to ensure that the State meets the conditions in §§ 300.101 through 300.176.

FAPE Requirements

Sec. 300.101 Free appropriate public education (FAPE).

(a) General. A free appropriate public education must be available to all children residing in the State between the ages of 3 and 21, inclusive, including children with disabilities who have been suspended or expelled from school, as provided for in § 300.530(d).

(b) FAPE for children beginning at age 3.

(1) Each State must ensure that —

(i) The obligation to make FAPE available to each eligible child residing in the State begins no later than the child's third birthday; and

(ii) An IEP or an IFSP is in effect for the child by that date, in accordance with § 300.323(b).

(2) If a child's third birthday occurs during the summer, the child's IEP Team shall determine the date when services under the IEP or IFSP will begin.

(c) Children advancing from grade to grade.

(1) Each State must ensure that FAPE is available to any individual child with a disability who needs special education and related services, even though the child has not failed or been retained in a course or grade, and is advancing from grade to grade.

(2) The determination that a child described in paragraph (a) of this section is eligible under this part, must be made on an individual basis by the group responsible within the child's LEA for making eligibility determinations.

Sec. 300.102 Limitation — exception to FAPE for certain ages.

(a) General. The obligation to make FAPE available to all children with disabilities does not apply with respect to the following:

(1) Children aged 3, 4, 5, 18, 19, 20, or 21 in a State to the extent that its application to those children would be inconsistent with State law or practice, or the order of any court, respecting the provision of public education to children of those ages.

(2) (i) Children aged 18 through 21 to the extent that State law does not require that special education and related services under Part B of the Act be provided to students with disabilities who, in the last educational placement prior to their incarceration in an adult correctional facility —

(A) Were not actually identified as being a child with a disability under § 300.8; and

(B) Did not have an IEP under Part B of the Act.

(ii) The exception in paragraph (a)(2)(i) of this section does not apply to children with disabilities, aged 18 through 21, who —

(A) Had been identified as a child with a disability under § 300.8 and had received services in accordance with an IEP, but who left school prior to their incarceration; or

(B) Did not have an IEP in their last educational setting, but who had actually been identified as a child with a disability under § 300.8.

(3) (i) Children with disabilities who have graduated from high school with a regular high school diploma.

(ii) The exception in paragraph (a)(3)(i) of this section does not apply to children who have graduated from high school but have not been awarded a regular high school diploma.

(iii) Graduation from high school with a regular high school diploma constitutes a change in placement, requiring written prior notice in accordance with § 300.503.

(iv) As used in paragraphs (a)(3)(i) through (a)(3)(iii) of this section, the term regular high school diploma does not include an alternative degree that is not fully aligned with the State's academic standards, such as a certificate or a general educational development credential (GED).

(4) Children with disabilities who are eligible under subpart H of this part, but who receive early intervention services under Part C of the Act.

(b)   Documents relating to exceptions. The State must assure that the information it has provided to the Secretary regarding the exceptions in paragraph (a) of this section, as required by § 300.700 (for purposes of making grants to States under this part), is current and accurate.

Other FAPE Requirements

Sec. 300.103   FAPE — methods and payments.

(a) Each State may use whatever State, local, Federal, and private sources of support that are available in the State to meet the requirements of this part. For example, if it is necessary to place a child with a disability in a residential facility, a State could use joint agreements between the agencies involved for sharing the cost of that placement.

(b) Nothing in this part relieves an insurer or similar third party from an otherwise valid obligation to provide or to pay for services provided to a child with a disability.

(c) Consistent with § 300.323(c), the State must ensure that there is no delay in implementing a child's IEP, including any case in which the payment source for providing or paying for special education and related services to the child is being determined.

Sec. 300.104   Residential placement

If placement in a public or private residential program is necessary to provide special education and related services to a child with a disability, the program, including non-medical care and room and board, must be at no cost to the parents of the child.

Sec. 300.105   Assistive technology.

(a) Each public agency must ensure that assistive technology devices or assistive technology services, or both, as those terms are defined in §§ 300.5 and 300.6, respectively, are made available to a child with a disability if required as a part of the child's —

(1) Special education under § 300.36;

(2) Related services under § 300.34; or

(3) Supplementary aids and services under §§ 300.38 and 300.114(a)(2)(ii).

(b) On a case-by-case basis, the use of school-purchased assistive technology devices in a child's home or in other settings is required if the child's IEP Team determines that the child needs access to those devices in order to receive FAPE.

Sec. 300.106 Extended school year services.

(a) General.

(1) Each public agency must ensure that extended school year services are available as necessary to provide FAPE, consistent with paragraph (a)(2) of this section.

(2) Extended school year services must be provided only if a child's IEP Team determines, on an individual basis, in accordance with §§ 300.320 through 300.324, that the services are necessary for the provision of FAPE to the child.

(3) In implementing the requirements of this section, a public agency may not —

(i) Limit extended school year services to particular categories of disability; or

(ii) Unilaterally limit the type, amount, or duration of those services.

(b) Definition. As used in this section, the term extended school year services means special education and related services that —

(1) Are provided to a child with a disability —

(i) Beyond the normal school year of the public agency;

(ii) In accordance with the child's IEP; and

(iii) At no cost to the parents of the child; and

(2) Meet the standards of the SEA.

Sec. 300.107 Nonacademic services.

The State must ensure the following:

(a) Each public agency must take steps, including the provision of supplementary aids and services determined appropriate and necessary by the child's IEP Team, to provide nonacademic and extracurricular services and activities in the manner necessary to afford children with disabilities an equal opportunity for participation in those services and activities.

(b) Nonacademic and extracurricular services and activities may include counseling services, athletics, transportation, health services, recreational activities, special interest groups or clubs sponsored by the public agency, referrals to agencies that provide assistance to individuals with disabilities, and employment of students, including both employment by the public agency and assistance in making outside employment available.

Sec. 300.108 Physical education.

The State must ensure that public agencies in the State comply with the following:

(a) General. Physical education services, specially designed if necessary, must be made available to every child with a disability receiving FAPE, unless the public agency enrolls children without disabilities and does not provide physical education to children without disabilities in the same grades.

(b) Regular physical education. Each child with a disability must be afforded the opportunity to participate in the regular physical education program available to nondisabled children unless —

(1) The child is enrolled full time in a separate facility; or

(2) The child needs specially designed physical education, as prescribed in the child's IEP.

(c) Special physical education. If specially designed physical education is prescribed in a child's IEP, the public agency responsible for the education of that child must provide the services directly or make arrangements for those services to be provided through other public or private programs.

(d) Education in separate facilities. The public agency responsible for the education of a child with a disability who is enrolled in a separate facility must ensure that the child receives appropriate physical education services in compliance with this section.

Sec. 300.109 Full educational opportunity goal (FEOG).

The State must have in effect policies and procedures to demonstrate that the State has established a goal of providing full educational opportunity to all children with disabilities, aged birth through 21, and a detailed timetable for accomplishing that goal.

Sec. 300.110 Program options.

The State must ensure that each public agency takes steps to ensure that its children with disabilities have available to them the variety of educational programs and services available to nondisabled children in the area served by the agency, including art, music, industrial arts, consumer and homemaking education, and vocational education.

Sec. 300.111 Child find.

(a) General.

(1) The State must have in effect policies and procedures to ensure that —

(i) All children with disabilities residing in the State, including children with disabilities who are homeless children or are wards of the State, and children with disabilities attending private schools, regardless of the severity of their disability, and who are in need of special education and related services, are identified, located, and evaluated; and

(ii) A practical method is developed and implemented to determine which children are currently receiving needed special education and related services.

(b) Use of term developmental delay. The following provisions apply with respect to implementing the child find requirements of this section:

(1) A State that adopts a definition of developmental delay under § 300.8(b) determines whether the term applies to children aged three through nine, or to a subset of that age range (e.g., ages three through five).

(2) A State may not require an LEA to adopt and use the term developmental delay for any children within its jurisdiction.

(3) If an LEA uses the term developmental delay for children described in § 300.8(b), the

LEA must conform to both the State's definition of that term and to the age range that has been adopted by the State.

(4) If a State does not adopt the term developmental delay, an LEA may not independently use that term as a basis for establishing a child's eligibility under this part.

(c)   Other children in child find. Child find also must include —

(1) Children who are suspected of being a child with a disability under § 300.8 and in need of special education, even though they are advancing from grade to grade; and

(2) Highly mobile children, including migrant children.

(d)   Construction. Nothing in the Act requires that children be classified by their disability so long as each child who has a disability that is listed in § 300.8 and who, by reason of that disability, needs special education and related services is regarded as a child with a disability under Part B of the Act.

Sec. 300.112   Individualized education programs (IEP).

The State must ensure that an IEP, or an IFSP that meets the requirements of section 636(d) of the Act, is developed, reviewed, and revised for each child with a disability in accordance with §§ 300.320 through 300.324, except as provided in § 300.300(b)(3)(ii).

Sec. 300.113   Routine checking of hearing aids and external components of surgically implanted medical devices.

(a)   Hearing aids. Each public agency must ensure that hearing aids worn in school by children with hearing impairments, including deafness, are functioning properly.

(b) External components of surgically implanted medical devices.

(1) Subject to paragraph (b)(2) of this section, each public agency must ensure that the external components of surgically implanted medical devices are functioning properly.

(2) For a child with a surgically implanted medical device who is receiving special education and related services under this part, a public agency is not responsible for the post-surgical maintenance, programming, or replacement of the medical device that has been surgically implanted (or of an external component of the surgically implanted medical device).

Least Restrictive Environment (LRE)

Sec. 300.114   LRE requirements.

(a)   General.

(1) Except as provided in § 300.324(d)(2) (regarding children with disabilities in adult prisons), the State must have in effect policies and procedures to ensure that public agencies in the State meet the LRE requirements of this section and §§ 300.115 through 300.120.

(2) Each public agency must ensure that —

(i) To the maximum extent appropriate, children with disabilities, including children in public or private institutions or other care facilities, are educated with children who are nondisabled; and

(ii) Special classes, separate schooling, or other removal of children with disabilities from the regular educational environment occurs only if the nature or severity of the disability is such that education in regular classes with the use of supplementary aids and services cannot be achieved satisfactorily.

(b) Additional requirement — State funding mechanism —

(1) General.

(i) A State funding mechanism must not result in placements that violate the requirements of paragraph (a) of this section; and

(ii) A State must not use a funding mechanism by which the State distributes funds on the basis of the type of setting in which a child is served that will result in the failure to provide a child with a disability FAPE according to the unique needs of the child, as described in the child's IEP.

(2) Assurance. If the State does not have policies and procedures to ensure compliance with paragraph (b)(1) of this section, the State must provide the Secretary an assurance that the State will revise the funding mechanism as soon as feasible to ensure that the mechanism does not result in placements that violate that paragraph.

Sec. 300.115   Continuum of alternative placements.

(a) Each public agency must ensure that a continuum of alternative placements is available to meet the needs of children with disabilities for special education and related services.

(b) The continuum required in paragraph (a) of this section must —

(1) Include the alternative placements listed in the definition of special education under § 300.38 (instruction in regular classes, special classes, special schools, home instruction, and instruction in hospitals and institutions); and

(2) Make provision for supplementary services (such as resource room or itinerant instruction) to be provided in conjunction with regular class placement.

Sec. 300.116   Placements.

In determining the educational placement of a child with a disability, including a preschool child with a disability, each public agency must ensure that —

(a) The placement decision —

(1) Is made by a group of persons, including the parents, and other persons knowledgeable about the child, the meaning of the evaluation data, and the placement options; and

(2) Is made in conformity with the LRE provisions of this subpart, including §§ 300.114 through 300.118;

(b) The child's placement —

(1) Is determined at least annually;

(2) Is based on the child's IEP; and

(3) Is as close as possible to the child's home;

(c) Unless the IEP of a child with a disability requires some other arrangement, the child is educated in the school that he or she would attend if nondisabled;

(d) In selecting the LRE, consideration is given to any potential harmful effect on the child or on the quality of services that he or she needs; and

(e) A child with a disability is not removed from education in age-appropriate regular classrooms solely because of needed modifications in the general education curriculum.

Sec. 300.117   Nonacademic settings.

In providing or arranging for the provision of nonacademic and extracurricular services and activities, including meals, recess periods, and the services and activities set forth in § 300.107, each public agency must ensure that each child with a disability participates with nondisabled children in the extracurricular services and activities to the maximum extent appropriate to the needs of that child. The public agency must ensure that each child with a disability has the supplementary aids and services determined by the child's IEP Team to be appropriate and necessary for the child to participate in nonacademic settings.

Sec. 300.118   Children in public or private institutions.

Except as provided in § 300.149(d) (regarding agency responsibility for general supervision of some individuals in adult prisons), an SEA must ensure that § 300.114 is effectively implemented, including, if necessary, making arrangements with public and private institutions (such as a memorandum of agreement or special implementation procedures).

Additional Eligibility Requirements

Sec. 300.121   Procedural safeguards.

(a)   General. The State must have procedural safeguards in effect to ensure that each public agency in the State meets the requirements of §§ 300.500 through 300.536.

(b)   Procedural safeguards identified. Children with disabilities and their parents must be afforded the procedural safeguards identified in paragraph (a) of this section.

Sec. 300.123   Confidentiality of personally identifiable information.

The State must have policies and procedures in effect to ensure that public agencies in the State comply with §§ 300.610 through 300.626 related to protecting the confidentiality of any personally identifiable information collected, used, or maintained under Part B of the Act.

Sec. 300.124   Transition of children from the Part C program to preschool programs.

The State must have in effect policies and procedures to ensure that —

(a) Children participating in early intervention programs assisted under Part C of the Act, and who will participate in preschool programs assisted under Part B of the Act, experience a smooth and effective transition to those preschool programs in a manner consistent with section 637(a)(9) of the Act;

(b) By the third birthday of a child described in paragraph (a) of this section, an IEP or, if consistent with § 300.323(b) and section 636(d) of the Act, an IFSP, has been developed and is being implemented for the child consistent with Sec. 300.101(b); and

(c) Each affected LEA will participate in transition planning conferences arranged by the designated lead agency under section 635(a)(10) of the Act.

Children With Disabilities Enrolled by Their Parents in Private Schools

Sec. 300.130   Definition of parentally-placed private school children with disabilities.

Parentally-placed private school children with disabilities means children with disabilities enrolled by their parents in private, including religious, schools or facilities that meet the definition of elementary school in § 300.13 or secondary school in § 300.36, other than children with disabilities covered under §§ 300.145 through 300.147.

Sec. 300.131   Child find for parentally-placed private school children with disabilities.

(a)   General. Each LEA must locate, identify, and evaluate all children with disabilities who are enrolled by their parents in private, including religious, elementary schools and secondary schools located in the school district served by the LEA, in accordance with paragraphs (b) through (e) of this section, and §§ 300.111 and 300.201.

(b)   Child find design. The child find process must be designed to ensure —

(1) The equitable participation of parentally-placed private school children; and

(2) An accurate count of those children.

(c)   Activities. In carrying out the requirements of this section, the LEA, or, if applicable, the SEA, must undertake activities similar to the activities undertaken for the agency's public school children.

(d)   Cost. The cost of carrying out the child find requirements in this section, including individual evaluations, may not be considered in determining if an LEA has met its obligation under § 300.133.

(e)   Completion period. The child find process must be completed in a time period comparable to that for students attending public schools in the LEA consistent with § 300.301.

(f)   Out-of-State children. Each LEA in which private, including religious, elementary schools and secondary schools are located must, in carrying out the child find requirements in this section, include parentally-placed private school children who reside in a State other than the State in which the private schools that they attend are located.

Sec. 300.132   Provision of services for parentally-placed private school children with disabilities — basic requirement.

(a)   General. To the extent consistent with the number and location of children with disabilities who are enrolled by their parents in private, including religious, elementary schools and secondary schools located in the school district served by the LEA, provision is made for the participation of those children in the program assisted or carried out under Part B of the Act by providing them with special education and related services, including direct services determined in accordance with § 300.137, unless the Secretary has arranged for services to those children under the by-pass provisions in §§ 300.190 through 300.198.

(b) Services plan for parentally-placed private school children with disabilities. In accordance with paragraph (a) of this section and §§ 300.137 through 300.139, a services plan must be developed and implemented for each private school child with a disability who has been designated by the LEA in which the private school is located to receive special education and related services under this part.

(c)   Record keeping. Each LEA must maintain in its records, and provide to the SEA, the following information related to parentally-placed private school children covered under §§ 300.130 through 300.144:

(1) The number of children evaluated;

(2) The number of children determined to be children with disabilities; and

(3) The number of children served.

Sec. 300.137   Equitable services determined.

(a)   No individual right to special education and related services. No parentally-placed private school child with a disability has an individual right to receive some or all of the special education and related services that the child would receive if enrolled in a public school.

(b)   Decisions.

(1) Decisions about the services that will be provided to parentally-placed private school children with disabilities under §§ 300.130 through 300.144 must be made in accordance with paragraph (c) of this section and § 300.134(d).

(2) The LEA must make the final decisions with respect to the services to be provided to eligible parentally-placed private school children with disabilities.

(c) Services plan for each child served under §§ 300.130 through 300.144. If a child with a disability is enrolled in a religious or other private school by the child's parents and will receive special education or related services from an LEA, the LEA must —

(1) Initiate and conduct meetings to develop, review, and revise a services plan for the child, in accordance with § 300.138(b); and

(2) Ensure that a representative of the religious or other private school attends each meeting. If the representative cannot attend, the LEA shall use other methods to ensure participation by the religious or other private school, including individual or conference telephone calls.

Sec. 300.138   Equitable services provided.

(a)   General.

(1) The services provided to parentally-placed private school children with disabilities must be provided by personnel meeting the same standards as personnel providing services in the public schools, except that private elementary school and secondary school teachers who are providing equitable services to parentally-placed private school children with disabilities do not have to meet the highly qualified special education teacher requirements of § 300.18.

(2) Parentally-placed private school children with disabilities may receive a different amount of services than children with disabilities in public schools.

(b) Services provided in accordance with a services plan.

(1) Each parentally-placed private school child with a disability who has been designated to receive services under § 300.132 must have a services plan that describes the specific

special education and related services that the LEA will provide to the child in light of the services that the LEA has determined, through the process described in §§ 300.134 and 300.137, it will make available to parentally-placed private school children with disabilities.

(2) The services plan must, to the extent appropriate —

(i) Meet the requirements of § 300.320, or for a child ages three through five, meet the requirements of § 300.323(b) with respect to the services provided; and

(ii) Be developed, reviewed, and revised consistent with §§ 300.321 through 300.324.

(c)   Provision of equitable services.

(1) The provision of services pursuant to this section and §§ 300.139 through 300.143 must be provided:

(i) By employees of a public agency; or

(ii) Through contract by the public agency with an individual, association, agency, organization, or other entity.

(2) Special education and related services provided to parentally-placed private school children with disabilities, including materials and equipment, must be secular, neutral, and nonideological.

Sec. 300.139   Location of services and transportation.

(a)   Services on private school premises. Services to parentally-placed private school children with disabilities may be provided on the premises of private, including religious, schools, to the extent consistent with law.

(b)   Transportation —

(1)   General.

(i) If necessary for the child to benefit from or participate in the services provided under this part, a parentally-placed private school child with a disability must be provided transportation —

(A) From the child's school or the child's home to a site other than the private school; and

(B) From the service site to the private school, or to the child's home, depending on the timing of the services.

(ii) LEAs are not required to provide transportation from the child's home to the private school.

(2)   Cost of transportation. The cost of the transportation described in paragraph (b)(1)(i) of this section may be included in calculating whether the LEA has met the requirement of § 300.133.

Sec. 300.140   Due process complaints and State complaints.

(a)   Due process not applicable, except for child find.

(1) Except as provided in paragraph (b) of this section, the procedures in §§ 300.504 through 300.519 do not apply to complaints that an LEA has failed to meet the requirements

of §§ 300.132 through 300.139, including the provision of services indicated on the child's services plan.

(b) Child find complaints — to be filed with the LEA in which the private school is located.

(1) The procedures in §§ 300.504 through 300.519 apply to complaints that an LEA has failed to meet the child find requirements in §§ 300.131, including the requirements in §§ 300.300 through 300.311.

(2) Any due process complaint regarding the child find requirements (as described in paragraph (b)(1) of this section) must be filed with the LEA in which the private school is located and a copy must be forwarded to the SEA.

(c)   State complaints.

(1) Any complaint that an SEA or LEA has failed to meet the requirements in §§ 300.132 through 300.135 and 300.137 through 300.144 must be filed in accordance with the procedures described in §§ 300.151 through 300.153.

(2) A complaint filed by a private school official under § 300.136(a) must be filed with the SEA in accordance with the procedures in § 300.136(b).

Sec. 300.141   Requirement that funds not benefit a private school.

(a) An LEA may not use funds provided under section 611 or 619 of the Act to finance the existing level of instruction in a private school or to otherwise benefit the private school.

(b) The LEA must use funds provided under Part B of the Act to meet the special education and related services needs of parentally-placed private school children with disabilities, but not for meeting —

(1) The needs of a private school; or

(2) The general needs of the students enrolled in the private school.

Sec. 300.142   Use of personnel.

(a)   Use of public school personnel. An LEA may use funds available under sections 611 and 619 of the Act to make public school personnel available in other than public facilities —

(1) To the extent necessary to provide services under §§ 300.130 through 300.144 for parentally-placed private school children with disabilities; and

(2) If those services are not normally provided by the private school.

(b)   Use of private school personnel. An LEA may use funds available under sections 611 and 619 of the Act to pay for the services of an employee of a private school to provide services under §§ 300.130 through 300.144 if —

(1) The employee performs the services outside of his or her regular hours of duty; and

(2) The employee performs the services under public supervision and control.

Sec. 300.143   Separate classes prohibited.

An LEA may not use funds available under section 611 or 619 of the Act for classes that are organized separately on the basis of school enrollment or religion of the children if —

(a) The classes are at the same site; and

(b) The classes include children enrolled in public schools and children enrolled in private schools.

Sec. 300.144   Property, equipment, and supplies.

(a) A public agency must control and administer the funds used to provide special education and related services under §§ 300.137 through 300.139, and hold title to and administer materials, equipment, and property purchased with those funds for the uses and purposes provided in the Act.

(b) The public agency may place equipment and supplies in a private school for the period of time needed for the Part B program.

(c) The public agency must ensure that the equipment and supplies placed in a private school —

(1) Are used only for Part B purposes; and

(2) Can be removed from the private school without remodeling the private school facility.

(d) The public agency must remove equipment and supplies from a private school if

(1) The equipment and supplies are no longer needed for Part B purposes; or

(2) Removal is necessary to avoid unauthorized use of the equipment and supplies for other than Part B purposes.

(e) No funds under Part B of the Act may be used for repairs, minor remodeling, or construction of private school facilities.

Children With Disabilities in Private Schools Placed or Referred by Public Agencies

Sec. 300.145   Applicability of §§ 300.146 through 300.147.

Sections 300.146 through 300.147 apply only to children with disabilities who are or have been placed in or referred to a private school or facility by a public agency as a means of providing special education and related services.

Sec. 300.146   Responsibility of SEA.

Each SEA must ensure that a child with a disability who is placed in or referred to a private school or facility by a public agency —

(a) Is provided special education and related services —

(1) In conformance with an IEP that meets the requirements of §§ 300.320 through 300.325; and

(2) At no cost to the parents;

(b) Is provided an education that meets the standards that apply to education provided by the SEA and LEAs including the requirements of this part, except for § 300.18 and § 300.156(c); and

(c) Has all of the rights of a child with a disability who is served by a public agency.

Sec. 300.147   Implementation by SEA.

In implementing § 300.146, the SEA must —

(a) Monitor compliance through procedures such as written reports, on-site visits, and parent questionnaires;

(b) Disseminate copies of applicable standards to each private school and facility to which a public agency has referred or placed a child with a disability; and

(c) Provide an opportunity for those private schools and facilities to participate in the development and revision of State standards that apply to them.

Children With Disabilities Enrolled by Their Parents in Private Schools When FAPE Is at Issue

Sec. 300.148   Placement of children by parents when FAPE is at issue.

(a)   General. This part does not require an LEA to pay for the cost of education, including special education and related services, of a child with a disability at a private school or facility if that agency made FAPE available to the child and the parents elected to place the child in a private school or facility. However, the public agency must include that child in the population whose needs are addressed consistent with §§ 300.131 through 300.144.

(b)   Disagreements about FAPE. Disagreements between the parents and a public agency regarding the availability of a program appropriate for the child, and the question of financial reimbursement, are subject to the due process procedures in §§ 300.504 through 300.520.

(c)   Reimbursement for private school placement. If the parents of a child with a disability, who previously received special education and related services under the authority of a public agency, enroll the child in a private preschool, elementary school, or secondary school without the consent of or referral by the public agency, a court or a hearing officer may require the agency to reimburse the parents for the cost of that enrollment if the court or hearing officer finds that the agency had not made FAPE available to the child in a timely manner prior to that enrollment and that the private placement is appropriate. A parental placement may be found to be appropriate by a hearing officer or a court even if it does not meet the State standards that apply to education provided by the SEA and LEAs.

(d)   Limitation on reimbursement. The cost of reimbursement described in paragraph (c) of this section may be reduced or denied —

(1) If —

(i) At the most recent IEP Team meeting that the parents attended prior to removal of the child from the public school, the parents did not inform the IEP Team that they were rejecting the placement proposed by the public agency to provide FAPE to their child, including stating their concerns and their intent to enroll their child in a private school at public expense; or

(ii) At least ten (10) business days (including any holidays that occur on a business day) prior to the removal of the child from the public school, the parents did not give written notice to the public agency of the information described in paragraph (d)(1)(i) of this section;

(2) If, prior to the parents' removal of the child from the public school, the public agency informed the parents, through the notice requirements described in § 300.503(a)(1), of its intent to evaluate the child (including a statement of the purpose of the evaluation that was appropriate and reasonable), but the parents did not make the child available for the evaluation; or

(3) Upon a judicial finding of unreasonableness with respect to actions taken by the parents.

(e) Exception. Notwithstanding the notice requirement in paragraph (d)(1) of this section, the cost of reimbursement —

(1) Must not be reduced or denied for failure to provide the notice if —

(i) The school prevented the parents from providing the notice;

(ii) The parents had not received notice, pursuant to § 300.504, of the notice requirement in paragraph (d)(1) of this section; or

(iii) Compliance with paragraph (d)(1) of this section would likely result in physical harm to the child; and

(2) May, in the discretion of the court or a hearing officer, not be reduced or denied for failure to provide this notice if —

(i) The parents are not literate or cannot write in English; or

(ii) Compliance with paragraph (d)(1) of this section would likely result in serious emotional harm to the child.

SEA Responsibility for General Supervision and Implementation of Procedural Safeguards

Sec. 300.149 SEA responsibility for general supervision.

(a) The SEA is responsible for ensuring —

(1) That the requirements of this part are carried out; and

(2) That each educational program for children with disabilities administered within the State, including each program administered by any other State or local agency (but not including elementary schools and secondary schools for Indian children operated or funded by the Secretary of the Interior) —

(i) Is under the general supervision of the persons responsible for educational programs for children with disabilities in the SEA; and

(ii) Meets the educational standards of the SEA (including the requirements of this part).

(3) In carrying out this part with respect to homeless children, the requirements of subtitle B of title VII of the McKinney-Vento Homeless Assistance Act (42 U.S.C. 11431 et seq.) are met.

(b) The State must have in effect policies and procedures to ensure that it complies with the monitoring and enforcement requirements in §§ 300.600 through 300.602 and §§ 300.606 through 300.608.

(c) Part B of the Act does not limit the responsibility of agencies other than educational agencies for providing or paying some or all of the costs of FAPE to children with disabilities in the State.

(d) Notwithstanding paragraph (a) of this section, the Governor (or another individual pursuant to State law) may assign to any public agency in the State the responsibility of ensuring that the requirements of Part B of the Act are met with respect to students with disabilities who are convicted as adults under State law and incarcerated in adult prisons.

Sec. 300.150 SEA implementation of procedural safeguards.

The SEA (and any agency assigned responsibility pursuant to § 300.149(d)) must have in effect procedures to inform each public agency of its responsibility for ensuring effective implementation of procedural safeguards for the children with disabilities served by that public agency.

State Complaint Procedures

Sec. 300.151 Adoption of State complaint procedures.

(a)   General. Each SEA must adopt written procedures for —

(1) Resolving any complaint, including a complaint filed by an organization or individual from another State, that meets the requirements of § 300.153 by —

(i) Providing for the filing of a complaint with the SEA; and

(ii) At the SEA's discretion, providing for the filing of a complaint with a public agency and the right to have the SEA review the public agency's decision on the complaint; and

(2) Widely disseminating to parents and other interested individuals, including parent training and information centers, protection and advocacy agencies, independent living centers, and other appropriate entities, the State procedures under §§ 300.151 through 300.153.

(b)   Remedies for denial of appropriate services. In resolving a complaint in which the SEA has found a failure to provide appropriate services, an SEA, pursuant to its general supervisory authority under Part B of the Act, must address —

(1) The failure to provide appropriate services, including corrective action appropriate to address the needs of the child (such as compensatory services or monetary reimbursement); and

(2) Appropriate future provision of services for all children with disabilities.

Sec. 300.152 Minimum State complaint procedures.

(a)   Time limit; minimum procedures. Each SEA must include in its complaint procedures a time limit of 60 days after a complaint is filed under § 300.153 to —

(1) Carry out an independent on-site investigation, if the SEA determines that an investigation is necessary;

(2) Give the complainant the opportunity to submit additional information, either orally or in writing, about the allegations in the complaint;

(3) Provide the public agency with the opportunity to respond to the complaint, including,

at a minimum —

(i) At the discretion of the public agency, a proposal to resolve the complaint; and

(ii) An opportunity for a parent who has filed a complaint and the public agency to voluntarily engage in mediation consistent with § 300.506;

(4) Review all relevant information and make an independent determination as to whether the public agency is violating a requirement of Part B of the Act or of this part; and

(5) Issue a written decision to the complainant that addresses each allegation in the complaint and contains —

(i) Findings of fact and conclusions; and

(ii) The reasons for the SEA's final decision.

(b) Time extension; final decision; implementation. The SEA's procedures described in paragraph (a) of this section also must —

(1) Permit an extension of the time limit under paragraph (a) of this section only if —

(i) Exceptional circumstances exist with respect to a particular complaint; or

(ii) The parent (or individual or organization, if mediation or other alternative means of dispute resolution is available to the individual or organization under State procedures) and the public agency involved agree to extend the time to engage in mediation pursuant to paragraph (a)(3)(ii) of this section, or to engage in other alternative means of dispute resolution, if available in the State; and

(2) Include procedures for effective implementation of the SEA's final decision, if needed, including —

(i) Technical assistance activities;

(ii) Negotiations; and

(iii) Corrective actions to achieve compliance.

(c) Complaints filed under this section and due process hearings under § 300.507 and §§ 300.530 through 300.532.

(1) If a written complaint is received that is also the subject of a due process hearing under § 300.507 or §§ 300.530 through 300.532, or contains multiple issues of which one or more are part of that hearing, the State must set aside any part of the complaint that is being addressed in the due process hearing until the conclusion of the hearing. However, any issue in the complaint that is not a part of the due process action must be resolved using the time limit and procedures described in paragraphs (a) and (b) of this section.

(2) If an issue raised in a complaint filed under this section has previously been decided in a due process hearing involving the same parties —

(i) The due process hearing decision is binding on that issue; and

(ii) The SEA must inform the complainant to that effect.

(3) A complaint alleging a public agency's failure to implement a due process hearing decision must be resolved by the SEA.

Sec. 300.153 Filing a complaint.

(a) An organization or individual may file a signed written complaint under the procedures described in §§ 300.151 through 300.152.

(b) The complaint must include —

(1) A statement that a public agency has violated a requirement of Part B of the Act or of this part;

(2) The facts on which the statement is based;

(3) The signature and contact information for the complainant; and

(4) If alleging violations with respect to a specific child —

(i) The name and address of the residence of the child;

(ii) The name of the school the child is attending;

(iii) In the case of a homeless child or youth (within the meaning of section 725(2) of the McKinney-Vento Homeless Assistance Act (42 U.S.C. 11434a(2)), available contact information for the child, and the name of the school the child is attending;

(iv) A description of the nature of the problem of the child, including facts relating to the problem; and

(v) A proposed resolution of the problem to the extent known and available to the party at the time the complaint is filed.

(c) The complaint must allege a violation that occurred not more than one year prior to the date that the complaint is received in accordance with § 300.151.

(d) The party filing the complaint must forward a copy of the complaint to the LEA or public agency serving the child at the same time the party files the complaint with the SEA.

Methods of Ensuring Services

Sec. 300.154 Methods of ensuring services.

(a) Establishing responsibility for services. The Chief Executive Officer of a State or designee of that officer must ensure that an interagency agreement or other mechanism for interagency coordination is in effect between each noneducational public agency described in paragraph (b) of this section and the SEA, in order to ensure that all services described in paragraph (b)(1) of this section that are needed to ensure FAPE are provided, including the provision of these services during the pendency of any dispute under paragraph (a)(3) of this section. The agreement or mechanism must include the following:

(1) An identification of, or a method for defining, the financial responsibility of each agency for providing services described in paragraph (b)(1) of this section to ensure FAPE to children with disabilities. The financial responsibility of each noneducational public agency described in paragraph (b) of this section, including the State Medicaid agency and other public insurers of children with disabilities, must precede the financial responsibility of the LEA (or the State agency responsible for developing the child's IEP).

(2) The conditions, terms, and procedures under which an LEA must be reimbursed by

other agencies.

(3) Procedures for resolving interagency disputes (including procedures under which LEAs may initiate proceedings) under the agreement or other mechanism to secure reimbursement from other agencies or otherwise implement the provisions of the agreement or mechanism.

(4) Policies and procedures for agencies to determine and identify the interagency coordination responsibilities of each agency to promote the coordination and timely and appropriate delivery of services described in paragraph (b)(1) of this section.

(b)   Obligation of noneducational public agencies.

(1) (i) If any public agency other than an educational agency is otherwise obligated under Federal or State law, or assigned responsibility under State policy or pursuant to paragraph (a) of this section, to provide or pay for any services that are also considered special education or related services (such as, but not limited to, services described in § 300.5 relating to assistive technology devices, § 300.6 relating to assistive technology services, § 300.34 relating to related services, § 300.41 relating to supplementary aids and services, and § 300.42 relating to transition services) that are necessary for ensuring FAPE to children with disabilities within the State, the public agency must fulfill that obligation or responsibility, either directly or through contract or other arrangement pursuant to paragraph (a) of this section or an agreement pursuant to paragraph (c) of this section.

(ii) A noneducational public agency described in paragraph (b)(1)(i) of this section may not disqualify an eligible service for Medicaid reimbursement because that service is provided in a school context.

(2) If a public agency other than an educational agency fails to provide or pay for the special education and related services described in paragraph (b)(1) of this section, the LEA (or State agency responsible for developing the child's IEP) must provide or pay for these services to the child in a timely manner. The LEA or State agency is authorized to claim reimbursement for the services from the noneducational public agency that failed to provide or pay for these services and that agency must reimburse the LEA or State agency in accordance with the terms of the interagency agreement or other mechanism described in paragraph (a) of this section.

(c)   Special rule. The requirements of paragraph (a) of this section may be met through —

(1) State statute or regulation;

(2) Signed agreements between respective agency officials that clearly identify the responsibilities of each agency relating to the provision of services; or

(3) Other appropriate written methods as determined by the Chief Executive Officer of the State or designee of that officer and approved by the Secretary.

(d)   Children with disabilities who are covered by public benefits or insurance.

(1) A public agency may use the Medicaid or other public benefits or insurance programs in which a child participates to provide or pay for services required under this part, as permitted under the public benefits or insurance program, except as provided in paragraph (d)(2) of this section.

(2) With regard to services required to provide FAPE to an eligible child under this part, the public agency —

(i) May not require parents to sign up for or enroll in public benefits or insurance programs in order for their child to receive FAPE under Part B of the Act;

(ii) May not require parents to incur an out-of-pocket expense such as the payment of a deductible or co-pay amount incurred in filing a claim for services provided pursuant to this part, but pursuant to paragraph (g)(2) of this section, may pay the cost that the parents otherwise would be required to pay;

(iii) May not use a child's benefits under a public benefits or insurance program if that use would —

(A) Decrease available lifetime coverage or any other insured benefit;

(B) Result in the family paying for services that would otherwise be covered by the public benefits or insurance program and that are required for the child outside of the time the child is in school;

(C) Increase premiums or lead to the discontinuation of benefits or insurance; or

(D) Risk loss of eligibility for home and community-based waivers, based on aggregate health-related expenditures; and

(iv) (A) Must obtain parental consent, consistent with § 300.9, each time that access to public benefits or insurance is sought; and

(B) Notify parents that the parents' refusal to allow access to their public benefits or insurance does not relieve the public agency of its responsibility to ensure that all required services are provided at no cost to the parents.

(e)   Children with disabilities who are covered by private insurance.

(1) With regard to services required to provide FAPE to an eligible child under this part, a public agency may access the parents' private insurance proceeds only if the parents provide consent consistent with § 300.9.

(2) Each time the public agency proposes to access the parents' private insurance proceeds, the agency must —

(i) Obtain parental consent in accordance with paragraph (e)(1) of this section; and

(ii) Inform the parents that their refusal to permit the public agency to access their private insurance does not relieve the public agency of its responsibility to ensure that all required services are provided at no cost to the parents.

(f)   Use of Part B funds.

(1) If a public agency is unable to obtain parental consent to use the parents' private insurance, or public benefits or insurance when the parents would incur a cost for a specified service required under this part, to ensure FAPE the public agency may use its Part B funds to pay for the service.

(2) To avoid financial cost to parents who otherwise would consent to use private insurance, or public benefits or insurance if the parents would incur a cost, the public agency may use its Part B funds to pay the cost that the parents otherwise would have to pay to use the

parents' benefits or insurance (e.g., the deductible or co-pay amounts).

(g) Proceeds from public benefits or insurance or private insurance.

(1) Proceeds from public benefits or insurance or private insurance will not be treated as program income for purposes of 34 CFR 80.25.

(2) If a public agency spends reimbursements from Federal funds (e.g., Medicaid) for services under this part, those funds will not be considered "State or local" funds for purposes of the maintenance of effort provisions in §§ 300.163 and 300.203.

(h) Construction. Nothing in this part should be construed to alter the requirements imposed on a State Medicaid agency, or any other agency administering a public benefits or insurance program by Federal statute, regulations or policy under title XIX, or title XXI of the Social Security Act, 42 U.S.C. 1396 through 1396v and 42 U.S.C. 1397aa through 1397jj, or any other public benefits or insurance program.

Additional Eligibility Requirements

Sec. 300.155 Hearings relating to LEA eligibility.

The SEA must not make any final determination that an LEA is not eligible for assistance under Part B of the Act without first giving the LEA reasonable notice and an opportunity for a hearing under 34 CFR 76.401(d).

Sec. 300.157 Performance goals and indicators.

The State must —

(a) Have in effect established goals for the performance of children with disabilities in the State that —

(1) Promote the purposes of this part, as stated in § 300.1;

(2) Are the same as the State's objectives for progress by children in its definition of adequate yearly progress, including the State's objectives for progress by children with disabilities, under section 1111(b)(2)(C) of the ESEA, 20 U.S.C. 6311;

(3) Address graduation rates and dropout rates, as well as such other factors as the State may determine; and

(4) Are consistent, to the extent appropriate, with any other goals and academic standards for children established by the State;

(b) Have in effect established performance indicators the State will use to assess progress toward achieving the goals described in paragraph (a) of this section, including measurable annual objectives for progress by children with disabilities under section 1111(b)(2)(C)(v)(II)(cc) of the ESEA, 20 U.S.C. 6311; and

(c) Annually report to the Secretary and the public on the progress of the State, and of children with disabilities in the State, toward meeting the goals established under paragraph (a) of this section, which may include elements of the reports required under section 1111(h) of the ESEA.

Sec. 300.160 Participation in assessments.

(a) General. A State must ensure that all children with disabilities are included in all general State and district-wide assessment programs, including assessments described under section 1111 of the ESEA, 20 U.S.C. 6311, with appropriate accommodations and alternate assessments, if necessary, as indicated in their respective IEPs.

(b) Accommodation guidelines.

(1) A State (or, in the case of a district-wide assessment, an LEA) must develop guidelines for the provision of appropriate accommodations.

(2) The State's (or, in the case of a district-wide assessment, the LEA's) guidelines must —

(i) Identify only those accommodations for each assessment that do not invalidate the score; and

(ii) Instruct IEP Teams to select, for each assessment, only those accommodations that do not invalidate the score.

(c) Alternate assessments.

(1) A State (or, in the case of a district-wide assessment, an LEA) must develop and implement alternate assessments and guidelines for the participation of children with disabilities in alternate assessments for those children who cannot participate in regular assessments, even with accommodations, as indicated in their respective IEPs, as provided in paragraph (a) of this section.

(2) For assessing the academic progress of students with disabilities under Title I of the ESEA, the alternate assessments and guidelines in paragraph (c)(1) of this section must provide for alternate assessments that —

(i) Are aligned with the State's challenging academic content standards and challenging student academic achievement standards;

(ii) If the State has adopted modified academic achievement standards permitted in 34 CFR 200.1(e), measure the achievement of children with disabilities meeting the State's criteria under Sec. 200.1(e)(2) against those standards; and

(iii) If the State has adopted alternate academic achievement standards permitted in 34 CFR 200.1(d), measure the achievement of children with the most significant cognitive disabilities against those standards.

(d) Explanation to IEP Teams. A State (or in the case of a district-wide assessment, an LEA) must provide IEP Teams with a clear explanation of the differences between assessments based on grade-level academic achievement standards and those based on modified or alternate academic achievement standards, including any effects of State or local policies on the student's education resulting from taking an alternate assessment based on alternate or modified academic achievement standards (such as whether only satisfactory performance on a regular assessment would qualify a student for a regular high school diploma).

(e) Inform parents. A State (or in the case of a district-wide assessment, an LEA) must ensure that parents of students selected to be assessed based on alternate or modified academic achievement standards are informed that their child's achievement will be measured based on alternate or modified academic achievement standards.

(f)   Reports. An SEA (or, in the case of a district-wide assessment, an LEA) must make available to the public, and report to the public with the same frequency and in the same detail as it reports on the assessment of nondisabled children, the following:

(1) The number of children with disabilities participating in regular assessments, and the number of those children who were provided accommodations (that did not result in an invalid score) in order to participate in those assessments.

(2) The number of children with disabilities, if any, participating in alternate assessments based on grade-level academic achievement standards.

(3) The number of children with disabilities, if any, participating in alternate assessments based on modified academic achievement standards.

(4) The number of children with disabilities, if any, participating in alternate assessments based on alternate academic achievement standards.

(5) Compared with the achievement of all children, including children with disabilities, the performance results of children with disabilities on regular assessments, alternate assessments based on grade-level academic achievement standards, alternate assessments based on modified academic achievement standards, and alternate assessments based on alternate academic achievement standards if —

(i) The number of children participating in those assessments is sufficient to yield statistically reliable information; and

(ii) Reporting that information will not reveal personally identifiable information about an individual student on those assessments.

(g)   Universal design. An SEA (or, in the case of a district-wide assessment, an LEA) must, to the extent possible, use universal design principles in developing and administering any assessments under this section.

Other Provisions Required for State Eligibility

Sec. 300.170   Suspension and expulsion rates.

(a)   General. The SEA must examine data, including data disaggregated by race and ethnicity, to determine if significant discrepancies are occurring in the rate of long-term suspensions and expulsions of children with disabilities —

(1) Among LEAs in the State; or

(2) Compared to the rates for nondisabled children within those agencies.

(b)   Review and revision of policies. If the discrepancies described in paragraph (a) of this section are occurring, the SEA must review and, if appropriate, revise (or require the affected State agency or LEA to revise) its policies, procedures, and practices relating to the development and implementation of IEPs, the use of positive behavioral interventions and supports, and procedural safeguards, to ensure that these policies, procedures, and practices comply with the Act.

Sec. 300.172   Access to instructional materials.

(a)   General. The State must —

(1) Adopt the National Instructional Materials Accessibility Standard (NIMAS), published as appendix C to part 300, for the purposes of providing instructional materials to blind persons or other persons with print disabilities, in a timely manner after publication of the NIMAS in the Federal Register on July 19, 2006 (71 FR 41084); and

(2) Establish a State definition of "timely manner" for purposes of paragraphs (b)(2) and (b)(3) of this section if the State is not coordinating with the National Instructional Materials Access Center (NIMAC) or (b)(3) and (c)(2) of this section if the State is coordinating with the NIMAC.

(b)   Rights and responsibilities of SEA.

(1) Nothing in this section shall be construed to require any SEA to coordinate with the NIMAC.

(2) If an SEA chooses not to coordinate with the NIMAC, the SEA must provide an assurance to the Secretary that it will provide instructional materials to blind persons or other persons with print disabilities in a timely manner.

(3) Nothing in this section relieves an SEA of its responsibility to ensure that children with disabilities who need instructional materials in accessible formats, but are not included under the definition of blind or other persons with print disabilities in § 300.172(e)(1)(i) or who need materials that cannot be produced from NIMAS files, receive those instructional materials in a timely manner.

(4) In order to meet its responsibility under paragraphs (b)(2), (b)(3), and (c) of this section to ensure that children with disabilities who need instructional materials in accessible formats are provided those materials in a timely manner, the SEA must ensure that all public agencies take all reasonable steps to provide instructional materials in accessible formats to children with disabilities who need those instructional materials at the same time as other children receive instructional materials.

(c)   Preparation and delivery of files. If an SEA chooses to coordinate with the NIMAC, as of December 3, 2006, the SEA must —

(1) As part of any print instructional materials adoption process, procurement contract, or other practice or instrument used for purchase of print instructional materials, enter into a written contract with the publisher of the print instructional materials to —

(i) Require the publisher to prepare and, on or before delivery of the print instructional materials, provide to NIMAC electronic files containing the contents of the print instructional materials using the NIMAS; or

(ii) Purchase instructional materials from the publisher that are produced in, or may be rendered in, specialized formats.

(2) Provide instructional materials to blind persons or other persons with print disabilities in a timely manner.

(d)   Assistive technology. In carrying out this section, the SEA, to the maximum extent possible, must work collaboratively with the State agency responsible for assistive technology programs.

(e) Definitions.

(1) In this section and § 300.210 —

(i) Blind persons or other persons with print disabilities means children served under this part who may qualify to receive books and other publications produced in specialized formats in accordance with the Act entitled "An Act to provide books for adult blind," approved March 3, 1931, 2 U.S.C. 135a;

(ii) National Instructional Materials Access Center or NIMAC means the center established pursuant to section 674(e) of the Act;

(iii) National Instructional Materials Accessibility Standard or NIMAS has the meaning given the term in section 674(e)(3)(B) of the Act;

(iv) Specialized formats has the meaning given the term in section 674(e)(3)(D) of the Act.

(2) The definitions in paragraph (e)(1) of this section apply to each State and LEA, whether or not the State or LEA chooses to coordinate with the NIMAC.

Sec. 300.173   Overidentification and disproportionality.

The State must have in effect, consistent with the purposes of this part and with section 618(d) of the Act, policies and procedures designed to prevent the inappropriate overidentification or disproportionate representation by race and ethnicity of children as children with disabilities, including children with disabilities with a particular impairment described in § 300.8.

Sec. 300.174   Prohibition on mandatory medication.

(a) General. The SEA must prohibit State and LEA personnel from requiring parents to obtain a prescription for substances identified under schedules I, II, III, IV, or V in section 202(c) of the Controlled Substances Act (21 U.S.C. 812(c)) for a child as a condition of attending school, receiving an evaluation under §§ 300.300 through 300.311, or receiving services under this part.

(b) Rule of construction. Nothing in paragraph (a) of this section shall be construed to create a Federal prohibition against teachers and other school personnel consulting or sharing classroom-based observations with parents or guardians regarding a student's academic and functional performance, or behavior in the classroom or school, or regarding the need for evaluation for special education or related services under § 300.111 (related to child find).

Sec. 300.177   States' sovereign immunity and positive efforts to employ and advance qualified individuals with disabilities.

(a) States' sovereign immunity.

(1) A State that accepts funds under this part waives its immunity under the 11th amendment of the Constitution of the United States from suit in Federal court for a violation of this part.

(2) In a suit against a State for a violation of this part, remedies (including remedies both at law and in equity) are available for such a violation in the suit against any public entity

other than a State.

(3) Paragraphs (a)(1) and (a)(2) of this section apply with respect to violations that occur in whole or part after the date of enactment of the Education of the Handicapped Act Amendments of 1990.

Sec. 300.209   Treatment of charter schools and their students.

(a)   Rights of children with disabilities. Children with disabilities who attend public charter schools and their parents retain all rights under this part.

(b)   Charter schools that are public schools of the LEA.

(1) In carrying out Part B of the Act and these regulations with respect to charter schools that are public schools of the LEA, the LEA must —

(i) Serve children with disabilities attending those charter schools in the same manner as the LEA serves children with disabilities in its other schools, including providing supplementary and related services on site at the charter school to the same extent to which the LEA has a policy or practice of providing such services on the site to its other public schools; and

(ii) Provide funds under Part B of the Act to those charter schools —

(A) On the same basis as the LEA provides funds to the LEA's other public schools, including proportional distribution based on relative enrollment of children with disabilities; and

(B) At the same time as the LEA distributes other Federal funds to the LEA's other public schools, consistent with the State's charter school law.

(2) If the public charter school is a school of an LEA that receives funding under § 300.705 and includes other public schools —

(i) The LEA is responsible for ensuring that the requirements of this part are met, unless State law assigns that responsibility to some other entity; and

(ii) The LEA must meet the requirements of paragraph (b)(1) of this section.

(c)   Public charter schools that are LEAs. If the public charter school is an LEA, consistent with § 300.28, that receives funding under § 300.705, that charter school is responsible for ensuring that the requirements of this part are met, unless State law assigns that responsibility to some other entity.

(d) Public charter schools that are not an LEA or a school that is part of an LEA.

(1) If the public charter school is not an LEA receiving funding under § 300.705, or a school that is part of an LEA receiving funding under § 300.705, the SEA is responsible for ensuring that the requirements of this part are met.

(2) Paragraph (d)(1) of this section does not preclude a State from assigning initial responsibility for ensuring the requirements of this part are met to another entity. However, the SEA must maintain the ultimate responsibility for ensuring compliance with this part, consistent with § 300.149.

Subpart D   Evaluations, Eligibility Determinations, Individualized Education Programs, and Educational Placements

Parental Consent

Sec. 300.300   Parental consent.

(a)   Parental consent for initial evaluation.

(1) (i) The public agency proposing to conduct an initial evaluation to determine if a child qualifies as a child with a disability under § 300.8 must, after providing notice consistent with §§ 300.503 and 300.504, obtain informed consent, consistent with § 300.9, from the parent of the child before conducting the evaluation.

(ii) Parental consent for initial evaluation must not be construed as consent for initial provision of special education and related services.

(iii) The public agency must make reasonable efforts to obtain the informed consent from the parent for an initial evaluation to determine whether the child is a child with a disability.

(2) For initial evaluations only, if the child is a ward of the State and is not residing with the child's parent, the public agency is not required to obtain informed consent from the parent for an initial evaluation to determine whether the child is a child with a disability if —

(i) Despite reasonable efforts to do so, the public agency cannot discover the whereabouts of the parent of the child;

(ii) The rights of the parents of the child have been terminated in accordance with State law; or

(iii) The rights of the parent to make educational decisions have been subrogated by a judge in accordance with State law and consent for an initial evaluation has been given by an individual appointed by the judge to represent the child.

(3) (i) If the parent of a child enrolled in public school or seeking to be enrolled in public school does not provide consent for initial evaluation under paragraph (a)(1) of this section, or the parent fails to respond to a request to provide consent, the public agency may, but is not required to, pursue the initial evaluation of the child by utilizing the procedural safeguards in subpart E of this part (including the mediation procedures under § 300.506 or the due process procedures under §§ 300.507 through 300.516), if appropriate, except to the extent inconsistent with State law relating to such parental consent.

(ii) The public agency does not violate its obligation under § 300.111 and §§ 300.301 through 300.311 if it declines to pursue the evaluation.

(b)   Parental consent for services.

(1) A public agency that is responsible for making FAPE available to a child with a disability must obtain informed consent from the parent of the child before the initial provision of special education and related services to the child.

(2) The public agency must make reasonable efforts to obtain informed consent from the

parent for the initial provision of special education and related services to the child.

(3) If the parent of a child fails to respond to a request for, or refuses to consent to, the initial provision of special education and related services, the public agency —

(i) May not use the procedures in subpart E of this part (including the mediation procedures under § 300.506 or the due process procedures under §§ 300.507 through 300.516) in order to obtain agreement or a ruling that the services may be provided to the child;

(ii) Will not be considered to be in violation of the requirement to make FAPE available to the child because of the failure to provide the child with the special education and related services for which the parent refuses to or fails to provide consent; and

(iii) Is not required to convene an IEP Team meeting or develop an IEP under §§ 300.320 and 300.324 for the child.

(4) If, at any time subsequent to the initial provision of special education and related services, the parent of a child revokes consent in writing for the continued provision of special education and related services, the public agency —

(i) May not continue to provide special education and related services to the child, but must provide prior written notice in accordance with § 300.503 before ceasing the provision of special education and related services;

(ii) May not use the procedures in subpart E of this part (including the mediation procedures under § 300.506 or the due process procedures under §§ 300.507 through 300.516) in order to obtain agreement or a ruling that the services may be provided to the child;

(iii) Will not be considered to be in violation of the requirement to make FAPE available to the child because of the failure to provide the child with further special education and related services; and

(iv) Is not required to convene an IEP Team meeting or develop an IEP under §§ 300.320 and 300.324 for the child for further provision of special education and related services.

(c)   Parental consent for reevaluations.

(1) Subject to paragraph (c)(2) of this section, each public agency —

(i) Must obtain informed parental consent, in accordance with § 300.300(a)(1), prior to conducting any reevaluation of a child with a disability.

(ii) If the parent refuses to consent to the reevaluation, the public agency may, but is not required to, pursue the reevaluation by using the consent override procedures described in paragraph (a)(3) of this section.

(iii) The public agency does not violate its obligation under § 300.111 and §§ 300.301 through 300.311 if it declines to pursue the evaluation or reevaluation.

(2) The informed parental consent described in paragraph (c)(1) of this section need not be obtained if the public agency can demonstrate that —

(i) It made reasonable efforts to obtain such consent; and

(ii) The child's parent has failed to respond.

(d)   Other consent requirements.

(1) Parental consent is not required before —

(i) Reviewing existing data as part of an evaluation or a reevaluation; or

(ii) Administering a test or other evaluation that is administered to all children unless, before administration of that test or evaluation, consent is required of parents of all children.

(2) In addition to the parental consent requirements described in paragraphs (a), (b), and (c) of this section, a State may require parental consent for other services and activities under this part if it ensures that each public agency in the State establishes and implements effective procedures to ensure that a parent's refusal to consent does not result in a failure to provide the child with FAPE.

(3) A public agency may not use a parent's refusal to consent to one service or activity under paragraphs (a), (b), (c), or (d)(2) of this section to deny the parent or child any other service, benefit, or activity of the public agency, except as required by this part.

(4) (i) If a parent of a child who is home schooled or placed in a private school by the parents at their own expense does not provide consent for the initial evaluation or the reevaluation, or the parent fails to respond to a request to provide consent, the public agency may not use the consent override procedures (described in paragraphs (a)(3) and (c)(1) of this section); and

(ii) The public agency is not required to consider the child as eligible for services under §§ 300.132 through 300.144.

(5) To meet the reasonable efforts requirement in paragraphs (a)(1)(iii), (a)(2)(i), (b)(2), and (c)(2)(i) of this section, the public agency must document its attempts to obtain parental consent using the procedures in § 300.322(d).

Evaluations and Reevaluations

Sec. 300.301   Initial evaluations.

(a)   General. Each public agency must conduct a full and individual initial evaluation, in accordance with §§ 300.304 through 300.306, before the initial provision of special education and related services to a child with a disability under this part.

(b)   Request for initial evaluation. Consistent with the consent requirements in § 300.300, either a parent of a child or a public agency may initiate a request for an initial evaluation to determine if the child is a child with a disability.

(c)   Procedures for initial evaluation. The initial evaluation —

(1) (i) Must be conducted within 60 days of receiving parental consent for the evaluation; or

(ii) If the State establishes a timeframe within which the evaluation must be conducted, within that timeframe; and

(2) Must consist of procedures —

(i) To determine if the child is a child with a disability under § 300.8; and

(ii) To determine the educational needs of the child.

(d)   Exception. The timeframe described in paragraph (c)(1) of this section does not apply to a public agency if —

(1) The parent of a child repeatedly fails or refuses to produce the child for the evaluation; or

(2) A child enrolls in a school of another public agency after the relevant timeframe in paragraph (c)(1) of this section has begun, and prior to a determination by the child's previous public agency as to whether the child is a child with a disability under § 300.8.

(e) The exception in paragraph (d)(2) of this section applies only if the subsequent public agency is making sufficient progress to ensure a prompt completion of the evaluation, and the parent and subsequent public agency agree to a specific time when the evaluation will be completed.

Sec. 300.302   Screening for instructional purposes is not evaluation.

The screening of a student by a teacher or specialist to determine appropriate instructional strategies for curriculum implementation shall not be considered to be an evaluation for eligibility for special education and related services.

Sec. 300.303   Reevaluations.

(a)   General. A public agency must ensure that a reevaluation of each child with a disability is conducted in accordance with §§ 300.304 through 300.311 —

(1) If the public agency determines that the educational or related services needs, including improved academic achievement and functional performance, of the child warrant a reevaluation; or

(2) If the child's parent or teacher requests a reevaluation.

(b)   Limitation. A reevaluation conducted under paragraph (a) of this section —

(1) May occur not more than once a year, unless the parent and the public agency agree otherwise; and

(2) Must occur at least once every 3 years, unless the parent and the public agency agree that a reevaluation is unnecessary.

Sec. 300.304   Evaluation procedures.

(a)   Notice. The public agency must provide notice to the parents of a child with a disability, in accordance with § 300.503, that describes any evaluation procedures the agency proposes to conduct.

(b)   Conduct of evaluation. In conducting the evaluation, the public agency must —

(1) Use a variety of assessment tools and strategies to gather relevant functional, developmental, and academic information about the child, including information provided by the parent, that may assist in determining —

(i) Whether the child is a child with a disability under § 300.8; and

(ii) The content of the child's IEP, including information related to enabling the child to be involved in and progress in the general education curriculum (or for a preschool child, to participate in appropriate activities);

(2) Not use any single measure or assessment as the sole criterion for determining whether a child is a child with a disability and for determining an appropriate educational program for the child; and

(3) Use technically sound instruments that may assess the relative contribution of cognitive and behavioral factors, in addition to physical or developmental factors.

(c) Other evaluation procedures. Each public agency must ensure that —

(1) Assessments and other evaluation materials used to assess a child under this part —

(i) Are selected and administered so as not to be discriminatory on a racial or cultural basis;

(ii) Are provided and administered in the child's native language or other mode of communication and in the form most likely to yield accurate information on what the child knows and can do academically, developmentally, and functionally, unless it is clearly not feasible to so provide or administer;

(iii) Are used for the purposes for which the assessments or measures are valid and reliable;

(iv) Are administered by trained and knowledgeable personnel; and

(v) Are administered in accordance with any instructions provided by the producer of the assessments.

(2) Assessments and other evaluation materials include those tailored to assess specific areas of educational need and not merely those that are designed to provide a single general intelligence quotient.

(3) Assessments are selected and administered so as best to ensure that if an assessment is administered to a child with impaired sensory, manual, or speaking skills, the assessment results accurately reflect the child's aptitude or achievement level or whatever other factors the test purports to measure, rather than reflecting the child's impaired sensory, manual, or speaking skills (unless those skills are the factors that the test purports to measure).

(4) The child is assessed in all areas related to the suspected disability, including, if appropriate, health, vision, hearing, social and emotional status, general intelligence, academic performance, communicative status, and motor abilities;

(5) Assessments of children with disabilities who transfer from one public agency to another public agency in the same school year are coordinated with those children's prior and subsequent schools, as necessary and as expeditiously as possible, consistent with § 300.301(d)(2) and (e), to ensure prompt completion of full evaluations.

(6) In evaluating each child with a disability under §§ 300.304 through 300.306, the evaluation is sufficiently comprehensive to identify all of the child's special education and related services needs, whether or not commonly linked to the disability category in which the child has been classified.

(7) Assessment tools and strategies that provide relevant information that directly assists

persons in determining the educational needs of the child are provided.

Sec. 300.305 Additional requirements for evaluations and reevaluations.

(a)   Review of existing evaluation data. As part of an initial evaluation (if appropriate) and as part of any reevaluation under this part, the IEP Team and other qualified professionals, as appropriate, must —

(1) Review existing evaluation data on the child, including —

(i) Evaluations and information provided by the parents of the child;

(ii) Current classroom-based, local, or State assessments, and classroom-based observations; and

(iii) Observations by teachers and related services providers; and

(2) On the basis of that review, and input from the child's parents, identify what additional data, if any, are needed to determine —

(i) (A) Whether the child is a child with a disability, as defined in § 300.8, and the educational needs of the child; or

(B) In case of a reevaluation of a child, whether the child continues to have such a disability, and the educational needs of the child;

(ii) The present levels of academic achievement and related developmental needs of the child;

(iii) (A) Whether the child needs special education and related services; or

(B) In the case of a reevaluation of a child, whether the child continues to need special education and related services; and

(iv) Whether any additions or modifications to the special education and related services are needed to enable the child to meet the measurable annual goals set out in the IEP of the child and to participate, as appropriate, in the general education curriculum.

(b)   Conduct of review. The group described in paragraph (a) of this section may conduct its review without a meeting.

(c)   Source of data. The public agency must administer such assessments and other evaluation measures as may be needed to produce the data identified under paragraph (a) of this section.

(d)   Requirements if additional data are not needed.

(1) If the IEP Team and other qualified professionals, as appropriate, determine that no additional data are needed to determine whether the child continues to be a child with a disability, and to determine the child's educational needs, the public agency must notify the child's parents of —

(i) That determination and the reasons for the determination; and

(ii) The right of the parents to request an assessment to determine whether the child continues to be a child with a disability, and to determine the child's educational needs.

(2) The public agency is not required to conduct the assessment described in paragraph

(d)(1)(ii) of this section unless requested to do so by the child's parents.

(e)   Evaluations before change in eligibility.

(1) Except as provided in paragraph (e)(2) of this section, a public agency must evaluate a child with a disability in accordance with §§ 300.304 through 300.311 before determining that the child is no longer a child with a disability.

(2) The evaluation described in paragraph (e)(1) of this section is not required before the termination of a child's eligibility under this part due to graduation from secondary school with a regular diploma, or due to exceeding the age eligibility for FAPE under State law.

(3) For a child whose eligibility terminates under circumstances described in paragraph (e)(2) of this section, a public agency must provide the child with a summary of the child's academic achievement and functional performance, which shall include recommendations on how to assist the child in meeting the child's postsecondary goals.

Sec. 300.306   Determination of eligibility.

(a)   General. Upon completion of the administration of assessments and other evaluation measures —

(1) A group of qualified professionals and the parent of the child determines whether the child is a child with a disability, as defined in § 300.8, in accordance with paragraph (c) of this section and the educational needs of the child; and

(2) The public agency provides a copy of the evaluation report and the documentation of determination of eligibility at no cost to the parent.

(b)   Special rule for eligibility determination. A child must not be determined to be a child with a disability under this part —

(1) If the determinant factor for that determination is —

(i) Lack of appropriate instruction in reading, including the essential components of reading instruction (as defined in section 1208(3) of the ESEA);

(ii) Lack of appropriate instruction in math; or

(iii) Limited English proficiency; and

(2) If the child does not otherwise meet the eligibility criteria under § 300.8(a).

(c)   Procedures for determining eligibility and educational need.

(1) In interpreting evaluation data for the purpose of determining if a child is a child with a disability under § 300.8, and the educational needs of the child, each public agency must —

(i) Draw upon information from a variety of sources, including aptitude and achievement tests, parent input, and teacher recommendations, as well as information about the child's physical condition, social or cultural background, and adaptive behavior; and

(ii) Ensure that information obtained from all of these sources is documented and carefully considered.

(2) If a determination is made that a child has a disability and needs special education and related services, an IEP must be developed for the child in accordance with §§ 300.320 through 300.324.

Additional Procedures for Identifying Children With Specific Learning Disabilities

Sec. 300.307   Specific learning disabilities.

(a)   General. A State must adopt, consistent with § 300.309, criteria for determining whether a child has a specific learning disability as defined in § 300.8(c)(10). In addition, the criteria adopted by the State —

(1) Must not require the use of a severe discrepancy between intellectual ability and achievement for determining whether a child has a specific learning disability, as defined in § 300.8(c)(10);

(2) Must permit the use of a process based on the child's response to scientific, research-based intervention; and

(3) May permit the use of other alternative research-based procedures for determining whether a child has a specific learning disability, as defined in § 300.8(c)(10).

(b)   Consistency with State criteria. A public agency must use the State criteria adopted pursuant to paragraph (a) of this section in determining whether a child has a specific learning disability.

Sec. 300.308   Additional group members.

The determination of whether a child suspected of having a specific learning disability is a child with a disability as defined in § 300.8, must be made by the child's parents and a team of qualified professionals, which must include —

(a) (1) The child's regular teacher; or

(2) If the child does not have a regular teacher, a regular classroom teacher qualified to teach a child of his or her age; or

(3) For a child of less than school age, an individual qualified by the SEA to teach a child of his or her age; and

(b) At least one person qualified to conduct individual diagnostic examinations of children, such as a school psychologist, speech-language pathologist, or remedial reading teacher.

Sec. 300.309   Determining the existence of a specific learning disability.

(a) The group described in § 300.306 may determine that a child has a specific learning disability, as defined in § 300.8(c)(10), if —

(1) The child does not achieve adequately for the child's age or to meet State-approved grade-level standards in one or more of the following areas, when provided with learning experiences and instruction appropriate for the child's age or State-approved grade-level standards:

(i) Oral expression.

(ii) Listening comprehension.

(iii) Written expression.

(iv) Basic reading skill.

(v) Reading fluency skills.

(vi) Reading comprehension.

(vii) Mathematics calculation.

(viii) Mathematics problem solving.

(2) (i) The child does not make sufficient progress to meet age or State-approved grade-level standards in one or more of the areas identified in paragraph (a)(1) of this section when using a process based on the child's response to scientific, research-based intervention; or

(ii) The child exhibits a pattern of strengths and weaknesses in performance, achievement, or both, relative to age, State-approved grade-level standards, or intellectual development, that is determined by the group to be relevant to the identification of a specific learning disability, using appropriate assessments, consistent with §§ 300.304 and 300.305; and

(3) The group determines that its findings under paragraphs (a)(1) and (2) of this section are not primarily the result of —

(i) A visual, hearing, or motor disability;

(ii) Mental retardation;

(iii) Emotional disturbance;

(iv) Cultural factors;

(v) Environmental or economic disadvantage; or

(vi) Limited English proficiency.

(b) To ensure that underachievement in a child suspected of having a specific learning disability is not due to lack of appropriate instruction in reading or math, the group must consider, as part of the evaluation described in §§ 300.304 through 300.306 —

(1) Data that demonstrate that prior to, or as a part of, the referral process, the child was provided appropriate instruction in regular education settings, delivered by qualified personnel; and

(2) Data-based documentation of repeated assessments of achievement at reasonable intervals, reflecting formal assessment of student progress during instruction, which was provided to the child's parents.

(c) The public agency must promptly request parental consent to evaluate the child to determine if the child needs special education and related services, and must adhere to the timeframes described in §§ 300.301 and 300.303, unless extended by mutual written agreement of the child's parents and a group of qualified professionals, as described in § 300.306(a)(1) —

(1) If, prior to a referral, a child has not made adequate progress after an appropriate period of time when provided instruction, as described in paragraphs (b)(1) and (b)(2) of this section; and

(2) Whenever a child is referred for an evaluation.

Sec. 300.310 Observation.

(a) The public agency must ensure that the child is observed in the child's learning environment (including the regular classroom setting) to document the child's academic performance and behavior in the areas of difficulty.

(b) The group described in § 300.306(a)(1), in determining whether a child has a specific learning disability, must decide to —

(1) Use information from an observation in routine classroom instruction and monitoring of the child's performance that was done before the child was referred for an evaluation; or

(2) Have at least one member of the group described in § 300.306(a)(1) conduct an observation of the child's academic performance in the regular classroom after the child has been referred for an evaluation and parental consent, consistent with § 300.300(a), is obtained.

(c) In the case of a child of less than school age or out of school, a group member must observe the child in an environment appropriate for a child of that age.

Sec. 300.311 Specific documentation for the eligibility determination.

(a) For a child suspected of having a specific learning disability, the documentation of the determination of eligibility, as required in § 300.306(a)(2), must contain a statement of —

(1) Whether the child has a specific learning disability;

(2) The basis for making the determination, including an assurance that the determination has been made in accordance with § 300.306(c)(1);

(3) The relevant behavior, if any, noted during the observation of the child and the relationship of that behavior to the child's academic functioning;

(4) The educationally relevant medical findings, if any;

(5) Whether —

(i) The child does not achieve adequately for the child's age or to meet State-approved grade-level standards consistent with § 300.309(a)(1); and

(ii) (A) The child does not make sufficient progress to meet age or State-approved grade-level standards consistent with § 300.309(a)(2)(i); or

(B) The child exhibits a pattern of strengths and weaknesses in performance, achievement, or both, relative to age, State-approved grade level standards or intellectual development consistent with § 300.309(a)(2)(ii);

(6) The determination of the group concerning the effects of a visual, hearing, or motor disability; mental retardation; emotional disturbance; cultural factors; environmental or economic disadvantage; or limited English proficiency on the child's achievement level; and

(7) If the child has participated in a process that assesses the child's response to scientific, research-based intervention —

(i) The instructional strategies used and the student-centered data collected; and

(ii) The documentation that the child's parents were notified about —

(A) The State's policies regarding the amount and nature of student performance data that would be collected and the general education services that would be provided;

(B) Strategies for increasing the child's rate of learning; and

(C) The parents' right to request an evaluation.

(b) Each group member must certify in writing whether the report reflects the member's conclusion. If it does not reflect the member's conclusion, the group member must submit a separate statement presenting the member's conclusions.

Individualized Education Programs

Sec. 300.320 Definition of individualized education program.

(a) General. As used in this part, the term individualized education program or IEP means a written statement for each child with a disability that is developed, reviewed, and revised in a meeting in accordance with §§ 300.320 through 300.324, and that must include —

(1) A statement of the child's present levels of academic achievement and functional performance, including —

(i) How the child's disability affects the child's involvement and progress in the general education curriculum (i.e., the same curriculum as for nondisabled children); or

(ii) For preschool children, as appropriate, how the disability affects the child's participation in appropriate activities;

(2) (i) A statement of measurable annual goals, including academic and functional goals designed to —

(A) Meet the child's needs that result from the child's disability to enable the child to be involved in and make progress in the general education curriculum; and

(B) Meet each of the child's other educational needs that result from the child's disability;

(ii) For children with disabilities who take alternate assessments aligned to alternate academic achievement standards, a description of benchmarks or short-term objectives;

(3) A description of —

(i) How the child's progress toward meeting the annual goals described in paragraph (2) of this section will be measured; and

(ii) When periodic reports on the progress the child is making toward meeting the annual goals (such as through the use of quarterly or other periodic reports, concurrent with the issuance of report cards) will be provided;

(4) A statement of the special education and related services and supplementary aids and services, based on peer-reviewed research to the extent practicable, to be provided to the child, or on behalf of the child, and a statement of the program modifications or supports for school personnel that will be provided to enable the child —

(i) To advance appropriately toward attaining the annual goals;

(ii) To be involved in and make progress in the general education curriculum in accordance with paragraph (a)(1) of this section, and to participate in extracurricular and other nonacademic activities; and

(iii) To be educated and participate with other children with disabilities and nondisabled children in the activities described in this section;

(5) An explanation of the extent, if any, to which the child will not participate with nondisabled children in the regular class and in the activities described in paragraph (a)(4) of this section;

(6) (i) A statement of any individual appropriate accommodations that are necessary to measure the academic achievement and functional performance of the child on State and districtwide assessments consistent with section 612(a)(16) of the Act; and

(ii) If the IEP Team determines that the child must take an alternate assessment instead of a particular regular State or districtwide assessment of student achievement, a statement of why —

(A) The child cannot participate in the regular assessment; and

(B) The particular alternate assessment selected is appropriate for the child; and

(7) The projected date for the beginning of the services and modifications described in paragraph (a)(4) of this section, and the anticipated frequency, location, and duration of those services and modifications.

(b)   Transition services. Beginning not later than the first IEP to be in effect when the child turns 16, or younger if determined appropriate by the IEP Team, and updated annually, thereafter, the IEP must include —

(1) Appropriate measurable postsecondary goals based upon age appropriate transition assessments related to training, education, employment, and, where appropriate, independent living skills; and

(2) The transition services (including courses of study) needed to assist the child in reaching those goals.

(c)   Transfer of rights at age of majority. Beginning not later than one year before the child reaches the age of majority under State law, the IEP must include a statement that the child has been informed of the child's rights under Part B of the Act, if any, that will transfer to the child on reaching the age of majority under § 300.520.

(d)   Construction. Nothing in this section shall be construed to require —

(1) That additional information be included in a child's IEP beyond what is explicitly required in section 614 of the Act; or

(2) The IEP Team to include information under one component of a child's IEP that is already contained under another component of the child's IEP.

Sec. 300.321   IEP Team.

(a)   General. The public agency must ensure that the IEP Team for each child with a disability includes —

(1) The parents of the child;

(2) Not less than one regular education teacher of the child (if the child is, or may be, participating in the regular education environment);

(3) Not less than one special education teacher of the child, or where appropriate, not less than one special education provider of the child;

(4) A representative of the public agency who —

(i) Is qualified to provide, or supervise the provision of, specially designed instruction to meet the unique needs of children with disabilities;

(ii) Is knowledgeable about the general education curriculum; and

(iii) Is knowledgeable about the availability of resources of the public agency.

(5) An individual who can interpret the instructional implications of evaluation results, who may be a member of the team described in paragraphs (a)(2) through (a)(6) of this section;

(6) At the discretion of the parent or the agency, other individuals who have knowledge or special expertise regarding the child, including related services personnel as appropriate; and

(7) Whenever appropriate, the child with a disability.

(b)   Transition services participants.

(1) In accordance with paragraph (a)(7) of this section, the public agency must invite a child with a disability to attend the child's IEP Team meeting if a purpose of the meeting will be the consideration of the postsecondary goals for the child and the transition services needed to assist the child in reaching those goals under § 300.320(b).

(2) If the child does not attend the IEP Team meeting, the public agency must take other steps to ensure that the child's preferences and interests are considered.

(3) To the extent appropriate, with the consent of the parents or a child who has reached the age of majority, in implementing the requirements of paragraph (b)(1) of this section, the public agency must invite a representative of any participating agency that is likely to be responsible for providing or paying for transition services.

(c)   Determination of knowledge and special expertise. The determination of the knowledge or special expertise of any individual described in paragraph (a)(6) of this section must be made by the party (parents or public agency) who invited the individual to be a member of the IEP Team.

(d)   Designating a public agency representative. A public agency may designate a public agency member of the IEP Team to also serve as the agency representative, if the criteria in paragraph (a)(4) of this section are satisfied.

(e)   IEP Team attendance. (1) A member of the IEP Team described in paragraphs (a)(2) through (a)(5) of this section is not required to attend an IEP Team meeting, in whole or in part, if the parent of a child with a disability and the public agency agree, in writing, that the attendance of the member is not necessary because the member's area of the curriculum or related services is not being modified or discussed in the meeting.

(2) A member of the IEP Team described in paragraph (e)(1) of this section may be

excused from attending an IEP Team meeting, in whole or in part, when the meeting involves a modification to or discussion of the member's area of the curriculum or related services, if —

(i) The parent, in writing, and the public agency consent to the excusal; and

(ii) The member submits, in writing to the parent and the IEP Team, input into the development of the IEP prior to the meeting.

(f) Initial IEP Team meeting for child under Part C. In the case of a child who was previously served under Part C of the Act, an invitation to the initial IEP Team meeting must, at the request of the parent, be sent to the Part C service coordinator or other representatives of the Part C system to assist with the smooth transition of services.

Sec. 300.322   Parent participation.

(a)   Public agency responsibility — general. Each public agency must take steps to ensure that one or both of the parents of a child with a disability are present at each IEP Team meeting or are afforded the opportunity to participate, including —

(1) Notifying parents of the meeting early enough to ensure that they will have an opportunity to attend; and

(2) Scheduling the meeting at a mutually agreed on time and place.

(b)   Information provided to parents.

(1) The notice required under paragraph (a)(1) of this section must —

(i) Indicate the purpose, time, and location of the meeting and who will be in attendance; and

(ii) Inform the parents of the provisions in § 300.321(a)(6) and (c) (relating to the participation of other individuals on the IEP Team who have knowledge or special expertise about the child), and Sec. 300.321(f) (relating to the participation of the Part C service coordinator or other representatives of the Part C system at the initial IEP Team meeting for a child previously served under Part C of the Act).

(2) For a child with a disability beginning not later than the first IEP to be in effect when the child turns 16, or younger if determined appropriate by the IEP Team, the notice also must —

(i) Indicate —

(A) That a purpose of the meeting will be the consideration of the postsecondary goals and transition services for the child, in accordance with § 300.320(b); and

(B) That the agency will invite the student; and

(ii) Identify any other agency that will be invited to send a representative.

(c)   Other methods to ensure parent participation. If neither parent can attend an IEP Team meeting, the public agency must use other methods to ensure parent participation, including individual or conference telephone calls, consistent with § 300.328 (related to alternative means of meeting participation).

(d)   Conducting an IEP Team meeting without a parent in attendance. A meeting may be conducted without a parent in attendance if the public agency is unable to convince the parents that they should attend. In this case, the public agency must keep a record of its attempts to arrange a mutually agreed on time and place, such as —

(1) Detailed records of telephone calls made or attempted and the results of those calls;

(2) Copies of correspondence sent to the parents and any responses received; and

(3) Detailed records of visits made to the parent's home or place of employment and the results of those visits.

(e)   Use of interpreters or other action, as appropriate. The public agency must take whatever action is necessary to ensure that the parent understands the proceedings of the IEP Team meeting, including arranging for an interpreter for parents with deafness or whose native language is other than English.

(f)   Parent copy of child's IEP. The public agency must give the parent a copy of the child's IEP at no cost to the parent.

Sec. 300.323   When IEPs must be in effect.

(a)   General. At the beginning of each school year, each public agency must have in effect, for each child with a disability within its jurisdiction, an IEP, as defined in § 300.320.

(b)   IEP or IFSP for children aged three through five.

(1) In the case of a child with a disability aged three through five (or, at the discretion of the SEA, a two-year-old child with a disability who will turn age three during the school year), the IEP Team must consider an IFSP that contains the IFSP content (including the natural environments statement) described in section 636(d) of the Act and its implementing regulations (including an educational component that promotes school readiness and incorporates pre-literacy, language, and numeracy skills for children with IFSPs under this section who are at least three years of age), and that is developed in accordance with the IEP procedures under this part. The IFSP may serve as the IEP of the child, if using the IFSP as the IEP is —

(i) Consistent with State policy; and

(ii) Agreed to by the agency and the child's parents.

(2) In implementing the requirements of paragraph (b)(1) of this section, the public agency must —

(i) Provide to the child's parents a detailed explanation of the differences between an IFSP and an IEP; and

(ii) If the parents choose an IFSP, obtain written informed consent from the parents.

(c)   Initial IEPs; provision of services. Each public agency must ensure that —

(1) A meeting to develop an IEP for a child is conducted within 30 days of a determination that the child needs special education and related services; and

(2) As soon as possible following development of the IEP, special education and related services are made available to the child in accordance with the child's IEP.

(d)   Accessibility of child's IEP to teachers and others. Each public agency must ensure that

—

(1) The child's IEP is accessible to each regular education teacher, special education teacher, related services provider, and any other service provider who is responsible for its implementation; and

(2) Each teacher and provider described in paragraph (d)(1) of this section is informed of —

(i) His or her specific responsibilities related to implementing the child's IEP; and

(ii) The specific accommodations, modifications, and supports that must be provided for the child in accordance with the IEP.

(e)   IEPs for children who transfer public agencies in the same State. If a child with a disability (who had an IEP that was in effect in a previous public agency in the same State) transfers to a new public agency in the same State, and enrolls in a new school within the same school year, the new public agency (in consultation with the parents) must provide FAPE to the child (including services comparable to those described in the child's IEP from the previous public agency), until the new public agency either —

(1) Adopts the child's IEP from the previous public agency; or

(2) Develops, adopts, and implements a new IEP that meets the applicable requirements in §§ 300.320 through 300.324.

(f)   IEPs for children who transfer from another State. If a child with a disability (who had an IEP that was in effect in a previous public agency in another State) transfers to a public agency in a new State, and enrolls in a new school within the same school year, the new public agency (in consultation with the parents) must provide the child with FAPE (including services comparable to those described in the child's IEP from the previous public agency), until the new public agency —

(1) Conducts an evaluation pursuant to §§ 300.304 through 300.306 (if determined to be necessary by the new public agency); and

(2) Develops, adopts, and implements a new IEP, if appropriate, that meets the applicable requirements in §§ 300.320 through 300.324.

(g)   Transmittal of records. To facilitate the transition for a child described in paragraphs (e) and (f) of this section —

(1) The new public agency in which the child enrolls must take reasonable steps to promptly obtain the child's records, including the IEP and supporting documents and any other records relating to the provision of special education or related services to the child, from the previous public agency in which the child was enrolled, pursuant to 34 CFR 99.31(a)(2); and

(2) The previous public agency in which the child was enrolled must take reasonable steps to promptly respond to the request from the new public agency.

Development of IEP

Sec. 300.324   Development, review, and revision of IEP.

(a) Development of IEP —

(1) General. In developing each child's IEP, the IEP Team must consider —

(i) The strengths of the child;

(ii) The concerns of the parents for enhancing the education of their child;

(iii) The results of the initial or most recent evaluation of the child; and

(iv) The academic, developmental, and functional needs of the child.

(2)   Consideration of special factors. The IEP Team must —

(i) In the case of a child whose behavior impedes the child's learning or that of others, consider the use of positive behavioral interventions and supports, and other strategies, to address that behavior;

(ii) In the case of a child with limited English proficiency, consider the language needs of the child as those needs relate to the child's IEP;

(iii) In the case of a child who is blind or visually impaired, provide for instruction in Braille and the use of Braille unless the IEP Team determines, after an evaluation of the child's reading and writing skills, needs, and appropriate reading and writing media (including an evaluation of the child's future needs for instruction in Braille or the use of Braille), that instruction in Braille or the use of Braille is not appropriate for the child;

(iv) Consider the communication needs of the child, and in the case of a child who is deaf or hard of hearing, consider the child's language and communication needs, opportunities for direct communications with peers and professional personnel in the child's language and communication mode, academic level, and full range of needs, including opportunities for direct instruction in the child's language and communication mode; and

(v) Consider whether the child needs assistive technology devices and services.

(3)   Requirement with respect to regular education teacher. A regular education teacher of a child with a disability, as a member of the IEP Team, must, to the extent appropriate, participate in the development of the IEP of the child, including the determination of —

(i) Appropriate positive behavioral interventions and supports and other strategies for the child; and

(ii) Supplementary aids and services, program modifications, and support for school personnel consistent with § 300.320(a)(4).

(4)   Agreement.

(i) In making changes to a child's IEP after the annual IEP Team meeting for a school year, the parent of a child with a disability and the public agency may agree not to convene an IEP Team meeting for the purposes of making those changes, and instead may develop a written document to amend or modify the child's current IEP.

(ii) If changes are made to the child's IEP in accordance with paragraph (a)(4)(i) of this section, the public agency must ensure that the child's IEP Team is informed of those changes.

(5)   Consolidation of IEP Team meetings. To the extent possible, the public agency must encourage the consolidation of reevaluation meetings for the child and other IEP Team meetings for the child.

(6)   Amendments. Changes to the IEP may be made either by the entire IEP Team at an IEP Team meeting, or as provided in paragraph (a)(4) of this section, by amending the IEP rather than by redrafting the entire IEP. Upon request, a parent must be provided with a revised copy of the IEP with the amendments incorporated.

(b) Review and revision of IEPs —

(1)   General. Each public agency must ensure that, subject to paragraphs (b)(2) and (b)(3) of this section, the IEP Team —

(i) Reviews the child's IEP periodically, but not less than annually, to determine whether the annual goals for the child are being achieved; and

(ii) Revises the IEP, as appropriate, to address —

(A) Any lack of expected progress toward the annual goals described in § 300.320(a)(2), and in the general education curriculum, if appropriate;

(B) The results of any reevaluation conducted under § 300.303;

(C) Information about the child provided to, or by, the parents, as described under § 300.305(a)(2);

(D) The child's anticipated needs; or

(E) Other matters.

(2)   Consideration of special factors. In conducting a review of the child's IEP, the IEP Team must consider the special factors described in paragraph (a)(2) of this section.

(3)   Requirement with respect to regular education teacher. A regular education teacher of the child, as a member of the IEP Team, must, consistent with paragraph (a)(3) of this section, participate in the review and revision of the IEP of the child.

(c) Failure to meet transition objectives —

(1)   Participating agency failure. If a participating agency, other than the public agency, fails to provide the transition services described in the IEP in accordance with § 300.320(b), the public agency must reconvene the IEP Team to identify alternative strategies to meet the transition objectives for the child set out in the IEP.

(2)   Construction. Nothing in this part relieves any participating agency, including a State vocational rehabilitation agency, of the responsibility to provide or pay for any transition service that the agency would otherwise provide to children with disabilities who meet the eligibility criteria of that agency.

(d) Children with disabilities in adult prisons —

(1)   Requirements that do not apply. The following requirements do not apply to children with disabilities who are convicted as adults under State law and incarcerated in adult prisons:

(i) The requirements contained in section 612(a)(16) of the Act and § 300.320(a)(6) (relating to participation of children with disabilities in general assessments).

(ii) The requirements in § 300.320(b) (relating to transition planning and transition services) do not apply with respect to the children whose eligibility under Part B of the Act will end, because of their age, before they will be eligible to be released from prison based on consideration of their sentence and eligibility for early release.

(2) Modifications of IEP or placement.

(i) Subject to paragraph (d)(2)(ii) of this section, the IEP Team of a child with a disability who is convicted as an adult under State law and incarcerated in an adult prison may modify the child's IEP or placement if the State has demonstrated a bona fide security or compelling penological interest that cannot otherwise be accommodated.

(ii) The requirements of §§ 300.320 (relating to IEPs), and 300.112 (relating to LRE), do not apply with respect to the modifications described in paragraph (d)(2)(i) of this section.

Sec. 300.325 Private school placements by public agencies.

(a) Developing IEPs.

(1) Before a public agency places a child with a disability in, or refers a child to, a private school or facility, the agency must initiate and conduct a meeting to develop an IEP for the child in accordance with §§ 300.320 and 300.324.

(2) The agency must ensure that a representative of the private school or facility attends the meeting. If the representative cannot attend, the agency must use other methods to ensure participation by the private school or facility, including individual or conference telephone calls.

(b) Reviewing and revising IEPs.

(1) After a child with a disability enters a private school or facility, any meetings to review and revise the child's IEP may be initiated and conducted by the private school or facility at the discretion of the public agency.

(2) If the private school or facility initiates and conducts these meetings, the public agency must ensure that the parents and an agency representative —

(i) Are involved in any decision about the child's IEP; and

(ii) Agree to any proposed changes in the IEP before those changes are implemented.

(c) Responsibility. Even if a private school or facility implements a child's IEP, responsibility for compliance with this part remains with the public agency and the SEA.

Sec. 300.327 Educational placements.

Consistent with § 300.501(c), each public agency must ensure that the parents of each child with a disability are members of any group that makes decisions on the educational placement of their child.

Sec. 300.328 Alternative means of meeting participation.

When conducting IEP Team meetings and placement meetings pursuant to this subpart, and subpart E of this part, and carrying out administrative matters under section 615 of the Act (such as scheduling, exchange of witness lists, and status conferences), the parent of a child with a disability and a public agency may agree to use alternative means of meeting participation, such as video conferences and conference calls.

Subpart E Procedural Safeguards Due Process Procedures for Parents and Children

Sec. 300.500 Responsibility of SEA and other public agencies.

Each SEA must ensure that each public agency establishes, maintains, and implements procedural safeguards that meet the requirements of §§ 300.500 through 300.536.

Sec. 300.501 Opportunity to examine records; parent participation in meetings.

(a) Opportunity to examine records. The parents of a child with a disability must be afforded, in accordance with the procedures of §§ 300.613 through 300.621, an opportunity to inspect and review all education records with respect to —

(1) The identification, evaluation, and educational placement of the child; and

(2) The provision of FAPE to the child.

(b) Parent participation in meetings.

(1) The parents of a child with a disability must be afforded an opportunity to participate in meetings with respect to —

(i) The identification, evaluation, and educational placement of the child; and

(ii) The provision of FAPE to the child.

(2) Each public agency must provide notice consistent with § 300.322(a)(1) and (b)(1) to ensure that parents of children with disabilities have the opportunity to participate in meetings described in paragraph (b)(1) of this section.

(3) A meeting does not include informal or unscheduled conversations involving public agency personnel and conversations on issues such as teaching methodology, lesson plans, or coordination of service provision. A meeting also does not include preparatory activities that public agency personnel engage in to develop a proposal or response to a parent proposal that will be discussed at a later meeting.

(c) Parent involvement in placement decisions.

(1) Each public agency must ensure that a parent of each child with a disability is a member of any group that makes decisions on the educational placement of the parent's child.

(2) In implementing the requirements of paragraph (c)(1) of this section, the public agency must use procedures consistent with the procedures described in § 300.322(a) through (b)(1).

(3) If neither parent can participate in a meeting in which a decision is to be made relating to the educational placement of their child, the public agency must use other methods to ensure their participation, including individual or conference telephone calls, or video conferencing.

(4) A placement decision may be made by a group without the involvement of a parent, if the public agency is unable to obtain the parent's participation in the decision. In this case, the public agency must have a record of its attempt to ensure their involvement.

Sec. 300.502   Independent educational evaluation.

(a)   General.

(1) The parents of a child with a disability have the right under this part to obtain an independent educational evaluation of the child, subject to paragraphs (b) through (e) of this section.

(2) Each public agency must provide to parents, upon request for an independent educational evaluation, information about where an independent educational evaluation may be obtained, and the agency criteria applicable for independent educational evaluations as set forth in paragraph (e) of this section.

(3) For the purposes of this subpart —

(i) Independent educational evaluation means an evaluation conducted by a qualified examiner who is not employed by the public agency responsible for the education of the child in question; and

(ii) Public expense means that the public agency either pays for the full cost of the evaluation or ensures that the evaluation is otherwise provided at no cost to the parent, consistent with § 300.103.

(b)   Parent right to evaluation at public expense.

(1) A parent has the right to an independent educational evaluation at public expense if the parent disagrees with an evaluation obtained by the public agency, subject to the conditions in paragraphs (b)(2) through (4) of this section.

(2) If a parent requests an independent educational evaluation at public expense, the public agency must, without unnecessary delay, either —

(i) File a due process complaint to request a hearing to show that its evaluation is appropriate; or

(ii) Ensure that an independent educational evaluation is provided at public expense, unless the agency demonstrates in a hearing pursuant to §§ 300.507 through 300.513 that the evaluation obtained by the parent did not meet agency criteria.

(3) If the public agency files a due process complaint notice to request a hearing and the final decision is that the agency's evaluation is appropriate, the parent still has the right to an independent educational evaluation, but not at public expense.

(4) If a parent requests an independent educational evaluation, the public agency may ask for the parent's reason why he or she objects to the public evaluation. However, the public agency may not require the parent to provide an explanation and may not unreasonably delay either providing the independent educational evaluation at public expense or filing a due process complaint to request a due process hearing to defend the public evaluation.

(5) A parent is entitled to only one independent educational evaluation at public expense each time the public agency conducts an evaluation with which the parent disagrees.

(c)   Parent-initiated evaluations. If the parent obtains an independent educational evaluation at public expense or shares with the public agency an evaluation obtained at private expense, the results of the evaluation —

(1) Must be considered by the public agency, if it meets agency criteria, in any decision made with respect to the provision of FAPE to the child; and

(2) May be presented by any party as evidence at a hearing on a due process complaint under subpart E of this part regarding that child.

(d)   Requests for evaluations by hearing officers. If a hearing officer requests an independent educational evaluation as part of a hearing on a due process complaint, the cost of the evaluation must be at public expense.

(e)   Agency criteria.

(1) If an independent educational evaluation is at public expense, the criteria under which the evaluation is obtained, including the location of the evaluation and the qualifications of the examiner, must be the same as the criteria that the public agency uses when it initiates an evaluation, to the extent those criteria are consistent with the parent's right to an independent educational evaluation.

(2) Except for the criteria described in paragraph (e)(1) of this section, a public agency may not impose conditions or timelines related to obtaining an independent educational evaluation at public expense.

Sec. 300.503   Prior notice by the public agency; content of notice.

(a)   Notice. Written notice that meets the requirements of paragraph (b) of this section must be given to the parents of a child with a disability a reasonable time before the public agency —

(1) Proposes to initiate or change the identification, evaluation, or educational placement of the child or the provision of FAPE to the child; or

(2) Refuses to initiate or change the identification, evaluation, or educational placement of the child or the provision of FAPE to the child.

(b)   Content of notice. The notice required under paragraph (a) of this section must include —

(1) A description of the action proposed or refused by the agency;

(2) An explanation of why the agency proposes or refuses to take the action;

(3) A description of each evaluation procedure, assessment, record, or report the agency used as a basis for the proposed or refused action;

(4) A statement that the parents of a child with a disability have protection under the procedural safeguards of this part and, if this notice is not an initial referral for evaluation, the means by which a copy of a description of the procedural safeguards can be obtained;

(5) Sources for parents to contact to obtain assistance in understanding the provisions of this part;

(6) A description of other options that the IEP Team considered and the reasons why those options were rejected; and

(7) A description of other factors that are relevant to the agency's proposal or refusal.

(c) Notice in understandable language.

(1) The notice required under paragraph (a) of this section must be —

(i) Written in language understandable to the general public; and

(ii) Provided in the native language of the parent or other mode of communication used by the parent, unless it is clearly not feasible to do so.

(2) If the native language or other mode of communication of the parent is not a written language, the public agency must take steps to ensure —

(i) That the notice is translated orally or by other means to the parent in his or her native language or other mode of communication;

(ii) That the parent understands the content of the notice; and

(iii) That there is written evidence that the requirements in paragraphs (c)(2)(i) and (ii) of this section have been met.

Sec. 300.504 Procedural safeguards notice.

(a) General. A copy of the procedural safeguards available to the parents of a child with a disability must be given to the parents only one time a school year, except that a copy also must be given to the parents —

(1) Upon initial referral or parent request for evaluation;

(2) Upon receipt of the first State complaint under §§ 300.151 through 300.153 and upon receipt of the first due process complaint under § 300.507 in a school year;

(3) In accordance with the discipline procedures in § 300.530(h); and

(4) Upon request by a parent.

(b) Internet Web site. A public agency may place a current copy of the procedural safeguards notice on its Internet Web site if a Web site exists.

(c) Contents. The procedural safeguards notice must include a full explanation of all of the procedural safeguards available under § 300.148, §§ 300.151 through 300.153, § 300.300, §§ 300.502 through 300.503, §§ 300.505 through 300.518, §§ 300.530 through 300.536 and §§ 300.610 through 300.625 relating to —

(1) Independent educational evaluations;

(2) Prior written notice;

(3) Parental consent;

(4) Access to education records;

(5) Opportunity to present and resolve complaints through the due process complaint and State complaint procedures, including —

(i) The time period in which to file a complaint;

(ii) The opportunity for the agency to resolve the complaint; and

(iii) The difference between the due process complaint and the State complaint procedures, including the jurisdiction of each procedure, what issues may be raised, filing and decisional timelines, and relevant procedures;

(6) The availability of mediation;

(7) The child's placement during the pendency of any due process complaint;

(8) Procedures for students who are subject to placement in an interim alternative educational setting;

(9) Requirements for unilateral placement by parents of children in private schools at public expense;

(10) Hearings on due process complaints, including requirements for disclosure of evaluation results and recommendations;

(11) State-level appeals (if applicable in the State);

(12) Civil actions, including the time period in which to file those actions; and

(13) Attorneys' fees.

(d) Notice in understandable language. The notice required under paragraph (a) of this section must meet the requirements of § 300.503(c).

Sec. 300.505 Electronic mail.

A parent of a child with a disability may elect to receive notices required by §§ 300.503, 300.504, and 300.508 by an electronic mail communication, if the public agency makes that option available.

Sec. 300.506 Mediation.

(a) General. Each public agency must ensure that procedures are established and implemented to allow parties to disputes involving any matter under this part, including matters arising prior to the filing of a due process complaint, to resolve disputes through a mediation process.

(b) Requirements. The procedures must meet the following requirements:

(1) The procedures must ensure that the mediation process —

(i) Is voluntary on the part of the parties;

(ii) Is not used to deny or delay a parent's right to a hearing on the parent's due process complaint, or to deny any other rights afforded under Part B of the Act; and

(iii) Is conducted by a qualified and impartial mediator who is trained in effective mediation techniques.

(2) A public agency may establish procedures to offer to parents and schools that choose not to use the mediation process, an opportunity to meet, at a time and location convenient to the parents, with a disinterested party —

(i) Who is under contract with an appropriate alternative dispute resolution entity, or a parent training and information center or community parent resource center in the State established under section 671 or 672 of the Act; and

(ii) Who would explain the benefits of, and encourage the use of, the mediation process to the parents.

(3) (i) The State must maintain a list of individuals who are qualified mediators and knowledgeable in laws and regulations relating to the provision of special education and related services.

(ii) The SEA must select mediators on a random, rotational, or other impartial basis.

(4) The State must bear the cost of the mediation process, including the costs of meetings described in paragraph (b)(2) of this section.

(5) Each session in the mediation process must be scheduled in a timely manner and must be held in a location that is convenient to the parties to the dispute.

(6) If the parties resolve a dispute through the mediation process, the parties must execute a legally binding agreement that sets forth that resolution and that —

(i) States that all discussions that occurred during the mediation process will remain confidential and may not be used as evidence in any subsequent due process hearing or civil proceeding; and

(ii) Is signed by both the parent and a representative of the agency who has the authority to bind such agency.

(7) A written, signed mediation agreement under this paragraph is enforceable in any State court of competent jurisdiction or in a district court of the United States.

(8) Discussions that occur during the mediation process must be confidential and may not be used as evidence in any subsequent due process hearing or civil proceeding of any Federal court or State court of a State receiving assistance under this part.

(c) Impartiality of mediator.

(1) An individual who serves as a mediator under this part —

(i) May not be an employee of the SEA or the LEA that is involved in the education or care of the child; and

(ii) Must not have a personal or professional interest that conflicts with the person's objectivity.

(2) A person who otherwise qualifies as a mediator is not an employee of an LEA or State agency described under § 300.228 solely because he or she is paid by the agency to serve as a mediator.

Sec. 300.507   Filing a due process complaint.

(a)   General.

(1) A parent or a public agency may file a due process complaint on any of the matters described in § 300.503(a)(1) and (2) (relating to the identification, evaluation or educational placement of a child with a disability, or the provision of FAPE to the child).

(2) The due process complaint must allege a violation that occurred not more than two years before the date the parent or public agency knew or should have known about the alleged action that forms the basis of the due process complaint, or, if the State has an

explicit time limitation for filing a due process complaint under this part, in the time allowed by that State law, except that the exceptions to the timeline described in § 300.511(f) apply to the timeline in this section.

(b) Information for parents. The public agency must inform the parent of any free or low-cost legal and other relevant services available in the area if —

(1) The parent requests the information; or

(2) The parent or the agency files a due process complaint under this section.

Sec. 300.508 Due process complaint.

(a) General.

(1) The public agency must have procedures that require either party, or the attorney representing a party, to provide to the other party a due process complaint (which must remain confidential).

(2) The party filing a due process complaint must forward a copy of the due process complaint to the SEA.

(b) Content of complaint. The due process complaint required in paragraph (a)(1) of this section must include —

(1) The name of the child;

(2) The address of the residence of the child;

(3) The name of the school the child is attending;

(4) In the case of a homeless child or youth (within the meaning of section 725(2) of the McKinney-Vento Homeless Assistance Act (42 U.S.C. 11434a(2)), available contact information for the child, and the name of the school the child is attending;

(5) A description of the nature of the problem of the child relating to the proposed or refused initiation or change, including facts relating to the problem; and

(6) A proposed resolution of the problem to the extent known and available to the party at the time.

(c) Notice required before a hearing on a due process complaint. A party may not have a hearing on a due process complaint until the party, or the attorney representing the party, files a due process complaint that meets the requirements of paragraph (b) of this section.

(d) Sufficiency of complaint.

(1) The due process complaint required by this section must be deemed sufficient unless the party receiving the due process complaint notifies the hearing officer and the other party in writing, within 15 days of receipt of the due process complaint, that the receiving party believes the due process complaint does not meet the requirements in paragraph (b) of this section.

(2) Within five days of receipt of notification under paragraph (d)(1) of this section, the hearing officer must make a determination on the face of the due process complaint of whether the due process complaint meets the requirements of paragraph (b) of this section, and must immediately notify the parties in writing of that determination.

(3) A party may amend its due process complaint only if —

(i) The other party consents in writing to the amendment and is given the opportunity to resolve the due process complaint through a meeting held pursuant to § 300.510; or

(ii) The hearing officer grants permission, except that the hearing officer may only grant permission to amend at any time not later than five days before the due process hearing begins.

(4) If a party files an amended due process complaint, the timelines for the resolution meeting in § 300.510(a) and the time period to resolve in § 300.510(b) begin again with the filing of the amended due process complaint.

(e) LEA response to a due process complaint.

(1) If the LEA has not sent a prior written notice under § 300.503 to the parent regarding the subject matter contained in the parent's due process complaint, the LEA must, within 10 days of receiving the due process complaint, send to the parent a response that includes —

(i) An explanation of why the agency proposed or refused to take the action raised in the due process complaint;

(ii) A description of other options that the IEP Team considered and the reasons why those options were rejected;

(iii) A description of each evaluation procedure, assessment, record, or report the agency used as the basis for the proposed or refused action; and

(iv) A description of the other factors that are relevant to the agency's proposed or refused action.

(2) A response by an LEA under paragraph (e)(1) of this section shall not be construed to preclude the LEA from asserting that the parent's due process complaint was insufficient, where appropriate.

(f) Other party response to a due process complaint. Except as provided in paragraph (e) of this section, the party receiving a due process complaint must, within 10 days of receiving the due process complaint, send to the other party a response that specifically addresses the issues raised in the due process complaint.

Sec. 300.509 Model forms.

(a) Each SEA must develop model forms to assist parents and public agencies in filing a due process complaint in accordance with §§ 300.507(a) and 300.508(a) through (c) and to assist parents and other parties in filing a State complaint under §§ 300.151 through 300.153. However, the SEA or LEA may not require the use of the model forms.

(b) Parents, public agencies, and other parties may use the appropriate model form described in paragraph (a) of this section, or another form or other document, so long as the form or document that is used meets, as appropriate, the content requirements in § 300.508(b) for filing a due process complaint, or the requirements in § 300.153(b) for filing a State complaint.

Sec. 300.510   Resolution process.

(a)   Resolution meeting.

(1) Within 15 days of receiving notice of the parent's due process complaint, and prior to the initiation of a due process hearing under § 300.511, the LEA must convene a meeting with the parent and the relevant member or members of the IEP Team who have specific knowledge of the facts identified in the due process complaint that —

(i) Includes a representative of the public agency who has decision-making authority on behalf of that agency; and

(ii) May not include an attorney of the LEA unless the parent is accompanied by an attorney.

(2) The purpose of the meeting is for the parent of the child to discuss the due process complaint, and the facts that form the basis of the due process complaint, so that the LEA has the opportunity to resolve the dispute that is the basis for the due process complaint.

(3) The meeting described in paragraph (a)(1) and (2) of this section need not be held if —

(i) The parent and the LEA agree in writing to waive the meeting; or

(ii) The parent and the LEA agree to use the mediation process described in Sec. 300.506.

(4) The parent and the LEA determine the relevant members of the IEP Team to attend the meeting.

(b)   Resolution period.

(1) If the LEA has not resolved the due process complaint to the satisfaction of the parent within 30 days of the receipt of the due process complaint, the due process hearing may occur.

(2) Except as provided in paragraph (c) of this section, the timeline for issuing a final decision under § 300.515 begins at the expiration of this 30-day period.

(3) Except where the parties have jointly agreed to waive the resolution process or to use mediation, notwithstanding paragraphs (b)(1) and (2) of this section, the failure of the parent filing a due process complaint to participate in the resolution meeting will delay the timelines for the resolution process and due process hearing until the meeting is held.

(4) If the LEA is unable to obtain the participation of the parent in the resolution meeting after reasonable efforts have been made (and documented using the procedures in § 300.322(d)), the LEA may, at the conclusion of the 30-day period, request that a hearing officer dismiss the parent's due process complaint.

(5) If the LEA fails to hold the resolution meeting specified in paragraph (a) of this section within 15 days of receiving notice of a parent's due process complaint or fails to participate in the resolution meeting, the parent may seek the intervention of a hearing officer to begin the due process hearing timeline.

(c)   Adjustments to 30-day resolution period. The 45-day timeline for the due process hearing in § 300.515(a) starts the day after one of the following events:

(1) Both parties agree in writing to waive the resolution meeting;

(2) After either the mediation or resolution meeting starts but before the end of the 30-day period, the parties agree in writing that no agreement is possible;

(3) If both parties agree in writing to continue the mediation at the end of the 30-day resolution period, but later, the parent or public agency withdraws from the mediation process.

(d)   Written settlement agreement. If a resolution to the dispute is reached at the meeting described in paragraphs (a)(1) and (2) of this section, the parties must execute a legally binding agreement that is —

(1) Signed by both the parent and a representative of the agency who has the authority to bind the agency; and

(2) Enforceable in any State court of competent jurisdiction or in a district court of the United States, or, by the SEA, if the State has other mechanisms or procedures that permit parties to seek enforcement of resolution agreements, pursuant to § 300.537.

(e)   Agreement review period. If the parties execute an agreement pursuant to paragraph (d) of this section, a party may void the agreement within 3 business days of the agreement's execution.

Sec. 300.511   Impartial due process hearing.

(a)   General. Whenever a due process complaint is received under § 300.507 or § 300.532, the parents or the LEA involved in the dispute must have an opportunity for an impartial due process hearing, consistent with the procedures in §§ 300.507, 300.508, and 300.510.

(b)   Agency responsible for conducting the due process hearing. The hearing described in paragraph (a) of this section must be conducted by the SEA or the public agency directly responsible for the education of the child, as determined under State statute, State regulation, or a written policy of the SEA.

(c)   Impartial hearing officer.

(1) At a minimum, a hearing officer —

(i) Must not be —

(A) An employee of the SEA or the LEA that is involved in the education or care of the child; or

(B) A person having a personal or professional interest that conflicts with the person's objectivity in the hearing;

(ii) Must possess knowledge of, and the ability to understand, the provisions of the Act, Federal and State regulations pertaining to the Act, and legal interpretations of the Act by Federal and State courts;

(iii) Must possess the knowledge and ability to conduct hearings in accordance with appropriate, standard legal practice; and

(iv) Must possess the knowledge and ability to render and write decisions in accordance with appropriate, standard legal practice.

(2) A person who otherwise qualifies to conduct a hearing under paragraph (c)(1) of this section is not an employee of the agency solely because he or she is paid by the agency to serve as a hearing officer.

(3) Each public agency must keep a list of the persons who serve as hearing officers. The list must include a statement of the qualifications of each of those persons.

(d) Subject matter of due process hearings. The party requesting the due process hearing may not raise issues at the due process hearing that were not raised in the due process complaint filed under § 300.508(b), unless the other party agrees otherwise.

(e) Timeline for requesting a hearing. A parent or agency must request an impartial hearing on their due process complaint within two years of the date the parent or agency knew or should have known about the alleged action that forms the basis of the due process complaint, or if the State has an explicit time limitation for requesting such a due process hearing under this part, in the time allowed by that State law.

(f) Exceptions to the timeline. The timeline described in paragraph (e) of this section does not apply to a parent if the parent was prevented from filing a due process complaint due to —

(1) Specific misrepresentations by the LEA that it had resolved the problem forming the basis of the due process complaint; or

(2) The LEA's withholding of information from the parent that was required under this part to be provided to the parent.

Sec. 300.512 Hearing rights.

(a) General. Any party to a hearing conducted pursuant to §§ 300.507 through 300.513 or §§ 300.530 through 300.534, or an appeal conducted pursuant to § 300.514, has the right to —

(1) Be accompanied and advised by counsel and by individuals with special knowledge or training with respect to the problems of children with disabilities, except that whether parties have the right to be represented by non-attorneys at due process hearings is determined under State law.

(2) Present evidence and confront, cross-examine, and compel the attendance of witnesses;

(3) Prohibit the introduction of any evidence at the hearing that has not been disclosed to that party at least five business days before the hearing;

(4) Obtain a written, or, at the option of the parents, electronic, verbatim record of the hearing; and

(5) Obtain written, or, at the option of the parents, electronic findings of fact and decisions.

(b) Additional disclosure of information.

(1) At least five business days prior to a hearing conducted pursuant to § 300.511(a), each party must disclose to all other parties all evaluations completed by that date and recommendations based on the offering party's evaluations that the party intends to use at the hearing.

(2) A hearing officer may bar any party that fails to comply with paragraph (b)(1) of this section from introducing the relevant evaluation or recommendation at the hearing without

the consent of the other party.

(c)   Parental rights at hearings. Parents involved in hearings must be given the right to

(1) Have the child who is the subject of the hearing present;

(2) Open the hearing to the public; and

(3) Have the record of the hearing and the findings of fact and decisions described in paragraphs (a)(4) and (a)(5) of this section provided at no cost to parents.

Sec. 300.513   Hearing decisions.

(a)   Decision of hearing officer on the provision of FAPE.

(1) Subject to paragraph (a)(2) of this section, a hearing officer's determination of whether a child received FAPE must be based on substantive grounds.

(2) In matters alleging a procedural violation, a hearing officer may find that a child did not receive a FAPE only if the procedural inadequacies —

(i) Impeded the child's right to a FAPE;

(ii) Significantly impeded the parent's opportunity to participate in the decision-making process regarding the provision of a FAPE to the parent's child; or

(iii) Caused a deprivation of educational benefit.

(3) Nothing in paragraph (a) of this section shall be construed to preclude a hearing officer from ordering an LEA to comply with procedural requirements under §§ 300.500 through 300.536.

(b)   Construction clause. Nothing in §§ 300.507 through 300.513 shall be construed to affect the right of a parent to file an appeal of the due process hearing decision with the SEA under § 300.514(b), if a State level appeal is available.

(c)   Separate request for a due process hearing. Nothing in §§ 300.500 through 300.536 shall be construed to preclude a parent from filing a separate due process complaint on an issue separate from a due process complaint already filed.

(d)   Findings and decision to advisory panel and general public. The public agency, after deleting any personally identifiable information, must —

(1) Transmit the findings and decisions referred to in § 300.512(a)(5) to the State advisory panel established under § 300.167; and

(2) Make those findings and decisions available to the public.

Sec. 300.514   Finality of decision; appeal; impartial review.

(a)   Finality of hearing decision. A decision made in a hearing conducted pursuant to §§ 300.507 through 300.513 or §§ 300.530 through 300.534 is final, except that any party involved in the hearing may appeal the decision under the provisions of paragraph (b) of this section and § 300.516.

(b)   Appeal of decisions; impartial review.

(1) If the hearing required by § 300.511 is conducted by a public agency other than the

SEA, any party aggrieved by the findings and decision in the hearing may appeal to the SEA.

(2) If there is an appeal, the SEA must conduct an impartial review of the findings and decision appealed. The official conducting the review must —

(i) Examine the entire hearing record.

(ii) Ensure that the procedures at the hearing were consistent with the requirements of due process;

(iii) Seek additional evidence if necessary. If a hearing is held to receive additional evidence, the rights in § 300.512 apply;

(iv) Afford the parties an opportunity for oral or written argument, or both, at the discretion of the reviewing official;

(v) Make an independent decision on completion of the review; and

(vi) Give a copy of the written, or, at the option of the parents, electronic findings of fact and decisions to the parties.

(c)   Findings and decision to advisory panel and general public. The SEA, after deleting any personally identifiable information, must —

(1) Transmit the findings and decisions referred to in paragraph (b)(2)(vi) of this section to the State advisory panel established under § 300.167; and

(2) Make those findings and decisions available to the public.

(d)   Finality of review decision. The decision made by the reviewing official is final unless a party brings a civil action under § 300.516.

Sec. 300.515   Timelines and convenience of hearings and reviews.

(a) The public agency must ensure that not later than 45 days after the expiration of the 30 day period under § 300.510(b), or the adjusted time periods described in § 300.510(c) —

(1) A final decision is reached in the hearing; and

(2) A copy of the decision is mailed to each of the parties.

(b) The SEA must ensure that not later than 30 days after the receipt of a request for a review —

(1) A final decision is reached in the review; and

(2) A copy of the decision is mailed to each of the parties.

(c) A hearing or reviewing officer may grant specific extensions of time beyond the periods set out in paragraphs (a) and (b) of this section at the request of either party.

(d) Each hearing and each review involving oral arguments must be conducted at a time and place that is reasonably convenient to the parents and child involved.

Sec. 300.516   Civil action.

(a)   General. Any party aggrieved by the findings and decision made under §§ 300.507 through 300.513 or §§ 300.530 through 300.534 who does not have the right to an appeal under

§ 300.514(b), and any party aggrieved by the findings and decision under § 300.514(b), has the right to bring a civil action with respect to the due process complaint notice requesting a due process hearing under § 300.507 or §§ 300.530 through 300.532. The action may be brought in any State court of competent jurisdiction or in a district court of the United States without regard to the amount in controversy.

(b)   Time limitation. The party bringing the action shall have 90 days from the date of the decision of the hearing officer or, if applicable, the decision of the State review official, to file a civil action, or, if the State has an explicit time limitation for bringing civil actions under Part B of the Act, in the time allowed by that State law.

(c)   Additional requirements. In any action brought under paragraph (a) of this section, the court —

(1) Receives the records of the administrative proceedings;

(2) Hears additional evidence at the request of a party; and

(3) Basing its decision on the preponderance of the evidence, grants the relief that the court determines to be appropriate.

(d)   Jurisdiction of district courts. The district courts of the United States have jurisdiction of actions brought under section 615 of the Act without regard to the amount in controversy.

(e)   Rule of construction. Nothing in this part restricts or limits the rights, procedures, and remedies available under the Constitution, the Americans with Disabilities Act of 1990, title V of the Rehabilitation Act of 1973, or other Federal laws protecting the rights of children with disabilities, except that before the filing of a civil action under these laws seeking relief that is also available under section 615 of the Act, the procedures under §§ 300.507 and 300.514 must be exhausted to the same extent as would be required had the action been brought under section 615 of the Act.

Sec. 300.517   Attorneys' fees.

(a)   In general.

(1) In any action or proceeding brought under section 615 of the Act, the court, in its discretion, may award reasonable attorneys' fees as part of the costs to —

(i) The prevailing party who is the parent of a child with a disability;

(ii) To a prevailing party who is an SEA or LEA against the attorney of a parent who files a complaint or subsequent cause of action that is frivolous, unreasonable, or without foundation, or against the attorney of a parent who continued to litigate after the litigation clearly became frivolous, unreasonable, or without foundation; or

(iii) To a prevailing SEA or LEA against the attorney of a parent, or against the parent, if the parent's request for a due process hearing or subsequent cause of action was presented for any improper purpose, such as to harass, to cause unnecessary delay, or to needlessly increase the cost of litigation.

(2) Nothing in this subsection shall be construed to affect section 327 of the District of Columbia Appropriations Act, 2005.

(b)   Prohibition on use of funds.

(1) Funds under Part B of the Act may not be used to pay attorneys' fees or costs of a party related to any action or proceeding under section 615 of the Act and subpart E of this part.

(2) Paragraph (b)(1) of this section does not preclude a public agency from using funds under Part B of the Act for conducting an action or proceeding under section 615 of the Act.

(c)   Award of fees. A court awards reasonable attorneys' fees under section 615(i)(3) of the Act consistent with the following:

(1) Fees awarded under section 615(i)(3) of the Act must be based on rates prevailing in the community in which the action or proceeding arose for the kind and quality of services furnished. No bonus or multiplier may be used in calculating the fees awarded under this paragraph.

(2) (i) Attorneys' fees may not be awarded and related costs may not be reimbursed in any action or proceeding under section 615 of the Act for services performed subsequent to the time of a written offer of settlement to a parent if —

(A) The offer is made within the time prescribed by Rule 68 of the Federal Rules of Civil Procedure or, in the case of an administrative proceeding, at any time more than 10 days before the proceeding begins;

(B) The offer is not accepted within 10 days; and

(C) The court or administrative hearing officer finds that the relief finally obtained by the parents is not more favorable to the parents than the offer of settlement.

(ii) Attorneys' fees may not be awarded relating to any meeting of the IEP Team unless the meeting is convened as a result of an administrative proceeding or judicial action, or at the discretion of the State, for a mediation described in § 300.506.

(iii) A meeting conducted pursuant to § 300.510 shall not be considered —

(A) A meeting convened as a result of an administrative hearing or judicial action; or

(B) An administrative hearing or judicial action for purposes of this section.

(3) Notwithstanding paragraph (c)(2) of this section, an award of attorneys' fees and related costs may be made to a parent who is the prevailing party and who was substantially justified in rejecting the settlement offer.

(4) Except as provided in paragraph (c)(5) of this section, the court reduces, accordingly, the amount of the attorneys' fees awarded under section 615 of the Act, if the court finds that —

(i) The parent, or the parent's attorney, during the course of the action or proceeding, unreasonably protracted the final resolution of the controversy;

(ii) The amount of the attorneys' fees otherwise authorized to be awarded unreasonably exceeds the hourly rate prevailing in the community for similar services by attorneys of reasonably comparable skill, reputation, and experience;

(iii) The time spent and legal services furnished were excessive considering the nature of the action or proceeding; or

(iv) The attorney representing the parent did not provide to the LEA the appropriate information in the due process request notice in accordance with § 300.508.

(5) The provisions of paragraph (c)(4) of this section do not apply in any action or proceeding if the court finds that the State or local agency unreasonably protracted the final resolution of the action or proceeding or there was a violation of section 615 of the Act.

Sec. 300.518 Child's status during proceedings.

(a) Except as provided in § 300.533, during the pendency of any administrative or judicial proceeding regarding a due process complaint notice requesting a due process hearing under § 300.507, unless the State or local agency and the parents of the child agree otherwise, the child involved in the complaint must remain in his or her current educational placement.

(b) If the complaint involves an application for initial admission to public school, the child, with the consent of the parents, must be placed in the public school until the completion of all the proceedings.

(c) If the complaint involves an application for initial services under this part from a child who is transitioning from Part C of the Act to Part B and is no longer eligible for Part C services because the child has turned three, the public agency is not required to provide the Part C services that the child had been receiving. If the child is found eligible for special education and related services under Part B and the parent consents to the initial provision of special education and related services under § 300.300(b), then the public agency must provide those special education and related services that are not in dispute between the parent and the public agency.

(d) If the hearing officer in a due process hearing conducted by the SEA or a State review official in an administrative appeal agrees with the child's parents that a change of placement is appropriate, that placement must be treated as an agreement between the State and the parents for purposes of paragraph (a) of this section.

Sec. 300.519 Surrogate parents.

(a)   General. Each public agency must ensure that the rights of a child are protected when —

(1) No parent (as defined in § 300.30) can be identified;

(2) The public agency, after reasonable efforts, cannot locate a parent;

(3) The child is a ward of the State under the laws of that State; or

(4) The child is an unaccompanied homeless youth as defined in section 725(6) of the McKinney-Vento Homeless Assistance Act (42 U.S.C. 11434a(6)).

(b)   Duties of public agency. The duties of a public agency under paragraph (a) of this section include the assignment of an individual to act as a surrogate for the parents. This must include a method —

(1) For determining whether a child needs a surrogate parent; and

(2) For assigning a surrogate parent to the child.

(c)   Wards of the State. In the case of a child who is a ward of the State, the surrogate parent alternatively may be appointed by the judge overseeing the child's case, provided that the surrogate meets the requirements in paragraphs (d)(2)(i) and (e) of this section.

(d)   Criteria for selection of surrogate parents.

(1) The public agency may select a surrogate parent in any way permitted under State law.

(2) Public agencies must ensure that a person selected as a surrogate parent —

(i) Is not an employee of the SEA, the LEA, or any other agency that is involved in the education or care of the child;

(ii) Has no personal or professional interest that conflicts with the interest of the child the surrogate parent represents; and

(iii) Has knowledge and skills that ensure adequate representation of the child.

(e)   Non-employee requirement; compensation. A person otherwise qualified to be a surrogate parent under paragraph (d) of this section is not an employee of the agency solely because he or she is paid by the agency to serve as a surrogate parent.

(f)   Unaccompanied homeless youth. In the case of a child who is an unaccompanied homeless youth, appropriate staff of emergency shelters, transitional shelters, independent living programs, and street outreach programs may be appointed as temporary surrogate parents without regard to paragraph (d)(2)(i) of this section, until a surrogate parent can be appointed that meets all of the requirements of paragraph (d) of this section.

(g)   Surrogate parent responsibilities. The surrogate parent may represent the child in all matters relating to —

(1) The identification, evaluation, and educational placement of the child; and

(2) The provision of FAPE to the child.

(h)   SEA responsibility. The SEA must make reasonable efforts to ensure the assignment of a surrogate parent not more than 30 days after a public agency determines that the child needs a surrogate parent.

Sec. 300.520   Transfer of parental rights at age of majority.

(a)   General. A State may provide that, when a child with a disability reaches the age of majority under State law that applies to all children (except for a child with a disability who has been determined to be incompetent under State law) —

(1) (i) The public agency must provide any notice required by this part to both the child and the parents; and

(ii) All rights accorded to parents under Part B of the Act transfer to the child;

(2) All rights accorded to parents under Part B of the Act transfer to children who are incarcerated in an adult or juvenile, State or local correctional institution; and

(3) Whenever a State provides for the transfer of rights under this part pursuant to paragraph (a)(1) or (a)(2) of this section, the agency must notify the child and the parents of the transfer of rights.

(b)   Special rule. A State must establish procedures for appointing the parent of a child with a disability, or, if the parent is not available, another appropriate individual, to represent the educational interests of the child throughout the period of the child's eligibility under Part B of the Act if, under State law, a child who has reached the age of majority, but has not been determined to be incompetent, can be determined not to have the ability to provide informed consent with respect to the child's educational program.

Discipline Procedures

Sec. 300.530   Authority of school personnel.

(a)   Case-by-case determination. School personnel may consider any unique circumstances on a case-by-case basis when determining whether a change in placement, consistent with the other requirements of this section, is appropriate for a child with a disability who violates a code of student conduct.

(b)   General.

(1) School personnel under this section may remove a child with a disability who violates a code of student conduct from his or her current placement to an appropriate interim alternative educational setting, another setting, or suspension, for not more than 10 consecutive school days (to the extent those alternatives are applied to children without disabilities), and for additional removals of not more than 10 consecutive school days in that same school year for separate incidents of misconduct (as long as those removals do not constitute a change of placement under § 300.536).

(2) After a child with a disability has been removed from his or her current placement for 10 school days in the same school year, during any subsequent days of removal the public agency must provide services to the extent required under paragraph (d) of this section.

(c)   Additional authority. For disciplinary changes in placement that would exceed 10 consecutive school days, if the behavior that gave rise to the violation of the school code is determined not to be a manifestation of the child's disability pursuant to paragraph (e) of this section, school personnel may apply the relevant disciplinary procedures to children with disabilities in the same manner and for the same duration as the procedures would be applied to children without disabilities, except as provided in paragraph (d) of this section.

(d)   Services.

(1) A child with a disability who is removed from the child's current placement pursuant to paragraphs (c), or (g) of this section must —

(i) Continue to receive educational services, as provided in § 300.101(a), so as to enable the child to continue to participate in the general education curriculum, although in another setting, and to progress toward meeting the goals set out in the child's IEP; and

(ii) Receive, as appropriate, a functional behavioral assessment, and behavioral intervention services and modifications, that are designed to address the behavior violation so that it does not recur.

(2) The services required by paragraph (d)(1), (d)(3), (d)(4), and (d)(5) of this section may be provided in an interim alternative educational setting.

(3) A public agency is only required to provide services during periods of removal to a child with a disability who has been removed from his or her current placement for 10 school days or less in that school year, if it provides services to a child without disabilities who is similarly removed.

(4) After a child with a disability has been removed from his or her current placement for

10 school days in the same school year, if the current removal is for not more than 10 consecutive school days and is not a change of placement under § 300.536, school personnel, in consultation with at least one of the child's teachers, determine the extent to which services are needed, as provided in § 300.101(a), so as to enable the child to continue to participate in the general education curriculum, although in another setting, and to progress toward meeting the goals set out in the child's IEP.

(5) If the removal is a change of placement under § 300.536, the child's IEP Team determines appropriate services under paragraph (d)(1) of this section.

(e) Manifestation determination.

(1) Within 10 school days of any decision to change the placement of a child with a disability because of a violation of a code of student conduct, the LEA, the parent, and relevant members of the child's IEP Team (as determined by the parent and the LEA) must review all relevant information in the student's file, including the child's IEP, any teacher observations, and any relevant information provided by the parents to determine —

(i) If the conduct in question was caused by, or had a direct and substantial relationship to, the child's disability; or

(ii) If the conduct in question was the direct result of the LEA's failure to implement the IEP.

(2) The conduct must be determined to be a manifestation of the child's disability if the LEA, the parent, and relevant members of the child's IEP Team determine that a condition in either paragraph (e)(1)(i) or (1)(ii) of this section was met.

(3) If the LEA, the parent, and relevant members of the child's IEP Team determine the condition described in paragraph (e)(1)(ii) of this section was met, the LEA must take immediate steps to remedy those deficiencies.

(f) Determination that behavior was a manifestation. If the LEA, the parent, and relevant members of the IEP Team make the determination that the conduct was a manifestation of the child's disability, the IEP Team must —

(1) Either —

(i) Conduct a functional behavioral assessment, unless the LEA had conducted a functional behavioral assessment before the behavior that resulted in the change of placement occurred, and implement a behavioral intervention plan for the child; or

(ii) If a behavioral intervention plan already has been developed, review the behavioral intervention plan, and modify it, as necessary, to address the behavior; and

(2) Except as provided in paragraph (g) of this section, return the child to the placement from which the child was removed, unless the parent and the LEA agree to a change of placement as part of the modification of the behavioral intervention plan.

(g) Special circumstances. School personnel may remove a student to an interim alternative educational setting for not more than 45 school days without regard to whether the behavior is determined to be a manifestation of the child's disability, if the child —

(1) Carries a weapon to or possesses a weapon at school, on school premises, or to or at a school function under the jurisdiction of an SEA or an LEA;

(2) Knowingly possesses or uses illegal drugs, or sells or solicits the sale of a controlled substance, while at school, on school premises, or at a school function under the jurisdiction of an SEA or an LEA; or

(3) Has inflicted serious bodily injury upon another person while at school, on school premises, or at a school function under the jurisdiction of an SEA or an LEA.

(h)   Notification. On the date on which the decision is made to make a removal that constitutes a change of placement of a child with a disability because of a violation of a code of student conduct, the LEA must notify the parents of that decision, and provide the parents the procedural safeguards notice described in § 300.504.

(i)   Definitions. For purposes of this section, the following definitions apply:

(1) Controlled substance means a drug or other substance identified under schedules I, II, III, IV, or V in section 202(c) of the Controlled Substances Act (21 U.S.C. 812(c)).

(2) Illegal drug means a controlled substance; but does not include a controlled substance that is legally possessed or used under the supervision of a licensed health-care professional or that is legally possessed or used under any other authority under that Act or under any other provision of Federal law.

(3) Serious bodily injury has the meaning given the term "serious bodily injury" under paragraph (3) of subsection (h) of section 1365 of title 18, United States Code.

(4) Weapon has the meaning given the term "dangerous weapon" under paragraph (2) of the first subsection (g) of section 930 of title 18, United States Code.

Sec. 300.531   Determination of setting.

The child's IEP Team determines the interim alternative educational setting for services under § 300.530(c), (d)(5), and (g).

Sec. 300.532   Appeal.

(a)   General. The parent of a child with a disability who disagrees with any decision regarding placement under §§ 300.530 and 300.531, or the manifestation determination under § 300.530(e), or an LEA that believes that maintaining the current placement of the child is substantially likely to result in injury to the child or others, may appeal the decision by requesting a hearing. The hearing is requested by filing a complaint pursuant to §§ 300.507 and 300.508(a) and (b).

(b)   Authority of hearing officer.

(1) A hearing officer under § 300.511 hears, and makes a determination regarding an appeal under paragraph (a) of this section.

(2) In making the determination under paragraph (b)(1) of this section, the hearing officer may —

(i) Return the child with a disability to the placement from which the child was removed if the hearing officer determines that the removal was a violation of § 300.530 or that the child's behavior was a manifestation of the child's disability; or

(ii) Order a change of placement of the child with a disability to an appropriate interim alternative educational setting for not more than 45 school days if the hearing officer determines that maintaining the current placement of the child is substantially likely to result in injury to the child or to others.

(3) The procedures under paragraphs (a) and (b)(1) and (2) of this section may be repeated, if the LEA believes that returning the child to the original placement is substantially likely to result in injury to the child or to others.

(c)   Expedited due process hearing.

(1) Whenever a hearing is requested under paragraph (a) of this section, the parents or the LEA involved in the dispute must have an opportunity for an impartial due process hearing consistent with the requirements of §§ 300.507 and 300.508(a) through (c) and §§ 300.510 through 300.514, except as provided in paragraph (c)(2) through (4) of this section.

(2) The SEA or LEA is responsible for arranging the expedited due process hearing, which must occur within 20 school days of the date the complaint requesting the hearing is filed. The hearing officer must make a determination within 10 school days after the hearing.

(3) Unless the parents and LEA agree in writing to waive the resolution meeting described in paragraph (c)(3)(i) of this section, or agree to use the mediation process described in § 300.506 —

(i) A resolution meeting must occur within seven days of receiving notice of the due process complaint; and

(ii) The due process hearing may proceed unless the matter has been resolved to the satisfaction of both parties within 15 days of the receipt of the due process complaint.

(4) A State may establish different State-imposed procedural rules for expedited due process hearings conducted under this section than it has established for other due process hearings, but, except for the timelines as modified in paragraph (c)(3) of this section, the State must ensure that the requirements in §§ 300.510 through 300.514 are met.

(5) The decisions on expedited due process hearings are appealable consistent with § 300.514.

Sec. 300.533   Placement during appeals.

When an appeal under § 300.532 has been made by either the parent or the LEA, the child must remain in the interim alternative educational setting pending the decision of the hearing officer or until the expiration of the time period specified in § 300.530(c) or (g), whichever occurs first, unless the parent and the SEA or LEA agree otherwise.

Sec. 300.534   Protections for children not determined eligible for special education and related services.

(a)   General. A child who has not been determined to be eligible for special education and related services under this part and who has engaged in behavior that violated a code of student conduct, may assert any of the protections provided for in this part if the public agency had knowledge (as determined in accordance with paragraph (b) of this section) that the child was a child with a disability before the behavior that precipitated the disciplinary action occurred.

(b)   Basis of knowledge. A public agency must be deemed to have knowledge that a child is a child with a disability if before the behavior that precipitated the disciplinary action occurred —

(1) The parent of the child expressed concern in writing to supervisory or administrative personnel of the appropriate educational agency, or a teacher of the child, that the child is in need of special education and related services;

(2) The parent of the child requested an evaluation of the child pursuant to §§ 300.300 through 300.311; or

(3) The teacher of the child, or other personnel of the LEA, expressed specific concerns about a pattern of behavior demonstrated by the child directly to the director of special education of the agency or to other supervisory personnel of the agency.

(c)   Exception. A public agency would not be deemed to have knowledge under paragraph (b) of this section if —

(1) The parent of the child —

(i) Has not allowed an evaluation of the child pursuant to §§ 300.300 through 300.311; or

(ii) Has refused services under this part; or

(2) The child has been evaluated in accordance with §§ 300.300 through 300.311 and determined to not be a child with a disability under this part.

(d)   Conditions that apply if no basis of knowledge.

(1) If a public agency does not have knowledge that a child is a child with a disability (in accordance with paragraphs (b) and (c) of this section) prior to taking disciplinary measures against the child, the child may be subjected to the disciplinary measures applied to children without disabilities who engage in comparable behaviors consistent with paragraph (d)(2) of this section.

(2) (i) If a request is made for an evaluation of a child during the time period in which the child is subjected to disciplinary measures under § 300.530, the evaluation must be conducted in an expedited manner.

(ii) Until the evaluation is completed, the child remains in the educational placement determined by school authorities, which can include suspension or expulsion without educational services.

(iii) If the child is determined to be a child with a disability, taking into consideration information from the evaluation conducted by the agency and information provided by the parents, the agency must provide special education and related services in accordance with this part, including the requirements of §§ 300.530 through 300.536 and section 612(a)(1)(A) of the Act.

Sec. 300.535   Referral to and action by law enforcement and judicial authorities.

(a)   Rule of construction. Nothing in this part prohibits an agency from reporting a crime committed by a child with a disability to appropriate authorities or prevents State law enforcement and judicial authorities from exercising their responsibilities with regard to the application of Federal and State law to crimes committed by a child with a disability.

(b)   Transmittal of records.

(1) An agency reporting a crime committed by a child with a disability must ensure that copies of the special education and disciplinary records of the child are transmitted for consideration by the appropriate authorities to whom the agency reports the crime.

(2) An agency reporting a crime under this section may transmit copies of the child's special education and disciplinary records only to the extent that the transmission is permitted by the Family Educational Rights and Privacy Act.

Sec. 300.536   Change of placement because of disciplinary removals.

(a) For purposes of removals of a child with a disability from the child's current educational placement under §§ 300.530 through 300.535, a change of placement occurs if —

(1) The removal is for more than 10 consecutive school days; or

(2) The child has been subjected to a series of removals that constitute a pattern —

(i) Because the series of removals total more than 10 school days in a school year;

(ii) Because the child's behavior is substantially similar to the child's behavior in previous incidents that resulted in the series of removals; and

(iii) Because of such additional factors as the length of each removal, the total amount of time the child has been removed, and the proximity of the removals to one another.

(b) (1) The public agency determines on a case-by-case basis whether a pattern of removals constitutes a change of placement.

(2) This determination is subject to review through due process and judicial proceedings.

Confidentiality of Information

Sec. 300.610   Confidentiality.

The Secretary takes appropriate action, in accordance with section 444 of GEPA, to ensure the protection of the confidentiality of any personally identifiable data, information, and records collected or maintained by the Secretary and by SEAs and LEAs pursuant to Part B of the Act, and consistent with §§ 300.611 through 300.627.

Sec. 300.611   Definitions.

As used in §§ 300.611 through 300.625 —

(a) Destruction means physical destruction or removal of personal identifiers from information so that the information is no longer personally identifiable.

(b) Education records means the type of records covered under the definition of "education records" in 34 CFR part 99 (the regulations implementing the Family Educational Rights and Privacy Act of 1974, 20 U.S.C. 1232g (FERPA)).

(c) Participating agency means any agency or institution that collects, maintains, or uses personally identifiable information, or from which information is obtained, under Part B of the Act.

Sec. 300.612   Notice to parents.

(a) The SEA must give notice that is adequate to fully inform parents about the requirements of § 300.123, including —

(1) A description of the extent that the notice is given in the native languages of the various population groups in the State;

(2) A description of the children on whom personally identifiable information is maintained, the types of information sought, the methods the State intends to use in gathering the information (including the sources from whom information is gathered), and the uses to be made of the information;

(3) A summary of the policies and procedures that participating agencies must follow regarding storage, disclosure to third parties, retention, and destruction of personally identifiable information; and

(4) A description of all of the rights of parents and children regarding this information, including the rights under FERPA and implementing regulations in 34 CFR part 99.

(b) Before any major identification, location, or evaluation activity, the notice must be published or announced in newspapers or other media, or both, with circulation adequate to notify parents throughout the State of the activity.

Sec. 300.613   Access rights.

(a) Each participating agency must permit parents to inspect and review any education records relating to their children that are collected, maintained, or used by the agency under this part. The agency must comply with a request without unnecessary delay and before any meeting regarding an IEP, or any hearing pursuant to § 300.507 or §§ 300.530 through 300.532, or resolution session pursuant to § 300.510, and in no case more than 45 days after the request has been made.

(b) The right to inspect and review education records under this section includes —

(1) The right to a response from the participating agency to reasonable requests for explanations and interpretations of the records;

(2) The right to request that the agency provide copies of the records containing the information if failure to provide those copies would effectively prevent the parent from exercising the right to inspect and review the records; and

(3) The right to have a representative of the parent inspect and review the records.

(c) An agency may presume that the parent has authority to inspect and review records relating to his or her child unless the agency has been advised that the parent does not have the authority under applicable State law governing such matters as guardianship, separation, and divorce.

Sec. 300.614   Record of access.

Each participating agency must keep a record of parties obtaining access to education records collected, maintained, or used under Part B of the Act (except access by parents and authorized employees of the participating agency), including the name of the party, the date access was given, and the purpose for which the party is authorized to use the records.

Sec. 300.615   Records on more than one child.

If any education record includes information on more than one child, the parents of those children have the right to inspect and review only the information relating to their child or to be informed of that specific information.

Sec. 300.616 List of types and locations of information.

Each participating agency must provide parents on request a list of the types and locations of education records collected, maintained, or used by the agency.

Sec. 300.617 Fees.

(a) Each participating agency may charge a fee for copies of records that are made for parents under this part if the fee does not effectively prevent the parents from exercising their right to inspect and review those records.

(b) A participating agency may not charge a fee to search for or to retrieve information under this part.

Sec. 300.618 Amendment of records at parent's request.

(a) A parent who believes that information in the education records collected, maintained, or used under this part is inaccurate or misleading or violates the privacy or other rights of the child may request the participating agency that maintains the information to amend the information.

(b) The agency must decide whether to amend the information in accordance with the request within a reasonable period of time of receipt of the request.

(c) If the agency decides to refuse to amend the information in accordance with the request, it must inform the parent of the refusal and advise the parent of the right to a hearing under § 300.619.

Sec. 300.619 Opportunity for a hearing.

The agency must, on request, provide an opportunity for a hearing to challenge information in education records to ensure that it is not inaccurate, misleading, or otherwise in violation of the privacy or other rights of the child.

Sec. 300.620 Result of hearing.

(a) If, as a result of the hearing, the agency decides that the information is inaccurate, misleading or otherwise in violation of the privacy or other rights of the child, it must amend the information accordingly and so inform the parent in writing.

(b) If, as a result of the hearing, the agency decides that the information is not inaccurate, misleading, or otherwise in violation of the privacy or other rights of the child, it must inform the parent of the parent's right to place in the records the agency maintains on the child a statement commenting on the information or setting forth any reasons for disagreeing with the decision of the agency.

(c) Any explanation placed in the records of the child under this section must —

(1) Be maintained by the agency as part of the records of the child as long as the record or contested portion is maintained by the agency; and

(2) If the records of the child or the contested portion is disclosed by the agency to any party, the explanation must also be disclosed to the party.

Sec. 300.621 Hearing procedures.

A hearing held under § 300.619 must be conducted according to the procedures in 34 CFR 99.22.

Sec. 300.622 Consent.

(a) Parental consent must be obtained before personally identifiable information is disclosed to parties, other than officials of participating agencies in accordance with paragraph (b)(1) of this section, unless the information is contained in education records, and the disclosure is authorized without parental consent under 34 CFR part 99.

(b) (1) Except as provided in paragraphs (b)(2) and (b)(3) of this section, parental consent is not required before personally identifiable information is released to officials of participating agencies for purposes of meeting a requirement of this part.

(2) Parental consent, or the consent of an eligible child who has reached the age of majority under State law, must be obtained before personally identifiable information is released to officials of participating agencies providing or paying for transition services in accordance with § 300.321(b)(3).

(3) If a child is enrolled, or is going to enroll in a private school that is not located in the LEA of the parent's residence, parental consent must be obtained before any personally identifiable information about the child is released between officials in the LEA where the private school is located and officials in the LEA of the parent's residence.

Sec. 300.623 Safeguards.

(a) Each participating agency must protect the confidentiality of personally identifiable information at collection, storage, disclosure, and destruction stages.

(b) One official at each participating agency must assume responsibility for ensuring the confidentiality of any personally identifiable information.

(c) All persons collecting or using personally identifiable information must receive training or instruction regarding the State's policies and procedures under § 300.123 and 34 CFR part 99.

(d) Each participating agency must maintain, for public inspection, a current listing of the names and positions of those employees within the agency who may have access to personally identifiable information.

Sec. 300.624 Destruction of information.

(a) The public agency must inform parents when personally identifiable information collected, maintained, or used under this part is no longer needed to provide educational services to the child.

(b) The information must be destroyed at the request of the parents. However, a permanent record of a student's name, address, and phone number, his or her grades, attendance record, classes attended, grade level completed, and year completed may be maintained without time limitation.

Sec. 300.625   Children's rights.

(a) The SEA must have in effect policies and procedures regarding the extent to which children are afforded rights of privacy similar to those afforded to parents, taking into consideration the age of the child and type or severity of disability.

(b) Under the regulations for FERPA in 34 CFR 99.5(a), the rights of parents regarding education records are transferred to the student at age 18.

(c) If the rights accorded to parents under Part B of the Act are transferred to a student who reaches the age of majority, consistent with § 300.520, the rights regarding educational records in §§ 300.613 through 300.624 must also be transferred to the student. However, the public agency must provide any notice required under section 615 of the Act to the student and the parents.

PART 303   EARLY INTERVENTION PROGRAM FOR INFANTS AND TODDLERS WITH DISABILITIES

Subpart A   General

Purpose, Eligibility, and Other General Provision

Sec. 303.1   Purpose of the early intervention program for infants and toddlers with disabilities.

The purpose of this part is to provide financial assistance to States to —

(a) Maintain and implement a statewide, comprehensive, coordinated, multidisciplinary, interagency system of early intervention services for infants and toddlers with disabilities and their families;

(b) Facilitate the coordination of payment for early intervention services from Federal, State, local, and private sources (including public and private insurance coverage);

(c) Enhance the States' capacity to provide quality early intervention services and expand and improve existing early intervention services being provided to infants and toddlers with disabilities and their families; and

(d) Enhance the capacity of State and local agencies and service providers to identify, evaluate, and meet the needs of historically underrepresented populations, particularly minority, low-income, inner-city, and rural populations.

Sec. 303.10   Developmental delay.

As used in this part, "developmental delay," when used with respect to an individual residing in a State, has the meaning given to that term under § 303.300.

Sec. 303.11   Early intervention program.

As used in this part, early intervention program means the total effort in a State that is directed at meeting the needs of children eligible under this part and their families.

Sec. 303.12   Early intervention services.

(a)   General. As used in this part, early intervention services means services that —

(1) Are designed to meet the developmental needs of each child eligible under this part

and the needs of the family related to enhancing the child's development;

(2) Are selected in collaboration with the parents;

(3) Are provided —

(i) Under public supervision;

(ii) By qualified personnel, as defined in § 303.21, including the types of personnel listed in paragraph (e) of this section;

(iii) In conformity with an individualized family service plan; and

(iv) At no cost, unless, subject to § 303.520(b)(3), Federal or State law provides for a system of payments by families, including a schedule of sliding fees; and

(4) Meet the standards of the State, including the requirements of this part.

(b) Natural environments. To the maximum extent appropriate to the needs of the child, early intervention services must be provided in natural environments, including the home and community settings in which children without disabilities participate.

(c) General role of service providers. To the extent appropriate, service providers in each area of early intervention services included in paragraph (d) of this section are responsible for —

(1) Consulting with parents, other service providers, and representatives of appropriate community agencies to ensure the effective provision of services in that area;

(2) Training parents and others regarding the provision of those services; and

(3) Participating in the multidisciplinary team's assessment of a child and the child's family, and in the development of integrated goals and outcomes for the individualized family service plan.

(d) Types of services; definitions. Following are types of services included under "early intervention services," and, if appropriate, definitions of those services:

(1) Assistive technology device means any item, piece of equipment, or product system, whether acquired commercially off the shelf, modified, or customized, that is used to increase, maintain, or improve the functional capabilities of children with disabilities. Assistive technology service means a service that directly assists a child with a disability in the selection, acquisition, or use of an assistive technology device. Assistive technology services include —

(i) The evaluation of the needs of a child with a disability, including a functional evaluation of the child in the child's customary environment;

(ii) Purchasing, leasing, or otherwise providing for the acquisition of assistive technology devices by children with disabilities;

(iii) Selecting, designing, fitting, customizing, adapting, applying, maintaining, repairing, or replacing assistive technology devices;

(iv) Coordinating and using other therapies, interventions, or services with assistive technology devices, such as those associated with existing education and rehabilitation plans and programs;

(v) Training or technical assistance for a child with disabilities or, if appropriate, that child's family; and

(vi) Training or technical assistance for professionals (including individuals providing early intervention services) or other individuals who provide services to or are otherwise substantially involved in the major life functions of individuals with disabilities.

(2) Audiology includes —

(i) Identification of children with auditory impairment, using at risk criteria and appropriate audiologic screening techniques;

(ii) Determination of the range, nature, and degree of hearing loss and communication functions, by use of audiological evaluation procedures;

(iii) Referral for medical and other services necessary for the habilitation or rehabilitation of children with auditory impairment;

(iv) Provision of auditory training, aural rehabilitation, speech reading and listening device orientation and training, and other services;

(v) Provision of services for prevention of hearing loss; and

(vi) Determination of the child's need for individual amplification, including selecting, fitting, and dispensing appropriate listening and vibrotactile devices, and evaluating the effectiveness of those devices.

(3) Family training, counseling, and home visits means services provided, as appropriate, by social workers, psychologists, and other qualified personnel to assist the family of a child eligible under this part in understanding the special needs of the child and enhancing the child's development.

(4) Health services (See § 303.13).

(5) Medical services only for diagnostic or evaluation purposes means services provided by a licensed physician to determine a child's developmental status and need for early intervention services.

(6) Nursing services includes —

(i) The assessment of health status for the purpose of providing nursing care, including the identification of patterns of human response to actual or potential health problems;

(ii) Provision of nursing care to prevent health problems, restore or improve functioning, and promote optimal health and development; and

(iii) Administration of medications, treatments, and regimens prescribed by a licensed physician.

(7) Nutrition services includes —

(i) Conducting individual assessments in —

(A) Nutritional history and dietary intake;

(B) Anthropometric, biochemical, and clinical variables;

(C) Feeding skills and feeding problems; and

(D) Food habits and food preferences;

(ii) Developing and monitoring appropriate plans to address the nutritional needs of children eligible under this part, based on the findings in paragraph (d)(7)(i) of this section; and

(iii) Making referrals to appropriate community resources to carry out nutrition goals.

(8) Occupational therapy includes services to address the functional needs of a child related to adaptive development, adaptive behavior and play, and sensory, motor, and postural development. These services are designed to improve the child's functional ability to perform tasks in home, school, and community settings, and include —

(i) Identification, assessment, and intervention;

(ii) Adaptation of the environment, and selection, design, and fabrication of assistive and orthotic devices to facilitate development and promote the acquisition of functional skills; and

(iii) Prevention or minimization of the impact of initial or future impairment, delay in development, or loss of functional ability.

(9) Physical therapy includes services to address the promotion of sensorimotor function through enhancement of musculoskeletal status, neurobehavioral organization, perceptual and motor development, cardiopulmonary status, and effective environmental adaptation. These services include —

(i) Screening, evaluation, and assessment of infants and toddlers to identify movement dysfunction;

(ii) Obtaining, interpreting, and integrating information appropriate to program planning to prevent, alleviate, or compensate for movement dysfunction and related functional problems; and

(iii) Providing individual and group services or treatment to prevent, alleviate, or compensate for movement dysfunction and related functional problems.

(10) Psychological services includes —

(i) Administering psychological and developmental tests and other assessment procedures;

(ii) Interpreting assessment results;

(iii) Obtaining, integrating, and interpreting information about child behavior, and child and family conditions related to learning, mental health, and development; and

(iv) Planning and managing a program of psychological services, including psychological counseling for children and parents, family counseling, consultation on child development, parent training, and education programs.

(11) Service coordination services means assistance and services provided by a service coordinator to a child eligible under this part and the child's family that are in addition to the functions and activities included under § 303.23.

(12) Social work services includes —

(i) Making home visits to evaluate a child's living conditions and patterns of parent-child interaction;

(ii) Preparing a social or emotional developmental assessment of the child within the family context;

(iii) Providing individual and family-group counseling with parents and other family members, and appropriate social skill-building activities with the child and parents;

(iv) Working with those problems in a child's and family's living situation (home, community, and any center where early intervention services are provided) that affect the child's maximum utilization of early intervention services; and

(v) Identifying, mobilizing, and coordinating community resources and services to enable the child and family to receive maximum benefit from early intervention services.

(13) Special instruction includes —

(i) The design of learning environments and activities that promote the child's acquisition of skills in a variety of developmental areas, including cognitive processes and social interaction;

(ii) Curriculum planning, including the planned interaction of personnel, materials, and time and space, that leads to achieving the outcomes in the child's individualized family service plan;

(iii) Providing families with information, skills, and support related to enhancing the skill development of the child; and

(iv) Working with the child to enhance the child's development.

(14) Speech-language pathology includes —

(i) Identification of children with communicative or oropharyngeal disorders and delays in development of communication skills, including the diagnosis and appraisal of specific disorders and delays in those skills;

(ii) Referral for medical or other professional services necessary for the habilitation or rehabilitation of children with communicative or oropharyngeal disorders and delays in development of communication skills; and

(iii) Provision of services for the habilitation, rehabilitation, or prevention of communicative or oropharyngeal disorders and delays in development of communication skills.

(15) Transportation and related costs includes the cost of travel (e.g., mileage, or travel by taxi, common carrier, or other means) and other costs (e.g., tolls and parking expenses) that are necessary to enable a child eligible under this part and the child's family to receive early intervention services.

(16) Vision services means —

(i) Evaluation and assessment of visual functioning, including the diagnosis and appraisal of specific visual disorders, delays, and abilities;

(ii) Referral for medical or other professional services necessary for the habilitation or rehabilitation of visual functioning disorders, or both; and

(iii) Communication skills training, orientation and mobility training for all environments, visual training, independent living skills training, and additional training necessary to activate visual motor abilities.

(e) Qualified personnel. Early intervention services must be provided by qualified personnel, including —

(1) Audiologists;

(2) Family therapists;

(3) Nurses;

(4) Nutritionists;

(5) Occupational therapists;

(6) Orientation and mobility specialists;

(7) Pediatricians and other physicians;

(8) Physical therapists;

(9) Psychologists;

(10) Social workers;

(11) Special educators; and

(12) Speech and language pathologists.

Sec. 303.13 Health services.

(a) As used in this part, health services means services necessary to enable a child to benefit from the other early intervention services under this part during the time that the child is receiving the other early intervention services.

(b) The term includes —

(1) Such services as clean intermittent catheterization, tracheostomy care, tube feeding, the changing of dressings or colostomy collection bags, and other health services; and

(2) Consultation by physicians with other service providers concerning the special health care needs of eligible children that will need to be addressed in the course of providing other early intervention services.

(c) The term does not include the following:

(1) Services that are —

(i) Surgical in nature (such as cleft palate surgery, surgery for club foot, or the shunting of hydrocephalus); or

(ii) Purely medical in nature (such as hospitalization for management of congenital heart ailments, or the prescribing of medicine or drugs for any purpose).

(2) Devices necessary to control or treat a medical condition.

(3) Medical-health services (such as immunizations and regular "well-baby" care) that are routinely recommended for all children.

Sec. 303.16 Infants and toddlers with disabilities.

(a) As used in this part, infants and toddlers with disabilities means individuals from birth through age two who need early intervention services because they —

(1) Are experiencing developmental delays, as measured by appropriate diagnostic instruments and procedures, in one or more of the following areas:

(i) Cognitive development.

(ii) Physical development, including vision and hearing.

(iii) Communication development.

(iv) Social or emotional development.

(v) Adaptive development; or

(2) Have a diagnosed physical or mental condition that has a high probability of resulting in developmental delay.

(b) The term may also include, at a State's discretion, children from birth through age two who are at risk of having substantial developmental delays if early intervention services are not provided.

Sec. 303.18 Natural environments.

As used in this part, natural environments means settings that are natural or normal for the child's age peers who have no disabilities.

Sec. 303.19 Parent.

(a) General. As used in this part, "parent" means —

(1) A natural or adoptive parent of a child;

(2) A guardian;

(3) A person acting in the place of a parent (such as a grandparent or stepparent with whom the child lives, or a person who is legally responsible for the child's welfare); or

(4) A surrogate parent who has been assigned in accordance with § 303.406.

(b) Foster parent. Unless State law prohibits a foster parent from acting as a parent, a State may allow a foster parent to act as a parent under Part C of the Act if —

(1) The natural parents' authority to make the decisions required of parents under the Act has been extinguished under State law; and

(2) The foster parent —

(i) Has an ongoing, long-term parental relationship with the child;

(ii) Is willing to make the decisions required of parents under the Act; and

(iii) Has no interest that would conflict with the interests of the child.

Sec. 303.23   Service coordination (case management).

(a)   General.

(1) As used in this part, except in § 303.12(d)(11), service coordination means the activities carried out by a service coordinator to assist and enable a child eligible under this part and the child's family to receive the rights, procedural safeguards, and services that are authorized to be provided under the State's early intervention program.

(2) Each child eligible under this part and the child's family must be provided with one service coordinator who is responsible for —

(i) Coordinating all services across agency lines; and

(ii) Serving as the single point of contact in helping parents to obtain the services and assistance they need.

(3) Service coordination is an active, ongoing process that involves —

(i) Assisting parents of eligible children in gaining access to the early intervention services and other services identified in the individualized family service plan;

(ii) Coordinating the provision of early intervention services and other services (such as medical services for other than diagnostic and evaluation purposes) that the child needs or is being provided;

(iii) Facilitating the timely delivery of available services; and

(iv) Continuously seeking the appropriate services and situations necessary to benefit the development of each child being served for the duration of the child's eligibility.

(b)   Specific service coordination activities. Service coordination activities include —

(1) Coordinating the performance of evaluations and assessments;

(2) Facilitating and participating in the development, review, and evaluation of individualized family service plans;

(3) Assisting families in identifying available service providers;

(4) Coordinating and monitoring the delivery of available services;

(5) Informing families of the availability of advocacy services;

(6) Coordinating with medical and health providers; and

(7) Facilitating the development of a transition plan to preschool services, if appropriate.

(c)   Employment and assignment of service coordinators.

(1) Service coordinators may be employed or assigned in any way that is permitted under State law, so long as it is consistent with the requirements of this part.

(2) A State's policies and procedures for implementing the statewide system of early intervention services must be designed and implemented to ensure that service coordinators are able to effectively carry out on an interagency basis the functions and services listed under paragraphs (a) and (b) of this section.

(d)   Qualifications of service coordinators. Service coordinators must be persons who, consistent with § 303.344(g), have demonstrated knowledge and understanding about —

(1) Infants and toddlers who are eligible under this part;

(2) Part C of the Act and the regulations in this part; and

(3) The nature and scope of services available under the State's early intervention program, the system of payments for services in the State, and other pertinent information.

Sec. 303.322   Evaluation and assessment.

(a)   General.

(1) Each system must include the performance of a timely, comprehensive, multidisciplinary evaluation of each child, birth through age two, referred for evaluation, and a family-directed identification of the needs of each child's family to appropriately assist in the development of the child.

(2) The lead agency shall be responsible for ensuring that the requirements of this section are implemented by all affected public agencies and service providers in the State.

(b)   Definitions of evaluation and assessment. As used in this part —

(1) Evaluation means the procedures used by appropriate qualified personnel to determine a child's initial and continuing eligibility under this part, consistent with the definition of "infants and toddlers with disabilities" in § 303.16, including determining the status of the child in each of the developmental areas in paragraph (c)(3)(ii) of this section.

(2) Assessment means the ongoing procedures used by appropriate qualified personnel throughout the period of a child's eligibility under this part to identify —

(i) The child's unique strengths and needs and the services appropriate to meet those needs; and

(ii) The resources, priorities, and concerns of the family and the supports and services necessary to enhance the family's capacity to meet the developmental needs of their infant or toddler with a disability.

(c)   Evaluation and assessment of the child. The evaluation and assessment of each child must —

(1) Be conducted by personnel trained to utilize appropriate methods and procedures;

(2) Be based on informed clinical opinion; and

(3) Include the following:

(i) A review of pertinent records related to the child's current health status and medical history.

(ii) An evaluation of the child's level of functioning in each of the following developmental areas:

(A) Cognitive development.

(B) Physical development, including vision and hearing.

(C) Communication development.

(D) Social or emotional development.

(E) Adaptive development.

(iii) An assessment of the unique needs of the child in terms of each of the developmental areas in paragraph (c)(3)(ii) of this section, including the identification of services appropriate to meet those needs.

(d)   Family assessment.

(1) Family assessments under this part must be family-directed and designed to determine the resources, priorities, and concerns of the family and the identification of the supports and services necessary to enhance the family's capacity to meet the developmental needs of the child.

(2) Any assessment that is conducted must be voluntary on the part of the family.

(3) If an assessment of the family is carried out, the assessment must —

(i) Be conducted by personnel trained to utilize appropriate methods and procedures;

(ii) Be based on information provided by the family through a personal interview; and

(iii) Incorporate the family's description of its resources, priorities, and concerns related to enhancing the child's development.

(e)   Timelines.

(1) Except as provided in paragraph (e)(2) of this section, the evaluation and initial assessment of each child (including the family assessment) must be completed within the 45-day time period required in § 303.321(e).

(2) The lead agency shall develop procedures to ensure that in the event of exceptional circumstances that make it impossible to complete the evaluation and assessment within 45 days (e.g., if a child is ill), public agencies will —

(i) Document those circumstances; and

(ii) Develop and implement an interim IFSP, to the extent appropriate and consistent with § 303.345 (b)(1) and (b)(2).

Sec. 303.323   Nondiscriminatory procedures.

Each lead agency shall adopt nondiscriminatory evaluation and assessment procedures. The procedures must provide that public agencies responsible for the evaluation and assessment of children and families under this part shall ensure, at a minimum, that —

(a) Tests and other evaluation materials and procedures are administered in the native language of the parents or other mode of communication, unless it is clearly not feasible to do so;

(b) Any assessment and evaluation procedures and materials that are used are selected and administered so as not to be racially or culturally discriminatory;

(c) No single procedure is used as the sole criterion for determining a child's eligibility under this part; and

(d) Evaluations and assessments are conducted by qualified personnel.

Individualized Family Service Plans (IFSPs)

Sec. 303.340   General.

(a) Each system must include policies and procedures regarding individualized family service plans (IFSPs) that meet the requirements of this section and §§ 303.341 through 303.346.

(b) As used in this part, individualized family service plan and IFSP mean a written plan for providing early intervention services to a child eligible under this part and the child's family. The plan must —

     (1) Be developed in accordance with §§ 303.342 and 303.343;

     (2) Be based on the evaluation and assessment described in § 303.322; and

     (3) Include the matters specified in § 303.344.

(c)   Lead agency responsibility. The lead agency shall ensure that an IFSP is developed and implemented for each eligible child, in accordance with the requirements of this part. If there is a dispute between agencies as to who has responsibility for developing or implementing an IFSP, the lead agency shall resolve the dispute or assign responsibility.

Sec. 303.342   Procedures for IFSP development, review, and evaluation.

(a) Meeting to develop initial IFSP — timelines. For a child who has been evaluated for the first time and determined to be eligible, a meeting to develop the initial IFSP must be conducted within the 45-day time period in § 303.321(e).

(b)   Periodic review.

     (1) A review of the IFSP for a child and the child's family must be conducted every six months, or more frequently if conditions warrant, or if the family requests such a review. The purpose of the periodic review is to determine —

         (i) The degree to which progress toward achieving the outcomes is being made; and

         (ii) Whether modification or revision of the outcomes or services is necessary.

     (2) The review may be carried out by a meeting or by another means that is acceptable to the parents and other participants.

(c)   Annual meeting to evaluate the IFSP. A meeting must be conducted on at least an annual basis to evaluate the IFSP for a child and the child's family, and, as appropriate, to revise its provisions. The results of any current evaluations conducted under § 303.322(c), and other information available from the ongoing assessment of the child and family, must be used in determining what services are needed and will be provided.

(d)   Accessibility and convenience of meetings.

     (1) IFSP meetings must be conducted —

         (i) In settings and at times that are convenient to families; and

         (ii) In the native language of the family or other mode of communication used by the family, unless it is clearly not feasible to do so.

     (2) Meeting arrangements must be made with, and written notice provided to, the family and other participants early enough before the meeting date to ensure that they will be able

to attend.

(e) Parental consent. The contents of the IFSP must be fully explained to the parents and informed written consent from the parents must be obtained prior to the provision of early intervention services described in the plan. If the parents do not provide consent with respect to a particular early intervention service or withdraw consent after first providing it, that service may not be provided. The early intervention services to which parental consent is obtained must be provided.

Sec. 303.343   Participants in IFSP meetings and periodic reviews.

(a) Initial and annual IFSP meetings.

(1) Each initial meeting and each annual meeting to evaluate the IFSP must include the following participants:

(i) The parent or parents of the child.

(ii) Other family members, as requested by the parent, if feasible to do so;

(iii) An advocate or person outside of the family, if the parent requests that the person participate.

(iv) The service coordinator who has been working with the family since the initial referral of the child for evaluation, or who has been designated by the public agency to be responsible for implementation of the IFSP.

(v) A person or persons directly involved in conducting the evaluations and assessments in § 303.322.

(vi) As appropriate, persons who will be providing services to the child or family.

(2) If a person listed in paragraph (a)(1)(v) of this section is unable to attend a meeting, arrangements must be made for the person's involvement through other means, including —

(i) Participating in a telephone conference call;

(ii) Having a knowledgeable authorized representative attend the meeting; or

(iii) Making pertinent records available at the meeting.

(b) Periodic review. Each periodic review must provide for the participation of persons in paragraphs (a)(1)(i) through (a)(1)(iv) of this section. If conditions warrant, provisions must be made for the participation of other representatives identified in paragraph (a) of this section.

Sec. 303.344   Content of an IFSP.

(a) Information about the child's status.

(1) The IFSP must include a statement of the child's present levels of physical development (including vision, hearing, and health status), cognitive development, communication development, social or emotional development, and adaptive development.

(2) The statement in paragraph (a)(1) of this section must be based on professionally acceptable objective criteria.

(b) Family information. With the concurrence of the family, the IFS must include a statement of the family's resources, priorities, and concerns related to enhancing the development of the child.

(c) Outcomes. The IFSP must include a statement of the major outcomes expected to be achieved for the child and family, and the criteria, procedures, and timeliness used to determine —

(1) The degree to which progress toward achieving the outcomes is being made; and

(2) Whether modifications or revisions of the outcomes or services are necessary.

(d) Early intervention services.

(1) The IFSP must include a statement of the specific early intervention services necessary to meet the unique needs of the child and the family to achieve the outcomes identified in paragraph (c) of this section, including —

(i) The frequency, intensity, and method of delivering the services;

(ii) The natural environments, as described in § 303.12(b), and § 303.18 in which early intervention services will be provided, and a justification of the extent, if any, to which the services will not be provided in a natural environment;

(iii) The location of the services; and

(iv) The payment arrangements, if any.

(2) As used in paragraph (d)(1)(i) of this section —

(i) Frequency and intensity mean the number of days or sessions that a service will be provided, the length of time the service is provided during each session, and whether the service is provided on an individual or group basis; and

(ii) Method means how a service is provided.

(3) As used in paragraph (d)(1)(iii) of this section, location means the actual place or places where a service will be provided.

(e) Other services.

(1) To the extent appropriate, the IFSP must include —

(i) Medical and other services that the child needs, but that are not required under this part; and

(ii) The funding sources to be used in paying for those services or the steps that will be taken to secure those services through public or private sources.

(2) The requirement in paragraph (e)(1) of this section does not apply to routine medical services (e.g., immunizations and "well-baby" care), unless a child needs those services and the services are not otherwise available or being provided.

(f) Dates; duration of services. The IFSP must include —

(1) The projected dates for initiation of the services in paragraph (d)(1) of this section as soon as possible after the IFSP meetings described in § 303.342; and

(2) The anticipated duration of those services.

(g) Service coordinator.

(1) The IFSP must include the name of the service coordinator from the profession most immediately relevant to the child's or family's needs (or who is otherwise qualified to carry out all applicable responsibilities under this part), who will be responsible for the implementation of the IFSP and coordination with other agencies and persons.

(2) In meeting the requirements in paragraph (g)(1) of this section, the public agency may —

(i) Assign the same service coordinator who was appointed at the time that the child was initially referred for evaluation to be responsible for implementing a child's and family's IFSP; or

(ii) Appoint a new service coordinator.

(3) As used in paragraph (g)(1) of this section, the term profession includes "service coordination."

(h) Transition from Part C services.

(1) The IFSP must include the steps to be taken to support the transition of the child, in accordance with § 303.148, to —

(i) Preschool services under Part B of the Act, to the extent that those services are appropriate; or

(ii) Other services that may be available, if appropriate.

(2) The steps required in paragraph (h)(1) of this section include —

(i) Discussions with, and training of, parents regarding future placements and other matters related to the child's transition;

(ii) Procedures to prepare the child for changes in service delivery, including steps to help the child adjust to, and function in, a new setting; and

(iii) With parental consent, the transmission of information about the child to the local educational agency, to ensure continuity of services, including evaluation and assessment information required in § 303.322, and copies of IFSPs that have been developed and implemented in accordance with §§ 303.340 through 303.346.

Sec. 303.345 Provision of services before evaluation and assessment are completed.

Early intervention services for an eligible child and the child's family may commence before the completion of the evaluation and assessment in § 303.322, if the following conditions are met:

(a) Parental consent is obtained.

(b) An interim IFSP is developed that includes —

(1) The name of the service coordinator who will be responsible, consistent with § 303.344(g), for implementation of the interim IFSP and coordination with other agencies and persons; and

(2) The early intervention services that have been determined to be needed immediately by the child and the child's family.

(c) The evaluation and assessment are completed within the time period required in

§ 303.322(e).

Sec. 303.346   Responsibility and accountability.

Each agency or person who has a direct role in the provision of early intervention services is responsible for making a good faith effort to assist each eligible child in achieving the outcomes in the child's IFSP. However, part C of the Act does not require that any agency or person be held accountable if an eligible child does not achieve the growth projected in the child's IFSP.

Subpart E   Procedural Safeguards

General

Sec. 303.400   General responsibility of lead agency for procedural safeguards.

Each lead agency shall be responsible for —

(a) Establishing or adopting procedural safeguards that meet the requirements of this subpart; and

(b) Ensuring effective implementation of the safeguards by each public agency in the State that is involved in the provision of early intervention services under this part.

Sec. 303.401   Definitions of consent, native language, and personally identifiable information.

As used in this subpart —

(a) Consent means that —

(1) The parent has been fully informed of all information relevant to the activity for which consent is sought, in the parent's native language or other mode of communication;

(2) The parent understands and agrees in writing to the carrying out of the activity for which consent is sought, and the consent describes that activity and lists the records (if any) that will be released and to whom; and

(3) The parent understands that the granting of consent is voluntary on the part of the parent and may be revoked at any time;

(b) Native language, where used with reference to persons of limited English proficiency, means the language or mode of communication normally used by the parent of a child eligible under this part;

(c) Personally identifiable means that information includes —

(1) The name of the child, the child's parent, or other family member;

(2) The address of the child;

(3) A personal identifier, such as the child's or parent's social security number; or

(4) A list of personal characteristics or other information that would make it possible to identify the child with reasonable certainty.

Sec. 303.402 Opportunity to examine records.

In accordance with the confidentiality procedures in the regulations under part B of the Act (34 CFR 300.560 through 300.576), the parents of a child eligible under this part must be afforded the opportunity to inspect and review records relating to evaluations and assessments, eligibility determinations, development and implementation of IFSPs, individual complaints dealing with the child, and any other area under this part involving records about the child and the child's family.

Sec. 303.403 Prior notice; native language.

(a) General. Written prior notice must be given to the parents of a child eligible under this part a reasonable time before a public agency or service provider proposes, or refuses, to initiate or change the identification, evaluation, or placement of the child, or the provision of appropriate early intervention services to the child and the child's family.

(b) Content of notice. The notice must be in sufficient detail to inform the parents about —

(1) The action that is being proposed or refused;

(2) The reasons for taking the action;

(3) All procedural safeguards that are available under §§ 303.401-303.460 of this part; and

(4) The State complaint procedures under §§ 303.510-303.512, including a description of how to file a complaint and the timelines under those procedures.

(c) Native language.

(1) The notice must be —

(i) Written in language understandable to the general public; and

(ii) Provided in the native language of the parents, unless it is clearly not feasible to do so.

(2) If the native language or other mode of communication of the parent is not a written language, the public agency, or designated service provider, shall take steps to ensure that —

(i) The notice is translated orally or by other means to the parent in the parent's native language or other mode of communication;

(ii) The parent understands the notice; and

(iii) There is written evidence that the requirements of this paragraph have been met.

(3) If a parent is deaf or blind, or has no written language, the mode of communication must be that normally used by the parent (such as sign language, braille, or oral communication).

Sec. 303.404 Parent consent.

(a) Written parental consent must be obtained before —

(1) Conducting the initial evaluation and assessment of a child under § 303.322; and

(2) Initiating the provision of early intervention services (see § 303.342(e)).

(b) If consent is not given, the public agency shall make reasonable efforts to ensure that the parent —

(1) Is fully aware of the nature of the evaluation and assessment or the services that would be available; and

(2) Understands that the child will not be able to receive the evaluation and assessment or services unless consent is given.

Sec. 303.405   Parent right to decline service.

The parents of a child eligible under this part may determine whether they, their child, or other family members will accept or decline any early intervention service under this part in accordance with State law, and may decline such a service after first accepting it, without jeopardizing other early intervention services under this part.

Sec. 303.406   Surrogate parents.

(a)   General. Each lead agency shall ensure that the rights of children eligible under this part are protected if —

(1) No parent (as defined in § 303.18) can be identified;

(2) The public agency, after reasonable efforts, cannot discover the whereabouts of a parent; or

(3) The child is a ward of the State under the laws of that State.

(b)   Duty of lead agency and other public agencies. The duty of the lead agency, or other public agency under paragraph (a) of this section, includes the assignment of an individual to act as a surrogate for the parent. This must include a method for —

(1) Determining whether a child needs a surrogate parent; and

(2) Assigning a surrogate parent to the child.

(c)   Criteria for selecting surrogates.

(1) The lead agency or other public agency may select a surrogate parent in any way permitted under State law.

(2) Public agencies shall ensure that a person selected as a surrogate parent —

(i) Has no interest that conflicts with the interests of the child he or she represents; and

(ii) Has knowledge and skills that ensure adequate representation of the child.

(d)   Non-employee requirement; compensation.

(1) A person assigned as a surrogate parent may not be —

(i) An employee of any State agency; or

(ii) A person or an employee of a person providing early intervention services to the child or to any family member of the child.

(2) A person who otherwise qualifies to be a surrogate parent under paragraph (d)(1) of this section is not an employee solely because he or she is paid by a public agency to serve as a surrogate parent.

(e)   Responsibilities. A surrogate parent may represent a child in all matters related to —

(1) The evaluation and assessment of the child;

(2) Development and implementation of the child's IFSPs, including annual evaluations and periodic reviews;

(3) The ongoing provision of early intervention services to the child; and

(4) Any other rights established under this part.

Mediation and Due Process Procedures for Parents and Children

Sec. 303.419   Mediation.

(a)   General. Each State shall ensure that procedures are established and implemented to allow parties to disputes involving any matter described in § 303.403(a) to resolve the disputes through a mediation process which, at a minimum, must be available whenever a hearing is requested under § 303.420. The lead agency may either use the mediation system established under Part B of the Act or establish its own system.

(b)   Requirements. The procedures must meet the following requirements:

(1) The procedures must ensure that the mediation process —

(i) Is voluntary on the part of the parties;

(ii) Is not used to deny or delay a parent's right to a due process hearing under § 303.420, or to deny any other rights afforded under Part C of the Act; and

(iii) Is conducted by a qualified and impartial mediator who is trained in effective mediation techniques.

(2) The State shall maintain a list of individuals who are qualified mediators and knowledgeable in laws and regulations relating to the provision of special education and related services.

(3) The State shall bear the cost of the mediation process, including the costs of meetings described in paragraph (c) of this section.

(4) Each session in the mediation process must be scheduled in a timely manner and must be held in a location that is convenient to the parties to the dispute.

(5) An agreement reached by the parties to the dispute in the mediation process must be set forth in a written mediation agreement.

(6) Discussions that occur during the mediation process must be confidential and may not be used as evidence in any subsequent due process hearings or civil proceedings, and the parties to the mediation process may be required to sign a confidentiality pledge prior to the commencement of the process.

(c)   Meeting to encourage mediation. A State may establish procedures to require parents who elect not to use the mediation process to meet, at a time and location convenient to the parents, with a disinterested party —

(1) Who is under contract with a parent training and information center or community parent resource center in the State established under sections 682 or 683 of the Act, or an appropriate alternative dispute resolution entity; and

(2) Who would explain the benefits of the mediation process and encourage the parents to use the process.

Sec. 303.420 Due process procedures.

Each system must include written procedures including procedures for mediation as described in § 303.419, for the timely administrative resolution of individual child complaints by parents concerning any of the matters in § 303.403(a). A State may meet this requirement by —

(a) Adopting the mediation and due process procedures in 34 CFR 300.506 through 300.512 and developing procedures that meet the requirements of § 303.425; or

(b) Developing procedures that —

(1) Meet the requirements in § 303.419 and §§ 303.421 through 303.425; and

(2) Provide parents a means of filing a complaint.

Sec. 303.421 Appointment of an impartial person.

(a) Qualifications and duties. An impartial person must be appointed to implement the complaint resolution process in this subpart. The person must —

(1) Have knowledge about the provisions of this part and the needs of, and services available for, eligible children and their families; and

(2) Perform the following duties:

(i) Listen to the presentation of relevant viewpoints about the complaint, examine all information relevant to the issues, and seek to reach a timely resolution of the complaint.

(ii) Provide a record of the proceedings, including a written decision.

(b) Definition of impartial.

(1) As used in this section, impartial means that the person appointed to implement the complaint resolution process —

(i) Is not an employee of any agency or other entity involved in the provision of early intervention services or care of the child; and

(ii) Does not have a personal or professional interest that would conflict with his or her objectivity in implementing the process.

(2) A person who otherwise qualifies under paragraph (b)(1) of this section is not an employee of an agency solely because the person is paid by the agency to implement the complaint resolution process.

Sec. 303.422 Parent rights in administrative proceedings.

(a) General. Each lead agency shall ensure that the parents of children eligible under this part are afforded the rights in paragraph (b) of this section in any administrative proceedings carried out under § 303.420.

(b) Rights. Any parent involved in an administrative proceeding has the right to —

(1) Be accompanied and advised by counsel and by individuals with special knowledge or

training with respect to early intervention services for children eligible under this part;

(2) Present evidence and confront, cross-examine, and compel the attendance of witnesses;

(3) Prohibit the introduction of any evidence at the proceeding that has not been disclosed to the parent at least five days before the proceeding;

(4) Obtain a written or electronic verbatim transcription of the proceeding; and

(5) Obtain written findings of fact and decisions.

Sec. 303.423   Convenience of proceedings; timelines.

(a) Any proceeding for implementing the complaint resolution process in this subpart must be carried out at a time and place that is reasonably convenient to the parents.

(b) Each lead agency shall ensure that, not later than 30 days after the receipt of a parent's complaint, the impartial proceeding required under this subpart is completed and a written decision mailed to each of the parties.

Sec. 303.424   Civil action.

Any party aggrieved by the findings and decision regarding an administrative complaint has the right to bring a civil action in State or Federal court under section 639(a)(1) of the Act.

Sec. 303.425   Status of a child during proceedings.

(a) During the pendency of any proceeding involving a complaint under this subpart, unless the public agency and parents of a child otherwise agree, the child must continue to receive the appropriate early intervention services currently being provided.

(b) If the complaint involves an application for initial services under this part, the child must receive those services that are not in dispute.

APPENDIX OF MAJOR CASES[1]

TABLE OF CONTENTS

PENNSYLVANIA ASSOCIATION FOR RETARDED CHILDREN, Nancy Beth Bowman, et al., Plaintiffs, v. COMMONWEALTH OF PENNSYLVANIA, David H. Kurtzman, et al.
334 F. Supp. 1257 (E.D. Pa. 1971)

Before ADAMS, CIRCUIT JUDGE, and MASTERSON and BRODERICK, DISTRICT JUDGES.

ORDER, INJUNCTIONS AND CONSENT AGREEMENT

And now, this 7th day of October, 1971, the parties having consented through their counsel to certain findings and conclusions and to the relief to be provided to the named plaintiffs and to the members of their class, the provisions of the Consent Agreement between the parties set out below are hereby approved and adopted and it is hereby so ordered.

And for the reasons set out below it is ordered that defendants . . . hereby are enjoined as follows:

(a)   from applying Section 1304 of the Public School Code of 1949, 24 Purd. Stat. Sec. 13-1304, so as to postpone or in any way to deny to any mentally retarded child access to a free public program of education and training;

(b)   from applying Section 1326 or Section 1330(2) of the School Code of 1949, 24 Purd.Stat. Secs. 13-1326, 13-1330(2) so as to postpone, to terminate or in any way to

---

[1] This is an edited version of these cases. Deletions to footnotes have been made without the use of ellipses. Footnote numbering has been retained. Internal citations have been edited without ellipses. Minor typographical errors have been corrected and formatting has been modified to conserve space. The cases have been listed in chronological order to provide the reader with a sense of the development of the law of special education over time.

deny to any mentally retarded child access to a free public program of education and training;

(c)   from applying Section 1371(1) of the School Code of 1949, 24 Purd.Stat. Sec. 13-1371(1) so as to deny to any mentally retarded child access to a free public program of education and training;

(d)   from applying Section 1376 of the School Code of 1949, 24 Purd.Stat. Sec. 13-1376, so as to deny tuition or tuition and maintenance to any mentally retarded person except on the same terms as may be applied to other exceptional children, including brain damaged children generally;

(e)   from denying homebound instruction under Section 1372(3) of the School Code of 1949, 24 Purd.Stat. Sec. 13-1372(3) to any mentally retarded child merely because no physical disability accompanies the retardation or because retardation is not a short-term disability.

(f)   from applying Section 1375 of the School Code of 1949, 24 Purd.Stat. Sec. 13-1375, so as to deny to any mentally retarded child access to a free public program of education and training;

(g)   to immediately re-evaluate the named plaintiffs, and to accord to each of them, as soon as possible but in no event later than October 13, 1971, access to a free public program of education and training appropriate to his learning capacities;

(h)   to provide, as soon as possible but in no event later than September 1, 1972, to every retarded person between the ages of six and twenty-one years as of the date of this Order and thereafter, access to a free public program of education and training appropriate to his learning capacities;

(i)   to provide, as soon as possible but in no event later than September 1, 1972, wherever defendants provide a pre-school program of education and training for children aged less than six years of age, access to a free public program of education and training appropriate to his learning capacities to every mentally retarded child of the same age.

* * *

CONSENT AGREEMENT
* * *

Now, therefore, this 7th of October 1971, the parties being desirous of effecting an amicable settlement of this action, the parties by their counsel agree, subject to the approval and Order of this Court, as follows:

I.

1. This action may and hereby shall be maintained by plaintiffs as a class action on behalf of all mentally retarded persons, residents of the Commonwealth of Pennsylvania, who have been, are being, or may be denied access to a free public program of education and training while they are, or were, less than twenty-one years of age.

It is expressly understood, subject to the provisions of Paragraph 44 below, that the immediate relief hereinafter provided shall be provided to those persons less than twenty-one years of age as of the date of the Order of the Court herein.

2. This action may and hereby shall be maintained against defendant school districts and intermediate units as a class action against all of the School Districts and Intermediate Units of the Commonwealth of Pennsylvania.

3. Pursuant to Rule 23, Fed.R.Civ.P., notice of the extent of the Consent Agreement and the proposed Order approving this Consent Agreement, in the form set out in Appendix A, shall be given as follows:

(a)   to the class of defendants, by the Secretary of Education, by mailing immediately a copy of this proposed Order and Consent Agreement to the Superintendent and the Director of Special Education of each School District and Intermediate Unit in the Commonwealth of Pennsylvania;

(b)   to the class of plaintiffs, (i) by the Pennsylvania Association for Retarded Children, by immediately mailing a copy of this proposed Order and Consent Agreement to each of its Chapters in fifty-four counties of Pennsylvania; (ii) by the Department of Justice, by causing an advertisement in the form set out in Appendix A, to be placed in one newspaper of general circulation in each County in the Commonwealth; and (iii) by delivery of a joint press release of the parties to the television and radio stations, newspapers, and wire services in the Commonwealth.

II.

4. Expert testimony in this action indicates that all mentally retarded persons are capable of benefiting from a program of education and training; that the greatest number of retarded persons, given such education and training, are capable of achieving self-sufficiency, and the remaining few, with such education and training, are capable of achieving some degree of self-care; that the earlier such education and training begins, the more thoroughly and the more efficiently a mentally retarded person will benefit from it; and, whether begun early or not, that a mentally retarded person can benefit at any point in his life and development from a program of education and training.

5. The Commonwealth of Pennsylvania has undertaken to provide a free public education to all of its children between the ages of six and twenty-one years, and, even more specifically, has undertaken to provide education and training for all of its exceptional children.

6. Having undertaken to provide a free public education to all of its children, including its exceptional children, the Commonwealth of Pennsylvania may not deny any mentally retarded child access to a free public program of education and training.

7. It is the Commonwealth's obligation to place each mentally retarded child in a free, public program of education and training appropriate to the child's capacity, within the context of a presumption that, among the alternative programs of education and training required by statute to be available, placement in a regular public school class is preferable to placement in a special public school class and placement in a special public school class is preferable to placement in any other type of program of education and training.

III.
Section 1304

8. Section 1304 of the School Code of 1949, as amended, 24 Purd.Stat. Sec. 13-1304, provides:

"Admission of beginners

The admission of beginners to the public schools shall be confined to the first two weeks of the annual school term in districts operating on an annual promotion basis, and to the first two weeks of either the first or the second semester of the school term to districts operating on a semi-annual promotion basis. Admission shall be limited to beginners who have attained the age of five years and seven months before the first day of September if they are to be admitted in the fall, and to those who have attained the age of five years and seven months before the first day of February if they are to be admitted at the beginning of the second semester. The board of school directors of any school district may admit beginners who are less than five years and seven months of age, in accordance with standards prescribed by the State Board of Education. The board of school directors may refuse to accept or retain beginners who have not attained a mental age of five years, as determined by the supervisor of special education or a properly certificated public school psychologist in accordance with standards prescribed by the State Board of Education.

"The term 'beginners,' as used in this section, shall mean any child that should enter the lowest grade of the primary school or the lowest primary class above the kindergarten level."

9. The [defendants] agree that they shall cease and desist from applying Section 1304 so as to postpone or in any way to deny access to a free public program of education and training to any mentally retarded child.

10. The Attorney General of the Commonwealth of Pennsylvania (hereinafter "the Attorney General") agrees to issue an Opinion declaring that Section 1304 means *only* that a school district may refuse to accept into or to retain in the lowest grade of the *regular* primary school or the lowest *regular* primary class above the kindergarten level, any child who has not attained a mental age of five years.

11. The Attorney General of the Commonwealth of Pennsylvania shall issue an Opinion thus construing Section 1304, and the State Board of Education (hereinafter "the Board") shall issue regulations to implement said construction and to supersede Sections 5-200 of the Pupil Attendance Regulations, copies of which Opinion and Regulations shall be filed with the Court and delivered to counsel for plaintiffs on or before October 25, 1971, and they shall be issued and promulgated respectively on or before October 27, 1971.

12. The aforementioned Opinion and Regulations shall (a) provide for notice and an opportunity for a hearing as set out in this Court's Order of June 18, 1971, before a child's admission as a beginner in the lowest grade of a regular primary school, or the lowest regular primary class above kindergarten, may be postponed; (b) require the automatic re-evaluation every two years of any educational assignment other than to a regular class, and (c) provide for an annual re-evaluation at the request of the child's parent or guardian, and (d) provide upon each such re-evaluation for notice and an opportunity for a hearing as set out in this Court's Order of June 18, 1971.

13. The aforementioned Opinion and Regulations shall also require the timely placement of any child whose admission to regular primary school or to the lowest regular primary class above kindergarten is postponed, or who is not retained in such school or class, in a free public program of education and training pursuant to Sections 1371 through 1382 of the School Code of 1949, as amended 24 Purd.Stat. Sec. 13-1371 through Sec. 13-1382.

Section 1326

14. Section 1326 of the School Code of 1949, as amended, 24 Purd.Stat. Sec. 13-1326, provides:

"Definitions

The term 'compulsory school age,' as hereinafter used, shall mean the period of a child's life from the time the child's parents elect to have the child enter school, which shall be not later than at the age of eight (8) years, until the age of seventeen (17) years. The term shall not include any child who holds a certificate of graduation from a regularly accredited senior high school."

15. The [Defendants] agree that they shall cease and desist from applying Section 1326 so as to postpone, to terminate, or in any way to deny access to a free public program of education and training to any mentally retarded child.

16. The Attorney General agrees to issue an Opinion declaring that Section 1326 means *only* that parents of a child have a compulsory duty while the child is between eight and seventeen years of age to assure his attendance in a program of education and training; and Section 1326 does not limit the ages between which a child must be granted access to a free, public program of education and training. Defendants are bound by Section 1301 of the School Code of 1949, 24 Purd.Stat. Sec. 13-1301, to provide free public education to all children six to twenty-one years of age. In the event that a parent elects to exercise the right of a child six through eight years and/or seventeen through twenty-one years of age to a free public education, defendants may not deny such child access to a program of education and training. Furthermore, if a parent does not discharge the duty of compulsory attendance with regard to any mentally retarded child between eight and seventeen years of age, defendants must and shall take those steps necessary to compel the child's attendance pursuant to Section 1327 of the School Code of 1949, 24 Purd.Stat. Sec. 13-1327, and related provisions of the School Code, and to the relevant regulations with regard to compulsory attendance promulgated by the Board.

17. The Attorney General shall issue an Opinion thus construing Section 1326, and related Sections, and the Board shall promulgate Regulations to implement said construction, copies of which Opinion and Regulations shall be filed with the Court and delivered to plaintiffs' counsel on or before October 25, 1971, and they shall be issued and promulgated respectively on or before October 27, 1971.

Section 1330(2)

18. Section 1330(2) of the School Code of 1949, as amended, 24 Purd.Stat. Sec. 13-1330(2) provides:

"Exceptions to compulsory attendance.

The provisions of this act requiring regular attendance shall not apply to any child who:

(2) Has been examined by an approved mental clinic or by a person certified as a public school psychologist or psychological examiner, and has been found to be unable to profit from further public school attendance, and who has been reported to the board of school directors and excused, in accordance with regulations prescribed by the State Board of Education."

19. The [Defendants] agree that they shall cease and desist from applying Section 1330(2) so as to terminate or in any way to deny access to a free public program of education and training to any mentally retarded child.

20. The Attorney General agrees to issue an Opinion declaring that Section 1330(2) means *only* that a parent may be excused from liability under the compulsory attendance provisions of the School Code when, with the approval of the local school board and the Secretary of Education and a finding by an approved clinic or public school psychologist or psychological examiner, the parent elects to withdraw the child from attendance. Section 1330(2) may not be invoked by defendants, contrary to the parents' wishes, to terminate or in any way to deny access to a free public program of education and training to any mentally retarded child. Furthermore, if a parent does not discharge the duty of compulsory attendance with regards to any mentally retarded child between eight and seventeen years of age, defendants must and shall take those steps necessary to compel the child's attendance pursuant to Section 1327 and related provisions of the School Code and to the relevant regulations with regard to compulsory attendance promulgated by the Board.

21. The Attorney General shall issue an Opinion so construing Section 1330(2) and related provisions and the Board shall promulgate Regulations to implement said construction and to supersede Section 5-400 of the Pupil Attendance Regulations, a copy of which Opinion and Regulations shall be filed with the Court and delivered to counsel for plaintiff on or before October 25, 1971, and they shall be issued and promulgated respectively on or before October 27, 1971.

Pre-School Education

22. Defendants . . . shall cease and desist from applying Section 1371(1) of the School Code of 1949, as amended, 24 Purd.Stat. Sec. 13-1371(1) so as to deny access to a free public program of education and training to any mentally retarded child, and they further agree that wherever the Department of Education through its instrumentalities, the School Districts and Intermediate Units, or the Department of Public Welfare through any of its instrumentalities provides a pre-school program of education and training to children below the age of six, they shall also provide a program of education and training appropriate to their learning capacities to all retarded children of the same age.

23. Section 1371(1) of the School Code of 1949, as amended, 24 Purd.Stat. Sec. 13-1371(1), provides:

"Definition of exceptional children; reports; examination

(1) The term 'exceptional children' shall mean children of school age who deviate from the average in physical, mental, emotional or social characteristics to such an extent that they require special educational facilities or services and shall include all children in detention homes."

24. The Attorney General agrees to issue an Opinion declaring that the phrase "children of school age" as used in Section 1371 means children aged six to twenty-one and also, whenever the Department of Education through any of its instrumentalities, the local School District, Intermediate Unit, or the Department of Public Welfare, through any of its instrumentalities, provides a pre-school program of education or training for children below the age of six, whether kindergarten or however so called, means all mentally retarded children who have reached the age less than six at which pre-school programs are available to others.

25. The Attorney General shall issue an Opinion thus construing Section 1371 and the Board shall issue regulations to implement said construction, copies of which Opinion and Regulations hall be filed with the Court and delivered to counsel for plaintiffs on or before October 25, 1971, and they shall be issued and promulgated respectively on or before October 27, 1971.

Tuition and Tuition and Maintenance

26. The [Defendants] shall cease and desist from applying Section 1376 of the School Code of 1949, as amended, 24 Purd.Stat. Sec. 13-1376, so as to deny tuition or tuition and maintenance to any mentally retarded person.

27. The Attorney General agrees to issue an Opinion, and the Council of Basic Education of the State Board of Education agrees to promulgate Regulations, construing the term "brain damage" as used in Section 1376 and as defined in the Board's "Criteria for Approval . . . of Reimbursement" so as to include thereunder all mentally retarded persons, thereby making available to them tuition for day school and tuition and maintenance for residential school up to the maximum sum available for day school or residential school, whichever provides the more appropriate program of education and training. Copies of the aforesaid Opinion and Regulations shall be filed with the Court and delivered to counsel for plaintiff on or before October 25, 1971, and they shall be issued and promulgated respectively on or before October 27, 1971.

28. Defendants may deny or withdraw payments of tuition or tuition and maintenance whenever the school district or intermediate unit in which a mentally retarded child resides provides a program of special education and training appropriate to the child's learning capacities into which the child may be placed.

29. The decision of defendants to deny or withdraw payments of tuition or tuition and maintenance shall be deemed a change in educational assignment as to which notice shall be given and an opportunity for a hearing afforded as set out in this Court's order of June 18, 1971.

Homebound Instruction

30. Section 1372(3) of the School Code of 1949, as amended, 24 Purd.Stat. Sec. 13-1372(3), provides in relevant part:

"Standards; plans; special classes or schools

(3) Special Classes or Schools Established and Maintained by School Districts.

*** If *** it is not feasible to form a special class in any district or to provide such education for any [exceptional] child in the public schools of the district, the board of school directors of the district shall secure such proper education and training outside the public schools of the district or in special institutions, or by providing for teaching the child in his home. ***"

31. The [Defendants] shall cease and desist from denying homebound instruction under Section 1372(3) to mentally retarded children merely because no physical disability accompanies the retardation or because retardation is not a short-term disability.

32. The Attorney General agrees to issue an Opinion declaring that a mentally retarded child, whether or not physically disabled, may receive homebound instruction and the State Board of Education and/or the Secretary of Education agrees to promulgate revised Regulations and forms in accord therewith, superseding the "Homebound Instruction Manual" (1970) insofar as it concerns mentally retarded children.

33. The aforesaid Opinion and Regulations shall also provide:

(a) that homebound instruction is the least preferable of the programs of education and training administered by the Department of Education and a mentally retarded child shall not be assigned to it unless it is the program most appropriate to the child's capacities;

(b) that homebound instruction shall involve education and training for at least five hours a week;

(c) that an assignment to homebound instruction shall be re-evaluated not less than every three months, and notice of the re-evaluation and an opportunity for a hearing thereon shall be accorded to the parent or guardian, as set out in the Order of this Court dated June 18, 1971;

34. Copies of the aforementioned Opinion and Regulations shall be filed with the Court and delivered to counsel for plaintiffs on or before October 25, 1971, and they shall be issued and promulgated respectively on or before October 27, 1971.

Section 1375

35. Section 1375 of the School Code of 1949, as amended, 24 Purd.Stat. Sec. 13-1375, provides:

"Uneducable children provided for by Department of Public Welfare

"The State Board of Education shall establish standards for temporary or permanent exclusion from the public school of children who are found to be uneducable and untrainable in the public schools. Any child who is reported by a person who is certified as a public school psychologist as being uneducable and untrainable in the public schools, may be reported by the board of school directors to the Superintendent of Public Instruction and when approved by him, in accordance with the standards of the State Board of Education, shall be certified to the Department of Public Welfare as a child who is uneducable and untrainable in the public schools. When a child is thus certified, the public schools shall be relieved of the obligation of providing education or training for such child. The Department of Public Welfare shall thereupon arrange for the care, training and supervision of such child in a manner not inconsistent with the laws governing mentally defective individuals."

36. Defendants the Commonwealth of Pennsylvania, the Secretary of Education, the State Board of Education, the named School Districts and Intermediate Units, on their own behalf and on behalf of all School Districts and Intermediate Units in the Commonwealth of Pennsylvania, and the Secretary of Public Welfare, each of them, for themselves, their officers, employees, agents and successors agree that they shall cease and desist from applying Section 1375 so as to deny access to a free public program of education and training to any mentally retarded child.

37. The Attorney General agrees to issue an Opinion declaring that since all children are capable of benefiting from a program of education and training, Section 1375 means that insofar as the Department of Public Welfare is charged to "arrange for the care, training and supervision" of a child certified to it, the Department of Public Welfare must provide a program of education and training appropriate to the capacities of that child.

38. The Attorney General agrees to issue an Opinion declaring that Section 1375 means that when it is found, on the recommendation of a public school psychologist and upon the approval of the local board of school directors and the Secretary of Education, as reviewed in the due process hearing as set out in the Order of this Court dated June 18, 1971, that a mentally retarded child would benefit more from placement in a program of education and training administered by the Department of Public Welfare than he would from any program of education and training administered by the Department of Education, he shall be certified to the Department of Public Welfare for placement in a program of education and training.

39. To assure that any program of education and training administered by the Department of Public Welfare shall provide education and training appropriate to a child's capacities the plan referred to in Paragraph 49 below shall specify, *inter alia*,

(a) the standards for hours of instruction, pupil-teacher ratios, curriculum, facilities, and teacher qualifications that shall be met in programs administered by the Department of Public Welfare;

(b) the standards which will qualify any mentally retarded person who completes a program administered by the Department of Public Welfare for a High School Certificate or a Certificate of Attendance as contemplated in Sections 8-132 and 8-133 of the Special Education Regulations;

(c) the reports which will be required in the continuing discharge by the Department of Education of its duty under Section 1302(1) of the Administrative Code of 1929, as amended, 71 P.S. Sec. 352(1), to inspect and to require reports of programs of education and training administered by the Department of Public Welfare, which reports shall include, for each child in such programs an annual statement of educational strategy (as defined in Section 8-123 of the Special Education Regulations) for the coming year and at the close of the year an evaluation of that strategy;

(d) that the Department of Education shall exercise the power under Section 1926 of the School Code of 1949, as amended, 24 Purd.Stat. Sec. 19-1926 to supervise the programs of education and training in all institutions wholly or partly supported by the Department of Public Welfare, and the procedures to be adopted therefor.

40. The Attorney General agrees to issue an Opinion so construing Section 1375 and the Board to promulgate Regulations implementing said construction, which Opinion and Regulations shall also provide:

(a) that the Secretary of Education shall be responsible for assuring that every mentally retarded child is placed in a program of education and training appropriate to his learning capacities, and to that end, by Rules of Procedure requiring that reports of the annual census and evaluation, under Section 1371(2) of the School Code of 1949, as amended, 24 Purd.Stat. 13-1371(2), be made to him, he shall be informed as to the identity, condition, and educational status of every mentally retarded child within the various school districts.

(b) that should it appear that the provisions of the School Code relating to the proper education and training of mentally retarded children have not been complied with or the needs of the mentally retarded child are not being adequately served in any program administered by the Department of Public Welfare, the Department of Education shall provide such education and training pursuant to Section 1372(5) of the School Code of 1949, as amended, 21 Purd.Stat. Sec. 13-1372(5).

(c) that the same right to notice and an opportunity for a hearing as is set out in the Order of this Court of June 18, 1971, shall be accorded on any change in educational assignment among the programs of education and training administered by the Department of Public Welfare.

(d) that not less than every two years the assignment of any mentally retarded child to a program of education and training administered by the Department of Public Welfare shall be re-evaluated by the Department of Education and upon such re-evaluation, notice and an opportunity to be heard shall be accorded as set out in the Order of this Court, dated June 18, 1971.

40. Copies of the aforesaid Opinion and Regulations shall be filed with the Court and delivered to counsel for plaintiffs on or before October 25, 1971, and they shall be issued and promulgated respectively on or before October 27, 1971.

IV.

41. Each of the named plaintiffs shall be immediately re-evaluated by defendants and, as soon as possible, but in no event later than October 13, 1971, shall be accorded access to a free public program of education and training appropriate to his learning capacities.

42. Every retarded person between the ages of six and twenty-one years as of the date of this Order and thereafter shall be provided access to a free public program of education and training appropriate to his capacities as soon as possible but in no event later than September 1, 1972.

43. Wherever defendants provide a pre-school program of education and training for children less than six years of age, whether kindergarten or howsoever called, every mentally retarded child of the same age as of the date of this Order and hereafter shall be provided access to a free public program of education and training appropriate to his capacities as soon

as possible but in no event later than September 1, 1972.

44. The parties explicitly reserve their right to hearing and argument on the question of the obligation of defendants to accord compensatory educational opportunity to members of the plaintiff class of whatever age who were denied access to a free public program of education and training without notice and without a due process hearing while they were aged six years to twenty-one years, for a period equal to the period of such wrongful denial.

45. To implement the aforementioned relief and to assure that it is extended to all members of the class entitled to it, Dr. Herbert Goldstein and Dennis E. Haggerty, Esquire are appointed Masters for the purpose of overseeing a process of identification, evaluation, notification, and compliance hereinafter described.

46. Notice of this Order and of the Order of June 18, 1971, in form to be agreed upon by counsel for the parties, shall be given by defendants to the parents and guardian of every mentally retarded person, and of every person thought by defendants to be mentally retarded, of the ages specified in Paragraphs 42 and 43 above, now resident in the Commonwealth of Pennsylvania, who while he was aged four years to twenty-one years was not accorded access to a free public program of education and training, whether as a result of exclusion, postponement, excusal, or in any other fashion, formal or informal.

47. Within thirty days of the date of this Order, defendants shall formulate and shall submit to the Masters for their approval a satisfactory plan to identify, locate, evaluate and give notice of all the persons described in the foregoing paragraph, and to identify all persons described in Paragraph 44, which plan shall include, but not be limited to, a search of the records of the local school districts, of the intermediate units, of County MH/MR units, of the State Schools and Hospitals, including the waiting lists for admission thereto, and of interim care facilities, and, to the extent necessary, publication in newspapers and the use of radio and television in a manner calculated to reach the persons described in the foregoing paragraph. A copy of the proposed plan shall be delivered to counsel for plaintiffs who shall be accorded a right to be heard thereon.

48. Within ninety days of the date of this Order, defendants shall identify and locate all persons described in paragraph 46 above, give them notice and provide for their evaluation, and shall report to the Masters the names, circumstances, the educational histories and the educational diagnosis of all persons so identified.

49. By February 1, 1972, defendants shall formulate and submit to the Masters for their approval a plan, to be effectuated by September 1, 1972, to commence or recommence a free public program of education and training for all mentally retarded persons described in Paragraph 46 above and aged between four and twenty-one years as of the date of this Order, and for all mentally retarded persons of such ages hereafter. The plan shall specify the range of programs of education and training, their kind and number, necessary to provide an appropriate program of education and training to all mentally retarded children, where they shall be conducted, arrangements for their financing, and, if additional teachers are found to be necessary, the plan shall specify recruitment, hiring, and training arrangements. The plan shall specify such additional standards and procedures, including but not limited to those specified in Paragraph 39 above, as may be consistent with this Order and necessary to its effectuation. A copy of the proposed plan will be delivered to counsel for plaintiffs who shall be accorded a right to be heard thereon.

50. If by September 1, 1972, any local school district or intermediate unit is not providing a

free public education to all mentally retarded persons 4 to 21 years of age within its responsibility, the Secretary of Education, pursuant to Section 1372(5) of the Public School Code of 1949, 24 Purd.Stat. 1372(5) shall directly provide, maintain, administer, supervise, and operate programs for the education and training of these children.

51. The Masters shall hear any members of the plaintiff class who may be aggrieved in the implementation of this Order.

52. The Masters shall be compensated by defendants.

53. This Court shall retain jurisdiction of the matter until it has heard the final report of the Masters on or before October 15, 1972.

* * *

APPENDIX A (omitted)

Peter MILLS et al., Plaintiffs, v. BOARD OF EDUCATION OF the DISTRICT OF COLUMBIA et al., Defendants.

348 F. Supp. 866 (D.D.C. 1972)

MEMORANDUM OPINION, JUDGMENT AND DECREE

WADDY, DISTRICT JUDGE.

This is a civil action brought on behalf of seven children of school age by their next friends in which they seek a declaration of rights and to enjoin the defendants from excluding them from the District of Columbia Public Schools and/or denying them publicly supported education and to compel the defendants to provide them with immediate and adequate education and educational facilities in the public schools or alternative placement at public expense. They also seek additional and ancillary relief to effectuate the primary relief. They allege that although they can profit from an education either in regular classrooms with supportive services or in special classes adopted to their needs, they have been labeled as behavioral problems, mentally retarded, emotionally disturbed or hyperactive, and denied admission to the public schools or excluded therefrom after admission, with no provision for alternative educational placement or periodic review. The action was certified as a class action under Rule 23(b)(1) and (2) of Federal Rules of Civil Procedure by order of the Court dated December 17, 1971.

The defendants are the Board of Education of the District of Columbia and its members, the Superintendent of Schools for the District of Columbia and subordinate school officials, the Commissioner of the District of Columbia and certain subordinate officials and the District of Columbia.

THE PROBLEM

The genesis of this case is found (1) in the failure of the District of Columbia to provide publicly supported education and training to plaintiffs and other "exceptional" children, members of their class, and (2) the excluding, suspending, expelling, reassigning and transferring of "exceptional" children from regular public school classes without affording them due process of law.

The problem of providing special education for "exceptional" children (mentally retarded, emotionally disturbed, physically handicapped, hyperactive and other children with behavioral problems) is one of major proportions in the District of Columbia. The precise number of such children cannot be stated because the District has continuously failed to comply with Section 31-208 of the District of Columbia Code which requires a census of all children aged 3 to 18 in the District to be taken. Plaintiffs estimate that there are ". . . 22,000 retarded, emotionally disturbed, blind, deaf, and speech or learning disabled children, and perhaps as many as 18,000 of these children are not being furnished with programs of specialized education." According to data prepared by the Board of Education, Division of Planning, Research and Evaluation, the District of Columbia provides publicly supported special education programs of various descriptions to at least 3880 school age children. However, in a 1971 report to the Department of Health, Education and Welfare, the District of Columbia Public Schools admitted that an estimated 12,340 handicapped children were not to be served in the 1971-72 school year.

Each of the minor plaintiffs in this case qualifies as an "exceptional" child.

Plaintiffs allege in their complaint and defendants admit as follows:

PETER MILLS is twelve years old, black, and a committed dependent ward of the District of Columbia resident at Junior Village. He was excluded from the Brent Elementary School on March 23, 1971, at which time he was in the fourth grade. Peter allegedly was a 'behavior problem' and was recommended and approved for exclusion by the principal. Defendants have not provided him with a full hearing or with a timely and adequate review of his status. Furthermore, Defendants have failed to provide for his reenrollment in the District of Columbia Public Schools or enrollment in private school. On information and belief, numerous other dependent children of school attendance age at Junior Village are denied a publicly-supported education. Peter remains excluded from any publicly-supported education.

DUANE BLACKSHEARE is thirteen years old, black, resident at Saint Elizabeth's Hospital, Washington, D. C., and a dependent committed child. He was excluded from the Giddings Elementary School in October, 1967, at which time he was in the third grade. Duane allegedly was a "behavior problem." Defendants have not provided him with a full hearing or with a timely and adequate review of his status. Despite repeated efforts by his mother, Duane remained largely excluded from all publicly-supported education until February, 1971. Education experts at the Child Study Center examined Duane and found him to be capable of returning to regular class if supportive services were provided. Following several articles in the Washington Post and Washington Star, Duane was placed in a regular seventh grade classroom on a two-hour a day basis without any catch-up assistance and without an evaluation or diagnostic interview of any kind. Duane has remained on a waiting list for a tuition grant and is now excluded from all publicly-supported education.

GEORGE LIDDELL, JR., is eight years old, black, resident with his mother, Daisy Liddell, at 601 Morton Street, N. W., Washington, D. C., and an AFDC recipient. George has never attended public school because of the denial of his application to the Maury Elementary School on the ground that he required a special class. George allegedly was retarded. Defendants have not provided him with a full hearing or with a timely and adequate review of his status. George remains excluded from all publicly-supported education, despite a medical opinion that he is capable of profiting from schooling, and despite his mother's efforts to secure a tuition grant from Defendants.

STEVEN GASTON is eight years old, black, resident with his mother, Ina Gaston, at 714 9th Street, N. E., Washington, D. C. and unable to afford private instruction. He has been excluded from the Taylor Elementary School since September, 1969, at which time he was in the first grade. Steven allegedly was slightly brain-damaged and hyperactive, and was excluded because he wandered around the classroom. Defendants have not provided him with a full hearing or with a timely and adequate review of his status. Steven was accepted in the Contemporary School, a private school, provided that tuition was paid in full in advance. Despite the efforts of his parents, Steven has remained on a waiting list for the requisite tuition grant from Defendant school system and excluded from all publicly-supported education.

MICHAEL WILLIAMS is sixteen years old, black, resident at Saint Elizabeth's Hospital, Washington, D. C., and unable to afford private instruction. Michael is epileptic and allegedly slightly retarded. He has been excluded from the Sharpe Health School since October, 1969, at which time he was temporarily hospitalized. Thereafter Michael was excluded from school because of health problems and school absences. Defendants have not provided him with a full hearing or with a timely and adequate review of his status. Despite his mother's efforts, and his attending physician's medical opinion that he could attend school, Michael has remained on a waiting list for a tuition grant and excluded from all publicly-supported education.

JANICE KING is thirteen years old, black, resident with her father, Andrew King, at 233 Anacostia Avenue, N. E., Washington, D. C., and unable to afford private instruction. She has been denied access to public schools since reaching compulsory school attendance age, as a result of the rejection of her application, based on the lack of an appropriate educational program. Janice is brain-damaged and retarded, with right hemiplegia, resulting from a childhood illness. Defendants have not provided her with a full hearing or with a timely and adequate review of her status. Despite repeated efforts by her parents, Janice has been excluded from all publicly-supported education.

JEROME JAMES is twelve years old, black, resident with his mother, Mary James, at 2512 Ontario Avenue, N. W., Washington, D. C., and an AFDC recipient. Jerome is a retarded child and has been totally excluded from public school. Defendants have not given him a full hearing or a timely and adequate review of his status. Despite his mother's efforts to secure either public school placement or a tuition grant, Jerome has remained on a waiting list for a tuition grant and excluded from all publicly supported education.

Although all of the named minor plaintiffs are identified as Negroes the class they represent is not limited by their race. They sue on behalf of and represent all other District of Columbia residents of school age who are eligible for a free public education and who have been, or may be, excluded from such education or otherwise deprived by defendants of access to publicly supported education.

Minor plaintiffs are poor and without financial means to obtain private instruction. There has been no determination that they may not benefit from specialized instruction adapted to their needs. Prior to the beginning of the 1971-72 school year minor plaintiffs, through their representatives, sought to obtain publicly supported education and certain of them were assured by the school authorities that they would be placed in programs of publicly supported education and certain others would be recommended for special tuition grants at private schools. However, none of the plaintiff children were placed for the 1971 Fall term and they continued to be entirely excluded from all publicly supported education. After thus trying unsuccessfully to obtain relief from the Board of Education the plaintiffs filed this action on September 24, 1971.

THERE IS NO GENUINE ISSUE OF MATERIAL FACT

Congress has decreed a system of publicly supported education for the children of the District of Columbia. The Board of Education has the responsibility of administering that system in accordance with law and of providing such publicly supported education to all of the children of the District, including these "exceptional" children.

Defendants have admitted in these proceedings that they are under an affirmative duty to provide plaintiffs and their class with publicly supported education suited to each child's needs, including special education and tuition grants, and also, a constitutionally adequate prior hearing and periodic review. They have also admitted that they failed to supply plaintiffs with such publicly supported education and have failed to afford them adequate prior hearing and periodic review. On December 20, 1971 the plaintiffs and defendants agreed to and the Court signed an interim stipulation and order which provided in part as follows:

Upon consent and stipulation of the parties, it is hereby ORDERED that:

1. Defendants shall provide plaintiffs Peter Mills, Duane Blacksheare, Steven Gaston and Michael Williams with a publicly-supported education suited to their (plaintiffs') needs by January 3, 1972.

2. Defendants shall provide counsel for plaintiffs, by January 3, 1972, a list showing, for every child of school age then known not to be attending a publicly-supported educational program because of suspension, expulsion, exclusion, or any other denial of placement, the name of the child's parent or guardian, the child's name, age, address and telephone number, the date of his suspension, expulsion, exclusion or denial of placement and, without attributing a particular characteristic to any specific child, a breakdown of such list, showing the alleged causal characteristics for such nonattendance and the number of children possessing such alleged characteristics.

3. By January 3, 1972, defendants shall initiate efforts to identify remaining members of the class not presently known to them, and also by that date, shall notify counsel for plaintiffs of the nature and extent of such efforts. Such efforts shall include, at a minimum, a system-wide survey of elementary and secondary schools, use of the mass written and electronic media, and a survey of District of Columbia agencies who may have knowledge pertaining to such remaining members of the class. By February 1, 1972, defendants shall provide counsel for plaintiffs with the names, addresses and telephone numbers of such remaining members of the class then known to them.

4. Pending further action by the Court herein, the parties shall consider the selection and compensation of a master for determination of special questions arising out of this action with regard to the placement of children in a publicly-supported educational program suited to their needs.

On February 9, 1972, the Board of Education passed a Resolution which included the following:

Special Education

1. All vacant authorized special education positions, whether in the regular, Impact Aid, or other Federal budgets, shall be filled as rapidly as possible within the capability of the Special Education Department. Regardless of the capability of the Department to fill vacant positions, all funds presently appropriated or allotted for special education, whether in the regular, Impact Aid, or other Federal budgets, shall be spent solely for special education.

2. The Board requests the Corporation Counsel to ask the United States District Court for an extension of time within which to file a response to plaintiffs' motion for

summary judgment in Mills v. Board of Education on the grounds that (a) the Board intends to enter into a consent judgment declaring the rights of children in the District of Columbia to a public education; and (b) the Board needs time (not in excess of 30 days) to obtain from the Associate Superintendent for Special Education a precise projection on a monthly basis the cost of fulfilling those budgets.

3. The Board directs the Rules Committee to devise as soon as possible for the purpose of Mills v. Board of Education rules defining and providing for due process and fair hearings; and requests the Corporation Counsel to lend such assistance to the Board as may be necessary in devising such rules in a form whichwill meet the requirements of Mills v. Board of Education.

4. It is the intention of the Board to submit for approval by the Court in Mills v. Board of Education a Memorandum of Understanding setting forth a comprehensive plan for the education, treatment and care of physically or mentally impaired children in the age range from three to twenty-one years. It is hoped that the various other District of Columbia agencies concerned will join with the Board in the submission of this plan.

It is the further intention of the Board to establish procedures to implement the finding that all children can benefit from education and, have a right to it, by providing for comprehensive health and psychological appraisal of children and the provision for each child of any special education which he may need. The Board will further require that no change in the kind of education provided for a child will be made against his wishes or the wishes of his parent or guardian unless he has been accorded a full hearing on the matter consistent with due process."

Defendants failed to comply with that consent order and there is now pending before the Court a motion of the plaintiffs to require defendants to show cause why they should not be held in contempt for such failure to comply.

On January 21, 1972 the plaintiffs filed a motion for summary judgment and a proposed order and decree for implementation of the proposed judgment and requested a hearing. On March 1, 1972 the defendants responded as follows:

1. The District of Columbia and its officers who are named defendants to this complaint consent to the entrance of a judgment declaring the rights of the plaintiff class to the effect prayed for in the complaint, as specified below, such rights to be prospectively effective as of March 1, 1972:

That no child eligible for a publicly supported education in the District of Columbia public schools shall be excluded from a regular public school assignment by a Rule, policy, or practice of the Board of Education of the District of Columbia or its agents unless such child is provided (a) adequate alternative educational services suited to the child's needs, which may include special education or tuition grants, and (b) a constitutionally adequate prior hearing and periodic review of the child's status, progress, and the adequacy of any educational alternative.

It is submitted that the entrance of a declaratory judgment to this effect renders plaintiffs' motion for summary judgment moot.

2. For response to plaintiffs' motion for a hearing, defendants respectfully request that this Court hold a hearing as soon as practicable at which defendants will present

a plan to implement the above declaratory judgment and at which the Court may decide whether further relief is appropriate.

The Court set the date of March 24, 1972, for the hearing that both parties had requested and specifically ordered the defendants to submit a copy of their proposed implementation plan no later than March 20, 1972.

On March 24, 1972, the date of the hearing, the defendants not only had failed to submit their implementation plan as ordered but were also continuing in their violation of the provisions of the Court's order of December 20, 1971. At the close of the hearing on March 24, 1972, the Court found that there existed no genuine issue of a material fact; orally granted plaintiffs' motion for summary judgment, and directed defendants to submit to the Court any proposed plan they might have on or before March 31, 1972. The defendants, other than Cassell, failed to file any proposal within the time directed. However, on April 7, 1972, there was sent to the Clerk of the Court on behalf of the Board of Education and its employees who are defendants in this case the following documents:

1. A proposed form of Order to be entered by the Court.

2. An abstract of a document titled "A District of Columbia Plan for Identification, Assessment, Evaluation, and Placement of Exceptional Children".

3. A document titled "A District of Columbia Plan for Identification, Assessment, Evaluation, and Placement of Exceptional Children".

4. Certain Attachments and Appendices to this Plan.

The letter accompanying the documents contained the following paragraph:

"These documents express the position of the Board of Education and its employees as to what should be done to implement the judgment of the Honorable Joseph C. Waddy, the District Judge presiding over this civil action. The contents of these documents have not been endorsed by the other defendants in this case."

None of the other defendants have filed a proposed order or plan. Nor has any of them adopted the proposal submitted by the Board of Education. Throughout these proceedings it has been obvious to the Court that the defendants have no common program or plan for the alleviation of the problems posed by this litigation and that this lack of communication, cooperation and plan is typical and contributes to the problem.

PLAINTIFFS ARE ENTITLED TO RELIEF

Plaintiffs' entitlement to relief in this case is clear. The applicable statutes and regulations and the Constitution of the United States require it.

Statutes and Regulations

Section 31-201 of the District of Columbia Code requires that:

"Every parent, guardian, or other person residing [permanently or temporarily] in the District of Columbia who has custody or control of a child between the ages of seven and sixteen years shall cause said child to be regularly instructed in a public school or in a private or parochial school or instructed privately during the period of each year in which the public schools of the District of Columbia are in session . . ."

Under Section 31-203, a child may be "excused" from attendance only when ". . . . upon examination ordered by . . . [the Board of Education of the District of Columbia], [the child] is found to be unable mentally or physically to profit from attendance at school: Provided, however, That if such examination shows that such child may benefit from specialized instruction adapted to his needs, he shall attend upon such instruction."

Failure of a parent to comply with Section 31-201 constitutes a criminal offense. D.C.Code 31-207. The Court need not belabor the fact that requiring parents to see that their children attend school under pain of criminal penalties presupposes that an educational opportunity will be made available to the children. The Board of Education is required to make such opportunity available. It has adopted rules and regulations consonant with the statutory direction. Chapter XIII of the Board Rules contains the following:

1.1-All children of the ages hereinafter prescribed who are bona fide residents of the District of Columbia are entitled to admission and free tuition in the Public Schools of the District of Columbia, subject to the rules, regulations, and orders of the Board of Education and the applicable statutes.

14.1-Every parent, guardian, or other person residing permanently or temporarily in the District of Columbia who has custody or control of a child residing in the District of Columbia between the ages of seven and sixteen years shall cause said child to be regularly instructed in a public school or in a private or parochial school or instructed privately during the period of each year in which the Public Schools of the District of Columbia are in session, provided that instruction given in such private or parochial school, or privately, is deemed reasonably equivalent by the Board of Education to the instruction given in the Public Schools.

14.3-The Board of Education of the District of Columbia may, upon written recommendation of the Superintendent of Schools, issue a certificate excusing from attendance at school a child who, upon examination by the Department of Pupil Appraisal, Study and Attendance or by the Department of Public Health of the District of Columbia, is found to be unable mentally or physically to profit from attendance at school: Provided, however, that if such examination shows that such child may benefit from specialized instruction adapted to his needs, he shall be required to attend such classes.

Thus the Board of Education has an obligation to provide whatever specialized instruction that will benefit the child. By failing to provide plaintiffs and their class the publicly supported specialized education to which they are entitled, the Board of Education violates the above statutes and its own regulations.

The Constitution-Equal Protection and Due Process

The Supreme Court in Brown v. Board of Education, 347 U.S. 483, 493 (1954) stated:

Today, education is perhaps the most important function of state and local governments. Compulsory school attendance laws and the great expenditures for education both demonstrate our recognition of the importance of education to our democratic society. It is required in the performance of our most basic public responsibilities, even service in the armed forces. It is the very foundation of good citizenship. Today it is a principal instrument in awakening the child to cultural values, in preparing him for later professional training, and in helping him to adjust normally to his environment. In these days, it is doubtful that any child may reasonably be expected to succeed in life if he is denied the opportunity of an education. *Such an opportunity, where the state has undertaken to provide it, is a right which must be made available to all on equal terms.*(emphasis supplied)

Bolling v. Sharpe, 347 U.S. 497 (1954) decided the same day as *Brown*, applied the *Brown* rationale to the District of Columbia public schools by finding that:

"Segregation in public education is not reasonably related to any proper governmental objective, and thus it imposes on Negro children of the District of Columbia a burden than constitutes an arbitrary deprivation of their liberty in violation of the Due Process Clause."

In Hobson v. Hansen, 269 F.Supp. 401 (D.D.C.1967) Circuit Judge J. Skelly Wright considered the pronouncements of the Supreme Court in the intervening years and stated that ". . . the Court has found the due process clause of the Fourteenth Amendment elastic enough to embrace not only the First and Fourth Amendments, but the self-incrimination clause of the Fifth, the speedy trial, confrontation and assistance of counsel clauses of the Sixth, and the cruel and unusual clause of the Eighth." (269 F.Supp. 401 at 493, citations omitted). Judge Wright concluded "(F)rom these considerations the court draws the conclusion that the doctrine of equal educational opportunity-the equal protection clause in its application to public school education-is in its full sweep a component of due process binding on the District under the due process clause of the Fifth Amendment."

In Hobson v. Hansen, *supra*, Judge Wright found that denying poor public school children educational opportunities equal to that available to more affluent public school children was violative of the Due Process Clause of the Fifth Amendment. *A fortiori*, the defendants' conduct here, denying plaintiffs and their class not just an equal publicly supported education but all publicly supported education while providing such education to other children, is violative of the Due Process Clause.

Not only are plaintiffs and their class denied the publicly supported education to which they are entitled many are suspended or expelled from regular schooling or specialized instruction or reassigned without any prior hearing and are given no periodic review thereafter. Due process of law requires a hearing prior to exclusion, termination of classification into a special program.

The Defense

The Answer of the defendants to the Complaint contains the following:

These defendants say that it is impossible to afford plaintiffs the relief they request unless:

(a) The Congress of the United States appropriates millions of dollars to improve special education services in the District of Columbia; or

(b) These defendants divert millions of dollars from funds already specifically appropriated for other educational services in order to improve special educational services. These defendants suggest that to do so would violate an Act of Congress and would be inequitable to children outside the alleged plaintiff class.

This Court is not persuaded by that contention.

The defendants are required by the Constitution of the United States, the District of Columbia Code, and their own regulations to provide a publicly-supported education for these "exceptional" children. Their failure to fulfill this clear duty to include and retain these children in the public school system, or otherwise provide them with publicly-supported education, and their failure to afford them due process hearing and periodical review, cannot be excused by the claim that there are insufficient funds. In Goldberg v. Kelly, 397 U.S. 254 (1969) the Supreme Court, in a case that involved the right of a welfare recipient to a hearing before termination of his benefits, held that Constitutional rights must be afforded citizens despite the greater expense involved. The Court stated at page 266, that "the State's interest that his [welfare recipient] payments not be erroneously terminated, clearly outweighs the State's competing concern to prevent any increase in its fiscal and administrative burdens." Similarly the District of Columbia's interest in educating the excluded children clearly must outweigh its interest in preserving its financial resources. If sufficient funds are not available to finance all of the services and programs that are needed and desirable in the system then the available funds must be expended equitably in such a manner that no child is entirely excluded from a publicly supported education consistent with his needs and ability to benefit therefrom. The inadequacies of the District of Columbia Public School System whether occasioned by insufficient funding or administrative inefficiency, certainly cannot be permitted to bear more heavily on the "exceptional" or handicapped child than on the normal child.

IMPLEMENTATION OF JUDGMENT

This Court has pointed out that Section 31-201 of the District of Columbia Code requires that every person residing in the District of Columbia ". . . who has custody or control of a child between the ages of seven and sixteen years shall cause said child to be regularly instructed in a public school or in a private or parochial school or instructed privately . . . ." It is the responsibility of the Board of Education to provide the opportunities and facilities for such instruction.

The Court has determined that the Board likewise has the responsibility for implementation of the judgment and decree of this Court in this case. Section 31-103 of the District of Columbia Code clearly places this responsibility upon the Board. It provides:

"The Board shall determine all questions of general policy relating to the schools, shall appoint the executive officers hereinafter provided for, define their duties, and direct expenditures."

The lack of communication and cooperation between the Board of Education and the other defendants in this action shall not be permitted to deprive plaintiffs and their class of publicly supported education.

* * *

If the District of Columbia Government and the Board of Education cannot jointly develop the procedures and programs necessary to implement this Court's order then it shall be the responsibility of the Board of Education to present the irresolvable issue to the Court for resolution in a timely manner so that plaintiffs and their class may be afforded their constitutional and statutory rights. If any dispute should arise between the defendants which requires for its resolution a degree of expertise in the field of education not possessed by the Court, the Court will appoint a special master pursuant to the provisions of Rule 53 of the Federal Rules of Civil Procedure to assist the Court in resolving the issue.

Inasmuch as the Board of Education has presented for adoption by the Court a proposed "Order and Decree" embodying its present plans for the identification of "exceptional" children and providing for their publicly supported education, including a time table, and further requiring the Board to formulate and file with the Court a more comprehensive plan, the Court will not now appoint a special master as was requested by plaintiffs. Despite the defendants' failure to abide by the provisions of the Court's previous orders in this case and despite the defendants' continuing failure to provide an education for these children, the Court is reluctant to arrogate to itself the responsibility of administering this or any other aspect of the Public School System of the District of Columbia through the vehicle of a special master. Nevertheless, inaction or delay on the part of the defendants, or failure by the defendants to implement the judgment and decree herein within the time specified therein will result in the immediate appointment of a special master to oversee and direct such implementation under the direction of this Court. The Court will include as a part of its judgment the proposed "Order and Decree" submitted by the Board of Education, as modified in minor part by the Court, and will retain jurisdiction of the cause to assure prompt implementation of the judgment. Plaintiffs' motion to require certain defendants to show cause why they should not be adjudged in contempt will be held in abeyance for 45 days.

JUDGMENT AND DECREE

Plaintiffs having filed their verified complaint seeking an injunction and declaration of rights as set forth more fully in the verified complaint and the prayer for relief contained therein; and having moved this Court for summary judgment pursuant to Rule 56 of the Federal Rules of Civil Procedure, and this Court having reviewed the record of this cause including plaintiffs' Motion, pleadings, affidavits, and evidence and arguments in support thereof, and defendants' affidavit, pleadings, and evidence and arguments in support thereof, and the proceedings of pre-trial conferences on December 17, 1971, and January 14, 1972, it is hereby ordered, adjudged and decreed that summary judgment in favor of plaintiffs and against defendants be, and hereby is, granted, and judgment is entered in this action as follows:

1. That no child eligible for a publicly supported education in the District of Columbia public schools shall be excluded from a regular public school assignment by a Rule, policy, or practice of the Board of Education of the District of Columbia or its agents unless such child is provided (a) adequate alternative educational services suited to the child's needs, which may include special education or tuition grants, and (b) a constitutionally adequate prior hearing and periodic review of the child's status, progress, and the adequacy of any educational alternative.

2. The defendants, their officers, agents, servants, employees, and attorneys and all those in active concert or participation with them are hereby enjoined from maintaining, enforcing or otherwise continuing in effect any and all rules, policies and practices which exclude plaintiffs and the members of the class they represent from a regular public school assignment without providing them at public expense (a) adequate and immediate alternative education or tuition grants, consistent with their needs, and (b) a constitutionally adequate prior hearing and periodic review of their status, progress and the adequacy of any educational alternatives; and it is further ORDERED that:

3. The District of Columbia shall provide to each child of school age a free and suitable publicly-supported education regardless of the degree of the child's mental, physical or emotional disability or impairment. Furthermore, defendants shall not exclude any child resident in the District of Columbia from such publicly-supported education on the basis of a claim of insufficient resources.

4. Defendants shall not suspend a child from the public schools for disciplinary reasons for any period in excess of two days without affording him a hearing pursuant to the provisions of Paragraph 13.f., below, and without providing for his education during the period of any such suspension.

5. Defendants shall provide each identified member of plaintiff class with a publicly-supported education suited to his needs within thirty (30) days of the entry of this order. With regard to children who later come to the attention of any defendant, within twenty (20) days after he becomes known, the evaluation (case study approach) called for in paragraph 9 below shall be completed and within 30 days after completion of the evaluation, placement shall be made so as to provide the child with a publicly supported education suited to his needs.

In either case, if the education to be provided is not of a kind generally available during the summer vacation, the thirty-day limit may be extended for children evaluated during summer months to allow their educational programs to begin at the opening of school in September.

6. Defendants shall cause announcements and notices to be placed in the Washington Post, Washington Star-Daily News, and the Afro-American, in all issues published for a three week period commencing within five (5) days of the entry of this order, and thereafter at quarterly intervals, and shall cause spot announcements to be made on television and radio stations for twenty (20) consecutive days, commencing within five (5) days of the entry of this order, and thereafter at quarterly intervals, advising residents of the District of Columbia that all children, regardless of any handicap or other disability, have a right to a publicly-supported education suited to their needs, and informing the parents or guardians of such children of the procedures required to enroll their children in an appropriate educational program. Such announcements should include the listing of a special answering service telephone number to be established by defendants in order to (a) compile the names, addresses, phone numbers of such children who are presently not attending school and (b) provide further information to their parents or guardians as to the procedures required to enroll their children in an appropriate educational program.

7. Within twenty-five (25) days of the entry of this order, defendants shall file with the Clerk of this Court, an up-to-date list showing, for every additional identified child, the name of the child's parent or guardian, the child's name, age, address and telephone number, the date of his suspension, expulsion, exclusion or denial of placement and, without attributing a particular characteristic to any specific child, a breakdown of such list, showing the alleged causal characteristics for such nonattendance (e. g., educable mentally retarded, trainable mentally retarded, emotionally disturbed, specific learning disability, crippled/other health impaired, hearing impaired, visually impaired, multiple handicapped) and the number of children possessing each such alleged characteristic.

8. Notice of this order shall be given by defendants to the parent or guardian of each child resident in the District of Columbia who is now, or was during the 1971-72 school year or the 1970-71 school year, excluded, suspended or expelled from publicly-supported educational programs or otherwise denied a full and suitable publicly-supported education for any period

in excess of two days. Such notice shall include a statement that each such child has the right to receive a free educational assessment and to be placed in a publicly-supported educational program suited to his needs. Such notice shall be sent by registered mail within five (5) days of the entry of this order, or within five (5) days after such child first becomes known to any defendant. Provision of notification for non-reading parents or guardians will be made.

9. a. Defendants shall utilize public or private agencies to evaluate the educational needs of all identified "exceptional" children and, within twenty (20) days of the entry of this order, shall file with the Clerk of this Court their proposal for each individual placement in a suitable educational program, including the provision of compensatory educational services where required.

b. Defendants, within twenty (20) days of the entry of this order, shall, also submit such proposals to each parent or guardian of such child, respectively, along with a notification that if they object to such proposed placement within a period of time to be fixed by the parties or by the Court, they may have their objection heard by a Hearing Officer in accordance with procedures required in Paragraph 13.e., below.

10. a. Within forty-five (45) days of the entry of this order, defendants shall file with the Clerk of the Court, with copy to plaintiffs' counsel, a comprehensive plan which provides for the identification, notification, assessment, and placement of class members. Such plan shall state the nature and extent of efforts which defendants have undertaken or propose to undertake to

(1) describe the curriculum, educational objectives, teacher qualifications, and ancillary services for the publicly-supported educational programs to be provided to class members; and,

(2) formulate general plans of compensatory education suitable to class members in order to overcome the present effects of prior educational deprivations,

(3) institute any additional steps and proposed modifications designed to implement the matters decreed in paragraph 5 through 7 hereof and other requirements of this judgment.

11. The defendants shall make an interim report to this Court on their performance within forty-five (45) days of the entry of this order. Such report shall show:

(1) The adequacy of Defendants' implementation of plans to identify, locate, evaluate and give notice to all members of the class.

(2) The number of class members who have been placed, and the nature of their placements.

(3) The number of contested hearings before the Hearing Officers, if any, and the findings and determinations resulting therefrom.

12. Within forty-five (45) days of the entry of this order, defendants shall file with this Court a report showing the expunction from or correction of all official records of any plaintiff with regard to past expulsions, suspensions, or exclusions effected in violation of the procedural rights set forth in Paragraph 13 together with a plan for procedures pursuant to which parents, guardians, or their counsel may attach to such students' records any clarifying or explanatory information which the parent, guardian or counsel may deem appropriate.

13. Hearing Procedures.

a. Each member of the plaintiff class is to be provided with a publicly-supported educational program suited to his needs, within the context of a presumption that among the alternative programs of education, placement in a regular public school class with appropriate ancillary services is preferable to placement in a special school class.

b. Before placing a member of the class in such a program, defendants shall notify his parent or guardian of the proposed educational placement, the reasons therefore and the right to a hearing before a Hearing Officer if there is an objection to the placement proposed. Any such hearing shall be held in accordance with the provisions of Paragraph 13.e., below

c. Hereinafter, children who are residents of the District of Columbia and are thought by any of the defendants, or by officials, parents or guardians, to be in need of a program of special education, shall neither be placed in, transferred from or to, nor denied placement in such a program unless defendants shall have first notified their parents or guardians of such proposed placement, transfer or denial, the reasons therefore, and of the right to a hearing before a Hearing Officer if there is an objection to the placement, transfer or denial of placement. Any such hearings shall be held in accordance with the provisions of Paragraph 13.e., below.

d. Defendants shall not, on grounds of discipline, cause the exclusion, suspension, expulsion, postponement, interschool transfer, or any other denial of access to regular instruction in the public schools to any child for more than two days without first notifying the child's parent or guardian of such proposed action, the reasons therefore, and of the hearing before a Hearing Officer in accordance with the provisions of Paragraph 13.f., below.

e. Whenever defendants take action regarding a child's placement, denial of placement, or transfer, as described in Paragraphs 13.b. or 13.c., above, the following procedures shall be followed.

(1) Notice required hereinbefore shall be given in writing by registered mail to the parent or guardian of the child.

(2) Such notice shall:

(a) describe the proposed action in detail;

(b) clearly state the specific and complete reasons for the proposed action, including the specification of any tests or reports upon which such action is proposed;

(c) describe any alternative educational opportunities available on a permanent or temporary basis;

(d) inform the parent or guardian of the right to object to the proposed action at a hearing before the Hearing Officer;

(e) inform the parent or guardian that the child is eligible to receive, at no charge, the services of a federally or locally funded diagnostic center for an independent medical, psychological and educational evaluation and shall specify the name, address and telephone number of an appropriate local diagnostic center;

(f) inform the parent or guardian of the right to be represented at the hearing by legal counsel; to examine the child's school records before the hearing, including any tests or reports upon which the proposed action may be based, to present evidence, including expert medical, psychological and educational testimony; and, to confront and cross-examine any school official, employee, or agent of the school district or public department who may have evidence upon which the proposed action was based.

(3) The hearing shall be at a time and place reasonably convenient to such parent or guardian.

(4) The hearing shall be scheduled not sooner than twenty (20) days waivable by parent or child, nor later than forty-five (45) days after receipt of a request from the parent or guardian.

(5) The hearing shall be a closed hearing unless the parent or guardian requests an open hearing.

(6) The child shall have the right to a representative of his own choosing, including legal counsel. If a child is unable, through financial inability, to retain counsel, defendants shall advise child's parents or guardians of available voluntary legal assistance including the Neighborhood Legal Services Organization, the Legal Aid Society, the Young Lawyers Section of the D. C. Bar Association, or from some other organization.

(7) The decision of the Hearing Officer shall be based solely upon the evidence presented at the hearing.

(8) Defendants shall bear the burden of proof as to all facts and as to the appropriateness of any placement, denial of placement or transfer.

(9) A tape recording or other record of the hearing shall be made and transcribed and, upon request, made available to the parent or guardian or his representative.

(10) At a reasonable time prior to the hearing, the parent or guardian, or his counsel, shall be given access to all public school system and other public office records pertaining to the child, including any tests or reports upon which the proposed action may be based.

(11) The independent Hearing Officer shall be an employee of the District of Columbia, but shall not be an officer, employee or agent of the Public School System.

(12) The parent or guardian, or his representative, shall have the right to have the attendance of any official, employee or agent of the public school system or any public employee who may have evidence upon which the proposed action may be based and to confront, and to cross-examine any witness testifying for the public school system.

(13) The parent or guardian, or his representative, shall have the right to present evidence and testimony, including expert medical, psychological or educational testimony.

(14) Within thirty (30) days after the hearing, the Hearing Officer shall render a decision in writing. Such decision shall include findings of fact and conclusions of law and shall be filed with the Board of Education and the Department of Human Resources and sent by registered mail to the parent or guardian and his counsel.

(15) Pending a determination by the Hearing Officer, defendants shall take no action described in Paragraphs 13.b. or 13.c., above, if the child's parent or guardian objects to such action. Such objection must be in writing and postmarked within five (5) days of the date of receipt of notification hereinabove described.

f. Whenever defendants propose to take action described in Paragraph 13.d., above, the following procedures shall be followed.

(1) Notice required hereinabove shall be given in writing and shall be delivered in person or by registered mail to both the child and his parent or guardian.

(2) Such notice shall

(a) describe the proposed disciplinary action in detail, including the duration thereof;

(b) state specific, clear and full reasons for the proposed action, including the specification of the alleged act upon which the disciplinary action is to be based and the reference to the regulation subsection under which such action is proposed;

(c) describe alternative educational opportunities to be available to the child during the proposed suspension period;

(d) inform the child and the parent or guardian of the time and place at which the hearing shall take place;

(e) inform the parent or guardian that if the child is thought by the parent or guardian to require special education services, that such child is eligible to receive, at no charge, the services of a public or private agency for a diagnostic medical, psychological or educational evaluation;

(f) inform the child and his parent or guardian of the right to be represented at the hearing by legal counsel; to examine the child's school records before the hearing, including any tests or reports upon which the proposed action may be based; to present evidence of his own; and to confront and cross-examine any witnesses or any school officials, employees or agents who may have evidence upon which the proposed action may be based.

(3) The hearing shall be at a time and place reasonably convenient to such parent or guardian.

(4) The hearing shall take place within four (4) school days of the date upon which written notice is given, and may be postponed at the request of the child's parent or guardian for no more than five (5) additional school days where necessary for preparation.

(5) The hearing shall be a closed hearing unless the child, his parent or guardian requests an open hearing.

(6) The child is guaranteed the right to a representative of his own choosing, including legal counsel. If a child is unable, through financial inability, to retain counsel, defendants shall advise child's parents or guardians of available voluntary legal assistance including the Neighborhood Legal Services Organization, the Legal Aid Society, the Young Lawyers Section of the D. C. Bar Association, or from some other organization.

(7) The decision of the Hearing Officer shall be based solely upon the evidence presented at the hearing.

(8) Defendants shall bear the burden of proof as to all facts and as to the appropriateness of any disposition and of the alternative educational opportunity to be provided during any suspension.

(9) A tape recording or other record of the hearing shall be made and transcribed and, upon request, made available to the parent or guardian or his representative.

(10) At a reasonable time prior to the hearing, the parent or guardian, or the child's counsel or representative, shall be given access to all records of the public school system and any other public office pertaining to the child, including any tests or reports upon which the proposed action may be based.

(11) The independent Hearing Officer shall be an employee of the District of Columbia, but shall not be an officer, employee or agent of the Public School System.

(12) The parent or guardian, or the child's counsel or representative, shall have the right to have the attendance of any public employee who may have evidence upon which the proposed action may be based and to confront and to cross-examine any witness testifying for the public school system.

(13) The parent or guardian, or the child's counsel or representative, shall have the right to present evidence and testimony.

(14) Pending the hearing and receipt of notification of the decision, there shall be no change in the child's educational placement unless the principal (responsible to the Superintendent) shall warrant that the continued presence of the child in his current program would endanger the physical well-being of himself or others. In such exceptional cases, the principal shall be responsible for insuring that the child receives some form of educational assistance and/or diagnostic examination during the interim period prior to the hearing.

(15) No finding that disciplinary action is warranted shall be made unless the Hearing Officer first finds, by clear and convincing evidence, that the child committed a prohibited act upon which the proposed disciplinary action is based. After this finding has been made, the Hearing Officer shall take such disciplinary action as he shall deem appropriate. This action shall not be more severe than that recommended by the school official initiating the suspension proceedings.

(16) No suspension shall continue for longer than ten (10) school days after the date of the hearing, or until the end of the school year, whichever comes first. In such cases, the principal (responsible to the Superintendent) shall be responsible for insuring that the child receives some form of educational assistance and/or diagnostic examination during the suspension period.

(17) If the Hearing Officer determines that disciplinary action is not warranted, all school records of the proposed disciplinary action, including those relating to the incidents upon which such proposed action was predicated, shall be destroyed.

(18) If the Hearing Officer determines that disciplinary action is warranted, he shall give written notification of his findings and of the child's right to appeal his decision to the Board of Education, to the child, the parent or guardian, and the counsel or representative of the child, within three (3) days of such determination.

(19) An appeal from the decision of the Hearing Officer shall be heard by the Student Life and Community Involvement Committee of the Board of Education which shall provide the child and his parent or guardian with the opportunity for an oral hearing, at which the child may be represented by legal counsel, to review the findings of the Hearing Officer. At the conclusion of such hearing, the Committee shall determine the appropriateness of and may modify such decision. However, in no event may such Committee impose added or more severe restrictions on the child.

14. Whenever the foregoing provisions require notice to a parent or guardian, and the child in question has no parent or duly appointed guardian, notice is to be given to any adult with whom the child is actually living, as well as to the child himself, and every effort will be made to assure that no child's rights are denied for lack of a parent or duly appointed guardian. Again provision for such notice to non-readers will be made.

15. Jurisdiction of this matter is retained to allow for implementation, modification and enforcement of this Judgment and Decree as may be required.

Norval GOSS et al., Appellants, v. Eileen LOPEZ et al.
419 U.S. 565 (1975)

MR. JUSTICE WHITE delivered the opinion of the Court.

This appeal by various administrators of the Columbus, Ohio, Public School System (CPSS) challenges the judgment of a three-judge federal court, declaring that appellees — various high school students in the CPSS — were denied due process of law contrary to the command of the Fourteenth Amendment in that they were temporarily suspended from their high schools without a hearing either prior to suspension or within a reasonable time thereafter, and enjoining the administrators to remove all references to such suspensions from the students' records.

I

Ohio law, Rev.Code Ann. § 3313.64 (1972), provides for free education to all children between the ages of six and 21. Section 3313.66 of the Code empowers the principal of an Ohio public school to suspend a pupil for misconduct for up to 10 days or to expel him. In either case, he must notify the student's parents within 24 hours and state the reasons for his action. A pupil who is expelled, or his parents, may appeal the decision to the Board of Education and in connection therewith shall be permitted to be heard at the board meeting. The Board may reinstate in pupil following the hearing. No similar procedure is provided in § 3313.66 or any other provision of state law for a suspended student. Aside from a regulation tracking the statute, at the time of the imposition of the suspensions in this case the CPSS itself had not issued any written procedure applicable to suspensions. Nor, so far as the record reflects, had any of the individual high schools involved in this case. Each, however, had formally or informally described the conduct for which suspension could be imposed.

The nine named appellees, each of whom alleged that he or she had been suspended from public high school in Columbus for up to 10 days without a hearing pursuant to § 3313.66, filed an action under 42 U.S.C. § 1983 against the Columbus Board of Education and various administrators of the CPSS. The complaint sought a declaration that § 3313.66 was unconstitutional in that it permitted public school administrators to deprive plaintiffs of their rights to an education without a hearing of any kind, in violation of the procedural due process component of the Fourteenth Amendment. It also sought to enjoin the public school officials from issuing future suspensions pursuant to § 3313.66 and to require them to remove references to the past suspensions from the records of the students in question.

The proof below established that the suspensions arose out of a period of widespread student unrest in the CPSS during February and March 1971. Six of the named plaintiffs, Rudolph Sutton, Tyrone Washington, Susan Cooper, Deborah Fox, Clarence Byars, and Bruce Harris, were students at the Marion-Franklin High School and were each suspended for 10 days on account of disruptive or disobedient conduct committed in the presence of the school administrator who ordered the suspension. One of these, Tyrone Washington, was among a group of students demonstrating in the school auditorium while a class was being conducted there. He was ordered by the school principal to leave, refused to do so, and was suspended. Rudolph Sutton, in the presence of the principal, physically attacked a police officer who was attempting to remove Tyrone Washington from the auditorium. He was immediately suspended. The other four Marion-Franklin students were suspended for similar conduct. None was given a hearing to determine the operative facts underlying the suspension, but each, together with his or her parents, was offered the opportunity to attend a conference, subsequent to the effective date of the suspension, to discuss the student's future.

Two named plaintiffs, Dwight Lopez and Betty Crome, were students at the Central High School and McGuffey Junior High School, respectively. The former was suspended in connection with a disturbance in the lunchroom which involved some physical damage to school property. Lopez testified that at least 75 other students were suspended from his school on the same day. He also testified below that he was not a party to the destructive conduct but was instead an innocent bystander. Because no one from the school testified with regard to this incident, there is no evidence in the record indicating the official basis for concluding otherwise. Lopez never had a hearing.

Betty Crome was present at a demonstration at a high school other than the one she was attending. There she was arrested together with others, taken to the police station, and released without being formally charged. Before she went to school on the following day, she was notified that she had been suspended for a 10-day period. Because no one from the school testified with respect to this incident, the record does not disclose how the McGuffey Junior High School principal went about making the decision to suspend Crome, nor does it disclose on what information the decision was based. It is clear from the record that no hearing was ever held.

There was no testimony with respect to the suspension of the ninth named plaintiff, Carl Smith. The school files were also silent as to his suspension, although as to some, but not all, of the other named plaintiffs the files contained either direct references to their suspensions or copies of letters sent to their parents advising them of the suspension.

On the basis of this evidence, the three-judge court declared that plaintiffs were denied due process of law because they were "suspended without hearing prior to suspension or within a reasonable time thereafter," and that Ohio Rev.Code Ann. § 3313.66 (1972) and regulations issued pursuant thereto were unconstitutional in permitting such suspensions. It was ordered that all references to plaintiffs' suspensions be removed from school files.

Although not imposing upon the Ohio school administrators any particular disciplinary procedures and leaving them "free to adopt regulations providing for fair suspension procedures which are consonant with the educational goals of their schools and reflective of the characteristics of their school and locality," the District Court declared that there were "minimum requirements of notice and a hearing prior to suspension, except in emergency situations." In explication, the court stated that relevant case authority would: (1) permit "[i]mmediate removal of a student whose conduct disrupts the academic atmosphere of the school, endangers fellow students, teachers or school officials, or damages property"; (2) require notice of suspension proceedings to be sent to the students' parents within 24 hours of the decision to conduct them; and (3) require a hearing to be held, with the student present, within 72 hours of his removal. Finally, the court stated that, with respect to the nature of the hearing, the relevant cases required that statements in support of the charge be produced, that the student and others be permitted to make statements in defense or mitigation, and that the school need not permit attendance by counsel.

The defendant school administrators have appealed the three-judge court's decision. Because the order below granted plaintiffs' request for an injunction-ordering defendants to expunge their records-this Court has jurisdiction of the appeal pursuant to 28 U.S.C. § 1253. We affirm.

II

At the outset, appellants contend that because there is no constitutional right to an education at public expense, the Due Process Clause does not protect against expulsions from the public school system. This position misconceives the nature of the issue and is refuted by prior decisions. The Fourteenth Amendment forbids the State to deprive any person of life, liberty, or property without due process of law. Protected interests in property are normally "not created by the Constitution. Rather, they are created and their dimensions are defined" by an independent source such as state statutes or rules entitling the citizen to certain benefits. *Board of Regents v. Roth*, 408 U.S. 564, 577 (1972).

Accordingly, a state employee who under state law, or rules promulgated by state officials, has a legitimate claim of entitlement to continued employment absent sufficient cause for discharge may demand the procedural protections of due process. So may welfare recipients who have statutory rights to welfare as long as they maintain the specified qualifications. *Goldberg v. Kelly*, 397 U.S. 254 (1970). *Morrissey v. Brewer*, 408 U.S. 471 (1972), applied the limitations of the Due Process Clause to governmental decisions to revoke parole, although a parolee has no constitutional right to that status. In like vein was *Wolff v. McDonnell*, 418 U.S. 539 (1974), where the procedural protections of the Due Process Clause were triggered by official cancellation of a prisoner's good-time credits accumulated under state law, although those benefits were not mandated by the Constitution.

Here, on the basis of state law, appellees plainly had legitimate claims of entitlement to a public education. Ohio Rev.Code Ann. §§ 3313.48 and 3313.64 (1972 and Supp.1973) direct local authorities to provide a free education to all residents between five and 21 years of age, and a compulsory-attendance law requires attendance for a school year of not less than 32 weeks. Ohio Rev.Code Ann. § 3321.04 (1972). It is true that § 3313.66 of the Code permits school principals to suspend students for up to 10 days; but suspensions may not be imposed without any grounds whatsoever. All of the schools had their own rules specifying the grounds for expulsion or suspension. Having chosen to extend the right to an education to people of appellees' class generally, Ohio may not withdraw that right on grounds of misconduct absent, fundamentally fair procedures to determine whether the misconduct has occurred. *Arnett v. Kennedy, supra* at 164, (Powell, J., concurring), 171(White, J., concurring and dissenting), 206 (Marshall, J., dissenting).

Although Ohio may not be constitutionally obligated to establish and maintain a public school system, it has nevertheless done so and has required its children to attend. Those young people do not "shed their constitutional rights" at the schoolhouse door. *Tinker v. Des Moines Independent Community School Dist.*, 393 U.S. 503, 506 (1969). "The Fourteenth Amendment, as now applied to the States, protects the citizen against the State itself and all of its creatures-Boards of Education not excepted." *West Virginia Board of Education v. Barnette*, 319 U.S. 624, 637 (1943). The authority possessed by the State to prescribe and enforce standards of conduct in its schools, although concededly very broad, must be exercised consistently with constitutional safeguards. Among other things, the State is constrained to recognize a student's legitimate entitlement to a public education as a property interest which is protected by the Due Process Clause and which may not be taken away for misconduct without adherence to the minimum procedures required by that Clause.

The Due Process Clause also forbids arbitrary deprivations of liberty. "Where a person's good name, reputation, honor, or integrity is at stake because of what the government is doing to him," the minimal requirements of the Clause must be satisfied. School authorities here suspended appellees from school for periods of up to 10 days based on charges of misconduct. If sustained and recorded, those charges could seriously damage the students' standing with their fellow pupils and their teachers as well as interfere with later opportunities for higher education and employment. It is apparent that the claimed right of the State to determine unilaterally and without process whether that misconduct has occurred immediately collides with the requirements of the Constitution.

Appellants proceed to argue that even if there is a right to a public education protected by the Due Process Clause generally, the Clause comes into play only when the State subjects a student to a "severe detriment or grievous loss." The loss of 10 days, it is said, is neither severe nor grievous and the Due Process Clause is therefore of no relevance. Appellants' argument is again refuted by our prior decisions; for in determining 'whether due process requirements apply in the first place, we must look not to the "weight" but to the nature of the interest at stake." *Board of Regents v. Roth, supra,* at 570-571. Appellees were excluded from school only temporarily, it is true, but the length and consequent severity of a deprivation, while another factor to weigh in determining the appropriate form of hearing, "is not decisive of the basic right" to a hearing of some kind. *Fuentes v. Shevin,* 407 U.S. 67, 86 (1972). The Court's view has been that as long as a property deprivation is not de minimis, its gravity is irrelevant to the question whether account must be taken of the Due Process Clause. A 10-day suspension from school is not de minimis in our view and may not be imposed in complete disregard of the Due Process Clause.

A short suspension is, of course, a far milder deprivation than expulsion. But, "education is perhaps the most important function of state and local governments," *Brown v. Board of Education,* 347 U.S. 483, 493 (1954), and the total exclusion from the educational process for more than a trivial period, and certainly if the suspension is for 10 days, is a serious event in the life of the suspended child. Neither the property interest in educational benefits temporarily denied nor the liberty interest in reputation, which is also implicated, is so insubstantial that suspensions may constitutionally be imposed by any procedure the school chooses, no matter how arbitrary.

III

"Once it is determined that due process applies, the question remains what process is due." *Morrissey v. Brewer,* 408 U.S., at 481. We turn to that question, fully realizing as our cases regularly do that the interpretation and application of the Due Process Clause are intensely practical matters and that "(t)he very nature of due process negates any concept of inflexible procedures universally applicable to every imaginable situation." *Cafeteria Workers v. McElroy,* 367 U.S. 886, 895 (1961). We are also mindful of our own admonition: "Judicial interposition in the operation of the public school system of the Nation raises problems requiring care and restraint. . . . By and large, public education in our Nation is committed to the control of state and local authorities." *Epperson v. Arkansas,* 393 U.S. 97, 104 (1968).

There are certain bench marks to guide us, however. *Mullane v. Central Hanover Trust Co.,* 339 U.S. 306 (1950), a case often invoked by later opinions, said that "(m)any controversies have raged about the cryptic and abstract words of the Due Process Clause but there can be no doubt that at a minimum they require that deprivation of life, liberty or property by adjudication be preceded by notice and opportunity for hearing appropriate to the nature of the case." Id., at 313, 70 S.Ct. at 657. "The fundamental requisite of due process of law is the opportunity to be heard," *Grannis v. Ordean*, 234 U.S. 385, 394 (1914), a right that "has little reality or worth unless one is informed that the matter is pending and can choose for himself whether to . . . contest." *Mullane v. Central Hanover Trust Co., supra*, 339 U.S. at 314. At the very minimum, therefore, students facing suspension and the consequent interference with a protected property interest must be given some kind of notice and afforded some kind of hearing. "Parties whose rights are to be affected are entitled to be heard; and in order that they may enjoy that right they must first be notified." *Baldwin v. Hale*, 1 Wall. 223, 233 (1864).

It also appears from our cases that the timing and content of the notice and the nature of the hearing will depend on appropriate accommodation of the competing interests involved. *Cafeteria Workers v. McElroy, supra*, 367 U.S. at 895; *Morrissey v. Brewer, supra*, 408 U.S. at 481. The student's interest is to avoid unfair or mistaken exclusion from the educational process, with all of its unfortunate consequences. The Due Process Clause will not shield him from suspensions properly imposed, but it disserves both his interest and the interest of the State if his suspension is in fact unwarranted. The concern would be mostly academic if the disciplinary process were a totally accurate, unerring process, never mistaken and never unfair. Unfortunately, that is not the case, and no one suggests that it is. Disciplinarians, although proceeding in utmost good faith, frequently act on the reports and advice of others; and the controlling facts and the nature of the conduct under challenge are often disputed. The risk of error is not at all trivial, and it should be guarded against if that may be done without prohibitive cost or interference with the educational process.

The difficulty is that our schools are vast and complex. Some modicum of discipline and order is essential if the educational function is to be performed. Events calling for discipline are frequent occurrences and sometimes require immediate, effective action. Suspension is considered not only to be a necessary tool to maintain order but a valuable educational device. The prospect of imposing elaborate hearing requirements in every suspension case is viewed with great concern, and many school authorities may well prefer the untrammeled power to act unilaterally, unhampered by rules about notice and hearing. But it would be a strange disciplinary system in an educational institution if no communication was sought by the disciplinarian with the student in an effort to inform him of his dereliction and to let him tell his side of the story in order to make sure that an injustice is not done. "[F]airness can rarely be obtained by secret, one-sided determination of facts decisive of rights. . . ." "Secrecy is not congenial to truth-seeking and self-righteousness gives too slender an assurance of rightness. No better instrument has been devised for arriving at truth than to give a person in jeopardy of serious loss notice of the case against him and opportunity to meet it." *Joint Anti-Fascist Committee v. McGrath, supra*, 341 U.S., at 170, 172-173 (Frankfurter, J., concurring).

We do not believe that school authorities must be totally free from notice and hearing requirements if their schools are to operate with acceptable efficiency. Students facing temporary suspension have interests qualifying for protection of the Due Process Clause, and due process requires, in connection with a suspension of 10 days or less, that the student be given oral or written notice of the charges against him and, if he denies them, an explanation of the evidence the authorities have and an opportunity to present his side of the story. The Clause requires at least these rudimentary precautions against unfair or mistaken findings of misconduct and arbitrary exclusion from school.

There need be no delay between the time "notice" is given and the time of the hearing. In the great majority of cases the disciplinarian may informally discuss the alleged misconduct with the student minutes after it has occurred. We hold only that, in being given an opportunity to explain his version of the facts at this discussion, the student first be told what he is accused of doing and what the basis of the accusation is. Lower courts which have addressed the question of the nature of the procedures required in short suspension cases have reached the same conclusion. *Tate v. Board of Education*, 453 F.2d 975, 979 (8th Cir. 1972); Vail v. Board of Education, 354 F.Supp. 592, 603 (D.N.H. 1973). Since the hearing may occur almost immediately following the misconduct, it follows that as a general rule notice and hearing should precede removal of the student from school. We agree with the District Court, however, that there are recurring situations in which prior notice and hearing cannot be insisted upon. Students whose presence poses a continuing danger to persons or property or an ongoing threat of disrupting the academic process may be immediately removed from school. In such cases, the necessary notice and rudimentary hearing should follow as soon as practicable, as the District Court indicated.

In holding as we do, we do not believe that we have imposed procedures on school disciplinarians which are inappropriate in a classroom setting. Instead we have imposed requirements which are, if anything, less than a fair-minded school principal would impose upon himself in order to avoid unfair suspensions. Indeed, according to the testimony of the principal of Marion-Franklin High School, that school had an informal procedure, remarkably similar to that which we now require, applicable to suspensions generally but which was not followed in this case. Similarly, according to the most recent memorandum applicable to the entire CPSS, see n. 1, *supra*, school principals in the CPSS are now required by local rule to provide at least as much as the constitutional minimum which we have described.

We stop short of construing the Due Process Clause to require, countrywide, that hearings in connection with short suspensions must afford the student the opportunity to secure counsel, to confront and cross-examine witnesses supporting the charge, or to call his own witnesses to verify his version of the incident. Brief disciplinary suspensions are almost countless. To impose in each such case even truncated trial-type procedures might well overwhelm administrative facilities in many places and, by diverting resources, cost more than it would save in educational effectiveness. Moreover, further formalizing the suspension process and escalating its formality and adversary nature may not only make it too costly as a regular disciplinary tool but also destroy its effectiveness as part of the teaching process.

On the other hand, requiring effective notice and informal hearing permitting the student to give his version of the events will provide a meaningful hedge against erroneous action. At least the disciplinarian will be alerted to the existence of disputes about facts and arguments about cause and effect. He may then determine himself to summon the accuser, permit cross-examination, and allow the student to present his own witnesses. In more difficult cases, he may permit counsel. In any event, his discretion will be more informed and we think the risk of error substantially reduced.

Requiring that there be at least an informal give-and-take between student and discipli-narian, preferably prior to the suspension, will add little to the factfinding function where the disciplinarian himself has witnessed the conduct forming the basis for the charge. But things are not always as they seem to be, and the student will at least have the opportunity to characterize his conduct and put it in what he deems the proper context.

We should also make it clear that we have addressed ourselves solely to the short suspension, not exceeding 10 days. Longer suspensions or expulsions for the remainder of the school term, or permanently, may require more formal procedures. Nor do we put aside the possibility that in unusual situations, although involving only a short suspension, something more than the rudimentary procedures will be required.

IV

The District Court found each of the suspensions involved here to have occurred without a hearing, either before or after the suspension, and that each suspension was therefore invalid and the statute unconstitutional insofar as it permits such suspensions without notice or hearing. Accordingly, the judgment is

Affirmed.

Mr. Justice POWELL, with whom THE CHIEF JUSTICE, Mr. Justice BLACKMUN, and Mr. Justice REHNQUIST join, dissenting.

* * *

One of the more disturbing aspects of today's decision is its indiscriminate reliance upon the judiciary, and the adversary process, as the means of resolving many of the most routine problems arising in the classroom. In mandating due process procedures the Court misapprehends the reality of the normal teacher-pupil relationship. There is an ongoing relationship, one in which the teacher must occupy many roles — educator, adviser, friend, and, at times, parent-substitute. It is rarely adversary in nature except with respect to the chronically disruptive or insubordinate pupil whom the teacher must be free to discipline without frustrating formalities.

The Ohio statute, providing as it does for due notice both to parents and the Board, is compatible with the teacher-pupil relationship and the informal resolution of mistaken disciplinary action. We have relied for generations upon the experience, good faith and dedication of those who staff our public schools, and the nonadversary means of airing grievances that always have been available to pupils and their parents. One would have thought before today's opinion that this informal method of resolving differences was more compatible with the interests of all concerned than resort to any constitutionalized procedure, however blandly it may be defined by the Court.

* * *

No one can foresee the ultimate frontiers of the new "thicket" the Court now enters. Today's ruling appears to sweep within the protected interest in education a multitude of discretionary decisions in the educational process. Teachers and other school authorities are required to make many decisions that may have serious consequences for the pupil. They must decide, for example, how to grade the student's work, whether a student passes or fails a course, whether he is to be promoted, whether he is required to take certain subjects, whether he may be excluded from interscholastic athletics or other extracurricular activities, whether he may be removed from one school and sent to another, whether he may be bused long distances when available schools are nearby, and whether he should be placed in a "general," "vocational," or "college-preparatory" track.

In these and many similar situations claims of impairment of one's educational entitlement identical in principle to those before the Court today can be asserted with equal or greater justification. Likewise, in many of these situations, the pupil can advance the same types of speculative and subjective injury given critical weight in this case. The District Court, relying upon generalized opinion evidence, concluded that a suspended student may suffer psychological injury in one or more of the ways set forth in the margin below. The Court appears to adopt this rationale.

It hardly need be said that if a student, as a result of a day's suspension, suffers "a blow" to his "self esteem," "feels powerless," views "teachers with resentment," or feels "stigmatized by his teachers," identical psychological harms will flow from many other routine and necessary school decisions. The student who is given a failing grade, who is not promoted, who is excluded from certain extracurricular activities, who is assigned to a school reserved for children of less than average ability, or who is placed in the "vocational" rather than the "college preparatory" track, is unlikely to suffer any less psychological injury than if he were suspended for a day for a relatively minor infraction.

If, as seems apparent, the Court will now require due process procedures whenever such routine school decisions are challenged, the impact upon public education will be serious indeed. The discretion and judgment of federal courts across the land often will be substituted for that of the 50-state legislatures, the 14,000 school boards, and the 2,000,000 teachers who heretofore have been responsible for the administration of the American public school system. If the Court perceives a rational and analytically sound distinction between the discretionary decision by school authorities to suspend a pupil for a brief period, and the types of discretionary school decisions described above, it would be prudent to articulate it in today's opinion. Otherwise, the federal courts should prepare themselves for a vast new role in society.

IV

Not so long ago, state deprivations of the most significant forms of state largesse were not thought to require due process protection on the ground that the deprivation resulted only in the loss of a state-provided "benefit." *E.g., Bailey v. Richardson*, 182 F.2d 46 (1950), aff'd by an equally divided Court, 341 U.S. 918 (1951). In recent years the Court, wisely in my view, has rejected the "wooden distinction" between "rights" and "privileges," *Board of Regents v. Roth*, 408 U.S., at 571, and looked instead to the significance of the state-created or state-enforced right and to the substantiality of the alleged deprivation. Today's opinion appears to abandon this reasonable approach by holding in effect that government infringement of any interest to which a person is entitled, no matter what the interest or how inconsequential the infringement, requires constitutional protection. As it is difficult to think of any less consequential infringement than suspension of a junior high school student for a single day, it is equally difficult to perceive any principled limit to the new reach of procedural due process.

BOARD OF EDUCATION OF the HENDRICK HUDSON CENTRAL SCHOOL DISTRICT, WESTCHESTER COUNTY, et al., Petitioners v. Amy ROWLEY, by her parents and natural guardians, Clifford and Nancy Rowley etc.
458 U.S. 176 (1982)

JUSTICE REHNQUIST delivered the opinion of the Court.

This case presents a question of statutory interpretation. Petitioners contend that the Court of Appeals and the District Court misconstrued the requirements imposed by Congress upon States which receive federal funds under the Education of the Handicapped Act. We agree and reverse the judgment of the Court of Appeals.

I

The Education of the Handicapped Act (Act), 84 Stat. 175, as amended, 20 U.S.C. § 1401 *et seq.* (1976 ed. and Supp.IV), provides federal money to assist state and local agencies in educating handicapped children, and conditions such funding upon a State's compliance with extensive goals and procedures. The Act represents an ambitious federal effort to promote the education of handicapped children, and was passed in response to Congress' perception that a majority of handicapped children in the United States "were either totally excluded from schools or [were] sitting idly in regular classrooms awaiting the time when they were old enough to 'drop out.'" H.R.Rep.No. 94-332, p. 2 (1975) (H.R.Rep.). The Act's evolution and major provisions shed light on the question of statutory interpretation which is at the heart of this case.

Congress first addressed the problem of educating the handicapped in 1966 when it amended the Elementary and Secondary Education Act of 1965 to establish a grant program "for the purpose of assisting the States in the initiation, expansion, and improvement of programs and projects . . . for the education of handicapped children." Pub.L. 89-750, § 161, 80 Stat. 1204. That program was repealed in 1970 by the Education of the Handicapped Act, Pub.L. 91-230, 84 Stat. 175, Part B of which established a grant program similar in purpose to the repealed legislation. Neither the 1966 nor the 1970 legislation contained specific guidelines for state use of the grant money; both were aimed primarily at stimulating the States to develop educational resources and to train personnel for educating the handicapped.

Dissatisfied with the progress being made under these earlier enactments, and spurred by two District Court decisions holding that handicapped children should be given access to a public education, Congress in 1974 greatly increased federal funding for education of the handicapped and for the first time required recipient States to adopt "a goal of providing full educational opportunities to all handicapped children." Pub.L. 93-380, 88 Stat. 579, 583 (1974 statute). The 1974 statute was recognized as an interim measure only, adopted "in order to give the Congress an additional year in which to study what if any additional Federal assistance [was] required to enable the States to meet the needs of handicapped children." H.R.Rep., at 4. The ensuing year of study produced the Education for All Handicapped Children Act of 1975.

In order to qualify for federal financial assistance under the Act, a State must demonstrate that it "has in effect a policy that assures all handicapped children the right to a free appropriate public education." 20 U.S.C. § 1412(1) . . . . The Act broadly defines "handicapped children" to include "mentally retarded, hard of hearing, deaf, speech impaired, visually handicapped, seriously emotionally disturbed, orthopedically impaired, [and] other health impaired children, [and] children with specific learning disabilities." § 1401(1).

The "free appropriate public education" required by the Act is tailored to the unique needs of the handicapped child by means of an "individualized educational program" (IEP). § 1401(18). The IEP, which is prepared at a meeting between a qualified representative of the local educational agency, the child's teacher, the child's parents or guardian, and, where appropriate, the child, consists of a written document containing:

> (A) a statement of the present levels of educational performance of such child, (B) a statement of annual goals, including short-term instructional objectives, (C) a statement of the specific educational services to be provided to such child, and the extent to which such child will be able to participate in regular educational programs, (D) the projected date for initiation and anticipated duration of such services, and (E) appropriate objective criteria and evaluation procedures and schedules for determining, on at least an annual basis, whether instructional objectives are being achieved.§ 1401(19).

Local or regional educational agencies must review, and where appropriate revise, each child's IEP at least annually. § 1414(a)(5). See also § 1413(a)(11).

In addition to the state plan and the IEP already described, the Act imposes extensive procedural requirements upon States receiving federal funds under its provisions. Parents or guardians of handicapped children must be notified of any proposed change in "the identification, evaluation, or educational placement of the child or the provision of a free appropriate public education to such child," and must be permitted to bring a complaint about "any matter relating to" such evaluation and education. §§ 1415(b)(1)(D) and (E). Complaints brought by parents or guardians must be resolved at "an impartial due process hearing," and appeal to the state educational agency must be provided if the initial hearing is held at the local or regional level. §§ 1415(b)(2) and (c). Thereafter, "[a]ny party aggrieved by the findings and decision" of the state administrative hearing has "the right to bring a civil action with respect to the complaint . . . in any State court of competent jurisdiction or in a district court of the United States without regard to the amount in controversy." § 1415(e)(2).

Thus, although the Act leaves to the States the primary responsibility for developing and executing educational programs for handicapped children, it imposes significant requirements to be followed in the discharge of that responsibility. Compliance is assured by provisions permitting the withholding of federal funds upon determination that a participating state or local agency has failed to satisfy the requirements of the Act, §§ 1414(b)(2)(A), 1416, and by the provision for judicial review. At present, all States except New Mexico receive federal funds under the portions of the Act at issue today.

II

This case arose in connection with the education of Amy Rowley, a deaf student at the Furnace Woods School in the Hendrick Hudson Central School District, Peekskill, N.Y. Amy has minimal residual hearing and is an excellent lipreader. During the year before she began attending Furnace Woods, a meeting between her parents and school administrators resulted in a decision to place her in a regular kindergarten class in order to determine what supplemental services would be necessary to her education. Several members of the school administration prepared for Amy's arrival by attending a course in sign-language interpretation, and a teletype machine was installed in the principal's office to facilitate communication with her parents who are also deaf. At the end of the trial period it was determined that Amy should remain in the kindergarten class, but that she should be provided with an FM hearing aid which would amplify words spoken into a wireless receiver by the teacher or fellow students during certain classroom activities. Amy successfully completed her kindergarten year.

As required by the Act, an IEP was prepared for Amy during the fall of her first-grade year. The IEP provided that Amy should be educated in a regular classroom at Furnace Woods, should continue to use the FM hearing aid, and should receive instruction from a tutor for the deaf for one hour each day and from a speech therapist for three hours each week. The Rowleys agreed with parts of the IEP, but insisted that Amy also be provided a qualified sign-language interpreter in all her academic classes in lieu of the assistance proposed in other parts of the IEP. Such an interpreter had been placed in Amy's kindergarten class for a 2-week experimental period, but the interpreter had reported that Amy did not need his services at that time. The school administrators likewise concluded that Amy did not need such an interpreter in her first-grade classroom. They reached this conclusion after consulting the school district's Committee on the Handicapped, which had received expert evidence from Amy's parents on the importance of a sign-language interpreter, received testimony from Amy's teacher and other persons familiar with her academic and social progress, and visited a class for the deaf.

When their request for an interpreter was denied, the Rowleys demanded and received a hearing before an independent examiner. After receiving evidence from both sides, the examiner agreed with the administrators' determination that an interpreter was not necessary because "Amy was achieving educationally, academically, and socially" without such assistance. App. to Pet. for Cert. F-22. The examiner's decision was affirmed on appeal by the New York Commissioner of Education on the basis of substantial evidence in the record. *Id.*, at E-4. Pursuant to the Act's provision for judicial review, the Rowleys then brought an action in the United States District Court for the Southern District of New York, claiming that the administrators' denial of the sign-language interpreter constituted a denial of the "free appropriate public education" guaranteed by the Act.

The District Court found that Amy "is a remarkably well-adjusted child" who interacts and communicates well with her classmates and has "developed an extraordinary rapport" with her teachers. 483 F.Supp. 528, 531 (1980). It also found that "she performs better than the average child in her class and is advancing easily from grade to grade," *id.*, at 534, but "that she understands considerably less of what goes on in class than she could if she were not deaf" and thus "is not learning as much, or performing as well academically, as she would without her handicap," *id.*, at 532. This disparity between Amy's achievement and her potential led the court to decide that she was not receiving a "free appropriate public education," which the court defined as "an opportunity to achieve [her] full potential commensurate with the opportunity provided to other children." *Id.*, at 534. According to the District Court, such a standard "requires that the potential of the handicapped child be measured and compared to his or her performance, and that the resulting differential or 'shortfall' be compared to the shortfall experienced by nonhandicapped children." *Ibid.* The District Court's definition arose from its assumption that the responsibility for "giv [ing] content to the requirement of an 'appropriate education'" had "been left entirely to the [federal] courts and the hearing officers." *Id.*, at 533.

A divided panel of the United States Court of Appeals for the Second Circuit affirmed. The

Court of Appeals "agree[d] with the [D]istrict [C]ourt's conclusions of law," and held that its "findings of fact [were] not clearly erroneous." 632 F.2d 945, 947 (1980).

We granted certiorari to review the lower courts' interpretation of the Act. 454 U.S. 961 (1981). Such review requires us to consider two questions: What is meant by the Act's requirement of a "free appropriate public education"? And what is the role of state and federal courts in exercising the review granted by 20 U.S.C. § 1415? We consider these questions separately.

III

A

This is the first case in which this Court has been called upon to interpret any provision of the Act. As noted previously, the District Court and the Court of Appeals concluded that "[t]he Act itself does not define 'appropriate education,' " 483 F.Supp., at 533, but leaves "to the courts and the hearing officers" the responsibility of "giv[ing] content to the requirement of an 'appropriate education.' " *Ibid.* See also 632 F.2d, at 947. Petitioners contend that the definition of the phrase "free appropriate public education" used by the courts below overlooks the definition of that phrase actually found in the Act. Respondents agree that the Act defines "free appropriate public education," but contend that the statutory definition is not "functional" and thus "offers judges no guidance in their consideration of controversies involving 'the identification, evaluation, or educational placement of the child or the provision of a free appropriate public education.' " Brief for Respondents 28. The United States, appearing as *amicus curiae* on behalf of respondents, states that "[a]lthough the Act includes definitions of a 'free appropriate public education' and other related terms, the statutory definitions do not adequately explain what is meant by 'appropriate.' " Brief for United States as *Amicus Curiae* 13.

We are loath to conclude that Congress failed to offer any assistance in defining the meaning of the principal substantive phrase used in the Act. It is beyond dispute that, contrary to the conclusions of the courts below, the Act does expressly define "free appropriate public education":

> The term 'free appropriate public education' means *special education* and *related services* which (A) have been provided at public expense, under public supervision and direction, and without charge, (B) meet the standards of the State educational agency, (C) include an appropriate preschool, elementary, or secondary school education in the State involved, and (D) are provided in conformity with the individualized education program required under section 1414(a)(5) of this title. § 1401(18) (emphasis added).

"Special education," as referred to in this definition, means "specially designed instruction, at no cost to parents or guardians, to meet the unique needs of a handicapped child, including classroom instruction, instruction in physical education, home instruction, and instruction in hospitals and institutions." § 1401(16). "Related services" are defined as "transportation, and such developmental, corrective, and other supportive services . . . as may be required to assist a handicapped child to benefit from special education." § 1401(17).

Like many statutory definitions, this one tends toward the cryptic rather than the comprehensive, but that is scarcely a reason for abandoning the quest for legislative intent.

Whether or not the definition is a "functional" one, as respondents contend it is not, it is the principal tool which Congress has given us for parsing the critical phrase of the Act. We think more must be made of it than either respondents or the United States seems willing to admit.

According to the definitions contained in the Act, a "free appropriate public education" consists of educational instruction specially designed to meet the unique needs of the handicapped child, supported by such services as are necessary to permit the child "to benefit" from the instruction. Almost as a checklist for adequacy under the Act, the definition also requires that such instruction and services be provided at public expense and under public supervision, meet the State's educational standards, approximate the grade levels used in the State's regular education, and comport with the child's IEP. Thus, if personalized instruction is being provided with sufficient supportive services to permit the child to benefit from the instruction, and the other items on the definitional checklist are satisfied, the child is receiving a "free appropriate public education" as defined by the Act.

Other portions of the statute also shed light upon congressional intent. Congress found that of the roughly eight million handicapped children in the United States at the time of enactment, one million were "excluded entirely from the public school system" and more than half were receiving an inappropriate education. 89 Stat. 774, note following § 1401. In addition, as mentioned in Part I, the Act requires States to extend educational services first to those children who are receiving no education and second to those children who are receiving an "inadequate education." § 1412(3). When these express statutory findings and priorities are read together with the Act's extensive procedural requirements and its definition of "free appropriate public education," the face of the statute evinces a congressional intent to bring previously excluded handicapped children into the public education systems of the States and to require the States to adopt *procedures* which would result in individualized consideration of and instruction for each child.

Noticeably absent from the language of the statute is any substantive standard prescribing the level of education to be accorded handicapped children. Certainly the language of the statute contains no requirement like the one imposed by the lower courts-that States maximize the potential of handicapped children "commensurate with the opportunity provided to other children." 483 F.Supp., at 534. That standard was expounded by the District Court without reference to the statutory definitions or even to the legislative history of the Act. Although we find the statutory definition of "free appropriate public education" to be helpful in our interpretation of the Act, there remains the question of whether the legislative history indicates a congressional intent that such education meet some additional substantive standard. For an answer, we turn to that history.

B

(i)

As suggested in Part I, federal support for education of the handicapped is a fairly recent development. Before passage of the Act some States had passed laws to improve the educational services afforded handicapped children, but many of these children were excluded completely from any form of public education or were left to fend for themselves in classrooms designed for education of their nonhandicapped peers. As previously noted, the House Report begins by emphasizing this exclusion and misplacement, noting that millions of handicapped children "were either totally excluded from schools or [were] sitting idly in regular classrooms awaiting the time when they were old enough to 'drop out.' " H.R.Rep., at 2. See also S.Rep., at 8. One of the Act's two principal sponsors in the Senate urged its passage in similar terms:

"While much progress has been made in the last few years, we can take no solace in that progress until all handicapped children are, in fact, receiving an education. The most recent statistics provided by the Bureau of Education for the Handicapped estimate that . . . 1.75 million handicapped children do not receive any educational services, and 2.5 million handicapped children are not receiving an appropriate education." 121 Cong.Rec. 19486 (1975) (remarks of Sen. Williams).

This concern, stressed repeatedly throughout the legislative history, confirms the impression conveyed by the language of the statute: By passing the Act, Congress sought primarily to make public education available to handicapped children. But in seeking to provide such access to public education, Congress did not impose upon the States any greater substantive educational standard than would be necessary to make such access meaningful. Indeed, Congress expressly "recognize[d] that in many instances the process of providing special education and related services to handicapped children is not guaranteed to produce any particular outcome." S.Rep., at 11, U.S.Code Cong. & Admin.News 1975, p. 1435. Thus, the intent of the Act was more to open the door of public education to handicapped children on appropriate terms than to guarantee any particular level of education once inside.

Both the House and the Senate Reports attribute the impetus for the Act and its predecessors to two federal-court judgments rendered in 1971 and 1972. As the Senate Report states, passage of the Act "followed a series of landmark court cases establishing in law the right to education for all handicapped children." S.Rep., at 6, U.S.Code Cong. & Admin.News 1975, p. 1430. The first case, *Pennsylvania Assn. for Retarded Children v. Commonwealth*, 334 F.Supp. 1257 (Ed Pa.1971) and 343 F.Supp. 279 (1972) (*PARC*), was a suit on behalf of retarded children challenging the constitutionality of a Pennsylvania statute which acted to exclude them from public education and training. The case ended in a consent decree which enjoined the State from "deny[ing] to any mentally retarded child *access* to a free public program of education and training." 334 F.Supp., at 1258 (emphasis added).

PARC was followed by *Mills v. Board of Education of District of Columbia*, 348 F.Supp. 866 (D.C.1972), a case in which the plaintiff handicapped children had been excluded from the District of Columbia public schools. The court's judgment, quoted in S.Rep., at 6, provided that

"no [handicapped] child eligible for a publicly supported education in the District of Columbia public schools shall be *excluded* from a regular school assignment by a Rule, policy, or practice of the Board of Education of the District of Columbia or its agents unless such child is provided (a) *adequate* alternative educational services suited to the child's needs, which may include special education or tuition grants, and (b) a constitutionally adequate prior hearing and periodic review of the child's status, progress, and the *adequacy* of any educational alternative." 348 F.Supp., at 878 (emphasis added).

Mills and *PARC* both held that handicapped children must be given *access* to an adequate, publicly supported education. Neither case purports to require any particular substantive level of education. Rather, like the language of the Act, the cases set forth extensive procedures to be followed in formulating personalized educational programs for handicapped children. See 348 F.Supp., at 878-883; 334 F.Supp., at 1258-1267. The fact that both *PARC* and *Mills* are discussed at length in the legislative Reports suggests that the principles which they established are the principles which, to a significant extent, guided the drafters of the Act. Indeed, immediately after discussing these cases the Senate Report describes the 1974 statute as having "incorporated the major principles of the right to education cases." S.Rep., at 8, U.S.Code Cong. & Admin.News 1975, p. 1432. Those principles in turn became the basis of the Act, which itself was designed to effectuate the purposes of the 1974 statute. H.R.Rep., at 5.

That the Act imposes no clear obligation upon recipient States beyond the requirement that handicapped children receive some form of specialized education is perhaps best demonstrated by the fact that Congress, in explaining the need for the Act, equated an "appropriate education" to the receipt of some specialized educational services. The Senate Report states: "[T]he most recent statistics provided by the Bureau of Education for the Handicapped estimate that of the more than 8 million children . . . with handicapping conditions requiring special education and related services, only 3.9 million such children are receiving an appropriate education." S.Rep., at 8, U.S.Code Cong. & Admin.News 1975, p. 1432. This statement, which reveals Congress' view that 3.9 million handicapped children were "receiving an appropriate education" in 1975, is followed immediately in the Senate Report by a table showing that 3.9 million handicapped children were "served" in 1975 and a slightly larger number were "unserved." A similar statement and table appear in the House Report. H.R.Rep., at 11-12.

It is evident from the legislative history that the characterization of handicapped children as "served" referred to children who were receiving some form of specialized educational services from the States, and that the characterization of children as "unserved" referred to those who were receiving no specialized educational services. For example, a letter sent to the United States Commissioner of Education by the House Committee on Education and Labor, signed by two key sponsors of the Act in the House, asked the Commissioner to identify the number of handicapped "children served" in each State. The letter asked for statistics on the number of children "being served" in various types of "special education program[s]" and the number of children who were not "receiving educational services." Hearings on S. 6 before the Subcommittee on the Handicapped of the Senate Committee on Labor and Public Welfare, 94th Cong., 1st Sess., 205-207 (1975). Similarly, Senator Randolph, one of the Act's principal sponsors in the Senate, noted that roughly one-half of the handicapped children in the United States "are receiving special educational services." *Id.*, at 1. By characterizing the 3.9 million handicapped children who were "served" as children who were "receiving an appropriate education," the Senate and House Reports unmistakably disclose Congress' perception of the type of education required by the Act: an "appropriate education" is provided when personalized educational services are provided.

(ii)

Respondents contend that "the goal of the Act is to provide each handicapped child with an equal educational opportunity." Brief for Respondents 35. We think, however, that the requirement that a State provide specialized educational services to handicapped children generates no additional requirement that the services so provided be sufficient to maximize each child's potential "commensurate with the opportunity provided other children." Respondents and the United States correctly note that Congress sought "to provide assistance to the States in carrying out their responsibilities under . . . the Constitution of the United States to provide equal protection of the laws." S.Rep., at 13, U.S.Code Cong. & Admin.News 1975, p.

1437. But we do not think that such statements imply a congressional intent to achieve strict equality of opportunity or services.

The educational opportunities provided by our public school systems undoubtedly differ from student to student, depending upon a myriad of factors that might affect a particular student's ability to assimilate information presented in the classroom. The requirement that States provide "equal" educational opportunities would thus seem to present an entirely unworkable standard requiring impossible measurements and comparisons. Similarly, furnishing handicapped children with only such services as are available to nonhandicapped children would in all probability fall short of the statutory requirement of "free appropriate public education"; to require, on the other hand, the furnishing of every special service necessary to maximize each handicapped child's potential is, we think, further than Congress intended to go. Thus to speak in terms of "equal" services in one instance gives less than what is required by the Act and in another instance more. The theme of the Act is "free appropriate public education," a phrase which is too complex to be captured by the word "equal" whether one is speaking of opportunities or services.

The legislative conception of the requirements of equal protection was undoubtedly informed by the two District Court decisions referred to above. But cases such as *Mills* and *PARC* held simply that handicapped children may not be excluded entirely from public education. In *Mills*, the District Court said:

> "If sufficient funds are not available to finance all of the services and programs that are needed and desirable in the system then the available funds must be expended equitably in such a manner that no child is entirely excluded from a publicly supported education consistent with his needs and ability to benefit therefrom." 348 F.Supp., at 876.

The *PARC* court used similar language, saying "[i]t is the commonwealth's obligation to place each mentally retarded child in a free, public program of education and training appropriate to the child's capacity. . . ." 334 F.Supp., at 1260. The right of access to free public education enunciated by these cases is significantly different from any notion of absolute equality of opportunity regardless of capacity. To the extent that Congress might have looked further than these cases which are mentioned in the legislative history, at the time of enactment of the Act this Court had held at least twice that the Equal Protection Clause of the Fourteenth Amendment does not require States to expend equal financial resources on the education of each child.

In explaining the need for federal legislation, the House Report noted that "no congressional legislation has required a precise guarantee for handicapped children, i.e. a basic floor of opportunity that would bring into compliance all school districts with the constitutional right of equal protection with respect to handicapped children." H.R.Rep., at 14. Assuming that the Act was designed to fill the need identified in the House Report-that is, to provide a "basic floor of opportunity" consistent with equal protection-neither the Act nor its history persuasively demonstrates that Congress thought that equal protection required anything more than equal access. Therefore, Congress' desire to provide specialized educational services, even in furtherance of "equality," cannot be read as imposing any particular substantive educational standard upon the States.

The District Court and the Court of Appeals thus erred when they held that the Act requires New York to maximize the potential of each handicapped child commensurate with the opportunity provided nonhandicapped children. Desirable though that goal might be, it is not the standard that Congress imposed upon States which receive funding under the Act. Rather, Congress sought primarily to identify and evaluate handicapped children, and to provide them with access to a free public education.

(iii)

Implicit in the congressional purpose of providing access to a "free appropriate public education" is the requirement that the education to which access is provided be sufficient to confer some educational benefit upon the handicapped child. It would do little good for Congress to spend millions of dollars in providing access to a public education only to have the handicapped child receive no benefit from that education. The statutory definition of "free appropriate public education," in addition to requiring that States provide each child with "specially designed instruction," expressly requires the provision of "such . . . supportive services . . . as may be required to assist a handicapped child *to benefit* from special education." § 1401(17) (emphasis added). We therefore conclude that the "basic floor of opportunity" provided by the Act consists of access to specialized instruction and related services which are individually designed to provide educational benefit to the handicapped child.

The determination of when handicapped children are receiving sufficient educational benefits to satisfy the requirements of the Act presents a more difficult problem. The Act requires participating States to educate a wide spectrum of handicapped children, from the marginally hearing-impaired to the profoundly retarded and palsied. It is clear that the benefits obtainable by children at one end of the spectrum will differ dramatically from those obtainable by children at the other end, with infinite variations in between. One child may have little difficulty competing successfully in an academic setting with nonhandicapped children while another child may encounter great difficulty in acquiring even the most basic of self-maintenance skills. We do not attempt today to establish any one test for determining the adequacy of educational benefits conferred upon all children covered by the Act. Because in this case we are presented with a handicapped child who is receiving substantial specialized instruction and related services, and who is performing above average in the regular classrooms of a public school system, we confine our analysis to that situation.

The Act requires participating States to educate handicapped children with nonhandicapped children whenever possible. When that "mainstreaming" preference of the Act has been met and a child is being educated in the regular classrooms of a public school system, the system itself monitors the educational progress of the child. Regular examinations are administered, grades are awarded, and yearly advancement to higher grade levels is permitted for those children who attain an adequate knowledge of the course material. The grading and advancement system thus constitutes an important factor in determining educational benefit. Children who graduate from our public school systems are considered by our society to have been "educated" at least to the grade level they have completed, and access to an "education" for handicapped children is precisely what Congress sought to provide in the Act.[25]

---

[25] We do not hold today that every handicapped child who is advancing from grade to grade in a regular public school system is automatically receiving a "free appropriate public education." In this case, however, we find Amy's academic progress, when considered with the special services and professional consideration accorded by the Furnace Woods school administrators, to be dispositive.

C

When the language of the Act and its legislative history are considered together, the requirements imposed by Congress become tolerably clear. Insofar as a State is required to provide a handicapped child with a "free appropriate public education," we hold that it satisfies this requirement by providing personalized instruction with sufficient support services to permit the child to benefit educationally from that instruction. Such instruction and services must be provided at public expense, must meet the State's educational standards, must approximate the grade levels used in the State's regular education, and must comport with the child's IEP. In addition, the IEP, and therefore the personalized instruction, should be formulated in accordance with the requirements of the Act and, if the child is being educated in the regular classrooms of the public education system, should be reasonably calculated to enable the child to achieve passing marks and advance from grade to grade.

IV

A

As mentioned in Part I, the Act permits "[a]ny party aggrieved by the findings and decision" of the state administrative hearings "to bring a civil action" in "any State court of competent jurisdiction or in a district court of the United States without regard to the amount in controversy." § 1415(e)(2). The complaint, and therefore the civil action, may concern "any matter relating to the identification, evaluation, or educational placement of the child, or the provision of a free appropriate public education to such child." § 1415(b)(1)(E). In reviewing the complaint, the Act provides that a court "shall receive the record of the [state] administrative proceedings, shall hear additional evidence at the request of a party, and, basing its decision on the preponderance of the evidence, shall grant such relief as the court determines is appropriate." § 1415(e)(2).

The parties disagree sharply over the meaning of these provisions, petitioners contending that courts are given only limited authority to review for state compliance with the Act's procedural requirements and no power to review the substance of the state program, and respondents contending that the Act requires courts to exercise *de novo* review over state educational decisions and policies. We find petitioners' contention unpersuasive, for Congress expressly rejected provisions that would have so severely restricted the role of reviewing courts. In substituting the current language of the statute for language that would have made state administrative findings conclusive if supported by substantial evidence, the Conference Committee explained that courts were to make "independent decision[s] based on a preponderance of the evidence." S.Conf.Rep.No.94-455, p. 50 (1975), U.S.Code Cong. & Admin.News 1975, p. 1503.

But although we find that this grant of authority is broader than claimed by petitioners, we think the fact that it is found in § 1415, which is entitled "Procedural safeguards," is not without significance. When the elaborate and highly specific procedural safeguards embodied in § 1415 are contrasted with the general and somewhat imprecise substantive admonitions contained in the Act, we think that the importance Congress attached to these procedural safeguards cannot be gainsaid. It seems to us no exaggeration to say that Congress placed every bit as much emphasis upon compliance with procedures giving parents and guardians a large measure of participation at every stage of the administrative process, see, *e.g.*, §§ 1415(a)-(d), as it did upon the measurement of the resulting IEP against a substantive standard. We think that the congressional emphasis upon full participation of concerned parties throughout the development of the IEP, as well as the requirements that state and local plans be submitted to the Secretary for approval, demonstrates the legislative conviction that adequate compliance with the procedures prescribed would in most cases assure much if not all of what Congress wished in the way of substantive content in an IEP.

Thus the provision that a reviewing court base its decision on the "preponderance of the evidence" is by no means an invitation to the courts to substitute their own notions of sound educational policy for those of the school authorities which they review. The very importance which Congress has attached to compliance with certain procedures in the preparation of an IEP would be frustrated if a court were permitted simply to set state decisions at nought. The fact that § 1415(e) requires that the reviewing court "receive the records of the [state] administrative proceedings" carries with it the implied requirement that due weight shall be given to these proceedings. And we find nothing in the Act to suggest that merely because Congress was rather sketchy in establishing substantive requirements, as opposed to procedural requirements for the preparation of an IEP, it intended that reviewing courts should have a free hand to impose substantive standards of review which cannot be derived from the Act itself. In short, the statutory authorization to grant "such relief as the court determines is appropriate" cannot be read without reference to the obligations, largely procedural in nature, which are imposed upon recipient States by Congress.

Therefore, a court's inquiry in suits brought under § 1415(e)(2) is twofold. First, has the State complied with the procedures set forth in the Act? And second, is the individualized educational program developed through the Act's procedures reasonably calculated to enable the child to receive educational benefits? If these requirements are met, the State has complied with the obligations imposed by Congress and the courts can require no more.

B

In assuring that the requirements of the Act have been met, courts must be careful to avoid imposing their view of preferable educational methods upon the States. The primary responsibility for formulating the education to be accorded a handicapped child, and for choosing the educational method most suitable to the child's needs, was left by the Act to state and local educational agencies in cooperation with the parents or guardian of the child. The Act expressly charges States with the responsibility of "acquiring and disseminating to teachers and administrators of programs for handicapped children significant information derived from educational research, demonstration, and similar projects, and [of] adopting, where appropriate, promising educational practices and materials." § 1413(a)(3). In the face of such a clear statutory directive, it seems highly unlikely that Congress intended courts to overturn a State's choice of appropriate educational theories in a proceeding conducted pursuant to § 1415(e)(2).

We previously have cautioned that courts lack the "specialized knowledge and experience" necessary to resolve "persistent and difficult questions of educational policy." *San Antonio Independent School Dist. v. Rodriguez*, 411 U.S., at 42. We think that Congress shared that view when it passed the Act. As already demonstrated, Congress' intention was not that the Act displace the primacy of States in the field of education, but that States receive funds to assist them in extending their educational systems to the handicapped. Therefore, once a court determines that the requirements of the Act have been met, questions of methodology are for resolution by the States.

V

Entrusting a child's education to state and local agencies does not leave the child without protection. Congress sought to protect individual children by providing for parental involvement in the development of state plans and policies, *supra*, at 3038, and n. 6, and in the formulation of the child's individual educational program. As the Senate Report states:

> "The Committee recognizes that in many instances the process of providing special education and related services to handicapped children is not guaranteed to produce any particular outcome. By changing the language [of the provision relating to individualized educational programs] to emphasize the process of parent and child involvement and to provide a written record of reasonable expectations, the Committee intends to clarify that such individualized planning conferences are a way to provide parent involvement and protection to assure that appropriate services are provided to a handicapped child." S.Rep., at 11-12, U.S.Code Cong. & Admin.News 1975, p. 1435.

See also S.Conf.Rep.No.94-445, p. 30 (1975); 34 CFR § 300.345 (1981). As this very case demonstrates, parents and guardians will not lack ardor in seeking to ensure that handicapped children receive all of the benefits to which they are entitled by the Act.

VI

Applying these principles to the facts of this case, we conclude that the Court of Appeals erred in affirming the decision of the District Court. Neither the District Court nor the Court of Appeals found that petitioners had failed to comply with the procedures of the Act, and the findings of neither court would support a conclusion that Amy's educational program failed to comply with the substantive requirements of the Act. On the contrary, the District Court found that the "evidence firmly establishes that Amy is receiving an 'adequate' education, since she performs better than the average child in her class and is advancing easily from grade to grade." 483 F.Supp., at 534. In light of this finding, and of the fact that Amy was receiving personalized instruction and related services calculated by the Furnace Woods school administrators to meet her educational needs, the lower courts should not have concluded that the Act requires the provision of a sign-language interpreter. Accordingly, the decision of the Court of Appeals is reversed, and the case is remanded for further proceedings consistent with this opinion.

So ordered.

Justice BLACKMUN, concurring in the judgment. (omitted)

Justice WHITE, with whom Justice BRENNAN and Justice MARSHALL join, dissenting.

In order to reach its result in this case, the majority opinion contradicts itself, the language of the statute, and the legislative history. Both the majority's standard for a "free appropriate education" and its standard for judicial review disregard congressional intent.

I

* * *

I agree that the language of the Act does not contain a substantive standard beyond requiring that the education offered must be "appropriate." However, if there are limits not evident from the face of the statute on what may be considered an "appropriate education," they must be found in the purpose of the statute or its legislative history. The Act itself announces it will provide a *"full* educational opportunity to all handicapped children." 20 U.S.C. § 1412(2)(A) (emphasis added). This goal is repeated throughout the legislative history, in statements too frequent to be " 'passing references and isolated phrases.' " *Ante*, at 3049, n. 26, quoting *Department of State v. Washington Post Co.*, 456 U.S. 596, 600 (1982). These statements elucidate the meaning of "appropriate." According to the Senate Report, for example, the Act does "guarantee that handicapped children are provided *equal* educational opportunity." S.Rep.No.94-168, p. 9 (1975), U.S.Code Cong. & Admin.News 1975, p. 1433 (emphasis added). This promise appears throughout the legislative history. Indeed, at times the purpose of the Act was described as tailoring each handicapped child's educational plan to enable the child "to achieve his or her maximum potential." H.R.Rep.No.94-332, pp. 13, 19 (1975); see 121 Cong.Rec. 23709 (1975). Senator Stafford, one of the sponsors of the Act, declared: "We can all agree that education [given a handicapped child] should be equivalent, at least, to the one those children who are not handicapped receive." *Id.*, at 19483. The legislative history thus directly supports the conclusion that the Act intends to give handicapped children an educational opportunity commensurate with that given other children.

The majority opinion announces a different substantive standard, that "Congress did not impose upon the States any greater substantive educational standard than would be necessary to make such access meaningful." *Ante*, at 3043. While "meaningful" is no more enlightening than "appropriate," the Court purports to clarify itself. Because Amy was provided with *some* specialized instruction from which she obtained *some* benefit and because she passed from grade to grade, she was receiving a meaningful and therefore appropriate education.

This falls far short of what the Act intended. The Act details as specifically as possible the kind of specialized education each handicapped child must receive. It would apparently satisfy the Court's standard of "access to specialized instruction and related services which are individually designed to provide educational benefit to the handicapped child," *ante*, at 3048, for a deaf child such as Amy to be given a teacher with a loud voice, for she would benefit from that service. The Act requires more. It defines "special education" to mean "specifically designed instruction, at no cost to parents or guardians, to *meet the unique needs* of a handicapped child. . . ." § 1401(16) (emphasis added). Providing a teacher with a loud voice would not meet Amy's needs and would not satisfy the Act. The basic floor of opportunity is instead, as the courts below recognized, intended to eliminate the effects of the handicap, at least to the extent that the child will be given an equal opportunity to learn if that is reasonably possible. Amy Rowley, without a sign-language interpreter, comprehends less than half of what is said in the classroom-less than half of what normal children comprehend. This is hardly an equal opportunity to learn, even if Amy makes passing grades.

* * *

II

The Court's discussion of the standard for judicial review is as flawed as its discussion of a "free appropriate public education." . . . It is clear enough to me that Congress decided to reduce substantially judicial deference to state administrative decisions.

* * *

There is no doubt that the state agency itself must make substantive decisions. The legislative history reveals that the courts are to consider, *de novo*, the same issues. Senator Williams explicitly stated that the civil action permitted under the Act encompasses all matters related to the original complaint. *Id.*, at 37416.

Thus, the Court's limitations on judicial review have no support in either the language of the Act or the legislative history. Congress did not envision that inquiry would end if a showing is made that the child is receiving passing marks and is advancing from grade to grade. Instead, it intended to permit a full and searching inquiry into any aspect of a handicapped child's education. The Court's standard, for example, would not permit a challenge to part of the IEP; the legislative history demonstrates beyond doubt that Congress intended such challenges to be possible, even if the plan as developed is reasonably calculated to give the child some benefits.

Parents can challenge the IEP for failing to supply the special education and related services needed by the individual handicapped child. That is what the Rowleys did. . . . Because the standard of the courts below seems to me to reflect the congressional purpose and because their factual findings are not clearly erroneous, I respectfully dissent.

Mary Ann RONCKER On Behalf of Neill RONCKER, Individually and on behalf of all others similarly situated, Plaintiff-Appellant, v. Franklin B. WALTER, et al., Defendants-Appellees.
700 F.2d 1058 (6th Cir. 1983)

Before KENNEDY and CONTIE, Circuit Judges, and GORDON, Senior District Judge.[*]

CONTIE, CIRCUIT JUDGE.

In this appeal, the plaintiff challenges the placement of her retarded son under the Education for All Handicapped Children Act of 1975, 20 U.S.C. § 1401 *et seq.* . . . . In this case, we examine the Act's requirement that handicapped children be educated with non-handicapped children to the "maximum extent appropriate."

I

The plaintiff's son, Neill Roncker, is nine years old and is severely mentally retarded. He is classified as Trainable Mentally Retarded (TMR), a category of children with an IQ of below 50. Less severely retarded students are classified as Educable Mentally Retarded (EMR) and are generally educated in special classes within the regular public schools.

There is no dispute that Neill is severely retarded and has a mental age of two to three with regard to most functions. Neill also suffers from seizures but they are not convulsive and he takes medication to control them. No evidence indicates that Neill is dangerous to others but he does require almost constant supervision because of his inability to recognize dangerous situations.

In 1976, Neill was evaluated and recommended for the Arlitt Child Development Center. It was believed that he would benefit from contact with non-handicapped children. In the spring of 1979, a conference was held to evaluate Neill's Individual Education Plan (IEP) as required by the Act. Present at the conference were Neill's parents, school psychologists, and a member of the Hamilton County Board of Mental Retardation. After evaluating Neill, the school district decided to place him in a county school. Since these county schools were exclusively for mentally retarded children, Neill would have received no contact with non-handicapped children.

The county schools receive part of their funding through tuition for individual students, which is paid by the school district. The county schools also receive partial funding through the state by virtue of a mental retardation tax levy. Funds from this levy are not available to public schools.

The Ronckers refused to accept the placement and sought a due process hearing before an impartial hearing officer pursuant to the Act. 20 U.S.C. § 1415(b)(2). The hearing officer found that the school district had not satisfied its burden of proving that its proposed placement afforded the maximum appropriate contact with non-handicapped children. He ordered that

---

[*] The Honorable James F. Gordon, Senior Judge, United States District Court for the Western District of Kentucky, sitting by designation.

Neill "be placed within the appropriate special education class in the regular elementary school setting."

The school district appealed to the Ohio State Board of Education pursuant to 20 U.S.C. § 1415(c). The State Board found that Neill required the educational opportunities provided by the county school. It also found, however, that he needed interaction with non-handicapped children during lunch, recess and transportation to and from school. Accordingly, the State Board held that Neill should be placed in a county school so long as some provision was made for him to receive contact with non-handicapped children. The State Board did not indicate how this split program was to be administered.

While the dispute over placement continued, Neill began attending a class for the severely mentally retarded at Pleasant Ridge Elementary School in September 1979. Pleasant Ridge is a regular public school which serves both handicapped and non-handicapped children. Neill's contact with non-handicapped children at Pleasant Ridge is limited to lunch, gym and recess. Neill has remained at Pleasant Ridge during the pendency of this action.

In January 1980, Neill's mother filed this action against the state and the school district. The claims against the state were settled. Prior to trial, the district court denied class certification without a hearing.

At trial, both parties presented expert testimony. Both agreed that Neill required special instruction; he could not be placed in educational classes with non-handicapped children. The plaintiff, however, contended that Neill could be provided the special instruction he needed in a setting where he could have contact with non-handicapped children. The school district contended that Neill could not benefit significantly from mainstreaming and that any minimal benefits would be greatly outweighed by the educational benefits of the county school.

The district court found in favor of the school district. The court interpreted the Act's mainstreaming requirement as allowing school districts broad discretion in the placement of handicapped children. In this case, the district court found that the school district did not abuse its discretion in placing Neill Roncker in a school where he would receive no contact with non-handicapped children. This conclusion was supported by the district court's finding that Neill had made no significant progress after 18 months at Pleasant Ridge. Finally, the district court held that a class action was inappropriate because the educational placement of handicapped children requires individual determinations.

II

We find that the district court erred in reviewing the school district's placement decision under an "abuse of discretion" standard.

* * *

The first inquiry in the two-step test mandated by *Rowley* is whether the state has complied with the Act's procedural requirements. These requirements clearly have been satisfied in this case. The second inquiry is whether "the individualized educational program developed through the Act's procedures [is] reasonably calculated to enable the child to receive educational benefits?" *Id.* at 3051.

In *Rowley*, the Supreme Court found that the state had complied with the Act's procedural requirements and had developed an IEP reasonably calculated to lead to educational benefits. Accordingly, the Act was satisfied. The present case differs from *Rowley* in two significant ways.

First, this case involves the mainstreaming provision of the Act while *Rowley* involved a choice between two methods for educating a deaf student. In the latter case, the dispute is simply one of methodology and the Supreme Court has emphatically stated that such questions should be left to the states. *Id.* at 3051-52. In the present case, the question is not one of methodology but rather involves a determination of whether the school district has satisfied the Act's requirement that handicapped children be educated alongside non-handicapped children to the maximum extent appropriate. The states accept federal aid in return for compliance with the Act. Since Congress has decided that mainstreaming is appropriate, the states must accept that decision if they desire federal funds.

Second, in this case, the district court failed to give "due weight" to the state administrative proceedings. *Rowley*, 102 S.Ct. at 3051. Both the impartial hearing officer and the State Board of Education found that the school district's placement did not satisfy the Act's mainstreaming requirement. Under such circumstances, the district court erred in reviewing the school district's placement under the deferential abuse of discretion standard. Such a standard of review renders the administrative hearings provided for by the Act virtually meaningless. By way of contrast, in *Rowley*, the administrative hearings unanimously concurred with the original placement but the district court found the placement to be inappropriate.

In sum, the abuse of discretion standard of review utilized by the district court was improper under the Act. We further find that the standard of review as set out in *Rowley* requires a *de novo* review but that the district court should give due weight to the state administrative proceedings in reaching its decision.

III

Since the district court employed an improper standard of review, we remand this case in order to allow the district court to re-examine the mainstreaming issue in light of the proper standard of review.

The Act does not require mainstreaming in every case but its requirement that mainstreaming be provided to the *maximum* extent appropriate indicates a very strong congressional preference. The proper inquiry is whether a proposed placement is appropriate under the Act. In some cases, a placement which may be considered better for academic reasons may not be appropriate because of the failure to provide for mainstreaming. The perception that a segregated institution is academically superior for a handicapped child may reflect no more than a basic disagreement with the mainstreaming concept. Such a disagreement is not, of course, any basis for not following the Act's mandate. *Campbell v. Talladega City Bd. of Education*, 518 F.Supp. 47, 55 (N.D.Ala.1981). In a case where the segregated facility is considered superior, the court should determine whether the services which make that placement superior could be feasibly provided in a non-segregated setting. If they can, the placement in the segregated school would be inappropriate under the Act. Framing the issue in this manner accords the proper respect for the strong preference in favor of mainstreaming while still realizing the possibility that some handicapped children simply must be educated in segregated facilities either because the handicapped child would not benefit from mainstreaming, because any marginal benefits received from mainstreaming are far outweighed by the benefits gained from services which could not feasibly be provided in the non-segregated setting, or because the handicapped child is a disruptive force in the non-segregated setting. Cost is a proper factor to consider since excessive spending on one handicapped child deprives other handicapped children. *See Age v. Bullitt County Schools,* 673 F.2d 141, 145 (6th Cir.1982). Cost is no defense, however, if the school district has failed to use its funds to provide a proper continuum of alternative placements for handicapped children. The provision of such alternative placements benefits all handicapped children.

In the present case, the district court must determine whether Neill's educational, physical or emotional needs require some service which could not feasibly be provided in a class for handicapped children within a regular school or in the type of split program advocated by the State Board of Education. Although Neill's progress, or lack thereof, at Pleasant Ridge is a relevant factor in determining the maximum appropriate extent to which he can be mainstreamed, it is not dispositive since the district court must determine whether Neill could have been provided with additional services, such as those provided at the county schools, which would have improved his performance at Pleasant Ridge.

We recognize that the mainstreaming issue imposes a difficult burden on the district court. Since Congress has chosen to impose that burden, however, the courts must do their best to fulfill their duty. The district courts are not without guidance inasmuch as they have the benefit of two state administrative proceedings and may justifiably give due weight to those administrative findings.

IV (omitted)

The judgment of the district court is VACATED and the case is REMANDED for further proceedings consistent with this opinion.

CORNELIA G. KENNEDY, Circuit Judge, dissenting (omitted).

SCHOOL COMMITTEE OF the TOWN OF BURLINGTON, MASSACHUSETTS, et al., Petitioners v. DEPARTMENT OF EDUCATION OF the Commonwealth of MASSACHUSETTS et al.
471 U.S. 359 (1985)

JUSTICE REHNQUIST delivered the opinion of the Court.

The Education of the Handicapped Act (Act), 84 Stat. 175, as amended, 20 U.S.C. § 1401 *et seq.*, requires participating state and local educational agencies "to assure that handicapped children and their parents or guardians are guaranteed procedural safeguards with respect to the provision of free appropriate public education" to such handicapped children. § 1415(a). These procedures include the right of the parents to participate in the development of an "individualized education program" (IEP) for the child and to challenge in administrative and court proceedings a proposed IEP with which they disagree. §§ 1401(19), 1415(b), (d), (e). Where as in the present case review of a contested IEP takes years to run its course-years critical to the child's development-important practical questions arise concerning interim placement of the child and financial responsibility for that placement. This case requires us to address some of those questions.

Michael Panico, the son of respondent Robert Panico, was a first grader in the public school system of petitioner Town of Burlington, Mass., when he began experiencing serious difficulties in school. It later became evident that he had "specific learning disabilities" and thus was "handicapped" within the meaning of the Act, 20 U.S.C. § 1401(1). This entitled him to receive at public expense specially designed instruction to meet his unique needs, as well as related transportation. §§ 1401(16), 1401(17). The negotiations and other proceedings between the Town and the Panicos, thus far spanning more than eight years, are too involved to relate in full detail; the following are the parts relevant to the issues on which we granted certiorari.

In the spring of 1979, Michael attended the third grade of the Memorial School, a public school in Burlington, Mass., under an IEP calling for individual tutoring by a reading specialist for one hour a day and individual and group counseling. Michael's continued poor performance and the fact that Memorial School was not equipped to handle his needs led to much discussion between his parents and Town school officials about his difficulties and his future schooling. Apparently the course of these discussions did not run smoothly; the upshot was that the Panicos and the Town agreed that Michael was generally of above average to superior intelligence, but had special educational needs calling for a placement in a school other than Memorial. They disagreed over the source and exact nature of Michael's learning difficulties, the Town believing the source to be emotional and the parents believing it to be neurological.

In late June, the Town presented the Panicos with a proposed IEP for Michael for the 1979-1980 academic year. It called for placing Michael in a highly structured class of six children with special academic and social needs, located at another Town public school, the Pine Glen School. On July 3, Michael's father rejected the proposed IEP and sought review under § 1415(b)(2) by respondent Massachusetts Department of Education's Bureau of Special Education Appeals (BSEA). A hearing was initially scheduled for August 8, but was apparently postponed in favor of a mediation session on August 17. The mediation efforts proved unsuccessful.

Meanwhile the Panicos received the results of the latest expert evaluation of Michael by specialists at Massachusetts General Hospital, who opined that Michael's "emotional difficulties are secondary to a rather severe learning disorder characterized by perceptual difficulties" and recommended "a highly specialized setting for children with learning handicaps . . . such as the Carroll School," a state-approved private school for special education located in Lincoln, Mass.App. 26, 31. Believing that the Town's proposed placement of Michael at the Pine Glen School was inappropriate in light of Michael's needs, Mr. Panico enrolled Michael in the Carroll School in mid-August at his own expense, and Michael started there in September.

The BSEA held several hearings during the fall of 1979, and in January 1980 the hearing officer decided that the Town's proposed placement at the Pine Glen School was inappropriate and that the Carroll School was "the least restrictive adequate program within the record" for Michael's educational needs. The hearing officer ordered the Town to pay for Michael's tuition and transportation to the Carroll School for the 1979-1980 school year, including reimbursing the Panicos for their expenditures on these items for the school year to date.

The Town sought judicial review of the State's administrative decision in the United States District Court for the District of Massachusetts pursuant to 20 U.S.C. § 1415(e)(2) and a parallel state statute, naming Mr. Panico and the State Department of Education as defendants. In November 1980, the District Court granted summary judgment against the Town on the state-law claim under a "substantial evidence" standard of review, entering a final judgment on this claim under Federal Rule of Civil Procedure 54(b). The court also set the federal claim for future trial. The Court of Appeals vacated the judgment on the state-law claim, holding that review under the state statute was pre-empted by § 1415(e)(2), which establishes a "preponderance of the evidence" standard of review and which permits the reviewing court to hear additional evidence. 655 F.2d 428, 431-432 (1st Cir. 1981).

In the meantime, the Town had refused to comply with the BSEA order, the District Court had denied a stay of that order, and the Panicos and the State had moved for preliminary injunctive relief. The State also had threatened outside of the judicial proceedings to freeze all of the Town's special education assistance unless it complied with the BSEA order. Apparently in response to this threat, the Town agreed in February 1981 to pay for Michael's Carroll School placement and related transportation for the 1980-1981 term, none of which had yet been paid, and to continue paying for these expenses until the case was decided. But the Town persisted in refusing to reimburse Mr. Panico for the expenses of the 1979-1980 school year. When the Court of Appeals disposed of the state claim, it also held that under this status quo none of the parties could show irreparable injury and thus none was entitled to a preliminary injunction. The court reasoned that the Town had not shown that Mr. Panico would not be able to repay the tuition and related costs borne by the Town if he ultimately lost on the merits, and Mr. Panico had not shown that he would be irreparably harmed if not reimbursed immediately for past payments which might ultimately be determined to be the Town's responsibility.

On remand, the District Court entered an extensive pretrial order on the Town's federal claim. In denying the Town summary judgment, it ruled that 20 U.S.C. § 1415(e)(3) did not bar reimbursement despite the Town's insistence that the Panicos violated that provision by changing Michael's placement to the Carroll School during the pendency of the administrative proceedings. The court reasoned that § 1415(e)(3) concerned the physical placement of the child and not the right to tuition reimbursement or to procedural review of a contested IEP. The court also dealt with the problem that no IEP had been developed for the 1980-1981 or 1981-1982 school years. It held that its power under § 1415(e)(2) to grant "appropriate" relief upon reviewing the contested IEP for the 1979-1980 school year included the power to grant relief for subsequent school years despite the lack of IEPs for those years. In this connection, however, the court interpreted the statute to place the burden of proof on the Town to upset the BSEA decision that the IEP was inappropriate for 1979-1980 and on the Panicos and the State to show that the relief for subsequent terms was appropriate.

After a 4-day trial, the District Court in August 1982 overturned the BSEA decision, holding that the appropriate 1979-1980 placement for Michael was the one proposed by the Town in the IEP and that the parents had failed to show that this placement would not also have been appropriate for subsequent years. Accordingly, the court concluded that the Town was "not responsible for the cost of Michael's education at the Carroll School for the academic years 1979-80 through 1981-82."

In contesting the Town's proposed form of judgment embodying the court's conclusion, Mr. Panico argued that, despite finally losing on the merits of the IEP in August 1982, he should be reimbursed for his expenditures in 1979-1980, that the Town should finish paying for the recently completed 1981-1982 term, and that he should not be required to reimburse the Town for its payments to date, apparently because the school terms in question fell within the pendency of the administrative and judicial review contemplated by § 1415(e)(2). The case was transferred to another District Judge and consolidated with two other cases to resolve similar issues concerning the reimbursement for expenditures during the pendency of review proceedings.

In a decision on the consolidated cases, the court rejected Mr. Panico's argument that the Carroll School was the "current educational placement" during the pendency of the review proceedings and thus that under § 1415(e)(3) the Town was obligated to maintain that placement. *Doe v. Anrig*, 561 F.Supp. 121 (D. Mass. 1983). The court reasoned that the Panicos' unilateral action in placing Michael at the Carroll School without the Town's consent could not "confer thereon the imprimatur of continued placement," *id.*, at 129, n. 5, even though strictly speaking there was no actual placement in effect during the summer of 1979 because all parties agreed Michael was finished with the Memorial School and the Town itself proposed in the IEP to transfer him to a new school in the fall.

The District Court next rejected an argument, apparently grounded at least in part on a state regulation, that the Panicos were entitled to rely on the BSEA decision upholding their placement contrary to the IEP, regardless of whether that decision were ultimately reversed by a court. With respect to the payments made by the Town after the BSEA decision, under the State's threat to cut off funding, the court criticized the State for resorting to extrajudicial pressure to enforce a decision subject to further review. Because this "was not a case where the town was legally obliged under section 1415(e)(3) to continue payments preserving the status quo," the State's coercion could not be viewed as "the basis for a final decision on liability," and could only be "regarded as other than wrongful . . . on the assumption that the payments were to be returned if the order was ultimately reversed." *Id.*, at 130. The court entered a judgment ordering the Panicos to reimburse the Town for its payments for Michael's Carroll placement and related transportation in 1980-1981 and 1981-1982. The Panicos appealed.

In a broad opinion, most of which we do not review, the Court of Appeals for the First Circuit remanded the case a second time. 736 F.2d 773 (1st Cir. 1984). The court ruled, among other things, that the District Court erred in conducting a full trial *de novo*, that it gave insufficient weight to the BSEA findings, and that in other respects it did not properly evaluate the IEP. The court also considered several questions about the availability of reimbursement for interim placement. The Town argued that § 1415(e)(3) bars the Panicos from any reimbursement relief, even if on remand they were to prevail on the merits of the IEP, because of their unilateral change of Michael's placement during the pendency of the § 1415(e)(2) proceedings. The court held that such unilateral parental change of placement would not be "a bar to reimbursement of the parents if their actions are held to be appropriate at final judgment." *Id.*, at 799. In dictum the court suggested, however, that a lack of parental consultation with the Town or "attempt to achieve a negotiated compromise and agreement on a private placement," as contemplated by the Act, "may be taken into account in a district court's computation of an award of equitable reimbursement." *Ibid.* To guide the District Court on remand, the court stated that "whether to order reimbursement, and at what amount, is a question determined by balancing the equities." *Id.*, at 801. The court also held that the Panicos' reliance on the BSEA decision would estop the Town from obtaining reimbursement "for the period of reliance and requires that where parents have paid the bill for the period, they must be reimbursed." *Ibid.*

The Town filed a petition for a writ of certiorari in this Court challenging the decision of the Court of Appeals on numerous issues, including the scope of judicial review of the administrative decision and the relevance to the merits of an IEP of violations by local school authorities of the Act's procedural requirements. We granted certiorari, 469 U.S. 1071 (1984), only to consider the following two issues: whether the potential relief available under § 1415(e)(2) includes reimbursement to parents for private school tuition and related expenses, and whether § 1415(e)(3) bars such reimbursement to parents who reject a proposed IEP and place a child in a private school without the consent of local school authorities. We express no opinion on any of the many other views stated by the Court of Appeals.

* * *

The Act . . . provides for judicial review in state or federal court to "[a]ny party aggrieved by the findings and decision" made after the due process hearing. The Act confers on the reviewing court the following authority: "[T]he court shall receive the records of the administrative proceedings, shall hear additional evidence at the request of a party, and, basing its decision on the preponderance of the evidence, shall grant such relief as the court determines is appropriate." § 1415(e)(2).

The first question on which we granted certiorari requires us to decide whether this grant of authority includes the power to order school authorities to reimburse parents for their expenditures on private special education for a child if the court ultimately determines that such placement, rather than a proposed IEP, is proper under the Act.

We conclude that the Act authorizes such reimbursement. The statute directs the court to "grant such relief as [it] determines is appropriate." The ordinary meaning of these words confers broad discretion on the court. The type of relief is not further specified, except that it must be "appropriate." Absent other reference, the only possible interpretation is that the relief is to be "appropriate" in light of the purpose of the Act. As already noted, this is principally to provide handicapped children with "a free appropriate public education which emphasizes special education and related services designed to meet their unique needs." The Act contemplates that such education will be provided where possible in regular public schools, with the child participating as much as possible in the same activities as nonhandicapped children, but the Act also provides for placement in private schools at public expense where this is not possible. See § 1412(5); 34 CFR §§ 300.132, 300.227, 300.307(b), 300.347 1984). In a case where a court determines that a private placement desired by the parents was proper under the Act and that an IEP calling for placement in a public school was inappropriate, it seems clear beyond cavil that "appropriate" relief would include a prospective injunction directing the school officials to develop and implement at public expense an IEP placing the child in a private school.

If the administrative and judicial review under the Act could be completed in a matter of weeks, rather than years, it would be difficult to imagine a case in which such prospective injunctive relief would not be sufficient. As this case so vividly demonstrates, however, the review process is ponderous. A final judicial decision on the merits of an IEP will in most instances come a year or more after the school term covered by that IEP has passed. In the meantime, the parents who disagree with the proposed IEP are faced with a choice: go along with the IEP to the detriment of their child if it turns out to be inappropriate or pay for what they consider to be the appropriate placement. If they choose the latter course, which conscientious parents who have adequate means and who are reasonably confident of their assessment normally would, it would be an empty victory to have a court tell them several years later that they were right but that these expenditures could not in a proper case be reimbursed by the school officials. If that were the case, the child's right to a *free* appropriate public education, the parents' right to participate fully in developing a proper IEP, and all of the procedural safeguards would be less than complete. Because Congress undoubtedly did not intend this result, we are confident that by empowering the court to grant "appropriate" relief Congress meant to include retroactive reimbursement to parents as an available remedy in a proper case.

In this Court, the Town repeatedly characterizes reimbursement as "damages," but that simply is not the case. Reimbursement merely requires the Town to belatedly pay expenses that it should have paid all along and would have borne in the first instance had it developed a proper IEP. Such a *post hoc* determination of financial responsibility was contemplated in the legislative history:

> "If a parent contends that he or she has been forced, at that parent's own expense, to seek private schooling for the child because an appropriate program does not exist within the local educational agency responsible for the child's education and the local educational agency disagrees, that disagreement and *the question of who remains financially responsible* is a matter to which the due process procedures established under [the predecessor to § 1415] appl[y]." S.Rep. No. 94-168, p. 32 (1975), U.S.Code Cong. & Admin.News 1975, pp. 1425, 1456 (emphasis added).

See 34 CFR § 300.403(b) (1984) (disagreements and question of financial responsibility subject to the due process procedures).

Regardless of the availability of reimbursement as a form of relief in a proper case, the Town maintains that the Panicos have waived any right they otherwise might have to reimbursement because they violated § 1415(e)(3), which provides: "During the pendency of any proceedings conducted pursuant to [§ 1415], unless the State or local educational agency and the parents or guardian otherwise agree, the child shall remain in the then current educational placement of such child . . . ."

We need not resolve the academic question of what Michael's "then current educational placement" was in the summer of 1979, when both the Town and the parents had agreed that a new school was in order. For the purposes of our decision, we assume that the Pine Glen School, proposed in the IEP, was Michael's current placement and, therefore, that the Panicos did "change" his placement after they had rejected the IEP and had set the administrative review in motion. In so doing, the Panicos contravened the conditional command of § 1415(e)(3) that "the child shall remain in the then current educational placement."

As an initial matter, we note that the section calls for agreement by *either* the *State or* the *local educational agency*. The BSEA's decision in favor of the Panicos and the Carroll School placement would seem to constitute agreement by the State to the change of placement. The decision was issued in January 1980, so from then on the Panicos were no longer in violation of § 1415(e)(3). This conclusion, however, does not entirely resolve the instant dispute because the Panicos are also seeking reimbursement for Michael's expenses during the fall of 1979, prior to the State's concurrence in the Carroll School placement.

We do not agree with the Town that a parental violation of § 1415(e)(3) constitutes a waiver of reimbursement. The provision says nothing about financial responsibility, waiver, or parental right to reimbursement at the conclusion of judicial proceedings. Moreover, if the provision is interpreted to cut off parental rights to reimbursement, the principal purpose of the Act will in many cases be defeated in the same way as if reimbursement were never available. As in this case, parents will often notice a child's learning difficulties while the child is in a regular public school program. If the school officials disagree with the need for special education or the adequacy of the public school's program to meet the child's needs, it is unlikely they will agree to an interim private school placement while the review process runs its course. Thus, under the Town's reading of § 1415(e)(3), the parents are forced to leave the child in what may turn out to be an inappropriate educational placement or to obtain the appropriate placement only by sacrificing any claim for reimbursement. The Act was intended to give handicapped children both an appropriate education and a free one; it should not be interpreted to defeat one or the other of those objectives.

The legislative history supports this interpretation, favoring a proper interim placement pending the resolution of disagreements over the IEP: "The conferees are cognizant that an impartial due process hearing may be required to assure that the rights of the child have been completely protected. We did feel, however, that the placement, or change of placement should not be unnecessarily delayed while long and tedious administrative appeals were being exhausted. Thus the conference adopted a flexible approach to try to meet the needs of both the child and the State." 121 Cong.Rec. 37412 (1975) (Sen. Stafford).

We think at least one purpose of § 1415(e)(3) was to prevent school officials from removing a child from the regular public school classroom over the parents' objection pending completion of the review proceedings. As we observed in *Rowley*, 458 U.S., at 192, 102 S.Ct., at 3043, the impetus for the Act came from two federal-court decisions, *Pennsylvania Assn. for Retarded Children v. Commonwealth*, 334 F.Supp. 1257 (E.D. Pa. 1971), and 343 F.Supp. 279 (E.D. Pa. 1972), and *Mills v. Board of Education of District of Columbia*, 348 F.Supp. 866 (D. D.C. 1972), which arose from the efforts of parents of handicapped children to prevent the exclusion or expulsion of their children from the public schools. Congress was concerned about the apparently widespread practice of relegating handicapped children to private institutions or warehousing them in special classes. See § 1400(b)(4); 34 CFR § 300.347(a) (1984). We also note that § 1415(e)(3) is located in a section detailing procedural safeguards which are largely for the benefit of the parents and the child.

This is not to say that § 1415(e)(3) has no effect on parents. While we doubt that this provision would authorize a court to order parents to leave their child in a particular placement, we think it operates in such a way that parents who unilaterally change their child's placement during the pendency of review proceedings, without the consent of state or local school officials, do so at their own financial risk. If the courts ultimately determine that the IEP proposed by the school officials was appropriate, the parents would be barred from obtaining reimbursement for any interim period in which their child's placement violated § 1415(e)(3). This conclusion is supported by the agency's interpretation of the Act's application to private placements by the parents:

> "(a) If a handicapped child has available a free appropriate public education and the parents choose to place the child in a private school or facility, the public agency is not required by this part to pay for the child's education at the private school or facility. . . .

> "(b) Disagreements between a parent and a public agency regarding the availability of a program appropriate for the child, and the question of financial responsibility, are subject to the due process procedures under [§ 1415]." 34 CFR § 300.403 (1984).

We thus resolve the questions on which we granted certiorari; because the case is here in an interlocutory posture, we do not consider the estoppel ruling below or the specific equitable factors identified by the Court of Appeals for granting relief. We do think that the court was correct in concluding that "such relief as the court determines is appropriate," within the meaning of § 1415(e)(2), means that equitable considerations are relevant in fashioning relief.

The judgment of the Court of Appeals is

Affirmed.

Bill HONIG, California Superintendent of Public Instruction, Petitioner v. John DOE and Jack Smith.

484 U.S. 305 (1988)

JUSTICE BRENNAN delivered the opinion of the Court.

As a condition of federal financial assistance, the Education of the Handicapped Act requires States to ensure a "free appropriate public education" for all disabled children within their jurisdictions. In aid of this goal, the Act establishes a comprehensive system of procedural safeguards designed to ensure parental participation in decisions concerning the education of their disabled children and to provide administrative and judicial review of any decisions with which those parents disagree. Among these safeguards is the so-called "stay-put" provision, which directs that a disabled child "shall remain in [his or her] then current educational placement" pending completion of any review proceedings, unless the parents and state or local educational agencies otherwise agree. 20 U.S.C. § 1415(e)(3). Today we must decide whether, in the face of this statutory proscription, state or local school authorities may nevertheless unilaterally exclude disabled children from the classroom for dangerous or disruptive conduct growing out of their disabilities. In addition, we are called upon to decide whether a district court may, in the exercise of its equitable powers, order a State to provide educational services directly to a disabled child when the local agency fails to do so.

I

In the Education of the Handicapped Act (EHA or the Act), 84 Stat. 175, as amended, 20 U.S.C. § 1400 *et seq.*, Congress sought "to assure that all handicapped children have available to them . . . a free appropriate public education which emphasizes special education and related services designed to meet their unique needs, [and] to assure that the rights of handicapped children and their parents or guardians are protected." § 1400(c). When the law was passed in 1975, Congress had before it ample evidence that such legislative assurances were sorely needed: 21 years after this Court declared education to be "perhaps the most important function of state and local governments," *Brown v. Board of Education*, 347 U.S. 483, 493 (1954), congressional studies revealed that better than half of the Nation's 8 million disabled children were not receiving appropriate educational services. § 1400(b)(3). Indeed, one out of every eight of these children was excluded from the public school system altogether, § 1400(b)(4); many others were simply "warehoused" in special classes or were neglectfully shepherded through the system until they were old enough to drop out. See H.R.Rep. No. 94-332, p. 2 (1975). Among the most poorly served of disabled students were emotionally disturbed children: Congressional statistics revealed that for the school year immediately preceding passage of the Act, the educational needs of 82 percent of all children with emotional disabilities went unmet. See S.Rep. No. 94-168, p. 8 (1975), U.S.Code Cong. & Admin.News 1975, p. 1425 (hereinafter S.Rep.).

Although these educational failings resulted in part from funding constraints, Congress recognized that the problem reflected more than a lack of financial resources at the state and local levels. Two federal-court decisions, which the Senate Report characterized as "landmark," see *id.*, at 6, U.S.Code Cong. & Admin.News 1430, demonstrated that many disabled children were excluded pursuant to state statutes or local rules and policies, typically without any consultation with, or even notice to, their parents. See *Mills v. Board of Education of District of Columbia*, 348 F.Supp. 866 (D. D.C. 1972); *Pennsylvania Assn. for Retarded Children v. Pennsylvania*, 334 F.Supp. 1257 (E.D. Pa.1971), and 343 F.Supp. 279 (E.D. Pa. 1972) (*PARC*). Indeed, by the time of the EHA's enactment, parents had brought legal challenges to similar exclusionary practices in 27 other States. See S.Rep., at 6.

In responding to these problems, Congress did not content itself with passage of a simple funding statute. Rather, the EHA confers upon disabled students an enforceable substantive right to public education in participating States, see *Board of Education of Hendrick Hudson Central School Dist. v. Rowley*, 458 U.S. 176 (1982), and conditions federal financial assistance upon a State's compliance with the substantive and procedural goals of the Act. Accordingly, States seeking to qualify for federal funds must develop policies assuring all disabled children the "right to a free appropriate public education," and must file with the Secretary of Education formal plans mapping out in detail the programs, procedures, and timetables under which they will effectuate these policies. 20 U.S.C. §§ 1412(1), 1413(a). Such plans must assure that, "to the maximum extent appropriate," States will "mainstream" disabled children, *i.e.*, that they will educate them with children who are not disabled, and that they will segregate or otherwise remove such children from the regular classroom setting "only when the nature or severity of the handicap is such that education in regular classes . . . cannot be achieved satisfactorily." § 1412(5).

The primary vehicle for implementing these congressional goals is the "individualized educational program" (IEP), which the EHA mandates for each disabled child. Prepared at meetings between a representative of the local school district, the child's teacher, the parents or guardians, and, whenever appropriate, the disabled child, the IEP sets out the child's present educational performance, establishes annual and short-term objectives for improvements in that performance, and describes the specially designed instruction and services that will enable the child to meet those objectives. § 1401(19). The IEP must be reviewed and, where necessary, revised at least once a year in order to ensure that local agencies tailor the statutorily required "free appropriate public education" to each child's unique needs. § 1414(a)(5).

Envisioning the IEP as the centerpiece of the statute's education delivery system for disabled children, and aware that schools had all too often denied such children appropriate educations without in any way consulting their parents, Congress repeatedly emphasized throughout the Act the importance and indeed the necessity of parental participation in both the development of the IEP and any subsequent assessments of its effectiveness. See §§ 1400(c), 1401(19), 1412(7), 1415(b)(1)(A), (C), (D), (E), and 1415(b)(2). Accordingly, the Act establishes various procedural safeguards that guarantee parents both an opportunity for meaningful input into all decisions affecting their child's education and the right to seek review of any decisions they think inappropriate. These safeguards include the right to examine all relevant records pertaining to the identification, evaluation, and educational placement of their child; prior written notice whenever the responsible educational agency proposes (or refuses) to change the child's placement or program; an opportunity to present complaints concerning any aspect of the local agency's provision of a free appropriate public education; and an opportunity for "an impartial due process hearing" with respect to any such complaints. §§ 1415(b)(1), (2).

At the conclusion of any such hearing, both the parents and the local educational agency may seek further administrative review and, where that proves unsatisfactory, may file a civil action in any state or federal court. §§ 1415(c), (e)(2). In addition to reviewing the administrative record, courts are empowered to take additional evidence at the request of either party and to "grant such relief as [they] determine[ ] is appropriate." § 1415(e)(2). The "stay-put" provision at issue in this case governs the placement of a child while these often lengthy review procedures run their course. It directs that: "During the pendency of any proceedings conducted pursuant to [§ 1415], unless the State or local educational agency and the parents or guardian otherwise agree, the child shall remain in the then current educational placement of such child. . . ." § 1415(e)(3).

The present dispute grows out of the efforts of certain officials of the San Francisco Unified School District (SFUSD) to expel two emotionally disturbed children from school indefinitely for violent and disruptive conduct related to their disabilities. In November 1980, respondent John Doe assaulted another student at the Louise Lombard School, a developmental center for disabled children. Doe's April 1980 IEP identified him as a socially and physically awkward 17-year-old who experienced considerable difficulty controlling his impulses and anger. Among the goals set out in his IEP was "[i]mprovement in [his] ability to relate to [his] peers [and to] cope with frustrating situations without resorting to aggressive acts." App. 17. Frustrating situations, however, were an unfortunately prominent feature of Doe's school career: physical abnormalities, speech difficulties, and poor grooming habits had made him the target of teasing and ridicule as early as the first grade, *id.*, at 23; his 1980 IEP reflected his continuing difficulties with peers, noting that his social skills had deteriorated and that he could tolerate only minor frustration before exploding. *Id.*, at 15-16.

On November 6, 1980, Doe responded to the taunts of a fellow student in precisely the explosive manner anticipated by his IEP: he choked the student with sufficient force to leave abrasions on the child's neck, and kicked out a school window while being escorted to the principal's office afterwards. *Id.*, at 208. Doe admitted his misconduct and the school subsequently suspended him for five days. Thereafter, his principal referred the matter to the SFUSD Student Placement Committee (SPC or Committee) with the recommendation that Doe be expelled. On the day the suspension was to end, the SPC notified Doe's mother that it was proposing to exclude her child permanently from SFUSD and was therefore extending his suspension until such time as the expulsion proceedings were completed. The Committee further advised her that she was entitled to attend the November 25 hearing at which it planned to discuss the proposed expulsion.

After unsuccessfully protesting these actions by letter, Doe brought this suit against a host of local school officials and the State Superintendent of Public Instructions. Alleging that the suspension and proposed expulsion violated the EHA, he sought a temporary restraining order canceling the SPC hearing and requiring school officials to convene an IEP meeting. The District Judge granted the requested injunctive relief and further ordered defendants to provide home tutoring for Doe on an interim basis; shortly thereafter, she issued a preliminary injunction directing defendants to return Doe to his then current educational placement at Louise Lombard School pending completion of the IEP review process. Doe reentered school on December 15, 5 1/2 weeks, and 24 school-days, after his initial suspension.

Respondent Jack Smith was identified as an emotionally disturbed child by the time he entered the second grade in 1976. School records prepared that year indicated that he was unable "to control verbal or physical outburst[s]" and exhibited a "[s]evere disturbance in relationships with peers and adults." *Id.*, at 123. Further evaluations subsequently revealed that he had been physically and emotionally abused as an infant and young child and that, despite above average intelligence, he experienced academic and social difficulties as a result of extreme hyperactivity and low self-esteem. *Id.*, at 136, 139, 155, 176. Of particular concern was Smith's propensity for verbal hostility; one evaluator noted that the child reacted to stress by "attempt [ing] to cover his feelings of low self-worth through aggressive behavior [,] . . . primarily verbal provocations." *Id.*, at 136.

Based on these evaluations, SFUSD placed Smith in a learning center for emotionally disturbed children. His grandparents, however, believed that his needs would be better served in the public school setting and, in September 1979, the school district acceded to their requests and enrolled him at A.P. Giannini Middle School. His February 1980 IEP recommended placement in a Learning Disability Group, stressing the need for close supervision and a highly structured environment. *Id.*, at 111. Like earlier evaluations, the February 1980 IEP noted that Smith was easily distracted, impulsive, and anxious; it therefore proposed a half-day schedule and suggested that the placement be undertaken on a trial basis. *Id.*, at 112, 115.

At the beginning of the next school year, Smith was assigned to a full-day program; almost immediately thereafter he began misbehaving. School officials met twice with his grandparents in October 1980 to discuss returning him to a half-day program; although the grandparents agreed to the reduction, they apparently were never apprised of their right to challenge the decision through EHA procedures. The school officials also warned them that if the child continued his disruptive behavior-which included stealing, extorting money from fellow students, and making sexual comments to female classmates-they would seek to expel him. On November 14, they made good on this threat, suspending Smith for five days after he made further lewd comments. His principal referred the matter to the SPC, which recommended exclusion from SFUSD. As it did in John Doe's case, the Committee scheduled a hearing and extended the suspension indefinitely pending a final disposition in the matter. On November 28, Smith's counsel protested these actions on grounds essentially identical to those raised by Doe, and the SPC agreed to cancel the hearing and to return Smith to a half-day program at A.P. Giannini or to provide home tutoring. Smith's grandparents chose the latter option and the school began home instruction on December 10; on January 6, 1981, an IEP team convened to discuss alternative placements.

After learning of Doe's action, Smith sought and obtained leave to intervene in the suit. The District Court subsequently entered summary judgment in favor of respondents on their EHA claims and issued a permanent injunction. In a series of decisions, the District Judge found that the proposed expulsions and indefinite suspensions of respondents for conduct attributable to their disabilities deprived them of their congressionally mandated right to a free appropriate public education, as well as their right to have that education provided in accordance with the procedures set out in the EHA. The District Judge therefore permanently enjoined the school district from taking any disciplinary action other than a 2- or 5-day suspension against any disabled child for disability-related misconduct, or from effecting any other change in the educational placement of any such child without parental consent pending completion of any EHA proceedings. In addition, the judge barred the State from authorizing unilateral placement changes and directed it to establish an EHA compliance-monitoring system or, alternatively, to enact guidelines governing local school responses to disability-related miscon- duct. Finally, the judge ordered the State to provide services directly to disabled children when, in any individual case, the State determined that the local educational agency was unable or unwilling to do so.

On appeal, the Court of Appeals for the Ninth Circuit affirmed the orders with slight modifications. *Doe v. Maher*, 793 F.2d 1470 (9th Cir. 1986). Agreeing with the District Court that an indefinite suspension in aid of expulsion constitutes a prohibited "change in placement" under § 1415(e)(3), the Court of Appeals held that the stay-put provision admitted of no "dangerousness" exception and that the statute therefore rendered invalid those provisions of the California Education Code permitting the indefinite suspension or expulsion of disabled children for misconduct arising out of their disabilities. The court concluded, however, that fixed suspensions of up to 30 schooldays did not fall within the reach of § 1415(e)(3), and therefore upheld recent amendments to the state Education Code authorizing such suspensions. Lastly, the court affirmed that portion of the injunction requiring the State to provide services directly to a disabled child when the local educational agency fails to do so.

Petitioner Bill Honig, California Superintendent of Public Instruction, sought review in this Court, claiming that the Court of Appeals' construction of the stay-put provision conflicted with that of several other Courts of Appeals which had recognized a dangerousness exception . . . and that the direct services ruling placed an intolerable burden on the State. We granted certiorari to resolve these questions, 479 U.S. 1084 (1987), and now affirm.

II

* * *

Because we believe that respondent Smith has demonstrated both "a sufficient likelihood that he will again be wronged in a similar way," *Los Angeles v. Lyons*, 461 U.S., at 111, and that any resulting claim he may have for relief will surely evade our review, we turn to the merits of his case.

III

The language of § 1415(e)(3) is unequivocal. It states plainly that during the pendency of any proceedings initiated under the Act, unless the state or local educational agency and the parents or guardian of a disabled child otherwise agree, "the child *shall* remain in the then current educational placement." § 1415(e)(3) (emphasis added). Faced with this clear directive, petitioner asks us to read a "dangerousness" exception into the stay-put provision on the basis of either of two essentially inconsistent assumptions: first, that Congress thought the residual authority of school officials to exclude dangerous students from the classroom too obvious for comment; or second, that Congress inadvertently failed to provide such authority and this Court must therefore remedy the oversight. Because we cannot accept either premise, we decline petitioner's invitation to rewrite the statute.

Petitioner's arguments proceed, he suggests, from a simple, commonsense proposition: Congress could not have intended the stay-put provision to be read literally, for such a construction leads to the clearly unintended, and untenable, result that school districts must return violent or dangerous students to school while the often lengthy EHA proceedings run their course. We think it clear, however, that Congress very much meant to strip schools of the *unilateral* authority they had traditionally employed to exclude disabled students, particularly emotionally disturbed students, from school. In so doing, Congress did not leave school administrators powerless to deal with dangerous students; it did, however, deny school officials their former right to "self-help," and directed that in the future the removal of disabled students could be accomplished only with the permission of the parents or, as a last resort, the courts.

As noted above, Congress passed the EHA after finding that school systems across the country had excluded one out of every eight disabled children from classes. In drafting the law, Congress was largely guided by the recent decisions in *Mills v. Board of Education of District of Columbia*, 348 F.Supp. 866 (D. D.C. 1972), and *PARC*, 343 F.Supp. 279 (E.D. Pa. 1972), both of which involved the exclusion of hard-to-handle disabled students. *Mills* in particular demonstrated the extent to which schools used disciplinary measures to bar children from the classroom. There, school officials had labeled four of the seven minor plaintiffs "behavioral problems," and had excluded them from classes without providing any alternative education to them or any notice to their parents. 348 F.Supp., at 869-870. After finding that this practice was not limited to the named plaintiffs but affected in one way or another an estimated class of 12,000 to 18,000 disabled students, *id.*, at 868-869, 875, the District Court enjoined future exclusions, suspensions, or expulsions "on grounds of discipline." *Id.*, at 880.

Congress attacked such exclusionary practices in a variety of ways. It required participating States to educate *all* disabled children, regardless of the severity of their disabilities, 20 U.S.C. § 1412(2)(C), and included within the definition of "handicapped" those children with serious emotional disturbances. § 1401(1). It further provided for meaningful parental participation in all aspects of a child's educational placement, and barred schools, through the stay-put provision, from changing that placement over the parent's objection until all review proceedings were completed. Recognizing that those proceedings might prove long and tedious, the Act's drafters did not intend § 1415(e)(3) to operate inflexibly, see 121 Cong.Rec. 37412 (1975) (remarks of Sen. Stafford), and they therefore allowed for interim placements where parents and school officials are able to agree on one. Conspicuously absent from § 1415(e)(3), however, is any emergency exception for dangerous students. This absence is all the more telling in light of the injunctive decree issued in *PARC*, which permitted school officials unilaterally to remove students in " 'extraordinary circumstances.' " 343 F.Supp., at 301. Given the lack of any similar exception in *Mills*, and the close attention Congress devoted to these "landmark" decisions, see S.Rep., at 6, U.S.Code Cong. & Admin.News p. 1430, we can only conclude that the omission was intentional; we are therefore not at liberty to engraft onto the statute an exception Congress chose not to create.

Our conclusion that § 1415(e)(3) means what it says does not leave educators hamstrung. The Department of Education has observed that, "[w]hile the [child's] placement may not be changed [during any complaint proceeding], this does not preclude the agency from using its normal procedures for dealing with children who are endangering themselves or others." Comment following 34 CFR § 300.513 (1987). Such procedures may include the use of study carrels, timeouts, detention, or the restriction of privileges. More drastically, where a student poses an immediate threat to the safety of others, officials may temporarily suspend him or her for up to 10 schooldays. This authority, which respondent in no way disputes, not only ensures that school administrators can protect the safety of others by promptly removing the most dangerous of students, it also provides a "cooling down" period during which officials can initiate IEP review and seek to persuade the child's parents to agree to an interim placement. And in those cases in which the parents of a truly dangerous child adamantly refuse to permit any change in placement, the 10-day respite gives school officials an opportunity to invoke the aid of the courts under § 1415(e)(2), which empowers courts to grant any appropriate relief.

Petitioner contends, however, that the availability of judicial relief is more illusory than real, because a party seeking review under § 1415(e)(2) must exhaust time-consuming administrative remedies, and because under the Court of Appeals' construction of § 1415(e)(3), courts are as bound by the stay-put provision's "automatic injunction," 793 F.2d, at 1486, as are schools.

It is true that judicial review is normally not available under § 1415(e)(2) until all administrative proceedings are completed, but as we have previously noted, parents may bypass the administrative process where exhaustion would be futile or inadequate. See *Smith v. Robinson*, 468 U.S. 992, 1014, n. 17 (1984) (citing cases); see also 121 Cong.Rec. 37416 (1975) (remarks of Sen. Williams) ("[E]xhaustion . . . should not be required . . . in cases where such exhaustion would be futile either as a legal or practical matter"). While many of the EHA's procedural safeguards protect the rights of parents and children, schools can and do seek redress through the administrative review process, and we have no reason to believe that Congress meant to require schools alone to exhaust in all cases, no matter how exigent the circumstances. The burden in such cases, of course, rests with the school to demonstrate the futility or inadequacy of administrative review, but nothing in § 1415(e)(2) suggests that schools are completely barred from attempting to make such a showing. Nor do we think that § 1415(e)(3) operates to limit the equitable powers of district courts such that they cannot, in appropriate cases, temporarily enjoin a dangerous disabled child from attending school. As the EHA's legislative history makes clear, one of the evils Congress sought to remedy was the unilateral exclusion of disabled children by *schools*, not courts, and one of the purposes of § 1415(e)(3), therefore, was "to prevent *school* officials from removing a child from the regular public school classroom over the parents' objection pending completion of the review proceedings." *Burlington School Committee v. Massachusetts Dept. of Education*, 471 U.S., at 373 (emphasis added). The stay-put provision in no way purports to limit or pre-empt the authority conferred on courts by § 1415(e)(2), see *Doe v. Brookline School Committee*, 722 F.2d 910, 917 (CA1 1983); indeed, it says nothing whatever about judicial power.

In short, then, we believe that school officials are entitled to seek injunctive relief under § 1415(e)(2) in appropriate cases. In any such action, § 1415(e)(3) effectively creates a presumption in favor of the child's current educational placement which school officials can overcome only by showing that maintaining the child in his or her current placement is substantially likely to result in injury either to himself or herself, or to others. In the present case, we are satisfied that the District Court, in enjoining the state and local defendants from indefinitely suspending respondent or otherwise unilaterally altering his then current placement, properly balanced respondent's interest in receiving a free appropriate public education in accordance with the procedures and requirements of the EHA against the interests of the state and local school officials in maintaining a safe learning environment for all their students.

IV

We believe the courts below properly construed and applied § 1415(e)(3), except insofar as the Court of Appeals held that a suspension in excess of 10 schooldays does not constitute a "change in placement." We therefore affirm the Court of Appeals' judgment on this issue as modified herein. Because we are equally divided on the question whether a court may order a State to provide services directly to a disabled child where the local agency has failed to do so, we affirm the Court of Appeals' judgment on this issue as well.

Affirmed.

Chief Justice REHNQUIST, concurring (omitted).

Justice SCALIA, with whom Justice O'CONNOR joins, dissenting [argue that case is moot].

DANIEL R.R., Plaintiff-Appellant, v. STATE BOARD OF EDUCATION, et al., Defendants, El Paso Independent School District, Defendant-Appellee.

874 F.2d 1036 (5th Cir. 1989)

Before THORNBERRY, GEE and POLITZ, Circuit Judges.

GEE, CIRCUIT JUDGE:

Plaintiffs in this action, a handicapped boy and his parents, urge that a local school district failed to comply with the Education of the Handicapped Act. Specifically, they maintain that a school district's refusal to place the child in a class with nonhandicapped students violates the Act. The district court disagreed and, after a careful review of the record, we affirm the district court.

I. *Background*

A. General

In 1975, on a finding that almost half of the handicapped children in the United States were receiving an inadequate education or none at all, Congress passed the Education of the Handicapped Act (EHA or Act). See 20 U.S.C.A. § 1400(b) (West 1988 Supp.); S.Rep. No. 168, 94th Cong., 1st Sess. 8 (1975), *reprinted in* 1975 U.S.Code Cong. & Admin.News 1425, 1432. Before passage of the Act, as the Supreme Court has noted, many handicapped children suffered under one of two equally ineffective approaches to their educational needs: either they were excluded entirely from public education or they were deposited in regular education classrooms with no assistance, left to fend for themselves in an environment inappropriate for their needs. To entice state and local school officials to improve upon these inadequate methods of educating children with special needs, Congress created the EHA, having as its purpose providing handicapped children access to public education and requiring states to adopt procedures that will result in individualized consideration of and instruction for each handicapped child.

The Act is largely procedural. It mandates a "free appropriate public education" for each handicapped child and sets forth procedures designed to ensure that each child's education meets that requirement. 20 U.S.C.A. §§ 1412(1) and 1415(a)-(e). School officials are required to determine the appropriate placement for each child and must develop an Individualized Educational Plan (IEP) that tailors the child's education to his individual needs. The child's parents are involved at all stages of the process. *See generally* § 1415(b). In addition, the Act requires that handicapped children be educated in regular education classrooms, with nonhandicapped students-as opposed to special education classrooms with handicapped students only-to the greatest extent appropriate. § 1412(5)(B). Educating a handicapped child in a regular education classroom with nonhandicapped children is familiarly known as "mainstreaming," and the mainstreaming requirement is the source of the controversy between the parties before us today.

B. Particular

Daniel R. is a six year old boy who was enrolled, at the time this case arose, in the El Paso Independent School District (EPISD). A victim of Downs Syndrome, Daniel is mentally retarded and speech impaired. By September 1987, Daniel's developmental age was between two and three years and his communication skills were slightly less than those of a two year old.

In 1985, Daniel's parents, Mr. and Mrs. R., enrolled him in EPISD's Early Childhood Program, a half-day program devoted entirely to special education. Daniel completed one academic year in the Early Childhood Program. Before the 1986-87 school year began, Mrs. R. requested a new placement that would provide association with nonhandicapped children. Mrs. R. wanted EPISD to place Daniel in Pre-kindergarten-a half-day, regular education class. Mrs. R. conferred with Joan Norton, the Pre-kindergarten instructor, proposing that Daniel attend the half-day Pre-kindergarten class in addition to the half-day Early Childhood class. As a result, EPISD's Admission, Review and Dismissal (ARD) Committee met and designated the combined regular and special education program as Daniel's placement.

This soon proved unwise, and not long into the school year Mrs. Norton began to have reservations about Daniel's presence in her class. Daniel did not participate without constant, individual attention from the teacher or her aide, and failed to master any of the skills Mrs. Norton was trying to teach her students. Modifying the Pre-kindergarten curriculum and her teaching methods sufficiently to reach Daniel would have required Mrs. Norton to modify the curriculum almost beyond recognition. In November 1986, the ARD Committee met again, concluded that Pre-kindergarten was inappropriate for Daniel, and decided to change Daniel's placement. Under the new placement, Daniel would attend only the special education, Early Childhood class; would eat lunch in the school cafeteria, with nonhandicapped children, three days a week if his mother was present to supervise him; and would have contact with nonhandicapped students during recess. Believing that the ARD had improperly shut the door to regular education for Daniel, Mr. and Mrs. R. exercised their right to a review of the ARD Committee's decision.

As the EHA requires, Mr. and Mrs. R. appealed to a hearing officer who upheld the ARD Committee's decision. See § 1415(b)(2). After a hearing which consumed five days of testimony and produced over 2500 pages of transcript, the hearing officer concluded that Daniel could not participate in the Pre-kindergarten class without constant attention from the instructor because the curriculum was beyond his abilities. In addition, the hearing officer found, Daniel was receiving little educational benefit from Pre-kindergarten and was disrupting the class-not in the ordinary sense of the term, but in the sense that his needs absorbed most of the teacher's time and diverted too much of her attention away from the rest of the class. Finally, the instructor would have to downgrade 90 to 100 percent of the Pre-kindergarten curriculum to bring it to a level that Daniel could master. Thus, the hearing officer concluded, the regular education, Pre-kindergarten class was not the appropriate placement for Daniel.

Dissatisfied with the hearing officer's decision, Mr. and Mrs. R. proceeded to the next level of review by filing this action in the district court. See § 1415(e). Although the EHA permits the parties to supplement the administrative record, Daniel's representatives declined to do so; and the court conducted its de novo review on the basis of the administrative record alone. The district court decided the case on cross motions for summary judgment. Relying primarily on Daniel's inability to receive an educational benefit in regular education, the district court affirmed the hearing officer's decision.

Mr. and Mrs. R. again appeal, but before we turn to the merits of the appeal we must pause to consider an issue that neither of the parties raised but which we must consider on our own initiative.

II. *Mootness*

* * *

The ponderous administrative and judicial review did, as the Court predicted, outlive Daniel's placement and IEP, allowing them to evade review. As the case presents a live controversy, we turn to the merits of Daniel's appeal.

III. *Procedural Violations*

At the heart of the EHA lie detailed procedural provisions, processes designed to guarantee that each handicapped student's education is tailored to his unique needs and abilities. The EHA, and the regulations promulgated pursuant to it, contain procedures for determining whether the appropriate placement is regular or special education, for preparing an IEP once the child is placed, for changing the placement or the IEP, and for removing the child from regular education. 20 U.S.C.A. §§ 1412 and 1415; 34 C.F.R. §§ 300.300-300.576 (1986). The Act's procedural guarantees are not mere procedural hoops through which Congress wanted state and local educational agencies to jump. Rather, "the formality of the Act's procedures is itself a safeguard against arbitrary or erroneous decisionmaking." *Jackson v. Franklin County School Board*, 806 F.2d 623, 630 (5th Cir.1986). Indeed, a violation of the EHA's procedural guarantees may be a sufficient ground for holding that a school system has failed to provide a free appropriate public education and, thus, has violated the Act. *Id.* at 629; *Hall v. Vance County Board of Education*, 774 F.2d 629, 635 (4th Cir.1985). Daniel raises five claims of procedural error, each without merit.

First, Daniel contends that EPISD failed to give proper notice of a proposed change in his IEP, an assertion that misconstrues the nature of EPISD's proposed action.

* * *

Second, ignoring the events surrounding EPISD's decision, Daniel complains that EPISD did not evaluate him before removing him from regular education . . . . When a student and his parents agree with the school's current evaluation and refuse a new evaluation, they can scarcely be heard to complain of a procedural violation based upon the school's failure to conduct a new evaluation.

Third, Daniel asserts that EPISD failed to provide a continuum of educational services . . . . EPISD has provided a continuum of alternative placements and has demonstrated an admirable willingness to experiment with and to adjust Daniel's placement to arrive at the appropriate mix of educational environments.

Fourth, Daniel maintains that EPISD removed him from the regular classroom for disciplinary reasons but failed to follow the EHA's procedure for removals based on disciplinary problems. Again, Daniel has misconstrued the events leading to this appeal

. . . .Thus, EPISD's decision to remove Daniel from regular education did not trigger the EHA's disciplinary procedures.

Finally, Daniel suggests that EPISD did not follow the EHA's procedure for removing a child from regular education . . . . Daniel misunderstands the nature of this issue; it relates to the substantive question whether and to what extent Daniel should be mainstreamed, not to the procedural requirements of the EHA . . . . As we find no merit to Daniel's claims of procedural error, we turn to his substantive claims.

IV. *Substantive Violations*

A. Mainstreaming Under the EHA

The cornerstone of the EHA is the "free appropriate public education." As a condition of receiving federal funds, states must have "in effect a policy that assures all handicapped children the right to a free appropriate public education." § 1412(1). The Act defines a free appropriate public education in broad, general terms without dictating substantive educational policy or mandating specific educational methods. In *Rowley*, the Supreme Court fleshed out the Act's skeletal definition of its principal term: "a 'free appropriate public education' consists of educational instruction specially designed to meet the unique needs of the handicapped child, supported by such services as are necessary to permit the child 'to benefit' from the instruction." *Rowley*, 458 U.S. at 188-89. The Court's interpretation of the Act's language does not, however, add substance to the Act's vague terms; instruction specially designed to meet each student's unique needs is as imprecise a directive as the language actually found in the Act.

The imprecise nature of the EHA's mandate does not reflect legislative omission. Rather, it reflects two deliberate legislative decisions . . . . Ultimately, the Act mandates an education for each handicapped child that is responsive to his needs, but leaves the substance and the details of that education to state and local school officials.

In contrast to the EHA's vague mandate for a free appropriate public education lies one very specific directive prescribing the educational environment for handicapped children. Each state must establish:

> procedures to assure that, to the maximum extent appropriate, handicapped children . . . are educated with children who are not handicapped, and that special education, separate schooling or other removal of handicapped children from the regular educational environment occurs only when the nature or severity of the handicap is such that education in regular classes with the use of supplementary aids and services cannot be achieved satisfactorily.

§ 1412(5)(B). With this provision, Congress created a strong preference in favor of mainstreaming.

By creating a statutory preference for mainstreaming, Congress also created a tension between two provisions of the Act. School districts must both seek to mainstream handicapped children and, at the same time, must tailor each child's educational placement and program to his special needs. §§ 1412(1) and (5)(B). Regular classes, however, will not provide an education that accounts for each child's particular needs in every case. The nature or severity of some children's handicaps is such that only special education can address their needs. For these children, mainstreaming does not provide an education designed to meet their unique needs and, thus, does not provide a free appropriate public education. As a result, we cannot evaluate in the abstract whether a challenged placement meets the EHA's mainstreaming requirement. "Rather, that laudable policy objective must be weighed in tandem with the Act's principal goal of ensuring that the public schools provide handicapped children with a free appropriate public education." *Lachman*, 852 F.2d at 299; *Wilson v. Marana Unified School District*, 735 F.2d 1178, 1183 (9th Cir.1984) (citations omitted).

Although Congress preferred education in the regular education environment, it also recognized that regular education is not a suitable setting for educating many handicapped children. *Rowley*, 458 U.S. at 181 n. 4; *Lachman*, 852 F.2d at 295. Thus, the EHA allows school officials to remove a handicapped child from regular education or to provide special education if they cannot educate the child satisfactorily in the regular classroom. § 1412(5)(B). Even when school officials can mainstream the child, they need not provide for an exclusively mainstreamed environment; the Act requires school officials to mainstream each child only to the maximum extent appropriate. *Id.* In short, the Act's mandate for a free appropriate public education qualifies and limits its mandate for education in the regular classroom. Schools must provide a free appropriate public education and must do so, to the maximum extent appropriate, in regular education classrooms. But when education in a regular classroom cannot meet the handicapped child's unique needs, the presumption in favor of mainstreaming is overcome and the school need not place the child in regular education. *See Lachman*, 852 F.2d at 295; *A.W.*, 813 F.2d at 163; *Roncker*, 700 F.2d at 1063. The Act does not, however, provide any substantive standards for striking the proper balance between its requirement for mainstreaming and its mandate for a free appropriate public education.

B. Determining Compliance With the Mainstreaming Requirement

Determining the contours of the mainstreaming requirement is a question of first impression for us. In the seminal interpretation of the EHA, the Supreme Court posited a two-part test for determining whether a school has provided a free appropriate public education: "First, has the State complied with the procedures set forth in the Act. And second, is the individualized educational program developed through the Act's procedures reasonably calculated to enable the child to receive educational benefits." *Rowley*, 458 U.S. at 206-07 (footnotes omitted). Despite the attractive ease of this two part inquiry, it is not the appropriate tool for determining whether a school district has met its mainstreaming obligations. In *Rowley*, the handicapped student was placed in a regular education class; the EHA's mainstreaming requirement was not an issue presented for the Court's consideration. Indeed, the Court carefully limited its decision to the facts before it, noting that it was not establishing a single test that would determine "the adequacy of educational benefits conferred upon all children covered by the Act." *Id.* at 202. Faced with the same issue we face today, both the Sixth and the Eighth Circuit concluded that the *Rowley* test was not intended to decide mainstreaming issues. *A.W.*, 813 F.2d at 163; *Roncker*, 700 F.2d at 1063. Moreover, both Circuits noted that the *Rowley* Court's analysis is ill suited for evaluating compliance with the mainstreaming requirement. *A.W.*, 813 F.2d at 163; *Roncker*, 700 F.2d at 1062. As the Eighth Circuit explained, the *Rowley* test assumes that the state has met all of the requirements of the Act, including the mainstreaming requirement. *A.W.*, 813 F.2d at 163 n. 7 (citations omitted). The *Rowley* test thus assumes the answer to the question presented in a mainstreaming case. Given the *Rowley* Court's express limitation on its own opinion, we must agree with the Sixth and Eighth Circuits that the *Rowley* test does not advance our inquiry when the question presented is whether the

Act's mainstreaming requirement has been met.

Although we have not yet developed a standard for evaluating mainstreaming questions, we decline to adopt the approach that other circuits have taken. In *Roncker*, visiting the same question which we address today, the Sixth Circuit devised its own test to determine when and to what extent a handicapped child must be mainstreamed. According to the *Roncker* court,

> [t]he proper inquiry is whether a proposed placement is appropriate under the Act. . . . In a case where the segregated facility is considered superior, the court should determine whether the services which make that placement superior could be feasibly provided in a non-segregated setting. If they can, the placement in the segregated school would be inappropriate under the Act.

Roncker, 700 F.2d at 1063 (citation and footnote omitted); *accord, A.W.*, 813 F.2d at 163. We respectfully decline to follow the Sixth Circuit's analysis. Certainly, the *Roncker* test accounts for factors that are important in any mainstreaming case. We believe, however, that the test necessitates too intrusive an inquiry into the educational policy choices that Congress deliberately left to state and local school officials. Whether a particular service feasibly can be provided in a regular or special education setting is an administrative determination that state and local school officials are far better qualified and situated than are we to make. Moreover, the test makes little reference to the language of the EHA. Yet, as we shall see, we believe that the language of the Act itself provides a workable test for determining whether a state has complied with the Act's mainstreaming requirement.

Nor do we find the district court's approach to the issue the proper tool for analyzing the mainstreaming obligation. Relying primarily on whether Daniel could receive an educational benefit from regular education, the district court held that the special education class was the appropriate placement for Daniel. According to the court, "some children, even aided by supplemental aids and services in a regular education classroom, will never receive an educational benefit that approximates the level of skill and comprehension acquisition of nonhandicapped children." In these cases, regular education does not provide the child an appropriate education and the presumption in favor of mainstreaming is overcome. As no aspect of the Pre-kindergarten curriculum was within Daniel's reach, EPISD was not required to mainstream him. Given the nature and severity of Daniel's handicap at the time EPISD placed him, we agree with the district court's conclusion that EPISD was not required to mainstream Daniel. We disagree, however, with the court's analysis of the mainstreaming issue, finding it troublesome for two reasons: first, as a prerequisite to mainstreaming, the court would require handicapped children to learn at approximately the same level as their nonhandicapped classmates. Second, the court places too much emphasis on the handicapped student's ability to achieve an educational benefit.

First, requiring as a prerequisite to mainstreaming that the handicapped child be able to learn at approximately the same level as his nonhandicapped classmates fails to take into account the principles that the Supreme Court announced in *Rowley*. Our public school system tolerates a wide range of differing learning abilities; at the same time, it provides educational opportunities that do not necessarily account for all of those different capacities to learn. As the *Rowley* Court noted, "[t]he educational opportunities provided by our public school systems undoubtedly differ from student to student, depending upon a myriad of factors that might affect a particular student's ability to assimilate information presented in the classroom." *Rowley*, 458 U.S. at 198.

With the EHA, Congress extended the states' tolerance of educational differences to include tolerance of many handicapped children. States must accept in their public schools children whose abilities and needs differ from those of the average student. Moreover, some of those students' abilities are vastly different from those of their nonhandicapped peers:

> [t]he Act requires participating states to educate a wide spectrum of handicapped children, from the marginally hearing impaired to the profoundly retarded and palsied. It is clear that the benefits obtainable by children at one end of the spectrum will differ dramatically from those obtainable by children at the other end, with infinite variations in between. One child may have little difficulty competing successfully with nonhandicapped children while another child may encounter great difficulty in acquiring even the most basic of self maintenance skills.

Rowley, 458 U.S. at 202, 102 S.Ct. at 3048, 73 L.Ed.2d at 709. The *Rowley* court rejected the notion that the EHA requires states to provide handicapped children with educational opportunities that are equal to those provided to nonhandicapped students. *Id.* at 189. Thus, the Court recognized that the Act draws handicapped children into the regular education environment but, in the nature of things, cannot always offer them the same educational opportunities that regular education offers nonhandicapped children. States must tolerate educational differences; they need not perform the impossible: erase those differences by taking steps to equalize educational opportunities. As a result, the Act accepts the notion that handicapped students will participate in regular education but that some of them will not benefit as much as nonhandicapped students will. The Act requires states to tolerate a wide range of educational abilities in their schools and, specifically, in regular education-the EHA's preferred educational environment. Given the tolerance embodied in the EHA, we cannot predicate access to regular education on a child's ability to perform on par with nonhandicapped children.

We recognize that some handicapped children may not be able to master as much of the regular education curriculum as their nonhandicapped classmates. This does not mean, however, that those handicapped children are not receiving any benefit from regular education. Nor does it mean that they are not receiving all of the benefit that their handicapping condition will permit. If the child's individual needs make mainstreaming appropriate, we cannot deny the child access to regular education simply because his educational achievement lags behind that of his classmates.

Second, the district court placed too much emphasis on educational benefits. Certainly, whether a child will benefit educationally from regular education is relevant and important to our analysis. Congress's primary purpose in enacting the EHA was to provide access to education for handicapped children. *Rowley*, 458 U.S. at 192, 193 n. 15. Implicit in Congress's purpose to provide access is a purpose to provide meaningful access, access that is sufficient to confer some educational benefit on the child. *Id.* at 200. Thus, the decision whether to mainstream a child must include an inquiry into whether the student will gain any educational benefit from regular education. Our analysis cannot stop here, however, for educational benefits are not mainstreaming's only virtue. Rather, mainstreaming may have benefits in and of itself. For example, the language and behavior models available from nonhandicapped children may be essential or helpful to the handicapped child's development. In other words, although a handicapped child may not be able to absorb all of the regular education curriculum, he may benefit from nonacademic experiences in the regular education environment. As the Sixth Circuit explained "[i]n some cases, a placement which may be considered better for academic reasons may not be appropriate because of the failure to provide for mainstreaming." *Roncker*, 700 F.2d at 1063. As we are not comfortable with the district court or the Sixth Circuit's approach to the mainstreaming question, we return to the text of the EHA for guidance.

Ultimately, our task is to balance competing requirements of the EHA's dual mandate: a free appropriate public education that is provided, to the maximum extent appropriate, in the regular education classroom. As we begin our task we must keep in mind that Congress left the choice of educational policies and methods where it properly belongs-in the hands of state and local school officials. Our task is not to second-guess state and local policy decisions; rather, it is the narrow one of determining whether state and local school officials have complied with the Act. Adhering to the language of the EHA, we discern a two part test for determining compliance with the mainstreaming requirement. First, we ask whether education in the regular classroom, with the use of supplemental aids and services, can be achieved satisfactorily for a given child. *See* § 1412(5)(B). If it cannot and the school intends to provide special education or to remove the child from regular education, we ask, second, whether the school has mainstreamed the child to the maximum extent appropriate. *See id.* A variety of factors will inform each stage of our inquiry; the factors that we consider today do not constitute an exhaustive list of factors relevant to the mainstreaming issue. Moreover, no single factor is dispositive in all cases. Rather, our analysis is an individualized, fact-specific inquiry that requires us to examine carefully the nature and severity of the child's handicapping condition, his needs and abilities, and the schools' response to the child's needs.

In this case, several factors assist the first stage of our inquiry, whether EPISD can achieve education in the regular classroom satisfactorily. At the outset, we must examine whether the state has taken steps to accommodate the handicapped child in regular education. The Act requires states to provide supplementary aids and services and to modify the regular education program when they mainstream handicapped children. If the state has made no effort to take such accommodating steps, our inquiry ends, for the state is in violation of the Act's express mandate to supplement and modify regular education. If the state is providing supplementary aids and services and is modifying its regular education program, we must examine whether its efforts are sufficient. The Act does not permit states to make mere token gestures to accommodate handicapped students; its requirement for modifying and supplementing regular education is broad. Indeed, Texas expressly requires its local school districts to modify their regular education program when necessary to accommodate a handicapped child.

Although broad, the requirement is not limitless. States need not provide every conceivable supplementary aid or service to assist the child. *See generally Rowley*, 458 U.S. 176. Furthermore, the Act does not require regular education instructors to devote all or most of their time to one handicapped child or to modify the regular education program beyond recognition. If a regular education instructor must devote all of her time to one handicapped child, she will be acting as a special education teacher in a regular education classroom. Moreover, she will be focusing her attentions on one child to the detriment of her entire class, including, perhaps, other, equally deserving, handicapped children who also may require extra attention. Likewise, mainstreaming would be pointless if we forced instructors to modify the regular education curriculum to the extent that the handicapped child is not required to learn any of the skills normally taught in regular education. The child would be receiving special education instruction in the regular education classroom; the only advantage to such an arrangement would be that the child is sitting next to a nonhandicapped student.

Next, we examine whether the child will receive an educational benefit from regular education. This inquiry necessarily will focus on the student's ability to grasp the essential elements of the regular education curriculum. Thus, we must pay close attention to the nature and severity of the child's handicap as well as to the curriculum and goals of the regular education class. For example, if the goal of a particular program is enhancing the child's development, as opposed to teaching him specific subjects such as reading or mathematics, our inquiry must focus on the child's ability to benefit from the developmental lessons, not exclusively on his potential for learning to read. We reiterate, however, that academic achievement is not the only purpose of mainstreaming. Integrating a handicapped child into a nonhandicapped environment may be beneficial in and of itself. Thus, our inquiry must extend beyond the educational benefits that the child may receive in regular education.

We also must examine the child's overall educational experience in the mainstreamed environment, balancing the benefits of regular and special education for each individual child. For example, a child may be able to absorb only a minimal amount of the regular education program, but may benefit enormously from the language models that his nonhandicapped peers provide for him. In such a case, the benefit that the child receives from mainstreaming may tip the balance in favor of mainstreaming, even if the child cannot flourish academically. *Roncker*, 700 F.2d at 1063. On the other hand, placing a child in regular education may be detrimental to the child. In such a case, mainstreaming would not provide an education that is attuned to the child's unique needs and would not be required under the Act. Indeed, mainstreaming a child who will suffer from the experience would violate the Act's mandate for a free appropriate public education.

Finally, we ask what effect the handicapped child's presence has on the regular classroom environment and, thus, on the education that the other students are receiving. A handicapped child's placement in regular education may prove troublesome for two reasons. First, the handicapped child may, as a result of his handicap, engage in disruptive behavior. " '[W]here a handicapped child is so disruptive in a regular classroom that the education of other students is significantly impaired, the needs of the handicapped child cannot be met in that environment. Therefore regular placement would not be appropriate to his or her needs.' " 34 C.F.R. § 300.552 Comment (quoting 34 CFR Part 104-Appendix, Paragraph 24) Second, the child may require so much of the instructor's attention that the instructor will have to ignore the other student's needs in order to tend to the handicapped child. The Act and its regulations mandate that the school provide supplementary aids and services in the regular education classroom. A teaching assistant or an aide may minimize the burden on the teacher. If, however, the handicapped child requires so much of the teacher or the aide's time that the rest of the class suffers, then the balance will tip in favor of placing the child in special education.

If we determine that education in the regular classroom cannot be achieved satisfactorily, we next ask whether the child has been mainstreamed to the maximum extent appropriate. The EHA and its regulations do not contemplate an all-or-nothing educational system in which handicapped children attend either regular or special education. Rather, the Act and its regulations require schools to offer a continuum of services. 34 C.F.R. § 300.551; *Lachman*, 852 F.2d at 296 n. 7 (citing *Wilson v. Marana School District No. 6 of Pima County*, 735 F.2d 1178, 1183 (9th Cir.1984)). Thus, the school must take intermediate steps where appropriate, such as placing the child in regular education for some academic classes and in special education for others, mainstreaming the child for nonacademic classes only, or providing interaction with nonhandicapped children during lunch and recess. The appropriate mix will vary from child to child and, it may be hoped, from school year to school year as the child develops. If the school officials have provided the maximum appropriate exposure to non-handicapped students, they have fulfilled their obligation under the EHA.

C. EPISD's Compliance with the Mainstreaming Requirement

After a careful review of the voluminous administrative record, we must agree with the trial court that EPISD's decision to remove Daniel from regular education does not run afoul of the EHA's preference for mainstreaming. Accounting for all of the factors we have identified today, we find that EPISD cannot educate Daniel satisfactorily in the regular education classroom. Furthermore, EPISD has taken creative steps to provide Daniel as much access to nonhandicapped students as it can, while providing him an education that is tailored to his unique needs. Thus, EPISD has mainstreamed Daniel to the maximum extent appropriate.

EPISD cannot educate Daniel satisfactorily in the regular education classroom; each of the factors we identified today counsels against placing Daniel in regular education. First, EPISD took steps to modify the Pre-kindergarten program and to provide supplementary aids and services for Daniel-all of which constitute a sufficient effort. Daniel contends that EPISD took no such steps and that, as a result, we can never know whether Daniel could have been educated in a regular classroom. Daniel's assertion is not supported by the record. The Pre-kindergarten teacher made genuine and creative efforts to reach Daniel, devoting a substantial-indeed, a disproportionate-amount of her time to him and modifying the class curriculum to meet his abilities. Unfortunately, Daniel's needs commanded most of the Pre-kindergarten instructor's time and diverted much of her attention away from the rest of her students. Furthermore, the instructor's efforts to modify the Pre-kindergarten curriculum produced few benefits to Daniel. Indeed, she would have to alter 90 to 100 percent of the curriculum to tailor it to Daniel's abilities. Such an effort would modify the curriculum beyond recognition, an effort which we will not require in the name of mainstreaming.

Second, Daniel receives little, if any, educational benefit in Pre-kindergarten. Dr. Bonnie Fairall, EPISD's Director of Special Education, testified that the Pre-kindergarten curriculum is "developmental in nature; communication skills, gross motor [skills]" and the like. The curriculum in Kindergarten and other grades is an academic program; the developmental skills taught in Pre-kindergarten are essential to success in the academic classes. Daniel's handicap has slowed his development so that he is not yet ready to learn the developmental skills offered in Pre-kindergarten. Daniel does not participate in class activities; he cannot master most or all of the lessons taught in the class. Very simply, Pre-kindergarten offers Daniel nothing but an opportunity to associate with nonhandicapped students.

Third, Daniel's overall educational experience has not been entirely beneficial. As we explained, Daniel can grasp little of the Pre-kindergarten curriculum; the only value of regular education for Daniel is the interaction which he has with nonhandicapped students. Daniel asserts that the opportunity for interaction, alone, is a sufficient ground for mainstreaming him. When we balance the benefits of regular education against those of special education, we cannot agree that the opportunity for Daniel to interact with nonhandicapped students is a sufficient ground for mainstreaming him. Regular education not only offers Daniel little in the way of academic or other benefits, it also may be harming him. When Daniel was placed in Pre-kindergarten, he attended school for a full day; both Pre-kindergarten and Early Childhood were half-day classes. The experts who testified before the hearing officer indicated that the full day program is too strenuous for a child with Daniel's condition. Simply put, Daniel is exhausted and, as a result, he sometimes falls asleep at school. Moreover, the record indicates that the stress of regular education may be causing Daniel to develop a stutter. Special education, on the other hand, is an educational environment in which Daniel is making progress. Balancing the benefits of a program that is only marginally beneficial and is somewhat detrimental against the benefits of a program that is clearly beneficial, we must agree that the beneficial program provides the more appropriate placement.

Finally, we agree that Daniel's presence in regular Pre-kindergarten is unfair to the rest of the class. When Daniel is in the Pre-kindergarten classroom, the instructor must devote all or most of her time to Daniel. Yet she has a classroom filled with other, equally deserving students who need her attention. Although regular education instructors must devote extra attention to their handicapped students, we will not require them to do so at the expense of their entire class.

Alone, each of the factors that we have reviewed suggests that EPISD cannot educate Daniel satisfactorily in the regular education classroom. Together, they clearly tip the balance in favor of placing Daniel in special education. Thus, we turn to the next phase of our inquiry and conclude that EPISD has mainstreamed Daniel to the maximum extent appropriate. Finding that a placement that allocates Daniel's time equally between regular and special education is not appropriate, EPISD has taken the intermediate step of mainstreaming Daniel for lunch and recess. This opportunity for association with nonhandicapped students is not as extensive as Daniel's parents would like. It is, however, an appropriate step that may help to prepare Daniel for regular education in the future. As education in the regular classroom, with the use of supplementary aids and services cannot be achieved satisfactorily, and as EPISD has placed Daniel with nonhandicapped students to the maximum extent appropriate, we affirm the district court.

V. *EPISD's Request for Sanctions*

EPISD requests that we sanction Daniel's parents and his counsel for bringing a frivolous appeal, a course we decline to take.

* * *

VI. *Conclusion*

When a parent is examining the educational opportunities available for his handicapped child, he may be expected to focus primarily on his own child's best interest. Likewise, when state and local school officials are examining the alternatives for educating a handicapped child, the child's needs are a principal concern. But other concerns must enter into the school official's calculus. Public education of handicapped children occurs in the public school system, a public institution entrusted with the enormous task of serving a variety of often competing needs. In the eyes of the school official, each need is equally important and each child is equally deserving of his share of the school's limited resources. In this case, the trial court correctly concluded that the needs of the handicapped child and the needs of the nonhandicapped students in the Pre-kindergarten class tip the balance in favor of placing Daniel in special education. We thus

AFFIRM.

CEDAR RAPIDS COMMUNITY SCHOOL DISTRICT, Petitioner, v. GARRET F., a Minor By His Mother and Next Friend, CHARLENE F.
526 U.S. 66 (1999)

Justice Stevens delivered the opinion of the Court.

The Individuals with Disabilities Education Act (IDEA), 84 Stat. 175, as amended, was enacted, in part, "to assure that all children with disabilities have available to them . . . a free appropriate public education which emphasizes special education and related services designed to meet their unique needs." 20 U.S.C. § 1400(c). Consistent with this purpose, the IDEA authorizes federal financial assistance to States that agree to provide disabled children with special education and "related services." See §§ 1401(a)(18), 1412(1). The question presented in this case is whether the definition of "related services" in § 1401(a)(17) requires a public school district in a participating State to provide a ventilator-dependent student with certain nursing services during school hours.

I

Respondent Garret F. is a friendly, creative, and intelligent young man. When Garret was four years old, his spinal column was severed in a motorcycle accident. Though paralyzed from the neck down, his mental capacities were unaffected. He is able to speak, to control his motorized wheelchair through use of a puff and suck straw, and to operate a computer with a device that responds to head movements. Garret is currently a student in the Cedar Rapids Community School District (District), he attends regular classes in a typical school program, and his academic performance has been a success. Garret is, however, ventilator dependent,[2] and therefore requires a responsible individual nearby to attend to certain physical needs while he is in school.[3]

During Garret's early years at school his family provided for his physical care during the schoolday. When he was in kindergarten, his 18-year-old aunt attended him; in the next four years, his family used settlement proceeds they received after the accident, their insurance, and other resources to employ a licensed practical nurse. In 1993, Garret's mother requested the District to accept financial responsibility for the health care services that Garret requires during the schoolday. The District denied the request, believing that it was not legally obligated to provide continuous one-on-one nursing services.

---

[2] In his report in this case, the Administrative Law Judge explained: "Being ventilator dependent means that [Garret] breathes only with external aids, usually an electric ventilator, and occasionally by someone else's manual pumping of an air bag attached to his tracheotomy tube when the ventilator is being maintained. This later procedure is called ambu bagging." App. to Pet. for Cert. 19a.

[3] "He needs assistance with urinary bladder catheterization once a day, the suctioning of his tracheotomy tube as needed, but at least once every six hours, with food and drink at lunchtime, in getting into a reclining position for five minutes of each hour, and ambu bagging occasionally as needed when the ventilator is checked for proper functioning. He also needs assistance from someone familiar with his ventilator in the event there is a malfunction or electrical problem, and someone who can perform emergency procedures in the event he experiences autonomic hyperreflexia. Autonomic hyperreflexia is an uncontrolled visceral reaction to anxiety or a full bladder. Blood pressure increases, heart rate increases, and flushing and sweating may occur. Garret has not experienced autonomic hyperreflexia frequently in recent years, and it has usually been alleviated by catheterization. He has not ever experienced autonomic hyperreflexia at school. Garret is capable of communicating his needs orally or in another fashion so long as he has not been rendered unable to do so by an extended lack of oxygen." Id., at 20a.

Relying on both the IDEA and Iowa law, Garret's mother requested a hearing before the Iowa Department of Education. An Administrative Law Judge (ALJ) received extensive evidence concerning Garret's special needs, the District's treatment of other disabled students, and the assistance provided to other ventilator-dependent children in other parts of the country. In his 47-page report, the ALJ found that the District has about 17,500 students, of whom approximately 2,200 need some form of special education or special services. Although Garret is the only ventilator-dependent student in the District, most of the health care services that he needs are already provided for some other students. "The primary difference between Garret's situation and that of other students is his dependency on his ventilator for life support." App. to Pet. for Cert. 28a. The ALJ noted that the parties disagreed over the training or licensure required for the care and supervision of such students, and that those providing such care in other parts of the country ranged from nonlicensed personnel to registered nurses. However, the District did not contend that only a licensed physician could provide the services in question.

The ALJ explained that federal law requires that children with a variety of health impairments be provided with "special education and related services" when their disabilities adversely affect their academic performance, and that such children should be educated to the maximum extent appropriate with children who are not disabled. In addition, the ALJ explained that applicable federal regulations distinguish between "school health services," which are provided by a "qualified school nurse or other qualified person," and "medical services," which are provided by a licensed physician. See 34 C.F.R. §§ 300.16(a), (b)(4), (b)(11) (1998). The District must provide the former, but need not provide the latter (except, of course, those "medical services" that are for diagnostic or evaluation purposes, 20 U.S.C. § 1401(a)(17)). According to the ALJ, the distinction in the regulations does not just depend on "the title of the person providing the service"; instead, the "medical services" exclusion is limited to services that are "in the special training, knowledge, and judgment of a physician to carry out." App. to Pet. for Cert. 51a. The ALJ thus concluded that the IDEA required the District to bear financial responsibility for all of the services in dispute, including continuous nursing services.

The District challenged the ALJ's decision in Federal District Court, but that court approved the ALJ's IDEA ruling and granted summary judgment against the District. Id., at 9a, 15a. The Court of Appeals affirmed. 106 F.3d 822 (8th Cir. 1997). It noted that, as a recipient of federal funds under the IDEA, Iowa has a statutory duty to provide all disabled children a "free appropriate public education," which includes "related services." See id., at 824. The Court of Appeals read our opinion in Irving Independent School Dist. v. Tatro, 468 U.S. 883 (1984), to provide a two-step analysis of the "related services" definition in § 1401(a)(17)-asking first, whether the requested services are included within the phrase "supportive services"; and second, whether the services are excluded as "medical services." 106 F.3d, at 824-825. The Court of Appeals succinctly answered both questions in Garret's favor. The Court found the first step plainly satisfied, since Garret cannot attend school unless the requested services are available during the schoolday. Id., at 825. As to the second step, the court reasoned that Tatro "established a bright-line test: the services of a physician (other than for diagnostic and evaluation purposes) are subject to the medical services exclusion, but services that can be provided in the school setting by a nurse or qualified layperson are not." 106 F.3d, at 825.

In its petition for certiorari, the District challenged only the second step of the Court of Appeals' analysis. The District pointed out that some federal courts have not asked whether the requested health services must be delivered by a physician, but instead have applied a multifactor test that considers, generally speaking, the nature and extent of the services at issue. We granted the District's petition to resolve this conflict.

II

The District contends that § 1401(a)(17) does not require it to provide Garret with "continuous one-on-one nursing services" during the schoolday, even though Garret cannot remain in school without such care. Brief for Petitioner 10. However, the IDEA's definition of "related services," our decision in *Irving Independent School Dist. v. Tatro*, 468 U.S. 883 (1984), and the overall statutory scheme all support the decision of the Court of Appeals.

The text of the "related services" definition, see n. 1, *supra*, broadly encompasses those supportive services that "may be required to assist a child with a disability to benefit from special education." As we have already noted, the District does not challenge the Court of Appeals' conclusion that the in-school services at issue are within the covered category of "supportive services." As a general matter, services that enable a disabled child to remain in school during the day provide the student with "the meaningful access to education that Congress envisioned." *Tatro*, 468 U.S., at 891, 104 S.Ct. 3371 (" 'Congress sought primarily to make public education available to handicapped children' and 'to make such access meaningful' " (quoting *Board of Ed. of Hendrick Hudson Central School Dist., Westchester Cty. v. Rowley*, 458 U.S. 176, 192 (1982))).

This general definition of "related services" is illuminated by a parenthetical phrase listing examples of particular services that are included within the statute's coverage. § 1401(a)(17). "[M]edical services" are enumerated in this list, but such services are limited to those that are "for diagnostic and evaluation purposes." *Ibid.* The statute does not contain a more specific definition of the "medical services" that are excepted from the coverage of § 1401(a)(17).

The scope of the "medical services" exclusion is not a matter of first impression in this Court. In *Tatro* we concluded that the Secretary of Education had reasonably determined that the term "medical services" referred only to services that must be performed by a physician, and not to school health services. 468 U.S., at 892-894. Accordingly, we held that a specific form of health care (clean intermittent catheterization) that is often, though not always, performed by a nurse is not an excluded medical service. We referenced the likely cost of the services and the competence of school staff as justifications for drawing a line between physician and other services, *ibid.*, but our endorsement of that line was unmistakable. It is thus settled that the phrase "medical services" in § 1401(a)(17) does not embrace all forms of care that might loosely be described as "medical" in other contexts, such as a claim for an income tax deduction. See 26 U.S.C. § 213(d)(1) (1994 ed. and Supp. II) (defining "medical care").

The District does not ask us to define the term so broadly. Indeed, the District does not argue that any of the items of care that Garret needs, considered individually, could be excluded from the scope of 20 U.S.C. § 1401(a)(17). It could not make such an argument, considering that one of the services Garret needs (catheterization) was at issue in *Tatro*, and the others may be provided competently by a school nurse or other trained personnel. See App. to Pet. for Cert. 15a, 52a. As the ALJ concluded, most of the requested services are already provided by the District to other students, and the in-school care necessitated by Garret's ventilator dependency does not demand the training, knowledge, and judgment of a licensed physician. *Id.*, at 51a-52a. While more extensive, the in-school services Garret needs are no more "medical" than was the care sought in *Tatro*.

Instead, the District points to the combined and continuous character of the required care, and proposes a test under which the outcome in any particular case would "depend upon a series of factors, such as [1] whether the care is continuous or intermittent, [2] whether existing school health personnel can provide the service, [3] the cost of the service, and [4] the potential consequences if the service is not properly performed." Brief for Petitioner 11; see also *id.*, at 34-35.

The District's multifactor test is not supported by any recognized source of legal authority. The proposed factors can be found in neither the text of the statute nor the regulations that we upheld in *Tatro*. Moreover, the District offers no explanation why these characteristics make one service any more "medical" than another. The continuous character of certain services associated with Garret's ventilator dependency has no apparent relationship to "medical" services, much less a relationship of equivalence. Continuous services may be more costly and may require additional school personnel, but they are not thereby more "medical." Whatever its imperfections, a rule that limits the medical services exemption to physician services is unquestionably a reasonable and generally workable interpretation of the statute. Absent an elaboration of the statutory terms plainly more convincing than that which we reviewed in *Tatro*, there is no good reason to depart from settled law.

Finally, the District raises broader concerns about the financial burden that it must bear to provide the services that Garret needs to stay in school. The problem for the District in providing these services is not that its staff cannot be trained to deliver them; the problem, the District contends, is that the existing school health staff cannot meet all of their responsibilities and provide for Garret at the same time. Through its multifactor test, the District seeks to establish a kind of undue-burden exemption primarily based on the cost of the requested services. The first two factors can be seen as examples of cost-based distinctions: Intermittent care is often less expensive than continuous care, and the use of existing personnel is cheaper than hiring additional employees. The third factor-the cost of the service-would then encompass the first two. The relevance of the fourth factor is likewise related to cost because extra care may be necessary if potential consequences are especially serious.

The District may have legitimate financial concerns, but our role in this dispute is to interpret existing law. Defining "related services" in a manner that *accommodates* the cost concerns Congress may have had, cf. *Tatro*, 468 U.S., at 892, is altogether different from using cost *itself* as the definition. Given that § 1401(a)(17) does not employ cost in its definition of "related services" or excluded "medical services," accepting the District's cost-based standard as the sole test for determining the scope of the provision would require us to engage in judicial lawmaking without any guidance from Congress. It would also create some tension with the purposes of the IDEA. The statute may not require public schools to maximize the potential of disabled students commensurate with the opportunities provided to other children, see *Rowley*, 458 U.S., at 200; and the potential financial burdens imposed on participating States may be relevant to arriving at a sensible construction of the IDEA, see *Tatro*, 468 U.S., at 892. But Congress intended "to open the door of public education" to all qualified children and "require[d] participating States to educate handicapped children with nonhandicapped children whenever possible." *Rowley*, 458 U.S., at 192, 202.

This case is about whether meaningful access to the public schools will be assured, not the level of education that a school must finance once access is attained. It is undisputed that the services at issue must be provided if Garret is to remain in school. Under the statute, our precedent, and the purposes of the IDEA, the District must fund such "related services" in order to help guarantee that students like Garret are integrated into the public schools.

The judgment of the Court of Appeals is accordingly

Affirmed.

Justice THOMAS, with whom Justice KENNEDY joins, dissenting (omitted).

Brian SCHAFFER, a minor, by his parents and next friends, Jocelyn and Martin SCHAFFER, et vir, et al., Petitioners v. Jerry WEAST, Superintendent, Montgomery County Public Schools, et al.
546 U.S. 49 (2005)

JUSTICE O'CONNOR delivered the opinion of the Court.

The Individuals with Disabilities Education Act (IDEA or Act), 84 Stat. 175, as amended, 20 U.S.C. § 1400 *et seq.* (2000 ed. and Supp.V), is a Spending Clause statute that seeks to ensure that "all children with disabilities have available to them a free appropriate public education," § 1400(d)(1)(A) (2000 ed., Supp.V). Under IDEA, school districts must create an "individualized education program" (IEP) for each disabled child. § 1414(d). If parents believe their child's IEP is inappropriate, they may request an "impartial due process hearing." § 1415(f). The Act is silent, however, as to which party bears the burden of persuasion at such a hearing. We hold that the burden lies, as it typically does, on the party seeking relief.

I

A

Congress first passed IDEA as part of the Education of the Handicapped Act in 1970, 84 Stat. 175, and amended it substantially in the Education for All Handicapped Children Act of 1975, 89 Stat. 773. At the time the majority of disabled children in America were "either totally excluded from schools or sitting idly in regular classrooms awaiting the time when they were old enough to 'drop out,' " H.R.Rep. No. 94-332, p. 2 (1975). IDEA was intended to reverse this history of neglect. As of 2003, the Act governed the provision of special education services to nearly 7 million children across the country.

IDEA is "frequently described as a model of 'cooperative federalism.' " *Little Rock School Dist. v. Mauney*, 183 F.3d 816, 830 (8th Cir. 1999). It "leaves to the States the primary responsibility for developing and executing educational programs for handicapped children, [but] imposes significant requirements to be followed in the discharge of that responsibility." *Board of Ed. of Hendrick Hudson Central School Dist., Westchester Cty. v. Rowley*, 458 U.S. 176, 183 (1982). For example, the Act mandates cooperation and reporting between state and federal educational authorities. Participating States must certify to the Secretary of Education that they have "policies and procedures" that will effectively meet the Act's conditions. 20 U.S.C. § 1412(a). (Unless otherwise noted, all citations to the Act are to the pre-2004 version of the statute because this is the version that was in effect during the proceedings below. We note, however, that nothing in the recent 2004 amendments, 118 Stat. 2674, appears to materially affect the rule announced here.) State educational agencies, in turn, must ensure that local schools and teachers are meeting the State's educational standards. §§ 1412(a)(11), 1412(a)(15)(A). Local educational agencies (school boards or other administrative bodies) can receive IDEA funds only if they certify to a state educational agency that they are acting in accordance with the State's policies and procedures. § 1413(a)(1).

The core of the statute, however, is the cooperative process that it establishes between parents and schools. *Rowley, supra,* at 205-206, ("Congress placed every bit as much emphasis upon compliance with procedures giving parents and guardians a large measure of participation at every stage of the administrative process, . . . as it did upon the measurement of the resulting IEP against a substantive standard"). The central vehicle for this collaboration is the IEP process. State educational authorities must identify and evaluate disabled children, §§ 1414(a)-(c), develop an IEP for each one, § 1414(d)(2), and review every IEP at least once a year, § 1414(d)(4). Each IEP must include an assessment of the child's current educational performance, must articulate measurable educational goals, and must specify the nature of the special services that the school will provide. § 1414(d)(1)(A).

Parents and guardians play a significant role in the IEP process. They must be informed about and consent to evaluations of their child under the Act. § 1414(c)(3). Parents are included as members of "IEP teams." § 1414(d)(1)(B). They have the right to examine any records relating to their child, and to obtain an "independent educational evaluation of the[ir] child." § 1415(b)(1). They must be given written prior notice of any changes in an IEP, § 1415(b)(3), and be notified in writing of the procedural safeguards available to them under the Act, § 1415(d)(1). If parents believe that an IEP is not appropriate, they may seek an administrative "impartial due process hearing." § 1415(f). School districts may also seek such hearings, as Congress clarified in the 2004 amendments. See S.Rep. No. 108-185, p. 37 (2003). They may do so, for example, if they wish to change an existing IEP but the parents do not consent, or if parents refuse to allow their child to be evaluated. As a practical matter, it appears that most hearing requests come from parents rather than schools. Brief for Petitioners 7.

Although state authorities have limited discretion to determine who conducts the hearings, § 1415(f)(1), and responsibility generally for establishing fair hearing procedures, § 1415(a), Congress has chosen to legislate the central components of due process hearings. It has imposed minimal pleading standards, requiring parties to file complaints setting forth "a description of the nature of the problem," § 1415(b)(7)(B)(ii), and "a proposed resolution of the problem to the extent known and available . . . at the time," § 1415(b)(7)(B)(iii). At the hearing, all parties may be accompanied by counsel, and may "present evidence and confront, cross-examine, and compel the attendance of witnesses." §§ 1415(h)(1)-(2). After the hearing, any aggrieved party may bring a civil action in state or federal court. § 1415(i)(2). Prevailing parents may also recover attorney's fees. § 1415(i)(3)(B). Congress has never explicitly stated, however, which party should bear the burden of proof at IDEA hearings.

B

This case concerns the educational services that were due, under IDEA, to petitioner Brian Schaffer. Brian suffers from learning disabilities and speech-language impairments. From prekindergarten through seventh grade he attended a private school and struggled academically. In 1997, school officials informed Brian's mother that he needed a school that could better accommodate his needs. Brian's parents contacted respondent Montgomery County Public Schools System (MCPS) seeking a placement for him for the following school year.

MCPS evaluated Brian and convened an IEP team. The committee generated an initial IEP offering Brian a place in either of two MCPS middle schools. Brian's parents were not satisfied with the arrangement, believing that Brian needed smaller classes and more intensive services. The Schaffers thus enrolled Brian in another private school, and initiated a due process hearing challenging the IEP and seeking compensation for the cost of Brian's subsequent private education.

In Maryland, IEP hearings are conducted by administrative law judges (ALJs). See Md.

Educ.Code Ann. § 8-413(c) (Lexis 2004). After a 3-day hearing, the ALJ deemed the evidence close, held that the parents bore the burden of persuasion, and ruled in favor of the school district. The parents brought a civil action challenging the result. The United States District Court for the District of Maryland reversed and remanded, after concluding that the burden of persuasion is on the school district. *Brian S. v. Vance*, 86 F.Supp.2d 538 (D.Md.2000). Around the same time, MCPS offered Brian a placement in a high school with a special learning center. Brian's parents accepted, and Brian was educated in that program until he graduated from high school. The suit remained alive, however, because the parents sought compensation for the private school tuition and related expenses.

Respondents appealed to the United States Court of Appeals for the Fourth Circuit. While the appeal was pending, the ALJ reconsidered the case, deemed the evidence truly in "equipoise," and ruled in favor of the parents. The Fourth Circuit vacated and remanded the appeal so that it could consider the burden of proof issue along with the merits on a later appeal. The District Court reaffirmed its ruling that the school district has the burden of proof. 240 F. Supp.2d 396 (D.Md. 2002). On appeal, a divided panel of the Fourth Circuit reversed. Judge Michael, writing for the majority, concluded that petitioners offered no persuasive reason to "depart from the normal rule of allocating the burden to the party seeking relief." 377 F.3d 449, 453 (4th Cir. 2004). We granted certiorari, 543 U.S. 1145 (2005), to resolve the following question: At an administrative hearing assessing the appropriateness of an IEP, which party bears the burden of persuasion?

II

A

The term "burden of proof" is one of the "slipperiest member[s] of the family of legal terms." 2 J. Strong, McCormick on Evidence § 342, p. 433 (5th ed.1999) (hereinafter McCormick). Part of the confusion surrounding the term arises from the fact that historically, the concept encompassed two distinct burdens: the "burden of persuasion," *i.e.*, which party loses if the evidence is closely balanced, and the "burden of production," *i.e.*, which party bears the obligation to come forward with the evidence at different points in the proceeding. *Director, Office of Workers' Compensation Programs v. Greenwich Collieries*, 512 U.S. 267, 272 (1994). We note at the outset that this case concerns only the burden of persuasion, as the parties agree, Brief for Respondents 14; Reply Brief for Petitioners 15, and when we speak of burden of proof in this opinion, it is this to which we refer.

When we are determining the burden of proof under a statutory cause of action, the touchstone of our inquiry is, of course, the statute. The plain text of IDEA is silent on the allocation of the burden of persuasion. We therefore begin with the ordinary default rule that plaintiffs bear the risk of failing to prove their claims. McCormick § 337, at 412 ("The burdens of pleading and proof with regard to most facts have been and should be assigned to the plaintiff who generally seeks to change the present state of affairs and who therefore naturally should be expected to bear the risk of failure of proof or persuasion"); C. Mueller & L. Kirkpatrick, Evidence § 3.1, p. 104 (3d ed. 2003) ("Perhaps the broadest and most accepted idea is that the person who seeks court action should justify the request, which means that the plaintiffs bear the burdens on the elements in their claims").

Thus, we have usually assumed without comment that plaintiffs bear the burden of persuasion regarding the essential aspects of their claims . . . .

The ordinary default rule, of course, admits of exceptions. See McCormick § 337, at 412-415. For example, the burden of persuasion as to certain elements of a plaintiff's claim may be shifted to defendants, when such elements can fairly be characterized as affirmative defenses or exemptions. See, *e.g.*, *FTC v. Morton Salt Co.*, 334 U.S. 37, 44-45 (1948). Under some circumstances this Court has even placed the burden of persuasion over an entire claim on the defendant. See *Alaska Dept. of Environmental Conservation v. EPA*, 540 U.S. 461, 494 (2004). But while the normal default rule does not solve all cases, it certainly solves most of them. Decisions that place the *entire* burden of persuasion on the opposing party at the *outset* of a proceeding-as petitioners urge us to do here-are extremely rare. Absent some reason to believe that Congress intended otherwise, therefore, we will conclude that the burden of persuasion lies where it usually falls, upon the party seeking relief.

B

Petitioners contend first that a close reading of IDEA's text compels a conclusion in their favor. They urge that we should interpret the statutory words "due process" in light of their constitutional meaning, and apply the balancing test established by *Mathews v. Eldridge*, 424 U.S. 319 (1976). Even assuming that the Act incorporates constitutional due process doctrine, *Eldridge* is no help to petitioners because "[o]utside the criminal law area, where special concerns attend, the locus of the burden of persuasion is normally not an issue of federal constitutional moment." *Lavine v. Milne*, 424 U.S. 577, 585 (1976).

Petitioners next contend that we should take instruction from the lower court opinions of *Mills v. Board of Education*, 348 F.Supp. 866 (D.D.C.1972), and *Pennsylvania Association for Retarded Children v. Pennsylvania*, 334 F.Supp. 1257 (E.D.Pa.1971) (hereinafter *PARC*). IDEA's drafters were admittedly guided "to a significant extent" by these two landmark cases. *Rowley*, 458 U.S., at 194. As the court below noted, however, the fact that Congress "took a number of the procedural safeguards from *PARC* and *Mills* and wrote them directly into the Act" does not allow us to "conclude . . . that Congress intended to adopt the ideas that it failed to write into the text of the statute." 377 F.3d, at 455.

Petitioners also urge that putting the burden of persuasion on school districts will further IDEA's purposes because it will help ensure that children receive a free appropriate public education. In truth, however, very few cases will be in evidentiary equipoise. Assigning the burden of persuasion to school districts might encourage schools to put more resources into preparing IEPs and presenting their evidence. But IDEA is silent about whether marginal dollars should be allocated to litigation and administrative expenditures or to educational services. Moreover, there is reason to believe that a great deal is already spent on the administration of the Act. Litigating a due process complaint is an expensive affair, costing schools approximately $8,000-to-$12,000 per hearing. See Department of Education, J. Chambers, J. Harr, & A. Dhanani, What Are We Spending on Procedural Safeguards in Special Education 1999-2000, p. 8 (May 2003) (prepared under contract by American Institutes for Research, Special Education Expenditure Project). Congress has also repeatedly amended the Act in order to reduce its administrative and litigation-related costs. For example, in 1997 Congress mandated that States offer mediation for IDEA disputes. § 615(e) of IDEA, as added by § 101 of the Individuals with Disabilities Education Act Amendments of 1997, Pub.L. 105-17, 111 Stat. 90, 20 U.S.C. § 1415(e). In 2004, Congress added a mandatory "resolution session" prior to any due process hearing. § 615(f)(1)(B) of IDEA, as added by § 101 of the Individuals with Disabilities Education Improvement Act of 2004, Pub.L. 108-446, 118 Stat. 2720, 20 U.S.C.A. § 1415(f)(1)(B) (Supp.2005). It also made new findings that "[p]arents and schools should be given expanded opportunities to resolve their disagreements in positive and constructive ways," and that "[t]eachers, schools, local educational agencies, and States should be relieved of irrelevant and unnecessary paperwork burdens that do not lead to improved educational outcomes." §§ 1400(c)(8)-(9).

Petitioners in effect ask this Court to assume that every IEP is invalid until the school district demonstrates that it is not. The Act does not support this conclusion. IDEA relies heavily upon the expertise of school districts to meet its goals. It also includes a so-called "stay-put" provision, which requires a child to remain in his or her "then-current educational placement" during the pendency of an IDEA hearing. § 1415(j). Congress could have required that a child be given the educational placement that a parent requested during a dispute, but it did no such thing. Congress appears to have presumed instead that, if the Act's procedural requirements are respected, parents will prevail when they have legitimate grievances. See *Rowley, supra*, at 206, 102 S.Ct. 3034 (noting the "legislative conviction that adequate compliance with the procedures prescribed would in most cases assure much if not all of what Congress wished in the way of substantive content in an IEP").

Petitioners' most plausible argument is that "[t]he ordinary rule, based on considerations of fairness, does not place the burden upon a litigant of establishing facts peculiarly within the knowledge of his adversary." *United States v. New York, N.H. & H.R. Co.*, 355 U.S. 253, 256, n. 5 (1957). But this "rule is far from being universal, and has many qualifications upon its application." *Greenleaf's Lessee v. Birth*, 6 Pet. 302, 312, 8 L.Ed. 406 (1832); see also McCormick § 337, at 413 ("Very often one must plead and prove matters as to which his adversary has superior access to the proof"). School districts have a "natural advantage" in information and expertise, but Congress addressed this when it obliged schools to safeguard the procedural rights of parents and to share information with them. See *School Comm. of Burlington v. Department of Ed. of Mass.*, 471 U.S. 359, 368 (1985). As noted above, parents have the right to review all records that the school possesses in relation to their child. § 1415(b)(1). They also have the right to an "independent educational evaluation of the[ir] child." *Ibid.* The regulations clarify this entitlement by providing that a "parent has the right to an independent educational evaluation at public expense if the parent disagrees with an evaluation obtained by the public agency." 34 CFR § 300.502(b)(1) (2005). IDEA thus ensures parents access to an expert who can evaluate all the materials that the school must make available, and who can give an independent opinion. They are not left to challenge the government without a realistic opportunity to access the necessary evidence, or without an expert with the firepower to match the opposition.

Additionally, in 2004, Congress added provisions requiring school districts to answer the subject matter of a complaint in writing, and to provide parents with the reasoning behind the disputed action, details about the other options considered and rejected by the IEP team, and a description of all evaluations, reports, and other factors that the school used in coming to its decision. § 615(c)(2)(B)(i)(I) of IDEA, as added by § 101 of Pub.L. 108-446, 118 Stat. 2718, 20 U.S.C. § 1415(c)(2)(B)(i)(I) (2000 ed., Supp.V). Prior to a hearing, the parties must disclose evaluations and recommendations that they intend to rely upon. 20 U.S.C. § 1415(f)(2). IDEA hearings are deliberately informal and intended to give ALJs the flexibility that they need to ensure that each side can fairly present its evidence. IDEA, in fact, requires state authorities to organize hearings in a way that guarantees parents and children the procedural protections of the Act. See § 1415(a). Finally, and perhaps most importantly, parents may recover attorney's fees if they prevail. § 1415(i)(3)(B). These protections ensure that the school bears no unique informational advantage.

III

Finally, respondents and several States urge us to decide that States may, if they wish, override the default rule and put the burden always on the school district. Several States have laws or regulations purporting to do so, at least under some circumstances. See, *e.g.*, Minn.Stat. § 125A.091, subd. 16 (2004); Ala. Admin. Code Rule 290-8-9-.08(8)(c)(6) (Supp.2004); Alaska Admin. Code, tit. 4, § 52.550(e)(9) (2003); Del.Code Ann., Tit. 14, § 3140 (1999). Because no such law or regulation exists in Maryland, we need not decide this issue today. Justice BREYER contends that the allocation of the burden ought to be left *entirely* up to the States. But neither party made this argument before this Court or the courts below. We therefore decline to address it.

We hold no more than we must to resolve the case at hand: The burden of proof in an administrative hearing challenging an IEP is properly placed upon the party seeking relief. In this case, that party is Brian, as represented by his parents. But the rule applies with equal effect to school districts: If they seek to challenge an IEP, they will in turn bear the burden of persuasion before an ALJ. The judgment of the United States Court of Appeals for the Fourth Circuit is, therefore, affirmed.

It is so ordered.

THE CHIEF JUSTICE took no part in the consideration or decision of this case. Justice STEVENS, concurring (omitted).

Justice GINSBURG, dissenting.

* * *

The Court acknowledges that "[a]ssigning the burden of persuasion to school districts might encourage schools to put more resources into preparing IEPs." *Ante*, at 535. Curiously, the Court next suggests that resources spent on developing IEPs rank as "administrative expenditures" not as expenditures for "educational services." *Ibid.* Costs entailed in the preparation of suitable IEPs, however, are the very expenditures necessary to ensure each child covered by the IDEA access to a free appropriate education. These outlays surely relate to "educational services." Indeed, a carefully designed IEP may ward off disputes productive of large administrative or litigation expenses.

This case is illustrative. Not until the District Court ruled that the school district had the burden of persuasion did the school design an IEP that met Brian Schaffer's special educational needs. See *ante*, at 533; Tr. of Oral Arg. 21-22 (Counsel for the Schaffers observed that "Montgomery County . . . gave [Brian] the kind of services he had sought from the beginning . . . once [the school district was] given the burden of proof."). Had the school district, in the first instance, offered Brian a public or private school placement equivalent to the one the district ultimately provided, this entire litigation and its attendant costs could have been avoided.

Notably, nine States, as friends of the Court, have urged that placement of the burden of persuasion on the school district best comports with the IDEA's aim. See Brief for Commonwealth of Virginia et al. as *Amici Curiae*. If allocating the burden to school districts would saddle school systems with inordinate costs, it is doubtful that these States would have filed in favor of petitioners. Cf. Brief for United States as *Amicus Curiae* Supporting Appellees Urging Affirmance in No. 00-1471(CA4), p. 12 ("Having to carry the burden of proof regarding the adequacy of its proposed IEP . . . should not substantially increase the workload for the school.").[3]

One can demur to the Fourth Circuit's observation that courts "do not automatically assign the burden of proof to the side with the bigger guns," 377 F.3d, at 453, for no such reflexive action is at issue here. It bears emphasis that "the vast majority of parents whose children require the benefits and protections provided in the IDEA" lack "knowledg[e] about the educational resources available to their [child]" and the "sophisticat[ion]" to mount an effective case against a district-proposed IEP. *Id.*, at 458 (Luttig, J., dissenting); cf. 20 U.S.C. § 1400(c)(7)-(10). In this setting, "the party with the 'bigger guns' also has better access to information, greater expertise, and an affirmative obligation to provide the contested services." 377 F.3d, at 458 (Luttig, J., dissenting). Policy considerations, convenience, and fairness, I think it plain, point in the same direction. Their collective weight warrants a rule requiring a school district, in "due process" hearings, to explain persuasively why its proposed IEP satisfies the IDEA's standards. *Ibid.* I would therefore reverse the judgment of the Fourth Circuit.

Justice BREYER, dissenting.

* * *

Nothing in the Act suggests a need to fill every interstice of the Act's remedial scheme with a uniform federal rule. See *Kamen v. Kemper Financial Services, Inc.*, 500 U.S. 90, 98 (1991) (citations omitted). And should some such need arise-*i.e.*, if nonuniformity or a particular state approach were to prove problematic-the Federal Department of Education, expert in the area, might promulgate a uniform federal standard, thereby limiting state choice. 20 U.S.C. § 1406(a) (2000 ed., Supp.V).

Most importantly, Congress has made clear that the Act itself represents an exercise in "cooperative federalism." See *ante*, at 531-532 (opinion of the Court). Respecting the States' right to decide this procedural matter here, where education is at issue, where expertise matters, and where costs are shared, is consistent with that cooperative approach. See *Wisconsin Dept. of Health and Family Servs. v. Blumer*, 534 U.S. 473, 495 (2002) (when interpreting statutes "designed to advance cooperative federalism[,] . . . we have not been reluctant to leave a range of permissible choices to the States"). And judicial respect for such congressional determinations is important. Indeed, in today's technologically and legally complex world, whether court decisions embody that kind of judicial respect may represent the true test of federalist principle. See *AT & T Corp. v. Iowa Utilities Bd.*, 525 U.S. 366, 420 (1999) (BREYER, J., concurring in part and dissenting in part).

Maryland has no special state law or regulation setting forth a special IEP-related burden of persuasion standard. But it does have rules of state administrative procedure and a body of state administrative law. The state ALJ should determine how those rules, or other state law, applies to this case. Cf., *e.g.*, Ind. Admin. Code, tit. 511, Rule 7-30-3 (2003) (hearings under the

---

[3] Before the Fourth Circuit, the United States filed in favor of the Schaffers; in this Court, the United States supported Montgomery County.

Act conducted in accord with general state administrative law); 7 Ky. Admin. Regs., tit. 707, ch. 1:340, Section 7(4) (same). Because the state ALJ did not do this (*i.e.*, he looked for a federal, not a state, burden of persuasion rule), I would remand this case.

ARLINGTON CENTRAL SCHOOL DISTRICT BOARD OF EDUCATION, Petitioner, v. Pearl MURPHY et al.

548 U.S. 291 (2006)

JUSTICE ALITO delivered the opinion of the Court.

The Individuals with Disabilities Education Act (IDEA or Act) provides that a court "may award reasonable attorneys' fees as part of the costs" to parents who prevail in an action brought under the Act. 111 Stat. 92, 20 U.S.C. § 1415(i)(3)(B). We granted certiorari to decide whether this fee-shifting provision authorizes prevailing parents to recover fees for services rendered by experts in IDEA actions. We hold that it does not.

I

Respondents Pearl and Theodore Murphy filed an action under the IDEA on behalf of their son, Joseph Murphy, seeking to require petitioner Arlington Central School District Board of Education to pay for their son's private school tuition for specified school years. Respondents prevailed in the District Court, 86 F.Supp.2d 354 (S.D.N.Y.2000), and the Court of Appeals for the Second Circuit affirmed, 297 F.3d 195 (2nd Cir. 2002).

As prevailing parents, respondents then sought $29,350 in fees for the services of an educational consultant, Marilyn Arons, who assisted respondents throughout the IDEA proceedings. The District Court granted respondents' request in part. It held that only the value of Arons' time spent between the hearing request and the ruling in respondents' favor could properly be considered charges incurred in an "action or proceeding brought" under the Act, see 20 U.S.C. § 1415(i)(3)(B). 2003 WL 21694398, *9 (S.D.N.Y., July 22, 2003). This reduced the maximum recovery to $8,650. The District Court also held that Arons, a nonlawyer, could be compensated only for time spent on expert consulting services, not for time spent on legal representation, *id.*, at *4, but it concluded that all the relevant time could be characterized as falling within the compensable category, and thus allowed compensation for the full $8,650, *id.*, at *10.

The Court of Appeals for the Second Circuit affirmed. 402 F.3d 332 (2nd Cir. 2005). Acknowledging that other Circuits had taken the opposite view, the Court of Appeals for the Second Circuit held that "Congress intended to and did authorize the reimbursement of expert fees in IDEA actions." *Id.*, at 336. The court began by discussing two decisions of this Court holding that expert fees could not be recovered as taxed costs under particular cost- or fee-shifting provisions. According to these decisions, the court noted, a cost- or fee-shifting provision will not be read to permit a prevailing party to recover expert fees without " 'explicit statutory authority' indicating that Congress intended for that sort of fee-shifting." 402 F.3d, at 336.

Ultimately, though, the court was persuaded by a statement in the Conference Committee Report relating to 20 U.S.C. § 1415(i)(3)(B) and by a footnote in *Casey* that made reference to that Report. 402 F.3d, at 336-337 (citing H.R. Conf. Rep. No. 99-687, p. 5 (1986), U.S.Code Cong. & Admin.News, 1986, p. 1807). Based on these authorities, the court concluded that it was required to interpret the IDEA to authorize the award of the costs that prevailing parents incur in hiring experts. 402 F.3d, at 336.

We granted certiorari, 546 U.S. 1085 (2006), to resolve the conflict among the Circuits with respect to whether Congress authorized the compensation of expert fees to prevailing parents in IDEA actions. We now reverse.

II

Our resolution of the question presented in this case is guided by the fact that Congress enacted the IDEA pursuant to the Spending Clause. U.S. Const., Art. I, § 8, cl. 1. Like its statutory predecessor, the IDEA provides federal funds to assist state and local agencies in educating children with disabilities "and conditions such funding upon a State's compliance with extensive goals and procedures." *Board of Ed. of Hendrick Hudson Central School Dist., Westchester Cty. v. Rowley*, 458 U.S. 176, 179 (1982).

Congress has broad power to set the terms on which it disburses federal money to the States, see, *e.g.*, *South Dakota v. Dole*, 483 U.S. 203, 206-207 (1987), but when Congress attaches conditions to a State's acceptance of federal funds, the conditions must be set out "unambiguously," see *Pennhurst State School and Hospital v. Halderman*, 451 U.S. 1, 17 (1981); *Rowley, supra*, at 204, n. 26. "[L]egislation enacted pursuant to the spending power is much in the nature of a contract," and therefore, to be bound by "federally imposed conditions," recipients of federal funds must accept them "voluntarily and knowingly." *Pennhurst*, 451 U.S., at 17. States cannot knowingly accept conditions of which they are "unaware" or which they are "unable to ascertain." *Ibid.* Thus, in the present case, we must view the IDEA from the perspective of a state official who is engaged in the process of deciding whether the State should accept IDEA funds and the obligations that go with those funds. We must ask whether such a state official would clearly understand that one of the obligations of the Act is the obligation to compensate prevailing parents for expert fees. In other words, we must ask whether the IDEA furnishes clear notice regarding the liability at issue in this case.

III

A

In considering whether the IDEA provides clear notice, we begin with the text. We have "stated time and again that courts must presume that a legislature says in a statute what it means and means in a statute what it says there." *Connecticut Nat. Bank v. Germain*, 503 U.S. 249, 253-254, (1992). When the statutory "language is plain, the sole function of the courts-at least where the disposition required by the text is not absurd-is to enforce it according to its terms." *Hartford Underwriters Ins. Co. v. Union Planters Bank, N. A.*, 530 U.S. 1, 6, (2000).

The governing provision of the IDEA, 20 U.S.C. § 1415(i)(3)(B), provides that "[i]n any action or proceeding brought under this section, the court, in its discretion, may award reasonable attorneys' fees as part of the costs" to the parents of "a child with a disability" who is the "prevailing party." While this provision provides for an award of "reasonable attorneys' fees," this provision does not even hint that acceptance of IDEA funds makes a State responsible for reimbursing prevailing parents for services rendered by experts.

Respondents contend that we should interpret the term "costs" in accordance with its meaning in ordinary usage and that § 1415(i)(3)(B) should therefore be read to "authorize reimbursement of all costs parents incur in IDEA proceedings, including expert costs." Brief for Respondents 17.

This argument has multiple flaws. For one thing, as the Court of Appeals in this case acknowledged, " 'costs' is a term of art that generally does not include expert fees." 402 F.3d, at 336. The use of this term of art, rather than a term such as "expenses," strongly suggests that § 1415(i)(3)(B) was not meant to be an open-ended provision that makes participating States liable for all expenses incurred by prevailing parents in connection with an IDEA case-for example, travel and lodging expenses or lost wages due to time taken off from work. Moreover, contrary to respondents' suggestion, § 1415(i)(3)(B) does not say that a court may award "costs" to prevailing parents; rather, it says that a court may award reasonable attorney's fees "as part of the costs" to prevailing parents. This language simply adds reasonable attorney's fees incurred by prevailing parents to the list of costs that prevailing parents are otherwise entitled to recover. This list of otherwise recoverable costs is obviously the list set out in 28 U.S.C. § 1920, the general statute governing the taxation of costs in federal court, and the recovery of witness fees under § 1920 is strictly limited by § 1821, which authorizes travel reimbursement and a $40 per diem. Thus, the text of 20 U.S.C. § 1415(i)(3)(B) does not authorize an award of any additional expert fees, and it certainly fails to provide the clear notice that is required under the Spending Clause.

Other provisions of the IDEA point strongly in the same direction. While authorizing the award of reasonable attorney's fees, the Act contains detailed provisions that are designed to ensure that such awards are indeed reasonable. See §§ 1415(i)(3)(C)-(G). The absence of any comparable provisions relating to expert fees strongly suggests that recovery of expert fees is not authorized. Moreover, the lack of any reference to expert fees in § 1415(d)(2) gives rise to a similar inference. This provision, which generally requires that parents receive "a full explanation of the procedural safeguards" available under § 1415 and refers expressly to "attorneys' fees," makes no mention of expert fees.

B

Respondents contend that their interpretation of § 1415(i)(3)(B) is supported by a provision of the Handicapped Children's Protection Act of 1986 that required the General Accounting Office (GAO) to collect certain data, § 4(b)(3), 100 Stat. 797 (hereinafter GAO study provision), but this provision is of little significance for present purposes. The GAO study provision directed the Comptroller General, acting through the GAO, to compile data on, among other things: "(A) the specific amount of attorneys' fees, costs, and expenses awarded to the prevailing party" in IDEA cases for a particular period of time, and (B) "the number of hours spent by personnel, including attorneys and consultants, involved in the action or proceeding, and expenses incurred by the parents and the State educational agency and local educational agency." *Id.*, at 797-798.

Subparagraph (A) would provide some support for respondents' position if it directed the GAO to compile data on awards to prevailing parties of the expense of hiring consultants, but that is not what subparagraph (A) says. Subparagraph (A) makes no mention of consultants or experts or their fees.

Subparagraph (B) similarly does not help respondents. Subparagraph (B), which directs the GAO to study "the number of hours spent [in IDEA cases] by personnel, including . . . consultants," says nothing about the award of fees to such consultants. Just because Congress directed the GAO to compile statistics on the hours spent by consultants in IDEA cases, it does not follow that Congress meant for States to compensate prevailing parties for the fees billed by these consultants.

Respondents maintain that "Congress' direction to the GAO would be inexplicable if Congress did not anticipate that the expenses for 'consultants' would be recoverable," Brief for Respondents 19, but this is incorrect. There are many reasons why Congress might have wanted the GAO to gather data on expenses that were not to be taxed as costs. Knowing the costs incurred by IDEA litigants might be useful in considering future procedural amendments (which might affect these costs) or a future amendment regarding fee shifting. And, in fact, it is apparent that the GAO study provision covered expenses that could not be taxed as costs. For example, the GAO was instructed to compile statistics on the hours spent by all attorneys involved in an IDEA action or proceeding, even though the Act did not provide for the recovery of attorney's fees by a prevailing state or local educational agency. Similarly, the GAO was directed to compile data on "expenses incurred by the parents," not just those parents who prevail and are thus eligible to recover taxed costs.

In sum, the terms of the IDEA overwhelmingly support the conclusion that prevailing parents may not recover the costs of experts or consultants. Certainly the terms of the IDEA fail to provide the clear notice that would be needed to attach such a condition to a State's receipt of IDEA funds.

IV

Thus far, we have considered only the text of the IDEA, but perhaps the strongest support for our interpretation of the IDEA is supplied by our decisions and reasoning in *Crawford Fitting*, 482 U.S. 437, and *Casey*, 499 U.S. 83. In light of those decisions, we do not see how it can be said that the IDEA gives a State unambiguous notice regarding liability for expert fees.

In *Crawford Fitting*, the Court rejected an argument very similar to respondents' argument that the term "costs" in § 1415(i)(3)(B) should be construed as an open-ended reference to prevailing parents' expenses. It was argued in *Crawford Fitting* that Federal Rule of Civil Procedure 54(d), which provides for the award of "costs" to a prevailing party, authorizes the award of costs not listed in 28 U.S.C. § 1821. 482 U.S., at 439. The Court held, however, that Rule 54(d) does not give a district judge "discretion to tax whatever costs may seem appropriate"; rather, the term "costs" in Rule 54(d) is defined by the list set out in § 1920. *Id.*, at 441. Because the recovery of witness fees, see § 1920(3), is strictly limited by § 1821, the Court observed, a broader interpretation of Rule 54(d) would mean that the Rule implicitly effected a partial repeal of those provisions. *Id.*, at 442. But, the Court warned, "[w]e will not lightly infer that Congress has repealed §§ 1920 and 1821, either through Rule 54(d) or any other provision not referring explicitly to witness fees." *Id.*, at 445.

The reasoning of *Crawford Fitting* strongly supports the conclusion that the term "costs" in 20 U.S.C. § 1415(i)(3)(B), like the same term in Rule 54(d), is defined by the categories of expenses enumerated in 28 U.S.C. § 1920. This conclusion is buttressed by the principle, recognized in *Crawford Fitting*, that no statute will be construed as authorizing the taxation of witness fees as costs unless the statute "refer[s] explicitly to witness fees." 482 U.S., at 445; see also *ibid.* ("[A]bsent explicit statutory or contractual authorization for the taxation of the expenses of a litigant's witness as costs, federal courts are bound by the limitations set out in 28 U.S.C. § 1821 and § 1920").

Our decision in *Casey* confirms even more dramatically that the IDEA does not authorize an award of expert fees. In *Casey*, as noted above, we interpreted a fee-shifting provision, 42 U.S.C. § 1988, the relevant wording of which was virtually identical to the wording of 20 U.S.C.

§ 1415(i)(3)(B). Compare *ibid.* (authorizing the award of "reasonable attorneys' fees as part of the costs" to prevailing parents) with 42 U.S.C. § 1988 (1988 ed.) (permitting prevailing parties in certain civil rights actions to be awarded "a reasonable attorney's fee as part of the costs"). We held that § 1988 did not empower a district court to award expert fees to a prevailing party. *Casey, supra,* at 102. To decide in favor of respondents here, we would have to interpret the virtually identical language in 20 U.S.C. § 1415 as having exactly the opposite meaning. Indeed, we would have to go further and hold that the relevant language in the IDEA *unambiguously means* exactly the opposite of what the nearly identical language in 42 U.S.C. § 1988 was held to mean in *Casey.*

The Court of Appeals, as noted above, was heavily influenced by a *Casey* footnote, see 402 F.3d, at 336-337 (quoting 499 U.S., at 91-92, n. 5,), but the court misunderstood the footnote's meaning. The text accompanying the footnote argued, based on an analysis of several fee-shifting statutes, that the term "attorney's fees" does not include expert fees. *Id.,* at 88-91. In the footnote, we commented on petitioners' invocation of the Conference Committee Report relating to 20 U.S.C. § 1415(i)(3)(B), which stated: " 'The conferees intend[ed] that the term "attorneys' fees as part of the costs" include reasonable expenses and fees of expert witnesses and the reasonable costs of any test or evaluation which is found to be necessary for the preparation of the . . . case.' " 499 U.S., at 91-92, n. 5, 111 S.Ct. 1138 (quoting H.R. Conf. Rep. No. 99-687, at 5, U.S.Code Cong. & Admin.News, 1986, pp. 1807, 1808; ellipsis in original). This statement, the footnote commented, was "an apparent effort to *depart* from ordinary meaning and to define a term of art." 499 U.S., at 92, n. 5. The footnote did not state that the Conference Committee Report set out the correct interpretation of § 1415(i)(3)(B), much less that the Report was sufficient, despite the language of the statute, to provide the clear notice required under the Spending Clause. The thrust of the footnote was simply that the term "attorneys' fees," standing alone, is generally not understood as encompassing expert fees. Thus, *Crawford Fitting* and *Casey* strongly reinforce the conclusion that the IDEA does not unambiguously authorize prevailing parents to recover expert fees.

V

Respondents make several arguments that are not based on the text of the IDEA, but these arguments do not show that the IDEA provides clear notice regarding the award of expert fees.

Respondents argue that their interpretation of the IDEA furthers the Act's overarching goal of "ensur[ing] that all children with disabilities have available to them a free appropriate public education," 20 U.S.C. § 1400(d)(1)(A), as well as the goal of "safeguard[ing] the rights of parents to challenge school decisions that adversely affect their child." Brief for Respondents 20. These goals, however, are too general to provide much support for respondents' reading of the terms of the IDEA. The IDEA obviously does not seek to promote these goals at the expense of all other considerations, including fiscal considerations. Because the IDEA is not intended in all instances to further the broad goals identified by respondents at the expense of fiscal considerations, the goals cited by respondents do little to bolster their argument on the narrow question presented here.

Finally, respondents vigorously argue that Congress clearly intended for prevailing parents to be compensated for expert fees. They rely on the legislative history of § 1415 and in particular on the following statement in the Conference Committee Report, discussed above: "The conferees intend that the term 'attorneys' fees as part of the costs' include reasonable expenses and fees of expert witnesses and the reasonable costs of any test or evaluation which is found to be necessary for the preparation of the . . . case." H.R. Conf. Rep. No. 99-687, at 5, U.S.Code Cong. & Admin.News, 1986, pp. 1807, 1808.

Whatever weight this legislative history would merit in another context, it is not sufficient here. Putting the legislative history aside, we see virtually no support for respondents' position. Under these circumstances, where everything other than the legislative history overwhelmingly suggests that expert fees may not be recovered, the legislative history is simply not enough. In a Spending Clause case, the key is not what a majority of the Members of both Houses intend but what the States are clearly told regarding the conditions that go along with the acceptance of those funds. Here, in the face of the unambiguous text of the IDEA and the reasoning in *Crawford Fitting* and *Casey*, we cannot say that the legislative history on which respondents rely is sufficient to provide the requisite fair notice.

* * *

We reverse the judgment of the Court of Appeals for the Second Circuit and remand the case for further proceedings consistent with this opinion.

It is so ordered.

Justice GINSBURG, concurring in part and concurring in the judgment (omitted).

Justice SOUTER, dissenting.

I join Justice BREYER's dissent and add this word only to say outright what would otherwise be implicit, that I agree with the distinction he draws between this case and *Barnes v. Gorman*, 536 U.S. 181 (2002). See *post*, at 2471 (citing *Barnes, supra*, at 191, 122 S.Ct. 2097 (SOUTER, J., concurring)). Beyond that, I emphasize the importance for me of § 4 of the Handicapped Children's Protection Act of 1986, 100 Stat. 797, note following 20 U.S.C. § 1415 (1988 ed.), which mandated the study by what is now known as the Government Accountability Office. That section, of equal dignity with the fee-shifting provision enacted by the same statute, makes Justice BREYER's resort to the related Conference Report the reasonable course.

Justice BREYER, with whom Justice STEVENS and Justice SOUTER join, dissenting.

The Individuals with Disabilities Education Act (IDEA or Act), 20 U.S.C. § 1400 *et seq.* (2000 ed. and Supp.V), says that a court may "award reasonable attorneys' fees as part of the costs to the parents" who are prevailing parties. § 1415(i)(3)(B). Unlike the Court, I believe that the word "costs" includes, and authorizes payment of, the costs of experts. The word "costs" does not define its own scope. Neither does the phrase "attorneys' fees as part of costs." But Members of Congress did make clear their intent by, among other things, approving a Conference Report that specified that "the term 'attorneys' fees as part of the costs' include[s] reasonable expenses and fees of expert witnesses and the reasonable costs of any test or evaluation which is found to be necessary for the preparation of the parent or guardian's case in the action or proceeding." H.R. Conf. Rep. No. 99-687, p. 5 (1986), U.S.Code Cong. & Admin.News, 1986, pp. 1807, 1808, Appendix A, *infra*, at 2475-2476. No Senator or Representative voiced *any* opposition to this statement in the discussion preceding the vote on the Conference Report-the last vote on the bill before it was sent to the President. I can find no good reason for this Court to interpret the language of this statute as meaning the precise opposite of what Congress told us it intended.

I

There are two strong reasons for interpreting the statutory phrase to include the award of expert fees. First, that is what Congress said it intended by the phrase. Second, that interpretation furthers the IDEA's statutorily defined purposes.

* * *

The practical significance of the Act's participatory rights and procedural protections may be seriously diminished if parents are unable to obtain reimbursement for the costs of their experts. In IDEA cases, experts are necessary. cf. *Schaffer, supra*, at 66-67 (GINSBURG, J., dissenting) ("[T]he vast majority of parents whose children require the benefits and protections provided in the IDEA lack knowledge about the educational resources available to their child and the sophistication to mount an effective case against a district-proposed," individualized education program (IEP) (internal quotation marks and brackets omitted)).

Experts are also expensive. See Brief for Respondents 28, n. 17 (collecting District Court decisions awarding expert costs ranging from $200 to $7,600, and noting three reported cases in which expert awards exceeded $10,000). The costs of experts may not make much of a dent in a school district's budget, as many of the experts they use in IDEA proceedings are already on the staff. Cf. *Oberti v. Board of Ed. Clementon School Dist.*, 995 F.2d 1204, 1219 (3rd Cir. 1993). But to parents, the award of costs may matter enormously. Without potential reimbursement, parents may well lack the services of experts entirely.

In a word, the Act's statutory right to a "free" and "appropriate" education may mean little to those who must pay hundreds of dollars to obtain it. That is why this Court has previously avoided interpretations that would bring about this kind of result. See *School Comm. of Burlington v. Department of Ed. of Mass.*, 471 U.S. 359 (1985) (construing IDEA provision granting equitable authority to courts to include the power to order reimbursement for parents who switch their child to private schools if that decision later proves correct); *id.*, at 370 (without cost reimbursement for prevailing parents, "the child's right to a *free* appropriate public education, the parents' right to participate fully in developing a proper IEP, and all of the procedural safeguards would be less than complete"); *Florence County School Dist. Four v. Carter*, 510 U.S. 7, 13 (1993) (holding that prevailing parents are not barred from reimbursement for switching their child to a private school that does not meet the IDEA's definition of a free and appropriate education). In *Carter*, we explained: "IDEA was intended to ensure that children with disabilities receive an education that is both appropriate and free. To read the provisions of § 1401(a)(18) to bar reimbursement in the circumstances of this case would defeat this statutory purpose." *Id.*, at 13-14 (citation omitted).

To read the word "costs" as requiring successful parents to bear their own expenses for experts suffers from the same problem. Today's result will leave many parents and guardians "without an expert with the firepower to match the opposition," *Schaffer*, 546 U.S., at 61, a far cry from the level playing field that Congress envisioned.

* * *

III

For the reasons I have set forth, I cannot agree with the majority's conclusion. Even less can I agree with its failure to consider fully the statute's legislative history. That history makes Congress' purpose clear. And our ultimate judicial goal is to interpret language in light of the statute's purpose. Only by seeking that purpose can we avoid the substitution of judicial for legislative will. Only by reading language in its light can we maintain the democratic link between voters, legislators, statutes, and ultimate implementation, upon which the legitimacy of our constitutional system rests.

In my view, to keep faith with that interpretive goal, we must retain all traditional interpretive tools-text, structure, history, and purpose. And, because faithful interpretation is art as well as science, we cannot, through rule or canon, rule out the use of any of these tools, automatically and in advance. Cf. *Helvering v. Gregory*, 69 F.2d 809, 810-811 (2nd Cir. 1934) (L. Hand, J.).

Nothing in the Constitution forbids us to give significant weight to legislative history. By disregarding a clear statement in a legislative Report adopted without opposition in both Houses of Congress, the majority has reached a result no Member of Congress expected or overtly desired. It has adopted an interpretation that undercuts, rather than furthers, the statute's purpose, a "free" and "appropriate" public education for "all" children with disabilities. See *Circuit City Stores, Inc. v. Adams*, 532 U.S. 105, 133 (2001) (STEVENS, J., joined by SOUTER, GINSBURG, and BREYER, JJ., dissenting) ("A method of statutory interpretation that is deliberately uninformed, and hence unconstrained, may produce a result that is consistent with a court's own views of how things should be, but it may also defeat the very purpose for which a provision was enacted"). And it has adopted an approach that, I fear, divorces law from life. See *Duncan, supra*, at 193 (BREYER, J., joined by GINSBURG, J., dissenting).

For these reasons, I respectfully dissent. (Appendices omitted.)

Jacob WINKELMAN, a minor, by and through his parents and legal guardians, Jeff and Sandee WINKELMAN, et al., Petitioners, v. PARMA CITY SCHOOL DISTRICT

550 U.S. 516 (2007)

Justice Kennedy delivered the opinion of the Court.

Some four years ago, Mr. and Mrs. Winkelman, parents of five children, became involved in lengthy administrative and legal proceedings. They had sought review related to concerns they had over whether their youngest child, 6-year-old Jacob, would progress well at Pleasant Valley Elementary School, which is part of the Parma City School District in Parma, Ohio.

Jacob has autism spectrum disorder and is covered by the Individuals with Disabilities Education Act (Act or IDEA), 84 Stat. 175, as amended, 20 U.S.C. § 1400 *et seq.* (2000 ed. and Supp. IV). His parents worked with the school district to develop an individualized education program (IEP), as required by the Act. All concede that Jacob's parents had the statutory right to contribute to this process and, when agreement could not be reached, to participate in administrative proceedings including what the Act refers to as an "impartial due process hearing." § 1415(f)(1)(A) (2000 ed., Supp. IV).

The disagreement at the center of the current dispute concerns the procedures to be followed when parents and their child, dissatisfied with the outcome of the due process hearing, seek further review in a United States District Court. The question is whether parents, either on their own behalf or as representatives of the child, may proceed in court unrepresented by counsel though they are not trained or licensed as attorneys. Resolution of this issue requires us to examine and explain the provisions of IDEA to determine if it accords to parents rights of their own that can be vindicated in court proceedings, or alternatively, whether the Act allows them, in their status as parents, to represent their child in court proceedings.

I

Respondent Parma City School District, a participant in IDEA's educational spending program, accepts federal funds for assistance in the education of children with disabilities. As a condition of receiving funds, it must comply with IDEA's mandates. IDEA requires that the school district provide Jacob with a "free appropriate public education," which must operate in accordance with the IEP that Jacob's parents, along with school officials and other individuals, develop as members of Jacob's "IEP Team." Brief for Petitioners 3 (internal quotation marks omitted).

The school district proposed an IEP for the 2003-2004 school year that would have placed Jacob at a public elementary school. Regarding this IEP as deficient under IDEA, Jacob's nonlawyer parents availed themselves of the administrative review provided by IDEA. They filed a complaint alleging respondent had failed to provide Jacob with a free appropriate public education; they appealed the hearing officer's rejection of the claims in this complaint to a state-level review officer; and after losing that appeal they filed, on their own behalf and on behalf of Jacob, a complaint in the United States District Court for the Northern District of Ohio. In reliance upon 20 U.S.C. § 1415(i)(2) (2000 ed., Supp. IV) they challenged the administrative decision, alleging, among other matters: that Jacob had not been provided with a free appropriate public education; that his IEP was inadequate; and that the school district had failed to follow procedures mandated by IDEA. Pending the resolution of these challenges, the Winkelmans had enrolled Jacob in a private school at their own expense. They had also obtained counsel to assist them with certain aspects of the proceedings, although they filed their federal complaint, and later their appeal, without the aid of an attorney. The Winkelmans' complaint sought reversal of the administrative decision, reimbursement for private-school expenditures and attorney's fees already incurred, and, it appears, declaratory relief.

The District Court granted respondent's motion for judgment on the pleadings, finding it had provided Jacob with a free appropriate public education. Petitioners, proceeding without counsel, filed an appeal with the Court of Appeals for the Sixth Circuit. Relying on its recent decision in *Cavanaugh v. Cardinal Local School Dist.*, 409 F.3d 753 (6th Cir. 2005), the Court of Appeals entered an order dismissing the Winkelmans' appeal unless they obtained counsel to represent Jacob. See Order in No. 05-3886 (Nov. 4, 2005), App. A to Pet. for Cert. 1a. In *Cavanaugh* the Court of Appeals had rejected the proposition that IDEA allows nonlawyer parents raising IDEA claims to proceed *pro se* in federal court. The court ruled that the right to a free appropriate public education "belongs to the child alone," 409 F.3d, at 757, not to both the parents and the child. It followed, the court held, that "any right on which the [parents] could proceed on their own behalf would be derivative" of the child's right, *ibid.*, so that parents bringing IDEA claims were not appearing on their own behalf, *ibid.* See also 28 U.S.C. § 1654 (allowing parties to prosecute their own claims *pro se*). As for the parents' alternative argument, the court held, nonlawyer parents cannot litigate IDEA claims on behalf of their child because IDEA does not abrogate the common-law rule prohibiting nonlawyer parents from representing minor children. 409 F.3d, at 756. As the court in *Cavanaugh* acknowledged, its decision brought the Sixth Circuit in direct conflict with the First Circuit, which had concluded, under a theory of "statutory joint rights," that the Act accords to parents the right to assert IDEA claims on their own behalf. See *Maroni v. Pemi-Baker Regional School Dist.*, 346 F.3d 247, 249, 250 (1st Cir. 2003).

Petitioners sought review in this Court. In light of the disagreement among the Courts of Appeals as to whether a nonlawyer parent of a child with a disability may prosecute IDEA actions *pro se* in federal court, we granted certiorari. 549 U.S. 1190 (2006).

II

Our resolution of this case turns upon the significance of IDEA's interlocking statutory provisions. Petitioners' primary theory is that the Act makes parents real parties in interest to IDEA actions, not "mer[e] guardians of their children's rights." Brief for Petitioners 16. If correct, this allows Mr. and Mrs. Winkelman back into court, for there is no question that a party may represent his or her own interests in federal court without the aid of counsel. See 28 U.S.C. § 1654 ("In all courts of the United States the parties may plead and conduct their own cases personally or by counsel . . ."). Petitioners cannot cite a specific provision in IDEA mandating in direct and explicit terms that parents have the status of real parties in interest. They instead base their argument on a comprehensive reading of IDEA. Taken as a whole, they contend, the Act leads to the necessary conclusion that parents have independent, enforceable rights. Brief for Petitioners 14 (citing *Koons Buick Pontiac GMC, Inc. v. Nigh*, 543 U.S. 50, 60 (2004)). Respondent, accusing petitioners of "knit[ting] together various provisions pulled from the crevices of the statute" to support these claims, Brief for Respondent 19, reads the text of IDEA to mean that any redressable rights under the Act belong only to children, *id.*, at 19-40.

We agree that the text of IDEA resolves the question presented. We recognize, in addition, that a proper interpretation of the Act requires a consideration of the entire statutory scheme. See *Dolan v. Postal Service*, 546 U.S. 481, 486 (2006). Turning to the current version of IDEA, which the parties agree governs this case, we begin with an overview of the relevant statutory provisions.

A

The goals of IDEA include "ensur[ing] that all children with disabilities have available to them a free appropriate public education" and "ensur[ing] that the rights of children with disabilities and parents of such children are protected." 20 U.S.C. §§ 1400(d)(1)(A)-(B) (2000 ed., Supp. IV). To this end, the Act includes provisions governing four areas of particular relevance to the Winkelmans' claim: procedures to be followed when developing a child's IEP; criteria governing the sufficiency of an education provided to a child; mechanisms for review that must be made available when there are objections to the IEP or to other aspects of IDEA proceedings; and the requirement in certain circumstances that States reimburse parents for various expenses. See generally §§ 1412(a)(10), 1414, 1415. Although our discussion of these four areas does not identify all the illustrative provisions, we do take particular note of certain terms that mandate or otherwise describe parental involvement.

IDEA requires school districts to develop an IEP for each child with a disability, see §§ 1412(a)(4), 1414(d), with parents playing "a significant role" in this process, *Schaffer v. Weast*, 546 U.S. 49, 53. Parents serve as members of the team that develops the IEP. § 1414(d)(1)(B). The "concerns" parents have "for enhancing the education of their child" must be considered by the team. § 1414(d)(3)(A)(ii). IDEA accords parents additional protections that apply throughout the IEP process. See, *e.g.*, § 1414(d)(4)(A) (requiring the IEP Team to revise the IEP when appropriate to address certain information provided by the parents); § 1414(e) (requiring States to "ensure that the parents of [a child with a disability] are members of any group that makes decisions on the educational placement of their child"). The statute also sets up general procedural safeguards that protect the informed involvement of parents in the development of an education for their child. See, *e.g.*, § 1415(a) (requiring States to "establish and maintain procedures . . . to ensure that children with disabilities and their parents are guaranteed procedural safeguards with respect to the provision of a free appropriate public education"); § 1415(b)(1) (mandating that States provide an opportunity for parents to examine all relevant records). See generally §§ 1414, 1415. A central purpose of the parental protections is to facilitate the provision of a " 'free appropriate public education,' " § 1401(9), which must be made available to the child "in conformity with the [IEP]," § 1401(9)(D).

The Act defines a "free appropriate public education" pursuant to an IEP to be an educational instruction "specially designed . . . to meet the unique needs of a child with a disability," § 1401(29), coupled with any additional " 'related services' " that are "required to assist a child with a disability to benefit from [that instruction]," § 1401(26)(A). See also § 1401(9). The education must, among other things, be provided "under public supervision and direction," "meet the standards of the State educational agency," and "include an appropriate preschool, elementary school, or secondary school education in the State involved." *Ibid.* The instruction must, in addition, be provided at "no cost to parents." § 1401(29).

When a party objects to the adequacy of the education provided, the construction of the IEP, or some related matter, IDEA provides procedural recourse: It requires that a State provide "[a]n opportunity for any party to present a complaint . . . with respect to any matter relating to the identification, evaluation, or educational placement of the child, or the provision of a free appropriate public education to such child." § 1415(b)(6). By presenting a complaint a party is able to pursue a process of review that, as relevant, begins with a preliminary meeting "where the parents of the child discuss their complaint" and the local educational agency "is provided the opportunity to [reach a resolution]." § 1415(f)(1)(B)(i)(IV). If the agency "has not resolved the complaint to the satisfaction of the parents within 30 days," § 1415(f)(1)(B)(ii), the parents may request an "impartial due process hearing," § 1415(f)(1)(A), which must be conducted either by the local educational agency or by the state educational agency, *ibid.*, and where a hearing officer will resolve issues raised in the complaint, § 1415(f)(3).

IDEA sets standards the States must follow in conducting these hearings. Among other things, it indicates that the hearing officer's decision "shall be made on substantive grounds based on a determination of whether the child received a free appropriate public education," § 1415(f)(3)(E)(i), and that, "[i]n matters alleging a procedural violation," the officer may find a child "did not receive a free appropriate public education," § 1415(f)(3)(E)(ii), only if the violation

(I) impeded the child's right to a free appropriate public education;

(II) significantly impeded the parents' opportunity to participate in the decisionmaking process regarding the provision of a free appropriate public education to the parents' child; or

(III) caused a deprivation of educational benefits."

§§ 1415(f)(3)(E)(i)-(ii).

If the local educational agency, rather than the state educational agency, conducts this hearing, then "any party aggrieved by the findings and decision rendered in such a hearing may appeal such findings and decision to the State educational agency." § 1415(g)(1). Once the state educational agency has reached its decision, an aggrieved party may commence suit in federal court: "Any party aggrieved by the findings and decision made [by the hearing officer] shall have the right to bring a civil action with respect to the complaint." § 1415(i)(2)(A); see also § 1415(i)(1).

IDEA, finally, provides for at least two means of cost recovery that inform our analysis. First, in certain circumstances it allows a court or hearing officer to require a state agency "to reimburse the parents [of a child with a disability] for the cost of [private school] enrollment if the court or hearing officer finds that the agency had not made a free appropriate public education available to the child." § 1412(a)(10)(C)(ii). Second, it sets forth rules governing when and to what extent a court may award attorney's fees. See § 1415(i)(3)(B). Included in this section is a provision allowing an award "to a prevailing party who is the parent of a child with a disability." § 1415(i)(3)(B)(i)(I).

B

Petitioners construe these various provisions to accord parents independent, enforceable rights under IDEA. We agree. The parents enjoy enforceable rights at the administrative stage, and it would be inconsistent with the statutory scheme to bar them from continuing to assert these rights in federal court.

The statute sets forth procedures for resolving disputes in a manner that, in the Act's express terms, contemplates parents will be the parties bringing the administrative complaints. In addition to the provisions we have cited, we refer also to § 1415(b)(8) (requiring a state educational agency to "develop a model form to assist parents in filing a complaint"); § 1415(c)(2) (addressing the response an agency must provide to a "parent's due process complaint notice"); and § 1415(i)(3)(B)(i) (referring to "the parent's complaint"). A wide range of review is available: Administrative complaints may be brought with respect to "any matter relating to . . . the provision of a free appropriate public education." § 1415(b)(6)(A). Claims raised in these complaints are then resolved at impartial due process hearings, where, again, the statute makes clear that parents will be participating as parties. See generally *supra*, at 2001. See also § 1415(f)(3)(C) (indicating "[a] parent or agency shall request an impartial due process hearing" within a certain period of time); § 1415(e)(2)(A)(ii) (referring to "a parent's right to a due process hearing"). The statute then grants "[a]ny party aggrieved by the findings and decision made [by the hearing officer] . . . the right to bring a civil action with respect to the complaint." § 1415(i)(2)(A).

Nothing in these interlocking provisions excludes a parent who has exercised his or her own rights from statutory protection the moment the administrative proceedings end. Put another way, the Act does not *sub silentio* or by implication bar parents from seeking to vindicate the rights accorded to them once the time comes to file a civil action. Through its provisions for expansive review and extensive parental involvement, the statute leads to just the opposite result.

Respondent, resisting this line of analysis, asks us to read these provisions as contemplating parental involvement only to the extent parents represent their child's interests. In respondent's view IDEA accords parents nothing more than "collateral tools related to the child's underlying substantive rights-not freestanding or independently enforceable rights." Brief for Respondent 25.

This interpretation, though, is foreclosed by provisions of the statute. IDEA defines one of its purposes as seeking "to ensure that the rights of children with disabilities and parents of such children are protected." § 1400(d)(1)(B). The word "rights" in the quoted language refers to the rights of parents as well as the rights of the child; otherwise the grammatical structure would make no sense.

Further provisions confirm this view. IDEA mandates that educational agencies establish procedures "to ensure that children with disabilities and their parents are guaranteed procedural safeguards with respect to the provision of a free appropriate public education." § 1415(a). It presumes parents have rights of their own when it defines how States might provide for the transfer of the "rights accorded to parents" by IDEA, § 1415(m)(1)(B), and it prohibits the raising of certain challenges "[n]otwithstanding any other individual right of action that a parent or student may maintain under [the relevant provisions of IDEA]," §§ 1401(10)(E), 1412(a)(14)(E). To adopt respondent's reading of the statute would require an interpretation of these statutory provisions (and others) far too strained to be correct.

Defending its countertextual reading of the statute, respondent cites a decision by a Court of Appeals concluding that the Act's "references to parents are best understood as accommodations to the fact of the child's incapacity." *Doe v. Board of Ed. of Baltimore Cty.*, 165 F.3d 260, 263 (4th Cir. 1998); see also Brief for Respondent 30. This, according to respondent, requires us to interpret all references to parents' rights as referring in implicit terms to the child's rights-which, under this view, are the only enforceable rights accorded by IDEA. Even if we were inclined to ignore the plain text of the statute in considering this theory, we disagree that the sole purpose driving IDEA's involvement of parents is to facilitate vindication of a child's rights. It is not a novel proposition to say that parents have a recognized legal interest in the education and upbringing of their child. See, *e.g.*, *Pierce v. Society of Sisters*, 268 U.S. 510, 534-535 (1925) (acknowledging "the liberty of parents and guardians to direct the upbringing and education of children under their control"); *Meyer v. Nebraska*, 262 U.S. 390, 399-401 (1923). There is no necessary bar or obstacle in the law, then, to finding an intention by Congress to grant parents a stake in the entitlements created by IDEA. Without question a parent of a child with a disability has a particular and personal interest in fulfilling "our national policy of ensuring equality of opportunity, full participation, independent living, and economic self-sufficiency for individuals with disabilities." § 1400(c)(1).

We therefore find no reason to read into the plain language of the statute an implicit rejection of the notion that Congress would accord parents independent, enforceable rights concerning the education of their children. We instead interpret the statute's references to parents' rights to mean what they say: that IDEA includes provisions conveying rights to parents as well as to children.

A variation on respondent's argument has persuaded some Courts of Appeals. The argument is that while a parent can be a "party aggrieved" for aspects of the hearing officer's findings and decision, he or she cannot be a "party aggrieved" with respect to all IDEA-based challenges. Under this view the causes of action available to a parent might relate, for example, to various procedural mandates, see, *e.g.*, *Collinsgru*, 161 F.3d, at 233, and reimbursement demands, see, *e.g.*, § 1412(a)(10)(C)(ii). The argument supporting this conclusion proceeds as follows: Because a "party aggrieved" is, by definition, entitled to a remedy, and parents are, under IDEA, only entitled to certain procedures and reimbursements as remedies, a parent cannot be a "party aggrieved" with regard to any claim not implicating these limited matters.

This argument is contradicted by the statutory provisions we have recited. True, there are provisions in IDEA stating parents are entitled to certain procedural protections and reimbursements; but the statute prevents us from placing too much weight on the implications to be drawn when other entitlements are accorded in less clear language. We find little support for the inference that parents are excluded by implication whenever a child is mentioned, and vice versa. Compare, *e.g.*, § 1411(e)(3)(E) (barring States from using certain funds for costs associated with actions "brought on behalf of a child" but failing to acknowledge that actions might also be brought on behalf of a parent) with § 1415(i)(3)(B)(i) (allowing recovery of attorney's fees to a "prevailing party who is the parent of a child with a disability" but failing to acknowledge that a child might also be a prevailing party). Without more, then, the language in IDEA confirming that parents enjoy particular procedural and reimbursement-related rights does not resolve whether they are also entitled to enforce IDEA's other mandates, including the one most fundamental to the Act: the provision of a free appropriate public education to a child with a disability.

We consider the statutory structure. The IEP proceedings entitle parents to participate not only in the implementation of IDEA's procedures but also in the substantive formulation of their child's educational program. Among other things, IDEA requires the IEP Team, which includes the parents as members, to take into account any "concerns" parents have "for enhancing the education of their child" when it formulates the IEP. § 1414(d)(3)(A)(ii). The IEP, in turn, sets the boundaries of the central entitlement provided by IDEA: It defines a " 'free appropriate public education' " for that parent's child. § 1401(9).

The statute also empowers parents to bring challenges based on a broad range of issues. The parent may seek a hearing on "any matter relating to the identification, evaluation, or educational placement of the child, or the provision of a free appropriate public education to such child." § 1415(b)(6)(A). To resolve these challenges a hearing officer must make a decision based on whether the child "received a free appropriate public education." § 1415(f)(3)(E). When this hearing has been conducted by a local educational agency rather than a state educational agency, "any party aggrieved by the findings and decision rendered in such a hearing may appeal such findings and decision" to the state educational agency. § 1415(g)(1). Judicial review follows, authorized by a broadly worded provision phrased in the same terms used to describe the prior stage of review: "[a]ny party aggrieved" may bring "a civil action." § 1415(i)(2)(A).

These provisions confirm that IDEA, through its text and structure, creates in parents an independent stake not only in the procedures and costs implicated by this process but also in the substantive decisions to be made. We therefore conclude that IDEA does not differentiate, through isolated references to various procedures and remedies, between the rights accorded to children and the rights accorded to parents. As a consequence, a parent may be a "party aggrieved" for purposes of § 1415(i)(2) with regard to "any matter" implicating these rights. See § 1415(b)(6)(A). The status of parents as parties is not limited to matters that relate to procedure and cost recovery. To find otherwise would be inconsistent with the collaborative framework and expansive system of review established by the Act. Cf. *Cedar Rapids Community School Dist. v. Garret F.*, 526 U.S. 66, 73, 119 S.Ct. 992, 143 L.Ed.2d 154 (1999) (looking to IDEA's "overall statutory scheme" to interpret its provisions).

Our conclusion is confirmed by noting the incongruous results that would follow were we to accept the proposition that parents' IDEA rights are limited to certain nonsubstantive matters. The statute's procedural and reimbursement-related rights are intertwined with the substantive adequacy of the education provided to a child, see, e.g., § 1415(f)(3)(E), see also § 1412(a)(10)(C)(ii), and it is difficult to disentangle the provisions in order to conclude that some rights adhere to both parent and child while others do not. Were we nevertheless to recognize a distinction of this sort it would impose upon parties a confusing and onerous legal regime, one worsened by the absence of any express guidance in IDEA concerning how a court might in practice differentiate between these matters. It is, in addition, out of accord with the statute's design to interpret the Act to require that parents prove the substantive inadequacy of their child's education as a predicate for obtaining, for example, reimbursement under § 1412(a)(10)(C)(ii), yet to prevent them from obtaining a judgment mandating that the school district provide their child with an educational program demonstrated to be an appropriate one. The adequacy of the educational program is, after all, the central issue in the litigation. The provisions of IDEA do not set forth these distinctions, and we decline to infer them.

The bifurcated regime suggested by the courts that have employed it, moreover, leaves some parents without a remedy. The statute requires, in express terms, that States provide a child with a free appropriate public education "at public expense," § 1401(9)(A), including specially designed instruction "at no cost to parents," § 1401(29). Parents may seek to enforce this mandate through the federal courts, we conclude, because among the rights they enjoy is the right to a free appropriate public education for their child. Under the countervailing view, which would make a parent's ability to enforce IDEA dependant on certain procedural and reimbursement-related rights, a parent whose disabled child has not received a free appropriate public education would have recourse in the federal courts only under two circumstances: when the parent happens to have some claim related to the procedures employed; and when he or she is able to incur, and has in fact incurred, expenses creating a right to reimbursement. Otherwise the adequacy of the child's education would not be regarded as relevant to any cause of action the parent might bring; and, as a result, only the child could vindicate the right accorded by IDEA to a free appropriate public education.

The potential for injustice in this result is apparent. What is more, we find nothing in the statute to indicate that when Congress required States to provide adequate instruction to a child "at no cost to parents," it intended that only some parents would be able to enforce that mandate. The statute instead takes pains to "ensure that the rights of children with disabilities and parents of such children are protected." § 1400(d)(1)(B). See, *e.g.*, § 1415(e)(2) (requiring that States implement procedures to ensure parents are guaranteed procedural safeguards with respect to the provision of a free appropriate public education); § 1415(e)(2)(A)(ii) (requiring that mediation procedures not be "used to deny or delay a parent's right to a due process hearing . . . or to deny any other rights afforded under this subchapter"); cf. § 1400(c)(3) (noting IDEA's success in "ensuring children with disabilities and the families of such children access to a free appropriate public education").

We conclude IDEA grants parents independent, enforceable rights. These rights, which are not limited to certain procedural and reimbursement-related matters, encompass the entitlement to a free appropriate public education for the parents' child.

C

Respondent contends, though, that even under the reasoning we have now explained petitioners cannot prevail without overcoming a further difficulty. Citing our opinion in *Arlington Central School Dist. Bd. of Ed. v. Murphy*, 548 U.S. 291, 126 S.Ct. 2455, 165 L.Ed.2d 526 (2006), respondent argues that statutes passed pursuant to the Spending Clause, such as IDEA, must provide " 'clear notice' " before they can burden a State with some new condition, obligation, or liability. Brief for Respondent 41. Respondent contends that because IDEA is, at best, ambiguous as to whether it accords parents independent rights, it has failed to provide clear notice of this condition to the States. See *id.*, at 40–49.

Respondent's reliance on *Arlington* is misplaced. In *Arlington* we addressed whether IDEA required States to reimburse experts' fees to prevailing parties in IDEA actions. "[W]hen Congress attaches conditions to a State's acceptance of federal funds," we explained, "the conditions must be set out 'unambiguously.' " 548 U.S., at —, 126 S.Ct., at 2459 (quoting *Pennhurst State School and Hospital v. Halderman*, 451 U.S. 1, 17 (1981)). The question to be answered in *Arlington*, therefore, was whether IDEA "furnishes clear notice regarding the liability at issue." 548 U.S., at —, 126 S.Ct., at 2459. We found it did not.

The instant case presents a different issue, one that does not invoke the same rule. Our determination that IDEA grants to parents independent, enforceable rights does not impose any substantive condition or obligation on States they would not otherwise be required by law to observe. The basic measure of monetary recovery, moreover, is not expanded by recognizing that some rights repose in both the parent and the child. Were we considering a statute other than the one before us, the Spending Clause argument might have more force: A determination by the Court that some distinct class of people has independent, enforceable rights might result in a change to the States' statutory obligations. But that is not the case here.

Respondent argues our ruling will, as a practical matter, increase costs borne by the States as they are forced to defend against suits unconstrained by attorneys trained in the law and the rules of ethics. Effects such as these do not suffice to invoke the concerns under the Spending

Clause. Furthermore, IDEA does afford relief for the States in certain cases. The Act empowers courts to award attorney's fees to a prevailing educational agency whenever a parent has presented a "complaint or subsequent cause of action . . . for any improper purpose, such as to harass, to cause unnecessary delay, or to needlessly increase the cost of litigation." § 1415(i)(3)(B)(i)(III). This provision allows some relief when a party has proceeded in violation of these standards.

III

The Court of Appeals erred when it dismissed the Winkelmans' appeal for lack of counsel. Parents enjoy rights under IDEA; and they are, as a result, entitled to prosecute IDEA claims on their own behalf. The decision by Congress to grant parents these rights was consistent with the purpose of IDEA and fully in accord with our social and legal traditions. It is beyond dispute that the relationship between a parent and child is sufficient to support a legally cognizable interest in the education of one's child; and, what is more, Congress has found that "the education of children with disabilities can be made more effective by . . . strengthening the role and responsibility of parents and ensuring that families of such children have meaningful opportunities to participate in the education of their children at school and at home." § 1400(c)(5).

In light of our holding we need not reach petitioners' alternative argument, which concerns whether IDEA entitles parents to litigate their child's claims *pro se*.

The judgment of the Court of Appeals is reversed, and the case is remanded for further proceedings consistent with this opinion.

It is so ordered.

Justice SCALIA, with whom Justice THOMAS joins, concurring in the judgment in part and dissenting in part (omitted).

FOREST GROVE SCHOOL DISTRICT, Petitioner, v. T.A.
129 S.Ct. 2484 (2009)

JUSTICE STEVENS delivered the opinion of the Court.

The Individuals with Disabilities Education Act (IDEA or Act), 84 Stat. 175, as amended, 20 U.S.C. § 1400 *et seq.*, requires States receiving federal funding to make a "free appropriate public education" (FAPE) available to all children with disabilities residing in the State, § 1412(a)(1)(A). We have previously held that when a public school fails to provide a FAPE and a child's parents place the child in an appropriate private school without the school district's consent, a court may require the district to reimburse the parents for the cost of the private education. See *School Comm. of Burlington v. Department of Ed. of Mass.*, 471 U.S. 359, 370 (1985). The question presented in this case is whether the IDEA Amendments of 1997 (Amendments), 111 Stat. 37, categorically prohibit reimbursement for private-education costs if a child has not "previously received special education and related services under the authority of a public agency." § 1412(a)(10)(C)(ii). We hold that the Amendments impose no such categorical bar.

I

Respondent T.A. attended public schools in the Forest Grove School District (School District or District) from the time he was in kindergarten through the winter of his junior year of high school. From kindergarten through eighth grade, respondent's teachers observed that he had trouble paying attention in class and completing his assignments. When respondent entered high school, his difficulties increased.

In December 2000, during respondent's freshman year, his mother contacted the school counselor to discuss respondent's problems with his schoolwork. At the end of the school year, respondent was evaluated by a school psychologist. After interviewing him, examining his school records, and administering cognitive ability tests, the psychologist concluded that respondent did not need further testing for any learning disabilities or other health impairments, including attention deficit hyperactivity disorder (ADHD). The psychologist and two other school officials discussed the evaluation results with respondent's mother in June 2001, and all agreed that respondent did not qualify for special-education services. Respondent's parents did not seek review of that decision, although the hearing examiner later found that the School District's evaluation was legally inadequate because it failed to address all areas of suspected disability, including ADHD.

With extensive help from his family, respondent completed his sophomore year at Forest Grove High School, but his problems worsened during his junior year. In February 2003, respondent's parents discussed with the School District the possibility of respondent completing high school through a partnership program with the local community college. They also sought private professional advice, and in March 2003 respondent was diagnosed with ADHD and a number of disabilities related to learning and memory. Advised by the private specialist that respondent would do best in a structured, residential learning environment, respondent's parents enrolled him at a private academy that focuses on educating children with special needs.

Four days after enrolling him in private school, respondent's parents hired a lawyer to ascertain their rights and to give the School District written notice of respondent's private placement. A few weeks later, in April 2003, respondent's parents requested an administrative due process hearing regarding respondent's eligibility for special-education services. In June 2003, the District engaged a school psychologist to assist in determining whether respondent had a disability that significantly interfered with his educational performance. Respondent's parents cooperated with the District during the evaluation process. In July 2003, a multidisciplinary team met to discuss whether respondent satisfied IDEA's disability criteria and concluded that he did not because his ADHD did not have a sufficiently significant adverse impact on his educational performance. Because the School District maintained that respondent was not eligible for special-education services and therefore declined to provide an individualized education program (IEP), respondent's parents left him enrolled at the private academy for his senior year.

The administrative review process resumed in September 2003. After considering the parties' evidence, including the testimony of numerous experts, the hearing officer issued a decision in January 2004 finding that respondent's ADHD adversely affected his educational performance and that the School District failed to meet its obligations under IDEA in not identifying respondent as a student eligible for special-education services. Because the District did not offer respondent a FAPE and his private-school placement was appropriate under IDEA, the hearing officer ordered the District to reimburse respondent's parents for the cost of the private-school tuition.

The School District sought judicial review pursuant to § 1415(i)(2), arguing that the hearing officer erred in granting reimbursement. The District Court accepted the hearing officer's findings of fact but set aside the reimbursement award after finding that the 1997 Amendments categorically bar reimbursement of private-school tuition for students who have not "previously received special education and related services under the authority of a public agency." § 612(a)(10)(C)(ii), 111 Stat. 63, 20 U.S.C. § 1412(a)(10)(C)(ii). The District Court further held that, "[e]ven assuming that tuition reimbursement may be ordered in an extreme case for a student not receiving special education services, under general principles of equity where the need for special education was obvious to school authorities," the facts of this case do not support equitable relief. App. to Pet. for Cert. 53a.

The Court of Appeals for the Ninth Circuit reversed and remanded for further proceedings. The court first noted that, prior to the 1997 Amendments, "IDEA was silent on the subject of private school reimbursement, but courts had granted such reimbursement as 'appropriate' relief under principles of equity pursuant to 20 U.S.C. § 1415(i)(2)(C)." 523 F.3d 1078, 1085 (9th Cir. 2008) (citing *Burlington*, 471 U.S., at 370, 105 S.Ct. 1996). It then held that the Amendments do not impose a categorical bar to reimbursement when a parent unilaterally places in private school a child who has not previously received special-education services through the public school. Rather, such students "are eligible for reimbursement, to the same extent as before the 1997 amendments, as 'appropriate' relief pursuant to § 1415(i)(2)(C)." 523 F.3d, at 1087-1088.

The Court of Appeals also rejected the District Court's analysis of the equities as resting on two legal errors. First, because it found that § 1412(a)(10)(C)(ii) generally bars relief in these circumstances, the District Court wrongly stated that relief was appropriate only if the equities were sufficient to "'override'" that statutory limitation. The District Court also erred in asserting that reimbursement is limited to "'extreme'" cases. *Id.*, at 1088 (emphasis deleted). The Court of Appeals therefore remanded with instructions to reexamine the equities, including the failure of respondent's parents to notify the School District before removing respondent from public school. In dissent, Judge Rymer stated her view that reimbursement is not available as an equitable remedy in this case because respondent's parents did not request an IEP before removing him from public school and respondent's right to a FAPE was therefore not at issue.

Because the Courts of Appeals that have considered this question have reached inconsistent results, we granted certiorari to determine whether § 1412(a)(10)(C) establishes a categorical bar to tuition reimbursement for students who have not previously received special-education services under the authority of a public education agency. 555 U.S. —, 129 S.Ct. 987, 173 L.Ed.2d 171 (2009).

II

Justice Rehnquist's opinion for a unanimous Court in *Burlington* provides the pertinent background for our analysis of the question presented. In that case, respondent challenged the appropriateness of the IEP developed for his child by public-school officials. The child had previously received special-education services through the public school. While administrative review was pending, private specialists advised respondent that the child would do best in a specialized private educational setting, and respondent enrolled the child in private school without the school district's consent. The hearing officer concluded that the IEP was not adequate to meet the child's educational needs and that the school district therefore failed to provide the child a FAPE. Finding also that the private-school placement was appropriate under IDEA, the hearing officer ordered the school district to reimburse respondent for the cost of the private-school tuition.

We granted certiorari in *Burlington* to determine whether IDEA authorizes reimbursement for the cost of private education when a parent or guardian unilaterally enrolls a child in private school because the public school has proposed an inadequate IEP and thus failed to provide a FAPE. The Act at that time made no express reference to the possibility of reimbursement, but it authorized a court to "grant such relief as the court determines is appropriate." § 1415(i)(2)(C)(iii). In determining the scope of the relief authorized, we noted that "the ordinary meaning of these words confers broad discretion on the court" and that, absent any indication to the contrary, what relief is "appropriate" must be determined in light of the Act's broad purpose of providing children with disabilities a FAPE, including through publicly funded private-school placements when necessary. 471 U.S., at 369. Accordingly, we held that the provision's grant of authority includes "the power to order school authorities to reimburse parents for their expenditures on private special-education services if the court ultimately determines that such placement, rather than a proposed IEP, is proper under the Act." *Ibid.*

Our decision rested in part on the fact that administrative and judicial review of a parent's complaint often takes years. We concluded that, having mandated that participating States provide a FAPE for every student, Congress could not have intended to require parents to either accept an inadequate public-school education pending adjudication of their claim or bear the cost of a private education if the court ultimately determined that the private placement was proper under the Act. *Id.*, at 370. Eight years later, we unanimously reaffirmed the availability of reimbursement in *Florence County School Dist. Four v. Carter*, 510 U.S. 7 (1993) (holding that reimbursement may be appropriate even when a child is placed in a private school that has not been approved by the State).

The dispute giving rise to the present litigation differs from those in *Burlington* and *Carter* in that it concerns not the adequacy of a proposed IEP but the School District's failure to provide an IEP at all. And, unlike respondent, the children in those cases had previously received public special-education services. These differences are insignificant, however, because our analysis in the earlier cases depended on the language and purpose of the Act and not the particular facts involved. Moreover, when a child requires special-education services, a school district's failure to propose an IEP of any kind is at least as serious a violation of its responsibilities under IDEA as a failure to provide an adequate IEP. It is thus clear that the reasoning of *Burlington* and *Carter* applies equally to this case. The only question is whether the 1997 Amendments require a different result.

III

Congress enacted IDEA in 1970 to ensure that all children with disabilities are provided " 'a free appropriate public education which emphasizes special education and related services designed to meet their unique needs [and] to assure that the rights of [such] children and their parents or guardians are protected.' " *Burlington*, 471 U.S., at 367. After examining the States' progress under IDEA, Congress found in 1997 that substantial gains had been made in the area of special education but that more needed to be done to guarantee children with disabilities adequate access to appropriate services. See S.Rep. No. 105-17, p. 5 (1997). The 1997 Amendments were intended "to place greater emphasis on improving student performance and ensuring that children with disabilities receive a quality public education." *Id.*, at 3.

Consistent with that goal, the Amendments preserved the Act's purpose of providing a FAPE to all children with disabilities. And they did not change the text of the provision we considered in *Burlington*, § 1415(i)(2)(C)(iii), which gives courts broad authority to grant "appropriate" relief, including reimbursement for the cost of private special education when a school district fails to provide a FAPE. "Congress is presumed to be aware of an administrative or judicial interpretation of a statute and to adopt that interpretation when it re-enacts a statute without change." *Lorillard v. Pons*, 434 U.S. 575, 580 (1978). Accordingly, absent a clear expression elsewhere in the Amendments of Congress' intent to repeal some portion of that provision or to abrogate our decisions in *Burlington* and *Carter*, we will continue to read § 1415(i)(2)(C)(iii) to authorize the relief respondent seeks.

The School District and the dissent argue that one of the provisions enacted by the Amendments, § 1412(a)(10)(C), effects such a repeal. Section 1412(a)(10)(C) is entitled "Payment for education of children enrolled in private schools without consent of or referral by the public agency," and it sets forth a number of principles applicable to public reimbursement for the costs of unilateral private-school placements. Section 1412(a)(10)(C)(i) states that IDEA "does not require a local educational agency to pay for the cost of education . . . of a child with a disability at a private school or facility if that agency made a free appropriate public education available to the child" and his parents nevertheless elected to place him in a private school. Section 1412(a)(10)(C)(ii) then provides that a "court or hearing officer may require [a public] agency to reimburse the parents for the cost of [private-school] enrollment if the court or hearing officer finds that the agency had not made a free appropriate public education available" and the child has "previously received special education and related services under the authority of [the] agency." Finally, § 1412(a)(10)(C)(iii) discusses circumstances under which the "cost of reimbursement described in clause (ii) may be reduced or denied," as when a parent fails to give 10 days' notice before removing a child from public school or refuses to make a child available for evaluation, and § 1412(a)(10)(C)(iv) lists circumstances in which a parent's failure to give notice may or must be excused.

Looking primarily to clauses (i) and (ii), the School District argues that Congress intended § 1412(a)(10)(C) to provide the exclusive source of authority for courts to order reimbursement when parents unilaterally enroll a child in private school. According to the District, clause (i) provides a safe harbor for school districts that provide a FAPE by foreclosing reimbursement in those circumstances. Clause (ii) then sets forth the circumstance in which reimbursement is appropriate-namely, when a school district fails to provide a FAPE to a child who has previously received special-education services through the public school. The District contends that because § 1412(a)(10)(C) only discusses reimbursement for children who have previously received special-education services through the public school, IDEA only authorizes reimbursement in that circumstance. The dissent agrees.

For several reasons, we find this argument unpersuasive. First, the School District's reading of the Act is not supported by its text and context, as the 1997 Amendments do not expressly prohibit reimbursement under the circumstances of this case, and the District offers no evidence that Congress intended to supersede our decisions in *Burlington* and *Carter.* Clause (i)'s safe harbor explicitly bars reimbursement only when a school district makes a FAPE available by correctly identifying a child as having a disability and proposing an IEP adequate to meet the child's needs. The clause says nothing about the availability of reimbursement when a school district fails to provide a FAPE. Indeed, its statement that reimbursement *is not* authorized when a school district provides a FAPE could be read to indicate that reimbursement *is* authorized when a school district does not fulfill that obligation.

Clause (ii) likewise does not support the District's position. Because that clause is phrased permissively, stating only that courts "may require" reimbursement in those circumstances, it does not foreclose reimbursement awards in other circumstances. Together with clauses (iii) and (iv), clause (ii) is best read as elaborating on the general rule that courts may order reimbursement when a school district fails to provide a FAPE by listing factors that may affect a reimbursement award in the common situation in which a school district has provided a child with some special-education services and the child's parents believe those services are inadequate. Referring as they do to students who have previously received special-education services through a public school, clauses (ii) through (iv) are premised on a history of cooperation and together encourage school districts and parents to continue to cooperate in developing and implementing an appropriate IEP before resorting to a unilateral private placement. The clauses of § 1412(a)(10)(C) are thus best read as elucidative rather than exhaustive. Cf. *United States v. Atlantic Research Corp.,* 551 U.S. 128, 137 (2007) (noting that statutory language may "perfor[m] a significant function simply by clarifying" a provision's meaning).

This reading of § 1412(a)(10)(C) is necessary to avoid the conclusion that Congress abrogated *sub silentio* our decisions in *Burlington* and *Carter.* In those cases, we construed § 1415(i)(2)(C)(iii) to authorize reimbursement when a school district fails to provide a FAPE and a child's private-school placement is appropriate, without regard to the child's prior receipt of services. It would take more than Congress' failure to comment on the category of cases in which a child has not previously received special-education services for us to conclude that the Amendments substantially superseded our decisions and in large part repealed § 1415(i)(2)(C)(iii). See *Branch v. Smith,* 538 U.S. 254, 273 (2003) ("[A]bsent a clearly expressed congressional intention, repeals by implication are not favored" (internal quotation marks and citation omitted)). We accordingly adopt the reading of § 1412(a)(10)(C) that is consistent with those decisions.

The School District's reading of § 1412(a)(10)(C) is also at odds with the general remedial purpose underlying IDEA and the 1997 Amendments. The express purpose of the Act is to "ensure that all children with disabilities have available to them a free appropriate public education that emphasizes special education and related services designed to meet their unique needs," § 1400(d)(1)(A)-a factor we took into account in construing the scope of § 1415(i)(2)(C)(iii), see *Burlington*, 471 U.S., at 369. Without the remedy respondent seeks, a "child's right to a *free* appropriate education . . . would be less than complete." *Id.*, at 370. The District's position similarly conflicts with IDEA's "child find" requirement, pursuant to which States are obligated to "identif[y], locat [e], and evaluat[e]" "[a]ll children with disabilities residing in the State" to ensure that they receive needed special-education services. § 1412(a)(3)(A); see § 1412(a)(10)(A)(ii). A reading of the Act that left parents without an adequate remedy when a school district unreasonably failed to identify a child with disabilities would not comport with Congress' acknowledgment of the paramount importance of properly identifying each child eligible for services.

Indeed, by immunizing a school district's refusal to find a child eligible for special-education services no matter how compelling the child's need, the School District's interpretation of § 1412(a)(10)(C) would produce a rule bordering on the irrational. It would be particularly strange for the Act to provide a remedy, as all agree it does, when a school district offers a child inadequate special-education services but to leave parents without relief in the more egregious situation in which the school district unreasonably denies a child access to such services altogether. That IDEA affords parents substantial procedural safeguards, including the right to challenge a school district's eligibility determination and obtain prospective relief, see *post*, at 2503 - 2504, is no answer. We roundly rejected that argument in *Burlington*, observing that the "review process is ponderous" and therefore inadequate to ensure that a school's failure to provide a FAPE is remedied with the speed necessary to avoid detriment to the child's education. 471 U.S., at 370,. Like *Burlington*, see *ibid.*, this case vividly demonstrates the problem of delay, as respondent's parents first sought a due process hearing in April 2003, and the District Court issued its decision in May 2005-almost a year after respondent graduated from high school. The dissent all but ignores these shortcomings of IDEA's procedural safeguards.

IV

The School District advances two additional arguments for reading the Act to foreclose reimbursement in this case. First, the District contends that because IDEA was an exercise of Congress' authority under the Spending Clause, U.S. Const., Art. I, § 8, cl. 1, any conditions attached to a State's acceptance of funds must be stated unambiguously. See *Pennhurst State School and Hospital v. Halderman*, 451 U.S. 1, 17 (1981). Applying that principle, we held in *Arlington Central School Dist. Bd. of Ed. v. Murphy*, 548 U.S. 291, 304 (2006), that IDEA's fee-shifting provision, § 1415(i)(3)(B), does not authorize courts to award expert-services fees to prevailing parents in IDEA actions because the Act does not put States on notice of the possibility of such awards. But *Arlington* is readily distinguishable from this case. In accepting IDEA funding, States expressly agree to provide a FAPE to all children with disabilities. See § 1412(a)(1)(A). An order awarding reimbursement of private-education costs when a school district fails to provide a FAPE merely requires the district "to belatedly pay expenses that it should have paid all along." *Burlington*, 471 U.S., at 370-371. And States have in any event been on notice at least since our decision in *Burlington* that IDEA authorizes courts to order reimbursement of the costs of private special-education services in appropriate circumstances. *Pennhurst's* notice requirement is thus clearly satisfied.

Finally, the District urges that respondent's reading of the Act will impose a substantial financial burden on public school districts and encourage parents to immediately enroll their children in private school without first endeavoring to cooperate with the school district. The dissent echoes this concern. See *post*, at — For several reasons, those fears are unfounded. Parents "are entitled to reimbursement *only* if a federal court concludes both that the public placement violated IDEA and the private school placement was proper under the Act." *Carter*, 510 U.S., at 15. And even then courts retain discretion to reduce the amount of a reimbursement award if the equities so warrant-for instance, if the parents failed to give the school district adequate notice of their intent to enroll the child in private school. In considering the equities, courts should generally presume that public-school officials are properly performing their obligations under IDEA. See *Schaffer v. Weast*, 546 U.S. 49, 62-63 (2005) (STEVENS, J., concurring). As a result of these criteria and the fact that parents who " 'unilaterally change their child's placement during the pendency of review proceedings, without the consent of state or local school officials, do so at their own financial risk,' " *Carter*, 510 U.S., at 15, the incidence of private-school placement at public expense is quite small, see Brief for National Disability Rights Network et al. as *Amici Curiae* 13-14.

V

The IDEA Amendments of 1997 did not modify the text of § 1415(i)(2)(C)(iii), and we do not read § 1412(a)(10)(C) to alter that provision's meaning. Consistent with our decisions in *Burlington* and *Carter*, we conclude that IDEA authorizes reimbursement for the cost of private special-education services when a school district fails to provide a FAPE and the private-school placement is appropriate, regardless of whether the child previously received special education or related services through the public school.

When a court or hearing officer concludes that a school district failed to provide a FAPE and the private placement was suitable, it must consider all relevant factors, including the notice provided by the parents and the school district's opportunities for evaluating the child, in determining whether reimbursement for some or all of the cost of the child's private education is warranted. As the Court of Appeals noted, the District Court did not properly consider the equities in this case and will need to undertake that analysis on remand. Accordingly, the judgment of the Court of Appeals is affirmed.

It is so ordered.

(Appendix omitted)

Justice SOUTER, with whom Justice SCALIA and Justice THOMAS join, dissenting (omitted).

TABLE OF CASES

[References are to pages]

[References are to pages]

[References are to pages]

TABLE OF STATUTES

[References are to pages]

[References are to pages]

[References are to pages]

[References are to pages]

[References are to pages]

[References are to pages]

[References are to pages]

[References are to pages]

INDEX

[References are to chapters and sections.]

I-1

[References are to chapters and sections.]

[References are to chapters and sections.]

[References are to chapters and sections.]

[References are to chapters and sections.]